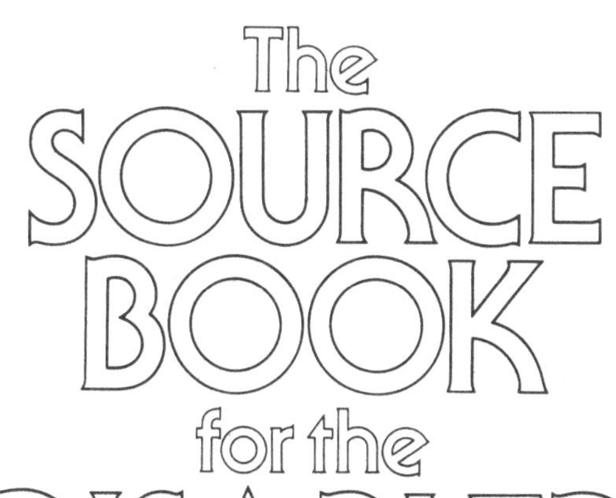
The
SOURCE
BOOK
for the
DISABLED

Edited by Glorya Hale

Contributors:
Pat Barr
Gertrude Buckman
Susan Goodman
Heather Jimenez
Vivian Naylor
George Seddon

The SOURCE BOOK for the DISABLED

An illustrated guide to easier and more independent living for physically disabled people, their families and friends

PADDINGTON PRESS LTD
NEW YORK & LONDON

The Source Book for the Disabled
was designed and edited by
Imprint Books Limited, London.

ART DIRECTOR: David Warner

Library of Congress Cataloging in Publication Data

Hale, Glorya.
The source book for the disabled.

Includes index.
1. Physically handicapped. 2. Self-help devices for the disabled. 3. Architecture and the physically handicapped. 4. Sex instruction for the physically handicapped. 5. Physically handicapped children—Care and treatment. 6. Handicapped services—United States. 7. Physically handicapped—Recreation. I. Title.
HV3011.H26 362.4 78-31463
ISBN 0 7092 0324 1
ISBN 0 7092 0327 6 (pbk)
U.S. and Canada only
ISBN 0 448 22426 7
ISBN 0 448 22429 1 (pbk)

Filmset in England by
SX Composing Ltd., Rayleigh, Essex
Origination and make-up by
Sarisberie Designs, Salisbury, Wilts.
Printed and bound in the United States.

IN THE UNITED STATES
PADDINGTON PRESS
Distributed by
GROSSET & DUNLAP

IN THE UNITED KINGDOM
PADDINGTON PRESS

IN CANADA
Distributed by
RANDOM HOUSE OF
CANADA LTD.

IN SOUTHERN AFRICA
Distributed by
ERNEST STANTON
(PUBLISHERS) (PTY.) LTD.

IN AUSTRALIA AND
NEW ZEALAND
Distributed by
A. H. & A. W. REED

Contents

Introduction

Physically disabled people—men, women and children who were born with a physical impairment or who have a physical limitation as the result of illness, injury, accident or age—represent the largest, although often hidden, minority in the world. In the United States alone, at least one out of every ten citizens is physically disabled. We do not need statistics, however, to tell us how far-reaching, and perhaps devastating, are the effects of our own disabilities or those of physically handicapped relatives or friends.

The Source Book for the Disabled has been created for those many millions who are physically disabled and for the millions more who care. It explains and explores the attitudes and available options and illustrates the kinds of aids which can make life fuller, more comfortable and more independent for every person who is disabled.

Increasingly, "the disabled" have become the subject of sociological surveys, of government reports and studies. Should we be expected to pay our way or settle for handouts? Is it advisable to encourage us to take our places in the work force or to keep us in sheltered employment? Should we be educated to raise our sights or be advised to lower our expectations? Should we be housed by state subsidies or looked after in institutions? Should our families bear the burden and if not, who should? How much can a government afford to spend on us when other, possibly more productive, citizens are clamoring for attention? How much does society owe its disabled members anyway?

Questions like these have prompted doctors, psychologists, educators, architects, social service personnel and rehabilitation experts, among others, to pay special attention to the needs and problems of people with disabilities. But like every other minority, disabled people themselves, together with their families and friends, have recognized the need to become advocates of their own causes and the importance of taking responsibility for their own lives. Although the life-styles, attitudes, opinions, backgrounds, tastes and temperaments of disabled people are as varied as those of other members of the community, we have joined together for a common cause.

Disabled people, individually as well as in groups, have sprung into action, fighting for civil rights, accessible transportation, buildings and educational facilities. We are learning, too, to challenge insensitive attitudes of the public who seem to assume all too often that physical impairment is synonymous with an inability to think or speak up. But despite all this activity, most people with physical limitations still feel that they have been collectively labeled "disabled" and wonder what the future holds for them as individuals with their own needs, ambitions and goals.

Today each person who is disabled must try to sort out hard fact from glib talk. What are government programs really achieving and to what do they entitle you? What are your rights? What are your options for sexual fulfillment? What can be done to ease the demands of everyday life? It is these questions and many others which this book will help you to answer.

The contributors, disabled and able-bodied, discuss the attitudes which can be helpful or hindering, explore im-

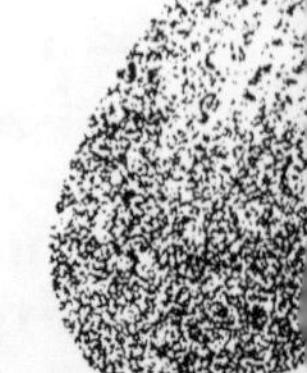

portant legislation and its implementation. The options of the individual are examined and emotions are shared. Aids for use in the home, for leisure activities and for personal needs are described and illustrated.

Throughout the book disabilities, rather than their causes, are referred to. Aids are suggested for the wheelchaired, for one-handed use or for weak grasp, for example, rather than for the paraplegic, the amputee or the arthritic. In the section The Disablers, however, specific medical conditions are defined. The Resources section at the end of the book lists leaflets, books and periodicals for further reading and gives addresses of organizations and government agencies, special interest groups and clubs and commercial sources of aids and equipment.

It is hoped that *The Source Book for the Disabled* will be an inspiring and practical guide to more independent living and more fulfilling lives for people of all ages with all degrees of physical limitations, as well as a valuable reference work, not only for the individual, but also for his or her family and friends.

Disabled or Handicapped?

The words we use reflect our attitudes; the use of the terms "the disabled" and "the handicapped" is particularly revealing. To many people they are objectionable. These terms are in effect labels which stereotype and categorize a diverse group of people who have nothing intrinsic in common. They are not descriptions of actual conditions and are really applicable only in such generalizations as in the title of a book or an act of legislation intended for people with all kinds of physical disabilities in all kinds of life situations.

Throughout this book we have tried, as far as possible, to avoid using these terms and have instead used the expressions "people with disabilities," "people who are disabled," "people with physical limitations." On occasion, too, to avoid awkwardness and repetition, we have referred to "disabled" or "handicapped people," although in fact few people are totally disabled or completely handicapped, as these terms might imply.

Then there are the words "disabled" and "handicapped" themselves, which are used interchangeably, as if they mean the same thing and by usage, have come to mean the same thing. But a physical disability, no matter how or by what it was caused, is a medically determined fact that can be defined and described explicitly. The word "handicap," originally used to denote a disadvantage in sports, is in effect a concept that's open to change as well as to interpretation.

Sometimes a handicap can be minimized or even completely eliminated. A man whose legs are paralyzed and depends totally on a wheelchair, is very handicapped if he lives and works in inaccessible buildings and cannot use public transportation. If, however, he moves to a ranch-style house, gets a job in a building which has an elevator and buys a car with hand controls, he is no longer handicapped since his disability no longer affects his ability to function. There are, too, disabilities which will seriously handicap a person in one situation and not in others. A concert pianist who loses two fingers is severely handicapped as far as her career is concerned, although she may not be

particularly handicapped in most of the other areas of her life.

In educational, occupational and recreational competition with people who are able-bodied, people with physical disabilities are often in the same position as the competitor in a sport who has been given a handicapping disadvantage that makes winning more difficult. There are two ways in which a person with a disability can mitigate his or her handicap. The first is through the use of suitable aids; the other is through constructive and realistic attitudes.

Aids, sophisticated or simple, can often make daily life infinitely easier. Aids save time and conserve energy, increase mobility and extend the ability to communicate. The space age has boosted the relatively new field of biomedical engineering, applying the knowledge gained in space technology to problems of disability. Included in the many new inventions are a heart pacemaker with a rechargeable battery that needs no surgical replacement, and a wheelchair that moves in response to a voice-activated mini-computer. With the increased momentum of applied research, aids that seemed possible only in science fiction may soon be a reality.

Many devices which are readily available are standard, inexpensive and easy to use; others are tailor-made for the individual and require professional counsel. Some people who are disabled discover ingenious ways to solve practical problems and to create their own aids. It takes imagination, knowledge and positive assistance from others to get the best out of the resources that are at hand, but the effort is worthwhile.

The extent to which you are handicapped by your disability can also depend on your attitudes. Surveys have shown that many people with severe physical limitations don't consider themselves to be particularly handicapped, while others, whose disabilities are relatively minor, think of themselves as severely handicapped. And such attitudes affect every area of the individual's life. Sometimes a person's view of his or her disability is more handicapping than the disability itself.

There are a number of common handicapping attitudes. Some people, for example, can't disassociate themselves from the able-bodied concept of "wholeness." They feel that they have to make up for being disabled and drive themselves relentlessly, often attempting to do far more than their capacities permit. Then, when they can't accomplish what is probably impossible, they feel frustrated, angry and, frequently, bitter. In their efforts to prove that they are as good as, or even better than, their able-bodied peers, they cannot accept their limitations and therefore do not take pleasure from their actual abilities and achievements.

Other people over-identify with the able-bodied world and try to "pass" as able-bodied. If their impairments are slight or hidden, they do without the aids and the help they really need and expend far too much energy keeping up their pretense. Although there is nothing wrong in playing down a disability, to deny it is to deny an aspect of oneself.

Some people with disabilities avoid others with similar problems. Although their excuse—that they have nothing in common—may have some truth in it, they are more strongly motivated by a fear of being identified as "one of them." This is a refusal to face oneself realistically. It is an attitude which often stops people from meeting many interesting men and women from all walks of life whose experiences of disability and whose common aims could be helpful and stimulating.

The opposite reaction is equally handicapping. While institutional living, special schools and architectural barriers all conspire to segregate people with disabilities, some people remain apart by choice. They cling to other people who are disabled for mutual support, creating a ghetto that's often barred to people who are able-bodied, as well as to those suffering from disabilities of a different kind.

Identifying the attitudes that can handicap—and understanding them—helps to change or control them so that a disability can be prevented from becoming a handicap.

Aids to Living

Inventors, engineers, designers, therapists and imaginative laypeople have devised a wide range of ingenious aids to extend the horizons of millions of disabled people. From a simple home-made reacher that retrieves dropped articles, to a sophisticated breath-controlled switch that operates a typewriter, these devices are designed to help people with disabilities to live more independent lives.

Aids can simplify eating, grooming, dressing, the basic tasks of daily living. They facilitate household chores—cleaning, cooking and laundering. Electronic systems, telephones, reading and writing contrivances augment communication. Automobile adaptations, special controls and transfer aids make driving possible. Wheelchairs, walkers, hoists, lifts and ramps increase outdoor and indoor mobility. A profusion of useful items and products are available that cover almost every area and activity of daily life—ranging from expensive equipment obtainable from specialist sources to simple gadgets illustrated in ordinary mail order catalogs.

Whether you avail yourself of any of these aids depends upon a number of factors. If you were ever treated in a rehabilitation unit, trained personnel probably assessed your capacities and suggested the devices best suited to help solve your particular problems at the time. But your life-style and, possibly, your condition may have changed and from time to time it's wise to go back for a reassessment. If you were not cared for by such specialists and want advice on aids, it is worth making an outpatient appointment at the nearest rehabilitation center or consulting the most knowledgeable doctor within traveling distance.

There are, however, always new aids on the market, some of which could simplify your life enormously or make it possible for you to do things you might never have attempted before. It's wise to do some detective work.

Consult your local library or get someone to go there for you. The librarian may have on file, or can get for you, copies of the numerous newsletters and magazines published by disabled people themselves or by organizations working on their behalf. Look through the Yellow Pages of your telephone book under the name of your disability or under headings that will lead you to such organizations. They often publish invaluable booklets and information sheets which illustrate aids and tell you where to get them. Catalogs from hospital supply companies frequently include very useful aids. Mail order catalogs are full of clever gadgets intended for the able-bodied that you might be able to put to good purpose.

Once you have tracked them down, the next problem is deciding which aids are best for you. To be effective, an aid must assist function and save energy. The interesting, mobile chair-table combination looks great in the picture, but will you really use it? Will you bother to unlock the tray from the side of the chair, lift it into position and lock it into place? Are you sure your old wheelchair lapboard isn't more convenient?

Whatever aids you choose must help, not worsen, your condition. A person with one weak arm might be tempted to favor it by using the good arm plus a gadget for one-armed use. But the weak arm might need exercising. If your doctor or physiotherapist hasn't mentioned one-arm devices there's probably a good reason. Check with the experts first. And keep in mind that many aids can be useless, or perhaps even damaging, if you haven't been instructed in their correct use.

Commercial catalogs often present a bewildering variety of products. Should you try the nontip mixing bowl with suction base or the nonskid place mat? Is the "no hands" book holder better than the frame that holds the book at any angle? Only trial and error will tell. Fortunately, these minor items are not very expensive so you can experiment occasionally.

Costly investments like car and van adaptations, ramps, wheelchairs and other hardware, need more serious consideration. Shop around and ask advice from others. Try the equipment before buying it or take it on a trial basis. The demonstrator may be helpful, but like any other salesperson is anxious to earn a commission. Make sure that the equipment you want carries a guarantee and that it can be quickly serviced.

Many aids can be copied or adapted and made at home. Those you buy should be well designed, well made and, if possible, mass-produced, with parts that are readily available and easily replaced, so that the cost is kept down. Keep these points in mind and take advantage of the best offers. Don't let yourself be conned just because you're a consumer with a disability.

People with handicaps find many novel and unorthodox solutions to outwit their limitations. Aids add extra ammunition. Of course you shouldn't use them if you don't need them, but keep an open mind and don't dismiss them just because you're accustomed to doing things in one particular way; there may be an easier or better solution and you'll never know if you don't experiment. The use of a new aid should never be considered an admission of defeat. Disability can creep up on you. You may get along for years without a kitchen chair on casters, but the day can come when having one doesn't seem like such a bad idea.

Included in this book are many everyday aids that you can make or buy (as well as ideas for alternative ways of doing things). They are just a sampling to spark your imagination. There are lots more on the market and others waiting to be invented—perhaps by you.

Asking for Help

Knowing when—and how—to ask for help doesn't come easily to most people. Some are so stubborn they can't admit that they are not able to do everything for themselves. Others have been inculcated since childhood with the attitude that every task they set out to do they must complete alone. Some people are simply unsure of themselves—so unsure that they dare not seek help for fear it will be interpreted as a sign of weakness. There are some, however, who take the opposite tack. They use, and reuse, the ploy of looking helpless until someone steps in and takes over.

We who have disabilities don't escape from these self-defeating patterns of behavior, if these traits happen to be part of our makeup. On the contrary, a physical disability provides a perfect excuse to pamper such proclivities. Those people who are passively dependent are in an unassailable position; since the world is all too ready to assume that they are dependent, help is offered whether it is needed or not. Those who are aggressively independent can have a field day, insisting on doing things for themselves that able-bodied friends or relatives could dispatch in half the time, brushing aside well-intentioned offers of help with snarls and generally hurting other peoples' feelings, as if by doing this they are proving that they are capable of looking after themselves.

Striking a balance between these two extremes is particularly difficult for a person with a disability. Most of us take pride in the way we have learned, or are learning, to cope. Most of us want to manage on our own. But striving for this goal may take so much determination and concentration that we lose perspective. We may consider that our need for help, from time to time, or all the time, is an admission of defeat. We may resent our need for help and, by extension, the people offering or giving the assistance. This can be hard on friends and relatives. If the roles were reversed would we handle the situation any better?

There is always, of course, the problem of well-meaning strangers who often do more harm than good. If you are blind they may startle you or make you lose your balance by grabbing your arm to steer you across the street. Or when they see you maneuvering your wheelchair down a curb they may, with all good intentions, seize it inexpertly and almost pitch you out. If you can't communicate they may shout as if you were deaf, and if you are deaf they may go into an embarrassing "Me Tarzan, you Jane" pantomime.

Don't turn against these well-wishers.

Why should they know how to help you? They're not professionals. They're just people who intend kindness. That's an impulse to be encouraged, so take the time to tell them how they can be helpful. It may make them realize how to offer help to another person with a disability another time.

Then there are the passersby who look the other way while you struggle up the steps with bags of groceries weighing down your crutches. This can be interpreted as indifference, but it is more likely to be diffidence. Many people don't want to offer assistance for fear that it won't be well received. Don't let false pride hold you back. They may only be waiting for a sign. Give it. Ask for a hand and accept it graciously. Help is by no means a one-way transaction. By allowing someone to help you, you may well be helping in return.

In all human exchanges the important thing is sending the right signals. Endless misunderstandings could be avoided if we were able to read each other's minds. The next best thing is to be open and honest about our needs in the hope that others will be the same. If we communicate our needs the people who know us well will know us better and those who pass through our lives, if only briefly, will be in a better position to cope with others who are disabled. Feeling free to ask for help when it is necessary and to offer help gladly is, after all, part of the give and take of everyday life.

Walking Aids

Only a doctor or a physiotherapist can properly assess your need for a walking aid, help you choose the correct one and teach you how to use it most effectively in the house and outdoors. An unsuitable walking aid can hinder progress and, in some cases, can be positively detrimental. Never, therefore, buy a walking aid without professional guidance.

You should also be taught how to instruct someone to give you effective assistance when you're walking. A helper often offers more physical support than is necessary. This makes walking more difficult because it disturbs the normal rhythms of body movement. You must learn how to enable a helper really to help you.

If you use a cane it should always have a rubber tip to grip the ground. These tips, which are available from pharmacies carrying convalescent aids, come in many designs and different sizes. Choose one with the largest ground-gripping surface; it should be at least one and a half inches (3 cm) in diameter. If your cane is too thin for the tip to fit securely, wrap adhesive tape around the end of the cane before putting the tip on.

Smooth-ended tips tend to slip and should not be used at all. A suction tip will not only grip the ground better, but will last longer than one made of pimpled rubber. A crutch tip with a flexible neck will grip the ground no matter what the angle of the cane. Ice-gripper cane tips are also available.

Be sure to keep the tip clean, for it will become dangerously slippery if it gets clogged with dirt. The tip should also be rotated regularly to keep it from wearing down unevenly. When a tip gets worn down, change it; it is no longer safe and is particularly hazardous when the ground is wet.

A variety of handles have been developed for canes to accommodate different grasps. Although the curved C-handle is most popular it may not always be comfortable. Wrapping the handle with foam rubber or cloth and covering it with tape or leather will build it up and cushion it.

One of the problems with a cane is where to put it when it's not in use. Some people who don't have to rely on canes all the time find folding canes useful. A leather thong attached to the handle of a cane, or an elastic loop around the handle plus a larger loop which goes around the wrist, leaves the hand free to grasp a railing or doorknob without fear of dropping the cane. If you are holding onto a banister, however, you must be careful not to let the dangling cane get caught in the stair rails or get in the way of your legs. It is often useful to keep an extra cane at the top of the staircase, held with a clip.

An ice-gripper cane tip is made of rubber and has a steel plate into which steel spikes are embedded.

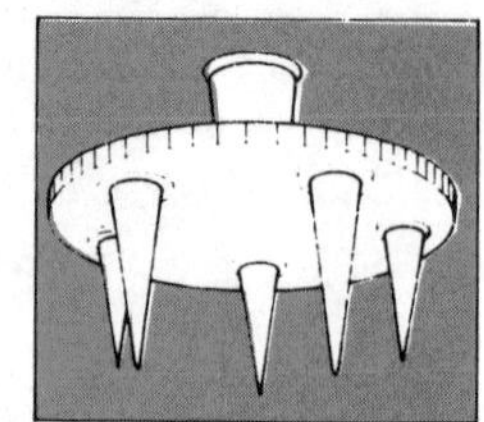

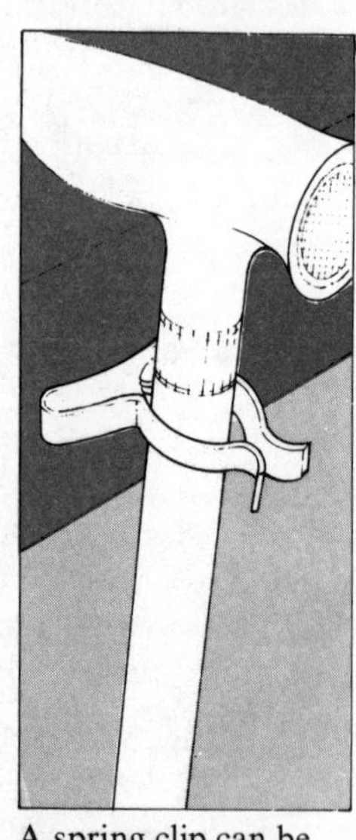

A spring clip can be attached to a table, a banister or a chair to hold a cane when it's not being used.

Far more stable than an ordinary cane is one with three or four widely splayed legs. It will stand alone when you are opening a door or sitting down. Usually, however, the legs are too widespread for such canes to be used on stairs.

Crutches are designed to carry much more of a person's weight than a cane. It is important that a therapist select the most suitable design, assess the correct length and the right position of the hand grips and teach you how to walk with the crutches.

Walking frames are very stable, but they take up a lot of room and this can limit their usefulness. The simplest kinds of walkers are solid units with built-up hand rests. The sides are moved alternately with the feet. Rubber tips on the legs prevent sliding. A reciprocating walker has jointed corners so that it angles to walk with you. Walkers with wheels on the front legs are designed for people who have difficulty lifting and maneuvering a conventional walking frame. Stair-walking frames can be used for going up or down stairs, as well as for level walking. Hemi-walkers, with a center hand grip adjustable to either hand, are useful for those people who are able to use only one hand. Some walking frames fold so that they can be easily put into a car or stored flat when not in use.

A sturdy tea wagon or serving cart can function both as a walking aid and a carrying aid. It must be strong enough so that you can lean on it without it tipping, with a handle at the right height for you and it should be fitted with reliable casters for easy steering. The casters should be cleaned and oiled regularly.

If there is not enough room for a tea wagon or if you don't have to carry much at one time, you can have ball bearing casters fitted on the legs of a plain wooden chair. It then makes a convenient walking and carrying aid.

The Manoy walking aid, a lightweight frame mounted on two nylon skids, is adjustable in height. Designed for indoor use, two models are available, one with bicycle-type handgrips, the other with forearm supports. It has a basket and an angled perch for sitting for a short time at a work surface or simply for having a brief rest while walking around the house.

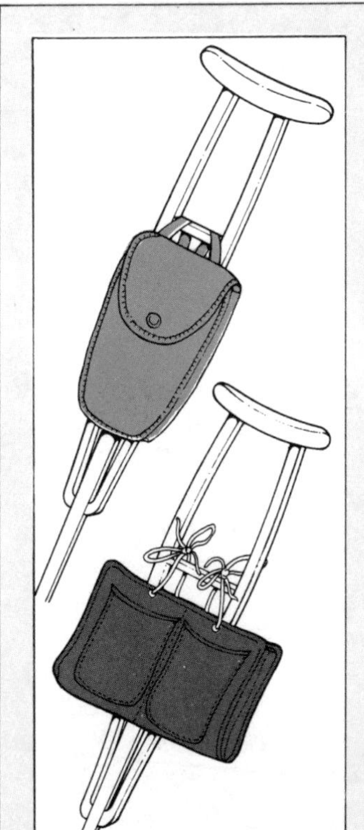

Detachable crutch bags are useful accessories which can be easily made. Things carried should be divided between a bag on each crutch.

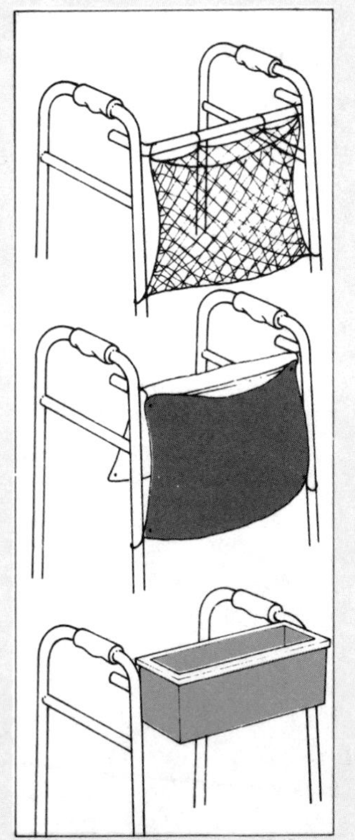

Available from self-help equipment firms, a carrier bag, pouch or basket which attaches to a walker adds greatly to its convenience.

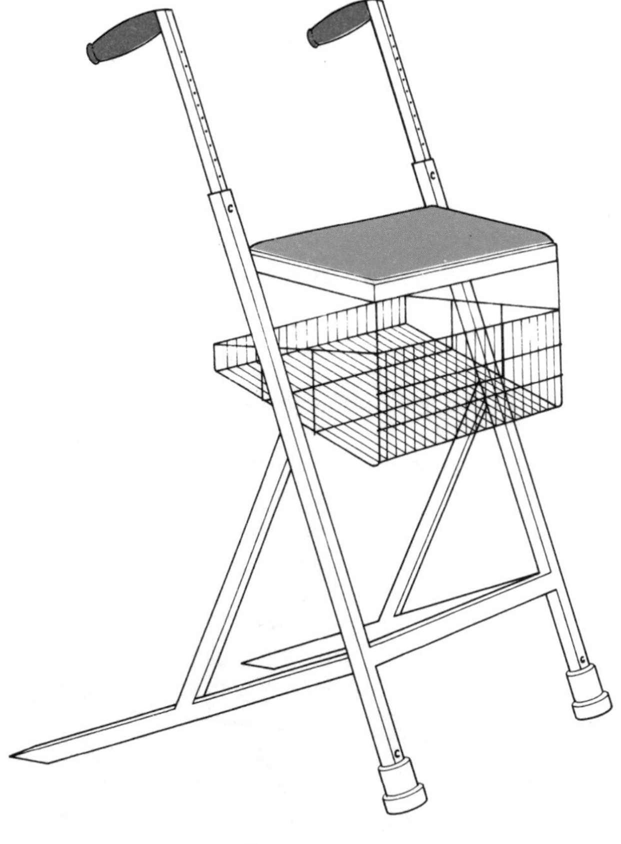

Wheelchairs

Most people who depend on wheelchairs consider them extensions of themselves —energy-saving, independence-giving substitutes for lost muscle power that help them to take their rightful places in the world around them.

Often, however, newly disabled people or those with degenerative disabilities don't understand this point of view, for they are still influenced by their earlier prejudices. Some able-bodied people equate wheelchairs with infirmity. They find it difficult to accept wheelchaired people as independent adults and tend to treat them like children or to talk down to them as though their minds as well as their bodies were affected.

When people with these attitudes become obliged to use wheelchairs they find it difficult to adjust. In their minds "taking to a wheelchair" represents a comedown or an admission of defeat. Such misconceptions inhibit many potential beneficiaries and account for the number of stubborn cane and crutch walkers who refuse wheelchairs on principle and whose mobility is as painful as it is restricted.

There should be no stigma attached to using a wheelchair; it is just another aid. Rather than a sign of weakness it is a symbol of independence which increases participation in life and does not diminish one's value as a person.

As important as coming to terms with being wheelchaired is getting the most appropriate wheelchair and then learning to utilize it as fully as possible. A doctor or therapist can help to choose the type of chair an individual needs, so buying without professional advice is not recommended. Your choice may be limited by medical considerations, or by the official agency that is providing the chair, but remember that once acquired it's you who will have to live with it.

If possible, rent before you buy. (Rental fees are sometimes deducted from the price of the chair that is finally bought.) The wheelchair that seemed suitable in the hospital or in the store may not be appropriate to your way of life. Don't be afraid to try chairs of different weights and sizes and those made by various manufacturers. And find out all you can about the options and extras which are available.

Manufacturers and suppliers of wheelchairs are listed in the Yellow Pages. Many of them offer illustrated catalogs. These may present what at first appears to be a bewildering array of manual and power-operated wheelchairs in a variety of models, sizes, weights and price ranges, and a confusing number of special features, extras and accessories. It's advisable to study the catalogs carefully, for it takes a careful eye to find the wheelchair you need, with the features you want, at a price you can afford to pay. Keep in mind that a higher price doesn't guarantee a better product, although the more you pay the more options you get. This is a guide to help you sort it all out.

The basic standard wheelchair for personal use has a straight back and arms that are fixed to the chair. It has large drive wheels in back, casters in front, brakes and, usually, removable footrests. For people who are unable to sit up straight the standard chair is also made with a fully reclining back which can be adjusted from an almost upright to a horizontal position.

Modified versions of the basic chair include: models designed for one-hand propelling with special double-rimmed wheels that can be mounted on either side; models for leg amputees with drive wheels set further back to compensate for the shift in weight; and models for hemiplegics which have a lower seat to permit foot propelling. (Some manufacturers make special attachments which convert their standard chairs for amputees and for one-handed propelling.)

In addition, most manufacturers make a streamlined "sportsman's" model, a small model for children as well as an adjustable chair for growing youngsters. For people who can't manage with the drive wheels in the normal position there are wheelchairs available with the drive wheels placed in front, but these chairs are only for indoor use.

The frames of most standard wheelchairs are made of nickel-plated steel;

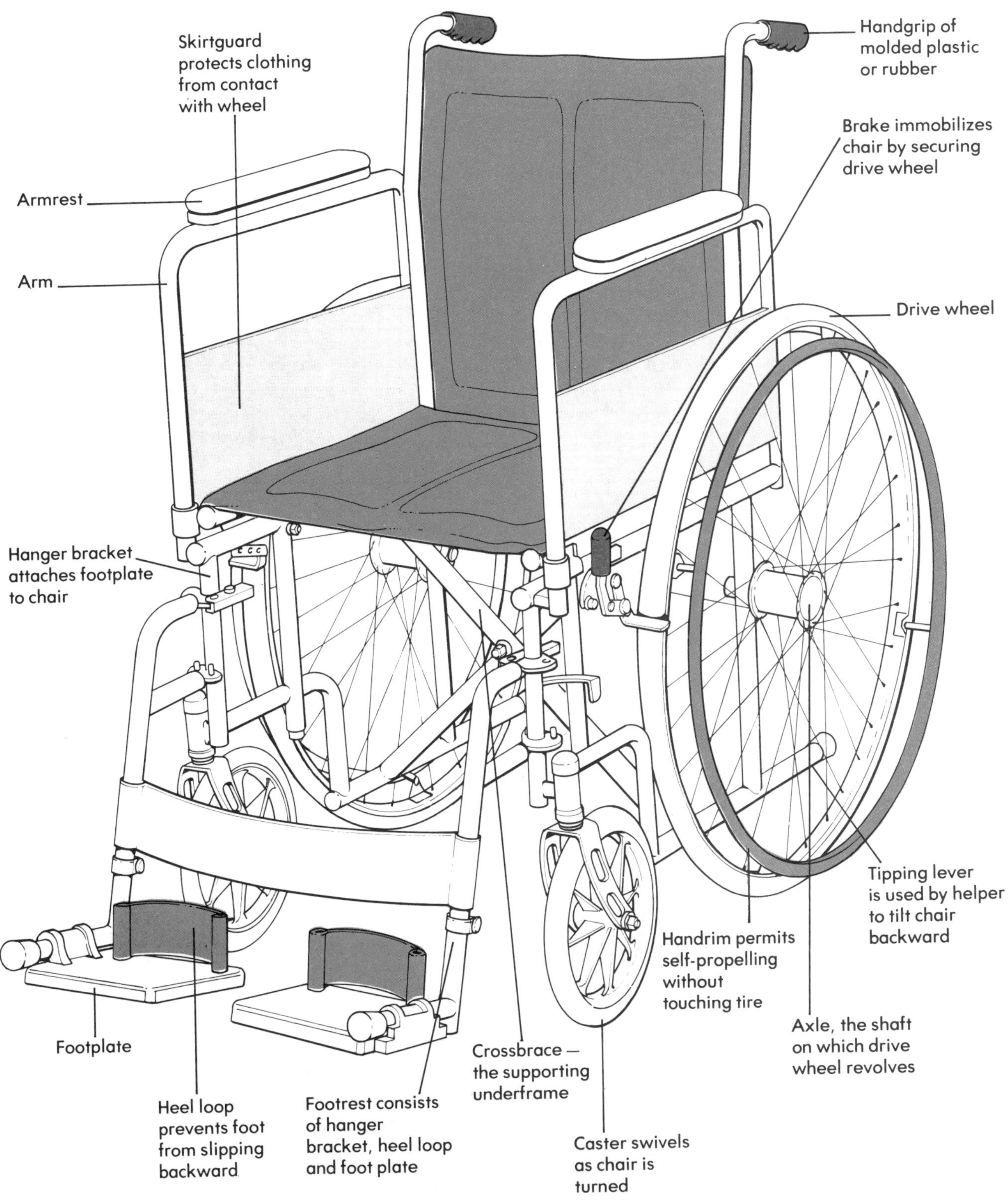
Skirtguard protects clothing from contact with wheel
Handgrip of molded plastic or rubber
Brake immobilizes chair by securing drive wheel
Armrest
Arm
Drive wheel
Hanger bracket attaches footplate to chair
Tipping lever is used by helper to tilt chair backward
Handrim permits self-propelling without touching tire
Axle, the shaft on which drive wheel revolves
Footplate
Crossbrace — the supporting underframe
Heel loop prevents foot from slipping backward
Footrest consists of hanger bracket, heel loop and foot plate
Caster swivels as chair is turned

the chairs weigh from forty to about fifty pounds (18 to 22 kg), depending on the model. There are also lightweight ranges. The frames of these chairs are made of lightweight aluminum and special alloyed metals so they weigh substantially less and are easier to transport, although not to maneuver and propel. There are also heavy-duty models which are reinforced at points of maximum stress. Heavy-duty parts can also be incorporated in a standard chair.

Wheelchairs come in certain standard sizes, although seat, back and arm dimensions can be custom modified, for a price. All manufacturers offer a "standard adult" and a "narrow adult" size wheelchair, as well as sizes for "juniors" (sometimes called "small adults") "tall" and "extra large" people. Dimensions vary slightly from one manufacturer to another, but the chair seat width of the "standard adult" chair is eighteen inches (45 cm) and the seat width of the "narrow adult" chair is sixteen inches (40 cm).

The overall width of a "standard adult" chair is several inches wider than that of a "narrow adult" chair. The actual measurements vary—from twenty-four and a half to twenty-six and a half inches (61 to 66 cm) on a "standard adult" to twenty-two to twenty-four and a half inches (55 to 61 cm) on a "narrow adult" chair—depending on the type of arms you choose.

Most people take it for granted that they are "standard adult" size. If you are slim try a "narrow adult" or a "junior" chair. You may be able to save yourself a few unnecessary inches—and every inch saved is important when it comes to getting through doorways.

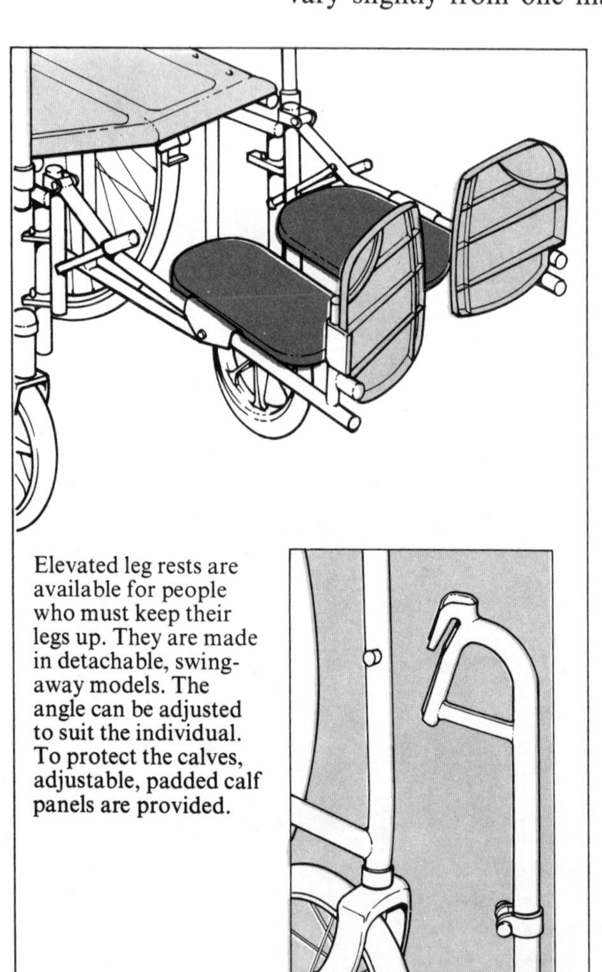

Elevated leg rests are available for people who must keep their legs up. They are made in detachable, swing-away models. The angle can be adjusted to suit the individual. To protect the calves, adjustable, padded calf panels are provided.

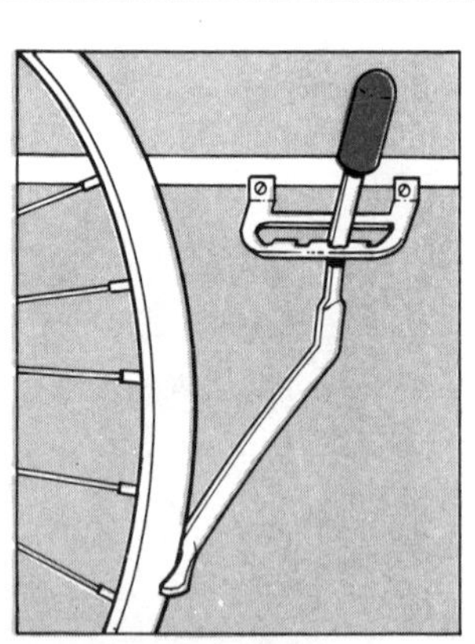

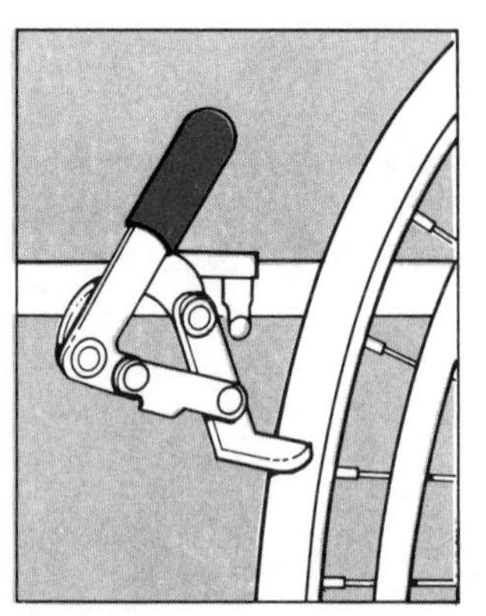

The lever-type wheelchair brake above can be placed in an on, off or in a partially on position, which helps to reduce acceleration. The toggle-type brake above has only the on and off positions.

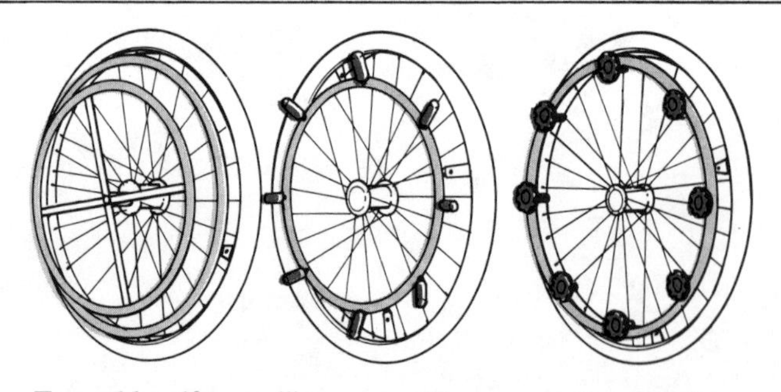

To enable self-propelling, a variety of special handrims are available. The double rim, above left, permits one-handed propulsion. When grasp is limited, a rim with oblique projections, center, permits propulsion through a pushing motion. When finger or hand movement is limited, contoured knobs, above right, are helpful.

Many optional features are available on all standard wheelchairs. Detachable arms, instead of fixed arms, usually add one and a half to two inches (3 to 5 cm) to the overall chair width, but they have many advantages. They permit sideways transfers—sliding from wheelchair to bed, to toilet and to car seat—with or without the help of a transfer board. They make the chair lighter to lift and carry and easier to stow away.

Full-length detachable arms give the same full forearm support that fixed arms do. Desk-length detachable arms are lower in the front so that the chair can be easily slid under desks and tables. They can also be turned back to front, making it possible to lean on the high end when transferring.

More expensive models come with full-length or desk-length arms in a "wraparound" design that saves one and a half inches (3 cm) in the overall width of the chair, a great help for maneuvering through narrow places. Since managing narrow places is a problem for most of us, this feature ought to be available in all price ranges. Adjustable detachable arms that can be raised or lowered are also available in some lines but not in others. An adjustable, detachable full-length arm, for example, can be lowered to give the same clearance under a desk or table as a detachable desk arm. Study all these arm options before choosing a wheelchair.

Some wheelchairs have adjustable height footrests and leg rests, but most standard models have removable, adjustable height footrests with folding footplates. These can be taken off to pack the chair, put it in a car, to propel it with the feet or to move as close as possible to the toilet, to a desk or to kitchen units. In addition, many footrests swing to one side, a very convenient feature.

Other useful optional footrest and leg-rest aids include a leg-rest panel to

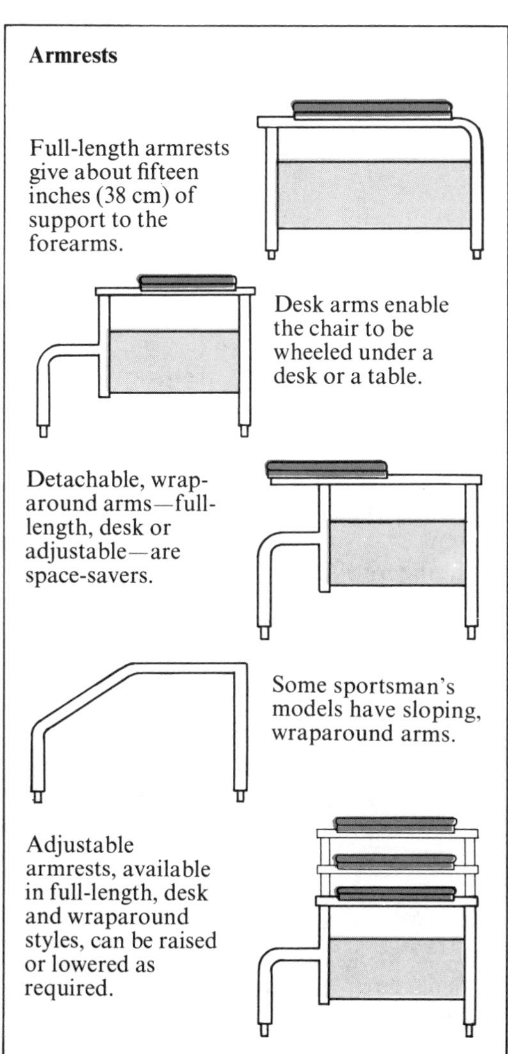

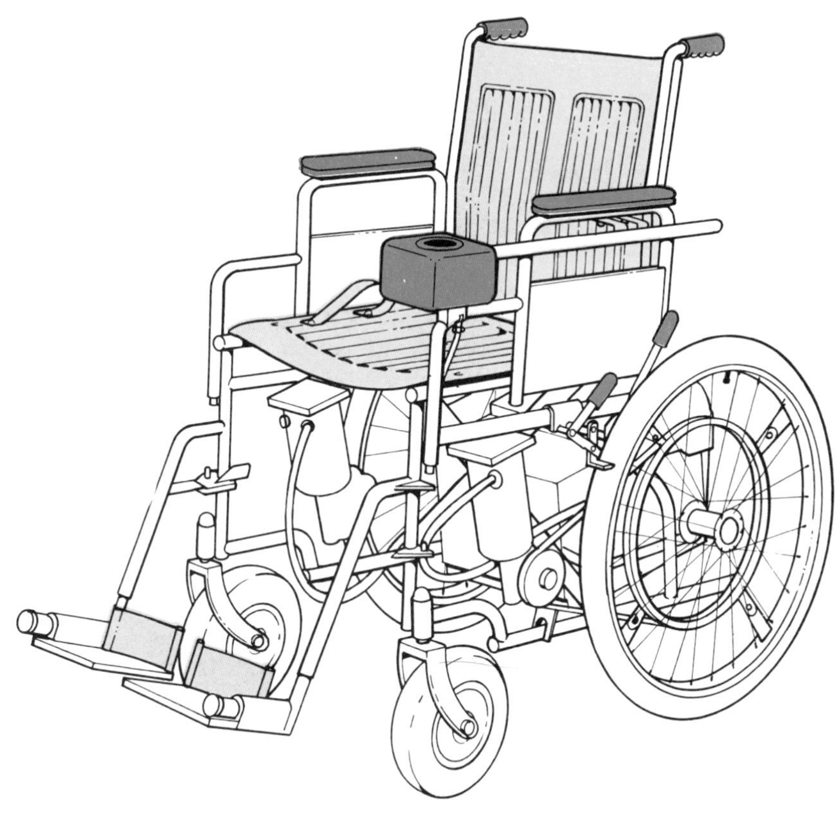

On most battery-operated wheelchairs, the carrier and batteries can be removed so that the chair can be folded. Power chairs, however, usually have heavy-duty features to support the weight of the motors and batteries. Even without batteries a chair weighs between seventy-five and eighty pounds (34 and 36 kg), so it is not very portable.

keep spastic or uncoordinated legs from slipping off the footplate, extra-large footplates, toe loops to keep feet in position and quad releases, aids that help weak fingers to release the swinging mechanisms on footrests and leg rests.

The brakes on wheelchairs work either on the lever or the toggle principle. Be sure that the wheelchair you choose comes with the kind of brake you can manage most easily. A brake extender, to extend the brake handle for easier grasp, can be made or bought. It should be removable so that it won't get in the way when transferring sideways.

Drive wheels usually have solid rubber tires which move easily over indoor floors, but are bumpy on rough surfaces. A number of different pneumatic tires are available that can be substituted for solid tires. They make the chair easier to propel outdoors. (A tire pump is needed for pneumatic tires. Sometimes it is included in the price of the tires, sometimes it's an "extra.")

The standard wheelchair is hand-propelled by the metal handrims that circle the drive wheels. For people whose grip is weak a rim is available which has rubber-tipped projections evenly spaced around it to assist the thrust.

Casters, the small front wheels, are usually eight inches (20 cm) in diameter. On some economy models, however, they are five inches (13 cm) in diameter and, consequently, less easily maneuvered. Pneumatic and semi-pneumatic casters are available. If it's necessary to keep the casters from moving while transferring, clamp-on swivel caster locks can be bought.

Solid seats with hinges to permit folding of the chair and a cushion to add height and comfort are available, but most chairs come with a slack seat, to which a seat board or foam rubber cushion can be added. Many different kinds of cushions are available for wheelchairs.

Standard chairs are upholstered in a vinyl-coated fabric, sometimes reinforced with canvas and padded with polyfoam. Some people prefer nylon upholstery that is not vinyl coated because they find it drier and cooler.

For people who are not able to propel a wheelchair by hand, four-wheel, manually operated chairs, which must be pushed by an attendant, are available. But most people who can't propel chairs themselves prefer battery-powered chairs.

A battery-powered wheelchair is designed like a manually controlled chair; the batteries are mounted on the back of the chair below seat level. The batteries will supply power for six to eight hours of continuous use, and can be charged overnight, using the charger supplied with the chair. There are two motor units, each of which drives one large wheel.

The controls can be placed for right or left hand use and respond not only to finger pressure but, if necessary, to chin or breath control. Self-contained portable power packs with control units are available in the United States. They attach to any standard wheelchair, to turn it into a powered chair.

For outdoor and indoor use there are many power-driven cars and scooters now being made. They look less institutional than wheelchairs, turn on a dime and are great fun to handle.

While your physical limitations will influence the prescription of the basic wheelchair for you, your own assessment of your life-style will help to determine the model and options which are best. If you are an active person, rushing around a college campus or the factory floor, you may want a heavy-duty model which will stand up to a lot of hard wear. If you're homebound or plan to keep the chair in an office, a lighter model might be preferable. If you travel a lot and want to take the chair along, you might decide on one that folds compactly, isn't too heavy and fits easily into the trunk of a car. For bumping over country roads a chair with maximum stability is a necessity. For getting in and out of city buildings a chair should be easy to maneuver and as narrow as possible. And a wide chair can be made slimmer by using a wheelchair narrower, a special cranking device that can be attached to fixed arms or to a detachable regular arm, narrows the chair temporarily and makes it possible to squeeze through narrow doorways.

Wheelchair Accessories

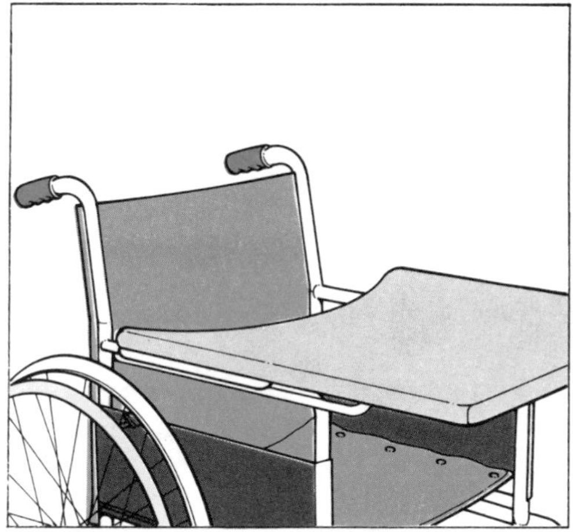

A utility tray or a lapboard, which attaches to the chair with strips of Velcro or with mounting brackets, is a useful accessory. A utility tray, like the one shown above, is placed on top of the armrests, while a lapboard rests on the skirt guard to provide a lower working surface.

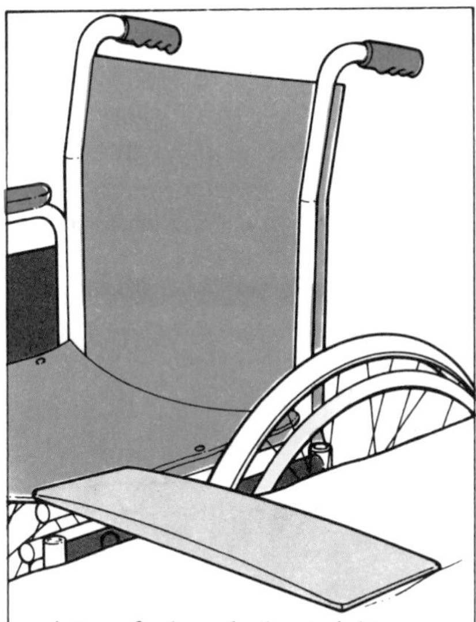

A transfer board, about eight inches (20 cm) by twenty-seven inches (68 cm) with tapered ends and rounded edges, facilitates transfers.

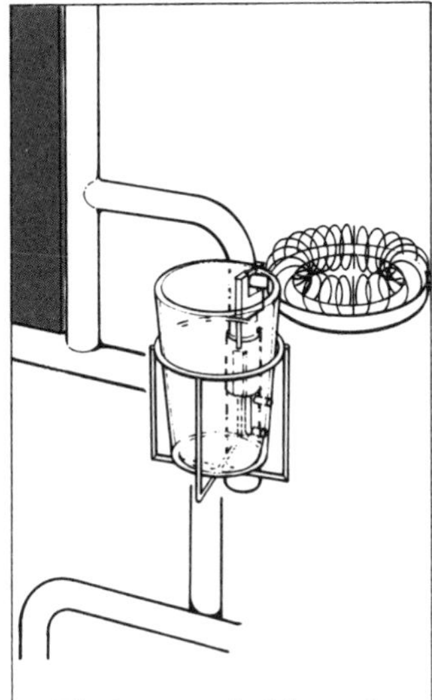

The beverage holder and the ashtray, which converts to a little utility tray, clip conveniently to the arm of a wheelchair.

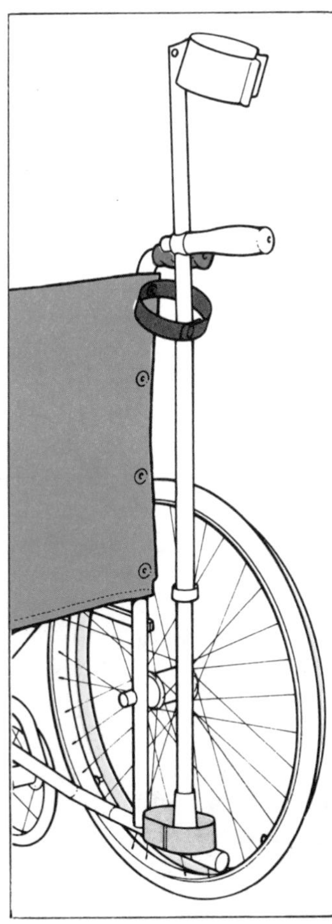

A receptacle, easily attached to the tipping lever, and a strap, attached to the upper chair, make an effective carrier for a cane or crutches.

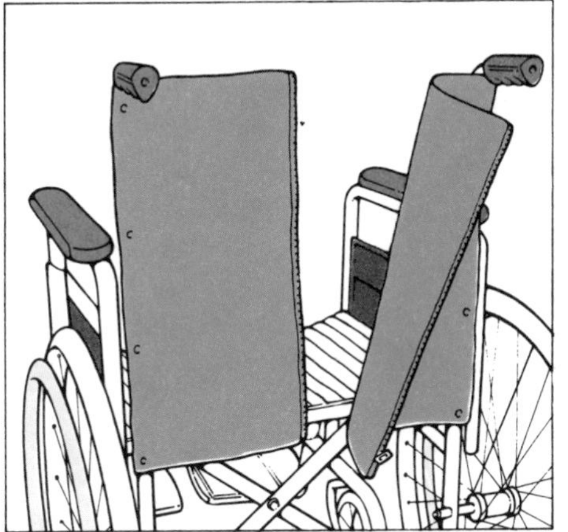

Zipper-back upholstery makes it possible to transfer to and from the rear of the wheelchair. The heavy-duty zipper keeps the back secure, yet it is easy to open.

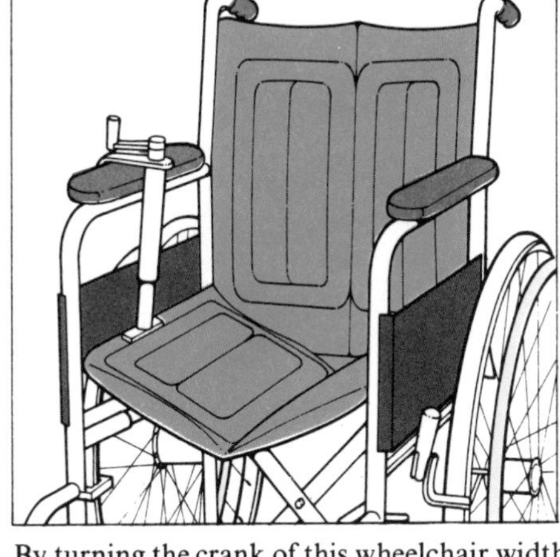

By turning the crank of this wheelchair width adjuster, the width of a folding chair, with X-frame construction, can be reduced as much as four inches (10 cm).

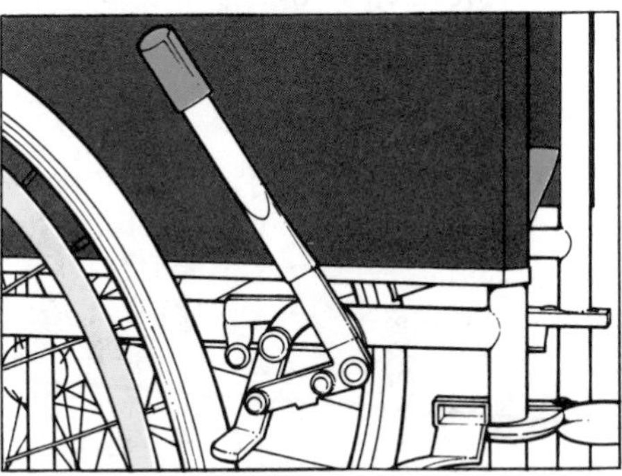

Various kinds of brake extenders are available from self-help equipment firms. The toggle brake extension handle shown above adds seven inches (18 cm) to the length of the brake and can be easily attached and removed.

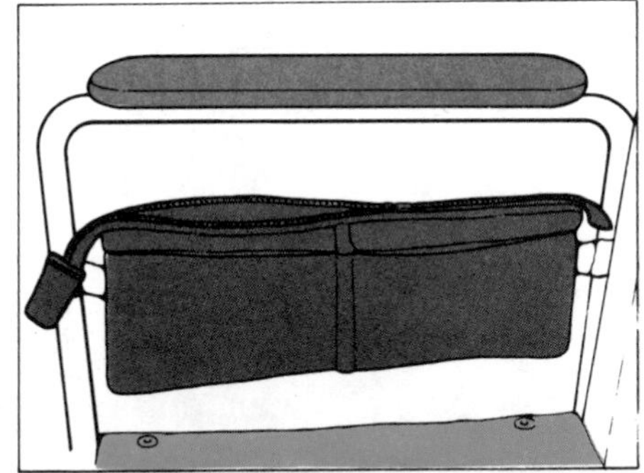

A wheelchair pouch, available in a variety of styles from self-help equipment firms, can be very helpful. The one shown above fits on a standard armrest and is six inches (15 cm) deep by sixteen inches (40 cm) wide.

No wheelchair is "all-purpose," no matter what the advertisements say, so be prepared to compromise. Unfortunately, too, manufacturers cater to a minority market. There is little incentive to improve design and durability, or supply of spare parts and servicing. Built-in obsolescence is as much a feature of wheelchair production as it is of any other modern product, and disabled consumers are literally sitting targets, in no position to shop around, boycott a manufacturer or return an unsatisfactory purchase.

In a 1976 survey on medical devices, The Disability Rights Center, a consumer group for disabled people, based in Washington, D.C. and funded by Ralph Nader's Public Citizen, Inc. and the Levenson Foundation, listed many consumer complaints about poor wheelchair construction. Slow servicing and undependable spare parts replacement was another common complaint. This is so widespread that such organizations as the Center for Independent Living in Berkeley, California, have set up their own twenty-four-hour curbside wheelchair repair service.

To protect yourself, check the manufacturer's warranty and try to find out whether the company has a good record for fast repairs and replacements. If you buy from a local dealer, make sure the outlet carries the spare parts you'll need, is responsible for repairs and will lend you another chair while yours is being fixed. Make friends, too, with the people who work in the nearest bicycle repair store. They can often do a fast and efficient repair job.

You can prolong your chair's life by keeping it dry and rustfree, by cleaning and oiling it regularly. paying special attention to joints and movable parts. Check regularly that the brakes are working properly, that pneumatic tires are at the correct pressure and that the handrims are securely bolted to the wheels.

If you follow these practical precautions and if you accept your wheelchair for what it is, an imperfect but invaluable vehicle, you'll be able to sit back and enjoy the freedom it brings without have the disillusioned feeling that you've been taken for a ride. Looking up at life from a seated position has its drawbacks and a wheelchair has its weaknesses, but as an alternative to immobility it's a small miracle.

Hints for Helpers

No matter how independent a wheelchair user is, inevitably there are situations where a helper is needed. These may be merely casual and momentary, or one or more people may be required to assist you regularly.

To help effectively, a helper who will give more than casual assistance needs help and guidance from you. You should explain the structure and mechanism of your wheelchair, the position and arrangement of wheels and brakes, the kind of armrests and footrests it has, whether they are movable, removable, retractable or fixed, and how everything works.

The person who helps should know your capabilities and your limitations and to what extent you can manage—and indeed prefer to manage—unaided. He or she should be told what you like to do by yourself and in your own time and that you appreciate being helped only where and when you ask for it.

A regular helper should be told gently, but firmly, that you may suffer discomfort, or even pain, if your wheelchair is handled awkwardly or, perhaps, that you lack sensation in arms or legs requiring positioning them safely to avoid an injury of which you would be unaware. Tell the helper that pushing the wheelchair too fast can be very unsettling, too slow quite boring; establish the speed that you prefer. Your pusher should be told, too, that clothing and blankets must be tucked in out of the way of the wheels, that a wheelchair is not a baby carriage and should not be rocked, that you want to be warned before the chair is pulled or turned around quickly. In fact, you will want the helper always to tell you what the next move is to be, to watch carefully for holes and uneven ground or roughly paved surfaces and to avoid pushing you suddenly into street traffic.

The helper should understand that, with both of you facing in the same direction, it may be difficult to hear each other over traffic noise, that you feel rudely excluded if a conversation with others is carried on outside your vision and that you have a different view and cannot always see what the helper may be pointing to.

There are of course right ways and wrong ways to handle a wheelchair. This check list of dos and don'ts will give some valuable tips to helpers.

Folding a Wheelchair

■ To fold most wheelchairs, remove the seat cushion first and, standing next to the chair, pull upward on the seat fabric at the center front and back.

■ Don't lift the chair by the armrests—they'll probably come right out in your hands.

Opening a Wheelchair

■ Keep fingers turned toward the middle of the seat and press with the heels of the hand on the two sides of the seat.

■ Don't put fingers between the chair frame and the seat—they'll be crushed.

Putting a Wheelchair Into a Car Trunk

■ Position the folded wheelchair close to and parallel with the trunk.

■ Don't bend your back—keep it straight and bend knees and hips.

■ Grasp struts of chair, not the wheels, armrests or movable parts. Keep one hand well forward, the other well back.

■ Lift the chair vertically by straightening your legs. Balance the chair on the edge of the trunk.

■ With the full weight being taken by the wheels resting on the trunk edge, tip the chair up. When it is almost horizontal, slide it into the trunk.

Pushing a Wheelchair Down a Curb

■ Place your foot on the tipping lever. Take firm hold of the handgrips, then tip the chair backward.

■ Gently lower the chair down the curb. You must now take some of the weight, so be sure to arch your back and bend your knees.

■ It is very important that both rear wheels hit the ground at the same time.

■ Another method is to turn the back of the chair toward the curb and lower the back wheels to ground level, then lower the front wheels.

Pushing a Wheelchair Up a Curb

■ Place foot on tipping lever and lift the chair off its front wheels, moving them forward onto the curb. Gauge the distance to the curb carefully; avoid forcing the front wheels against any ridge or unevenness.

■ A second person can help to lift the chair by grasping one handle of the wheelchair and the bar below the armrest. Movements should be made together on an agreed signal.

■ Sometimes the wheelchair passenger can help to control the chair by steadying the rear wheels.

Carrying a Wheelchair Up Stairs

■ Although a very light disabled person, or a child, can be lifted by one helper, two helpers are usually required.

■ Position the wheelchair squarely at the foot of the stairs with its back toward the steps. Tip chair backward.

■ Take a firm grip, place one foot up on the first step, throw the same shoulder slightly backward and pull the chair up onto the first step.

■ A second helper stands in front to steady and lift the chair when it rises upward over the step, holding the chair frame below the armrests.

■ Repeat for the second step. Make sure you are solidly balanced, throw your weight back, pull up again.

Carrying a Wheelchair Down Stairs

■ Don't try to take a wheelchair down a flight of stairs unless you are absolutely sure you can hold the weight of the person in it and maintain full control.

■ Grasp handgrips, slowly move the chair forward, control the forward and downward movement against the step's edge. Use your body as a brake at the top of the step. Don't wait until the chair drops to do so.

■ Stop for a rest between steps.

■ Use another helper, perhaps a passer-by, whenever available. The second helper stands below in front, holds the chair frame under the armrests, slowing and steadying the descent.

Communication

Our need to communicate with one another is a basic human instinct, as important to our survival as our need for food and shelter. But for many people with motor and sensory impairments the ability to communicate is limited. As a result, they are isolated, unable to express ideas, thoughts and feelings, unable to impart and receive information or distress signals, cut off from the normal sources of intellectual stimulation.

There are, however, many aids which can help the individual to break through communication barriers. They range from a simple rubber thimble which facilitates page turning to sophisticated electronic devices that permit breath-controlled typing.

Such aids are the tools that can make it possible to speak, write, read, hear, control the environment and function in safety. But, equally important, they can help many people with physical disabilities to expand their horizons, to participate in society and achieve successful independent living.

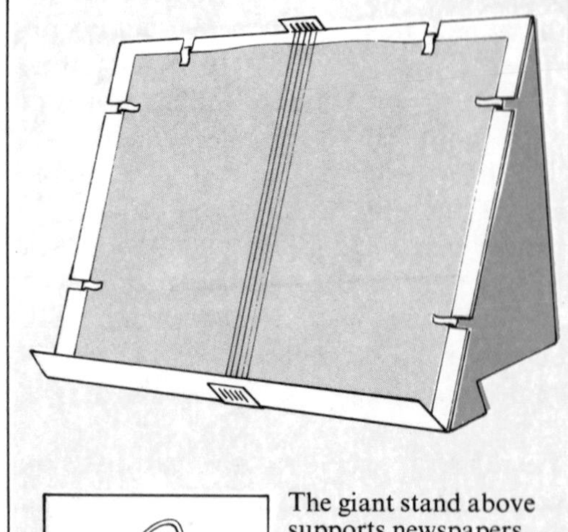

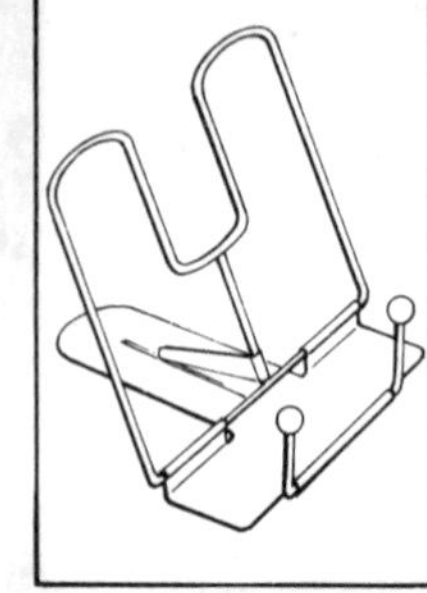

The giant stand above supports newspapers, magazines and oversize books. It fits on table edges or table top, has rods to separate sections of the reading material and plastic clips to hold the pages in place. The steel bookstand left adjusts in angle and folds flat when not in use.

Reading Aids

Books, newspapers and periodicals expand communication with the world of the past, of the present and even of the future. Fortunately, a variety of aids are available to hold reading matter, to turn pages and to bring written material to people who are blind, whose vision is impaired or who cannot read because of physical disabilities.

A book stand is not only useful when it is difficult or inadvisable to hold a book, but when vision is limited it may also help to position a book at a more convenient height or angle. A book stand should be sturdy and there must be sufficient adjustment to bring the book to the best position. When choosing a book stand the size of the material likely to be read must be taken into consideration. Some stands are unstable when they are used for heavier books. A larger stand is necessary for holding periodicals. A book stand which is used on a table can be made at home or purchased. An inexpensive model, which adjusts in angle and folds flat, for storage or for moving from place to place, is available from stationery stores and mail order companies.

A book stand which stands on the floor, much like a music stand, is useful for reading when seated in a chair. A model which is adjustable in height, so that it can be used with any chair, and has a top that tilts, may be extremely helpful.

A cantilever table can usually be tilted to act as a book stand. Some models are designed so that only part of the surface tilts, thus eliminating the need to remove everything from the table when you want to read.

People with weak or unsteady hands who have difficulty turning the pages of a book often find that an eraser-tipped pencil, a rubber thimble or two thimbles on adjacent figures solve the problem by creating more traction. Sometimes, when the fingers cannot be used but there is good control of the arm, pages can be turned with the side of the hand or the

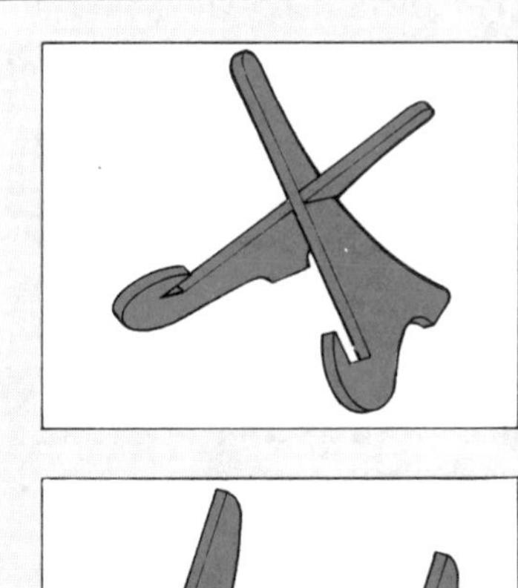
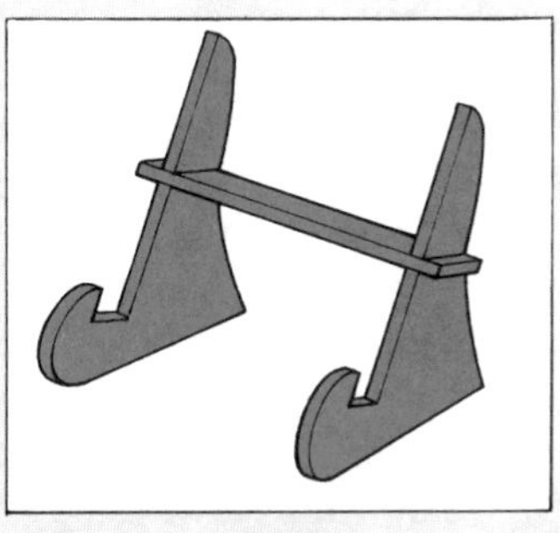
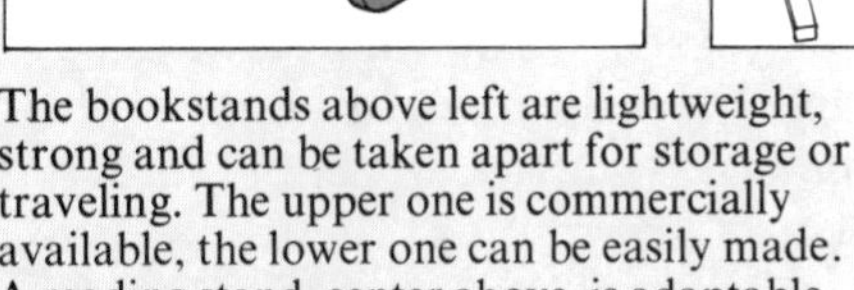
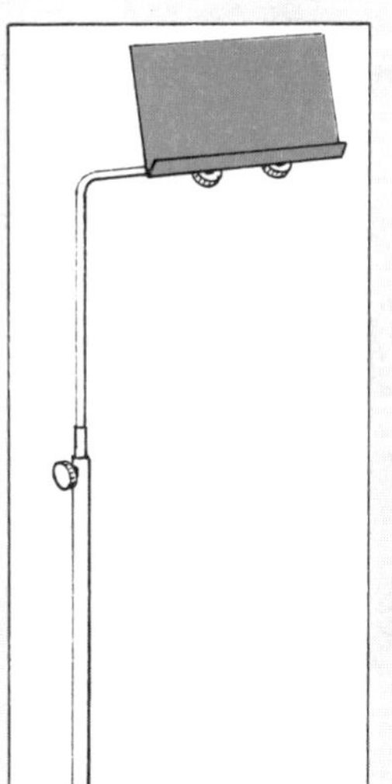
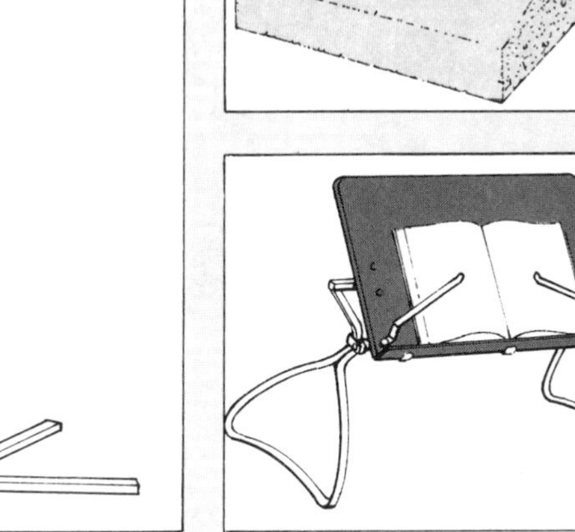

The bookstands above left are lightweight, strong and can be taken apart for storage or traveling. The upper one is commercially available, the lower one can be easily made. A reading stand, center above, is adaptable for use in a reclining, a sitting or a standing position. A plastic foam cushion, upper right, covered with an anti-slip fabric, makes a light support for a book held on the lap. The stand above is designed for reading in bed.

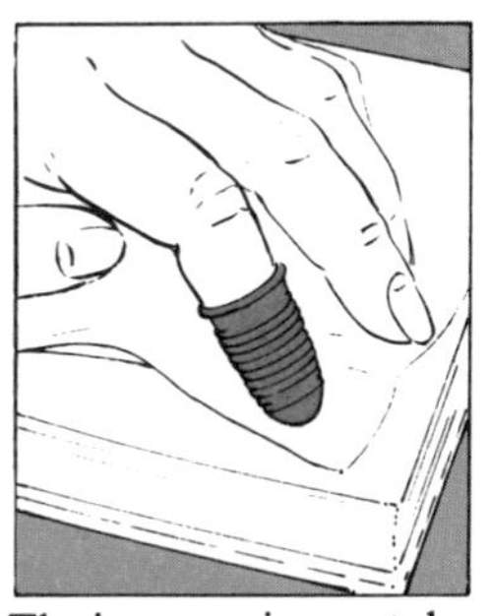

The inexpensive metal bookmark top above holds the pages of a book flat, but permits them to be turned with one hand. Two bookmarks can be used to keep the pages on both sides of the book flat when reading at an angle. A rubber thimble, above, creates friction and often makes it easier to turn pages.

elbow if a book or magazine is lying flat.

In some cases, it is possible to use a mouthstick to turn pages or to have a page turner attached to a headband. Such devices must be fitted by a doctor or a therapist with the help of a dental technician for the mouthstick.

Fairly elaborate, electric-powered page turners, which can be operated with a twitch of a toe, a nudge of an elbow or a gentle puff of breath, are available from hospital supply companies.

Prismatic glasses, which work rather like a periscope, make it possible to see things at right angles to the eyes when lying down. Such glasses often help to reduce eyestrain, too, when neck motion is limited. Prismatic glasses have no power of their own and may be worn over eyeglasses or can be made up with the suitable optical correction.

A magnifying glass can be helpful for reading small print, but should never be used extensively without medical consultation.

When you read or do close work, proper lighting is of great importance. The illumination should be of adequate intensity and located so that it falls properly and enough light is shed on the book or work surface. A reading lamp should adjust easily and have on-off controls within reach. If you use a small, high-intensity lamp, avoid eyestrain from sharp contrast in lighting by using additional general lighting in the room.

Large print editions of many books and some magazines are available in bookstores and in most public libraries in the United States and in the United Kingdom.

In the United States public libraries in many cities have microfilm projectors and films of books for loan free of charge. The machine projects pages of books on the ceiling or the wall so that it is possible to read while lying in bed. The units are produced by Projected Books, Inc., a nonprofit organization which will supply, on request, information and a catalog of titles. In the United Kingdom the National Fund for Research into Crippling Diseases sells, or hires out, a microfilm projector for filmed books which is controlled by a pneumatic switch and can be used from a bed or a chair.

In the United States the Library of Congress, Division for the Blind and

The portable, battery-operated, automatic page turner right holds books and magazines up to two inches (5 cm) thick and adjusts to any angle. The page turner below operates on electricity and accepts books of any size. Both of these page turners have sensitive switches and can be activated with hand, foot or chin. They are available from self-help equipment firms.

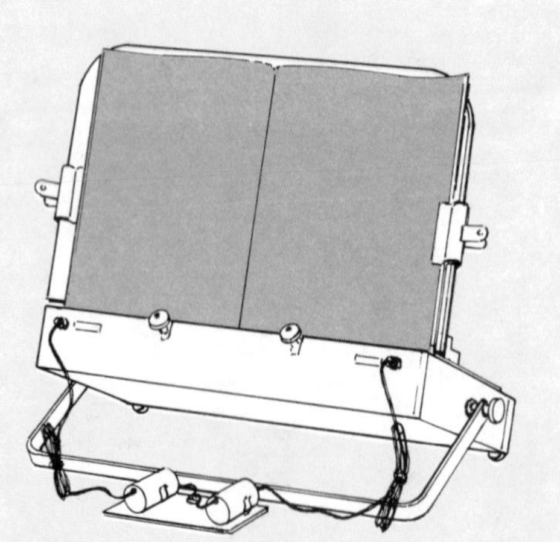

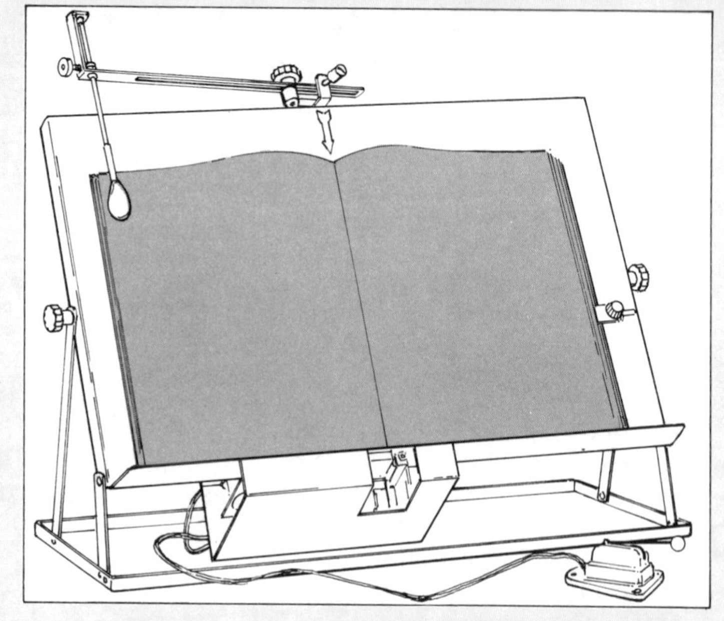

This magnifying glass doesn't have to be held. It may be placed over the reading matter and just pushed along. It folds for carrying.

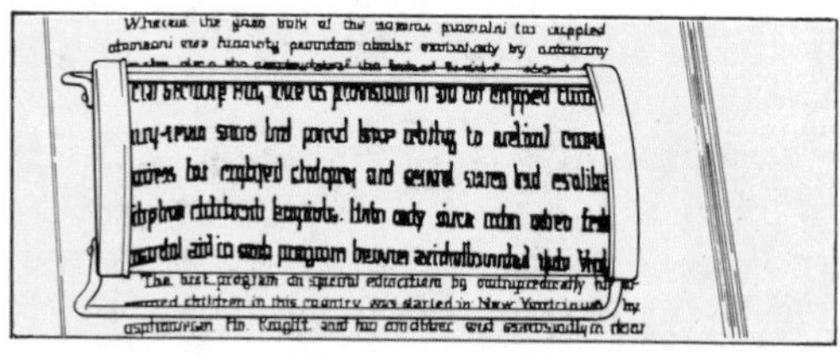

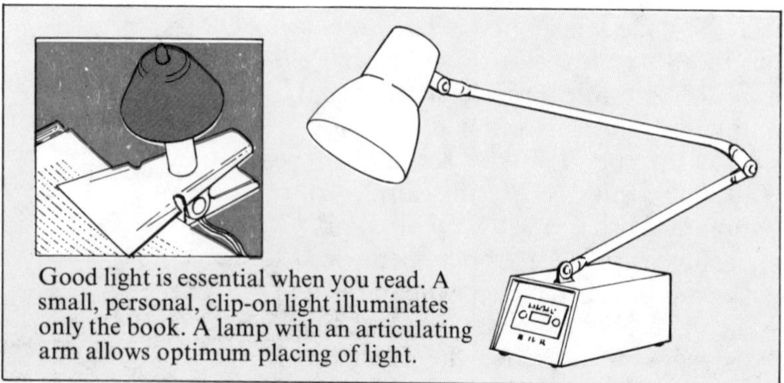

Good light is essential when you read. A small, personal, clip-on light illuminates only the book. A lamp with an articulating arm allows optimum placing of light.

Physically Handicapped, will send information on reading aids and the availability of recorded Talking Books to people who find it difficult, or impossible, to read because of visual limitations or inability to manage books physically. The books are sent by mail, postage free. A phonograph or tape recorder will be lent, free of charge, to anyone who does not have one, with special attachments if necessary. People who apply for this service also receive a free subscription to *Talking Book Topics*, a bimonthly magazine which lists newly available books.

Choice Magazine Listening is an American magazine on records for English-speaking people who are blind or who are unable to read normal type because of visual or physical handicap. Each "issue" is an audio anthology, on 8-rpm records, of eight hours of the best unabridged articles, fiction and poetry selected from more than fifty current periodicals including *The New Yorker*, *Harper's*, *Fortune*, the *Wall Street Journal*, *Esquire*, *Sports Illustrated*, the *Smithsonian* and BBC's *The Listener*. Published every two months, it is available free of charge as a project of Lucerna Fund, a nonprofit organization. A limited number of complete copies recorded at $16\frac{2}{3}$ rpm are available without charge for handicapped readers outside the United States. All subscribers are required to furnish certification of handicap, such as a letter from a doctor, social worker or agency.

In the United Kingdom, as well as the Talking Book Service for the Blind, there are various organizations which produce taped books on cassettes for people who are temporarily blind, partially sighted or who cannot physically manage books. An annual subscription is usually charged for the use of the tapes. The machine for playing the tapes can be hired, but the Social Services Department of the local authority may provide part or all of the cost.

The National Listening Library, headquartered in London, provides taped books on cassettes for playing back on a machine which is designed so that a large proportion of people with disabilities can operate it without difficulty.

Writing Aids

Always try to write at a desk or table which is the correct height for you to sit comfortably. The chair should be close enough to the table to permit the forearm to be fully supported. As the page is filled up it should be moved farther onto the table, instead of the forearm being moved toward the table edge.

It is easier to write on a large pad of paper than on loose sheets. There are, however, many ways to stabilize sheets of paper. A clipboard will hold the paper firmly, but the spring of the clip needs strong pressure to open it and help may be needed to insert the paper. A piece of metal sheet can be used as a writing board on which the paper can be held in place by small magnets. A paperweight can also be used to hold a sheet of paper down.

A magnetic ruler makes it easier to draw lines when only one hand is functional. A rubber strip on a ruler will keep it from sliding or a yardstick with weights placed on each end can be used instead of a ruler.

Felt tip pens need less pressure than ballpoint pens and soft lead pencils are preferable to those with hard lead. Giant pencils and ballpoint pens may be easier to grasp than implements of conventional size. Any pen or pencil can be made easier to grasp by increasing its diameter. This can be done by wrapping a piece of rubber or plastic foam around the shaft and securing it with tape.

A larger handgrip can be made by inserting the pen or pencil through a foam rubber ball, a block of plastic foam or a golf practice ball. The shaft of a pen or pencil can be made less slippery by twisting a rubber band around it or by glueing a piece of pimple rubber to it.

If finger muscles are weak, a wide, flat rubber band can be knotted around a pen or pencil in such a way as to provide loops for thumb and index fingers, thus reducing the need to grasp. Another method is to make a strap, with Velcro at the ends, which wraps around the fingers to stabilize the pen or pencil. Be sure the strap has sufficient overlap

A light, easily made, wedge-shaped writing board is a convenient aid for writing in bed. Much more elaborate, the aid right can be used for reading as well as for writing in a supine position. The vertical support bar clamps to the headboard, the swinging, overhead fixture rotates to any desired position and the easel adjusts to a wide range of angles.

For writing or drawing in bed, a simple, easel-type bed table can be made of plywood with wood or aluminum supports.

A magnetic writing board can be made from a piece of stainless-steel sheet backed with pimple rubber.

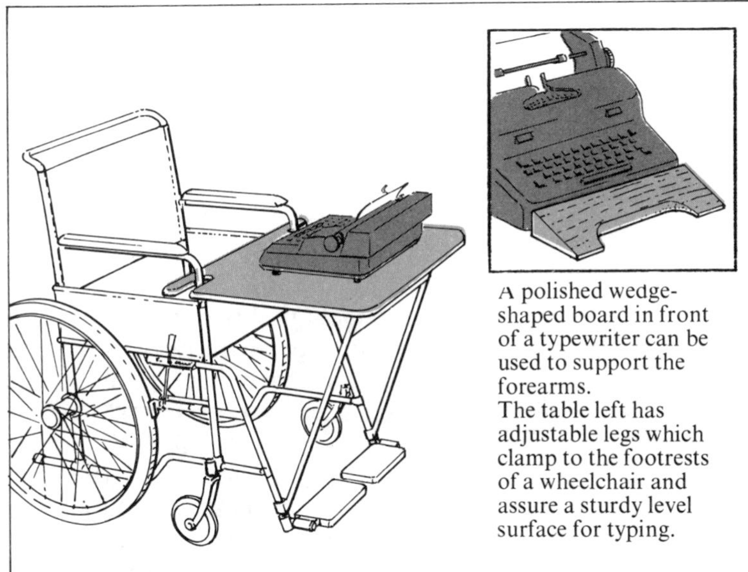

A polished wedge-shaped board in front of a typewriter can be used to support the forearms.
The table left has adjustable legs which clamp to the footrests of a wheelchair and assure a sturdy level surface for typing.

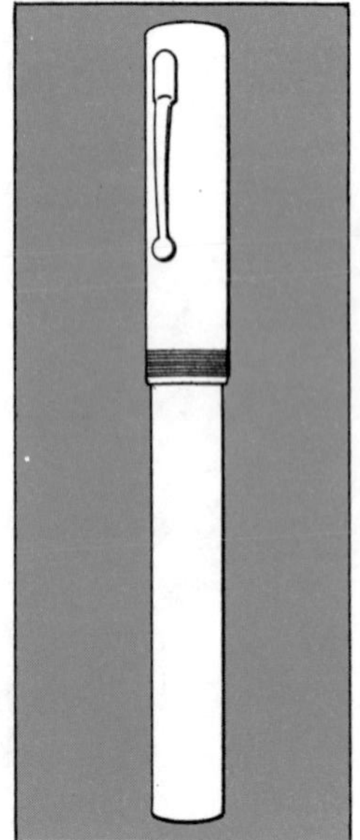
A ballpoint pen whose diameter is one and a half inches (3 cm) is easy to grasp and use.

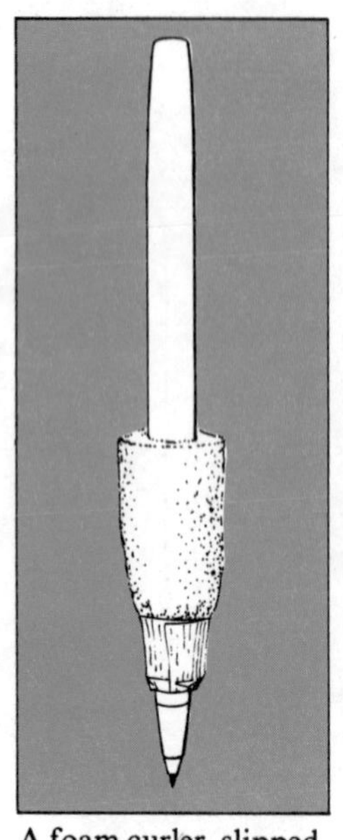
A foam curler, slipped over a pen or pencil and secured with tape, can improve grasp.

Push a pen or pencil through a practice golf ball to create a large grasping surface.

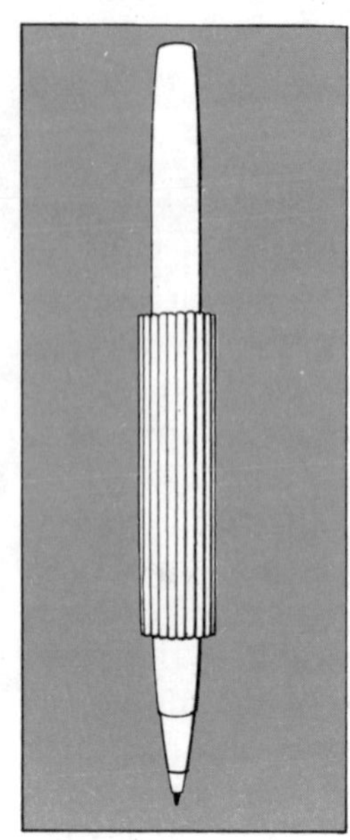
Corrugated rubber tubing slipped over a writing implement increases friction.

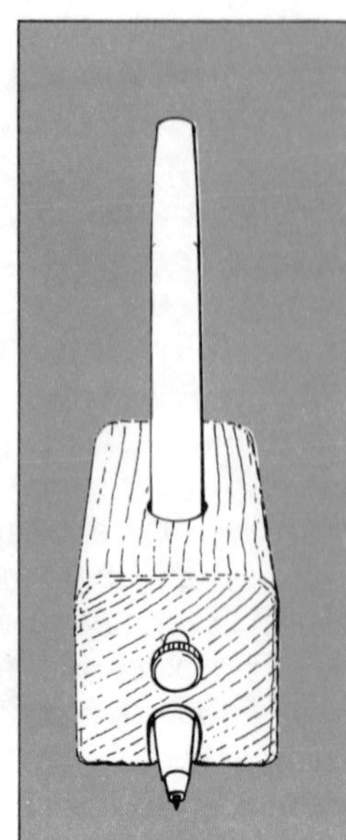
This writing aid is designed for people whose grasp is severely restricted.

Pencil Sharpeners

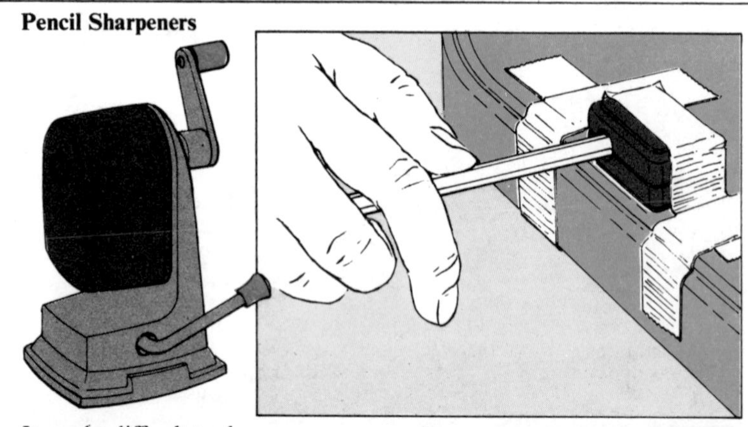

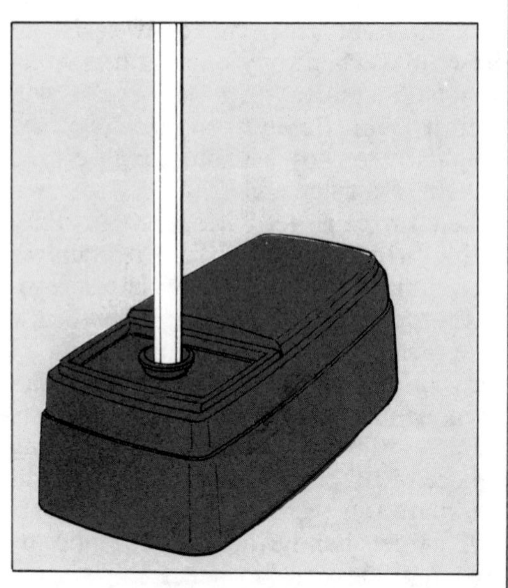

It can be difficult to sharpen a pencil with only one hand or with two weak hands. Various types of pencil sharpeners which are commercially available can make the job easier. The sharpener above left attaches firmly by suction to any nonporous surface. A battery-powered sharpener, right, works when a pencil is inserted and pressed lightly. When a small, twist-type sharpener is taped to a table edge, however, it can often be used with one hand.

to tighten it around two, three or four fingers, whichever feels most comfortable.

Some people find they are able to use a typewriter when writing with pen or pencil proves too difficult. An electric typewriter requires less physical exertion to operate than a manual typewriter and it types evenly however uneven the pressure on the keys. A motorized carriage eliminates the need to reach at the end of every line. It is possible to operate an electric typewriter using a stick attached to a mouthpiece, but it is important that the mouthpiece be made in consultation with a dentist. A typewriter can also be operated with the big toes, using a footboard to support the feet.

Line spacers, available in various models from office suppliers, hold copy at the same level for easier reading while typing. Also available from office suppliers are typewriter ribbons which allow corrections to be made without the use of erasers. If you make a mistake you only need to switch to the white half of the ribbon and type over the error, then backspace and retype the correct letters. A keyboard guard can be fitted to some typewriters to prevent hitting two keys at the same time.

It is not difficult to learn to type with one hand. *Type With One Hand*, a book published by South-Western Publishing Company, provides a keyboard approach which aids rapid learning and has separate sections for left and right hands.

For typing when lying in bed a great aid is a wedge-shaped stand which fits onto a bed table, tilts the typewriter forward and holds it in position for easy viewing.

When writing or typing is difficult or impossible, a tape recorder can be a valuable aid. It can be used to take notes and to study and many people find it just as satisfying to correspond by cassette as by letter.

It is usually easier to change a cassette than a reel of tape and this should be considered when selecting a machine. Of course, a long-playing machine requires a minimum of handling; some tape recorders record on four tracks, requiring only a push of a button to start a new track.

Telephoning Aids

In modern society the telephone is undoubtedly one of the most vital tools of communication. A telephone is essential for those who live alone and have to rely on it in emergencies as well as for social contact. For many people, too, the telephone may be the means of carrying on a business and earning a livelihood.

There are, however, disabling conditions which make it difficult, or impossible, to use a standard telephone. To compensate for many of these limitations a variety of aids have been developed. Advances in telephone design for general use have also proved applicable to the needs of some people who are disabled.

For someone who is unable to hold a handset for any length of time, a lightweight headset can be helpful. It plugs into a socket associated with a modified telephone which has press buttons to switch the headset on and off. Also available are units which allow you to speak directly into a microphone without holding a handset. A loudspeaker transmits the incoming call. The telephone itself is dialed as usual and the circuit is connected by a switch key. There are, too, various types of telephone arms which clamp to a desk or table top and hold the handset in a comfortable position leaving the hands free.

A telephone should be positioned for the most efficient and comfortable use, particularly when reach is limited. When the cord is not long enough to use the phone in a convenient place, the telephone company will install an extra long cord.

Many disabling conditions can make dialing a telephone difficult, if not impossible, without special equipment. For some people a simple dialing aid,

There is a great range of telephone equipment available to meet the needs of people with various disabilities. A lightweight headset, above, which plugs into a modified telephone, or the unit below which houses loudspeaker and microphone, are useful when it's difficult to hold a handset. An extra earpiece, left, permits a person with hearing loss to listen to incoming speech with both ears, thus reducing interference from other noises.

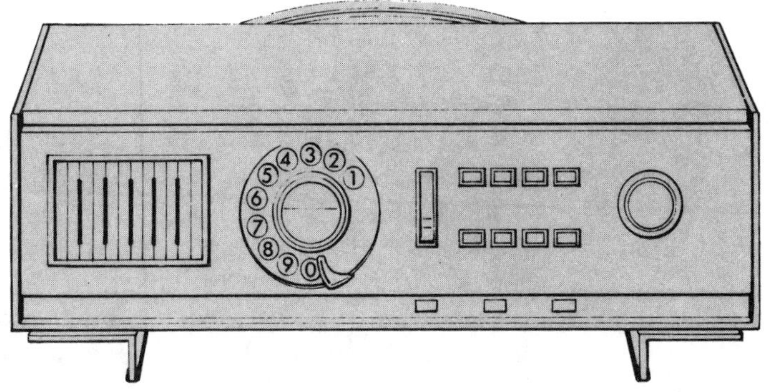

More strength is required to operate the buttons on the Touch-Tone phone left than to turn a dial, but some people find the pushing movement easier. It is more convenient to dial, particularly when confined to bed, if the dial is in the bottom of the telephone or is located within the handset.

A Card Dialer telephone eliminates the seven or more movements of the rotary dial, since dialing consists only of placing a card in the slot, pushing it down and pressing a bar.

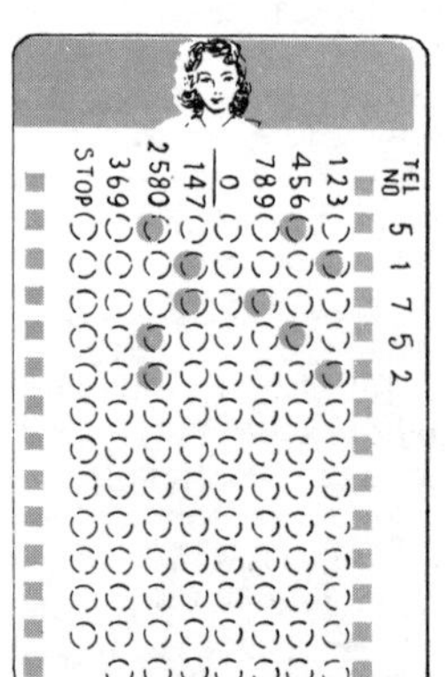
The cards of a Card Dialer telephone are themselves a directory which is easy to read. When names cannot be recognized, photos may be used for identifying the cards.

such as a pencil, can solve the problem, while for others more elaborate arrangements are necessary.

For someone who cannot use a telephone dial there is a device which, by pressing a button, connects the caller direct to the operator. Push button telephones, which are easier to operate than standard dials, are now available in most areas.

A Callmaker completely eliminates the need to dial, for it calls automatically at the press of a button or the insertion of a card into a slot. It can be pre-programmed with the telephone numbers the user calls most frequently, as well as emergency numbers. Calls can then be originated as often as required.

Callmakers are also helpful for people whose vision is impaired. For someone who is blind, braille markings can be used to help him or her locate easily the name of the person to be called. A blind person can rapidly locate the correct finger holes required to dial a number, from a pattern of finger positions. Instructions for dialing in this way are available from organizations for the blind.

For someone with a weak voice a faint-speech amplifier reduces the strain of trying to communicate effectively over the telephone. The unit amplifies outgoing speech to a normal level and can be switched on and off as required.

For people with hearing loss, a handset which contains a transistorized amplifier is available to replace the standard handset. By turning the volume control the sound in the earpiece can be increased from normal to the level which suits the user. Portable amplifiers for telephones are also commercially available. It's always best to try such a unit before buying one to be sure the amplification is right for you.

An extra earpiece enables a person to listen to an incoming call with both ears and so reduce interference from other noises. The earpiece can also be held

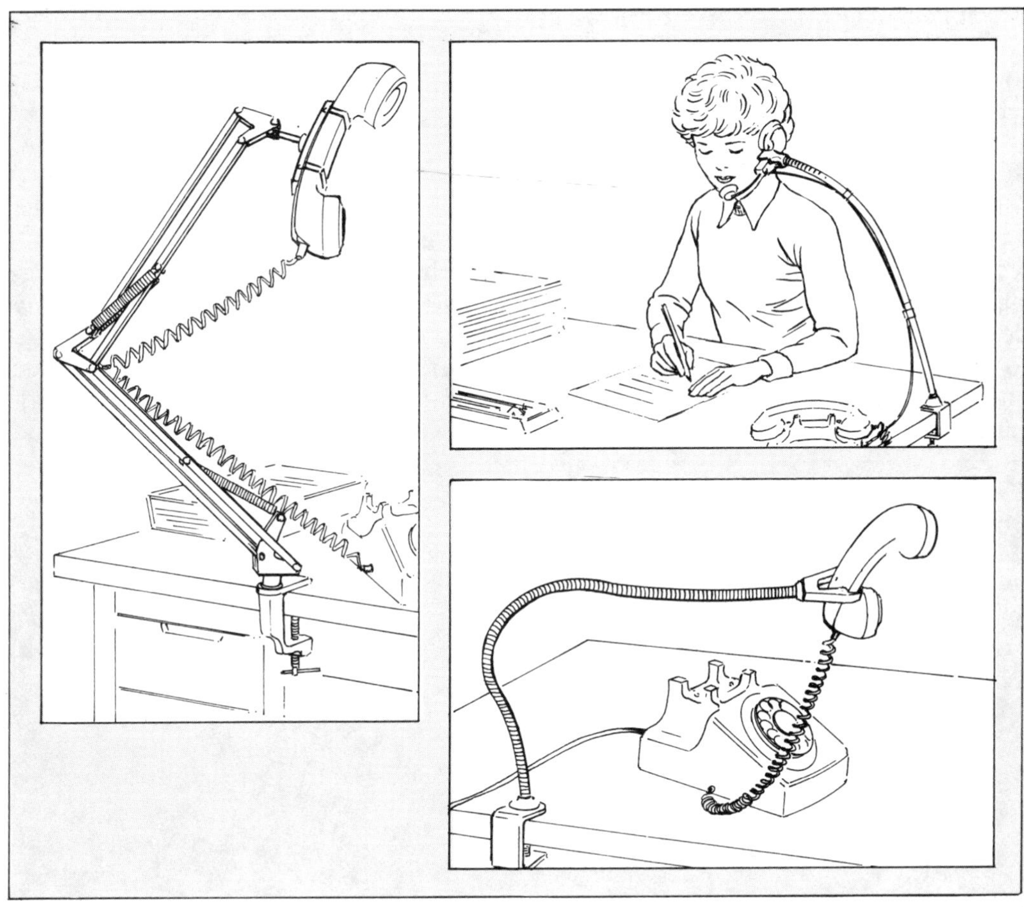

Holding the Handset
A stable device which holds the handset is a valuable aid for a person who cannot pick up the telephone, hold the receiver for any length of time or must use one good hand to take notes. Various telephone arms which clamp to a surface and hold the handset at a convenient angle are widely available.

against the microphone of certain types of hearing aid. The user listens through his or her hearing-aid earpiece while speaking into the handset transmitter in the usual manner. The extra earpiece can also be used to enable a person with normal hearing to listen to the incoming call and translate it so that it can be understood by sign or lip-reading.

If a person has difficulty in hearing the bell in the telephone an extension bell can be provided. The frequencies and tones people can hear vary widely. Therefore, a selection can be made from a range of bells of different frequencies and degrees of loudness.

Several different arrangements of lamp-signaling can be provided in addition to a bell. Part of the handset, or separate from the telephone, they can be adjusted to flash with the ringing tone or to light continuously until switched off or the call is answered. (A light signal can also be used in conjunction with the doorbell. Portable light signals are available that work on electricity and flash when the doorbell is pushed.)

The teletypewriter (TTY), a telephone for deaf people, permits typed messages to be transmitted through regular telephone services. It is now possible to attach an electronic typewriter keyboard, a teletypewriter, to any standard telephone, enabling two people with TTYs to type messages back and forth. The equipment ranges from large units, which utilize teletype keyboards and provide printed paper copies of the messages, to small portable units with typewriter keyboards, which elicit electronic displays of the letters on small screens. Only minimal typing skills are needed for basic TTY communication.

Teletypewriters have been used for many years by news services and telegraph offices to send printed information quickly between remote locations. It was not until 1965, however, when Robert Weitbrecht, a deaf American physicist,

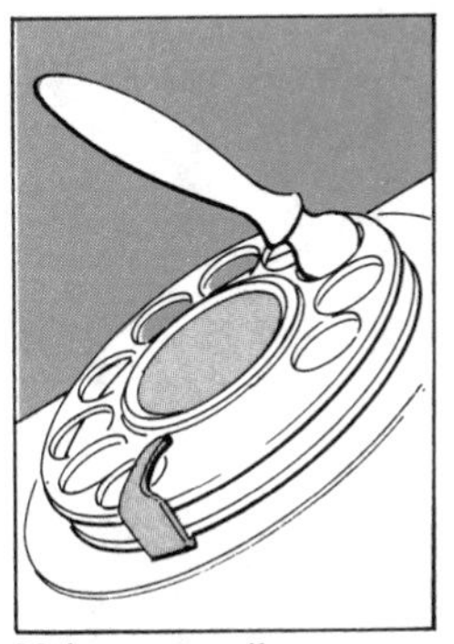

Using a pencil or a telephone dialing tool reduces stress on the finger joints. Dialing tools are available from department stores and can be built up to accommodate weak grasp.

developed an electronic device known as an acoustic coupler, that it was possible to connect teletypewriters to standard telephones.

Teletypewriters for the Deaf, Inc. (TDI), a nonprofit corporation, was formed in 1968 in the United States to acquire and recondition teletypewriters which large companies discarded as surplus and then to sell them at cost to deaf people. Today TTYs are beginning to open an extraordinary range of social and vocational opportunities for thousands of deaf people.

Speaking Aids

For people who are unable to speak, visual aids may assist in communication. Obviously, the advice and guidance of a speech therapist should be sought when there are speech difficulties.

Writing everything down can sometimes be a solution, but it is slow and only effective when communicating with one or perhaps two other people. For basic communication a spelling board, with letters of the alphabet, numerals and

The MCM Communications System is a mobile telecommunications device for people who are deaf or hearing impaired. Compatible with all TTY equipment, the MCM has a thirty-two character read-out of both sides of the conversation and a monitor lamp that indicates the status of the call—dial tone, telephone ringing, line or circuit busv.

Designed for people who are deaf or hearing impaired, and compatible with TTY equipment, the TVphone is a portable unit which has a standard typewriter-style keyboard. With the TVphone connected to the antenna of any household television set, telephone communication is provided by reading the typed conversation on the television screen.

some common words, or a picture chart, made from pictures cut from magazines, can be used with a pointer. A lightwriter, which is expensive and sophisticated, may, in some cases, be very helpful. It is a kind of typewriter, which weighs five and a half pounds (2.5 kg) and is battery operated. The lightwriter produces a luminous line of capital letters on a board which faces away from the typist so that it can be read by several people at the same time. As new letters are typed they displace the previous ones. When the typist wants to join in the conversation, he or she presses a buzzer and begins typing.

Blissymbols is a concise and logical communication system for children and adults who cannot speak as the result of various disabling conditions. A symbol language, Blissymbols was devised by Charles Bliss who, inspired by the picto-idiographic writing of China, used only one hundred basic symbols related in meaning rather than sound, and combined them to make thousands of meanings. Blissymbols can be adapted to suit the needs of the individual. For someone who cannot point to the symbols on a board, for example, a remote control device can be used.

In Canada and in the United States, several thousand people are now either using or exploring Blissymbols. Interest has been increasing in Britain where Action Research for the Crippled Child has sponsored the establishment of the Blissymbolics Communication Centre in Cardiff.

Deaf people can and do speak. The terms "deaf-mute" and "deaf and dumb" are archaic and are considered offensive by many people who are deaf. Most deaf

Just as languages which are spoken differ in each country, so do the sign languages which are used by people who are deaf. The illustrations below show the signs for the word "mother" used in six different countries. The tint denotes the beginning of the movement.

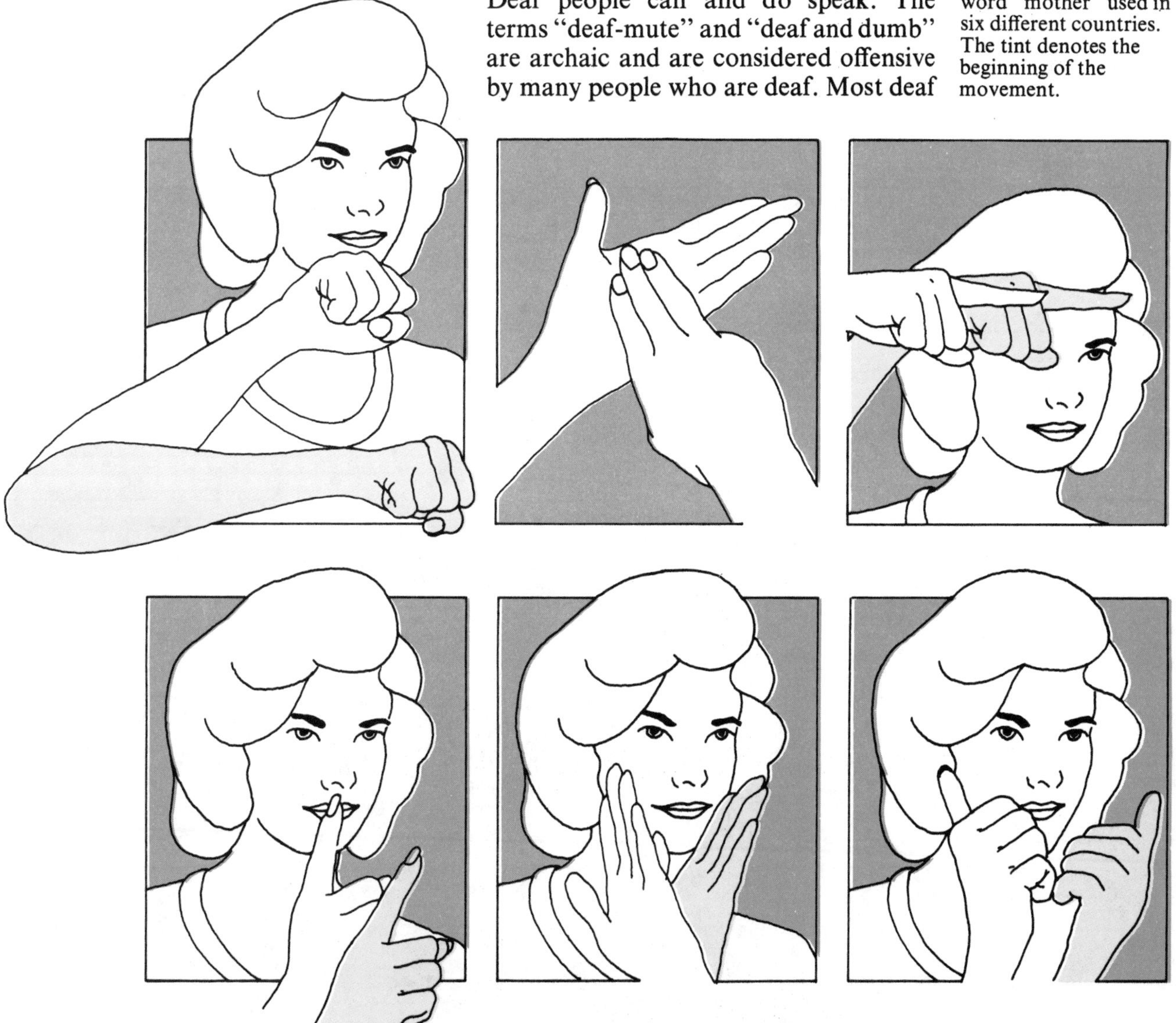

people have normal vocal chords but, because they are unable to hear their own voices, they cannot modulate them as hearing people can. Even after years of training they may still have speech that is initially difficult to understand.

The majority of deaf people use sign language as their preferred mode of social communication with other deaf people and with their hearing families and friends who have learned the language. In this visible language, movements of hands and arms take the place of spoken elements of language and the eyes, instead of the ears, receive the messages. These movements are gestures, developed beyond those used by people every day. They are symbols organized in a way that can be analyzed linguistically and combine in ways unique to the sign language. The individual gestures in the language are called signs.

Just as spoken languages differ from region to region and from country to country, so do sign languages. American Sign Language (Amsalan), therefore, has regional dialects and differs from the sign languages of other countries, including the United Kingdom, although in this case the spoken language is basically the same.

Fingerspelling refers to the system of using hand positions and configurations for the letters of the alphabet. Usually, fingerspelling is used in addition to signs. Fingerspelling is seldom used exclusively, but it is used when a proper name is mentioned for the first time in a conversation or for names of ideas or objects for which no signs exist. In the same way as there are different sign languages there are different manual alphabets. One hand is used for fingerspelling in the United States, while in the United Kingdom a two-handed manual alphabet is used. The World Federation of the Deaf has officially adopted the one-hand manual alphabet for use in its meetings.

One hand is used for fingerspelling in the United States. The illustrations right show how the handshapes look to the person speaking and how they look to the person who is reading them.

In the United Kingdom two hands are used for fingerspelling. It only takes a little time and a good memory for the American to learn British fingerspelling or for the Briton to learn the American manual alphabet.

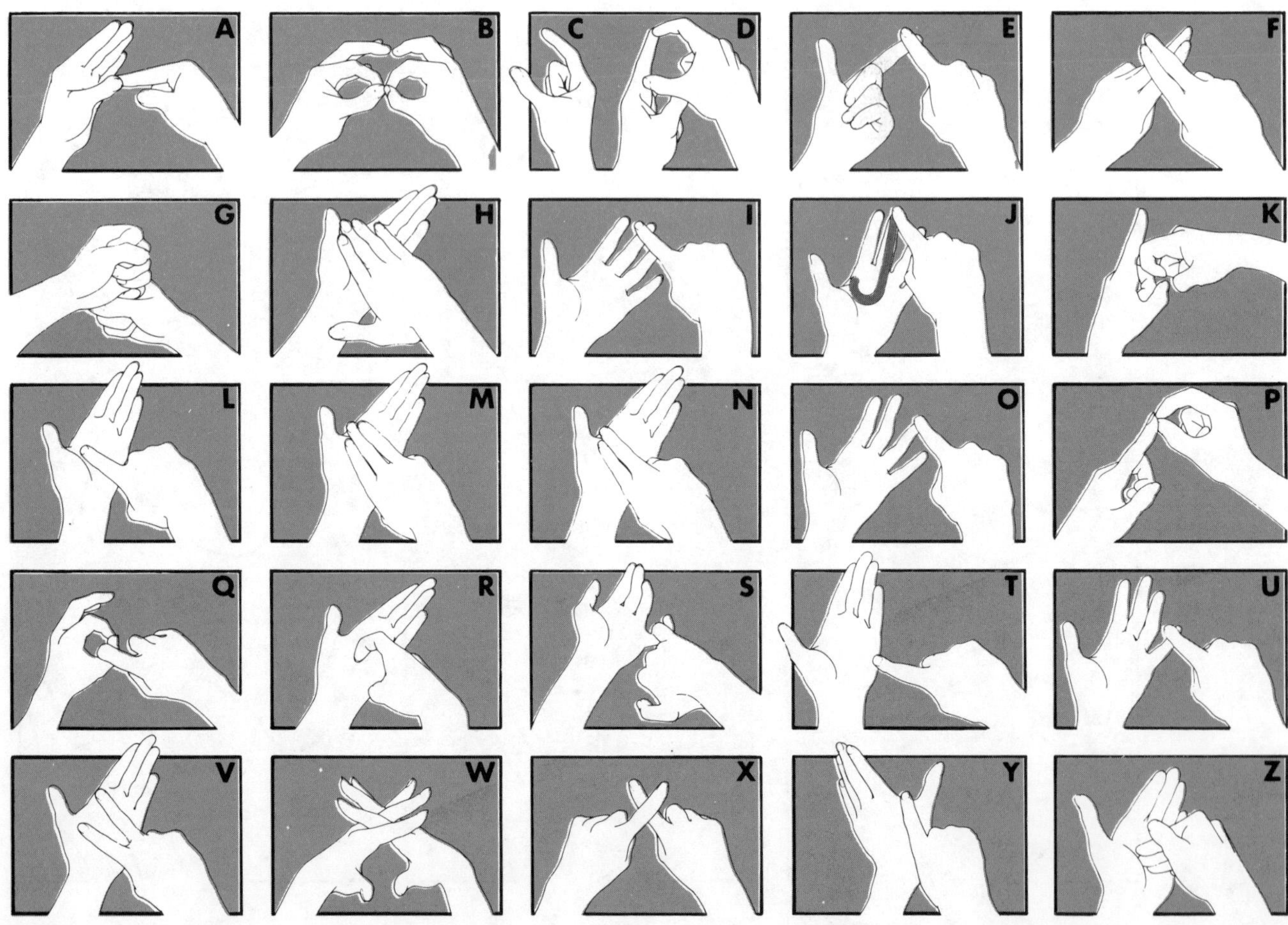

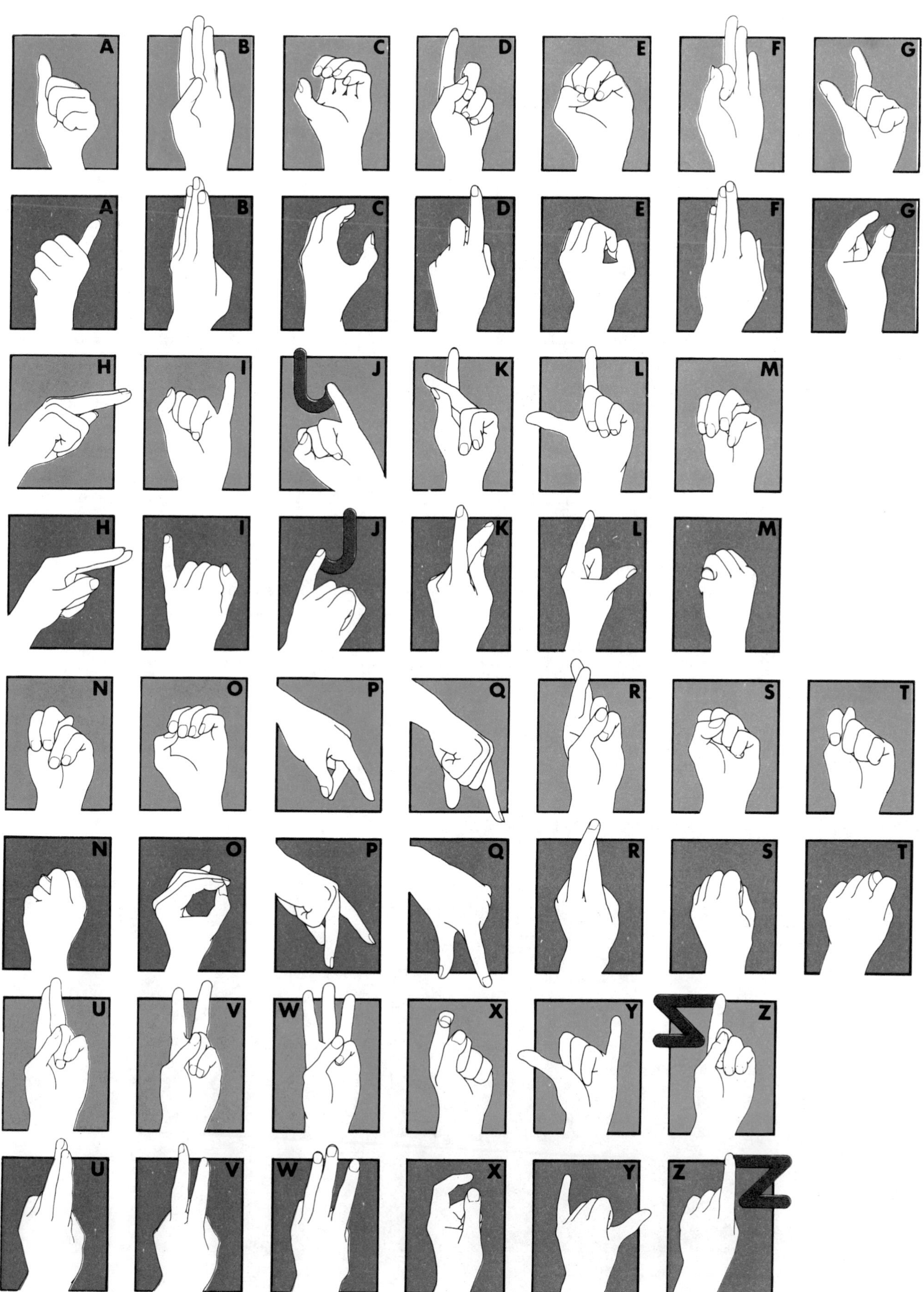
A B C D E F G
A B C D E F G
H I J K L M
H I J K L M
N O P Q R S T
N O P Q R S T
U V W X Y Z
U V W X Y Z

Electronic Aids

Much of the remote control equipment designed to increase the independence of severely disabled people is both sophisticated and expensive. Specialized help is necessary, too, to select the most suitable equipment and to adapt it to the requirements of the individual.

The Possum remote control system was developed in the United Kingdom and is now available in the United States. ("Possum" stands for Patient Operated Support System.) By either light pressure on a microswitch or simply by sucking on and blowing into a pneumatic tube, the person using the apparatus can operate and control up to eleven electrical devices. These include a tape recorder, a television set, a radio, an alarm system, a door-entry mechanism with intercom, a device for opening and closing the curtains, answering and dialing the telephone and controlling heating and lighting. A typewriter operated by this system has a capacity of up to one hundred words a minute.

A Possum remote control system is expensive. In the United Kingdom it can, in some cases, be obtained through the National Health Service, but only after careful assessment. The Possum Users Association in Bristol, England, assists users of Possum equipment and publishes a magazine, *Possability*.

There are several other systems available which utilize different methods of remote control. One system uses a light, which can be hand held or attached to a foot or to a specially designed headband. The light beam is shone onto a control panel and by minimal movement of hand, foot or head, can be moved along it onto a typewriter keyboard or a control panel. With another system, a microswitch or a sensor is activated by the tiniest muscular movement. A control panel lights up in sequence. When it reaches the required function the switch is activated to stop the light.

An important feature of the Possum system is the intercom and door lock which can be operated by remote control.

This Possum unit gives a person who is severely disabled control over the immediate environment and greater independence in the home. The system comprises an indicator panel, an electronic control unit and a sensitive microswitch or pneumatic switch. The switch operates the main unit which controls the electrical appliances. The Possum gives on and off control of appliances, such subsidiary switching functions as channel changes and volume control of television and radio, dialing control over a loud-speaking telephone and intercom links with key points in the house.

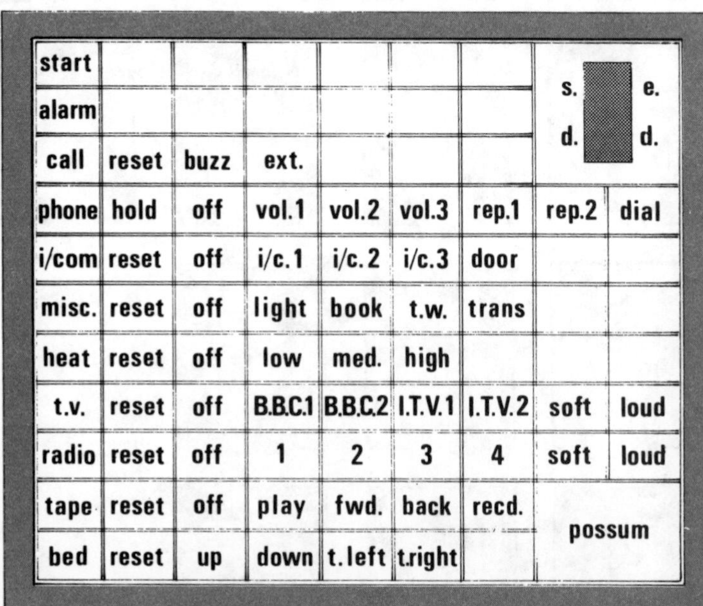

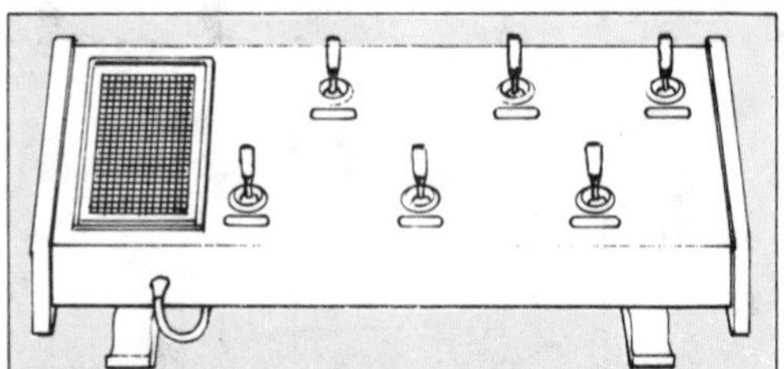

The Possum-Link consists of a switch panel, a distribution unit and a door lock intercom. It is operated by flicking one of six switches.

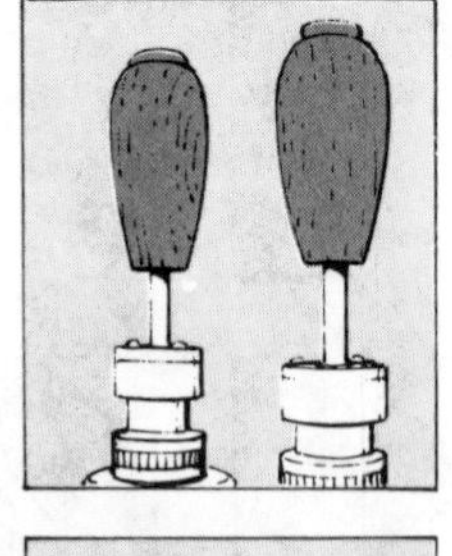

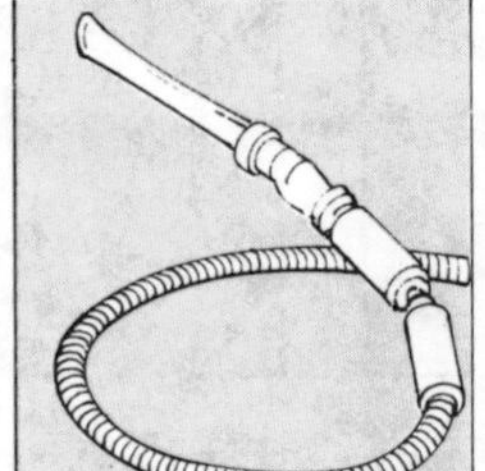

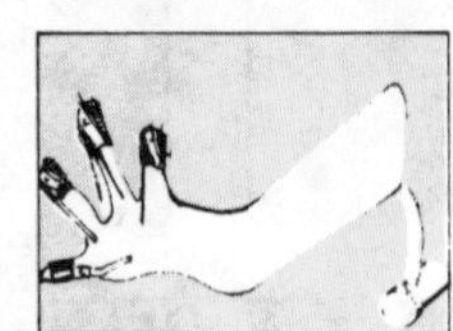

The Possum system can be operated by foot switches, pneumatic pressure and suction, by knocking wobblesticks or by microswitches mounted on a splint.

Far less complex is an inexpensive single microswitch, available from electronic firms, which can be operated by an almost imperceptible movement, such as expanding a cheek or twitching a toe. A microswitch can be attached to a single unit—a page turner, for example, or a television set—or hooked up to an electronic circuit system using coded taps to activate various devices.

Simpler still is a push-button remote control which enables you to turn appliances on and off without moving from your chair or bed. It plugs into an electric outlet and is then attached to the appliance. Small single controls are available from department stores and mail order companies.

For people with limited mobility, a two-way intercom system with a remote control device to open the front door can be useful. Some intercom systems work through the telephone, are installed by the local telephone company and charged on a monthly rate. In the United States, the Home Interphone, which consists of telephones with built-in microphones and loudspeakers combined with a door-answering unit, enables you to ascertain who is at the front door, to keep a remote eye on the children and to speak to other members of the family in far corners of the house, without moving. Two-way, hands-free conversation is made possible through a small sensitive microphone in the base of each telephone.

Alarm Systems

There are many alarm systems available, but none is ideal. Indeed, some are dangerous because they may not work in an emergency and therefore give a false sense of security. If you live alone the best alarm system is probably a good neighbor with whom an arrangement has been made for frequent and regular visits or phone calls.

Depression

People speak of being depressed, meaning that they feel low in spirit and perhaps, in energy. There are many realistic reasons for this kind of depression, which is usually of short duration. There is, too, the acute depression which may follow a bereavement or disablement. Depression can, however, also be an illness and can be medically treated as such.

Many of us have been brought up to consider it a sign of weakness to show that we are feeling low. Consequently, we tend always to fight this feeling. Our attitudes toward depression often come from early conditioning. No matter what is bothering us we're expected to keep smiling and be good sports—and we feel obliged to live up to these unrealistic standards. This makes it all the more difficult when we are involved in a traumatic situation—a situation in which we would probably be retreating into a dream world if we didn't feel some degree of depression.

Some societies recognize that illness and sorrow are as much a part of the fabric of living as happiness and good fortune. Our own society seems not to want to know. Tragedy is swept under the carpet, rather than acknowledged as a vital, common, human experience.

People with disabilities have to pay a heavy price for this attitude. They have to handle both their feelings of despair and their uneasy conviction that these emotions are somehow unnatural. If we consider the many realistic reasons to be depressed, someone with the added disadvantage of a disability need not struggle to remain immune—especially if that disability is progressive or subject to alternating remissions and relapses, or if it has struck overnight, transforming, at the tick of a clock, a free-moving individual into one who can't wiggle a toe. Even those born with physical infirmities have to learn to cope with their own limitations; the theory that a person doesn't miss what he or she doesn't know is nonsense. In such circumstances, it would be strange if someone didn't feel depressed from time to time.

Of course, a depression which goes on for any length of time and has no reasonable explanation ought not be regarded as an inevitable by-product of disablement. Depression can be symptomatic of any one of a number of ailments, or it can itself be a clinical condition. Consult your doctor if you suffer from prolonged depression.

Sudden disablement is almost always followed by devastating depression. As a result of an unexpected illness or an accident, your sound, familiar body has become incomplete and alien. Fate has stepped in to sever, mutilate or paralyze some part of you which you had always taken for granted. After the first sharp shock, suspension of belief sets in. This cannot be happening to you! But that state doesn't last for long; sooner or later you can no longer deny that from now on everything is going to be different. It is impossible to go on looking backward, remembering the safe, unimpaired past. It is equally impossible to look ahead—the future is unthinkable. The deep despair that follows has been compared to the pain of bereavement; nothing can make up for the loss. Everything is seen in the context of the missing person or, in the case of disability, the missing function.

That this state of mourning doesn't continue forever is a testament to the infinite adaptability and resilience of the human spirit. The change in outlook creeps up so gradually that you are hardly aware of it, but at a certain point you begin to understand that an upheaval in one area of your life has not necessarily affected all areas. You begin to realize that, despite what has happened to your body, you still retain your identity. Your mind—like your body—has assimilated and adjusted to your new circumstances. The depression has lifted. You are ready to face the future.

A more common state of depression, shared by able-bodied people, hits during certain periods when everything is going wrong. A job loss, family problems, a household crisis—any stress can trigger it off. For many people burdened with a handicap, an external setback combined with a chronic limitation saps the will to strive. But it's important to figure out whether the problems are the result of the disability or would have arisen in any case. It is all too tempting to take the easy way out and blame the disability, but that only confuses the issue at a time when every faculty must concentrate on tackling, not obscuring, the real problem.

Certain disabilities involve constant nagging pain. Discomfort, the erosion of strength and the struggle to keep going are depression-producing factors that can't be wished or willed away. They can, however, be recognized and allowed for. Fortitude, carried to extremes, does more harm than good, so don't be too hard on yourself. And don't bottle up your feelings. It might even be a revelation, as well as an education, to able-bodied friends and relatives to witness your justifiable anguish. Generally speaking, it is healthier to complain out loud than to resent suffering in silence.

A depression can sometimes be dissipated by action. Turn depression into useful aggression and fight the forces that you can control or affect—the man-made barriers, for example, that make daily life so difficult, or the social attitudes that spring from prejudice, lack of imagination or limited experience.

Common Sense

Not a subject that is taught in school, nor one that books are written about, common sense is, nevertheless, something which people with disabilities should try to develop to the full.

It takes common sense to know when to ask for help—and when to turn it down, when to say "Let me try" and when to say "I can't do it." It takes common sense to save your strength for important things—and to recognize the things that are important. It takes common sense to acknowledge your physical limitations—and to know when to discount them. It takes common sense to know when a failure is due to your disability—and when it's due to a failure in yourself.

Above all, it takes common sense to know when to suffer thoughtless remarks in silence ("How on earth do you bear it? I'd die if I couldn't walk . . .see . . . hear . . .speak.") and when to retaliate. And then there are the many times you have to deal kindly with somebody else's ideas of what's good for you. It seems to be a failing of some able-bodied people unthinkingly to equate impaired bodies with impaired judgement. Some of them are very quick to say, "I wouldn't try that if I were you." But they are not you and surely it's only common sense to point that out in a matter-of-fact and amiable way.

Fatigue

People with disabilities often tend to push themselves too hard. We often seem determined to prove that we can make it, whatever the impediments. This attitude is certainly better than giving up, but carried too far it becomes counter-productive—tiredness leads to loss of perspective.

Medical experts have a good idea of what can be expected of someone with a particular disability. Their advice on what you can expect to achieve without fatigue is based not only on your physical capacities, but also on your age and your general state of mental and physical health. But such estimates can't really take into account your life-style and the demands made upon you by others and by your own temperament. Nobody can calculate your threshold of fatigue better than you.

Some people are energetic by nature and others are easygoing. Some are overachievers, driven to prove themselves; others are content to let life take its course. Motivation is an important factor. When you're faced with an unrewarding task you're likely to tire quickly. When you're working toward a specific goal, whether it's learning to sit up by yourself or getting a college degree, fatigue lessens or becomes unimportant. Morale makes a huge difference, too. When the barometer is set for fair everything seems possible. But if your home life is beset by difficulties, you can't find suitable employment or there is a crisis in a personal relationship, just getting out of bed in the morning can be tiring.

People with disabilities go through most days like tightrope artists, keeping their balance between what they know is possible to achieve and what they can actually manage. One miscalculation and they slip, exhaustion sets in, defenses are down and everything seems too much.

Learn to conserve your strength by planning ahead and by pacing yourself. Don't overdo, and watch for the warning signs. Stop and rest before you get too tired and the joy has gone out of the day.

Medical Care

Physically disabled people are, more than any other group, at the mercy of the medical world. Most able-bodied people consult their doctors only at moments of crisis and the rest of the time are free to live their lives as they choose, ignoring or following medical advice as they see fit. That is also true of some people who are disabled, but for many others the doctor's office is a lifeline. Survival and the ability to function hang on professional decisions. In addition, disabling conditions usually require consultations with other members of the health-care team and people with disabilities are often processed from department to department, dependent on a variety of expert opinions.

All too often the quality of care and attention is related to financial means, geographic location, the particular disability and—occasionally—just plain luck. A throw of the dice could find a person in a shiny city complex, evaluated, exercised and advised by teams of experts. A turn of the wheel might find him or her waiting to be seen in a clinic where even the name of the disability, let alone the treatment, is open to question. This game of chance extends throughout the health-care system set up to serve us. It applies as well to the individuals who work within it.

Some of us may be fortunate enough to come across practitioners and personnel who hold no preconceived views on what disabled people can and cannot do. A few of us may be lucky enough to be in the care of one of that vanishing breed, the family doctor who knows the individual and does not judge the patient only on the basis of a disability. But many of us meet professionals who know nothing about us except the facts in our case histories. This should not stop them from seeing us as individuals, but it too often does. It's somehow easier to deal with a medical record than with a human being.

Able-bodied patients also suffer, of course, from this kind of professional myopia, but with any luck their situation is temporary. They don't have to surrender their autonomy for the rest of their lives. Sometimes, instead of being consulted as rational beings who happen to have physical limitations, people with disabilities may find themselves being treated like dependent children. This must not be permitted to happen, even if it means searching for a doctor with whom rapport is possible. who treats people with disabilities as thinking adults rather than as impaired people.

Yet another problem faces us. An entire discipline has developed to deal not only with our medical concerns, but with our psychological "balance," our "adjustment" and our "capabilities," but this sometimes has very little to do with our actual rehabilitation requirements or our personal goals.

It's all too easy to slip into the passive role assigned to us, to accept the assessments made about our "motivation" and our "adjustment capacities" and to leave decisions about our capabilities to those in charge. But in the long run we are the best judges of our own needs.

It takes determination to reassume responsibility for our physical selves. It takes courage to ask questions and to insist on getting answers. We, however, are the ones who have to live with our disabilities. This is an aspect of being disabled that the medical profession too often overlooks and that we would do well to remember.

Attendants

Many people who want to live independently, and as fully as their physical limitations permit, can only do so with the help of paid attendants. Frequently, too, when one partner is disabled a couple feels that it is preferable to hire an attendant to help with such activities of daily living as bathing and bowel care, rather than risk the respective feelings of guilt and resentment which can be created by dependency.

The requirements for such help vary and depend not only on the extent of the disability, but, equally important, on individual emotional needs. People who are severely disabled may need help with every aspect of their personal care, while those whose disabilities are less extensive can manage with limited assistance. And while some people don't mind, or even prefer, having one or several part-time attendants, others feel insecure if they don't have an attendant who lives with them.

It's not easy to find an attendant who has the ability to meet an individual's specialized requirements. Strength may not always be necessary, but patience, dependability and resourcefulness always are. Many people have found that the best attendants are those with disabilities different from their own. A blind man, for example, who needs someone to read to him several hours a day has had part-time wheelchaired attendants for years. A woman whose mobility is severely restricted has found that attendants who are mentally handicapped are able to help her with her personal care as well as with household chores and that their relationship is mutually rewarding. Sometimes, in return for room and board, students are happy to work for several hours a day as attendants.

There are several ways to go about looking for a suitable attendant. Often social service departments, vocational rehabilitation offices, regular employment agencies or local branches of organizations like the Red Cross and the Salvation Army can be helpful. Many people find, too, that they get suitable applicants by putting notices up on bulletin boards in neighborhood hospitals, churches and colleges.

Always interview applicants yourself, or at least be present during interviews. After all, you are the person most likely to be able to judge personal qualities, to ask appropriate questions and to give explicit information about the tasks that will have to be performed.

In the United Kingdom an attendance allowance may cover at least part of the salary of an attendant. In the United States there is the possibility that some part of the cost can be met out of Social Security or Medicaid benefits.

Loneliness

Being alone when you don't want to be alone is one definition of loneliness. The only loneliness-producing factors peculiar to people with disabilities are social attitudes and the practical problems that can make it difficult to reach out to others. These barriers do have to be considered, but there is almost always a way around them, a way to enrich the hours which are not filled with work or chores.

Some people gradually drop out and lose touch with old friends. Then, if they feel neglected, they blame their disabilities. It takes a distinct effort to lift the telephone, to invite people over, to signal that you're alive and available to participate in whatever is going on. But that effort has to be made if you don't want to remain alone.

Doing something for others is one way to counter loneliness. Many men and women have discovered that despite their own physical disabilities they can, through volunteer work, enrich both their own lives and the lives of others. Remedial reading with children or adults, recording books for the blind, helping with a youth group, working in a hospital gift shop or library are among the many volunteer jobs open to people with disabilities. Find out what's going on in your community and where you can fill a gap and you may be sure you will be warmly welcomed.

Even if you don't consider yourself a "joiner," you will find that joining a group of people with similar interests can be stimulating and enjoyable. If you're interested in politics contact your local party headquarters. Most churches sponsor a variety of social and educational activities and welcome new members. Adult education classes offer the opportunity to learn and to meet people at the same time. Disabled people are getting involved, too, in the fight to win their civil rights. If you feel strongly about these issues, contact the nearest activist group.

Even if you're housebound you don't have to be lonely. Many businesses are run from a bed and many civil rights activists are unable to leave their rooms.

But being busy isn't the only remedy for loneliness. Even if you can't leave your home, television and radio can bring the world to you; books and music can provide intellectual stimulation and entertainment; painting and writing can be creative outlets. People who have informed interests and lively curiosity use these resources to combat loneliness, even if they are often alone.

Love

We know that we are as capable of loving, and of being loved, as anyone else. And love, in all its aspects, is as important to us as it is to everyone else. Unfortunately, many people think that the right to love and to make love is the prerogative only of the physically sound. They react with distress and distaste to the idea that physically impaired people have the same emotional and sexual needs as they do. This is too disturbing an assumption for them to face. So they may dismiss the whole subject by thinking of disabled people as "different" from the rest of humanity and free from "normal" dreams and desires.

We realize that this is nonsense. Nevertheless, people with disabilities are sometimes brainwashed by these negative attitudes. They are afraid to express love and sometimes even to allow themselves to feel it, because they fear rejection. They inhibit their sexual desires because they've been told they shouldn't have any. And the practical barriers that limit the opportunities for meeting other people, the difficulties of getting out and around, compound their frustrations.

Every person's definition of love is different, and to confine ourselves to any one aspect is limiting. Some people, by choice or through circumstances, look for love not necessarily in the context of marriage but through other human relationships which include many close contacts beyond the immediate family circle. Some of us find our way to it through our church, through work, through political or community activities.

Able-bodied attitudes, environmental barriers and the degree of our disabilities may restrict our opportunities to seek love, but our own capacity to give love and to receive it is not diminished.

Independence

In modern society an individual's ability to be self-sufficient is usually encouraged from childhood. By the time we are adults we are supposed to have learned to depend upon ourselves, to be as quick on the draw as the next person and to be ready to hold our own in a more or less hostile world.

Independence is also considered a civic virtue, for self-reliance means pulling your own weight, paying your taxes and not being a burden on your hard-pressed fellow countryman. Quite unconsciously, many able-bodied people either write off their disabled brethren as parasites or else assume that we should be striving to be exactly like them. The emphasis in almost all medical rehabilitation is to retrain us for productive work. If this proves unfeasible, we may be considered useless and left to languish apart from the mainstream.

This attitude puts tremendous pressure on the disabled minority. Trying to keep our self-respect in a society that equates independence with physical well-being makes an already difficult situation almost intolerable; for we ourselves are generally persuaded to think the same way.

Such overemphasis on paying one's way seems to leave disabled people with only two alternatives—to knock themselves out trying to compete on able-bodied terms or to opt out entirely. This limited choice would not apply if society acknowledged other criteria of worth.

This is not to say that independence isn't admirable. Everyone, whatever his or her impairment, would surely prefer the freedom of choice that is synonymous with independence. Learning to dress yourself, to maneuver on crutches, to hold down a job or to cook for your family are all facets of independence and like learning to lip-read, to master braille or to dominate spasticity, are goals well worth a supreme effort.

But independence for the sake of independence shouldn't become an end in itself. If your sights are set on that goal alone, you are bound to feel frustrated if your physical condition deteriorates or if some other factor puts you out of the running. It's far better to cultivate other values, to adjust to your own limitations, to accept yourself as you are and to acknowledge your own virtues. Not all people with disabilities will be able to make it on their own. Those of us who can't should not feel guilty or devalued because of that. We must remember our essential worth and all the reasons for which we are entitled to self-esteem and the esteem of others.

It's important to realize that no individual can really exist alone. In a civilized society we are all interdependent. And, at best, physical independence is variable. Able-bodied or not, everyone experiences periods of dependence; illness and old age are undiscriminating. Moral independence, on the other hand, is indestructible.

Your Place in the Outside World

More than physical barriers stand between many people with disabilities and the outside world. There are also historical and attitudinal barriers. These may not be as tangible as the inaccessibility of buildings, trains and buses, but they are often as daunting and implacable. For too long we have been helpless before them, trapped in our own frustration and rage.

The rejection and isolation of people with disabilities have a long and deeply discouraging history. Participation in the ordinary activities of most of society was more or less closed to us. We were rarely seen in public places because it was too difficult, if not impossible, to get to most of them. Our plight, since it was unseen—or if observed, too painful for most people to acknowledge—was therefore easily ignored.

Neglect of our civil rights was universal. Although private organizations were formed to improve the lot of certain groups, governments generally regarded the problems presented to them as embarrassing anomalies, nasty things to be swept under the carpet and hidden from view.

That this situation has changed for the better—although by no means completely or at dizzying speed—reaffirms the maxim "In union there is strength." In many countries, including the United States, people with disabilities form one of the largest minorities (if not the largest single minority), and we have at last begun to exercise the power which is implicit in numbers as well as in concerted action.

It is true that the only thing "the disabled" have in common is physical limitation. Often, too, we are splintered into groups which deal with specific disabilities and this can result in competitive factionalism. Yet we must be bound together by our shared and paramount desire for equal rights in every area of our lives.

It is fortunate that we live in rapidly changing times. There is greater social mobility and no one has a predetermined place on the totem pole. Yesterday's assumptions are questioned today and many will be amended tomorrow. This works to our advantage. Not very long ago, people with physical disabilities were hidden away in attics and institutions. Now, at least on paper, no one questions our right to live as fully as everyone else.

This is a big step, but it is only a beginning. We all look forward to the time when architects would no more design buildings with doors too narrow for wheelchairs than they would design buildings without any doors at all. But it is only the disabled themselves, working together toward a common goal, who can achieve this. To be effective, our demands must be backed by the relentless, concerted pressure of advocacy groups and, on a personal level, by individual persuasive firmness in insisting that others be aware of our equal rights.

Pending full implementation of legislation of all kinds, we are obliged to tackle the world as we find it and to try to manage despite its imperfections. It is, above all, essential that we do everything possible to take full advantage of whatever resources are currently available to us. It is only by doing this that we can change our public image and gain genuine acceptance.

Now that we are making our presences felt more significantly, we are beginning to enjoy life more fully within a larger framework. Mobility, access, education, employment, travel and recreation are slowly becoming increasingly feasible for many of us. We now have more options open to us than ever before. There has been more realization and consideration of us as people like everyone else and we are seen not merely in the context of our disabilities. We are now beginning to be acknowledged as people who indeed have rights to richer lives than have been possible up to now.

These advances are certainly triumphs, but we must not let ourselves be fobbed off with token recognition. It is not enough that we have recorded some achievements of a high order. We must continue the struggle to assure that everyone who has the potential and the will can also have the opportunity and the encouragement.

Attitudes of the Public

At different times in their lives most people have felt themselves to be isolated, neglected, spurned or somehow stigmatized. Whatever the reasons for such feelings, the reactions are often acute and can range from a sense of inadequacy, self-pity or fear to despair and fury. Ironically, even we who have physical disabilities are guilty on occasion of behaving toward other handicapped people in exactly the ways we find most deplorable when we are the victims of such behavior.

Many social attitudes are irrational; such reactions as facial expressions are often unconscious or uncontrollable. Little as we may feel ourselves to be different, we can appreciate that to the unaccustomed eye we are. And if we feel painfully conspicuous we may regard others as more "normal" than ourselves and begin to believe that we are not entitled to be accepted on equal terms with the able-bodied.

There are still, amazingly, some able-bodied people who consider any kind of disablement a retribution for sin, an expression of the wrath of God. There are, too, people who are able to enjoy feelings of superiority only when they see others less fortunate than themselves. And there are those who view as somehow wrong the efforts of a disabled person to live as rich and unconstricted a life as possible.

Due in large part to the systematic barring of disabled people from integration into society, most able-bodied people, however, have never faced the problems of disability and may never have been in a position to observe or relate to a person with physical disabilities. They don't know, therefore, how to handle the most casual encounter. It calls for great inner strength on your part to face up to views so bigoted or limited, even if you understand the reasons behind them.

Your first impulse may be to react resentfully to a negative attitude. If you don't check that response and transform it into more positive behavior you are perpetuating misunderstanding. Repetition of such incidents can make life in the outside world increasingly difficult for all handicapped people. It is the disabled themselves who must make a positive effort to educate the able-bodied and establish empathy.

"Does he take sugar in his tea?" is the kind of query unthinking people will put to the companion of a disabled person, rather than to the tea drinker himself. Exaggerated heartiness or a blunt question like "What's the matter with you?" can be extremely irritating, but it might well be an innocent question or a cover-up for uneasiness. Try to be perceptive and answer as you would like to be answered. An aggressive reply will only set up another barrier.

The disturbing directness of small children is different. Their curiosity springs from natural innocent interest and any mature adult should be able to turn it to good account with an honest, matter-of-fact response. If a child shows curiosity about your wheelchair, for example, ignore the parent's obvious embarrassment and explain why you can't walk and that the chair serves as your legs. That child, after all, is tomorrow's adult.

The attitudes of the public toward people with disabilities are gradually changing, but there is still much more to be done. It is up to us to build a bridge of mutual understanding.

Integration

Modern medicine, increasingly sophisticated rehabilitation techniques, advanced technology, as well as enlightened legislation, have begun to make it easier for people with disabilities to share more fully in the world. Nevertheless, genuine across-the-board integration is still an ideal.

Such isolating factors as architectural barriers and archaic and inaccessible transportation are only very slowly being eliminated or modified. Employment opportunities are still restricted and may even be out of the question when the cost of medical care can only be adequately covered by unemployment or social security benefits. Many provisions specially made for people with disabilities impose a kind of segregation by their very nature. And there are, of course, many disabilities which themselves are so limiting that integration is not really possible.

Like everyone else, people with disabilities have the right to choose where they will go, how they will live, with whom they will associate and how they will be educated. Every person, disabled or able-bodied, has the right to contribute to society to the full extent of his or her talent and ability.

But undermined self-confidence and unencouraged motivation, underutilization of faculties and unenlightened public attitudes combine to screen people with disabilities from the community. And this sets a vicious circle to turning—the less visibility there is the more delayed will be accommodation and acceptance.

The basis for integration as stated in the Snowdon report *Integrating the Disabled* is "a society which palpably recognizes their common humanity with the handicapped." It is toward the laying of this foundation stone of a better society that we must strive.

The Media

Today the marvels of modern media are largely taken for granted. Television, radio, newspapers, books and magazines are part of most people's daily experience. Few would question the power exerted by the media over their lives as a continuing source of information, entertainment and education and as a molder of public opinion.

There can be no doubt that for many people with disabilities the media are the mainspring of their connection with the world and its infinitely varied activities. The deaf can read, the blind can listen and for the homebound the media help to combat isolation and provide intellectual stimulation. The media can also strongly influence attitudes by showing what the handicapped can achieve and by destroying the myths surrounding disablement.

Happily, there are signs of an increasingly positive approach in the presentation to the public of people who are disabled. Newspapers and magazines continually disseminate information about handicapping conditions. The blind insurance investigator, Longstreet, was a popular hero in an American television series, as was Ironside, the wheelchaired San Francisco cop. And such children's programs as *Sesame Street* and *Captain Kangaroo* have included material stressing the similarities between the disabled and able-bodied. *Crossroads*, a long-running serial on British television, includes among its central characters a young man who is a paraplegic.

In the United States and Britain there have been television documentaries which have dramatized the emotional needs of young people with disabilities. One excellent British documentary, presented during prime viewing time, showed the rehabilitation and eventual return to family life of a young pilot whose neck had been broken in a plane crash. In the 1978 American film *Coming Home*, Jon Voight plays a paraplegic Vietnam veteran and one hundred actual paraplegics appear as extras.

In Touch, the weekly British radio program for the blind, has been on the air for more than twenty years. It is concerned in such a down-to-earth way with the problems of the blind and the means of dealing with them, that it has a revelatory function for the sighted as well. And on both sides of the Atlantic there are now several weekly phone-in radio programs run by disabled people for the purpose of providing information in response to specific inquiries.

Feeling Free, an American public television six-part series aimed at children, was shown in 1978 and starred five disabled children. The programs were designed to ease the introduction of disabled children into the public school system throughout the United States, as directed in new federal legislation which guarantees an adequate public school education for all handicapped children.

Perhaps one of the most significant leaps forward, however, is *Link*, the weekly British television series which focuses on living with disability and is presented by the disabled themselves. A discussion program which stresses integration and has become increasingly hard-hitting, *Link* also offers current information on aids for daily living, vocational rehabilitation, legislation and recreational facilities. Audience response, suggestions and participation are welcomed. Program information sheets, compiled with the help of voluntary organizations, give details of the aids mentioned on the program, the books reviewed and the topics discussed; they are sent to viewers on request.

The fund-raising telethon, a uniquely American method of bringing the handicapped to the attention of the public, has incurred the wrathful disapproval of disabled activists. But while many feel that such programs, in their zeal to raise money for research and services, portray handicapped people as pitiable helpless creatures—an image that militates strongly against the more general aspiration to independence—others defend them because of the huge sums of money they raise along with the consciousness of a complacent public.

The President's Committee on Employment of the Handicapped offers a free guide to improving media effectiveness for disabled adults and for organizations working with people who are handicapped. This guide also has suggestions for improving telethons and making them less offensive to independent people with disabilities.

Because few handicapped people host programs which are not directly related to disability, or participate in those which might easily include them, such as talk shows, quiz programs and discussion panels, the handicapped minority cannot but feel that they have indeed been relegated to invisibility by those who "don't want to know."

Laws can only do so much. The media can do much more, much faster and much more effectively by showing the disabled to be as much individuals as everybody else. Television and radio producers will respond to pressure. Telephone or write to them and protest against programs which ignore the handicapped or misrepresent them.

Access

There are millions of people in the world who have mobility problems. Besides war casualties, those affected by various diseases and victims of sports and traffic accidents and industrial and natural disasters, the numbers everywhere are on the increase. Advances in medicine have ensured that a great proportion of severely injured people survive, hoping and expecting to resume independent lives and to make their contributions to society. Modern medicine has made it possible for those suffering from disabling diseases to participate more fully in the life of their communities. Despite these inescapable facts, modern building design and construction all over the world have for the most part been influenced more by aesthetic than by practical considerations.

Few able-bodied people can appreciate the intense feelings of frustration and even of humiliation induced by lack of access. Free movement in and out of houses, offices, theaters, schools and museums, which is a right taken for granted by the able-bodied, can present exasperating and often unpredictable difficulties for people who are on crutches or in wheelchairs. The helplessness and anger occasioned by thoughtlessly created environmental barriers can alter the character of the most routine excursion. Even a trip to the supermarket can involve detailed planning of a kind usually reserved for exploratory expeditions.

Architectural barriers more effectively threaten or curtail independence than a disability itself. True independence implies the ability to undertake normal activities with as little outside help as possible. A single step, almost unobserved by those able to negotiate it unthinkingly, can be as daunting an obstacle as an entire flight of stairs.

In the United States the first significant official recognition of the need for emendations in the building codes occurred in 1961 on the basis of recommendations by the President's Committee on the Employment of the Handicapped. Studies by this and other governmental agencies and socially concerned private groups clearly indicated the need for legislation covering such basic requirements as ground-level entrances, doorways of sufficient width to accommodate wheelchairs, ramps, handrails and special lavatory facilities. These studies did indeed provide the groundwork for such subsequent legislation as the Housing Act of 1964 and later acts in 1968, 1973 and 1974, which incorporated in-depth specifications. Federally funded and state-funded buildings, as well as privately funded projects, have since benefited from progressively realistic building codes.

The Architectural Barriers Act, passed by Congress in 1968, specified that all federally funded buildings must be designed and constructed to provide access to physically handicapped persons. This was the first United States effort at effective legislation; its strictures now apply to all construction other than private residences.

Compliance with the act, however, was less than effectively achieved during the six years that followed and, in 1974, with the formation of the Architectural and

Transportation Barriers Compliance Board, Section 502 of the previous year's Rehabilitation Act was amended. A quasi-independent agency composed of the heads of nine federal agencies, the board carries out investigations and holds public hearings. On its authority, moreover, federal funds may be withheld or suspended in the event that the construction of any building or facility has not been carried out in accordance with the act.

In principle at least there has been nationwide adoption, although with local modifications, of the so-called ANSI standard, specifying the elimination of architectural barriers in public buildings, set by the American Standards Association (now the American Standards Institute). New ANSI standards, issued in 1978, more thoroughly cover the needs of deaf and blind people as well as those who are wheelchaired. There is, nevertheless, considerable variance throughout the country in the extent and the means of enforcement as well as in the character and functions of the responsible agencies. Some states lack even the inspection mandate to ascertain conformance to the specifications, while other states employ their own engineers and architects to design barrier-free buildings.

At least seventeen other countries, including Great Britain, the Scandinavian countries, the Federal Republic of Germany, the Netherlands, Canada and Australia, have been alert to the necessity for similar legislation and, equally important, to its implementation.

In 1971 a clause was added to the Building Code of Sweden that "In all buildings those parts to which the general public is admitted or that constitutes working places shall be designed, as far as reasonable, in a manner making them accessible and usable for persons whose motor ability or ability of orientation is restricted by age, disability or sickness." This clause applies to new or reconstructed buildings and also covers schools.

In Israel the National Planning and Building Act of 1965 has been amended and now requires that not only must all new public buildings be barrier-free, but also that any structural changes in existing buildings must encompass the minimal requirements of accessibility for the disabled. In Australia government authorities have agreed to incorporate in all buildings erected by them the recommendations of the Australian Standards Association with regard to buildings, furniture and equipment.

The need for barrier-free design throughout the world is considered to be so important that it was the subject of a United Nations Expert Group Meeting held in June 1974. But, unfortunately, actual construction everywhere has not kept pace with the generally intensified awareness and good will, or even with actual governmental commitment. In many cases an insufficiency of public funds, or the inefficiency of their allocation, have resulted in the transfer of responsibility to private organizations.

There is also evidence of unbelievable lack of foresight, imagination or ordinary common sense in some installations or adaptations of facilities. An example of this is the elevator which was specifically built to accommodate wheelchaired students at the Student Union at the University of Texas. Only after it was installed was it found to be too small to accommodate an attendant as well as a wheelchaired passenger. Some public organizations and educational and company administrators protest at the soaring costs of meeting government construction requirements, while at the same time enormous amounts of money are misspent on faulty and inadequate construction.

Obviously it is more costly to modify existing structures than to incorporate modifications at the design stage, but older buildings must, nevertheless, be modified. And there is certainly no reason for any new building to be inaccessible. Research undertaken by various groups, including the National League of Cities in the United States, has shown that the cost of constructing from scratch a completely accessible building could amount to no more than one-half of one percent of the total cost—a negligible sum in terms of economy and human need.

Illogical thinking about accessibility often cancels the advantages of modern building design. Some locally implemented fire regulations, for example, deny those in wheelchairs access to upper floors, even when elevators are available. Yet people with other mobility disadvantages, including those who use crutches or canes, suffer no such restrictions, although the pace at which they move might well constitute a greater hazard in the event of fire than that of a person in an easily maneuverable wheelchair.

Seating arrangements in theaters and concert halls are often as illogically considered. If seats have not been removed to enable the wheelchaired to remain in their chairs, they must transfer into the fixed seats. Since these seats are invariably on the aisle, in case of fire, the disabled, together with the other people in these rows, could well be trapped—or at least dangerously delayed in making their exit, whereas if they remained in their wheelchairs their escape could be as rapid as anyone else's.

Too little consideration is also being given by many architects and builders to the socio-psychological aspects of disability. There is no reason, for example, not to construct a ramp in conjunction with the main staircase of a public building so that the disabled need not use a segregated entrance, which has the unfortunate effect of suggesting inferior or outcast status.

At an exhibit built by the Minnesota Society for Crippled Children and Adults, hundreds of city officials, architects and interested citizens were given the chance to experience for themselves, on a specially built "obstacle course," the architectural barriers encountered by disabled people in everyday situations and surroundings. The participants, seated in wheelchairs, tackled ramps, telephone booths, rest rooms and water fountains, and propelled themselves over the thresholds and through the rooms of a model house. Some accessible features were included, to point up the dramatic difference that even minor modifications can make.

Although some architects, designers and engineers are becoming increasingly aware of the ways in which simple adaptations can make access easier and more

comfortable, and can reduce the self-consciousness of people with disabilities, imaginative sympathy and resourcefulness are by no means universal. Recently, at a London hotel where a conference for a disabled pressure group was being held, the doors to some toilets, too narrow to accommodate wheelchairs, were temporary removed. But the next logical, considerate step had not been taken; no arrangements had been made to screen off the cubicles to shield the users from the public gaze.

In some American rest rooms, too, even in cases where the cubicles have been specifically designed to permit wheelchair entry, the design has often not been followed through so that the door can be closed behind the chair. The user must, therefore, first effect a transfer from the chair to the toilet, then push the chair outside the cubicle. In order to leave the cubicle help is usually required to push the chair back in. This can be difficult, as well as embarrassing—and of course it is altogether unnecessary.

The accessibility of individual buildings and of their amenities cannot often be separated from that of the surrounding terrain and the more general environment, including, of course, the streets we must travel and cross. Increasingly, curb cuts are being incorporated into new town planning and road construction, and adjustments are now being made to existing walkways—a development that has also proved a boon to thousands of people with no mobility problems.

Curb cuts, like ramps and wide doorways, actually offer benefits to all, including the elderly and mothers pushing baby carriages. When, recently, the designer of a shopping center in the north of England was congratulated by a group of handicapped people on its highly accessible and convenient construction, he was honest enough to admit that he had actually had only the elderly and mothers with young children in mind. The universal advantages were accidental!

Access guides are now issued for most major towns and cities in the United States and Europe and more and more public facilities display the access symbol. It was intended that the use of the symbol, which was adopted in 1969 by Rehabilitation International, a nongovernmental federation of national and international organizations concerned with all aspects of disability, would help to stimulate action to eliminate environmental barriers. According to the resolution on policy concerning its use, however, the standards of accessibility to be applied are "established by the responsible authorities in each country." Consequently, the extent of accessibility signified by display of the symbol varies considerably.

The regulations set out for hotels in the United States, for example, require adherence to "at least five out of eleven standards." These include several which are less than radical and are certainly not formidable to hotel managements, such as "special menus for diabetics or those on salt-free diets," "light switches in guest rooms in convenient bedside locations," and "reserved parking marked Handicapped Only."

It is within the power of people with disabilities to ensure the progressive improvement of the environment to meet general and specific needs. The greater our visibility and participation in the community and the more disseminated the acknowledgement of our problems, the greater are the opportunities for changes to be instigated. A need that is not seen or felt is not likely to be understood or met.

It is up to us to make our presence realized and to articulate objections to unnecessary man-made environmental barriers. We must consistently bring obstacles and hazards to the attention of responsible bodies or individuals—businessmen, storekeepers, restaurant owners, theater managers, museum directors, government officials. The most concerned attitudes and effective action can be implemented by the determined disabled, for we are the ones who suffer most keenly from the effects of inadequate access.

However reassuring the growing ubiquity of the access symbol may be, we should set our goal much higher. We should aim toward a future when every public building will as a matter of course be accessible and there will no longer be a need for any symbol.

Mobility

It is not possible to be truly independent without adequate transportation to work, schools, hospitals, stores and recreational facilities. More than ever, practical outdoor mobility is now a vital part of the business of living.

According to one survey in the United States, there are about thirteen million noninstitutionalized handicapped people who are not sufficiently mobile to use public transportation, yet there have been few advances in making available to these millions the means of personal mobility. A multiplicity of plans, many of them quite feasible, have been projected by technological dreamers, social idealists and disabled pressure groups. In some cases the plans have been brought to design stage and in others implemented by legislation. But in general, progress in the right direction has been so slow, so fragmented or so bureaucratically sidestepped that it has resulted in even more frustration for people with physical disabilities. Long-term, encompassing vision has been singularly lacking. As far as official action on mobility is concerned, the movement may be said to have been two steps forward and three back.

In the United Kingdom in 1947, when the National Health Service Act was passed, the government acknowledged its responsibility to solve personal mobility problems and undertook to provide special vehicles or other concessions to certain categories of people with physical disabilities.

Some people were given small cars. Disabled drivers who owned their own vehicles were given allowances and exemption from vehicle taxes. A small, three-wheeled, motorized vehicle, either electric or gasoline-powered, was developed and issued to other people. The "trike," although somewhat unimaginative and less than adequate, was nevertheless geared to some of the important needs of the country's disabled population. Despite successive refinements, however, the trike failed to meet international safety standards, according to the Secretary of State for Social Services, and in July 1976 its phase-out was announced, to the great distress of many disabled people.

For all its faults, for some people the trike had advantages over the mobility allowance which takes its place and the place of other concessions as well. Its size makes it suitable for urban traffic and easy to park. Its robin's egg blue body makes it instantly recognizable, so that help is readily available from passersby or police. It is economical for the individual to run, since the expenses of tax, insurance and servicing are underwritten by the government. The trike, however, was not designed (nor is it legally permissible) to carry a passenger. Because of this, as well as its conspicuousness, the argument has long raged among the disabled themselves about the desirability of a vehicle that many consider to be stigmatizing and segregating.

Despite this conflict of interests, it cannot be denied that the British Government has made a determined and unique effort to provide mobility assistance to those who need it. The mobility allowance, which is a cash benefit, is intended to help people who are virtually unable to walk, irrespective of whether or not they drive. It is given to the parents of disabled children age five and over and to adults of "working age"—under sixty-five for men and under sixty for women. The government is also encouraging car manufacturers and dealers to establish purchase concessions for recipients of mobility allowances.

In the United States Government's visions of glorious technological advances in transportation, no comparable concern has yet been manifested for the mobility needs of the handicapped. True, the United States has much less welfare state orientation than the United Kingdom and the government's stated policy of emphasis on employment opportunities that make the purchase of a private car practicable might even be considered more enlightened. Obviously, however, there needs to be a concomitant policy of providing either a means of private transportation or the kind of public transit system which will enable disabled people to get jobs in the first place.

Public Transportation

The right to be "abroad in the land" is a civil and personal right as valued as any other. This right is fully acknowledged internationally by individuals and governments. But making it practicable in everyday terms for people with physical disabilities and providing all the necessary services require radical rethinking, redesigning of vast networks of public transportation systems and enormous expenditures. The costs of constructing effective new transportation systems that would enable all citizens, able-bodied and disabled alike, to use them freely and with ease and comfort, would be staggering (although hardly on the same scale as the costs of the defense systems of most countries).

The cost factor has resulted in many compromises and only partial achievement of the goal of greater accessibility and convenience for the disabled traveler. Access guides and vacation and transportation information, ramps, handrails, accessible restaurants, rest rooms and other public facilities in stations and terminals, elevators, audio and visual information signals, wheelchairs, moving walkways for lengthy passageways in some terminals, personal assistance and free passage for attendants are among the positive innovations and advances. But without complete renovation of stations, terminals and public facilities, these remain compromises.

In the United States estimates of the number of people with some physical disability range from between twenty-eight and forty-six million. The number of disabled and elderly Americans who cannot use, or experience difficulty in using, existing transit systems is estimated at thirteen million. And at least four million of these are employable people who are unable to reach places where they could be working.

Despite the government's expenditure of billions of dollars on the rehabilitation of the handicapped, it was not until the late 1960s that any consideration was given to the lack of accessibility and suitability of public transportation for this considerable segment of the population. With the 1970 Biaggi Amendment to the 1964 Urban Mass Transportation Act came the first real legislative breakthrough. It made it national policy to grant the physically handicapped and elderly equal rights with other citizens to mass transportation facilities and services.

But while accessible public transportation would enable millions of Americans to enter the work force, or to take advantage of educational facilities and vocational training centers and thus eventually become contributing members of society, objections to such use of government funds have been raised on the grounds that, whatever the results, the very diverse transportation requirements of all disabled people are unlikely ever to be fully met. Although the general pronouncement of the 1973 Rehabilitation Act was that "no otherwise qualified handicapped individual in the United States . . . shall, by reason of his handicap, be excluded from participation in, be denied the benefits of, or be subjected to discrimination under any program or activity receiving federal financial assistance," public transit systems are still singularly inadequate. In part this is because implementation of the federal legislation concerning them is under the jurisdiction of individual cities and states.

A number of public transportation systems are nearly bankrupt and many cities have little or no public transportation at the present time. As of 1978 only Maryland had enacted legislation requiring all public transit accommodations supported by public funds to be made accessible and usable by the physically disabled. A number of cities are only now beginning to plan new barrier-free rail systems.

Accessibility, too, has not been the major priority of the Department of Transport in granting funds. The Urban Mass Transit Administration (UMTA) has funded a few research and demonstration projects, from which transbus, an accessible bus design, resulted, but until recently it had exerted little or no pressure on local transit bodies to achieve or even to work toward accessibility.

Federal funds have, however, created the Amtrak railroad system, which represents perhaps the most advanced approach to date in railroad planning. Its new rolling stock—Amfleet cars and the Turboliner equipment—is efficient and equitable. New stations and their rest rooms have been made accessible, cars are flush with platforms, entrances to all cars are wide enough for wheelchair entry and porters are usually available.

Long-distance trains, with bi-level cars, have accessible toilet facilities in each coach. Each long-distance train also has at least two special sleeping compartments with toilet facilities in the lower level.

Enlightened as these arrangements are, certain practical difficulties remain. Passengers are not permitted to travel in wheelchairs. On short-distance runs, the special toilet for the handicapped, which is large enough for wheelchair entry, is in the food service car, of which there is only one, and at most two, on each train. But given the basic restriction that no passenger may occupy a wheelchair, the disabled traveler who wishes to use the toilet must first retransfer to the wheelchair and then again out of it into the train seat.

The solitary passenger cannot expect more than minimal help from an Amtrak employee in transferring to a regular train seat, and the only seat on each train which has a removable arm to facilitate transfer from a wheelchair is also in the food service car. On most short-distance runs, including those from Boston to New York to Washington, there is no reserved seating—not even for the special seat in the food service car. Nevertheless, given advance notice, Amtrak staff claim that every effort will be made to accommodate the handicapped passenger.

The Amtrak system was designed with people with disabilities in mind, after consultation with organizations of the handicapped, but even its obvious superiority to most other railroads cannot permit unqualified praise.

In Britain, until recently, the wheelchaired who chose to travel anywhere by rail were obliged to sit in the unheated, drafty guard's van, with the luggage—a pleasure for which they paid the full second-class fare. The situation has improved considerably on some trains.

Most modern Inter-City coaches have wide entrance doors with handholds to facilitate entrance and exit. The newest coaches have, at the end of each first-class saloon, close to the entrance vestibule and toilet, a seat and table which can be removed to allow the position to be occupied by a disabled passenger in a wheelchair. Because this facility could not be incorporated into second-class coaches, British Rail only charge second-class single fares for each journey made for both the disabled passenger and accompanying attendant. (When a wheelchaired passenger and attendant still have to travel in the guard's van, British Rail now offer tickets at half the rate of the second-class single fare.)

In a further attempt to make rail travel easier for disabled passengers, folding wheelchairs are available at the main stations for use between taxis and trains and special narrow wheelchairs can be provided to take passengers through the coach to a seat. Most stations are equipped with Call for Aid signs, which incorporate the international access symbol and give information about the nearest point at which assistance can be given. *British Rail Guide for Disabled People* gives detailed information about more than two hundred and fifty stations.

The Council of Europe supports a program to establish among the eighteen member countries a higher uniform standard of facilities for the handicapped in all forms of public transportation. The aim is to introduce a European Card for "substantially disabled persons" that would be valid in all the participating countries and would provide—among other things—free facilities and assistance at airports and railroad stations, priority seating in public transportation vehicles and priority attention at check-in counters and baggage areas.

In the United States private commuter railroads are generally run with old stock and were originally designed without consideration of accessibility problems. Travel to most cities from exurbia is, therefore, out of the question for

many people with disabilities unless alternative transportation is available.

The subway and bus systems of such large American cities as New York, Chicago and Boston which—like the London Underground and the Paris Metro—were constructed long ago, are totally inaccessible to most people with disabilities. Some design modifications have recently been made to Paris's Metro and bus systems and special privileges are offered to disabled passengers.

Oslo, with a population of well under one million, is unusual in having a barrier-free underground railroad system which is generally accessible even to the wheelchaired. In Sweden there is government subsidy of the "demand responsive" taxi and minibus services which operate in many localities. (Such arrangements are available in some areas of the United States and were pushed by the federal government as alternatives to integrated public transportation. The disabled population, however, was against such services, except for the severely disabled, because they can never be as effective as public transportation, are not as economically viable and because they discriminate against and segregate the disabled.) In Canada, little consideration has been given to accessible public transportation. Only in 1977 was a national symposium held on Transportation Needs of the Disabled.

Most moves toward resolutions of the problems clearly do not effect dramatic, immediate or widespread changes. The Bay Area Transit System (BART) in San Francisco is one of the world's most effectively designed systems for use by the disabled. But despite its manifest superiority, even it suffers from having had accessibility provisions for stations and rolling stock forced on transportation officials by legislation after actual plans had been completed. As a result, there are long distances to be covered between some elevators and entrance gates and platforms. Help is sometimes necessary to get through turnstiles and there is no weekend service. Apart from such inadequacies, there remains the problem of coping at the terminal points.

The retroactive modifications to

BART sent construction costs ten million dollars above the original budget, and transit officials have complained that the use of the system by the handicapped is too limited to justify the expenditure. To some extent this is certainly because all the stations are not uniformly accessible.

In Washington, D.C., despite legal strictures, the Gallery Place Station of the vastly expensive Metro subway system was built with sixty steps leading steeply down into it. Only the action of the American Coalition of Citizens with Disabilities, climaxing a ten-year struggle to ensure the enforcement of the law, finally brought about the installation of elevators to the platforms. The Washington Metro system is now, however, being made completely accessible with elevators at each station and braille signs.

New underground systems are not being designed in Great Britain, and London is served by a network begun in the Victorian era. London Transport issues the *Guide to the Underground for the Disabled*, but few stations are accessible to the wheelchaired. Those stations which have lifts were certainly not designed with the disabled in mind; many of the lifts are flanked by long passages and staircases. Even the new extension to Heathrow Airport, which went into operation at the end of December, 1977, has no lifts—only escalators. The one positive advantage of the airport station is its provision of travelators—moving walkways.

The reduced fare systems for the elderly and handicapped generally in operation in the United States and the United Kingdom are helpful in intent, but the privilege applies to buses with entry steps that present an obstacle to many, and to subways that are equally, if not more, inaccessible. The discount, too, applies only to travel during the nonpeak hours, so that one aim, which is to offer economical transportation to places of employment, is more or less negated.

In the United States all urban mass transit buses purchased by transit authorities with UMTA funds after September 30, 1979 will have to meet transbus specifications. These include a stationary floor height of not more than twenty-two inches (57 cm), a front door which is forty-four inches (110 cm) wide, and a weatherproof, traction ramp that extends to the curb. Public transportation authorities in some American cities, including Philadelphia, Los Angeles and Miami, have already begun to purchase the transbus.

Earlier, some bus companies included modified "kneeling buses" in their fleets. But in New York, for example, bus company officials complained that the mechanisms were often faulty, frequently causing delays, and that the buses were insufficiently used by the very people for whom they were modified. Pressure groups of people with disabilities were critical of the modifications and pointed out that the buses were insufficiently used because the modifications were themselves insufficient.

In response to demand, UMTA sponsored the development by private industry of "the bus of the future." The perfect transbus envisioned by the Department of Transport thus became a reality. The improvements incorporated in the transbus will significantly advance the mass transportation of all persons, including the disabled and the elderly. Approximately four thousand new transbuses will be added to America's public mass transit system each year. Although the estimated production cost is 12.5 percent more than that of current buses it should be more than offset by increases in annual farebox revenues of between twenty-three million dollars and sixty-five million dollars from new ridership.

Greyhound Lines, a private bus company, has taken a significant step toward providing concessions and physical assistance to disabled passengers on its interstate service. The company issues a brochure giving detailed information about its Helping Hand operation, which includes free transportation for an attendant (a medical certificate is required), for guide dogs and for wheelchairs. These services are all very well, and a Greyhound bus often provides the cheapest interstate travel, but inaccessible rest rooms, both on board and at some terminals, can be a major deterrent.

Continental Trailways, which also requires a physician's letter for the attendant's concession, have a Good Samaritan Plan similar to Greyhound's Helping Hand and their fleet includes Silver Eagle Coaches that can transport motorized as well as manual wheelchairs. The company is also adapting and building terminals for easier access.

Air travel is perhaps the best bet for disabled travelers. Thanks to the recognition of the need for general facilities for the physically handicapped in many countries throughout the world, the accessibility of air travel has increased considerably in recent years. Following World War II, major airlines made the modifications necessary to enable disabled veterans to travel by plane. Since then thousands of disabled people, including many who are wheelchaired, have flown hundreds of thousands of miles.

Although some carriers still insist that handicapped passengers be accompanied by an able-bodied attendant, most major airlines ignore this requirement. In general, airline personnel are quite accustomed to meeting the needs of disabled passengers and often go to the utmost trouble to ensure that their flights are accomplished with a minimum of effort and discomfort. For someone who is not medically ill but merely has a mobility problem, the care and attention can even be excessive.

Facilities for the disabled passenger already exist in many large airports in the United States and in Europe. In the United States the Airport and Airway Development Act Amendment, made law in July 1976, affects the accessibility of all new airports and all renovations begun after the act's effective date. Access guides have been published for many major international airports.

For the severely disabled it is usually possible, particularly at major airports, if there is no level entry, to be conveyed into the aircraft directly by a fork lift truck and wheeled to the airplane seat. This considerably reduces the humiliation of being carried and the fear of being mishandled. Nevertheless, air travel still has its problems for handicapped passengers. Even on such large aircraft as the Boeing 747 and the DC 10, which have wider gangways and more leg room than most planes, toilets are still inaccessible to many. Often, too, airlines will not transport the wet cell batteries used for powered wheelchairs and passengers must make arrangements to have suitable batteries waiting at their destinations. Folding wheelchairs are, however, carried free of weight restriction. Blind passengers are permitted to keep guide dogs with them in the cabin.

It is always advisable to check out the policy of any airline you wish to use well in advance of travel, and this applies particularly to connecting airlines on which you are ticketed; they may have quota restrictions (as do Alitalia, Air New Zealand, Air Canada, British Airways, Eastern Airlines and TWA) or require medical certificates—sometimes for each leg of a journey. Hair-raising accounts have been given of handicapped travelers being turned down by a connecting airline and being stranded in mid-journey. When you make your reservations be sure to inform the airline of your particular limitations and requirements, including special diet.

Ultimately, strange as it may seem, it is the decision of the pilot as to who can fly in his aircraft, and he can deny passage to any person with a physical disability on the grounds that safety will be compromised. But because there is so little data available on actual crisis situations, the Federal Airlines Administration (FAA) has conducted tests on evacuation procedures for the disabled. These tests have indicated that handicapped passengers could be evacuated safely through exits with chutes without risk to themselves or to others.

Given the rate at which progress is being made in the domain of public transportation in general, it will be some time before people with physical disabilities can be completely carefree and relaxed about traveling, whether it be for a short or long distance. But there is definitely a new, positive quality to the attention and consideration being given to the mobility problems of the disabled and this is reassuring.

Private Transportation

Fully accessible public transportation is still decades away. Meanwhile, for people with physical disabilities, as for the population as a whole, the advantages of private transportation are immediately obvious. To many handicapped people, for whom mobility literally means independence and integration, a vehicle which is adapted to their needs, which able-bodied friends and relatives can also drive and which will accommodate passengers, is almost a necessity. Fortunately, improved technology has given more and more disabled people a new freedom and today even those with severe disabilities are able to drive themselves.

Many automotive aids are now available which make it possible for a disabled person to drive in safety and comfort as well as enter and leave a vehicle unassisted. The ingenuity of the devices and aids designed for almost every aspect of car travel and for almost every disability is heartening. Hand controls are even available in kits, for use on many of the car models offered for rental.

The question of road safety, often raised in connection with disabled drivers, has no validity. Many studies have shown that the safety record of registered disabled drivers is on a par with, and often considerably better than, that of the nondisabled. According to a Harvard study "the nonimpaired group of drivers sustained approximately twice as many accidents and were charged with approximately twice as many nonaccident violations as were the impaired." After another survey, Connecticut's Motor Vehicle Commissioner concluded that "the so-called average driver without a physical handicap could do well to enjoy the really remarkable, trouble-free traffic records attained by almost all of these physically handicapped drivers." Indeed it has been frequently pointed out that the physically handicapped, being more aware of their limitations, compensate for them by extra caution and consideration. Nevertheless, despite the arguments and the statistics, insurance companies often refuse to insure disabled drivers or insist on higher insurance rates for them.

In many countries handicapped citizens receive government assistance to buy cars. In the United States, however, no federal help is available to a disabled person toward the purchase of a car, except that the Veterans Administration grants disabled veterans an allowance toward a car's purchase and adaptation. In some states tax exemptions are granted to disabled drivers and they are also issued with special license plates and privileged parking stickers.

Whatever the difficulties of acquiring a special vehicle, it is nevertheless encouraging to see how much progress in automotive technology and specific adaptation has been made since the 1920s when a Model T Ford was modified for Franklin D. Roosevelt's use.

Power brakes and steering and automatic transmission are not only advantageous for specific disabilities, but have reduced the physical exertion needed for driving and have made it less tiring. Controls are less complicated and special installations are safer.

Special adaptations are now manufactured to enable people with disabilities to operate the various controls through mechanical connections. Hand levers can be installed to control steering, acceleration and braking. There are accessories which operate the brakes and the accelerator from the steering column, as well as one-lever "fingertip" controls which can be operated with safety. It is even possible to adapt a car so that it can be driven only with the feet.

When a handicapped person chooses a car, his or her specific needs and disability must be considered. Each disabled driver has individual problems and should seek competent help and advice when selecting automotive controls.

For some disabled drivers getting into and out of a car pose greater difficulties than driving itself. Opening the door, for example, can be a major obstacle. This can often be most easily accomplished by pressing the button with the side of the hand rather than with the thumb. There are also commercially available aids which some people find helpful.

Many modern cars have low clearance which seems even lower when they are parked next to curbs. A four-door car makes access to the back seat easier, but a two-door car allows much more room for getting into the front seats.

Some people find it easiest to get into a car backward, wriggle toward the center of the seat and then lift in their legs. Most car seats can be adapted to rotate through ninety degrees so that it's possible to turn the seat to face out of the door. When a seat cannot be adapted, a special rotating seat can be bought and installed. Some swiveling car seats will slide over the doorsill and clear of the car.

A standard hoist can be utilized for transfer to a car as well as to bed, bath and wheelchair. There are also hoists which can be attached to the roof of a car. One electric hoist runs off the car battery. Unfortunately, the driver cannot independently operate any of the currently available models.

To transfer from a wheelchair to a car

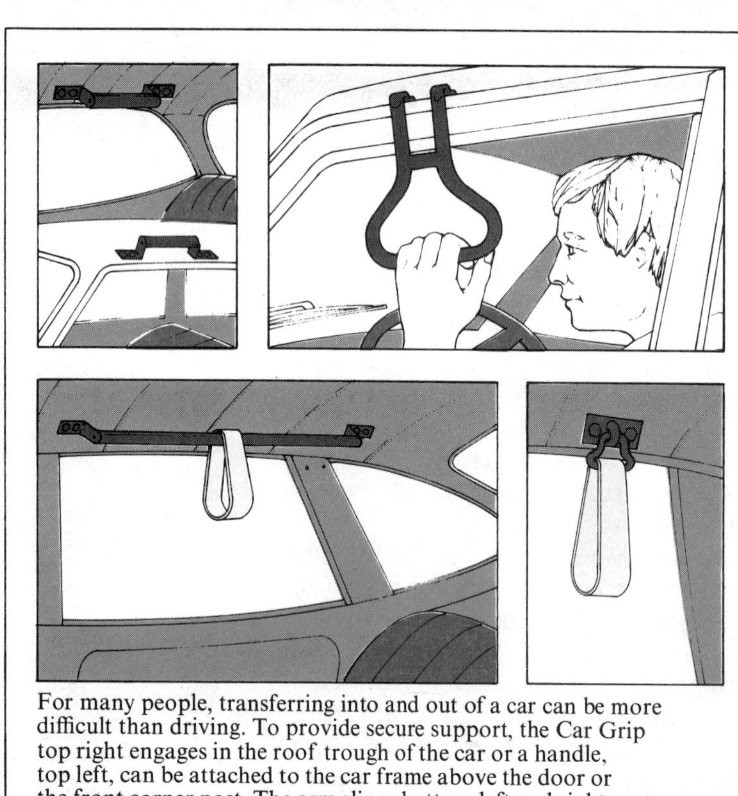

For many people, transferring into and out of a car can be more difficult than driving. To provide secure support, the Car Grip top right engages in the roof trough of the car or a handle, top left, can be attached to the car frame above the door or the front corner post. The arm slings bottom left and right are helpful if grasp is limited.

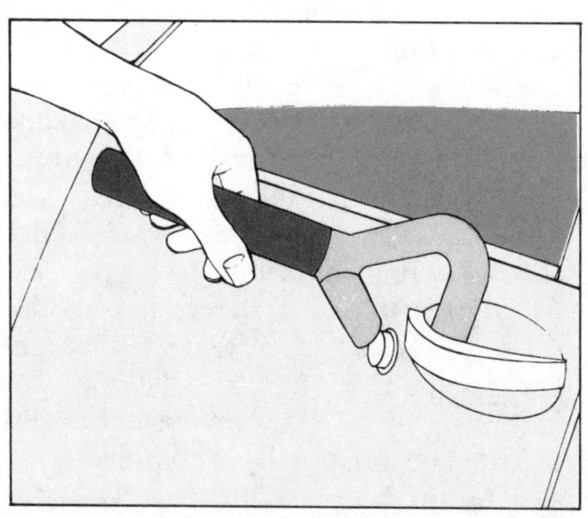

The car door opener right is designed to aid in opening and closing the push-button type of car door handle.

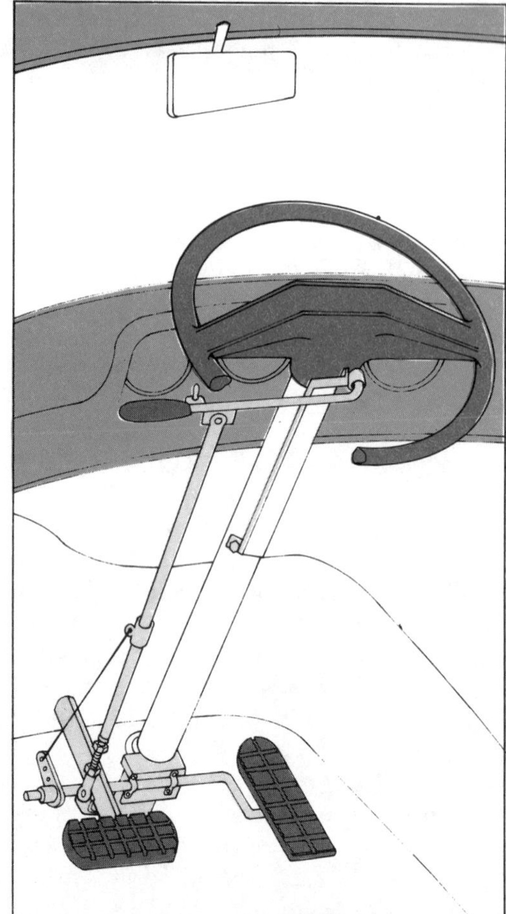

Hand control units for left-hand or right-hand operation all work on more or less the same principle and do not affect conventional use of the foot pedals. The brake is applied by pushing the control lever in one direction, the accelerator by moving the lever in the other direction. Desired driving speed can be maintained with light pressure. Such units are easy to install and the position of the hand lever and brake and accelerator movement are adjustable after installation.

without standing, a sliding board, to bridge the space between the wheelchair and the car seat, is the simplest aid. The board should be at least eight inches (20 cm) wide, one inch (2 cm) thick and thirty inches (76 cm) to thirty-six inches (90 cm) long. It should be tapered at each end and smoothly sanded and polished or covered with a slick material. For added safety, one end of the board can be notched to slip over the post of the chair and the other end can be cleated to keep it from slipping into the car.

Some people find that they have better balance when they transfer backward rather than sideways into and out of a car. In such cases the wheelchair must have a zippered or snap-fastened back.

Most independent drivers who are wheelchaired find the extra doorway space of a two-door car essential for getting the wheelchair into the car. The driver usually has to get into the car from the passenger side, fold the chair, transfer to the driver's side and then pull the wheelchair in. A wheelchair can usually be pulled more easily into a car by lifting in the small front wheels first and so

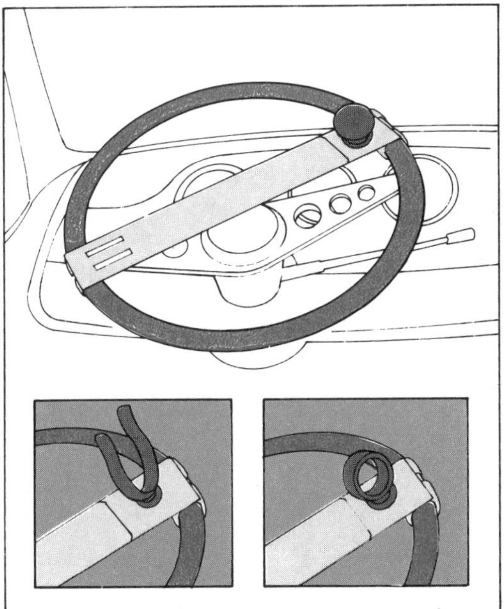

A spinner bar is a useful aid when it is difficult to grasp the steering wheel. The bar serves as a rigid platform for various devices, of which three are illustrated above. The attachments can be removed with just the touch of a button.

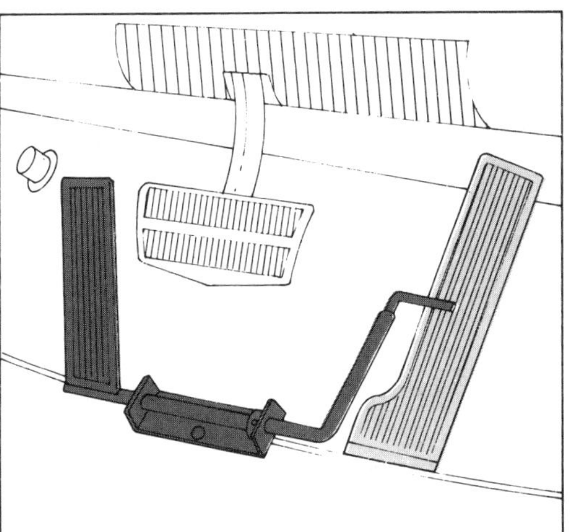

A left-foot accelerator can be easily attached to the car floor. When not in use it can be completely detached from the existing accelerator and folded forward. The cross bar telescopes to permit proper mounting on all makes of cars.

Built-up brake and accelerator pedals are available for people whose feet do not reach the pedals. The height of the pedals can be adjusted from one to six inches (2 to 15 cm).

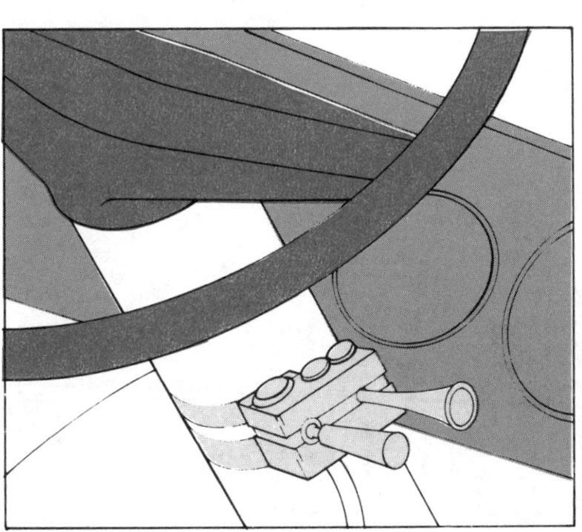

This dimmer switch, to control bright lights, attaches to the steering column and does not interfere with operation of the existing switch.

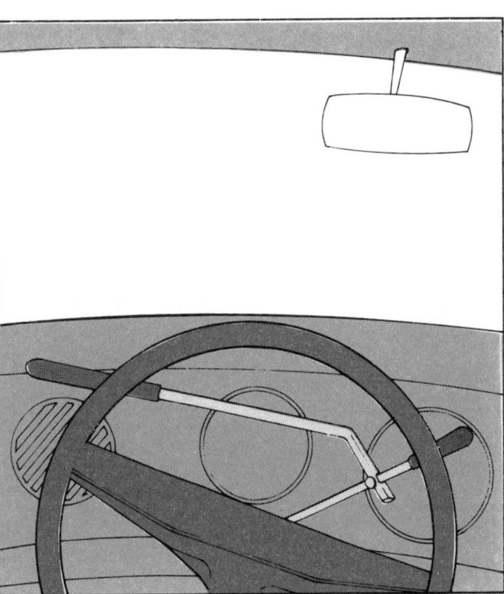

This device clamps to the existing shift lever and converts shift to left-hand use on American cars, right-hand use on British cars.

gaining leverage for the heavier end.

It is easier to pull a wheelchair into the back seat of a two-door car, than a four-door car, because there is no door post to get in the way. Some drivers prefer to pull the chair into the front seat beside them. In this case the wheelchair must have removable footrests and should be strapped into the seat so that it does not fall against the driver.

An aluminum ramp can be used to roll the chair up into the front or back seat. The ramp should be as wide as the wheels of the folded chair and have a small lip on either side to keep them on the track. A small hand-operated hoist is available which is helpful for lifting a folded wheelchair into the car. Filling in one depression in the back seat floor to make it level helps to get the chair in and out more easily.

It is possible to adapt a van to enable a wheelchaired driver to travel in his or her chair. To provide sufficient head room it may be necessary to raise the roof, lower the floor, or both. A lift or ramp has to be provided at the side. It is also necessary to have a means of locking the wheelchair in position to the floor of the van.

The disabled driver must always be prepared for emergencies. Emergency lights will serve not only to warn other cars, but can also bring help. Several units which are commercially available use standard batteries or power from the cigarette lighter socket and are magnetized to attach to the car.

For inclement weather a long-handled window scraper is easy to manage. A car defroster gun that plugs into the lighter socket is also good to have on hand. If reach is limited it is often wise to cover the windows of the parked car to eliminate entirely the need to scrape.

In the United Kingdom the Disabled Drivers' Association, in Ashwellthorpe, Norwich, and the Disabled Drivers' Motor Club in London will help and advise people with physical disabilities on all matters of mobility, including vehicles and conversions, insurance, legal requirements and government and local authority assistance.

In the United States the American Automobile Association publishes a pamphlet listing companies that manufacture vehicle controls and giving information about prices of adapted parts. Information is also given about installation of parts and any precautions that should be taken.

Economic Aspects of Disability

Disability is expensive. While the physical, psychological and emotional difficulties are, to some extent, understood, the costs of managing mundane everyday matters are difficult for the able-bodied to assess.

A variety of aids, including wheelchairs, may be needed to expand the range of mobility and functioning. In many European countries such aids are provided to the disabled; in the United States the cost must be assumed by the individual. The cost of drugs and pharmaceutical products can be a steady financial drain. Incontinence can double or treble laundry bills. Clothing snagged and worn through by braces or other appliances require frequent replacement.

It is expensive to adapt a home to the needs of a disabled person and even modest modifications are not cheap. Costly car adaptations or the purchase of a special van may be necessary and automobile insurance premiums may be unjustifiably increased. The services of an attendant, or even of a nurse, may be needed. Help may be required, too, to cope with shopping, housecleaning, gardening, cooking and a host of little household chores and repairs.

The newly disabled adult suffers an immediate diminishment, if not loss, of income. Coupled with reduced earnings and additional expenses are the obvious and unpredictable extra costs related to employment. And employment potential depends not only on the extent of a handicap and on individual ability and experience, but also on such limiting factors as adverse attitudes of potential employers and man-made barriers to accessibility. Sometimes the list of expenses and the extent of economic problems seem endless and quite daunting to anyone without a large, almost limitless, private income.

Today the governments of most countries recognize that they have an obligation to help alleviate some of these financial burdens. The extent and type of assistance varies from country to country, depending on governmental resources and social and political philosophy. It is the responsibility of every person with physical disabilities to discover what benefits are available and to take advantage of them. Such benefits are not charity; they are entitlements and should be claimed.

In the United States government programs that can benefit people with disabilities are not taxable and include Workers' Compensation, Social Security Disability Insurance, Medicare and Medicaid. As is the case in most countries, there is a variety of additional special provisions for disabled veterans.

Protection against loss of earnings because of disability became part of Social Security law in 1954. Determination of eligibility is complex, depending on medical evaluation and on the Social Security contributions of the disabled individual or his or her family. But don't let the prospect of unraveling a lot of red tape prevent you from applying at your local Social Security office for the benefits to which you may well be entitled. If notified, the Social Security office will send a representative to call on anyone who is hospitalized or housebound.

When people apply for Social Security Disability Insurance (SSDI) benefits they are asked for the names and addresses of doctors who have treated them and of the hospitals and clinics where they have gone for treatment. They may also be asked about the kind of work they have done and how their impairment affects their ability to work and to carry on their daily activities.

Under Social Security law, newly disabled adults or people disabled before the age of twenty-two are deemed disabled if they have physical or mental conditions which prevent them from doing any substantially gainful work, and if the disability is expected to last, or has lasted, for at least twelve months, or is expected to result in death. Even if they are not permanently disabled, but meet these requirements, they are eligible for payments until they have fully recovered and are physically and mentally able to resume gainful employment.

Whether or not they are considered to be eligible, all applicants for SSDI benefits are considered for services by the state vocational rehabilitation agency. Services include teaching of new employment skills, counseling, training in the use of prostheses and job placement. This in itself is a plus and makes it worthwhile to apply.

The SSDI program also enables a person to retain benefits for a twelve-month trial period after full-time employment has been secured. This is reassuring at a time when people are likely to be worried about their ability to cope with a job.

But before deciding in favor of employment, the person with disabilities must consider the financial risks involved. An individual who has been receiving benefits for two years has an automatic entitlement to Medicare coverage, which gives hospital and medical insurance protection. This, if the disability demands a great deal of medical attention, could be vital because there is no national health insurance program in the United States and private insurers can decline to insure a person who is disabled unless the person is employed and qualifies for insurance under his or her employer's insurance program. Private health insurance (for people who are ineligible for a "group" policy, which is usually available only through an employer) can be prohibitively expensive as well as quite limited in its coverage.

According to recent reports, a paraplegic, for example, would have to earn more than twelve thousand dollars a year to be able to afford the medical benefits provided by Social Security and Medicare. And someone who has a job could be in danger of being made redundant, or of being forced by illness to leave. Once an individual has come off SSDI he or she must wait a further six months and then go through the same lengthy process before benefits can be received again. And there is another two-year wait before the person can again be entitled to Medicare.

The decision, therefore, is not easy, especially for anyone eager to be self-sufficient. It is no wonder that many gifted and experienced people are sometimes forced to decide that they cannot possibly afford to work. Before a person makes the decision to return to work it is wise to seek the advice of doctors who are familiar with his or her condition, as well as from disabled people who have already faced and dealt with the problem.

In addition to SSDI benefits, beginning in 1974 certain categories of persons became entitled by law to receive income as a result of the Federal Supplemental Security Income program (SSI), which replaced the widely varied state welfare programs. The basic aim of SSI is to assure a minimum income, related to the cost of living, for individuals and couples by providing basic federal payments with supplements on the state level. This means, unfortunately, that SSI benefits vary considerably from state to state.

More than two million people who were participating in the federal-state old age, blind and disability assistance programs prior to January 1, 1974 were automatically transferred to SSI. It has been estimated, however, that an additional two and a half million people who are eligible for these benefits have not applied for them.

To be eligible for SSI payments a person must be sixty-five or older, or blind or disabled, a resident of one of the fifty states or the District of Columbia and either a United States citizen or a lawfully admitted alien, with limited income and resources. Not all income and assets are counted, however, in the determination of eligibility. It is possible, for example, to own one's own home or have some income and still receive payments. Most people who receive SSI benefits are entitled to free medical services under the Medicaid program.

People who are injured or become disabled on the job or while in a job-related activity are entitled to Workers' Compensation payments and benefits, which can include rehabilitation, job training, medical costs and the right to employment. Regular payments can be instituted for those people who are unable to return to work. Under certain conditions, these payments can be supplemented by SSDI. Workers' Compensation varies from state to state. Consequently, the amounts of payment vary, although the general protections (rehabilitation, medical expenses and income payments) are the same.

Unfortunately, some employers use Workers' Compensation as an excuse not to hire people with disabilities. Most state Workers' Compensation plans have a Second Injury Provision, however, to protect the employer in the event that a disabled employee becomes permanently handicapped because of a job-related injury. The American Mutual Insurance Alliance of Chicago, an association of private insurers which underwrites Workers' Compensation, maintains that hiring a disabled person does not affect an employer's Workers' Compensation rates and is, therefore, an invalid excuse for not hiring such a person.

Although the United States Congress has had on its agenda for years a bill that would allow a special extra exemption on income tax for people with physical disabilities, special exemption is still allowed only to the blind. A number of expenses of the handicapped are, however, often overlooked in the itemization of deductions on personal tax returns. Contact the advisory officer at your local Internal Revenue Service office to be sure that you are taking all the deductions to which you are entitled.

In the United Kingdom, with the introduction of the National Health Service in 1948, free health services have been available to the disabled and able-bodied alike. Although the standard of care varies from area to area and waiting lists for certain services, medical procedures and operations are long, nobody who requires medical care need suffer financial hardship.

The range of services is broad and includes remedial therapy, family planning clinics, advice from health visitors, home nursing by district nurses and child health clinics. Prostheses, surgical appliances, wheelchairs and other mobility aids, hearing aids, home nursing equipment, aids for the sight impaired and a limited number of environmental control units for the severely disabled, are available without cost when prescribed by a doctor.

As a result of several Acts of Parliament there are many other benefits, allowances and services available to people with disabilities. Local authorities are required to keep a register of disabled people in their areas and to give them practical assistance with, for example, housing, aids and adaptations required to bring daily living to a satisfactory standard of safety, comfort and convenience and such services in the home as Meals on Wheels and home-helps. There is, however, considerable variation in the extent to which local authorities provide help and some authorities are more generous than others. The assistance an individual receives depends on the residential area, personal income (which may determine whether payment must be made for certain kinds of help) and on the resources and priorities of the particular authority in charge of the case.

Most British workers must make weekly contributions to Social Security (the National Insurance scheme), but disablement pensions don't always depend on the record of contribution, nor is the sum of money granted based on individual earnings. The highest allowances, based on extent of injury, go to war veterans. The disability benefits received by people incapable of work because of an industrial illness or accident incurred on the job are somewhat lower and are based on a medical assessment of the degree of disability.

A person who has contributed a required amount to Social Security and whose disability is not work-related is entitled to a "civilian" disability pension which is less than either the war or industrial injury pension. To be eligible for it, an individual must have paid in a required amount of Social Security contribution.

In 1975 a noncontributory disability pension was introduced for people of working age who have been unable to work for some time, or who have never been able to work, and therefore don't qualify for an industrial injuries or Social Security disability benefit. Eligibility is based on medical proof of disability, not on the contribution record of spouse or family or on the individual's income.

In 1977 this noncontributory pension was extended to cover disabled married women who are incapable of carrying out their usual household duties and cannot do paid work. To receive it, however, a woman must be virtually unable to perform any normal household tasks even with the help of aids.

There are three more noncontributory benefits which are not means-tested and which recently came into law. The mobility allowance is a cash benefit designed to help people with disabilities who are virtually unable to walk or whose condition does not permit them to walk. An attendance allowance is paid to adults and children who need constant care because of severe physical or mental disability. There are two levels of payment—the higher for those who require attendance both day and night and the lower for those who need attendance during either the day or night.

The invalid care allowance is noncontributory for people of working age who can't go out to work because they must stay at home to care for severely disabled relatives who receive attendance allowances. The claimant must prove that thirty-five hours a week or more is spent in caring for a member of the family. The allowance is not given to a woman, living with or supported by a man, who must give up her job in order to take care of a disabled parent or child. Other than the mobility allowance, this is the only disability benefit that is taxable.

Everyone, including people with disabilities, whose income falls below a certain level is eligible to receive Supplementary Benefits. The amount of the payments is related to financial resources and needs. Recipients receive financial help to cover certain essential and special needs and are entitled to various free services. A claimant for Supplementary and other Social Security benefits has the right to appeal to independent tribunals if he or she is dissatisfied with the decision on a claim.

In the Netherlands financial provision for the disabled has, since October 1, 1976, been governed by two major pieces of legislation—the Disablement Insurance Act and the General Disablement Benefits Act. Under the Dutch Social Security system, no separate plan exists to cover accidents or occupational diseases suffered at work. Benefits are awarded on proof of reduced capacity to work, irrespective of cause.

The Disablement Insurance Act covers all employees up to the age of sixty-five. The General Disablement Act applies not only to employees up to the age of sixty-five, but also to the self-employed, the congenitally disabled and disabled children.

In the Netherlands a person with disabilities receives two types of benefit. The first is a cash payment as wage compensation or income replacement, plus those provisions which are meant to preserve, recover or improve the ability to work, enabling the individual still to receive an income. This might include the loan of a car to travel to work and the adaptation of machinery to help the individual achieve greater productivity. The second type of benefit is designed to improve living conditions and to compensate for the problems of disabled living.

Insurance under both acts is compulsory and benefits begin when a person's incapacity for work has lasted fifty-two weeks without interruption. (Any employee who permanently or temporarily has become unable to continue his own work receives sickness benefit at a rate of 80 percent of his normal wages. The entitlement lasts for fifty-two weeks.) Under the General Disablement Benefits Act, those who are congenitally handicapped and those who become handicapped before their eighteenth birthday are entitled to benefits on reaching their eighteenth birthdays.

Benefits under the Disablement Insurance Act are paid for by contributions and the act covers all insured employees. Contributions for the General Disablement Benefits Act are levied by the Tax Department. Those entitled to receive cash benefits under this scheme include married men and unmarried men and women. Children under eighteen, married women and widows are not entitled to cash benefits, but do receive provisions to help increase working capacity and to offset the problems of daily living. The benefits provided for uninsured people are paid out of public funds. The rate of benefit paid under both these acts is index-linked to average wages and rise in concert with them.

The Dutch tax system provides disabled people with the right to tax exemption and they are exempt from motor vehicle tax. As far as direct taxation is concerned, there is a plan for working incapacity relief by which a person with physical disabilities in any tax bracket is allowed a certain increase in tax-free income. Above a certain tax threshold, disabled people can be reimbursed for expenses of medical treatment, including drugs, costs of aids and adaptations, costs of transportation and extra domestic help.

In the Federal Republic of Germany perhaps the most striking feature of the provisions for the disabled is the diversity not only of the type of benefit awarded according to either the cause or result of the disability, but also of the insurance plans which exist for different sections of the working population—plans which are administered by more than one hundred separate and independent associations, not including the two thousand different sickness benefit funds through which the health insurance is administered. The lack of unity which exists in the West German social security structure is due in part to history and in part to policy. Social insurance has existed in Germany for almost one hundred years and it has been extended and improved piecemeal to meet particular situations. It is only since 1975 that any kind of unification has taken place.

In any event, the social policy of Germany has never been to create a welfare state, but rather to create particular remedies to meet particular situations with emphasis on the principles of individual self-help. The great mass of West German social legislation is based on principles of compulsory contributory insurance, rather than on the award of flat-rate, noncontributory benefits. On average, almost 18 percent of an employed person's earnings is withheld for purposes of social insurance.

The provisions for the disabled fall broadly into two categories—accident insurance, which provides for people disabled as the result of industrial injuries, and that part of general pensions insurance which deals with invalidity pensions for those whose disability arose in other circumstances. Under the Federal Social Assistance Act, allowances are given to people who are not entitled to invalidity pensions.

In Sweden a sickness insurance plan, compulsory for all adults over sixteen, covers medical treatment, hospital treatment, medicine and equipment. Separate disablement pensions exist for those who are disabled as the result of work accidents or occupational diseases and for those whose disability is not attributable to either of these causes. Both pensions are calculated on the basis of lost working capacity rather than medical criteria.

All working people, including the self-employed and certain students, are compulsorily insured against work injuries. Anyone whose working capacity is reduced by at least 15 percent as a result of an injury is entitled to a "life annuity." The amount of the annuity is directly proportional to the degree of the disability.

Disability pensions, which are subject to income tax, are awarded to all those whose working capacity is reduced by at least 50 percent for a considerable period of time because of illness, injury or any other reduction of capability. The extent of the pension depends on how much the working capacity has been reduced.

A disability allowance is payable to those people who need help to accomplish the necessary tasks of everyday life or work, or who have substantial extra costs. (People who are blind or deaf are always entitled to this allowance.) It is payable at three rates depending on the extent of need for help or the extent of the extra costs.

In Sweden the social services are promoted by extensive publicity encouraging people to take full advantage of the benefits and services offered. The publicity has a double purpose—to ensure that people get their entitlements and to remove any stigma attached to the receipt of public assistance.

Programs for people with disabilities tend to be multiple. In the United States, for example, they operate on federal, state and local levels. Research is, therefore, necessary if you are to be sure that you are getting everything to which you are entitled. Disability benefits are not charity. They are like insurance payments. You or your family have either worked for them or paid for them and you are entitled to collect them. But it's up to you to find out what they are.

Rehabilitation

The word rehabilitation means a good deal more today than it used to. Increasingly, the scope of social services for the disabled has expanded internationally. Now, in many countries, medical therapy, vocational training and retraining, counseling, educational and employment assessment and placement and even help in finding suitable housing, come under the umbrella of rehabilitation.

Rehabilitation services have been established primarily in response to society's emphasis on the value of economic as well as social status and security, rewards usually consequent on having well-paid employment with prospects of upward mobility. Apart from the moral obligation to people with physical disabilities, rehabilitation directed toward employment is desirable from any government's point of view because every person who is economically independent is also a contributing member of society in many important ways, not least of them financial.

Increasingly, governments are trying to develop, improve or restore to the fullest extent the personal effectiveness of all their disabled citizens, to give them, in every area of their lives, equal opportunity with the able-bodied in fact as well as in principle.

The government of the Federal Republic of Germany, for example, instituted for the 1970s an action program to expand and standardize the nation's network of rehabilitation facilities, benefits and services. It has backed the program with improved legislation, and research is being carried out to develop technical and orthopedic aids and better psychiatric care.

Model centers offer combined medical and vocational rehabilitation services for people with heart disease and circulatory disorders, for brain-damaged adolescents, for paraplegics and for those disabled by internal diseases. Twenty of these training centers and twenty centers for vocational retraining have been planned and some are already in operation. People who are not yet ready for placement in competitive employment are provided with employment opportunities in an expanding network of special workshops.

In the United Kingdom there are government Employment Rehabilitation Centres throughout the country whose aim is to restore the confidence of people with permanent, as well as temporary, disabilities, to help the individual adjust to a new handicap and to give vocational assessment, guidance and training. Financial benefits are given during the period of rehabilitation.

Disablement Resettlement Officers (DROs) work from local Employment Offices or Job Centres. They are responsible for finding appropriate jobs for people with disabilities, but their most important function is as liaison between the individual and everyone else involved in the rehabilitation picture. Backed by medical advisory and occupational guidance officers and psychologists as well as by other official rehabilitation schemes, they keep in close contact with employers, hospital personnel and the local social services.

Introduced in 1972, Britain's Training Opportunities Scheme (TOPS) has an extensive network of training arrangements. Free full-time courses, lasting from four weeks to a year, are offered at fifty Skillcentres, seven hundred colleges of further education and two hundred business establishments—and trainees are given allowances and other benefits. The courses cover more than five hundred occupations, among them craft and technical skills, clerical and secretarial work, business management and administration. The aim is to qualify men and women, ranging in age from sixteen to fifty-five, for different or better jobs—or even for first jobs. No previous training or skill is required; advice in course choice and help in finding employment are given. Through this scheme special arrangements, including residential training at specialized colleges, are made for disabled students.

In the United States, in recognition of the scope of rehabilitation, the word "vocational" was significantly omitted from the title of the 1973 Rehabilitation Act which is, perhaps, the greatest legislative breakthrough for people with disabilities anywhere. Despite this significant federal legislation, and the fact that prior to this Offices of Vocational Rehabilitation were established all over the country to serve all the legitimate needs of clients, the extent and the quality of rehabilitation vary from state to state.

In some states rehabilitation centers now offer a range of services, many in conjunction with specializing agencies or hospitals, and including medical care and physical therapy, social and psychological counseling, aptitude testing and higher education referral. Some offer vocational evaluation and training, the provision of necessary tools, uniforms, equipment or licenses, job placement and follow-up after employment. The services may even extend to counseling of other members of the family and to having accessibility modifications made at places of employment at no cost to the employer. In some cases, allowances are given for board, room and travel during rehabilitation.

A local Office of Vocational Rehabilitation is generally the best place to go for information about further education and its financing. Further education may be financed in part or in full by the rehabilitation service itself or by educational grant-awarding bodies, to which the office will

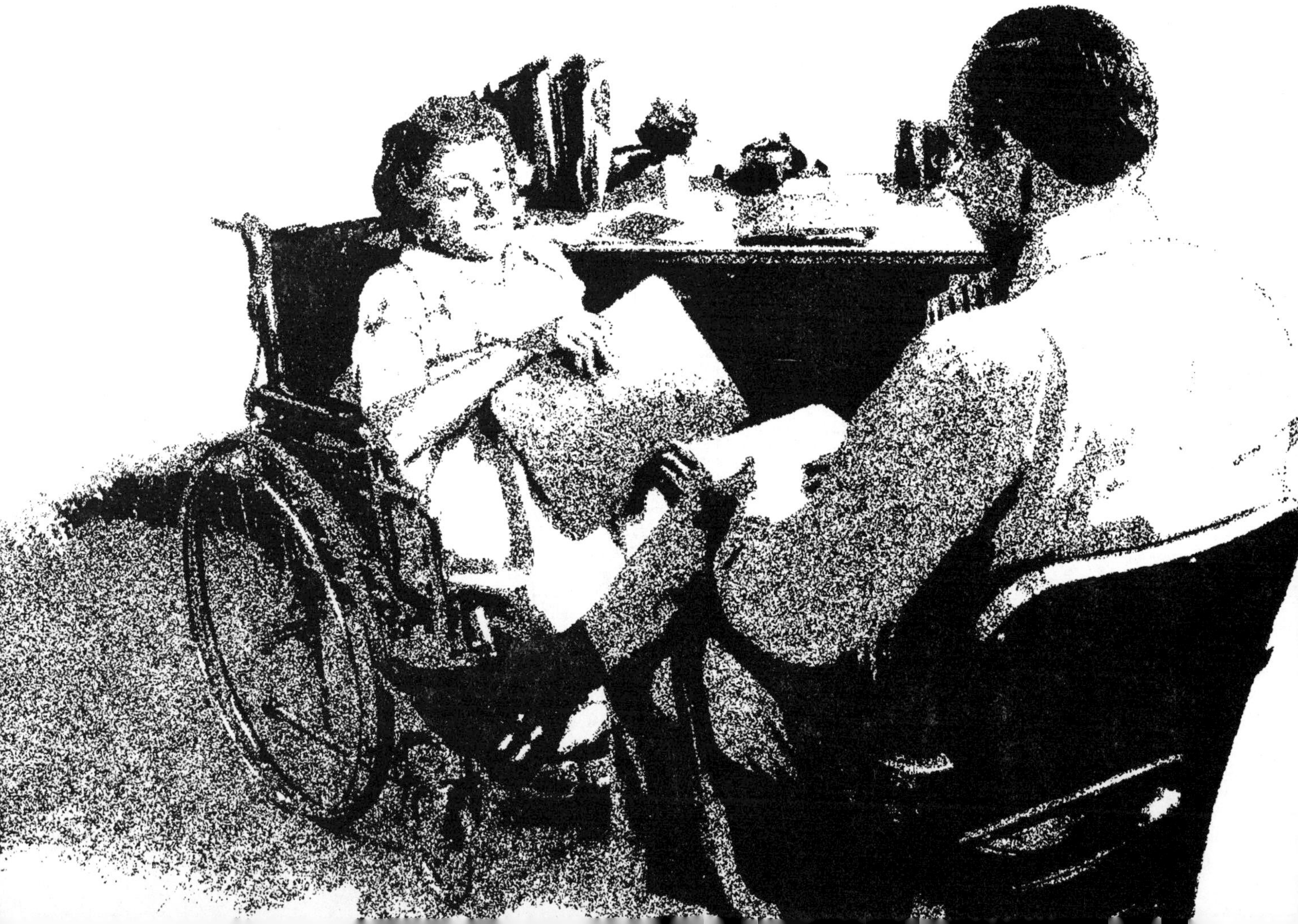

frequently refer the prospective student.

Since an office's success is usually rated by its number of case closures, there is, understandably, an emphasis on processing and completing cases as quickly as possible, and all too often along stereotyped lines. Unfortunately, the accuracy of evaluation and prognosis and the applicability of recommendations often depend on the sensitivity and resourcefulness of the individual counselor, who may be inadequately trained, have defeatist attitudes toward handicapped clients or have limited contact with community employers. Efforts are now being made to put the client in a position to exercise greater independence of judgment as well as to adopt procedures for arbitration between the client and the counselor when it is necessary.

To be eligible for rehabilitation in the United States, an individual must have a physical or mental disability which constitutes a substantial handicap to finding and keeping employment or to functioning as a homemaker. Eligibility has, however, been restricted and people above the age of fifty-five, the institutionalized, the severely disabled and the multihandicapped have been excluded, as have those with rapidly progressive diseases. So, too, have the homebound, except in cases where rehabilitation would free another member of the family for gainful employment.

In recent years, however, a number of states, most notably New York and Wisconsin, have taken steps toward radical changes in the assessment of eligibility and the extension of facilities to the homebound. The 1973 Rehabilitation Act mandates services for the severely disabled in an effort to prevent further exclusion of those people whose disabilities require longer term, more sophisticated and, consequently, more expensive, rehabilitation, and whose potential for independent living or employment is not promising.

Despite all the generally good and comprehensive rehabilitation services, the system has been a target for criticism on two major grounds. One is the bureaucratic administration, and the other is the tendency toward early placement in employment with little regard for the individual's career potential.

At the 1977 White House Conference on Handicapped Individuals the dismaying gap between the procedures of rehabilitation and of placement in inadequate or inappropriate employment was boldly attacked. Routine criticism of the shortcomings of individual rehabilitation officers and of the workings of the federal and state employment services were set aside and it was proposed that industry involve itself in the rehabilitation process from the time of the first diagnostic interview.

Actually this concept had, on a small scale, already been implemented. In 1970 the Department of Health, Education and Welfare funded eleven model programs to place handicapped people in competitive jobs. Called Projects with Industry (PWI), almost five hundred private industries were involved, representing most facets of American business. The companies included Sears Roebuck, IBM, Dupont, the Metropolitan Life Insurance Company, the Banker's Trust of New York, as well as the U.S.Civil Service Commission.

One such program was developed at the Human Resources Center, a private non-profit organization located on Long Island, New York. It was designed to obtain entry-level, white collar jobs in the local business community for severely disabled people between the ages of eighteen and sixty-five. The staff of the center worked in conjunction with a business advisory group to select and develop instruction manuals and training equipment. Evaluation at the center was limited to eleven weeks and each company assumed the responsibility for training the individual in the specific tasks of each job.

The advantages of such mutually productive arrangements are clear, and in fact nearly three out of every four handicapped people served by the PWI program found employment in the competitive labor market. They benefited from job training undertaken for a particular position and industry benefited from the "follow-along" services provided by the project, especially during the probationary work period. The amount of money returned to the government in taxes paid for the program many times over.

The Center for Independent Living (CIL) in Berkeley, California, is a non-residential, self-help program which provides people with disabilities with support and services to enable them to leave institutions, live independently and hold jobs. Established in 1972 by a group of handicapped people to make available services that were not provided by traditional rehabilitation agencies, CIL has been so successful that it now serves as a model for similar centers which are being established all over the country.

CIL's services range from transportation to legal assistance; from peer counseling and housing assistance to van modification and curbside wheelchair repair; from a college degree program to on-the-job training. One of its many services is an intensive nine-month computer training program which is funded by the State Department of Rehabilitation. Two instructors, both of whom are disabled, work with twenty students who, after their training, qualify as entry-level computer programmers.

The program's advisers come from the Department of Rehabilitation, from the local Community College and from the business community. A business advisory committee aids in course planning, provides lecturers from the field and arranges field trips so that students can see large computer systems at work. More than thirty firms and organizations, represented by the committee, help in the placement of graduates.

It has been estimated that for every one thousand dollars invested in rehabilitation in the United States, the economy is reimbursed by nine thousand dollars. This awesome return is made by the actual taxes paid by the rehabilitated individual when he or she gets a job, the elimination of welfare payments and the newly acquired purchasing power of this consumer.

Although the benefits of rehabilitation can almost always be measured in advantageous financial terms, the enrichment of a society by the participation of all its members is greater still.

Education

It is self-evident that education has a beneficial effect on the quality of an individual's life. It broadens cultural horizons, encourages independent thinking and helps to develop emotional maturity. When education is directed toward specific occupational goals it also helps to ensure financial security.

"Our pride should be in guaranteeing that every qualified person with a disability, whatever it may be, has the right to pursue the field of studies for which he is qualified and to which he aspires—with reasonable choice." This is the credo of Dr. Timothy J. Nugent, who pioneered the expansion of educational horizons for the physically disabled in the United States and influenced attitudes toward education for the disabled all over the world.

In 1947 Dr. Nugent took the initiative of admitting the first paraplegic student to the University of Illinois. During the next thirty years the campus buildings and facilities were made increasingly accessible with one-storied, ramped buildings, enclosed connecting corridors between buildings and campus buses equipped to carry wheelchaired passengers. The university now has a Rehabilitation Education Center, headed by Dr. Nugent, and an enrollment of several hundred handicapped students, more than one hundred of whom are wheelchaired. They participate fully in all academic, cultural, extramural and extracurricular activities and are given every opportunity for physical, emotional and social development.

By 1980 it will be mandatory for all American universities receiving financial assistance from the federal government to make their programs accessible to handicapped students and to provide such facilities as special equipment and adapted furniture for classrooms, libraries and dormitories, tape recorders, braillers, aural and visual indicators, grants for tuition, books, tutorial service and, when necessary, attendants, therapy and supportive counseling. Many colleges and universities are already providing some of these services. Gallaudet College in Washington, D.C., the only liberal arts college for the deaf in the world, is fully supported by the federal government; it maintains an extensive research program and is a training center for audiologists and teachers.

Handicapped Americans are beginning to avail themselves enthusiastically of the facilities for higher education that have opened to them. In 1970 one estimate put the number of severely handicapped students in American colleges at over thirty-four thousand, with more than seven thousand in New York State alone and about fifteen hundred in the San Diego Community College programs. When Fresno State College in California made its campus more accessible, enrollment of disabled students leaped from fifty to four hundred and fifty.

Increasingly, as architectural barriers are being modified or eliminated, students with disabilities are attending colleges all across the country. While it is a good idea for any student to visit the campus of the college in which he or she is interested in enrolling, such a preliminary visit is particularly important for a handicapped student. *The College Guide for Students with Disabilities* by Elinor Gollay and Alwina Bennet, is a valuable directory of higher education services, programs and college facilities accessible to handicapped American students. In addition, the President's Committee on Employment of the Handicapped has a number of free guides to accessible colleges and universities with descriptions of services to disabled students.

In the United States adult education is offered in different ways. Besides universities and colleges there are technical

colleges, education for the homebound for high school and college credit, for vocational advancement or simply for personal interest. More than seven hundred educational institutions offer home study courses in a wide range of subjects—academic, professional and technical. The courses include such diverse subjects as automation, motel management, small engine repair and journalism. Accreditation of a school or membership in the National Home Study Council or National University Extension Association helps to assure study under a competent faculty. Instruction is provided by a variety of means. These include correspondence, video cassettes, which are played through an ordinary television set, and home-to-class—and even hospital bed-to-class—telephone.

When Long Island University opened its enrollment to the handicapped there were seven disabled attending students and three hospital patients at a respirator center who were taking courses by telephone service. In three and a half years the enrollment of disabled students rose to two hundred and fifty-seven, of whom eighteen took courses by telephone communication.

The University Without Walls is an American program which makes it possible for the individual to receive "life experience" credit for past learning experience outside the classroom. It is possible, for example, to obtain political science credit for volunteer work in a political campaign or community program. Many courses are available for independent study credit. Information about this program and the names of participating colleges are available from the Union for Experimenting Colleges at Antioch College, Yellow Springs, Ohio.

The College Level Examination Program (CLEP) is one which makes it possible for the individual to receive credit toward a degree by demonstration—through examination—of knowledge of a subject. More than two thousand colleges and universities are affiliated with this program. Examinations are given monthly, for a fee, at eight hundred locations throughout the country.

The positive approach of the United States Government has been taken, to lesser degrees, by a number of other governments. In Denmark, for example, the conditions for admission to institutions of higher education apply without reservation to qualified handicapped individuals. In France the only restrictions are on admission to institutions which qualify students for professions that the handicapped are unable to exercise. The government provides such specific assistance as special equipment, transportation, career guidance and help in finding employment.

Disabled Israeli students are encouraged to continue their educations and are provided with grants and any necessary equipment. In the Netherlands the handicapped are given the same educational opportunities as the nonhandicapped and the government gives help with some mainly technical requirements. The Swedish Government provides various specific kinds of assistance, such as readers for the blind, books in braille, tape recordings, transportation facilities and hearing aids to students who have disabilities.

In the United Kingdom students with disabilities are eligible for special grants from local authorities and aids from local Education Authorities, but there is no legislation to facilitate their admission to universities. Most of the necessary advances are still in the study stage where the operative word is "should." The nongovernmental National Bureau of Handicapped Students gives advice and information on accessibility, available courses and grants. The universities themselves try to provide opportunities for students with the necessary ability, but many of them are highly inaccessible.

Since 1971, however, the Open University has offered degree courses to anyone in the United Kingdom, regardless of age, status or previous academic achievement. Tuition is by correspondence, textbook study, radio and television programs, individual tutoring, group seminars, summer school and, when required, field work. When attendance at a summer school is not possible, home counseling and tuition sessions may be given, or the student may be linked by home-to-school telephone to classroom discussions. Every effort is made to accommodate the individual needs of disabled students, from ensuring admission to otherwise oversubscribed courses to providing aids to communication and mobility. Grants are available to cover the expense of attendants and travel.

The initial enrollment of the Open University was twenty thousand students; within four years fifteen thousand of them, one hundred and thirteen of whom were handicapped, had been graduated. Although exact figures are difficult to gather, it is believed that today the Open University has more disabled students on its register than have all the universities and polytechnics throughout the country put together—and the numbers continue to rise.

The level of courses offered ranges from undergraduate and postgraduate courses to self-contained post-experience courses; previously earned credits are honored and degrees are earned on the basis of a credit system which enables students to work at their own pace and even to drop out and reenter later. Some courses can be transferred for completion at conventional universities.

By whatever method people with disabilities choose to study, their conditions, goals and available time and money will naturally influence the choice of program. Inspirational stories are legion of handicapped people who have achieved unusual success in a broad spectrum of careers and occupations, after pursuing studies as attending or home-based students.

Today, as never before, educational facilities and opportunities are available to people with physical disabilities. Strong motivation is necessary, however, for the achievement of a high level of education involves many more problems for the disabled than it does for the able-bodied. But it is never too late to learn to the full extent of your capacities, along the lines of your inclination and to reap the rewards of so doing.

Employment

Work can be both a means and an end. For many people employment is more than merely a means of livelihood; it provides a treasured sense of independence and self-respect, creates a reassuring framework of stable routine and offers the stimulation of daily personal exchange and incident. Although modern society tends, perhaps unfortunately, to put its highest values on the goals of money, power and prestige, for the most fortunate people their work is in itself a vocation, an essential gratification, rewarding because it permits productive expression of creative abilities and is of absorbing interest.

For many people with disabilities every inch of this terrain of motivation and accomplishment is fraught with difficulties. The kind and extent of the disability, the age at which it occurred, the level of education, the applicability and success of rehabilitation and counseling, the actual employment possibilities, the existing financial benefits of unemployment that cannot be matched by a salary and the individual's temperament and self-image, all bear on the problem. But governments' policies and barriers, both attitudinal and environmental, are of equal, or even greater, importance.

Many of these same factors have contributed to the deplorable unemployment, underemployment and misemployment of people with disabilities. As a result, millions of individuals have suffered considerably and nations have not only been deprived of valuable human resources, but have also had to bear the mounting costs of maintaining forced dependency and the consequent loss of consumer power.

In the United States the nation's sights first began to be focused on the problems of employment of the handicapped in 1945 when many disabled veterans needed and wanted jobs. It was then that the President's Committee on Employment of the Handicapped was set up. But because the committee lacks legal power its role has been essentially that of a public relations agency and a coordinator of the activities of organizations concerned with improving employment opportunities for the disabled. The federal government itself spends about twenty-one billion dollars a year to support those who are handicapped and unemployed and less than two billion dollars a year on rehabilitation and training.

Perhaps the most significant advance for the establishment of the disabled as citizens with equal rights has resulted from the 1973 Rehabilitation Act of which Sections 501, 503 and 504 are of the greatest importance in relation to job opportunities for the handicapped. Section 501 requires the federal government, one of the United States' largest employers, to take affirmative action in the hiring and promoting of people with disabilities. The Civil Service Commission is responsible for the implementation of Section 501.

Section 503 requires companies who do at least twenty-five hundred dollars worth of annual business with the federal government to take affirmative action to hire and to promote handicapped people or face the loss of federal contracts. This affects about two million companies and institutions that employ more than one-third of the country's work force.

The law requires the submission of an affirmative action plan for the removal of architectural barriers, the mounting of a recruiting campaign, the modification of job requirements and the training of unskilled disabled workers whenever possible. "Reasonable accommodation" must also be provided, a requirement which means that companies may have to make expensive changes in offices and factories and has understandably resulted in protest from some employers.

Under Section 503, each federal contract and subcontract must contain a clause declaring nondiscrimination against qualified handicapped employees (unless undue business hardship would result).

Section 504 requires that any organization receiving federal funds may not discriminate against the handicapped. This section affects most universities, public school systems, hospitals and nursing homes in the United States. It not only requires that these institutions take affirmative action in the hiring and promoting of people with disabilities, but it also requires these institutions to make their facilities and programs accessible to them.

Among the private organizations established to assist and encourage compliance with the 1973 Rehabilitation Act is Mainstream, Inc. Founded in 1976 and based in Washington, D.C., this non-profit organization has undertaken responsibility for consultation, education and public affairs programs aimed at getting the disabled into the mainstream of American life.

The Rehabilitation Act has established the fundamental rights of disabled American workers and has also set in motion the legal machinery which enables those unjustly treated to file official complaints with the Department of Labor under Section 503 or with the Department of Health, Education and Welfare under Section 504. Job discrimination charges have already been filed by disabled people against such companies as General Motors Corporation, R.C.A., U.S. Steel and International Business Machines.

In the United Kingdom companies with staffs of more than twenty people are required by law to employ at least 3 percent of their personnel from the registry of disabled persons. Since registration as a disabled person is voluntary this results in some anomalies. Fewer and fewer people with disabilities are registering with the Department of Employment because they do not feel they should be labeled and, naturally, because they want to be hired on their own merits, not merely to make up a quota. Although D.R.O.s must find work for all disabled people, employers are not obliged to hire anyone who is not registered; and a person cannot go to a sheltered workshop unless he or she is registered. The government itself, moreover, has set a poor example; only two out of nine government departments have been reported to have exceeded their quotas.

In the Federal Republic of Germany, on the other hand, employers, both private and public, with a minimum of sixteen employees are obliged by law to fulfill a 6 percent quota of severely handicapped people. Provision is made for the payment of a monthly compensatory contribution by employers for each unfilled vacancy in their quotas. The proceeds of these contributions are primarily used for the provision of rehabilitation, training and jobs suitable for the disabled.

Employers are, slowly, beginning to realize that it is to their advantage to hire people with disabilities. Surveys done by the U.S. Department of Labor indicate a better safety record for disabled workers than for the average able-bodied worker exposed to the same work hazards. The record of disabled people for attendance, job stability, as well as their performance rate, is excellent.

E. I. du Pont de Nemours and Company, America's sixteenth largest employer, spent eight months gathering data on 1,452 employees with physical handicaps. The key findings of the study were that there had been no increases in compensation costs or lost-time injuries; that 96 percent of handicapped workers rated average or better safety records both on and off the job and that more than 50 percent were above average; that handicapped workers wanted to be treated as regular employees with no special privileges; that 91 percent rated average or better on job performance; and that 79 percent rated average or better on attendance. The study also showed very little difference between handicapped and nonhandicapped workers with regard to their ability to work in harmony with supervisors and fellow employees.

With these facts as ammunition any handicapped person who wants a job should feel confident about going after one, particularly since there are very few jobs that require 100 percent physical fitness. Job seekers frequently become disheartened far too soon, usually because they have given insufficient consideration to the techniques of job application. Many interviewers in personnel departments don't know enough about physical handicaps to interview applicants with disabilities properly. Sometimes it is the applicant who has to put the interviewer at ease by referring to his or her physical limitations.

The President's Committee on Employment of the Handicapped has prepared a useful list of practical suggestions for job seekers.

Do:

- Learn ahead of time as much as you can about the company. Know what goods it produces or what services it sells.
- Apply in person and go alone. Mail or telephone contacts rarely get results.
- Be on time if you have a definite appointment—not too early, not late.
- Look your best, well-groomed and appropriately dressed.
- Apply for a specific kind of work.
- Speak clearly.
- Stress your qualifications for the job you want; review your past experience, training and skills which would fit you for the job; take a list of former employers, dates and periods of your past work history. If you have none, state any training or home study that is a qualifying point in getting the job.
- Stress the contribution you can make to the company.
- Answer questions honestly and enthusiastically.
- Briefly explain your physical limitations and be optimistic in your attitude.

Don't:

- Plead how much you need a job.
- Apologize for your handicap.
- Dwell on your disability or recount a lengthy medical history.
- Hedge in answering questions, misrepresent facts, bluff or be a know-it-all.
- Balk at a request to take a physical examination.
- Be discouraged if the first interview is unfavorable.
- Fail to exhaust all the community resources which exist for your benefit.

The committee also points out that if handicapped people feel truly qualified to do certain jobs, have the necessary transportation, are able to care for themselves independently throughout an entire working day to meet the demands of working outside the home, they should not be satisfied until they have found suitable employment.

Sheltered Employment

The transition from rehabilitation and training to employment involves a crucial adjustment in the life of a person with disabilities. It is not easy to set out, perhaps for the first time, to face the hazards of the physical environment and to confront the sometimes thoughtless curiosity of the able-bodied. It is no wonder that some people with disabilities prefer the security of sheltered employment.

For those whose disabilities are too severe to permit outside employment, a sheltered workshop can provide more than financial reward. It can also offer the theraupeutic advantages of getting out of the house, of occupying time constructively and of meeting other people.

There are different types of sheltered employment, operated by both government agencies and voluntary organizations. Some are limited to specific disabilities; many are intended as short-term transitional programs, giving on-the-job training and apprenticeships in such marketable skills as the mechanics of air-conditioning and television repair, in conditions closely resembling those of real working situations. Such experience helps to develop work tolerance and to increase the individual's capacity to meet the work standards of open industry.

The concept of sheltered employment does run counter to the desire of many people with disabilities for social integration and it has, therefore, its voluble and impassioned opponents who see it as a stigmatizing force. They also claim that such workshops underpay people for the work they do, condone a low standard of achievement and hence do nothing to encourage greater self-esteem. Nevertheless, nobody can deny that if a more satisfactory solution cannot be found, sheltered employment is preferable to total isolation, idleness and boredom.

Working from Home

Transportation problems, architectural barriers, lack of personal mobility, inability to use rest rooms and restaurant facilities or to care for oneself independently throughout a working day are among the many valid reasons for people with disabilities to choose the more feasible alternative of working from home.

The stimulation and fulfillment derived from having an occupation can be considerable even when the income is small, for a successful business venture need not be a full-time one, and the expectation of profit need not be the only reason for engaging in it. Part-time or seasonal work can also be absorbing and satisfying and at the same time can provide a little income. And working from home permits personal control of hours, output and demands on time and strength.

A lack of imagination about what they might do and the ways to go about doing it keep many people from embarking on a home-based occupation. There are a number of interesting possibilities, however, suited to a variety of personal needs, preferences and abilities.

Before deciding on an occupation it is essential to evaluate as objectively as possible your capacities as well as the market potential for the kind of product or service you can and would like to sell. You must also consider your handicap, as well as the help you may need and its availability and the space and facilities in your home.

Fortunately, a wealth of commercially available or easily homemade aids can make it possible even for those who are severely disabled to pursue a rewarding occupation with ease. Most people find, too, that the longer they work the more resourceful they become in devising ways to make things easier for themselves.

In the United Kingdom aids, including remote control apparatus, adapted typewriters, page turners, special chairs, sewing machines and braille micrometers, are supplied on indefinite loan to enable severely disabled people to work from home. In special cases, when all other possibilities of employment have been found unsuitable and where a suggested home-based business seems a viable economic proposition, adaptation of housing already occupied by a disabled person may be made for work purposes. Applications for such help should be made to the Disablement Resettlement Officer at a local Employment Office or Job Centre.

Many newly disabled people of professional attainments find that they can successfully and comfortably carry on their work from home. Architects, technical draftsmen and commercial artists may enjoy working away from the distracting activity and noise of an office. And many severely disabled people who might well be, and only a few years ago were, considered unemployable, are now lucratively employed—from home—in such professional fields as law, insurance, public relations, journalism and real estate. In the United Kingdom the Civil Service provides home employment for professionals, including engineers, lawyers and translators.

If you are not yet sure of the right occupation for yourself, a good way to begin is to make two parallel lists—one of the activities you enjoy pursuing and the other of the services or products most likely to be needed in your community. Remember, too, that a hobby can often become the basis for a money-making occupation.

Many current books and periodicals give explicit practical advice about the running of small home-based businesses. Consult them for information about procedures, outlets and suppliers, and for warnings about otherwise unpredictable crises and hazards. The librarian at your local library can help you to find material dealing with your field of interest, as well as specific guides to establishing a small business.

In the United States, Rehabilitation Offices are usually able to offer practical guidance and to refer clients to further sources of information. With the financial assistance of Small Business Administration loans, many handicapped people have been able to start small home-based businesses.

There are certain fundamental requirements for establishing even a very modest business. Once the nature of the business is decided upon it is important that time be taken to acquire not only the available information on the subject, but also the proper training when required in order to do the best possible job. It is necessary to plan ahead to organize the work and to arrange a schedule so that you will be sure to have the time, energy and flow of funds to carry on the business efficiently. If you will be selling things you make it is vital, before you actually go into business, to accumulate a stock of representative samples to show prospective customers.

Once you have decided on your business, have inexpensive business cards printed and send them, along with letters of explanation, to potentially interested firms and individuals in your area. Any service or product that you are able to offer can also, of course, be advertised in local newspapers, trade magazines or in neighborhood stores, on bulletin boards in schools and colleges or by mail to a list of people or companies selected from local directories or from rented mailing lists.

Clients are frequently acquired by word of mouth recommendation. If you please even one or two people you are likely soon to have more calls or orders for your service or product than you can deal with.

The following suggestions may enable you, or inspire you, to take a fresh look at the possibilities in your life for a home-based occupation.

Sufficient knowledge of almost any subject makes tutoring from home feasible. Those with language skills can offer private lessons to individuals or groups, or translation can be undertaken for publishers, technical magazines or business firms engaged in exporting or

importing. Trained remedial teachers can work at home with children who have learning difficulties.

Many clipping services employ home workers or a service can be set up which deals with people who are researching particular subjects or with those who are accumulating press notices about specific events, campaigns or personalities.

Copy typists are always at a premium. Typing can easily be done at home and accuracy is usually far more important than speed.

A good telephone manner and voice and the ability to sell are all that are needed to qualify for a telephone sales or market research job. With proper aids even people who are bedridden can and do run successful businesses by telephone. An employment agency for babysitters is an often needed but neglected service as, too, are wake-up, reminder and liaison services.

A general office service can be large or small. It can be restricted to one or two operations or can include typing, proofreading, mimeographing or photoduplicating, bookkeeping and envelope addressing.

There is an increasingly ready market for handmade articles and scrupulous finish usually ensures good prices and continued demand from individual customers as well as retailers. Ceramics, knitwear, embroidery, needlepoint and woven items can be produced according to personal taste or to customers' orders, designs or color schemes. It is not difficult to contact and interest store buyers, who are always on the lookout for something new. A few samples can bring in orders, or goods can be offered on consignment, which means that the retailer will display the work and take a percentage of the selling price.

People with mechanical ability and experience find that repairing small appliances at home can be a lucrative business.

The list of likely home-based occupations is long indeed. All it takes to get started is a little imagination and research and a lot of careful planning. You'll make mistakes; everyone does, but don't let that deter you.

Positive Action

Whatever their handicaps, people with physical disabilities are first and foremost individuals. Their only shared identity is that they are not able-bodied. As a group, however, they form a sizable minority which is legally entitled to the same protection as other minority groups and which can and must exert political and social pressure in its quest for civil rights in practice as well as in principle.

In the last decade, governmental and public awareness and concern for the plight of the handicapped has been growing. As the number of people disabled by wars, machinery, road accidents, age and disease increases, it becomes obvious that anyone can become disabled at any time. Individuals belonging to this large minority of the population should never again be stigmatized, demoralized or denied dignity. Nor need they ever again have to be grateful for scraps of mere charity or patronage.

Today there is a new breed of handicapped people who reject the almost traditional attitude of accepting discrimination, of quietly turning the other cheek and staying at home behind closed doors. The disabled are becoming justifiably self-assertive, insistent and strong in their demands for access to education, employment, independent living, family life, recreation and travel.

Hundreds of advocacy groups have been organized by disabled people to campaign for the rights of the handicapped and to inform and enlist the support of government and private agencies, business firms, the financial community, the media and the general public. The evident necessity for enlightened new approaches to the social problems of disablement has brought into being a backup army of dedicated professionals. Rehabilitation experts, educators, medical personnel, specialized architects, inventors and manufacturers, journalists and social reformers have joined with the disabled themselves in working toward the positive and permanent entry of people with disabilities into the mainstream of life.

In the United States the agitations of the dissident disabled have brought about important legislative advances in civil rights, environmental and transportation facilities, employment opportunities, services, benefits and representation. As the result of pressure from eight hundred handicapped groups and an all-night vigil by people in wheelchairs at the Lincoln Memorial, Congress passed the Rehabilitation Act of 1973, Section 504 of which prohibits any federally funded institution from excluding the handicapped from programs or facilities solely on the basis of handicap.

But enacting legislation and implementing it are two very different things. Four years after the passage of the act the Secretary of the Department of Health, Education and Welfare still had not signed the regulations required to make Section 504 effective. It was not until there was another sit-in by disabled people at the HEW offices that the adoption of the regulations took place.

New laws benefiting people with disabilities are only effective if they are understood and used and it is difficult for an individual to keep up with all the current legislative activity. There are, however, a number of information sources and publications which endeavor to keep disabled people abreast of developments as they occur.

In the United States the American Civil Liberties Union recently published a handbook, *The Rights of Physically Handicapped People*, which covers such subjects as the right to access, the right to transportation, the right to education, the right to integrated living and the right to employment. Sources of information on legislative developments in the United States include the National Center for Law and the Handicapped, Inc., in South Bend, Indiana and the National Center for Law and the Deaf in Washington, D.C.

In the United Kingdom, *Directory for the Disabled*, published in association with The Multiple Sclerosis Society of Great Britain and Northern Ireland, a handbook of information and opportunities for the handicapped, outlines and explains relevant legislation and lists advisory services and helpful organizations.

Pressure on vital issues can certainly be applied most effectively by committees and organizations. Nevertheless, the individual with physical disabilities must take responsibility and be alert to any opportunities to enforce personally the work of advocacy groups.

In recent years the handicapped, like the old, women and blacks before them, have begun to go to court to sue under the Constitution, the Rehabilitation Act and other federal laws. A woman who is a paraplegic sued the Los Angeles city council because she was unable to enter a polling place without assistance and was offered only an absentee ballot as an alternative. A disabled veteran sued a movie theater that would not permit him to enter in his wheelchair. A New York attorney brought legal action because he couldn't get his wheelchair into the municipal court to protest a parking ticket.

Everyday life provides many opportunities for the expression of opinion and for the correction of misrepresentation or prejudice. Make your political representative or the local authority aware of your position on a given issue. Write to the media. Respond critically or supportively to radio and television programs that touch on the problems of disablement. Complain when necessary to property owners, theater managements and storekeepers.

Above all, you can establish a line of natural, mutually cooperative contact with able-bodied people and make them aware of your intrinsic qualities. Public ignorance is still one of the greatest barriers to be eliminated and the people you win to understanding can become champions of the cause of the minority to which we belong.

This is a good fight and it must be fought on all fronts, neither hesitantly nor tentatively. It is incumbent on handicapped people, working cooperatively, to back it unremittingly with action. Given the present momentum, the situation can only improve—and we are the ones who can best speed the rate of improvement.

You and Your Home

Home is a concept with connotations that are universal and, in all but nomad societies, precious. With few exceptions, we all desire a place where we can be ourselves, feel at ease, where we can have our own special possessions about us—a place which serves as a base for excursions into the outside world and a haven to return to. A home gives shelter, but more than that, it provides comfort and the opportunity for self-expression and for independence.

People with disabilities may have an even greater need for the security of a home than able-bodied people since they are, by circumstance, if not necessarily by temperament, more vulnerable, less mobile and less certain of their way in life. For a disabled person, however, a home which is badly designed can be an additional handicap—or even an inhospitable prison.

In recognition of the need for suitable housing for people with disabilities, governments and private agencies, often in tandem, have devised a variety of solutions, some of which have provided genuine security and independence for many people. These range from large specialized housing projects which segregate people with disabilities from the community, to integration within the community in barrier-free housing.

In many countries there now exist complexes of purpose-built residential quarters which permit independent living backed by supportive services. One of the best known complexes of this kind is Het Dorp, in Arnhem, the Netherlands. Opened in 1966, it is a well-designed village community of four hundred severely disabled men and women. Each resident has his or her own self-contained apartment. Each group of ten apartments, of which one is occupied by a staff attendant, is a self-sufficient unit. To some people Het Dorp may seem a ghetto, but to the people who want and need its sheltered life it is a highly desirable alternative to institutionalization.

More and more disabled people themselves are becoming involved in planning their own integrated facilities as well as attendant services. But neither the scale nor the character of existing programs could possibly accommodate or appeal to every person with disabilities who is in need of some kind of special housing.

In the United Kingdom local authorities are required to consider the special housing needs and requirements of registered disabled people in their areas, to provide assistance for home adaptation and for any necessary extra facilities to secure the greater safety, comfort or convenience of these people. Local authorities vary widely, however, in their interpretation of disabled people's needs.

In Britain there is now more wheelchair housing, specially designed for people who are totally wheelchaired, and more mobility housing, which includes such features as ramped entrances and wide doors, being built in among general housing developments. This is a step, albeit a small one, toward integrating people with disabilities and helping them at the same time.

In the United States most residential construction is private enterprise with no involvement of federal funds. Consequently, legislation can do little about accessibility in housing. There is, however, a certain amount of federally funded housing construction and there are now about thirty thousand rent-subsidized housing units in which disabled people can live with their families. In 1977, the Department of Housing and Urban Development (HUD) established a new Office of Independent Living for the Disabled to deal with the special problems of people with disabilities and pledged that 5 percent of the department's funds would be allocated toward housing for disabled people.

The provision of special housing for people with disabilities, no matter how positive the trends, can never truly keep pace with the needs or the preferences of people who want to be able to live where and how they please, near their friends, with or without families and, above all, as independently as possible.

Although, generally, most new housing is being designed for greater accessibility and easier maintenance, most of us still have little choice and must make do with living in older buildings which were not designed with the convenience or the safety of the able-bodied in mind—let alone the needs of people with disabilities.

Some people with disabilities are beginning to regard the purchase of a specially designed mobile home as a relatively inexpensive and convenient solution to their housing problems. Many manufacturers of vans, travel trailers, or caravans, and motor-homes will produce a model built to individual specifications for a nominal additional charge or the individual can make his or her own alterations.

In the United States almost half of all single-family homes purchased in 1977 were mobile homes and 95 percent of homes selling for less than twenty thousand dollars are mobile homes. Gradually, the mobile-home industry is changing its name to "manufactured housing." This is, indeed, a more accurate name since only 10 percent of the homes are ever moved after they have been initially set up.

In the United Kingdom a range of purpose-designed mobile homes have been developed by Donnington Castle Caravans Ltd. The designer himself is wheelchaired and has given careful thought to many aspects of a disabled person's living requirements.

While some people are turning to mobile housing and others can afford to make major changes in their homes or even to buy a home designed to meet their specific needs, most people must have the necessary adaptations made on a limited budget. And in the case of a rented house or apartment, the adaptations must be made within the restrictions set by the owner or landlord.

Fortunately, as many of the ideas in this section show, making a home comfortable and manageable can often depend as much upon imaginative and resourceful planning and organization as upon expenditure. Equipment suitable for your use may cost no more than that of conventional design and may actually be more convenient and safer for able-bodied family and friends to use as well. Often, too, only modest adaptations can make the difference between frustration and satisfaction, uselessness and function.

Adapting Your Home

We all dream of a home that is geared to our specific needs. Reality, unfortunately, is usually less satisfactory. Extensive alterations are costly and in a rented house or apartment might not even be permitted. Nevertheless, there is probably much that can be done around your home to eliminate possible hazards, to increase your self-sufficiency and to make your life more comfortable and pleasant. Often quite minor modifications can go a long way toward achieving these aims. The first thing to do is to figure out how to make the most of what you have to work with. There may well be some relatively simple solutions for the problems you face in the present design of your home.

The Entrance

A few steps, or even one steep step, at the entrance to a house or an apartment building can keep a person with certain disabilities a virtual prisoner. The height of a high step that cannot be managed can be reduced by the addition of a half step. This is easiest to do if the step is wide. A railing will help you to gain leverage when you are going up and will provide balance when you are going down. A shelf at the front door, on which to put packages while you unlock the door, is helpful.

For someone who is wheelchaired and lives in an apartment or does much traveling, a portable ramp can be useful. The lightest of these consist of two pieces of metal channel grooves. They can be hooked onto the back of the wheelchair and when needed can be set down to accommodate the chair wheels. Available from self-help equipment firms, such ramps can be used on curbs and steps up to about nine inches (20 cm) high. Various portable folding ramps are also available.

When it is necessary to have a ramp built over a flight of steps it is important that the gradient be taken into consideration. The ratio should be no more than one foot (30 cm) of rise in twelve feet (360 cm). This means that for every one-foot rise there should be twelve feet in length. Steps that rise to three feet (90 cm) above ground level would, therefore, require a ramp thirty-six feet (1,080 cm) long. This is the steepest slope for propelling a wheelchair upward comfortably. Given sufficient space, a ramp with a one-foot (30-cm) rise in a fourteen-foot (420-cm) gradient is better.

A low guard rail or curb at the edge of the ramp is essential. On at least one side of the ramp there should also be a handrail of wood or nonslippery metal.

There must be a flat area at the top of the ramp where the wheelchair can stop. This area, which should be at least three feet (90 cm) deep if the door opens in and five feet (150 cm) deep if it opens out,

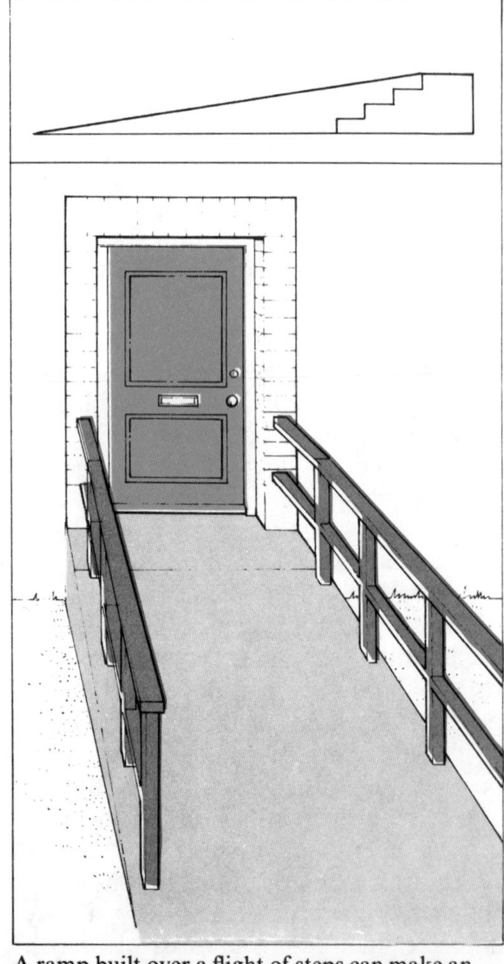

A ramp built over a flight of steps can make an entrance accessible, but the gradient of the ramp should never be less than twelve feet (360 cm) of length for every one foot (30 cm) of rise.

will make it possible to unlock the door without having to hold the chair in position on the ramp at the same time. It is difficult to put the brake on when on a ramp and releasing it is dangerous because of the possibility of rolling backward.

A ramp should be wide enough to allow for leeway in steering the chair. About a thirty-inch (75-cm) width is the minimum. If there is room, a width of three feet (90 cm) is better.

The surface of a ramp should be fireproof and nonslip even when it is wet. It can be made slip-proof with a coat of paint on which sand is sprinkled while it is still wet, by using a skid-resistant paint or by covering it with a rough surfaced roofing paper. In winter rock salt can be put down to melt snow and ice, but if a ramp is so exposed as to be seriously affected by frost or snow it should be enclosed, roofed or canopied.

When propelling a chair up a ramp it is safest to go slowly and to concentrate on going up in the middle in a straight line. Whether you are pushed or self-propelled lean slightly forward in the chair and always go up facing forward and go down backward.

When the installation of a ramp is not practical or safe, an alternative may be an outdoor wheelchair elevator or lift. Such lifts can be used independently by a wheelchaired person in any kind of weather.

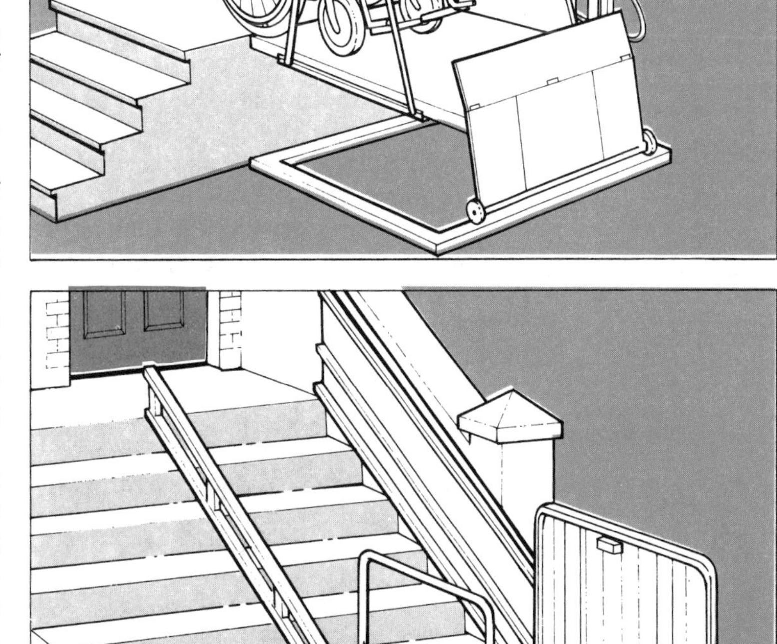

Outdoor wheelchair lifts, easy to operate independently, are available to go up and down a straight staircase or to be used to the side of the steps. An automatic ramp on the front of the platform ensures that the wheelchair cannot roll off when the lift is moving.

In the winter, a specially treated jute mat (widely available from department stores and mail order companies) will keep outside steps and path free of slippery snow and ice.

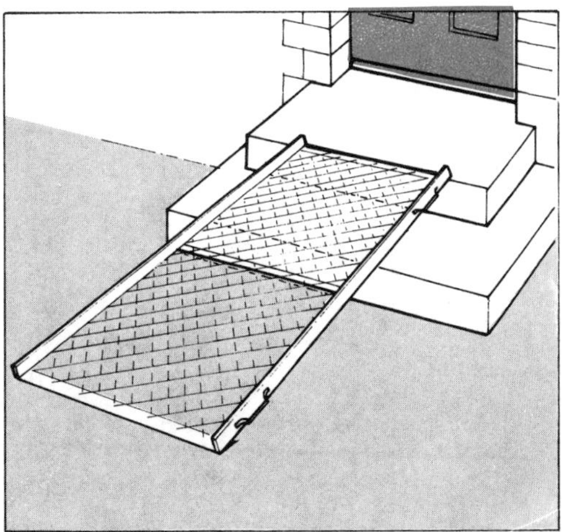

A removable ramp makes it possible to negotiate a few steps in a wheelchair. Although ramps like the one above fold for carrying, they tend to be too heavy to be really portable.

Doors

To permit free wheelchair clearance or passage with crutches or a walker, doors should be at least thirty inches (75 cm) and preferably thirty-six inches (90 cm) wide. To determine the extent of door clearance, measure the distance from the inner side of the door jamb to the point where the door itself comes inside the jamb on the hinged side. This is between one and a half inches (3 cm) and two inches (5 cm) less than the actual opening of the doorway.

If a doorway is just slightly too narrow for a wheelchair to get through, an inch or so can be gained by replacing the hinges with step-back hinges, available at most hardware stores, that swing the door free of the frame and allow it to lie flat against the wall.

Some people find that if they must go through a particularly narrow doorway in a wheelchair they avoid bruised knuckles by pulling on the door frame with both hands to get through, instead of keeping their hands on the wheels.

In some situations, in a very small bathroom, for example, it may be necessary to increase the width of the door to more than thirty-six inches (90 cm) to allow for turning the wheelchair. When the inside space is so limited that it is difficult to close the door, a folding door that hinges in the middle can be substituted.

When it is awkward to open a door it may be feasible to rehang it so that it opens the other way or to remove the door altogether and substitute a curtain, a sliding door or a folding door. A sliding door with top and bottom runners is easiest to operate from a wheelchair. A door held only on a top runner tends to twist when it is grasped low down from a wheelchair. The channel for the bottom runner must, however, be set into the floor so that it does not obstruct the wheelchair.

A folding door is easily opened, but it will take up four to six inches (10 to 15 cm) of valuable doorway space, so before buying one be sure the doorway is wide enough.

French doors—double doors that open from the center—provide the best access to closets as well as to rooms. They can be hung to swing either way and for easier opening and closing can be

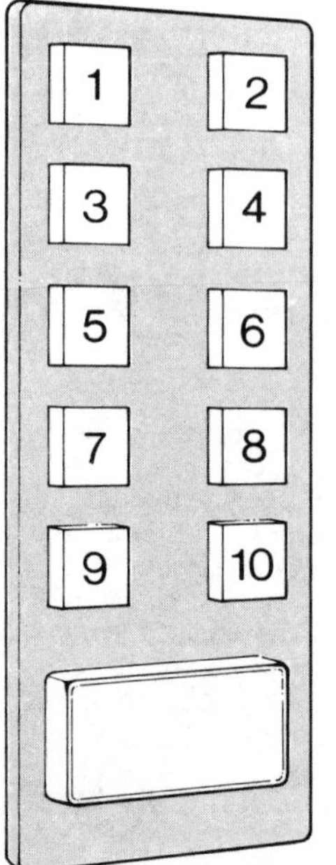

A keyless lock, which is operated by a combination of buttons pushed in a particular sequence, is often easier to manipulate than a key, although a certain amount of strength is required.

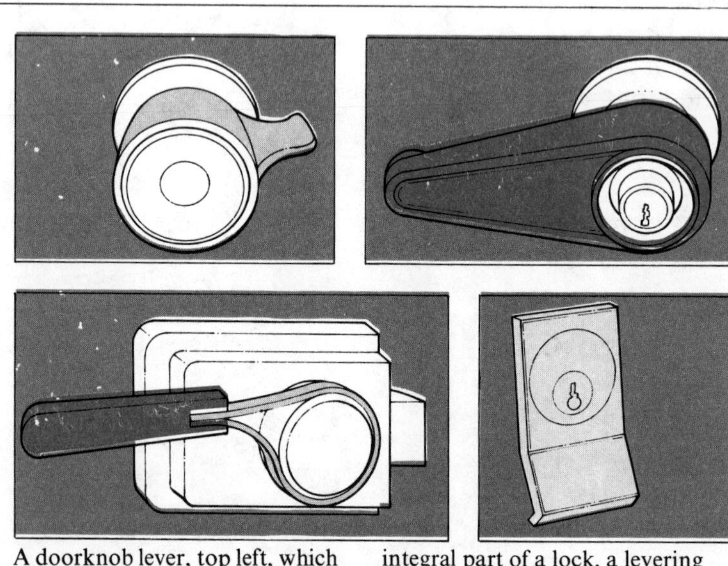

A doorknob lever, top left, which can be taped to a doorknob, makes it possible to open the latch with a minimum of strength and grasp. A gentle downward push on a rubber lever, top right, which fits over a round doorknob, releases the latch. When a knob is an integral part of a lock, a levering handle, made of a leather strip attached to a piece of wood, bottom left, can help to turn the knob. A finger hold fitted over a conventional cylinder lock, bottom right, is helpful when opening and closing the door.

When reach is limited, a latch can be easily released by pulling downward on a cord and dowel handle hung from a hole in a door lever.

equipped with any one of a variety of handholds to suit a particular disability. Such doors are also attractive; they are available louvered, with glass panels or made of solid wood.

When there is partial loss of grasp, metal lever door handles are easier to manage than round doorknobs. They fit on existing door-handle shafts and are available from most hardware stores. A round knob can be turned more easily if heavy rubber bands or the nonslip strips that are used in bathtubs are put around it. Sometimes a round doorknob can be turned more easily if the hand is put behind it, with the knob between index and middle fingers and the palm outward.

Doorknobs can be eliminated entirely, however, and replaced with spring roller catches which allow the doors to be opened and closed merely by pressure against the surface.

If a door handle cannot be reached, a simple extension can be made. Have a hole drilled in a lever handle through which a cord can be drawn and on which any suitable handle can be hung within reach. The cord can even be extended so that it can be operated by foot.

When a key is difficult to grasp, leverage can be increased by having a metal plate riveted to the key, by putting a piece of doweling through the hole in the key or by fitting the key into a slit in a wooden block and securing it with a screw.

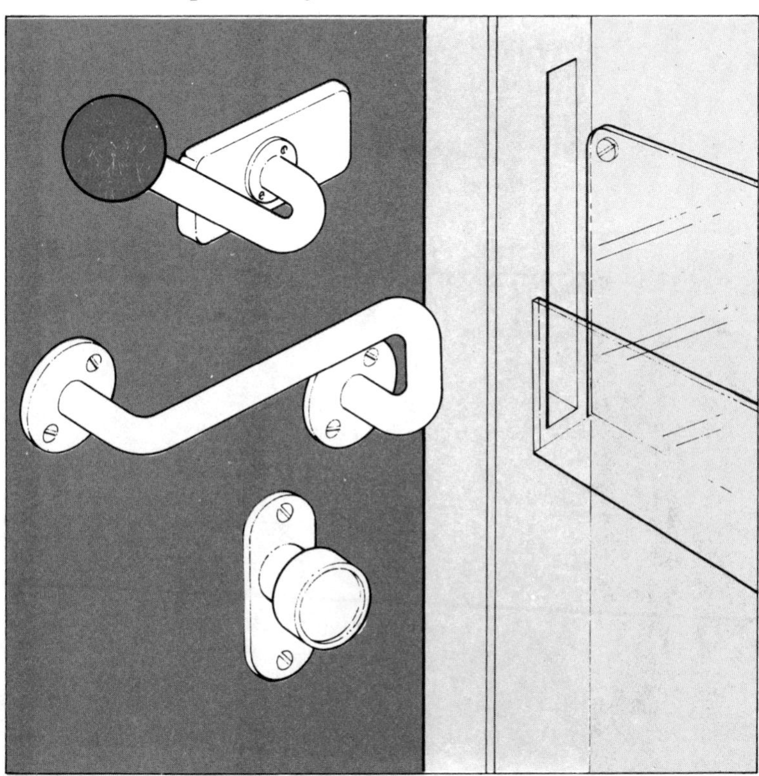

The handle on the front door left needs only the gentlest pressure to depress it and release the latch. The large grab handle is an added convenience, as is the tray next to the mail slot.

Stairs and Stair Lifts

The less you have to go up and down stairs the better, but if you live in a house with steps there are practical adjustments for making them easier to negotiate. Half steps, which can be constructed to reduce each step to half its height along about one-third of its width, are often helpful. This does entail climbing twice the number of steps, but each one will be easier to climb. The half steps should be made of wood and must be firmly screwed to each step.

A second banister rail can be very helpful. It gives additional support on a narrow staircase and for someone with only one useful hand it obviously offers support for going upstairs and for coming down. The hand on the rail should always be a step ahead of the feet so, ideally, the rail should extend beyond the staircase at both top and bottom by about eighteen inches (45 cm) to provide support when stepping off the top and bottom steps.

Stair carpeting should be fixed firmly in place. If there are worn patches, have the carpet runner moved so that they come on the risers and not on the treads. Vinyl or rubber stair treads increase traction. The treads should be deeply corrugated and tacked down securely.

A stair lift may be the most suitable solution for someone who cannot negotiate stairs. The expense of such an installation is substantial, but it is usually much less costly than moving, installing a full bathroom on the ground floor or remodeling a dining-room or other area to serve as a bedroom. Frequently, too, it is possible to rent a stair lift. In the United States a stair elevator is tax deductible as a medical expense when it is recommended by a physician, or the cost may be partially borne by the Social Rehabilitation Administration when its installation results in an individual's

There are many types of stair lifts available. The wall-mounted lift far right will carry a person who is in a wheelchair. For a wheelchair lift the staircase must be at least seven inches (18 cm) wider than the chair. The footrest on the stairnose mounted lift right folds upward when not in use. The seat of the wall-mounted lift below right folds up neatly so the lift can be used by a standing passenger, too.

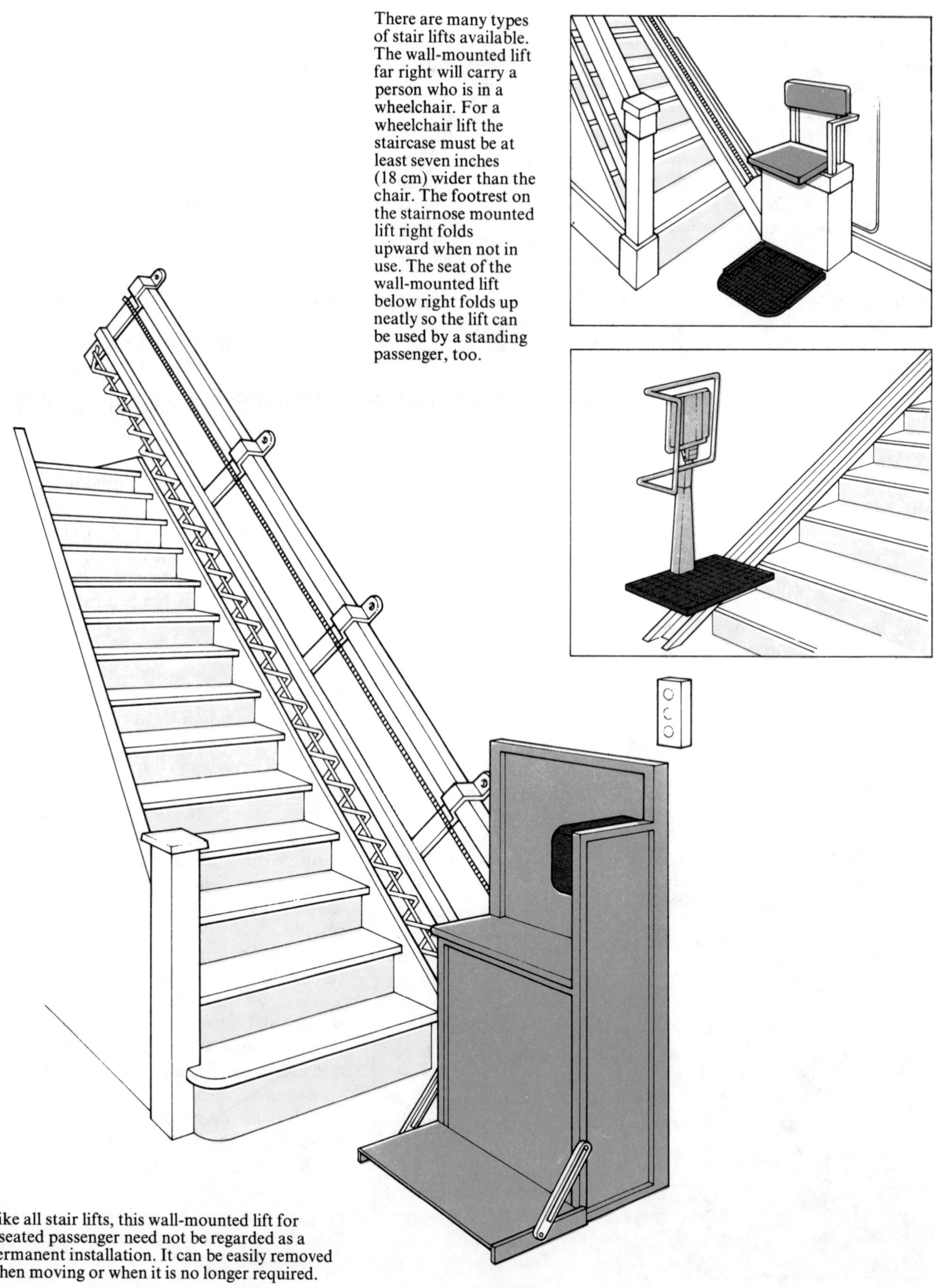

Like all stair lifts, this wall-mounted lift for a seated passenger need not be regarded as a permanent installation. It can be easily removed when moving or when it is no longer required.

self-sufficiency. In Britain local authorities may help with the cost.

A stair lift is a platform which travels up and down a staircase on tracks either on the stairs themselves or on the adjoining wall. An installation with the tracks on the wall is neater and leaves more of the stairs clear. Stair lifts fit various types of staircases and include such optional accessories as removable armrests, hand, foot or lever switches and a large footrest.

Some models have a fixed seat and others have a folding seat so that the user can either sit or stand. Others have only a standing platform with a support rail. The seat or the platform of most stair lifts fold back against the wall when not in use. Some models take a wheelchair.

Most stair lifts are designed to go up a straight staircase. If a staircase is made up of two long flights with a landing between, it would be necessary to install two stair lifts and cross the landing from one to the other. There are stair lifts, however, which have specially curved rails to negotiate turns, but these are far more expensive than straight lifts.

In some cases a vertical lift is the only feasible solution. Basically there are two different types of vertical lifts. One type is encased in a shaft and the other is open and runs on guide rails or wall tracks. In a large house it is often possible to fit a lift into the stair well; otherwise an opening has to be cut in the ceiling and in the floor of the level above. The installation of a vertical lift is likely to be much more expensive than that of a stair lift because of the building work involved.

Flooring

Floors should be smooth and level and must be kept in good repair. Chipped tiles, frayed carpets and loose boards can easily cause accidents. The flooring should also be slip-proof and easy to care for. Good nonslip surfaces are unglazed tiles, vinyl asbestos and unfinished wood.

Thick carpeting is fatiguing to walk on and propelling a wheelchair over it has been compared to trying to roll it through a mossy forest. If you have carpets they should be firmly woven and have minimum pile. Flat, smooth-surfaced commercial carpet is really the most suitable; not only is it easy to move around on, but it is long lasting and easy to keep clean.

Cork flooring provides a firm, smooth surface for a wheelchair and is warmer than vinyl. Cork flooring tiles have an anti-slip finish, are easily cleaned and do not require polishing.

Loose rugs are dangerous. If a small rug must be used, at an entrance, for example, be sure to make it secure. There are various types of rug grippers available from hardware stores. There is also a double-faced adhesive tape on the market which sticks to both rug and floor; when the rug needs to be lifted the tape can be peeled off and then replaced.

Windows

If they are in good repair all windows will open more easily. Casement windows are the easiest to manage, especially if the hinges and fastenings are free of paint and are oiled regularly so that they move freely. Handles or cranks can be built up to make them easier to grasp.

Windows that slide to the side require less strength and coordination than those that must be raised or rolled out. The lower half of an old-fashioned sash window can be opened and closed by using a pulley system. The top part can be opened more easily if a ring is screwed into the center of the top frame and a long pole with a hook on the end is used to pull it up and down.

Never put a large piece of furniture, such as a table or a sofa, in front of a window. However attractive the arrangement may be it's more important to be able to get to the window easily to open and close it.

A cord-operated curtain control that works on a pulley system is the easiest way to open and close curtains. Venetian blinds give privacy without obstructing much light or interfering with the view. They are almost as easy to handle as curtains, but cleaning them is hard work. A small motor can be fitted so that curtains as well as blinds can be opened and closed electrically by remote control.

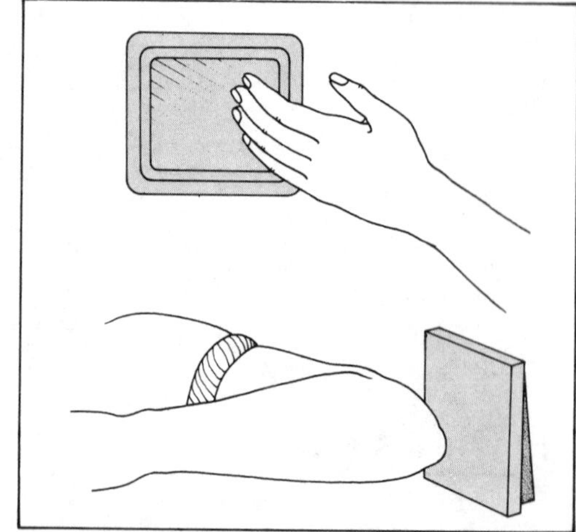

The two switches above are particularly easy to operate. The top one works when warmth from any part of the body touches it. The bottom one responds to the lightest pressure.

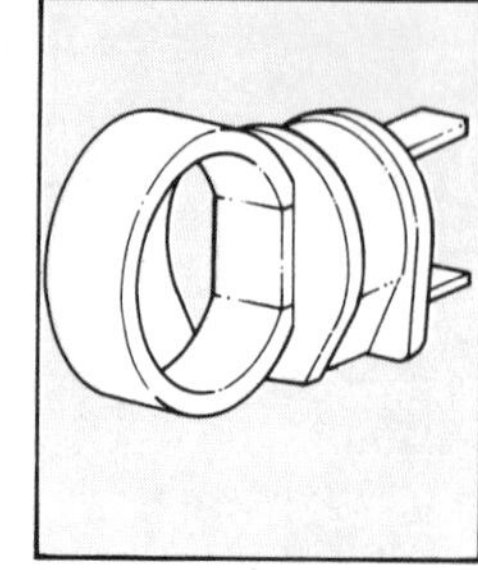

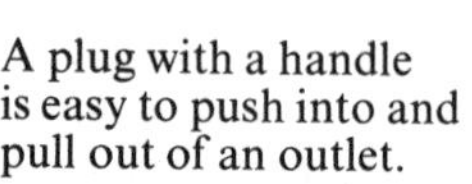

A plug with a handle is easy to push into and pull out of an outlet.

Lighting and Electrical Outlets

Good lighting and conveniently placed electrical outlets make a home more pleasant, efficient and safe. It is not difficult to make minor adjustments to existing light switches and electrical outlets and if any remodeling is being done electrical circuits should be taken into consideration.

A light switch should always be located so that any dark space can be illuminated before it is entered. Lighting in hallways and on the stairs should be adequate. If you are having light switches and other controls installed have them put in at a height which you can comfortably reach —not at the height which the contractor says is right. If you are wheelchaired, for example, you might find it most convenient to have switches next to doors, aligned horizontally with the door handles.

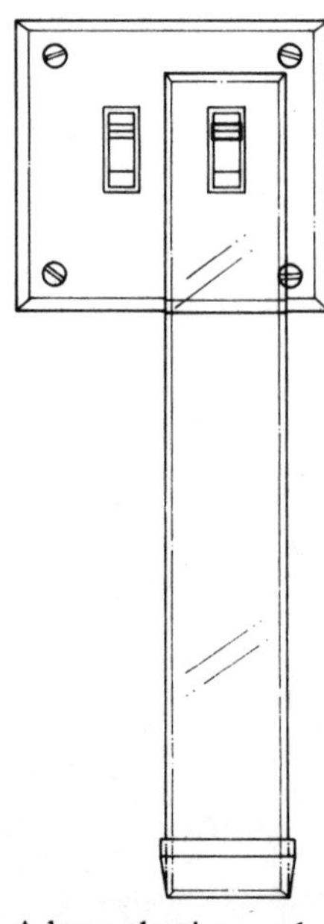

A long plastic panel, with a small slot cut in the top (available from mail order companies or improvised of wood) can be used to switch a light on and off when reach is limited.

Outlets for light plugs, too, can be fixed at any height most convenient to you. They should be at least eighteen inches (40 cm) from the floor to be comfortably reached from a sitting position. It has been found, however, that the best compromise height for able-bodied and disabled alike is thirty-nine inches (about 1 meter) above the floor. All electric outlets should be grounded for safety.

Two-way light switches make it possible to switch a light on and off from more than one point without having to go back across a room or down a corridor. Rocker action light switches, which require only a little pressure on a small area, are easier to operate than the old-fashioned dolly switches. There is also a switch available which responds to the warmth of any part of the body held against it. It is possible, too, to install a foot-press switch if it is difficult to operate a switch by hand. A cord ceiling switch can be fitted with a large ring at the bottom so that it can be operated by an arm movement. If grasp is weak, a large tassel or knob can be attached to the end of the cord.

With a remote control switch an electrical appliance can be turned on and off without having to go to the appliance. A remote control switch on an extension cord, which can be used to turn a lamp, radio or television on and off, is available from mail order companies and self-help equipment firms. There are also time switches available. They can be connected to lamps or to electrical appliances and preset to turn on and off automatically at certain times.

For table lamps, as well as other electrical appliances, low-pressure air switches can be installed. These can be operated by very light manual pressure or can be fitted with a mouthpiece and operated by blowing. For people who find it difficult to reach under a lamp-shade to pull the chain or flick the switch there is a unit on the market which attaches to any lamp so that the light can be turned on and off by slightly tipping the shade.

Trailing wires are extremely hazardous. If a lamp or an electrical appliance must be some distance from the socket outlet the wire should be long enough to be tacked along the baseboard. Electric wires should never be covered by carpeting or rugs.

If you have difficulty pulling a plug out of the socket, try using the heels and sides of both palms pressed together around the plug. Never pull on the cord for this can break the connection between plug and cord and is dangerous.

Reachers

All too often something you need is just out of reach on the floor, on a shelf or even at the foot of the bed. If you have the aid of a retrieving device your worries are over.

Reachers come in various styles. They are available from self-help equipment firms or a suitable aid can often be made at home. You may not even need a special reacher, for the crook of a cane can be used to pick up a handbag or can be hooked around the leg of a chair to move it and a magnet on a plant stake or a string can be used to retrieve hairpins, paper clips and other small, light, metal objects.

To be used effectively, some reachers require a stronger grasp than others. The design of the jaws also differs; a few have no more than a two-inch (5-cm) opening, which means that they can pick up only very light objects.

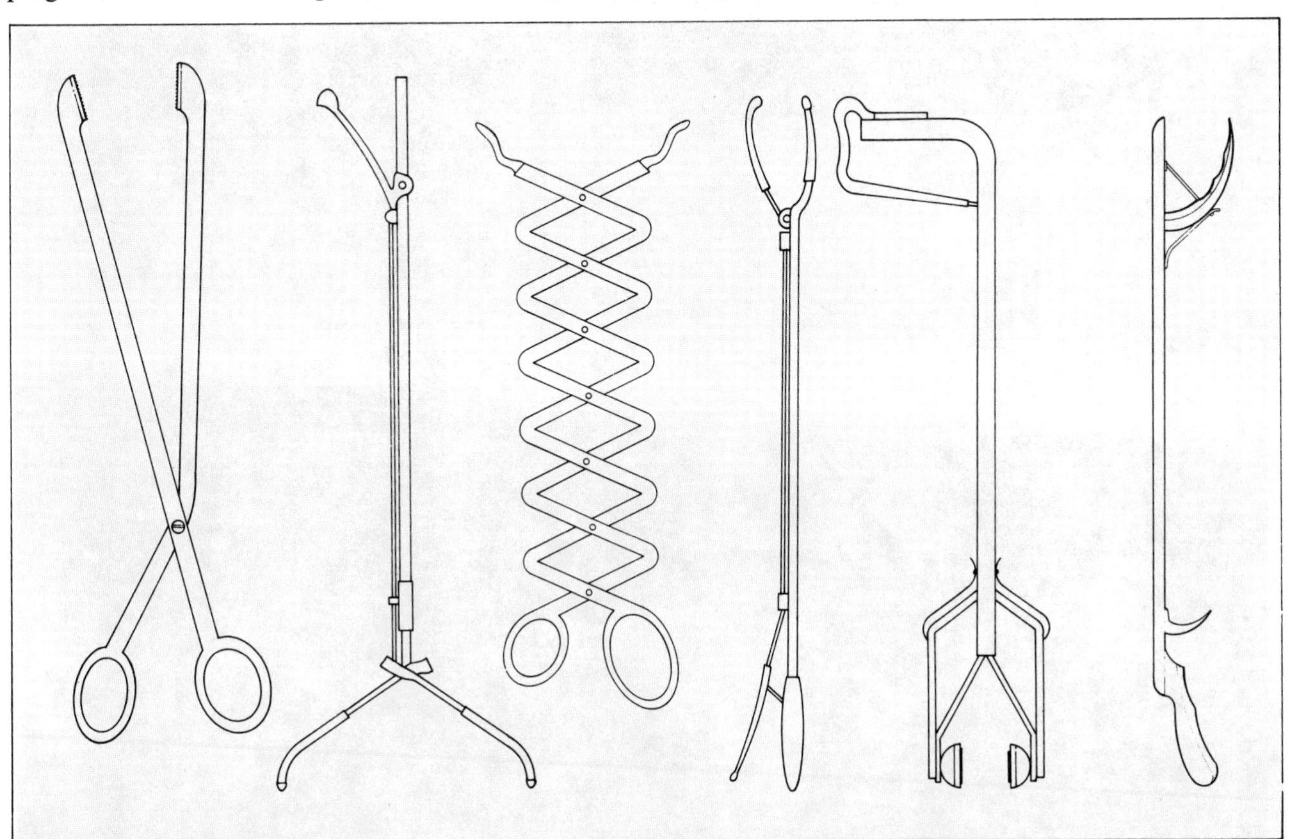

The six reachers illustrated above are only a few of the many types which are commercially available. Some reachers must be used with two hands, others are designed for one-handed use, but a few require good grasp to control the trigger mechanisms. Magnetic tips on many of the models aid in picking up small metal items. Although some reachers can lift objects of considerable weight, it is never advisable to store heavy objects beyond easy reach.

The correct length of a reacher depends mainly on whether it is going to be used from a sitting or a standing position. Less effort is required to pick things up with a shorter stick and the lifting process is easier to control. Longer models are also slightly heavier. The weight of a reacher must be considered, especially if it is a long one, for it has to be brought up through the horizontal position to a convenient height and will therefore feel heavier and will put a greater strain on the muscles. Reachers with the widest jaws are usually the heaviest. A device with a handle at an angle of about forty-five degrees to the shaft is likely to be more comfortable to use than one with a straight handle because it makes less demand on the wrist.

Most reachers can be attached with spring clips to a cane, a walking frame or a wheelchair.

A cantilever table can be used as a work surface, a book stand, as well as a bed table. Models are available with various shaped bases. A table with a U-shaped base, and some with H-shaped bases, cannot be used with a chair. A T-shaped base is the least stable. It is easiest to adjust the height when a table has only one pillar and one tightening knob.

The Right Furniture

Comfort, mobility and safety can all be increased by carefully selected and arranged furniture. A person who is wheelchaired requires turning space of at least four and one-half feet by four and one-half feet (1.4 m by 1.4 m)—800 percent more than an ambulant person.

Obviously seating is an important consideration. You should have in your living-room, and perhaps in your bed-room, too, a well-designed chair which provides good body support, allows you to relax and is high enough for adequate leverage when you rise.

The chair should be stable and strong because you may put all your weight on one side of it when you get up or you may fall back heavily when you sit down. It should have arms, to help you get up and down, and a fairly firm upholstered seat and back. The front edge of the seat should be padded so that it doesn't cut off circulation in the legs.

Sometimes a difference of only three or four inches (8 or 10 cm) can permit you to sit comfortably and to rise un-assisted from a chair. The height of a chair seat can be increased with blocks on the legs, with chair lifters, available from self-help equipment firms, or with a cushion. If you raise the seat by adding

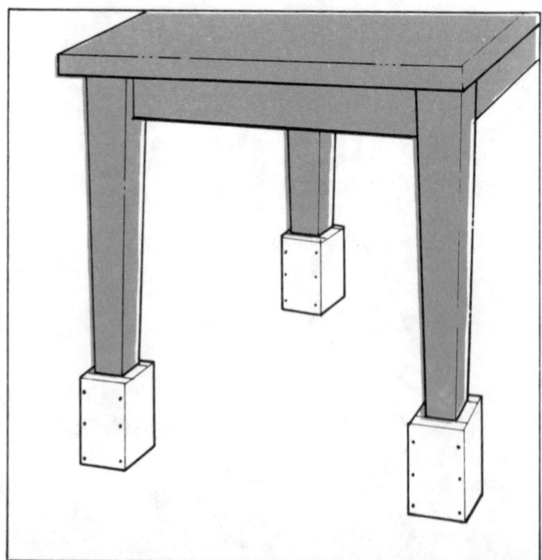

To raise the height of a table, a chair or a bed, four wooden blocks can be used. The blocks should be hollow for one-third of their height, so that the legs of the piece of furniture will fit firmly into them. Chair legs can be raised with

a cushion you can prevent it from slipping by inserting a piece of nonslip carpet underlay between the cushion and the seat. Often, however, raising the height in this way makes the arms too low.

A footstool may be used with a chair with a high seat if you need the extra height of the chair for rising, but find sitting in it uncomfortable because your feet do not touch the floor. The stool should be high enough to support the feet without putting pressure on the back of the thighs.

A footstool is, however, a hazard because it may be tripped over. Casters make it easier to move it around and it must be pushed out of the way before you get up and replaced after you sit down. A footstool with legs can be pulled into position with the crook of a cane.

A chair with a spring-assisted lifting seat, designed to adjust the seat from the horizontal to an angle of about forty-five degrees, can be helpful. Portable spring-driven cushion seats, which assist in rising or sitting and can be used in any chair, are available. Also on the market are electrically operated chairs which will raise you from a sitting to an upright position.

A backrest can be used if a chair seat is too soft or too deep for comfort. Spinal support backrests are available from hospital suppliers and mail order companies.

A chair for working should be adjustable to your needs. Casters make it possible to move around without getting up and down. You may well find that a standard office chair, available from office suppliers or secondhand office furniture stores, will be suitable.

A work table should be solid, stable and large enough to sit at comfortably. The height of the table should relate to the height of the chair and the person in it. Ideally, your elbows should be level with the table top when you're sitting down. A space of about eight inches (20 cm) between the chair seat and the underside of the table will ensure that the thighs are not compressed. A drop-leaf table installed against a wall can provide instant table space at just the right height when it is needed and be out of the way when it isn't. A height-adjustable cantilever table is versatile. For greatest usefulness, the table top should overlap the center of the chair or bed by at least eight inches (20 cm).

The standard height of most dining tables is twenty-eight inches (80 cm). This is a comfortable height for a wheelchair with desk arms. For standard wheelchair arms to get under the table there must be a minimum clearance of thirty-one inches (78 cm).

This lifting seat unit, which can be used on most chairs, has a lever-operated spring device, supplied to suit the individual user's weight. The unit locks automatically when the person is seated.

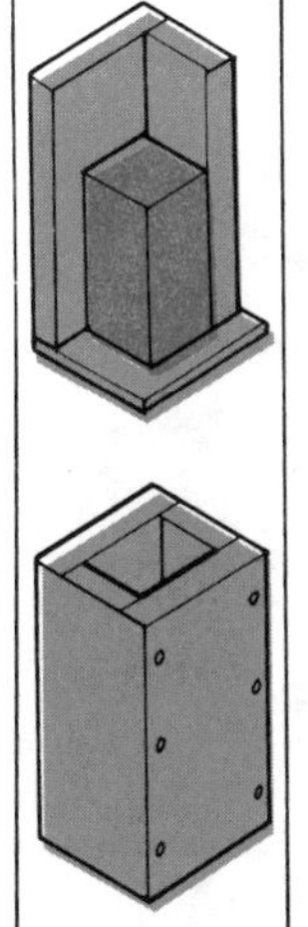

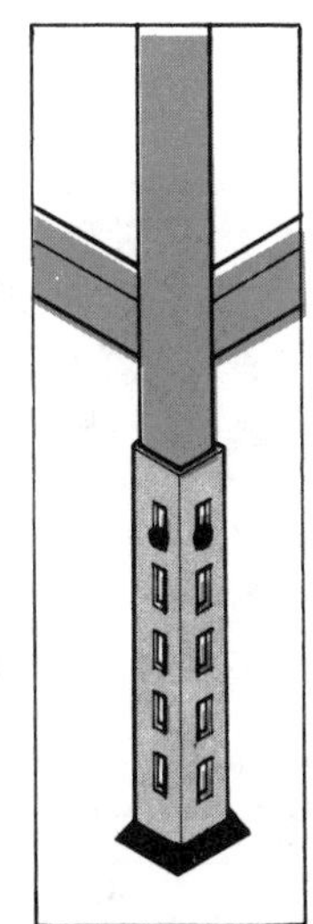

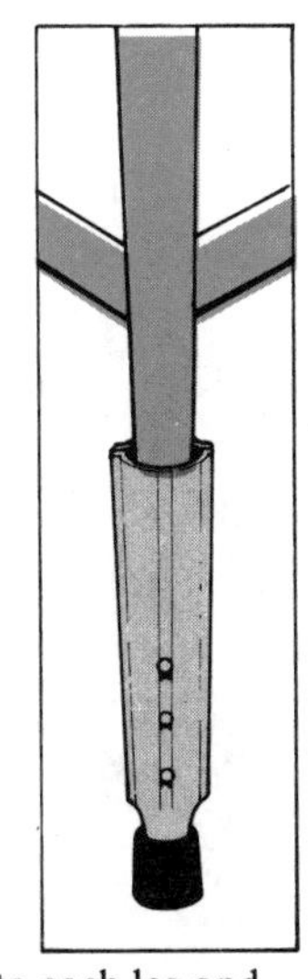

angle irons, center above, bolted to each leg and fitted with plastic or rubber caps to prevent them from sliding. Easily installed, plastic-tipped, steel chair leg lifts, above right, fit round or square legs and are available from mail order companies.

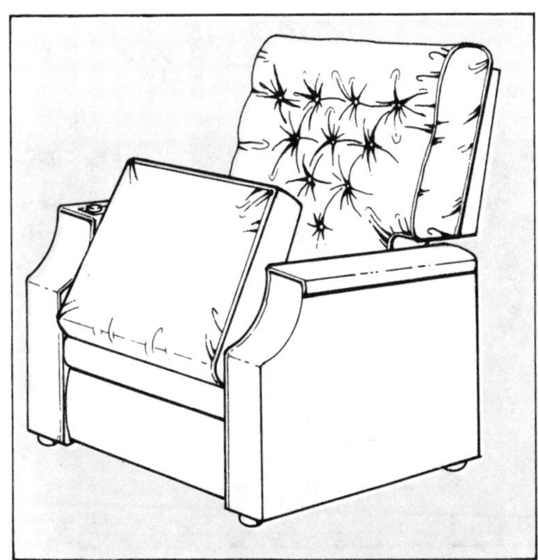

In addition to an elevating seat, which makes it easy to sit down and to get up, the electric reclining chair above has a footrest that rises automatically when the back is reclined. A hand control stops the back in the desired position.

General Storage

The multipurpose storage wall below combines units which are available from mail order companies, accessories from hardware stores and homemade adaptations. The upper shelves and drawers are for things seldom needed; everyday items are within easy reach. Jackets and short clothes are hung on the low rod; long-handled hangers make long clothes on the high rod reachable from below. The four pull-out units are simply wooden boxes on large casters. Storing clothes in wire baskets makes everything visible at a glance.

One of the most problematical aspects of any household is accessible storage space. If range of reach and extent of mobility are limited, finding the most convenient places to put things and the most efficient methods of storing them are challenges that demand very careful planning.

The first step is to be ruthless about possessions—when in doubt, throw them out! The next is to divide items into categories dictated by the frequency of use. Finally, the storage spaces that are handy must be maximized by using special units that can be attached to doors or will expand shelf space.

In a linen closet, for example, shallow shelving, with the shelves no more than eighteen inches (45 cm) deep, provide the best access. Whether you are ambulant or wheelchaired, frequently used linens should be placed on shelves not lower than knee level nor higher than shoulder level. Depending on your disability other linens that are used less often can be stored above or below that.

It is generally easiest, too, to reach drawers that are between knee and shoulder height. If you have the use of only one hand or need one hand to steady yourself, a centered drawer handle is best. Drawers can also be fitted with glides on either side so that they open and close freely. Hardware stores sell the units.

A lowered rod makes a clothes closet more convenient if you're in a wheelchair. Extension bars that attach to the regular closet rod can be adjusted to the best height for your use. They can be bought wherever closet equipment is sold.

You might find, too, that it's best to remove the doors from closets in narrow hallways and replace them with folding doors, a vinyl closing or—if you're very tidy—you can leave the shelves open.

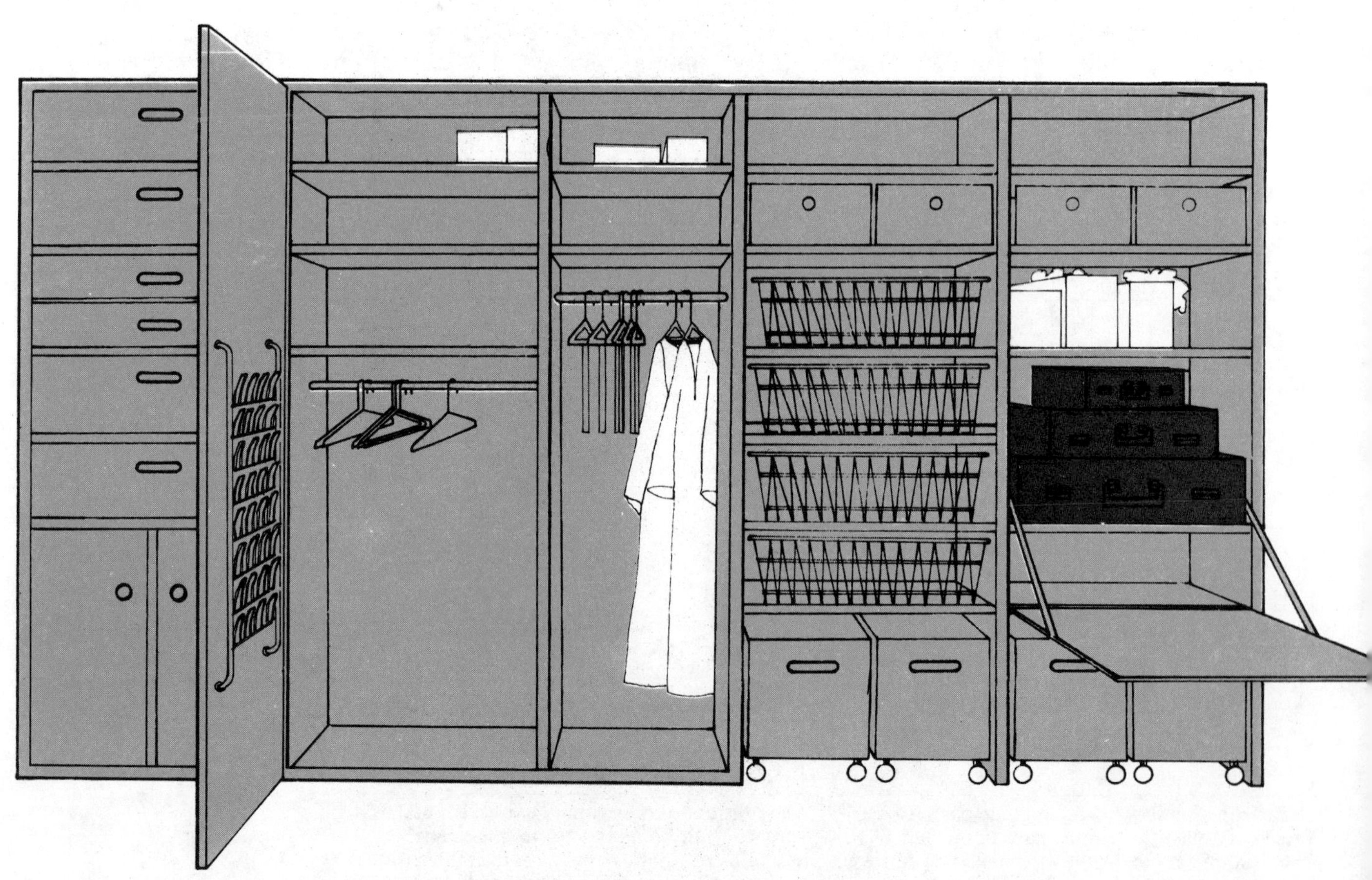

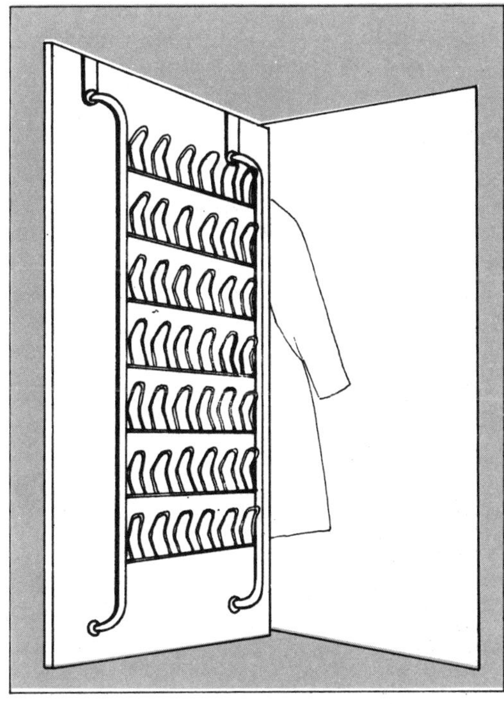

The back of a door can make a storage area not only for shoes but also for small accessories. Mail order companies offer a variety of attachable units which accommodate items of different sizes and shapes and keep everything tidy, visible and within easy reach.

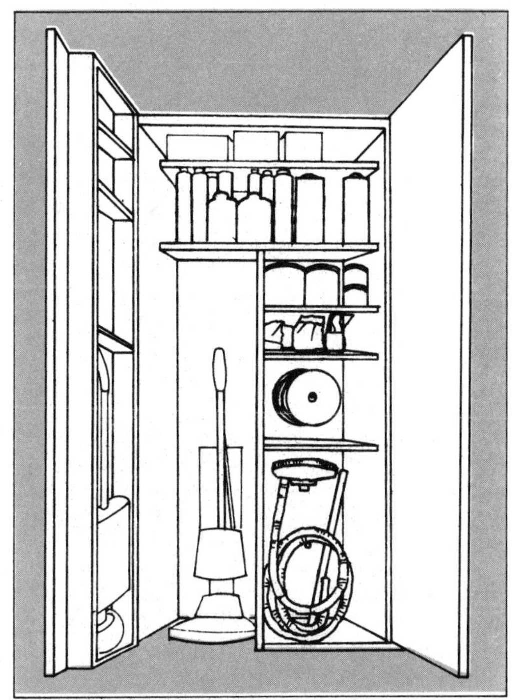

This specially built cleaning closet uses the backs of doors for specific items of equipment and has extra panels and shelves for cleaning supplies and miscellaneous boxes, cans and bottles. Everything can be seen and reached without taking other things out of the way.

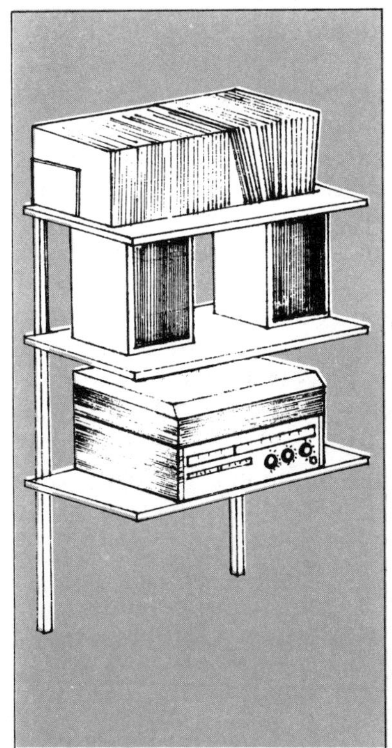

Items used frequently can be kept in a practical and attractive way in easily installed, adaptable storage walls. The strips and brackets are available from hardware and department stores.

A closet unit of the size of a chest of drawers can be bought already finished, or in kit form for assembly and finishing, from mail order companies and department stores. No higher than forty inches (100 cm), such a unit holds many suits and short garments.

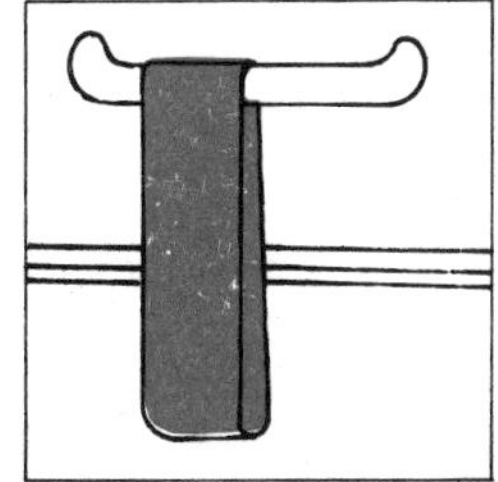

If hands are weak or painful, opening and closing drawers can be difficult. A knob can be changed to a handle and a leather loop can be pulled with the forearm.

The Bedroom

For many people the bedroom is the one room in the house that they consider to be their own. It is the room where they can go when they want to be alone and it is usually the room that reflects individual taste rather than the needs of the family.

To ensure your privacy you should be able to move freely around your bedroom. The storage space should be adequate and accessible and you should be able to control the lighting, heating and ventilation yourself. It is helpful to have a telephone beside the bed and, if necessary, an intercom or other call system. A battery-operated bell can be easily installed.

Some people find it useful to have a solid table next to the bed for leverage when getting into or out of bed. A stable bedside lamp that throws good light is a necessity. If you frequently have to get up during the night you might find a night light helps you to orientate yourself quickly.

Your bed is probably the most important piece of furniture you have. It is essential that it be comfortable, easy to get into and out of, easy to make and placed so that all the things you need are within comfortable reach. If you spend a lot of time in bed it should be sited to permit you to look out of a window or into the hallway.

Modern beds are usually between fifteen inches (38 cm) and twenty-two inches (55 cm) high. To transfer most easily from wheelchair to bed, the height of the bed must be as close to that of the chair as possible—usually about nineteen inches (47 cm) high. Someone with very stiff hips will need a bed which is even higher.

The best way to discover the optimum height for your bed is by trial. If possible try to get on and off beds of different heights in your home or at friends' homes, or have a second mattress put on your bed to see whether the added height would be better.

It is not difficult to increase the height of most beds. Screw-in legs on sofa beds are usually five inches (13 cm) high, but some manufacturers will provide longer legs. Blocks to put under the legs of the bed can be bought or made. Alternatively, you can use an extra mattress. If the mattress is covered in a slippery fabric a cotton cover should be put over it or a large piece of nonslip carpet underlay can be put between the two mattresses to keep the top one from sliding.

The legs of a bed that is higher than desired can be sawn off. If the bed is too high for comfortable transfer from a wheelchair, a cushion in the chair will lessen the difference. A transfer board, available from self-help equipment firms, makes it possible to slide from wheelchair to bed.

A footboard and headboard are often desirable to lean on when getting up and when making the bed.

If it is necessary to use a hoist to get into and out of bed, get expert advice from a physiotherapist on the type required and on its installation.

A firm mattress is the first requisite for correct body support, as well as for safe and smooth transfer. It is easier, too, to sit down and get up and to turn over if the mattress is firm, doesn't sag under your weight and has a firm edge.

A five-inch (13-cm) foam rubber mattress over a bed board provides firm support with adequate resilience. And a foam mattress has the advantage of not needing to be turned. A washable bed pad may be used to protect the mattress from soiling. A bed board, made at home or commercially available, can also be used to give solidity to a soft mattress and springs. Portable folding bed boards

When a lot of time is spent in bed, it's helpful to have necessities nearby. A bed butler, above, hangs at the side of the bed and is held in place by a thin board slipped between springs and mattress. A small metal shelf, right, clips onto the bed frame and brings things within closer reach. Both items are available from mail order companies.

Bed Aids
Many aids have been devised to make it easier to sit up or to change position in bed. A selection of such aids is shown below. Some of them can be made at home. Others, which are more elaborate, are available from hospital suppliers.

can be made of plywood or purchased from department stores or mail-order companies.

Special care must be given to protection of the skin during long periods of confinement to bed. Bedding, especially sheets, must be smooth and soft. A fitted bottom sheet won't wrinkle and the elasticized corners make daily bed-making easier. When rubber or plastic mattress covers are necessary they should be covered with thick padding. Fleece-lined elbow and heel protectors, available from mail-order companies, keep elbows and heels from becoming sore from rubbing. If you are prone to skin breakdown your doctor may advise the use of an alternating pressure mattress or pads.

Lying on a sheepskin also helps to prevent pressure sores. A sheepskin is used fleecy side up; the wool fibers distribute the weight over a large area and so reduce the tendency to produce localized pressure points. The deep pile lets air circulate and helps to keep the skin dry. The sheepskin will absorb up to its own weight in water before it begins to feel damp. Synthetic sheepskins, which are less expensive, lose their resilience and also tend to reflect heat rather than to absorb it. They are, however, easier to launder and sheepskins must be washed frequently.

Warmth in bed is an individual matter. Thermal-weave blankets provide warmth and ventilation and are lightweight. An electric blanket doesn't add much weight and is easily controlled. Continental-style quilts are warm and light and

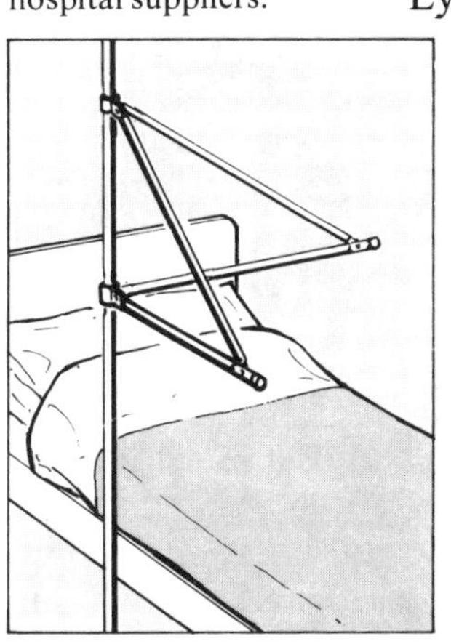

The bar on the assembly above swivels to assist a person from a lying, to a sitting, to a standing position.

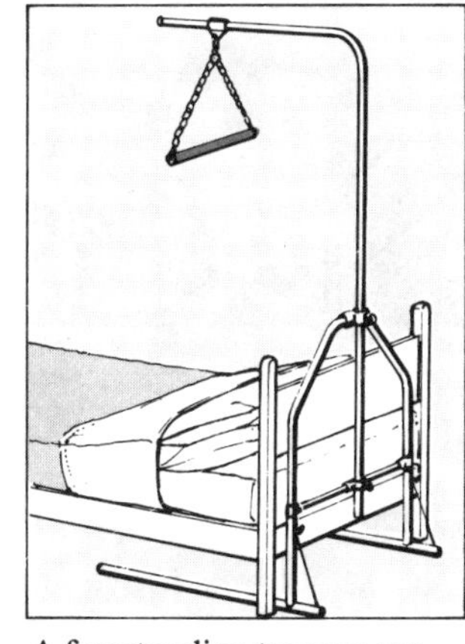

A freestanding trapeze can aid in sitting up, shifting weight, exercising and transferring to a wheelchair.

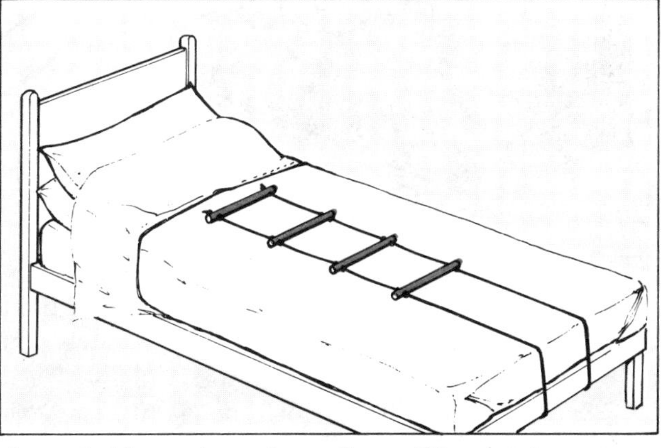

A rope ladder can be used to pull oneself from a lying to a sitting position. Such ladders are commercially available or can be made from heavy sash cord, or cotton webbing, and wooden dowels spaced to suit the individual.

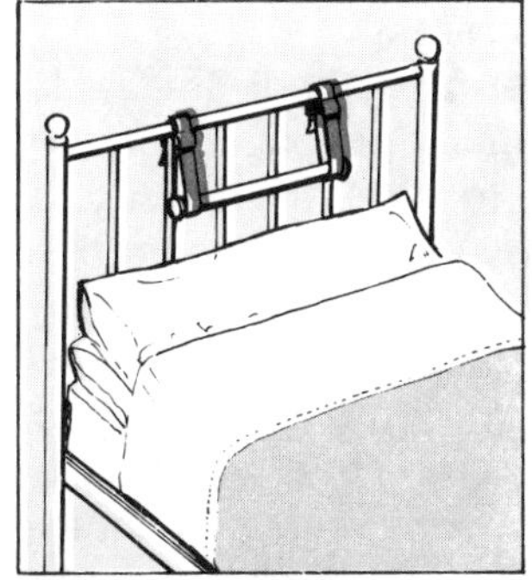

People who can reach over their heads often find that a heavy bar, attached to the bed head with adjustable straps, like the commercially available aid above, helps them to pull themselves up toward the head of the bed and to turn over.

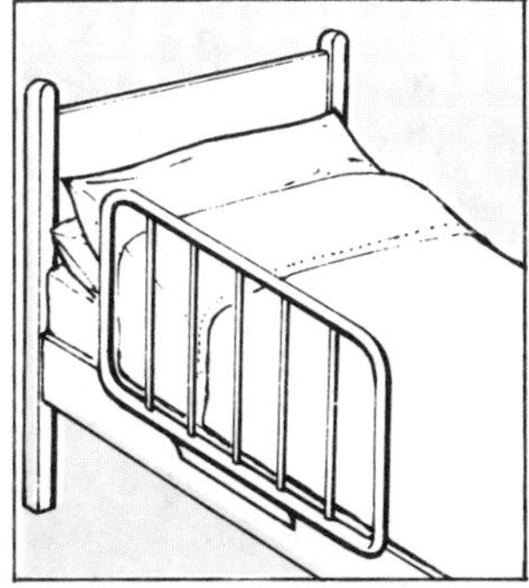

A bed rail gives stability when changing position or when getting up. Gradual leverage is obtained from the vertical posts. To allow space for swinging the legs over the edge of the bed, the rail should be no more than three-quarters of the bed's length.

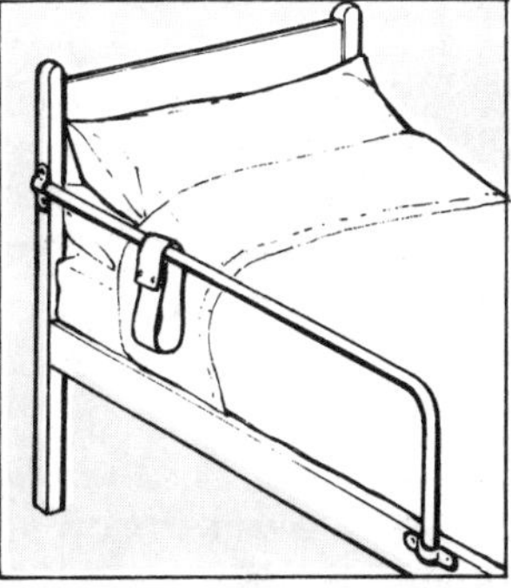

A simple hand rail can be made from metal tubing and attached to the bed with brackets. To accommodate weak grasp the rail can be built up with tape, or a loop of leather, into which the forearm can be slipped, may be riveted to the rail.

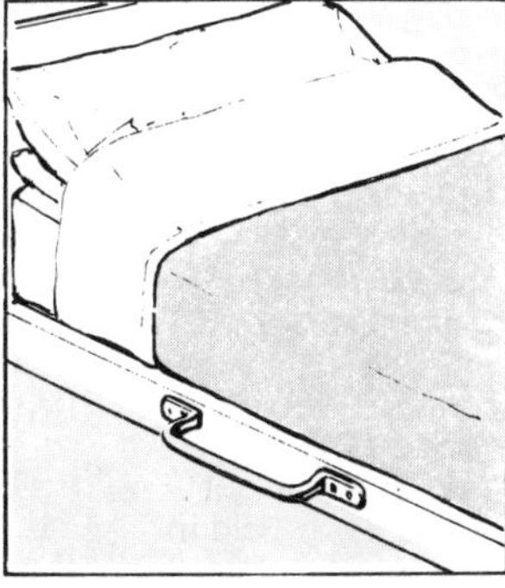

If grasp is good, grab handles, firmly bolted or screwed to the side frame on each side of the bed, are simple, and frequently helpful, aids for turning from lying on the back to lying on one side or the other.

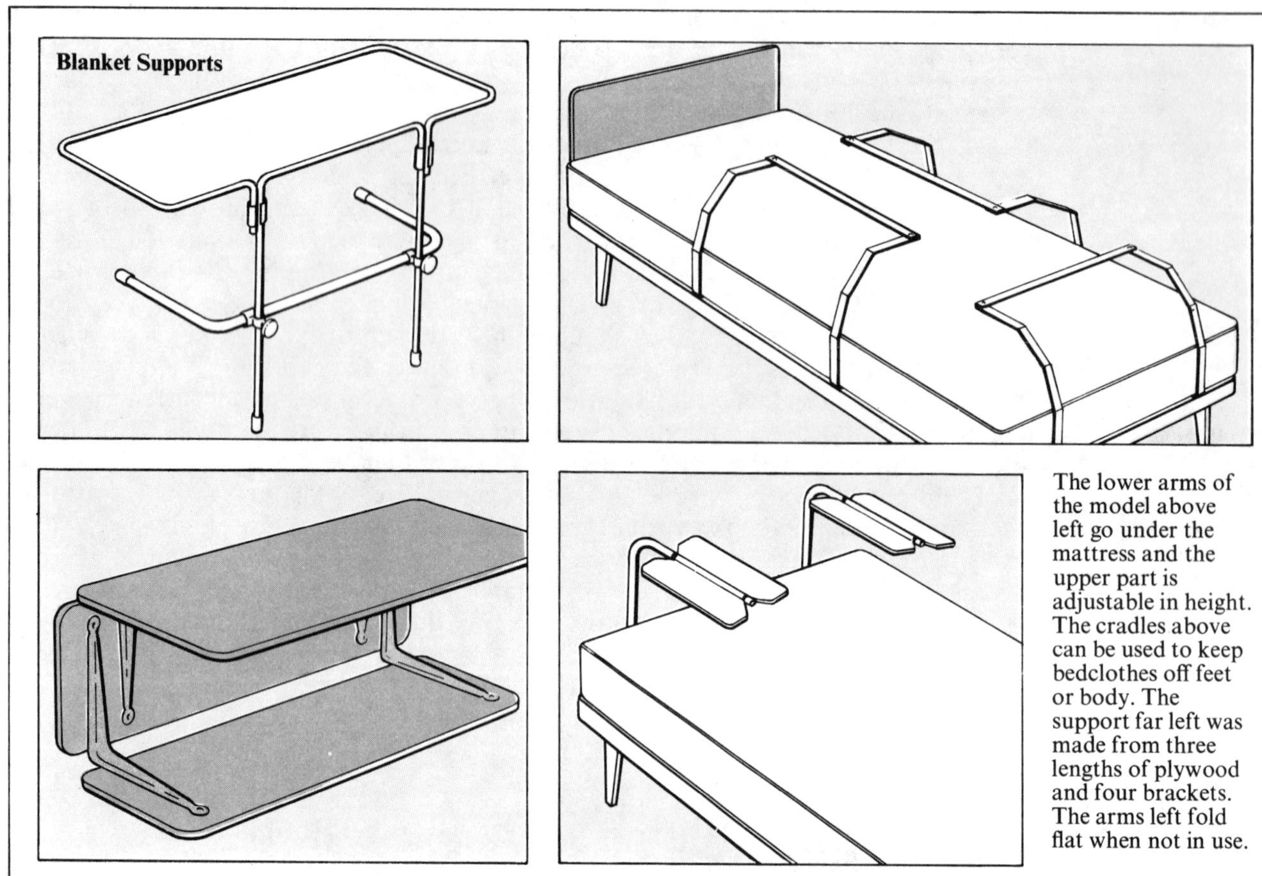

The lower arms of the model above left go under the mattress and the upper part is adjustable in height. The cradles above can be used to keep bedclothes off feet or body. The support far left was made from three lengths of plywood and four brackets. The arms left fold flat when not in use.

washable covers eliminate the need for a top sheet. Although these quilts don't tuck in they stay in place for all but the most restless sleepers. If necessary, however, flaps can be sewn on the bottom edge of the cover for tucking in.

A blanket support can be put under the bedclothes to take the weight of the bedding off the feet. The top sheet and blankets must be wide enough to go over the support and still tuck under the mattress. Such supports, which can be made at home or bought from self-help equipment firms, can be of the cantilever or hoop design. The cantilever type allows more freedom of movement because the feet can move sideways.

If you use pillows to prop yourself up in bed, they should be arranged under the shoulders so that your head is not forced forward. A large pile of pillows, resting one on top of the other, gives support and remains in position better than the more usual arrangement of two pillows set behind you at an angle.

An overbed table is a good investment for someone who spends a lot of time in bed. Most cantilevered tables are adjustable in height and are quite stable, but some move more easily than others on casters or glides. Some incorporate vanity mirrors. The hospital type of bed table, which slides over the bed along both sides, tends to inhibit movement and is more constricting.

While inexpensive methods and aids are adequate for many people, if you are confined to bed for long periods you may find an electric gatch bed preferable. An adjustable bed gives greater independence, for it makes it possible to change position frequently, to eat, read and write more comfortably. It also makes transfer easier. There are many different models available. The factors to consider before renting or buying an adjustable bed include versatility of position, the height of spring and mattress in relation to transfer, location and design of controls for ease of operation and the availability of an accessory manual control in case of power failure.

Adjustable Bed Boards

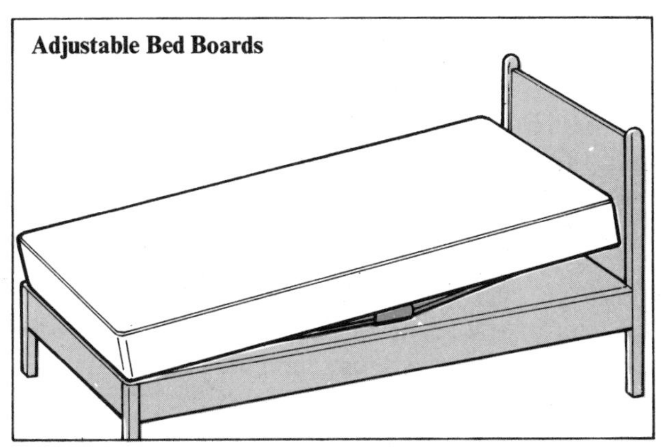

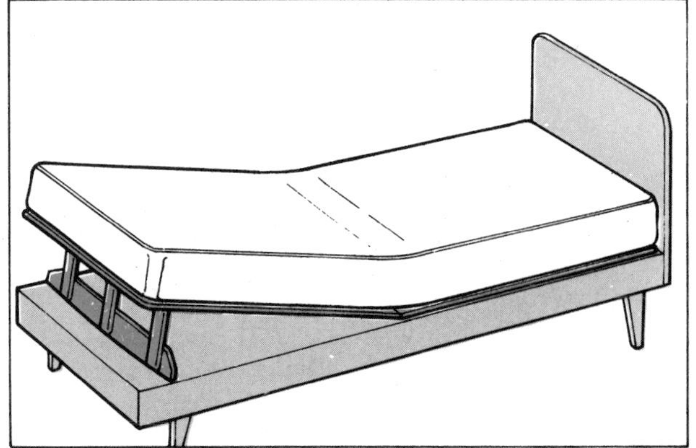

An adjustable bed board is sometimes an alternative to an electric gatch bed. The bed board above gives support at an incline when it is necessary to lie completely flat. The unit above right can be used to elevate head or feet. The board right can elevate the knees and feet and give support in a partial sitting position.

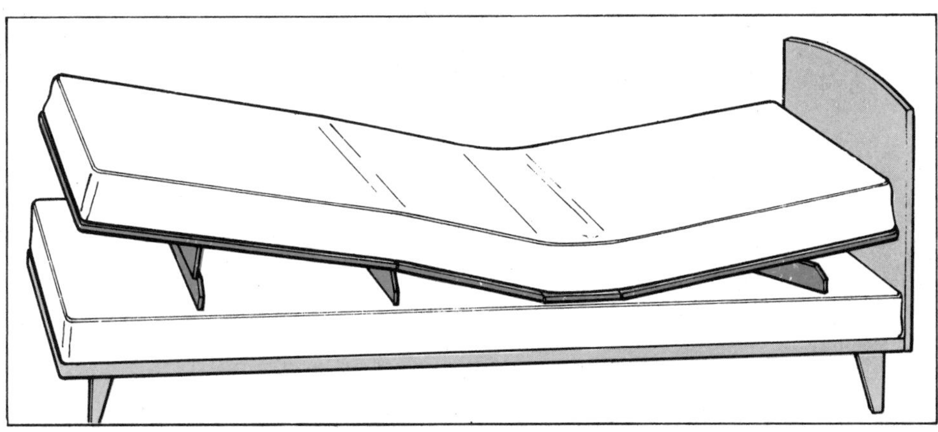

Sitting Up in Bed

A wedge-shaped foam pillow against the headboard and behind a pile of pillows gives comfortable support.

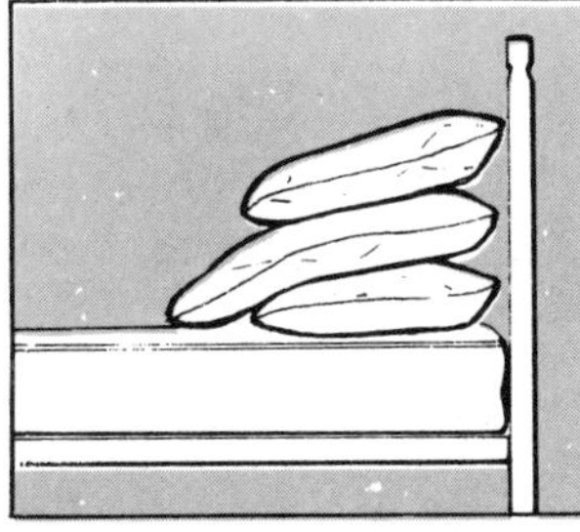

To keep the spine flat while raising the head, lay one pillow crosswise, one lengthwise and a third crosswise.

A triangular-shaped pillow can be adjusted to aid in partial sitting or to give armchair support.

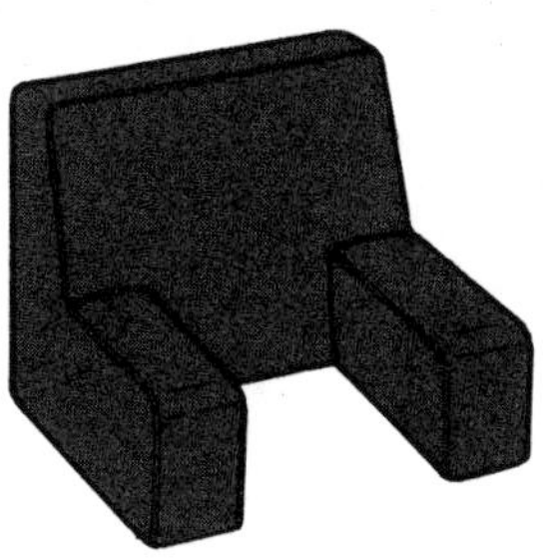

While a bed rest which is like the back and sides of an armchair looks comfortable, it is often ineffective. When sitting in bed, unlike sitting in an armchair, the knees are straight and so the body tends to slide forward and the armrests are no longer in a useful position.

A backrest can be used for sitting partially or fully erect. This one adjusts to three positions.

Adjustable in angle, this tubular steel support has a canvas cover which yields to body contours.

A backrest can be easily improvised by placing a straight chair upside down behind a pillow.

The Bathroom

This room, which might be considered the most essential room in the house, is often the most inaccessible. Usually the door is the narrowest in the house—possibly because the bathroom is the only room into which furniture never has to be moved. And even if the doorway is wide enough for wheelchair entry, the open space inside is frequently too small to permit transfer, turning or even closing the door for privacy.

The ideal wheelchair bathroom would have a door at least thirty-two inches (80 cm) wide that swings outward or slides. The clear floor space would be at least five feet by five feet (150 cm by 150 cm). The toilet would be of a height for convenient transfer with handrails placed nearby as needed. A sink would be high enough to clear the wheelchair arms so that the chair could be rolled under it and would have single lever water controls and insulated water pipes.

This freestanding toilet frame, available from hospital suppliers, is made of lightweight aluminum, has wide plastic armrests and is adjustable in height.

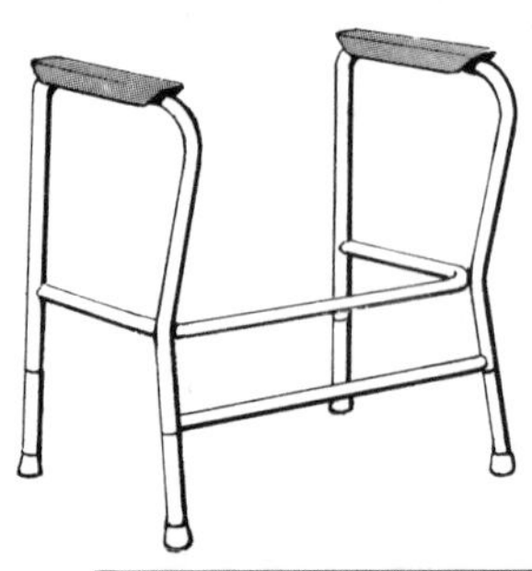

The bathtub would have a built-in transfer area, suitable handrails or a lift that could be used independently. The stall shower would be free of curbs and would have at least three and a half feet (105 cm) of clear interior space with a folding seat at wheelchair height, and a single-lever water control within easy reach. The water temperature would be thermostatically controlled. The medicine cabinet and the mirrors would be at a convenient height. There would be adequate and accessible storage. The floor would be slip-proof and there would be an alarm system easy to reach from bath, shower and toilet.

The ideal bathroom for someone who is ambulant, on the other hand, would have some different features. Whereas someone who is wheelchaired requires a lot of space, a disabled person who is ambulant often prefers a narrow room so that the solid fittings or the walls are within easy reach to provide stability when moving around.

The ideal bathroom is, sadly, rare.

Toilet Aids

Side grab bars must be chosen to suit individual needs and the design of the bathroom. Grab bars can only be used if the wall will support the stress of descending or rising with their help. A floor model, such as the one at bottom far right, fits any toilet. It stands free or can be clamped to the bowl, has hand grips adjustable to three levels and also adjusts in width and depth. The corrugated rubber keeps it from slipping.

Compromise is usually necessary and most people have to work out their own adaptations, but there are many fixtures and aids available which can help to increase independence.

The height of the toilet seat constitutes a problem for many people. The standard fifteen to seventeen inches (38 to 43 cm) is often too low. Elevating the seat from five to seven inches (13 to 18 cm) gives better leverage for regaining a standing position. For someone who is wheelchaired, the toilet seat must be at a convenient height for easy and safe transfer.

If you are remodeling or making plumbing changes in your bathroom, you might consider a wall-mounted toilet. It can be installed at whatever height is most convenient and, since there is no obstruction below, it allows closer approach in a wheelchair and also makes floor cleaning easier.

An existing toilet unit which is too low can be raised to a more comfortable height by mounting it on a wooden platform or block. The simplest solution, however, is to use a removable raised toilet seat, of which there are several types available. There are, as well, raised seats which are permanently fixed to the toilet assembly. Both the removable and permanent models are available with padded seats to prevent pressure sores.

Toilet safety bars or frames are necessary for support as well as for safety. Your individual needs, whether you need support to lift yourself off the seat, pull yourself to or from a wheelchair or maintain balance while seated, should be assessed by a therapist before a unit is chosen and installed. It must also be ascertained whether the wall will support the added stress of bars, or whether a floor model is necessary. It is important, too, that there be enough space for a clenched fist between the wall and the bar so that it is possible to free the hand and regrasp quickly if necessary. Towel bars, which are not designed to hold substantial weight, should never be substituted for safety bars.

Although various types of reachers are

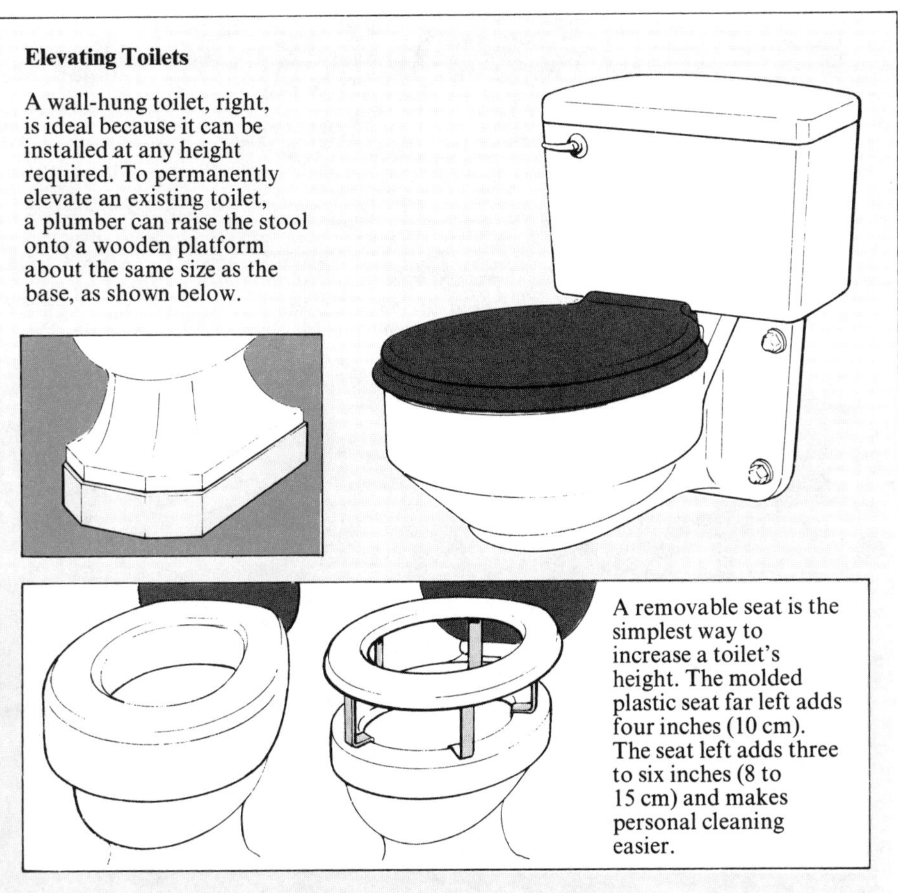

Elevating Toilets

A wall-hung toilet, right, is ideal because it can be installed at any height required. To permanently elevate an existing toilet, a plumber can raise the stool onto a wooden platform about the same size as the base, as shown below.

A removable seat is the simplest way to increase a toilet's height. The molded plastic seat far left adds four inches (10 cm). The seat left adds three to six inches (8 to 15 cm) and makes personal cleaning easier.

available as aids when self-cleaning is difficult, a bidet makes cleansing of the perineal area easier. A conventional bidet may create problems of transfer, but it can be installed at a higher than usual height, at approximately the same level as the toilet. Adjacent support rails will probably be necessary.

A combined bidet and toilet is, however, usually more convenient. Several models are available which attach to any standard toilet bowl, require no extra floor space and only an attachment to the water supply and an electric outlet are required for installation. A self-contained mechanism spray-washes with thermostatically controlled warm water and dries with a flow of warm air, thus eliminating the use of toilet paper and the need for hands. Controls can be operated with the hands, feet or even with the head.

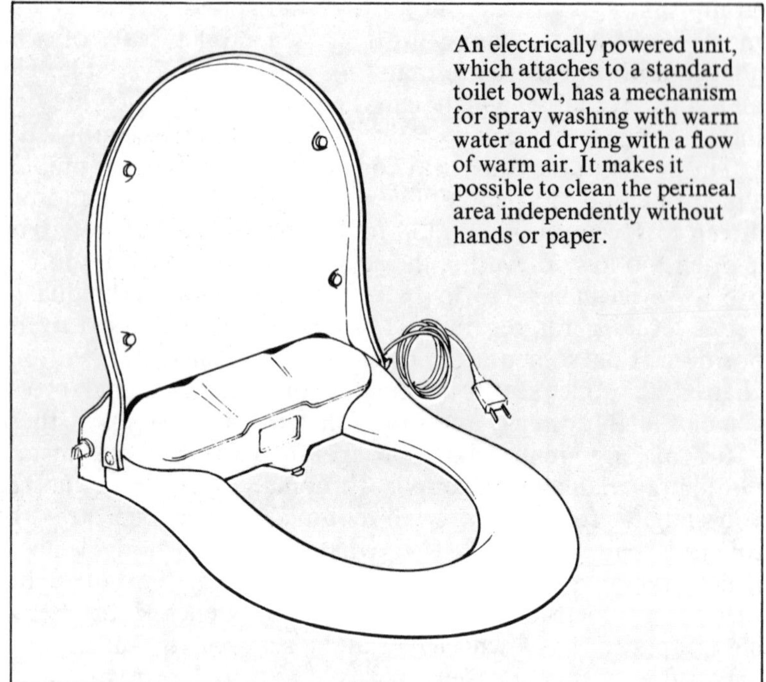

An electrically powered unit, which attaches to a standard toilet bowl, has a mechanism for spray washing with warm water and drying with a flow of warm air. It makes it possible to clean the perineal area independently without hands or paper.

There are several ways to solve some of the problems of a minuscule bathroom. A straight chair can, for example, be used as a bridge between the wheelchair and the toilet if the wheelchair will not fit into the bathroom. Fairly good balance is, however, required for this transfer feat.

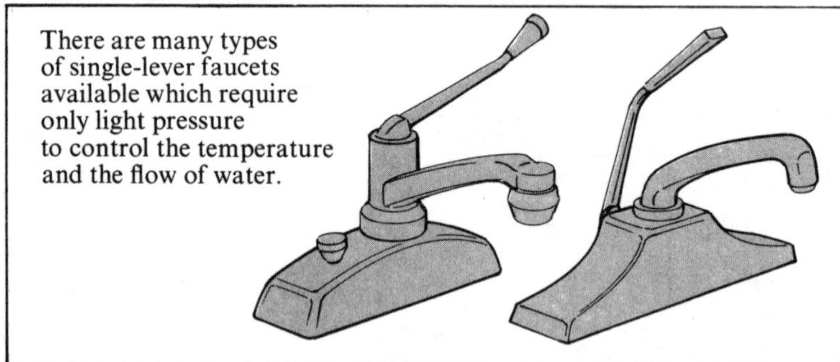

There are many types of single-lever faucets available which require only light pressure to control the temperature and the flow of water.

When lack of space prevents sideways transfer, a wheelchair with a removable back—with a zipper or snap fastening—makes it possible to shift backward to the toilet seat from the wheelchair. The two seats must be the same height.

A portable urinal can be a boon to both women and men because it will save trips to the bathroom. Portable urinals for women are contoured for proper fit and can be used when sitting or when lying down.

Commode chairs that conceal their purpose are available from hospital supply companies. Some flush and some look like modern armchairs. Commode chairs that roll over a toilet are also available. Developed for vans, motor homes and boats, chemical toilets are inexpensive and functional and can be used to make a corner of a bedroom or a closet into a bathroom.

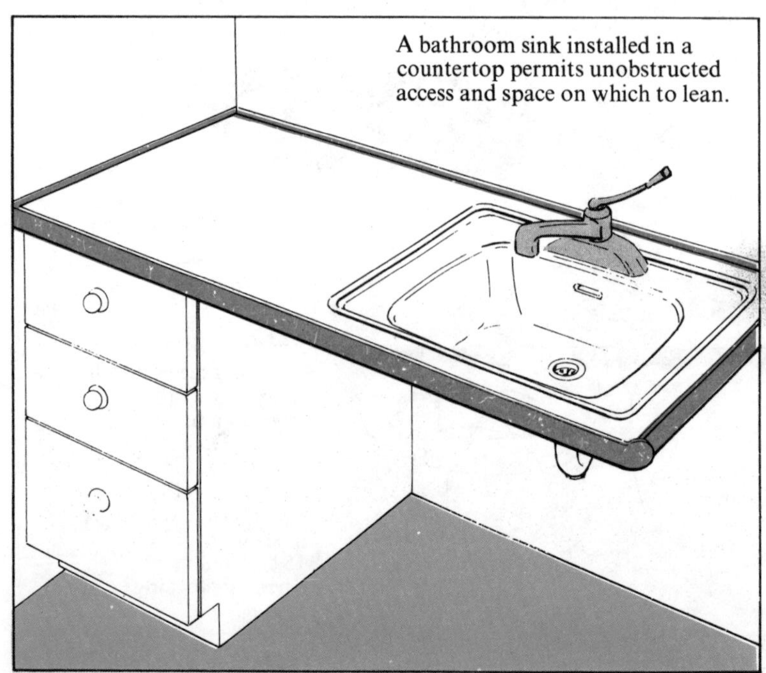

A bathroom sink installed in a countertop permits unobstructed access and space on which to lean.

The rim height of the bathroom sink should be about three feet (90 cm) for someone who is ambulant and about five inches (13 cm) lower for someone who is wheelchaired. When a sink is used by both ambulant and wheelchaired people, a good compromise is about two feet and eight inches (80 cm). To permit close access for a wheelchair it is best if the sink is wall-hung and does not have a pedestal. Sometimes it is necessary to set the sink out from the wall to allow room for wheelchair footrests. A wide wall-hung sink with two front legs or a sink built into a counter top provide space on which to lean and to keep toilet items. The pipes under the sink should be covered with asbestos or some other suitable insulating material.

Single-lever faucets, which require only light pressure, rather than the twisting needed to turn standard knobs on and off, are worth considering if plumbing changes are being made.

The first step toward managing a bath or shower with ease and independence is to organize the bathing area for safe entrance into or out of the shower or tub. A nonskid, foam-backed or latex-coated mat on the bathroom floor provides firm footing. Nonslip or suction mats or adhesive-backed, rubber-silicone treads in the tub or shower are a precaution against dangerous falls.

The tub or shower should be fitted with sturdy and properly fitted grab bars. When selecting and installing rails, it's important to consider the structure of the walls, the plumbing arrangements and the wall space. Many designs are available to meet specific leverage, space and plumbing situations. As with grab bars next to the toilet, there must be enough space for a clenched fist between the rail and the wall to permit fast regrasp of the rail if necessary. By spiraling an

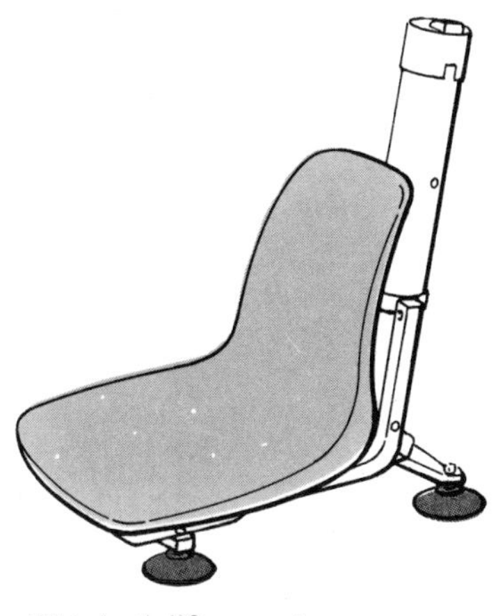

This bath lift operates on water pressure and can be used independently. The seat swings out over the tub edge; the bather sits, swings feet into the tub and glides into the bath to as low as three inches (8 cm).

Two U-shaped bars on the inner tub wall, one vertical and one horizontal, make a grasping area that is within convenient reach.

When getting into and out of the bathtub and changing position, an L-shaped bar at hand height supports the full weight.

Stable maneuverability when stepping over the tub rim and a secure hold when turning and showering is provided by a J-shaped bar.

A combined vertical-horizontal bar gives support when entering, changing position and leaving the tub and aids sitting balance.

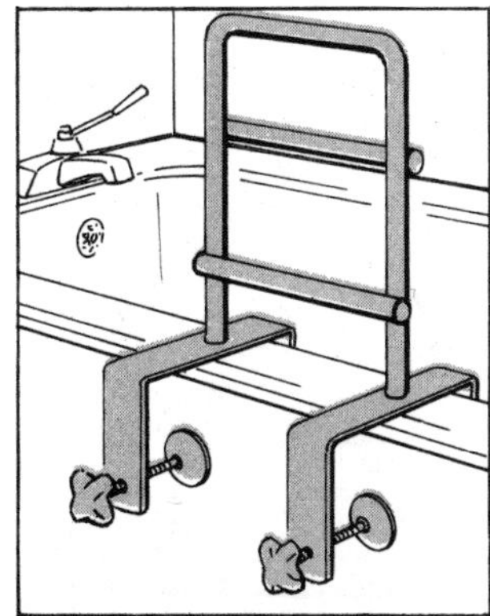

The three horizontal bars of the bathtub grip above were designed for wide-walled tubs and give extra security. The height of the tub rail right makes it unnecessary to stoop to get into the tub.

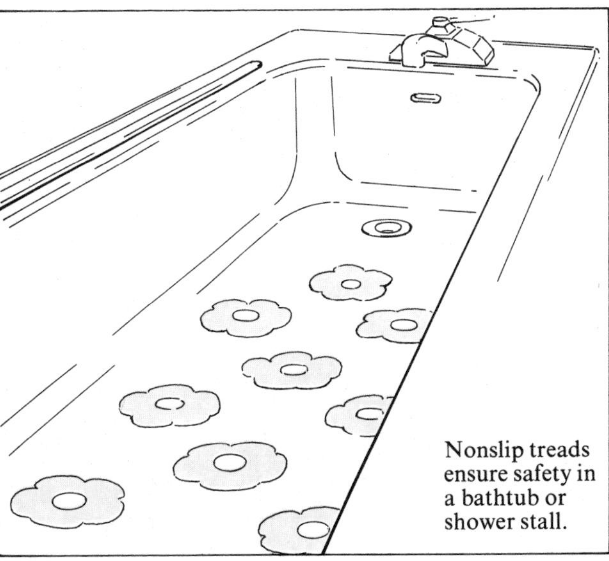

Nonslip treads ensure safety in a bathtub or shower stall.

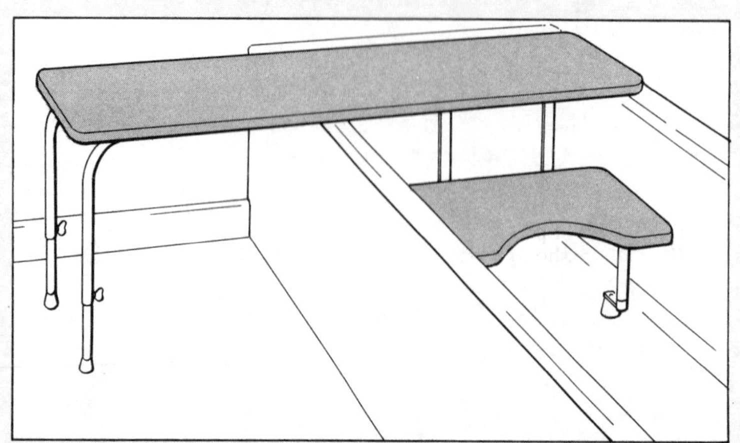

A bath bench used in conjunction with a bath seat and grab bars makes it easier to get into and out of the tub. The bath bench shown above can be assembled at either end of the tub and is adjustable in height. The seat is made of laminated board.

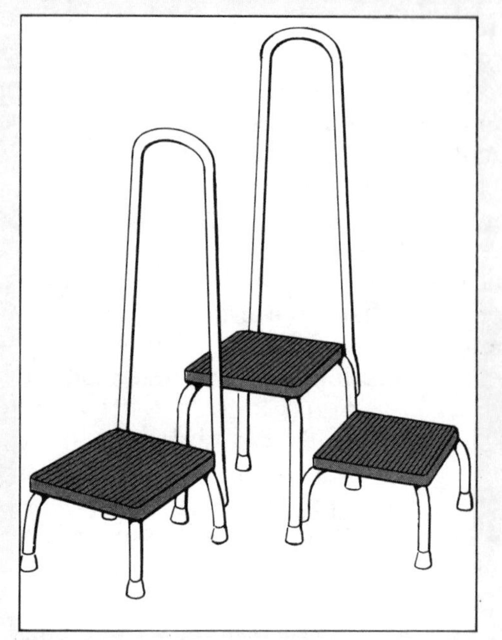

A step stool which is used in the bathroom should always have rubber-tipped legs and, preferably, a corrugated rubber surface, as do the stools shown right. A high handrail provides additional security when the stool is used to get into and out of the bathtub.

Bathtub Seats

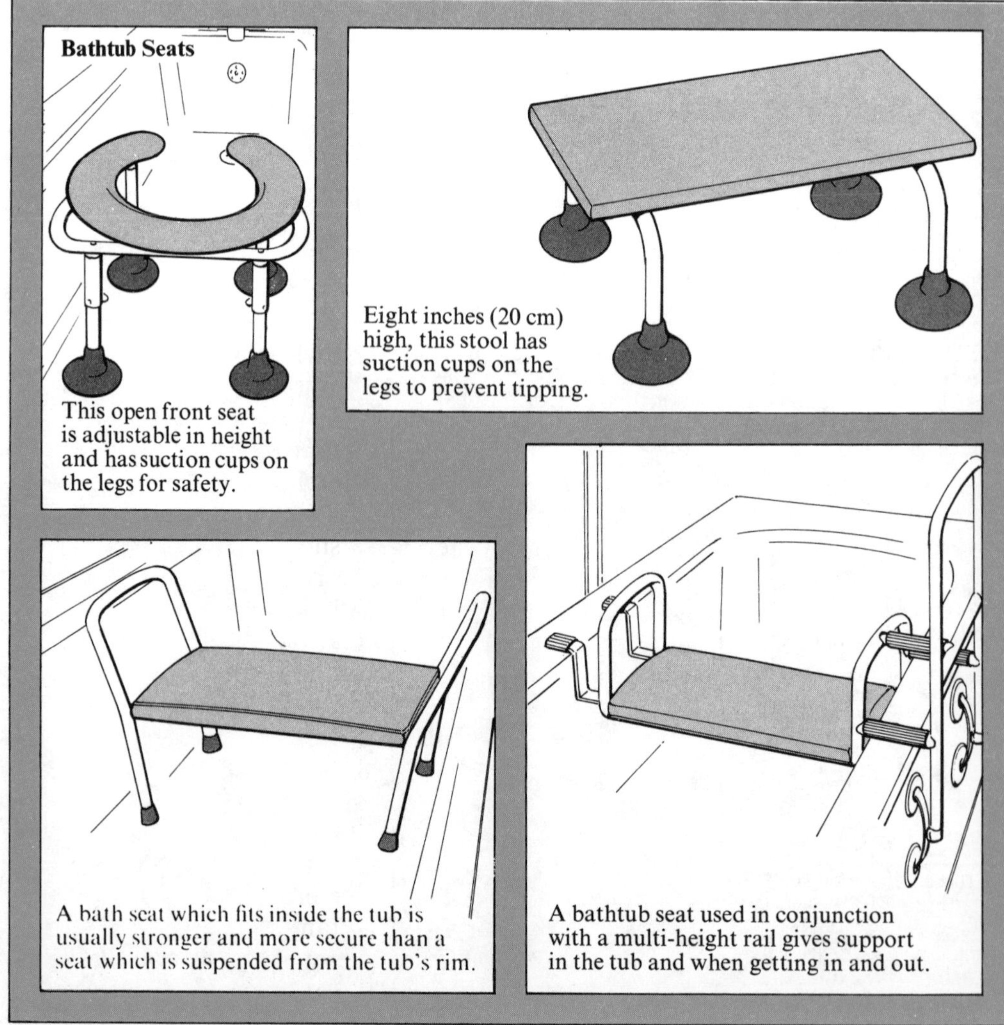

This open front seat is adjustable in height and has suction cups on the legs for safety.

Eight inches (20 cm) high, this stool has suction cups on the legs to prevent tipping.

A bath seat which fits inside the tub is usually stronger and more secure than a seat which is suspended from the tub's rim.

A bathtub seat used in conjunction with a multi-height rail gives support in the tub and when getting in and out.

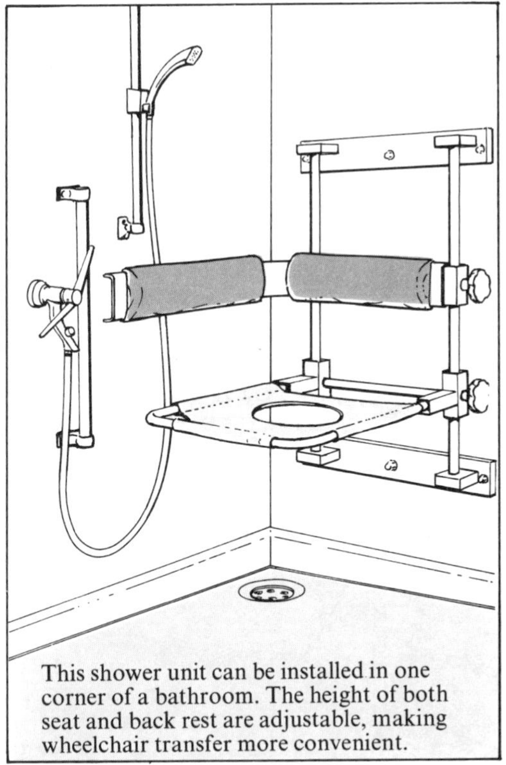

This shower unit can be installed in one corner of a bathroom. The height of both seat and back rest are adjustable, making wheelchair transfer more convenient.

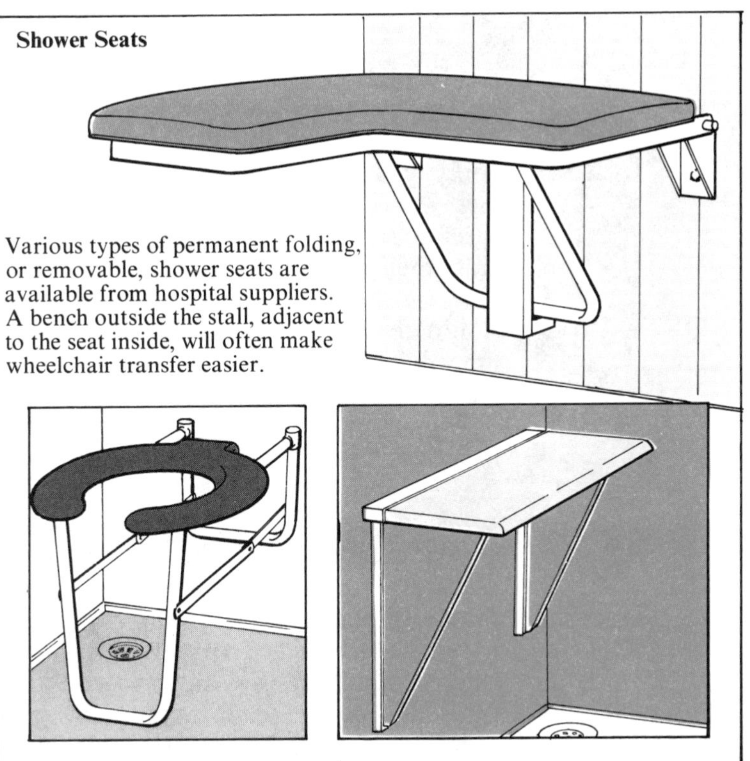

Shower Seats

Various types of permanent folding, or removable, shower seats are available from hospital suppliers. A bench outside the stall, adjacent to the seat inside, will often make wheelchair transfer easier.

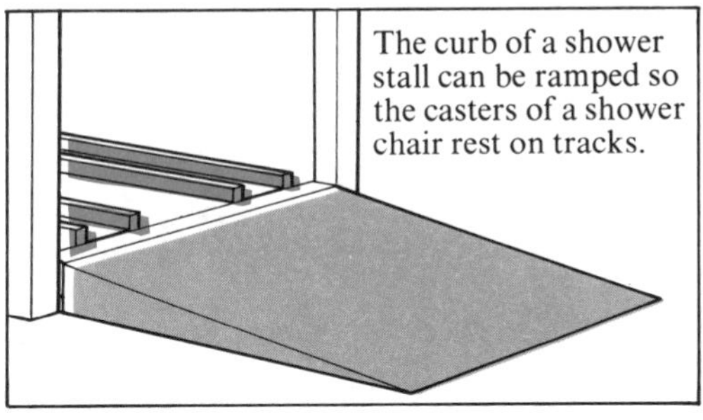

The curb of a shower stall can be ramped so the casters of a shower chair rest on tracks.

adhesive-backed safety tread around a grab rail a firm grasp can be assured. Never rely on a towel bar or a soap holder to support your weight.

Transfer to the bathtub can be assisted by the use of a tub chair or a bathtub seat which is lower than the edge of the tub. Bath lifters with hydraulically powered seats are commercially available for those who cannot transfer without assistance. Most lifters are manually operated by a hydraulic pump which elevates the seat and by a release mechanism which lowers it; some units are motorized. There are models which can be operated independently, but most require the assistance of an attendant. Since lifters are quite expensive and the choice of one is based on many factors, including space requirements, a doctor or physiotherapist should be consulted before purchase.

A stall shower is the simplest and safest way to bathe since it eliminates the need to step over a high tub rim or to lower your body into the water. A bathroom with a stall shower usually allows more room for maneuvering a wheelchair than does one with a tub and should, therefore, be considered when bathroom alterations are being planned.

A stall shower is also convenient because a chair or permanent folding bench can be placed inside it. A shower chair that rolls into the stall may be used instead. A shower stall into which a chair can be rolled must have the curb removed and the drain depressed in one corner to keep water from overflowing into the room.

A bath cabinet provides private independent bathing and eliminates the need for either bathtub or shower. Portable and stationary units are available. One fiberglass model has a two-way seat which moves in and out of the cabinet so that it can be entered from a wheelchair or from a standing position. The seat, which is operated by a lever, is powered by normal water pressure. The heat of the water is thermostatically controlled.

Single-control faucets are available for bathtub or shower, as well as for the sink. If necessary the lever can be built up so that it can be more easily grasped.

The Kitchen

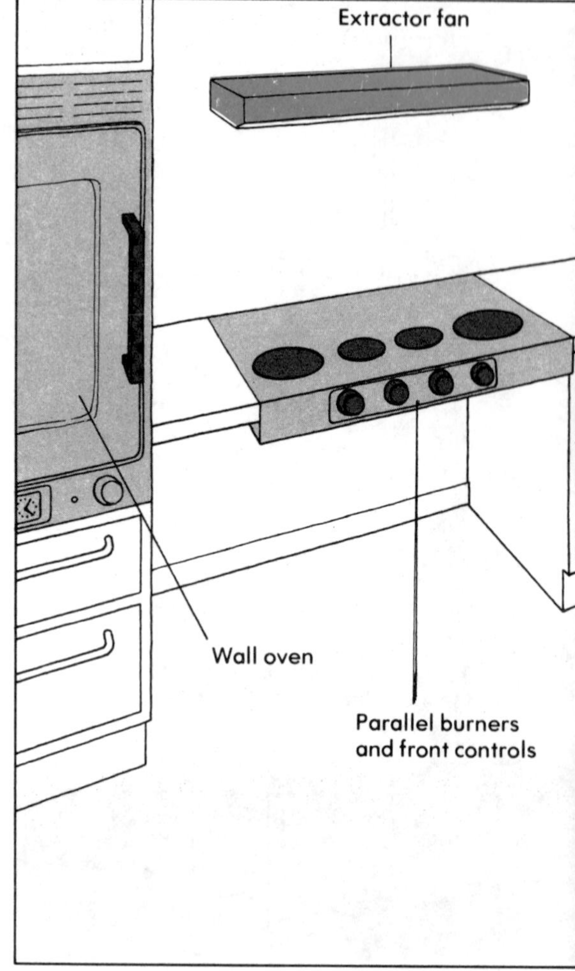

For maximum efficiency a kitchen need not be large or filled with expensive appliances and units. The proper arrangement of cabinets and appliances, the careful selection of equipment, the use of aids when necessary and the adoption of different methods of doing things can eliminate unnecessary movement, save time, simplify meal preparation and make cooking a pleasure.

The appliances must be properly located in relation to each other. There must be adequate counter space between appliances, and provisions and cooking utensils must be stored near their place of use and within easy reach. The layout should be based on the three-point work triangle which has been proved to be most efficient—refrigerator, sink and cooking facilities arranged from right to left for a right-handed person, left to right for someone who is left-handed. But, above all, the kitchen must be tailored to your individual needs.

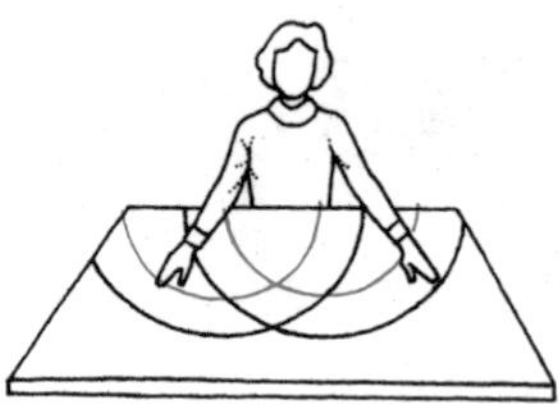

Before replanning your kitchen it is necessary to determine your comfortable and maximum horizontal reach ranges and vertical reach ranges from the position—either standing or sitting—in which you work.

The kitchen of someone who is wheelchaired requires lower work surfaces and somewhat different storage arrangements than the kitchen of someone who is ambulant. A removable, rigid wheelchair seat, apart from increasing comfort, can also raise a person of average height to a level at which standard-height kitchen equipment can be used.

People who are ambulant often find that they can work most efficiently in the kitchen from a comfortable chair that gives proper support. Often two chairs of different heights are necessary; one of standard height for use at a kitchen table and a higher chair for use at the sink and food preparation areas.

There are other factors, too, which must be considered when remodeling or adapting a kitchen. Well-organized work areas will save time and energy for anyone, but are most important for someone who is handicapped by a disability.

Storage facilities should be organized to accommodate cooking needs and also allow for limited mobility and reach or restricted bending capacity. If you rely on portable appliances, such as an electric skillet or blender, keep them permanently at the back of the counter top or on a table so they can be slid back and forth rather than lifted. Electric outlets for small appliances should be at counter level. Items most frequently used should be arranged so that they can be seen and can be reached easily.

Things should be stored so that they cannot fall, slip or harm you when you try to retrieve them. This means keeping heavy things low and knives in holders, rather than in the bottom of a drawer. Don't stack things, either; it may be difficult to get one item out from under the weight of others.

Group things according to usage. Keep ingredients for baking, for example, in the same area in which mixing bowls, rolling pin, cake pans and pie plates are stored. It is also a good idea to store utensils in the area where they are first used. Frying pans, for example, should

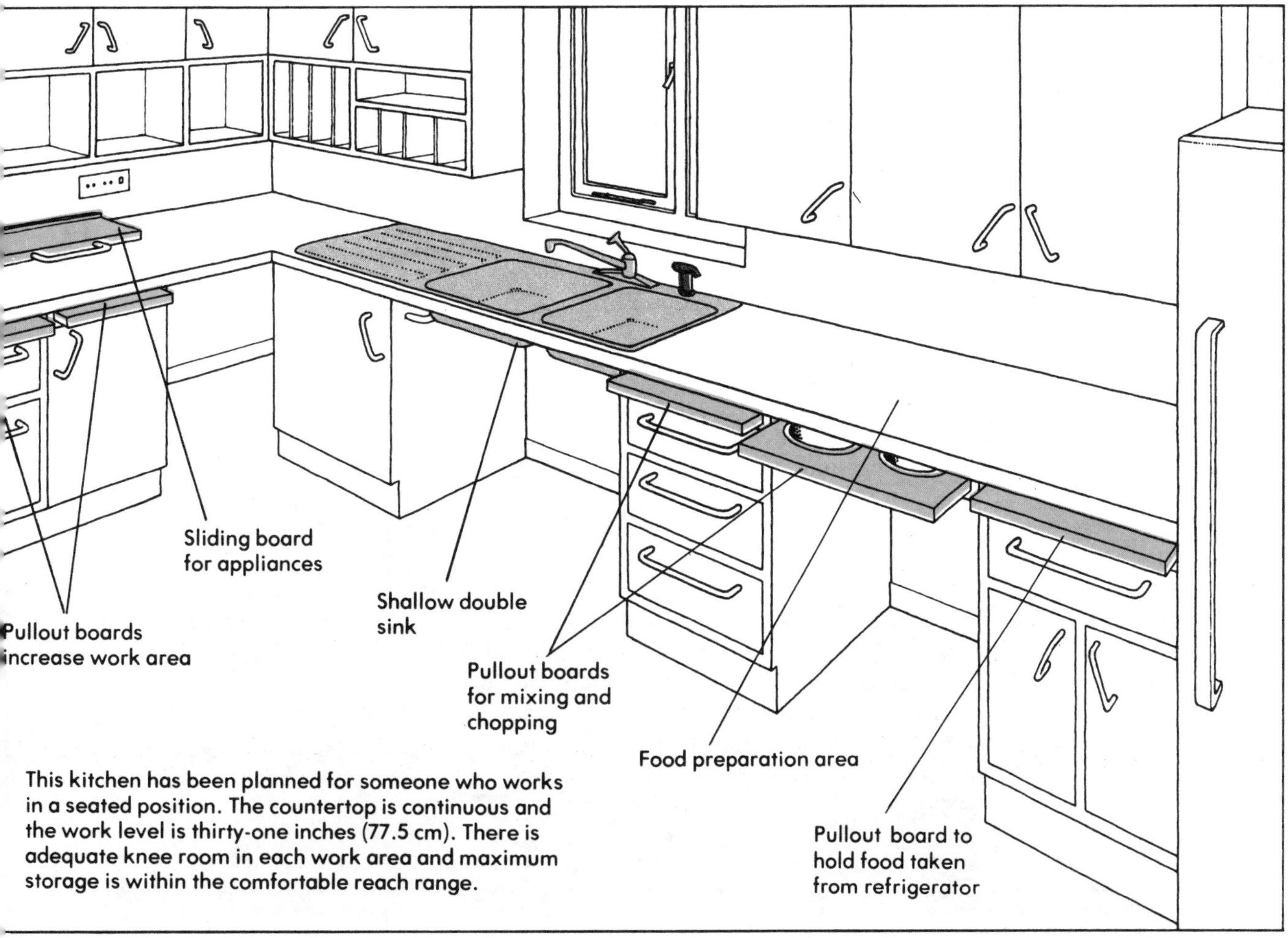

Sliding board for appliances

Pullout boards increase work area

Shallow double sink

Pullout boards for mixing and chopping

Food preparation area

Pullout board to hold food taken from refrigerator

This kitchen has been planned for someone who works in a seated position. The countertop is continuous and the work level is thirty-one inches (77.5 cm). There is adequate knee room in each work area and maximum storage is within the comfortable reach range.

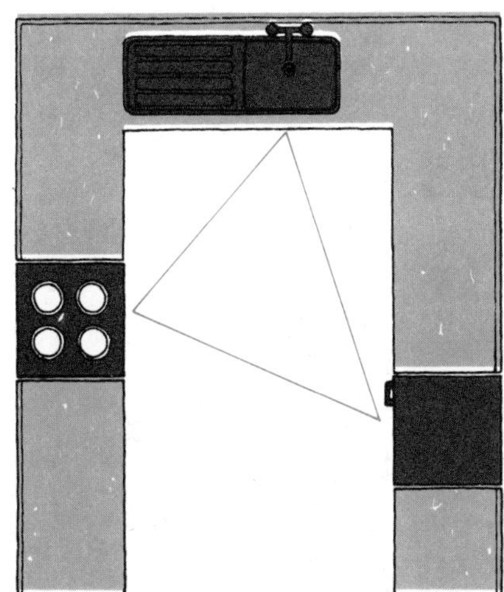

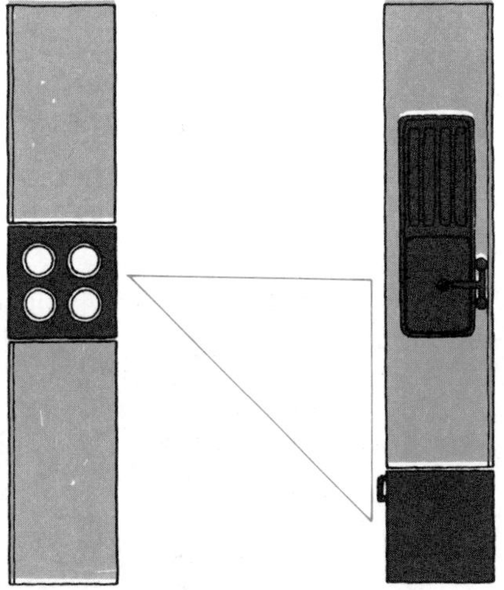

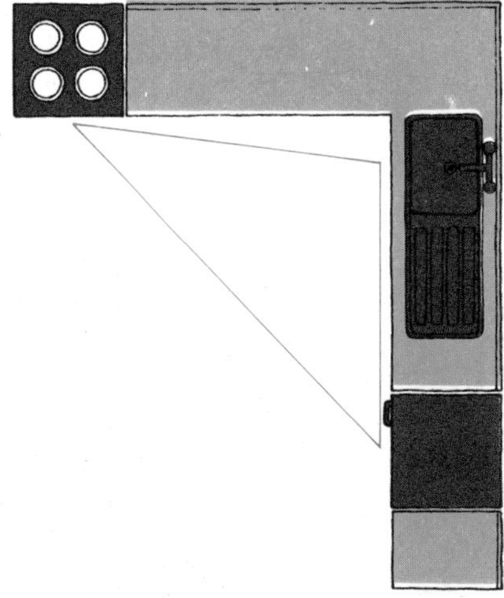

The kitchen layout should, ideally, be based on the three-point work triangle, with the refrigerator, sink and cooking facilities arranged in that order, which follows the sequence of food preparation—food is taken from the refrigerator, washed and put in a pan at the sink and then moved to the stove for cooking. The countertops should be unbroken so that whenever possible hot or heavy items can be slid, rather than carried, from area to area. Kitchen equipment can be arranged in a U shape, an L shape or in a corridor shape on two parallel walls. People who use a cane or crutches often find that the U-shaped arrangement saves steps and energy. An L-shaped layout is usually the most practical for someone who is wheelchaired, provided the countertops are ample. Although the corridor layout is not generally considered as desirable as the other two because of the breaks in the countertops, this is often the only arrangement which allows adequate space for a wheelchair to turn completely.

be stored near the cooking area, but saucepans, coffeepot and kettle are better stored near the sink, since the first step in using them usually involves getting water from the faucet. Have duplicates of such items as measuring cups, spoons and knives, which you use in different areas of the kitchen.

Kitchen Storage

Before you plan the storage and make any alterations in your present kitchen, test your reach and its limits carefully. You can then maximize the storage space accessible to you by taking advantage of various space-saving devices.

If you are wheelchaired, the upper shelves of most wall cabinets are probably inaccessible to you and most of what is conventionally stored on such shelves must be given space lower down. With the help of a reaching device some high shelves can become usable—but use them with discretion. They are fine for light unopened packages, baskets, plastic dishes and other unbreakables. Breakable or heavy items, like glassware or cans, should never be stored high up.

Storage will be further restricted if you are wheelchaired or sit when you wash dishes and prepare food, for the storage space usually available below the level of the counter in the area under the sink must be given up for knee space, as must at least one other space in the area where food is prepared.

There is, however, a great variety of devices and simple fixtures that, strategically placed, can expand the capacity of accessible storage space. Many simple and inexpensive "kitchen organizers" can be bought or made at home.

A lazy Susan brings cans and packages within easy reach and makes it possible for each item to be stored so that it can be retrieved with one hand without other items having to be lifted out of the way.

If hand function is limited, handles set at forty-five degrees are easiest to grasp.

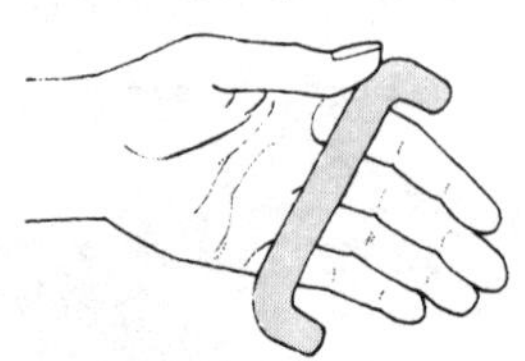

A revolving shelf unit, which has shelves that operate independently of each other, is useful in a deep cabinet.

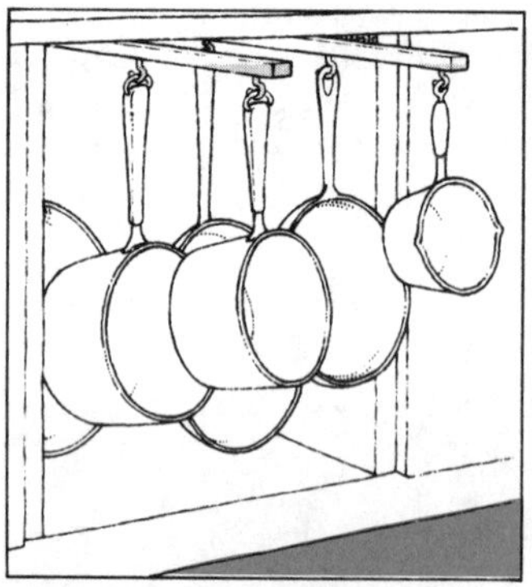

An efficient and accessible way to store pans in a deep cabinet is on sliding racks from which the pans hang.

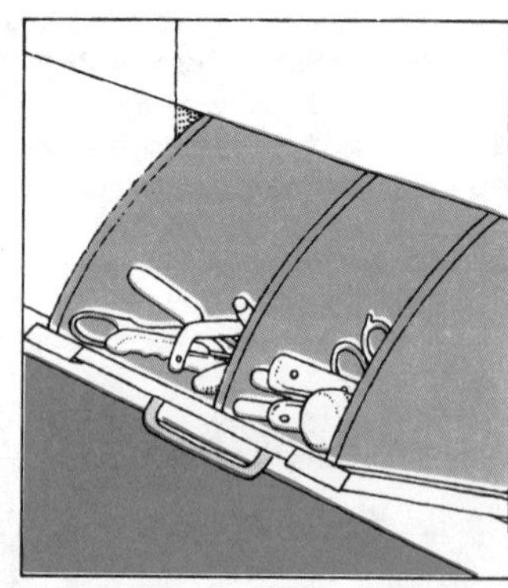

Everything stored in a pull-down drawer, which is hinged at the bottom, can be quickly seen and retrieved.

Vegetables and fruit which do not require refrigeration can be stored in a cabinet in large, pull out plastic bins.

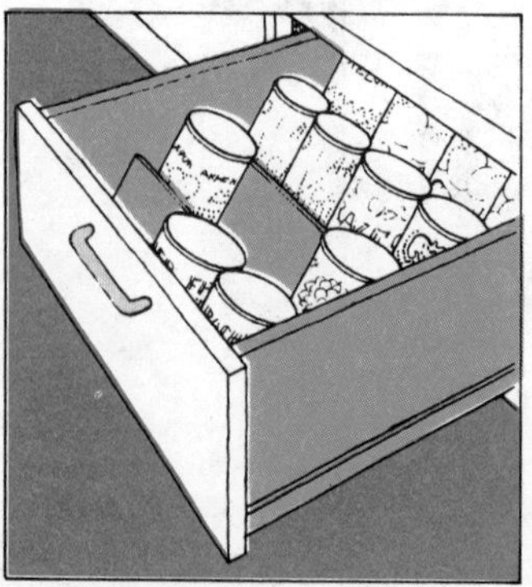

Inside a drawer, racks to hold cans make it possible to see all the cans at a glance and to remove each one easily.

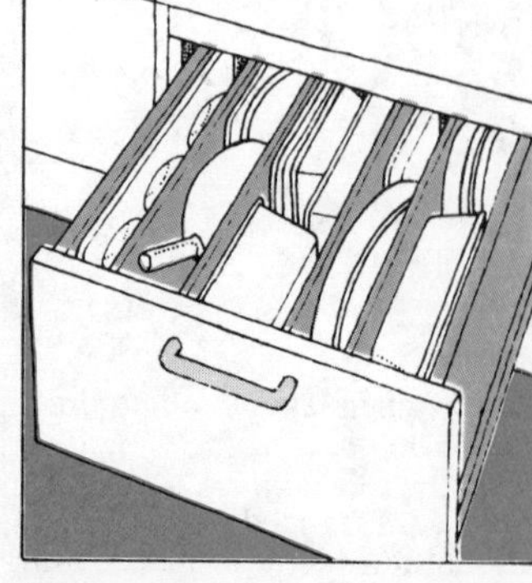

Bulky and awkwardly shaped kitchen equipment can be stored in a drawer which has vertical dividers.

Although rotating shelves can be built in, freestanding rotating shelves in various sizes are commercially available.

Pegboard panels can be used on any open wall space. Hangers for pegboards include hooks, with prongs that hold them firmly in place, brackets for shelves and holders for a variety of utensils and tools.

Deep-drawer dividers create vertical filing space for flat items so that one at a time can be selected without moving others. They provide excellent storage space for baking sheets, shallow baking dishes, muffin tins, cutting boards and pot lids. The dividers can be made of plywood and held in place with clips or metal brads at each end.

An existing unit can often be altered for more efficient use. A broom closet, for example, can be fitted with sliding shelves. If the shelves are shallow and set in from the edge, the broom, brushes and other cleaning supplies can be hung on the back of the door.

For the ambulant person who finds it difficult as well as inconvenient to reach lower storage, vertically divided drawers and back-of-door storage are particularly valuable.

Door backs can also be used for storage of canned goods and other items up to three and a half inches (9 cm) deep. Shelves can be built in, but adjustable shelf units are commercially available.

A raised edge or some kind of retaining bar will be needed on shelves on the inside of cabinet doors. The doors must have strong hinges (piano hinges are preferable), and heavy items should be stored only at the hinged end of the shelves.

If a shelf in an existing cabinet is too deep to reach into easily and cannot be fitted with a drawer, the back part should be blocked off so that things cannot get pushed out of reach. Goods stored on narrow shelves in single rows are more visible and accessible. Two shelves can be made where there was only one before.

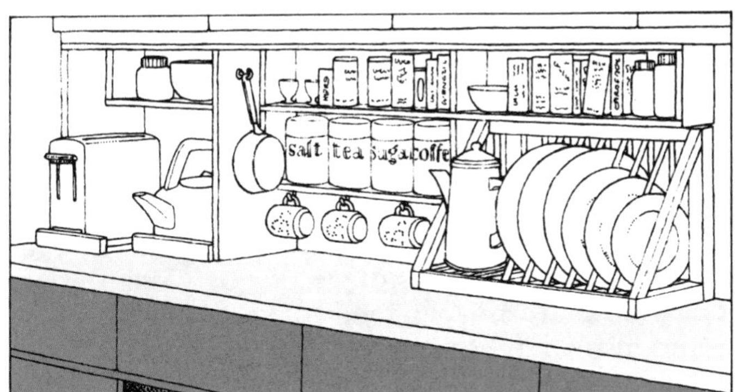

If you are wheelchaired you can use the often wasted back portion of the countertop for storage. Here dishes can be kept in vertical files and electrical appliances can be permanently installed, each on a pull out platform.

Pull out shelves in base cabinets make large utensils easily accessible from a wheelchair.

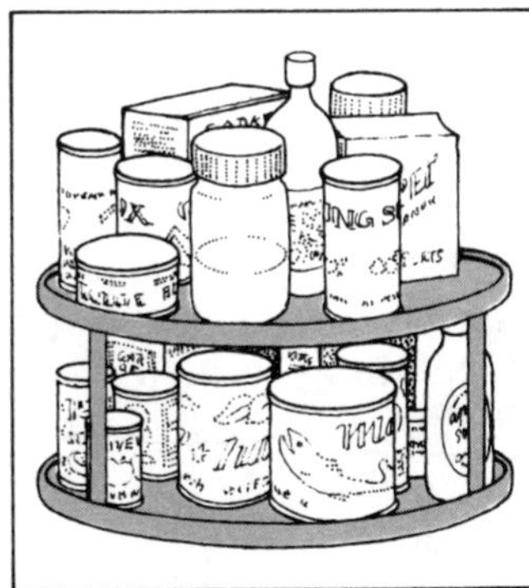

A lazy Susan provides high density and accessible storage on a countertop for small cans and bottles.

A specially constructed slide-out unit, or the back of a closet door, can be used to store items which are bulky and awkwardly shaped. Many utensils can be hung from pegboard and a bottom shelf accommodates others.

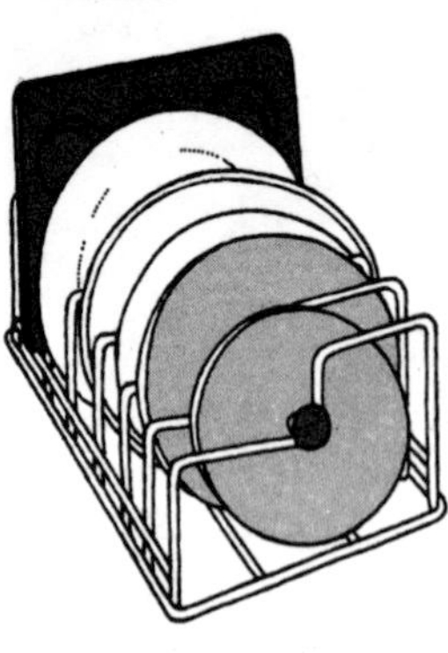

A rack for vertical filing serves as well for storage on a countertop as in a cabinet.

The back of a door can be used to store boxes, cans and bottles. Adjustable shelf units, which are easy to install, are available from mail order companies and department stores.

Low shallow shelving can be created to store cans and small boxes in single rows so that no item has to be lifted over another to be removed and everything is immediately seen.

The shelves can be close, one above the other, since there is no need to leave space for items at the back to be lifted over those in front.

A wheelchair user has available for storage the sometimes wasted back portion of the standard twenty-four inch (60 cm) counter top. Many people who are wheelchaired also find that drawers and slideout bins built into base cabinets are, if they are well made, generally more efficient, less wasteful of space and easier to manage than cabinets with doors enclosing fixed shelves.

If the doors of cabinets are removed they become open storage bins and space is also made for additional pull-out drawers and pull-out sliding racks for pots and pans and other utensils with handles.

When any remodeling is done the best hardware available should be used so that drawers, no matter how heavily laden, will glide in and out at a touch. Cabinet doors should have tap catches, which operate at a very light touch, or magnetic catches which offer minimum resistance. A horizontal handle at the bottom of each door will provide an easy grip.

The refrigerator is an important element in kitchen storage. Not only is this where perishable food is kept, but adequate refrigerator space makes frequent shopping trips unnecessary. Unfortunately, although refrigerators come in a great variety of designs and sizes, most of them are poorly designed for people who are wheelchaired or who have limited reach or difficulty in bending.

For someone who is wheelchaired, the upper shelves and the rear areas of most refrigerators are often beyond reach. A freezer compartment at the top with a down-dropping door is effectively barred to reach from below. And it is impossible from a wheelchair to use the top part of a refrigerator that has the freezer on the bottom.

People who use crutches or can't bend from the hips are not usually able to reach the back of the lower shelves of a model with a large freezer at the top and they

Vertically hinged, shallow shelves in a cabinet provide convenient and safe storage for large, heavy cans. Beading along the edges of the shelves prevents items falling off.

find it equally difficult to cope with a freezing compartment that is at the bottom of the refrigerator.

Most convenient for any disability is probably a side-by-side, double-door model which has a vertical freezer and refrigerator. Because both doors open from the center such refrigerators also require less floor space than conventional models.

Some small refrigerators are sufficient for a family and are quite accessible from a wheelchair. Slide-out shelves, revolving shelves and shelves on the door increase storage capacity as well as accessibility. Refrigerators are available with the door opening at the right or the left. It's important for the opening edge of the door to be next to counter space. Some refrigerators have a foot pedal and a hand control for opening the door. The pedal can be extended to the side so that it can be depressed by the wheel of a wheelchair.

An automatic ice-cube maker eliminates the sometimes awkward task of getting water-filled ice trays from the sink to the freezer compartment. The ice-cube making feature, however, requires a plumbing connection to the cold water intake. If you don't have an automatic ice-cube maker, remember that half-filled ice trays are easier to carry. And if you buy nonstick coated ice trays, or spray conventional trays with the nonstick spray that is used for cooking before you fill them, the ice cubes will pop right out.

A self-defrosting refrigerator saves one regular chore and the newer frost-free models also eliminate the laborious and sometimes impossible task of defrosting a heavily iced-up freezer compartment.

Putting a turntable on the lower shelves of a deep refrigerator makes the contents easier to reach. If your grasp is weak, position a wheeled table or the lapboard of the wheelchair as close to the refrigerator as possible. Keep heavier items on a shelf level with that surface so that they can be slid easily into and out of the refrigerator. Extra racks in the freezer will make it unnecessary to lift one thing to get another.

Food Preparation

As much thought as is given to the planning of storage must go into the organization of the area where food is prepared. If you work from a seated position, knee space under the counter is essential and should be a minimum of twenty-four inches (60 cm) wide and twenty-four inches (60 cm) high. The work surface should be thirty to thirty-two inches (75 to 80 cm) high, although for certain work, such as mixing and beating, a lower level, about twenty-seven inches (68 cm) high is usually better. This can be a pull out board. For stability and safety, especially for one-hand use, the board can have a cutout opening into which the mixing bowl can be placed. Such a pullout must, of course, have adequate support.

When work surfaces are too high and remodeling is out of the question, a fold-down table hinged to the wall, a

The food preparation area is often most functional if it is sited between the sink and the refrigerator. Pullout boards, which are lower than the countertop, provide additional work surfaces and are a better height for beating and mixing from a seated position. For one-handed use it can be helpful to have a pullout board with cutouts into which mixing bowls fit and are held steady. The incredients and utensils usually used in this area should be stored within easy reach.

folding table or a drop-leaf table can be used for food preparation. A wheeled table can be utilized to hold ingredients and utensils and also to serve as additional work space. A board supported by an open drawer, can be used as a lower work surface for mixing, as can the bottom of the sink or a wheelchair lapboard.

Choose your kitchenware with care—and keep it to a minimum. Buy equipment which will help you to overcome the limitations imposed by your disability and enable you to function more efficiently in your kitchen. Remember that the fewer utensils and pieces of equipment you use the less space you require for storing them and the handier they will be when you need them.

All your kitchen equipment should be as versatile as possible. A variety of cutting jobs can be done, for example, with a single knife that has a sharp, medium-length blade and a handle that can be grasped comfortably. A stiff brush will scrub dishes as well as fruit and vegetables. An attractive flameproof, ovenproof casserole with handles can be used for cooking on top of the stove, for baking in the oven and for serving.

Durability is important, too. Buy reliable brands to ensure quality. While price does not always determine quality, it is sometimes necessary to pay more for truly superior equipment. The handles of utensils should be firmly attached so that they will never become wobbly and unsafe and if the utensils are used on the stove the handles should be heatproof. A knife should be balanced and comfortable to grasp and to use. A shaped handle is easier to grip, a larger handle easier to hold. Handles can be adapted to special needs by a therapist. At least one-third of the length of the blade should extend into the handle and should be secured by a minimum of two rivets.

Everything you use in your kitchen should be easy to clean. Nonstick finishes make pans and utensils easy to care for. Decorative grooves and curlicues accu-

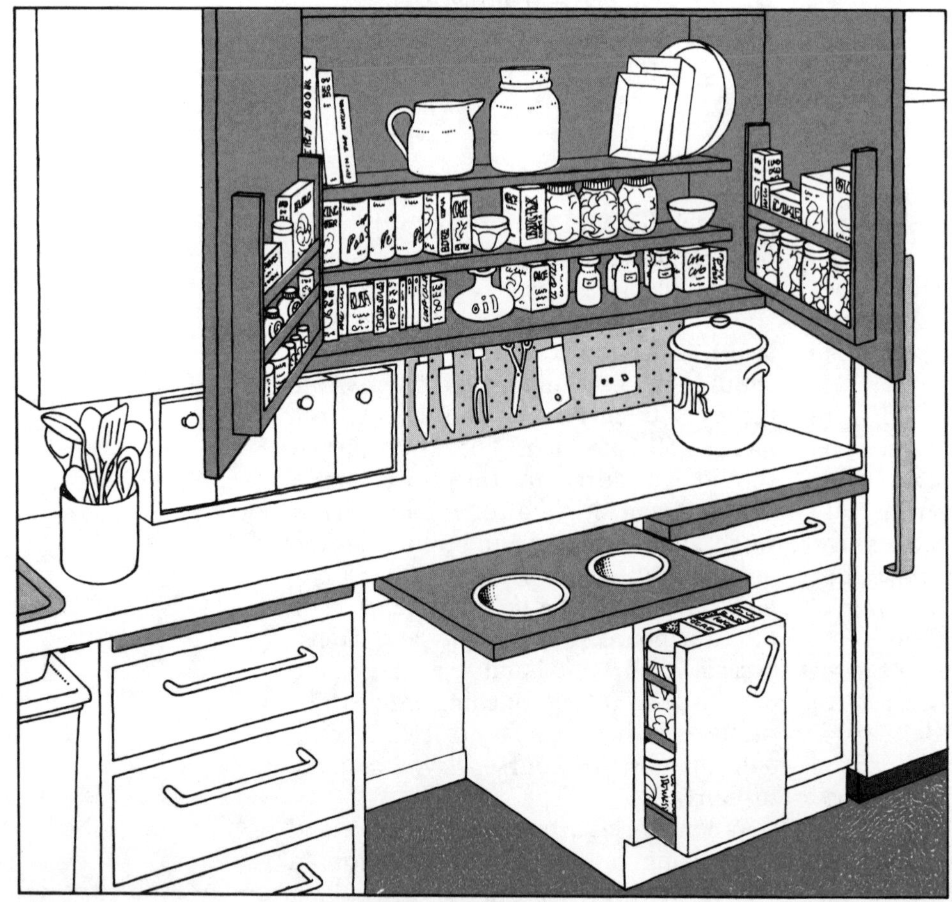

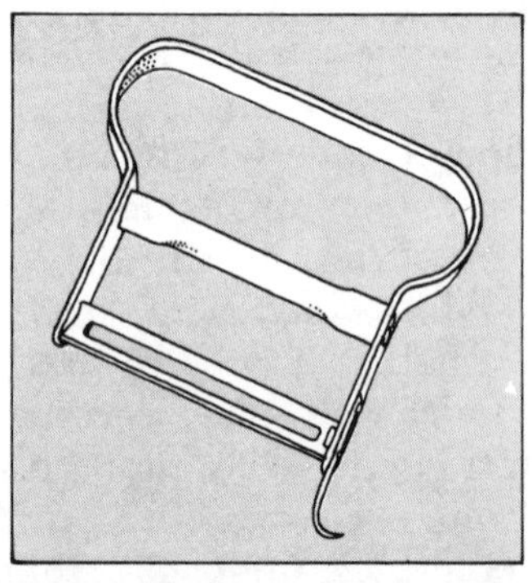

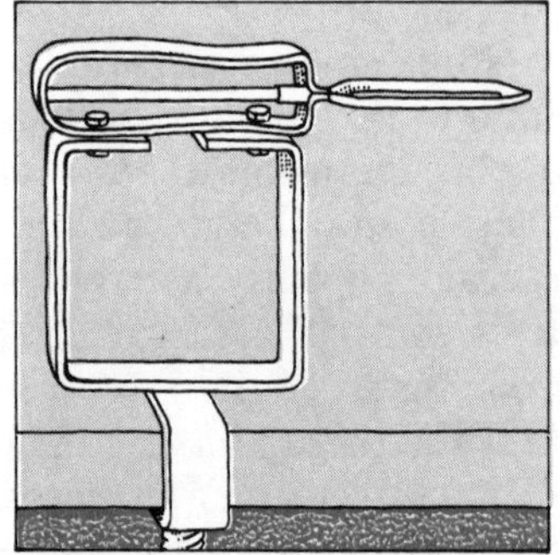

A floating blade peeler can be used with either hand, the handle can be built up or it can be fixed to a metal clamp. The large-loop peeler top is easy to hold with stiff or weak fingers and has a special point to remove potato eyes.

mulate grease and dirt and require extra scrubbing.

Almost every meal requires some cutting preparation. Knives are, therefore, probably the most frequently used kitchen tools and a good, solid cutting board is a necessity. Knives should always be kept sharp. A sharp knife requires less pressure to cut than one which is dull and is also less likely to slip. To control excess motion when cutting, keep the point of the blade down on the board.

It's often desirable to have a knife sharpener that can be operated with one hand. A small hand sharpener can be attached to the wall or to the side of a cabinet. One model has suction action, controlled by a small lever, so that it will adhere to a counter top.

Some people prefer to use a knife with a serrated blade since the toothed edge gives greater control, is less apt to slip than a straight blade and permits cutting with a slow, steady, sawing motion. Another advantage of a serrated knife is that the blade rarely requires sharpening. Other people find that scissors with long sharp blades are easier to use than a knife when cutting fish, meat and some vegetables.

A cordless, powered knife that works on rechargeable batteries can be useful. Although little pressure is required to use such a knife, good coordination is necessary to guide it. An electrically operated knife is potentially dangerous because of the trailing cord and should be avoided.

When peeling fruit and vegetables it is often safer and easier to use a peeler than a knife. The type with a "floating blade" can be used with the right or left hand and the handle can be built up for better grasp.

Holding vegetables and fruit steady for peeling and cutting can be difficult. A cutting board into which two stainless steel nails, about one inch (2 cm) apart, have been driven from below, will hold them firmly. A raised ledge in one corner of the board will stabilize a slice of bread

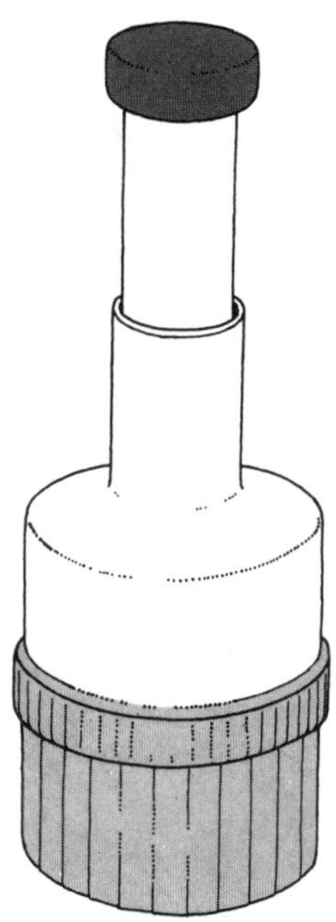

A one-handed food chopper works quickly and efficiently to chop almost any solid or leafy food with a simple action.

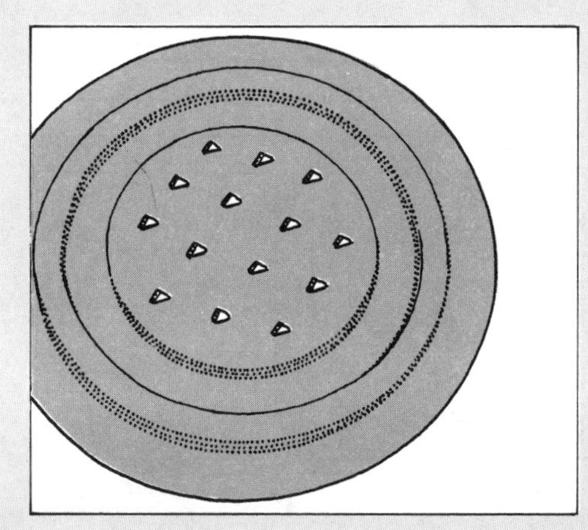

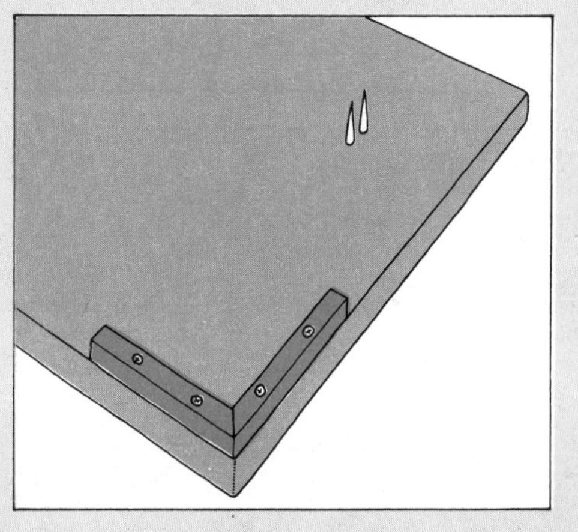

A cutting board with suction cups to hold it firmly on the work surface is convenient when working with one hand. The board left has small slender spikes which hold meat, bread and some vegetables. The hardwood board right has two stainless-steel nails to hold the food being cut and a right-angled ledge on one corner for spreading bread.

The plastic graters center and far right will grate food without cutting fingers. The model center has a rubber-rimmed base so it will not slip when used with one hand. The sharp metal grater right is attached to a wooden support which can be fixed firmly to the wall for one-handed use.

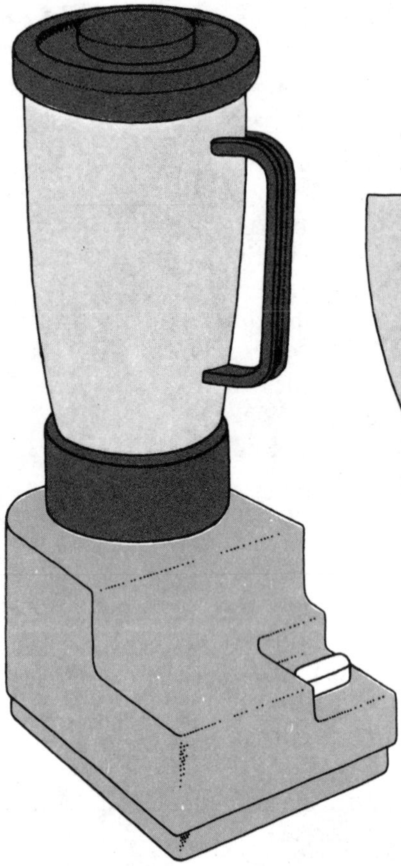

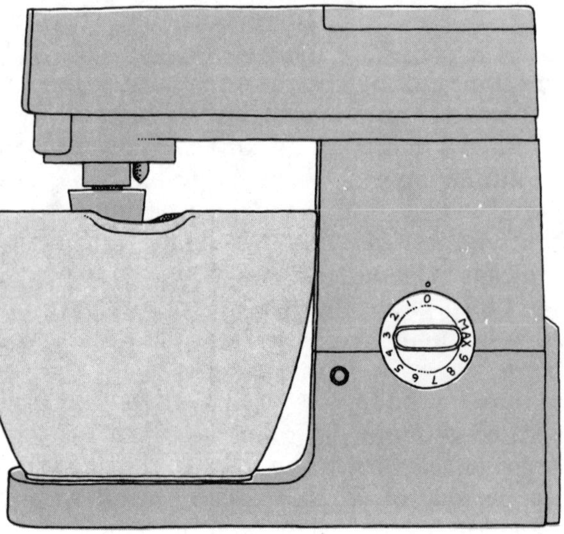

An electric mixer conserves energy and greatly reduces mixing time. A stationary unit, like the one left, is often preferable when hands are weak, but of course it must be easily accessible and the bowl must not be too heavy. While a blender, far left, will not do heavy mixing jobs, it can be used to beat batters and is very useful for pureeing fruit and vegetables.

A portable electric mixer requires good grasp in one hand, but it is a very versatile appliance for it can be used at the stove, on a lapboard or on a utility table. When choosing a portable mixer be sure you can easily manage the controls and the insertion and ejection of the beaters.

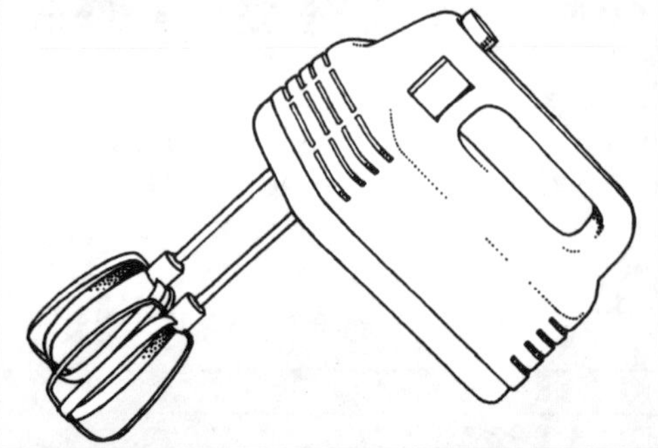

A hand beater can often be used for small mixing jobs. A wire whisk, right, beats more easily than a spoon and the handle can be built up if necessary. The lightweight beater far right has plastic blades and is easily operated by downward pressure with one hand.

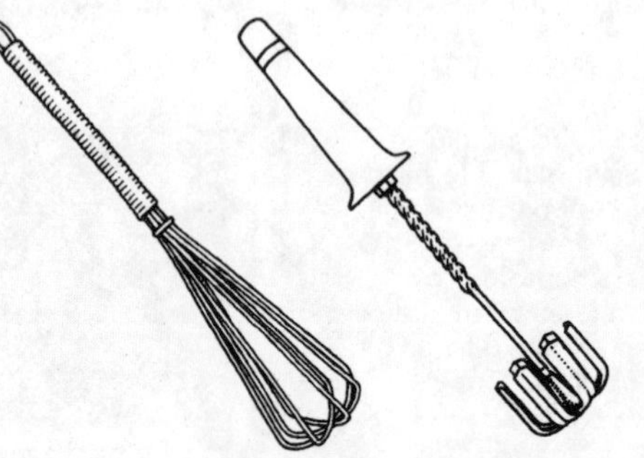

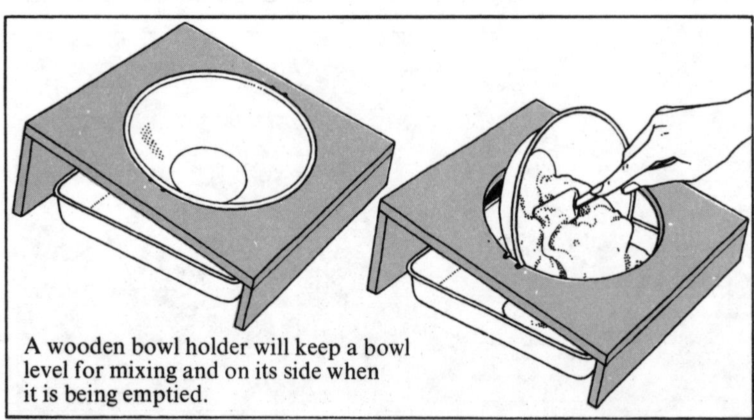

A wooden bowl holder will keep a bowl level for mixing and on its side when it is being emptied.

A double-sided suction base, top left, or a nonskid mat, above, can be used to keep a mixing bowl steady. A Grip'n Mix Bowl, above right, is also useful.

that is being spread or a sandwich that is being cut. Suction cups under the base keep the board from slipping. The board can be hung on the wall when not in use, with corks pushed onto the points of the nails to protect yourself from an accidental brush with them.

There are food processors, as well as attachments for food mixers, which shred and slice vegetables. Fitting the attachments and feeding in the vegetables could be difficult, so it's wise to experiment with the motions involved before investing in such equipment.

An electric blender, on the other hand, cuts, dices, chops and purees foods, mixes batters and requires a minimum of fuss. Designs vary so much that before buying one be sure that you can easily handle the controls and that the container is not too heavy for you to lift.

An electric mixer greatly reduces mixing time and using one involves little energy, although the bowls on some stationary models are quite heavy. A portable mixer can be used if you have good grasp capacity in one hand and is a versatile appliance, since it can be used at the stove, on a lowered work surface or on a lapboard.

A good can opener is one that cuts the lid out completely, leaving a smooth rim with no sharp edges. The lid of the can should also lift for easy removal. Whether the opener is hand-operated or electric, it should support the can while it is being opened so that it need not be held.

If you are buying an electric can opener—which does save muscle wear and tear—make an effort to try out your selection in the store before you buy it, to be sure you can use it. If it's not possible to test it in the store, be sure that you will be able to return it if it proves unsuitable after a trial at home.

Gadgets and equipment are not the whole answer to simplifying food preparation. Although there are many devices and methods which make chopping, mincing, cutting, grating, peeling and slicing easier, the best solution is to make use whenever possible of the convenience foods that eliminate these aspects of preparation entirely. Buy sliced bread. Have the butcher trim meat

A wedge-type opener which attaches to a wall or is fixed horizontally under a shelf makes it easier to open jars. Metal teeth grip corrugated or noncorrugated screw tops while the jar is twisted with one hand or with both hands.

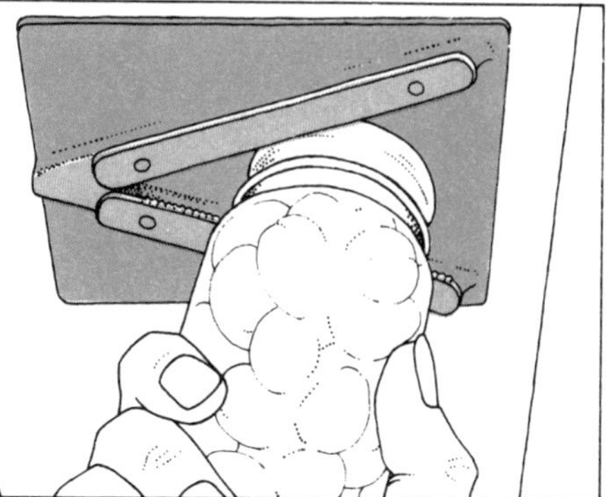

A hand-held electric can opener is often easier to use than one which is wall-mounted. Some models will open cans of any shape and can be used with one hand, although dexterity and good vision are necessary.

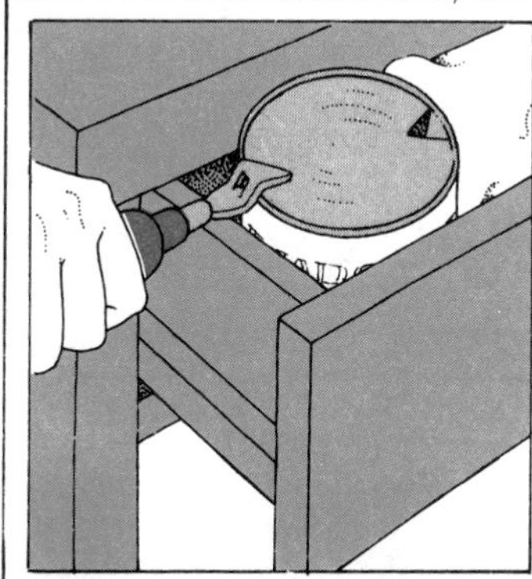

To open a can of liquid with one hand or two weak ones, wedge the can firmly in the corner of a drawer with a folded towel underneath to bring the top of the can above the side of the drawer.

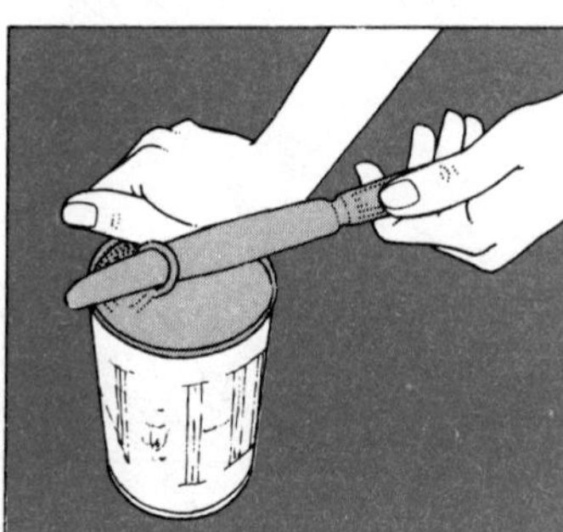

Use a table knife for leverage when opening a ring-topped can. To release the top, simply press down, then lever from the other side.

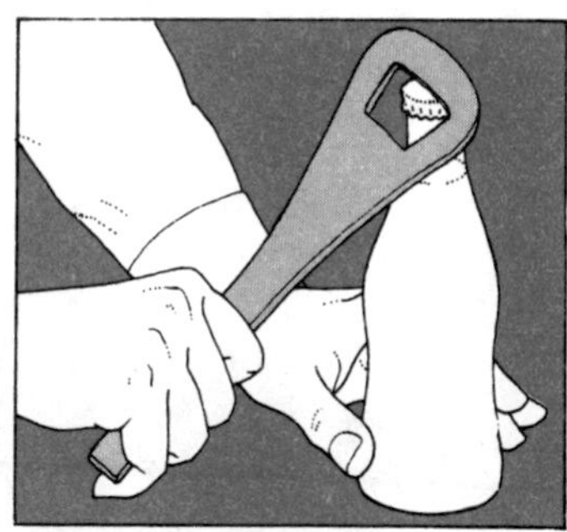

A giant bottle opener, available from gift shops, provides good leverage as well as a large gripping area for removing bottle caps.

Although presifted flour is now widely available, if flour must be sifted a lightweight sifter can be used with one hand.

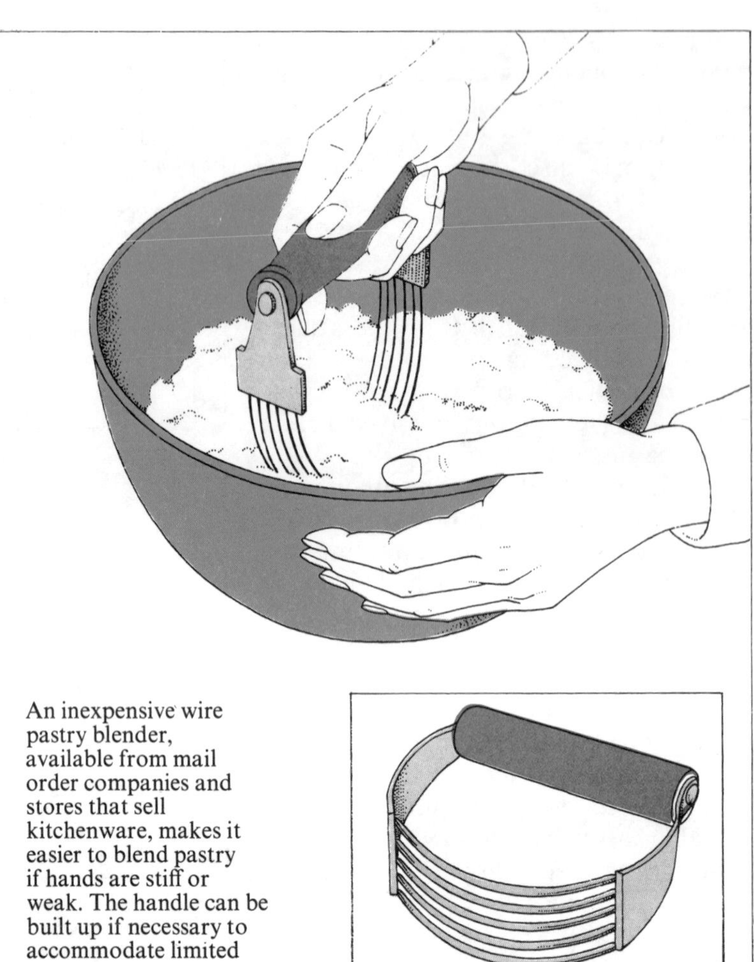

An inexpensive wire pastry blender, available from mail order companies and stores that sell kitchenware, makes it easier to blend pastry if hands are stiff or weak. The handle can be built up if necessary to accommodate limited grasp.

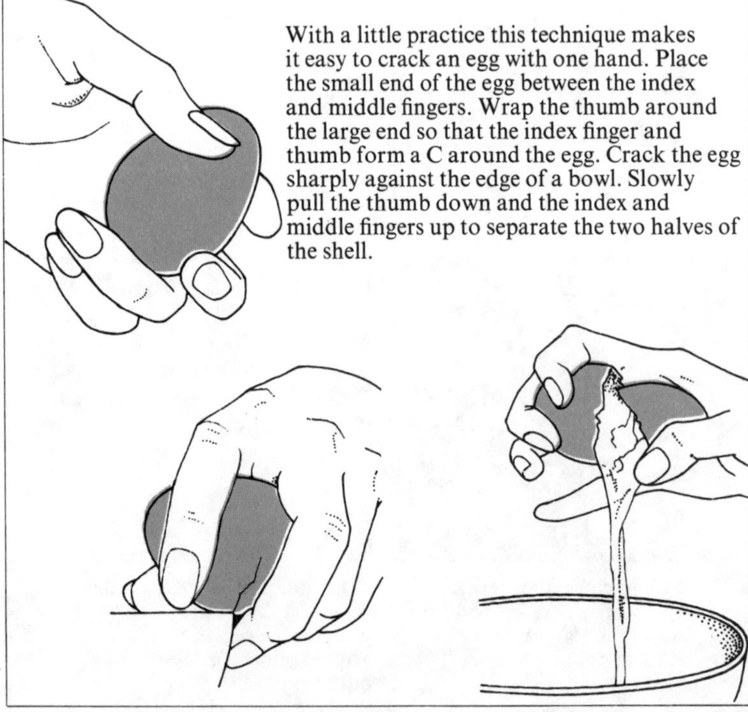

With a little practice this technique makes it easy to crack an egg with one hand. Place the small end of the egg between the index and middle fingers. Wrap the thumb around the large end so that the index finger and thumb form a C around the egg. Crack the egg sharply against the edge of a bowl. Slowly pull the thumb down and the index and middle fingers up to separate the two halves of the shell.

and cut it as you want it. Buy chicken parts and filleted fish. Some foods, including onions, green peppers, celery, carrots, parsley and garlic, can be bought dried, or cleaned, cut and frozen.

Different and previously unconsidered methods of doing things often prove very efficient. Here are a few tips, but with thought and a little ingenuity you will surely find many more shortcuts to make the preparation of meals easier.

Leave butter or margarine out of the refrigerator for at least thirty minutes before you need it; it will spread more easily than when it is used cold from the refrigerator.

Mix thin cake or pancake batters in a lightweight pitcher. The handle is easier to hold than the side of a bowl while you beat the batter and it is far easier to pour from.

Plastic or stainless steel bowls are lighter in weight and easier to lift than those

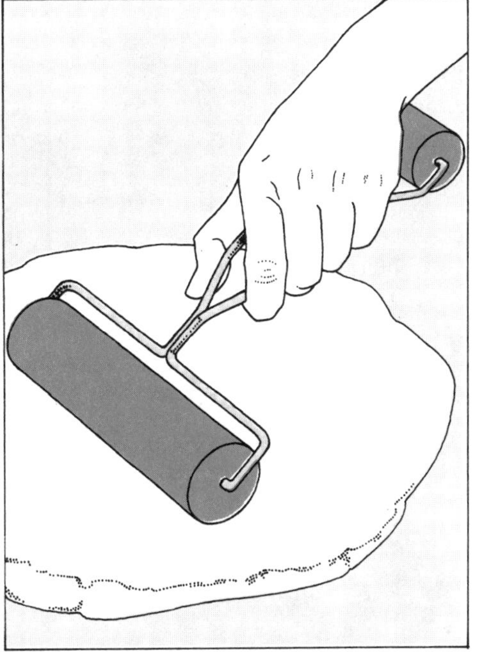

One-handed rolling pins are available from self-help equipment firms, but a conventional rolling pin can be adapted, above, or a small, double pizza roller, right, can be used.

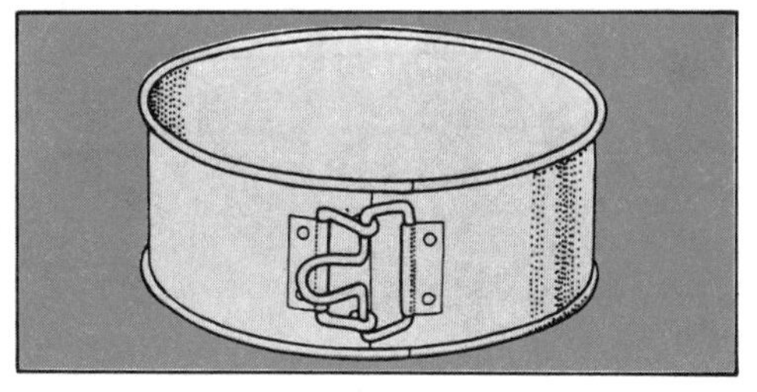

If a cake is baked in a spring-form pan, the removable rim can be easily opened with one hand to transfer it. Fold rolled pastry into quarters to transfer it to a pie plate with one hand.

If coordination is lacking a light cocktail shaker or a covered plastic tumbler can be used to mix thin batters and liquid ingredients.

made of glass or pottery. Some stainless steel bowls have handles on the sides.

Let a roast stand for about fifteen minutes before carving it. The meat will be firmer and easier to carve.

To coat fish, chicken or meat with flour or bread crumbs, put all the ingredients together in a paper or plastic bag and shake them.

Use a funnel to separate an egg white from the yolk.

Dough can be rolled with only one hand by pressing down on the center of the rolling pin instead of on the ends.

To transfer dough into a pie plate using only one hand, simply start at one end of the dough and roll it onto the rolling pin. Lift it over the rolling pin and roll it into the pie plate. Press the dough into place with your fingers.

A plastic or metal tumbler can be grasped more easily than a biscuit cutter and works equally well.

A three-sided box on ball bearings between two uprights, above, is a simple aid for pouring liquids. The box supports the bottle and makes it easy to handle.

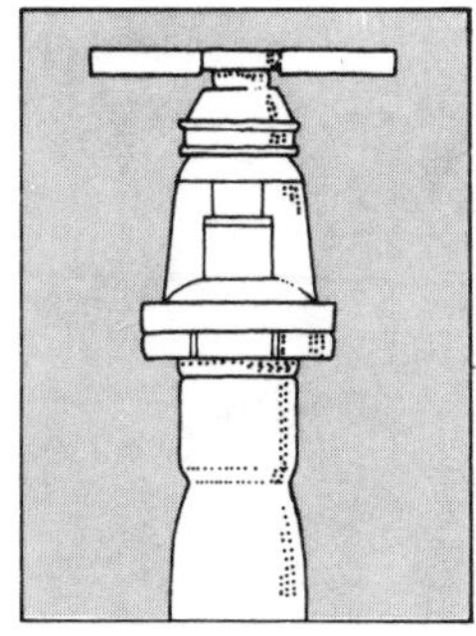

A liquor measure, right, is useful to control the amount of liquid poured.

Cooking and Baking

For a variety of reasons the free-standing gas or electric range with oven and broiler below is unusable by many people with disabilities. For someone who is wheelchaired, the conventional thirty-six-inch (90-cm) height can make moving heavy hot pans not only difficult, but actually dangerous. Checking the progress of cooking food, when the rim of the pan is above eye level, is impossible and stirring food in the pans on the rear burners is perilous since it is necessary to reach over the tops of the pans on the front burners. In addition, the conventional oven arrangement makes it necessary for the wheelchaired cook to work sideways.

For people who have limited reach or difficulty in bending, such ovens are usually too low to reach. Certainly the broiler of a gas range, which is usually close to the floor, is unreachable. And if the oven or broiler door opens downward, the contents are even farther out of reach.

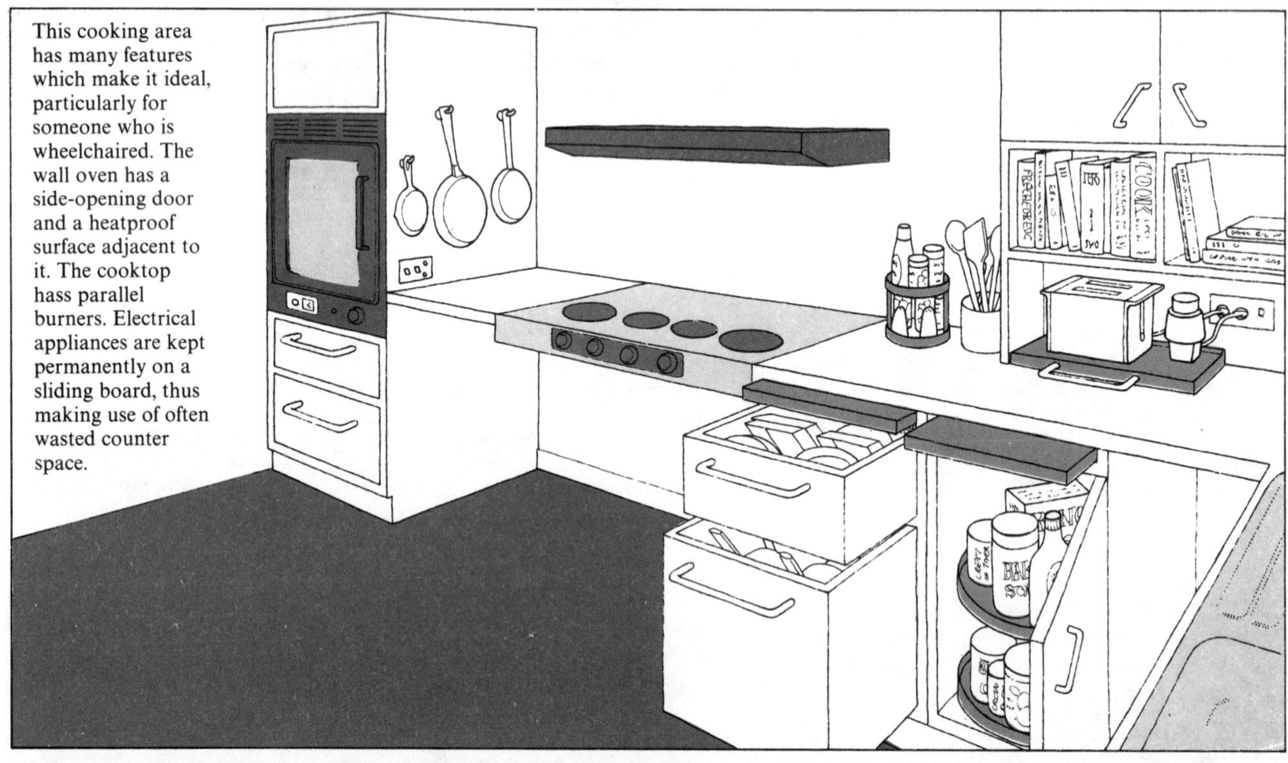

This cooking area has many features which make it ideal, particularly for someone who is wheelchaired. The wall oven has a side-opening door and a heatproof surface adjacent to it. The cooktop hass parallel burners. Electrical appliances are kept permanently on a sliding board, thus making use of often wasted counter space.

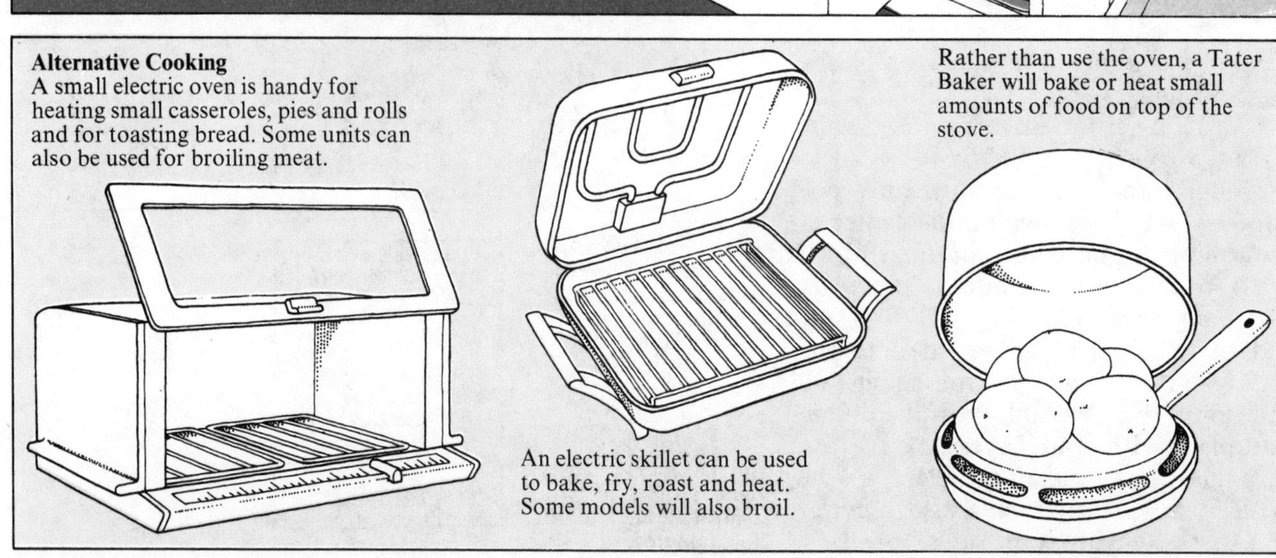

Alternative Cooking
A small electric oven is handy for heating small casseroles, pies and rolls and for toasting bread. Some units can also be used for broiling meat.

An electric skillet can be used to bake, fry, roast and heat. Some models will also broil.

Rather than use the oven, a Tater Baker will bake or heat small amounts of food on top of the stove.

Replacing the conventional free-standing range with a separate cooktop and a built-in wall oven brings cooking facilities to more convenient working heights. A variety of cooktop electric or gas units are available with two, three or four burners. The burners should be at counter level so that heavy pots can be slid rather than lifted. If there are three or four burners they should be set in a staggered pattern to reduce the danger of reaching over the front burners. Better still are two two-burner units which can be set end to end, parallel with the edge of the counter.

A wall oven can be installed at any convenient height. It is usually best to have the most used shelf of the oven level with the adjacent counter top. A door which opens to the side, rather than one which drops down, will make the oven space itself more accessible. On the other hand, the down-dropping door provides a shelf for sliding things in and out. In an electric model a pullout burn-proof shelf can be installed under a side-opening door. This is not possible with a gas model because the flames are at the bottom.

A wall oven may be located near the cooktop or elsewhere—but never next to the refrigerator, which the oven heat might affect. Wherever it is located the oven must have some heat-resistant counter space next to it. If the door of the oven is side-hinged it should open on the side of the counter space.

Some models with a side-opening door have a narrow broiler next to the oven which also has a side-hinged door. Others have the broiler underneath the oven where its height may be inconvenient for some and useless to those who cannot bend over to retrieve things.

Modern ovens have many excellent features, not the least attractive of which is the self-cleaning mechanism. If you choose an oven without the self-cleaning feature, select one with a removable door, for this can make cleaning much easier.

Some people who are wheelchaired find that they are able to use a standard height range, particularly if they use a removable rigid seat to increase their height. In such cases it is best to have pans with sides high enough to prevent spilling, but still low enough to make it possible to see into them to check cooking progress. A small mirror on a handle can be helpful there, too. Although it is frequently recommended that a large mirror be installed over the top of the burners to make it possible to look into the pans, this has proven to be unsatisfactory. Even a steam-proofed mirror tends to cloud over with grease and in any case is difficult to reach and clean.

When the standard height range is inaccessible and extensive kitchen re-

A microwave oven never gets hot, reduces cooking and baking time and permits you to heat food in serving dishes.

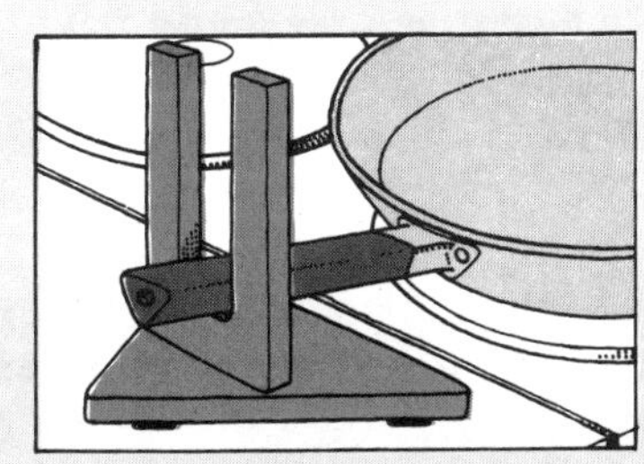

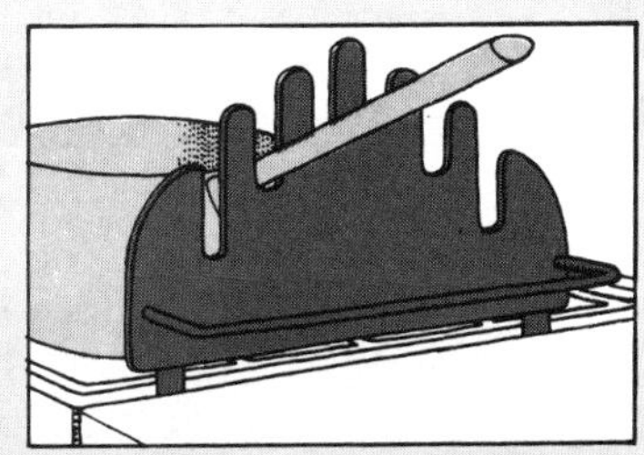

A pot stabilizer, easily made or commercially available, steadies a hot pan while the contents are being stirred. It should be placed on the same side as the stronger hand.

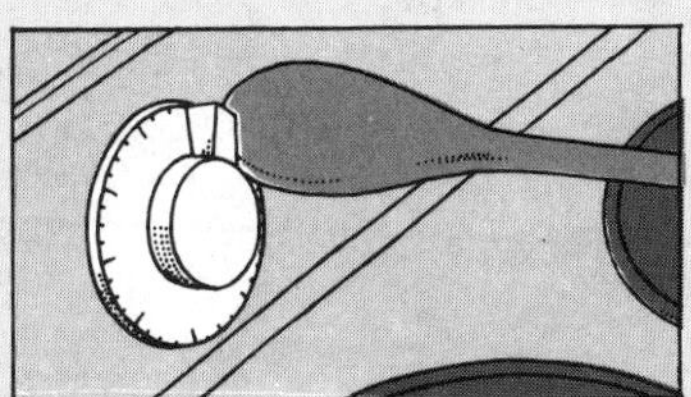

No one device or technique will work to manipulate the controls of all stoves. Sometimes a wooden spoon can be used to push a dial. In some cases turners can be made to fit the dials.

modeling is not possible, alternative counter top cooking appliances may provide a solution.

A two-burner electric hot plate or tabletop range is an inexpensive alternative. Although some lifting of pans is always necessary, unless the unit is set into a well in the counter top, it should nevertheless be low enough so that lifting is minimized. Tubular-type cooking elements, which lift up, are easier to clean and are safer than open wire coils. The unit should have large control knobs which are easy to manipulate and they should be at the front. The controls should have more than just high and low settings so that the cooking temperature can be easily adjusted.

An electric skillet is one of the most versatile appliances. It can fry, grill and roast, is excellent for heating leftovers and can be used in the kitchen or at the dining table. Models vary in weight. Before buying an electric skillet be sure that it's not too heavy and that the temperature control is located within easy reach. The immersible type is easiest to clean.

A good portable broiler-oven can often substitute for a conventional oven. A portable unit can be kept on a table or counter top at the most convenient height. There should be a resting area for pans in front of the unit, especially if carrying is difficult.

A microwave oven provides an accessible baking and cooking unit which reduces cooking time and makes it possible to heat food in serving dishes. And neither the oven nor the dishes holding the food get hot.

If you use a number of small electric appliances in the kitchen, it's a good idea to have a special heavy-duty outlet control center with its own on-off switch and several outlets which will permit you to keep the most frequently used appliances plugged in all the time, ready for use. The control center can be placed wherever it is most convenient.

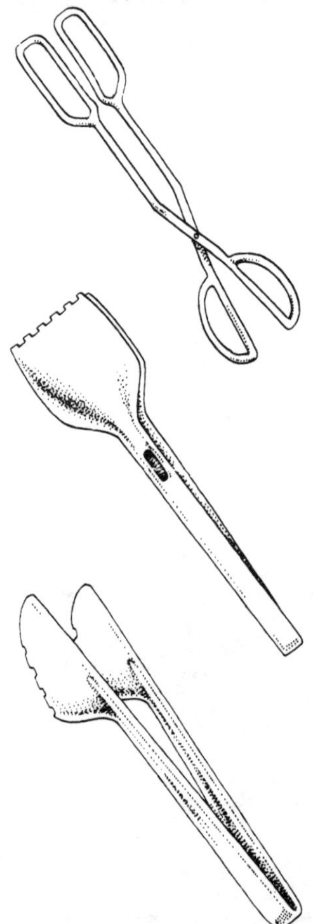

Tongs, which are available in many styles, can be used to remove vegetables from boiling liquid, potatoes from the oven and for turning frying food.

There are certain precautions you should take when you're cooking in order to avoid accidents.

- Don't reach over one burner to get at another or to reach the controls. Reach from the side or use a reaching device.
- Never pour water on a fat or grease fire—it will only spread it.
- A fat fire in an oven or broiler can be extinguished by turning off the heat and closing the door. By cutting off the air supply the flames are smothered.
- A fat or grease fire on top of the range can be smothered with large amounts of salt. Better still, keep a small carbon dioxide fire extinguisher near the cooking area. It is effective against grease fires, is harmless to food and leaves no residue.
- Never try to fight a spreading fire. Get out of the room and call for help.
- Always turn the handles of pans away from the front.
- Never use a pan with a loose handle.
- When handling a hot pan, always use asbestos-padded potholders. Oven gloves, or mitten-type potholders, are much safer to use than regular pothold-

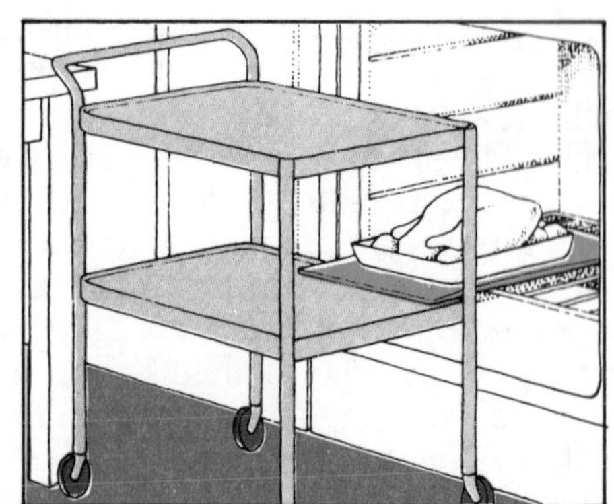

A smooth board, beveled on both ends, can be used for transferring food into and out of the oven.

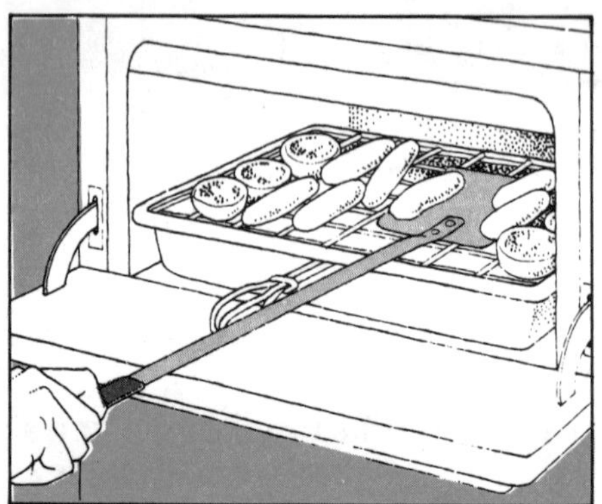

Long barbecue utensils extend reach and make it possible to turn food in the oven and keep hands away from the heat.

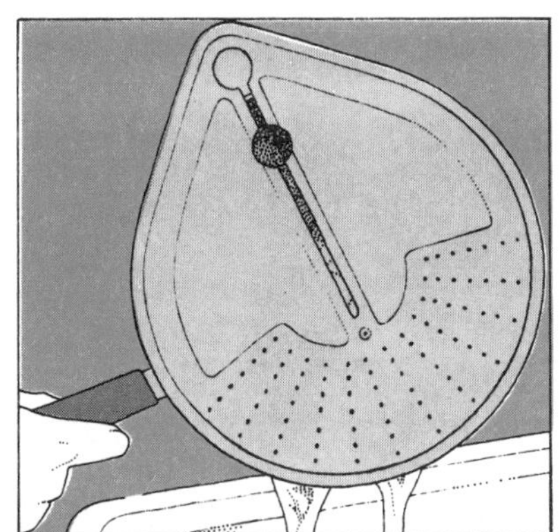
An adjustable strainer top that will clamp onto most pans makes it easier to drain off hot cooking liquid.

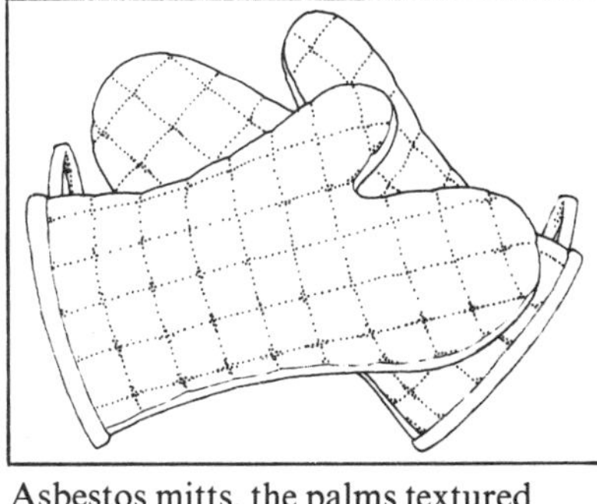
Asbestos mitts, the palms textured to prevent slipping, are often safer and easier to use than potholders.

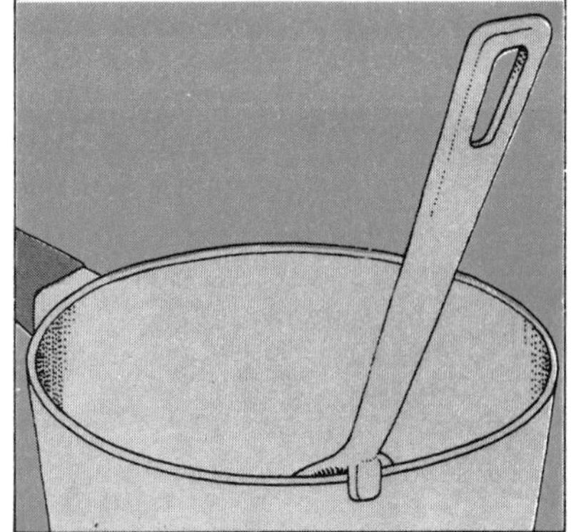
The handle of a safety spoon hooks over the side of the pan so it will stay cool and won't slide into the soup.

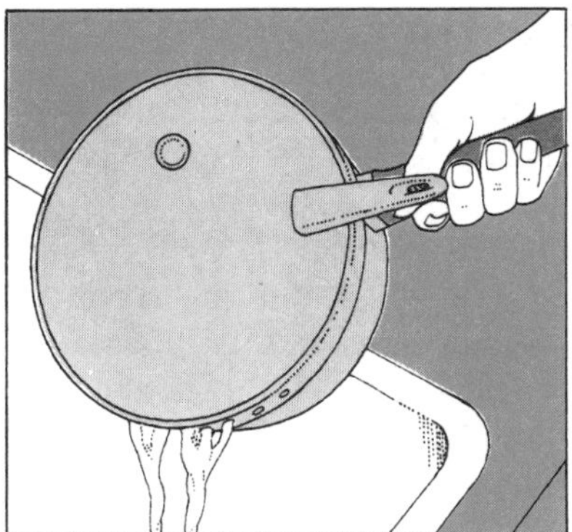
Food cooked in a pan with a lock-on lid can be safely drained using just one hand.

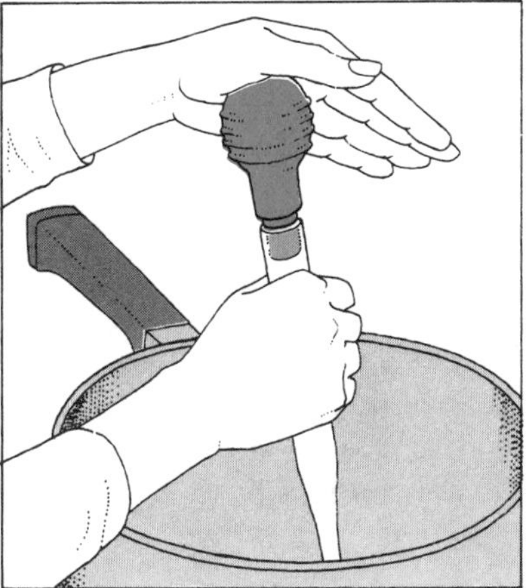
A baster can be used to transfer small quantities of hot liquid to and from a pan.

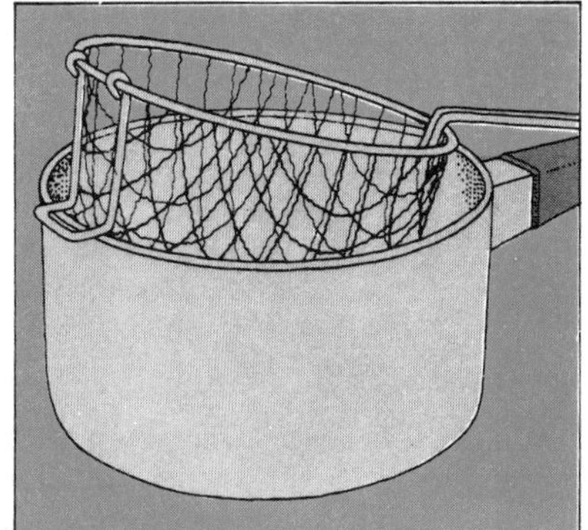
Vegetables cooked in a deep-frying basket eliminate the need to tip the pan to drain them.

ers; they cannot slip from your hands.

■ When reaching into the oven wear long insulated oven gloves.

■ Pans should have handles made of nonheat-conducting material. Baking pans with handles provide a surer grip.

■ The most difficult part of cooking vegetables is managing a heavy saucepan of water, especially when the water is hot. It's often best to put the pan on the burner and then to add water with a long hose from the sink or by pouring from a large, lightweight plastic pitcher.

■ Ladle hot liquids to prevent spilling.

■ Instead of lifting a pan to drain off the cooking liquid, remove the food from the liquid with a slotted spoon.

■ A nonautomatic gas burner can be safely lit with a flint sparking device or by striking a match, laying it across the gas jets and then turning on the gas. In this way, your fingers are out of the way and the gas has no chance to accumulate. A small piece of sandpaper taped to the counter top at one side of the range provides a handy striking surface.

■ Long fireplace or barbecue matches eliminate the need to bend when lighting a gas broiler or oven. A twelve-inch (30-cm) long match will reach almost all the way or can be held with a pair of tongs. Don't turn on the gas until the match is lit.

■ Long-handled barbecue tools make it easier to use a conventional broiler when bending is difficult.

■ To eliminate basting a roast, and having to take it out of the oven several times, cook it in a special plastic roasting bag which allows it to brown. This method also keeps the oven clean.

■ Putting a baking sheet under a cake pan or baking dish will make it easier to pull it out of the oven.

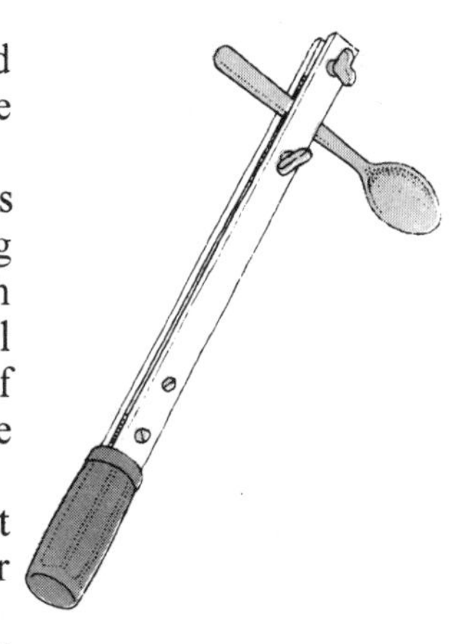
For working in hard-to-reach pans at the back of the stove, an extension can be made for a mixing spoon.

The Kitchen Sink

At least three-quarters of the time that anyone spends working in the kitchen is spent at the sink. Every activity at the sink, including washing dishes, can be accomplished from a sitting position, whether on a high chair, a standard kitchen chair or from a wheelchair. (A resilient mat underfoot lessens fatigue for those who must stand.)

For the person who works in a seated position, knee space can be created without extensive remodeling by removing the cabinet doors and floor molding under the sink. Sliding doors can be installed or a curtain hung across the opening.

For someone who is wheelchaired, or works from a standard height chair, the ideal sink should be shallow, about five and a half inches (14 cm) deep. This is easiest to reach into and is least likely to interfere with knee space below. A double sink with two shallow bowls can be even better, especially if there is a waste disposal unit.

For least intrusion into knee space, the drain should be at the rear, preferably in a corner. Hot pipes should be back out of the way and, for additional safety, should be covered with insulation. The underpart of the sink itself should also be insulated.

Ideally, the faucet should be the long swinging type. A mesh aerator in the faucet outlet will minimize splashing. A single-lever control permits both temperature and volume of flow to be managed with one hand. Since the lever moves differently for each function—from side to side for temperature control and up and down for volume—the temperature can be set first to avoid possible scalding when the flow is increased. If separate hot and cold controls are unavoidable, they should have large handles for easy grasp.

A long retractable spray hose—with an easy-to-work thumb-lever control—is invaluable. It makes it possible to fill pans on the counter top instead of lifting them out of the sink. It also makes rinsing vegetables and dishes and washing the sink far easier.

When you work at the sink in a seated position, adequate knee space is of prime importance. Since there is little room for cleaning supplies under the sink, they can be stored on shelves inside the door of an adjacent cabinet. It makes for greater efficiency, too, if vegetables which must be scrubbed before use are stored near the sink. It is of course ideal if the sink is shallow and there is a single-lever water control as well as a spray attachment.

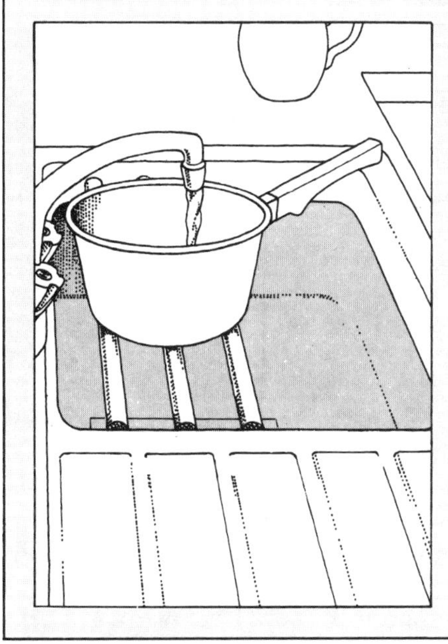

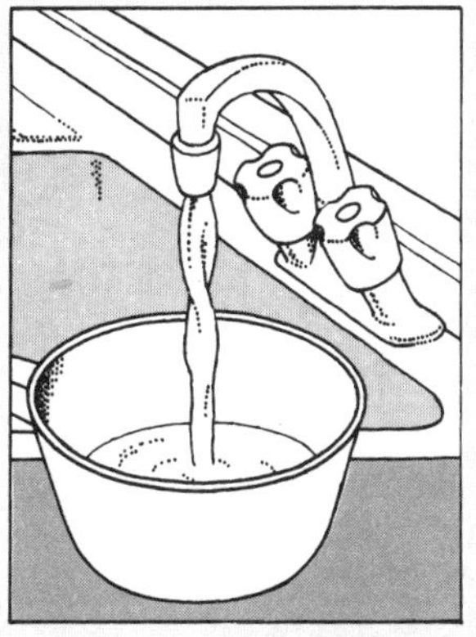

A raised, swivel, mixer-type tap fills pans and bowls on the work surface and eliminates the need to lift them when they are full. An alternative, left, is a platform made of lightweight, aluminum bars.

A strong, light tap turner, right, can be bought or made of wood, below, to fit a particular tap.

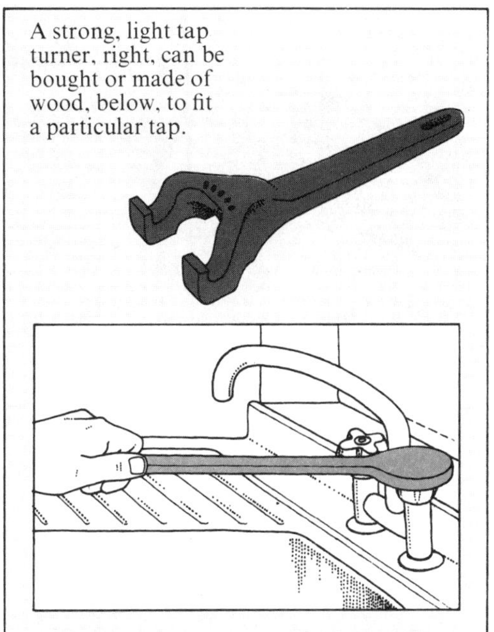

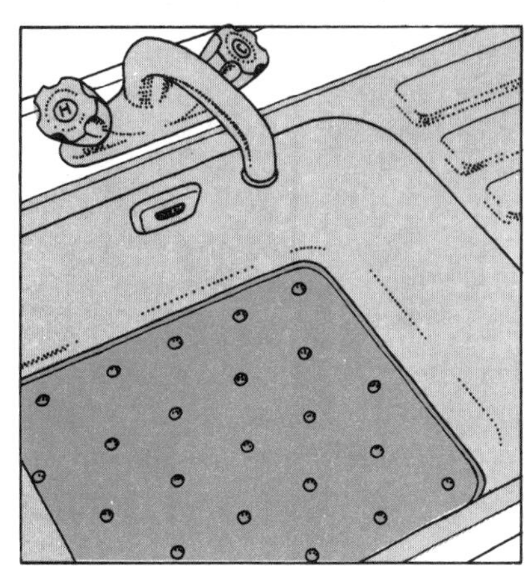

When working with one hand or if grasp is weak, a rubber or sponge mat at the bottom of the sink or dishpan reduces the risk of breakage.

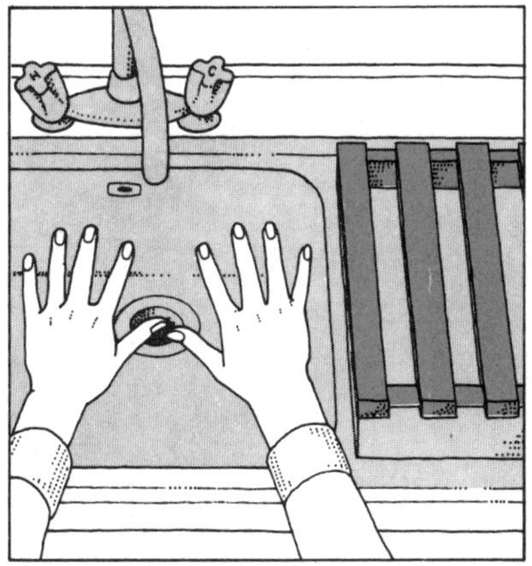

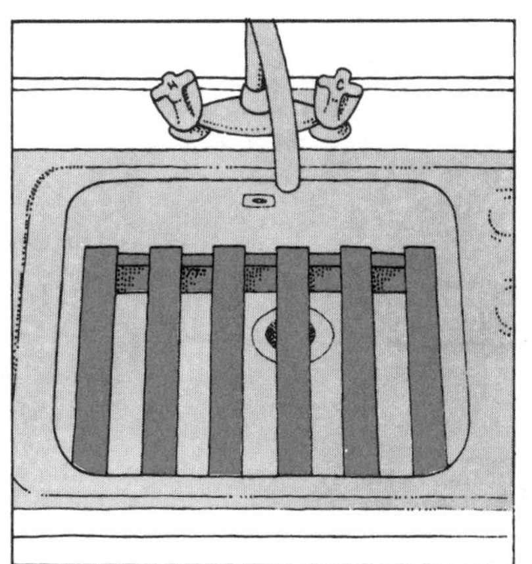

To establish the correct working height at the kitchen sink, when sitting or standing, stretch the palms of the hands toward the bottom of the sink without leaning forward. If the sink is too deep a wooden rack can be made to hold the dishpan at the proper height.

Dishwashing is a chore that may be unavoidable, but it can be simplified so that less time and energy need be expended. The first step is to organize your clean-up area so that you work methodically and logically in a flow from one side to the other—dirty dishes, wash water, rinse water, drying rack. If you work with only one hand the rinse water and dish rack should be next to the working hand. A sponge or rubber mat in the bottom of the sink or dishpan reduces risk of breakage.

Careful planning and a bit of ingenuity will enable you to use a minimum of utensils and to avoid as much scrubbing as possible. Instead of transferring food from cooking utensils to serving dishes, for example, use oven-to-table ware or serve directly from the pot. If you mix ingredients in a casserole itself you won't have to wash an extra mixing bowl.

Nonstick pans rinse clean without hard scrubbing, and if you use only recommended products for cleaning them the finish will last longer. When baking, cooking, roasting or broiling meat or fish, line the pan (but not the rack) with foil. Afterward you throw the foil away and the pan needs only a little washing.

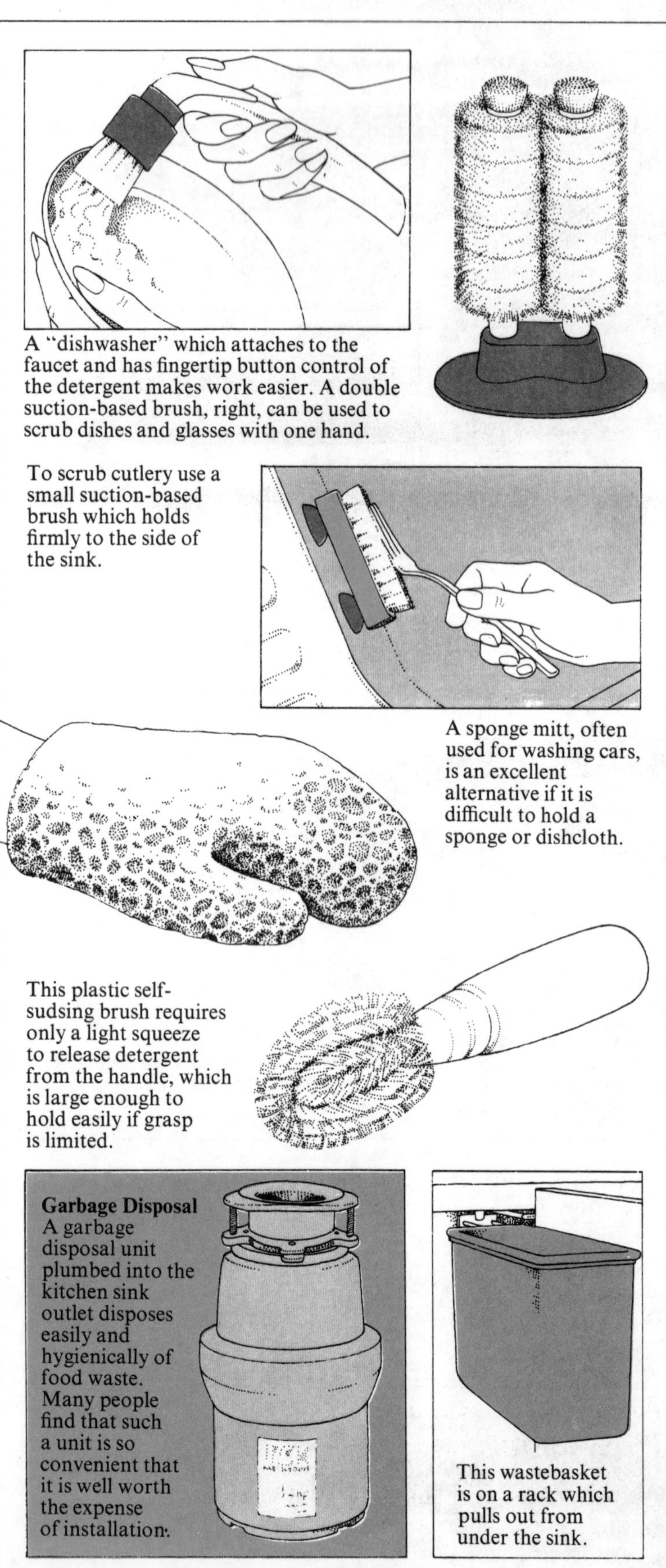

A "dishwasher" which attaches to the faucet and has fingertip button control of the detergent makes work easier. A double suction-based brush, right, can be used to scrub dishes and glasses with one hand.

To scrub cutlery use a small suction-based brush which holds firmly to the side of the sink.

A sponge mitt, often used for washing cars, is an excellent alternative if it is difficult to hold a sponge or dishcloth.

This plastic self-sudsing brush requires only a light squeeze to release detergent from the handle, which is large enough to hold easily if grasp is limited.

Garbage Disposal A garbage disposal unit plumbed into the kitchen sink outlet disposes easily and hygienically of food waste. Many people find that such a unit is so convenient that it is well worth the expense of installation.

This wastebasket is on a rack which pulls out from under the sink.

If you soak dirty utensils and pans properly in water and detergent immediately after you use them, scrubbing is almost completely eliminated. Fill pans used for starchy food, like oatmeal, milk or eggs, with cold water and those used for sugary or greasy foods with hot water.

Only silver, aluminum and cast iron need to be dried. Letting dishes and pans stand to air dry saves time and energy and is also considered more hygienic. For best results use liquid or powder detergents which rinse off completely.

An electric dishwasher is a great convenience. Unfortunately, standard machines are thirty-four to thirty-six inches (85 to 90 cm) high and, placed next to the sink as is most practical, could break a thirty-one inch (78 cm) high counter top at a crucial spot. There are, however, some models which can be lowered by removing the toe space and small portable dishwashers are available which sit on the counter or roll up to the sink and hook directly to the faucets.

When buying a dishwasher look for a model which loads from the front rather than from the top, has controls in front and racks that slide out independently of each other. A self-clearing drain is essential since a clogged drain generally cannot be reached from a wheelchair or by a person with limited reach or bending ability.

Garbage Disposal

For garbage and trash disposal, an ordinary container with a pedal lever is of little use to someone who is wheelchaired. One solution is a container mounted on the inside of a cabinet door, with a spring-mounted lid that pops up when the door is opened. It is higher and easier to reach than an ordinary garbage can and is out of sight when not in use. If there is sufficient floor space, a high swing-top bin, with a lid that removes for emptying, is a good height both for a wheelchair user and for someone who is ambulant and is large enough so that frequent emptying is not required. Such a bin can be lined with large plastic bags, which then need only be tied and removed to be ready for garbage collection.

Serving

With the increasing emphasis on informality, serving has become greatly simplified. No longer is it frowned upon to serve directly from the pot in which a dish has been cooked and ovenware is now available in the most attractive colors and designs.

Nevertheless, for someone with limited mobility, there is still the problem of getting food to the table at the correct serving temperature. This is best achieved by using a wheeled table which makes it possible to transport a whole meal at one time and to cut down on trips to the kitchen.

A simple wooden or metal table on wheels makes it possible to move a complete dinner to the dining table in one trip. Dirty dishes can be stacked on the lower shelf and moved back to the sink in one return trip.

Wheeled tables come in a variety of designs and sizes. When buying such a table look for one which is sturdy, has large casters, preferably with ball bearings, for ease in negotiating doorsills and corners. If the table is to be pushed from a wheelchair it should have ballbearing swivel casters which are at least three inches (8 cm) in diameter. If you are ambulant be sure that the table is high enough for you to push without bending.

The table should have heat resistant surfaces which are easy to clean. A small rim around the edges of the trays will collect crumbs, but also will keep things from slipping off. Rubber bumpers or adhesive-backed foam can be attached to the corners of the table to protect walls and furniture.

To keep food warm at the table a warming tray can be used. These are available in many models, some electric and some using heat candles. They range from a warmer for a single coffee-pot or casserole to an elaborate warming table on wheels.

This foldaway cart can be used half open for narrow places or the bottom shelf can be folded back so that it can be used as a typewriter table or an individual dining table. The cart folds completely to three inches (8 cm) wide for easy storage.

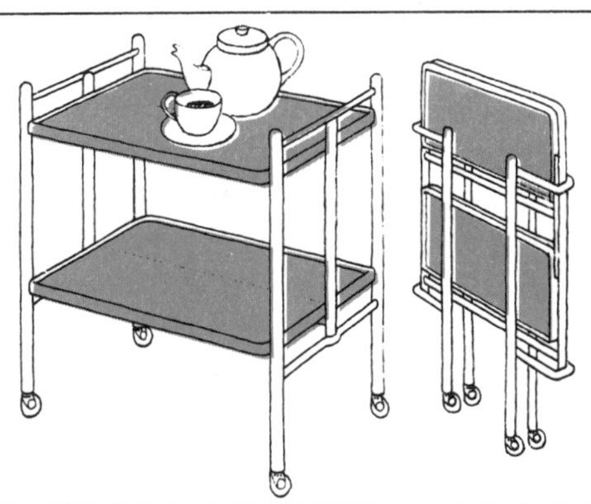

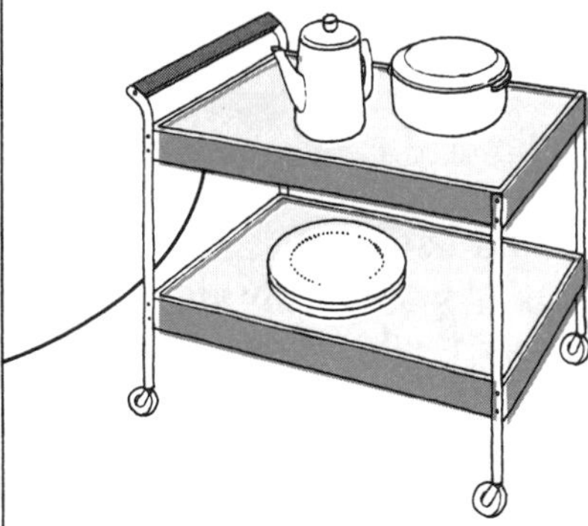

A serving cart and hot tray combined simplifies serving. The lower shelf holds cold food, dishes and other tableware; the upper shelf, which has an adjustable thermostatic control, keeps food hot.

A sturdy tubular steel cart with removable wire baskets is useful for transporting cleaning supplies and laundry from one room to another.

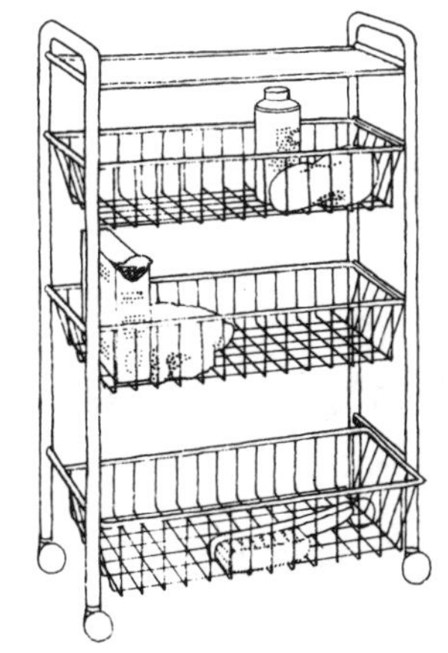

A cart which combines basket bins with a flat top surface can be used for serving and for moving cleaning supplies.

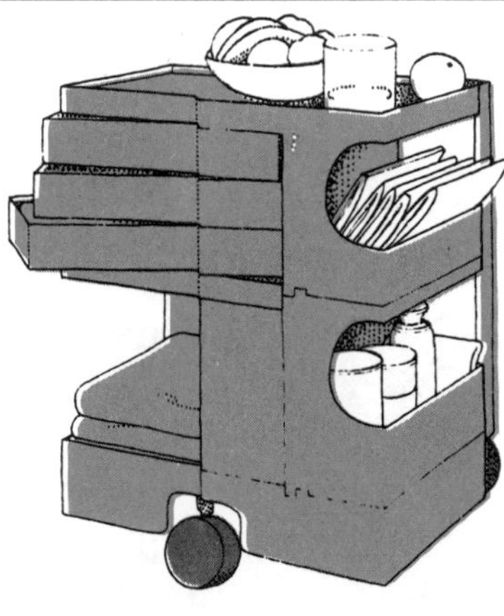

This attractive wheeled unit can be easily pushed from a wheelchair. It can be used for serving or as a utility table in the kitchen, bedroom or workroom.

Laundry

With a bit of ingenuity and planning laundry need be no more consuming of time and energy than other household tasks. The major part of the problem can be eliminated from the start by buying easy-care clothing and sheets that require little or no ironing. And many new laundry products, including prewash stain removers and fabric softeners, lessen or make unnecessary the need for hand scrubbing and for ironing.

To reduce the amount of laundry to be done at home, it may be worth the expense of sending such unwieldy items as sheets and bath towels and garments which require a lot of finishing, such as cotton shirts and dresses, to a commercial laundry. In some cases, this can prove to be less expensive than buying new laundry equipment.

If you do laundry at home, the proper equipment, installed at the right height, as well as adequate space, will permit you to work comfortably and efficiently. You should never have to stoop, bend or reach. To save steps and lifting, drying facilities should be close to the washing area.

A top-loading washing machine is usually most suitable for someone who works from a standing position. To avoid the need to bend, the basket for soiled laundry should be placed on a bench or low table so that the top of the basket is level with the washing machine. Since all dryers load from the front, the dryer should be installed on a platform or on top of the washing machine, low enough, however, so that the controls are comfortably within reach.

A front-loading washing machine permits someone who is wheelchaired, or who works from a sitting position, to get the clothes in and out easily and to transfer them to the dryer without strain.

Whether you work from a standing or a sitting position, both front-loading washing machine and dryer should have easy-to-use side-hinged doors. Doors that drop downward should be avoided. The controls should be at the front of the machines and easy to manipulate. If you are buying a new machine, try it out in the store if possible before making the purchase.

The position of the dryer in relation to the washing machine depends on the individual. Since articles move from the washing machine to the dryer, it is best for the dryer to be placed on the side of the stronger hand. If reach is limited, long-handled tongs can be used to get articles out of the machines.

A washer-dryer combination does away with the need to transfer clothes from one machine to the other and is also a great space-saver. It can be installed on a platform for greater accessibility.

If you have a washing machine, almost all hand washing can be eliminated by using a net laundry bag. Delicate garments, including lingerie, are put into it and the zippered bag and its contents are then washed in the machine. Net bags,

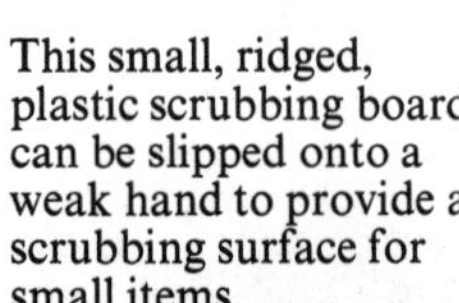

This small, ridged, plastic scrubbing board can be slipped onto a weak hand to provide a scrubbing surface for small items.

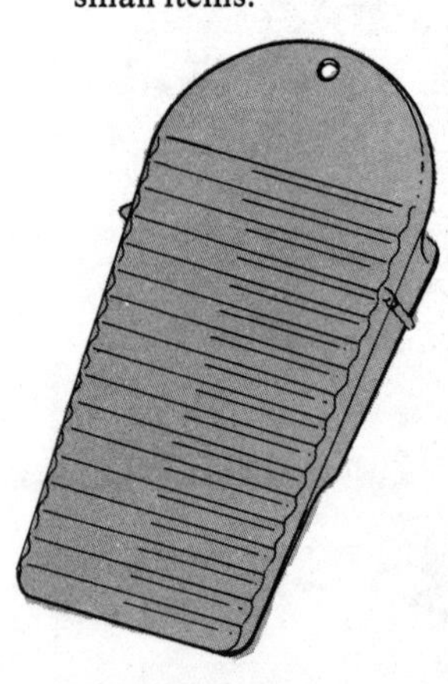

A wall-mounted clothes drier can make it easier to dry clothes indoors in a limited area. The arms of the drier above are conveniently notched

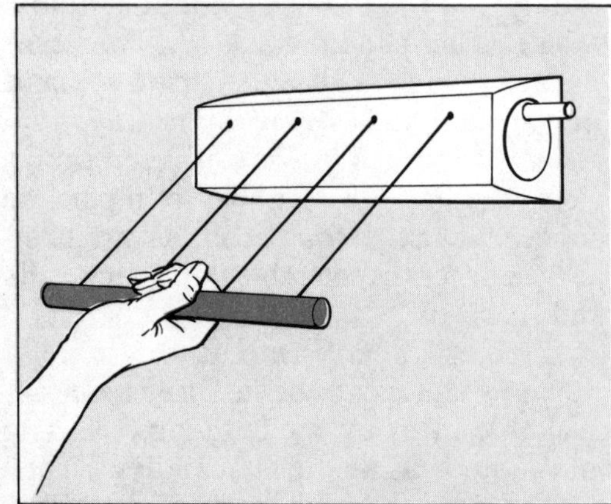

to hold clothes hung on hangers. The retractable clothesline neatly stores four, twelve-foot long (360-cm), nylon lines in the holder.

which hold up to three pounds of clothes, are available from housewares stores and mail order companies.

If you work with only one hand and have garments which you do not want to machine wash, soak them first and then use that old-fashioned device, a washboard. Now available in plastic, a washboard is a most effective aid for hand washing small articles of clothing. It can be stabilized by attaching suction cups to the back.

Drip-drying does away with the need for wringing hand-washed clothes. A garment is most easily placed on a hanger for drying while it is in the water. There are, however, several methods of wringing out articles with one hand or two weak ones. The simplest way is to drain the water from the sink and then press the items against the bottom. Small articles can be rolled in a large towel and kneaded so that excess moisture will be absorbed. Another method is to drape the article around the faucet, hold both ends and slowly twist until most of the water is out.

A washing machine, however convenient, is not necessary if there are only small amounts of laundry to be done. But since wringing and drying are often more of a problem than washing, a dryer may be the most useful item of laundry equipment to buy. Several small compact models, which require no special wiring or venting, are now on the market. Easy-care fabrics require little ironing if the clothes are taken from the dryer while they are still warm and are immediately smoothed, folded or hung up.

For air-drying clothes when there is a limited amount of laundry, several types of clotheslines and drying racks for indoor and outdoor use are available. For someone who uses only one hand, a "traveling" clothesline made of twisted elastic cord is particularly helpful. Light articles can be hung single-handed by inserting them between the twists. Such a line usually has a hook at each end and can be attached to convenient points indoors or out. If you do dry your washing out-of-doors, a plastic basket on wheels is useful for transporting it.

Easy-care fabrics, drip-drying or removing articles from the dryer while they are still warm, should eliminate the need to iron or reduce it to the barest minimum. But if you do iron, you should do so on a surface at which you can sit and work at a comfortable height—the height of your elbows when you are sitting upright.

Free-standing ironing boards that can be adjusted to a number of heights are readily available. The board selected should be easy to adjust and have adequate knee space. Models with curved legs usually have the most room underneath. An ironing board which pulls down from the wall is usually easier to set up and fold back after use, but it must be carefully positioned on the wall when installed so that it is at the proper working height.

You may find it most convenient, particularly if you don't do much ironing, to use a well-padded kitchen table or portable traveling board which can be set up on a table or over the arms of a wheelchair.

Heat, not pressure, does the work of ironing, so it's not necessary to have a heavy iron. There are many lightweight models available. Travel irons are lighter than household irons and some can be used on dry and steam. If, however, your hands are unsteady, you may find a heavier iron best since the weight helps to counteract the shakiness.

A steam iron eliminates the need for sprinkling equipment. A nonstick finish on the sole plate makes ironing smoother

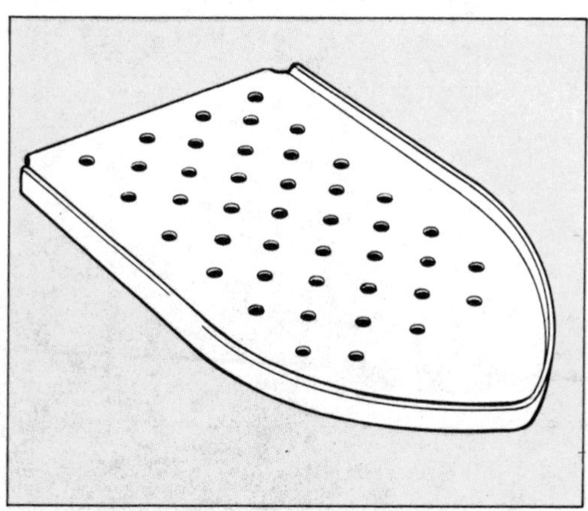

A steam-iron rest makes it unnecessary to upend the iron and collects excess steam after use so that the iron doesn't have to be emptied.

Ironing Boards

Ironing should always be done on a surface at which you can sit and work at a comfortable height. The adjustable ironing board right has offset legs which give sufficient knee room. A portable ironing board, which can be used on a table, is easy to manage. The table-top board below has legs which keep it firmly in position during use and fold flat for storage. The portable ironing board below right has two tops, for ironing large or small items. It locks in an upright position and folds for storage.

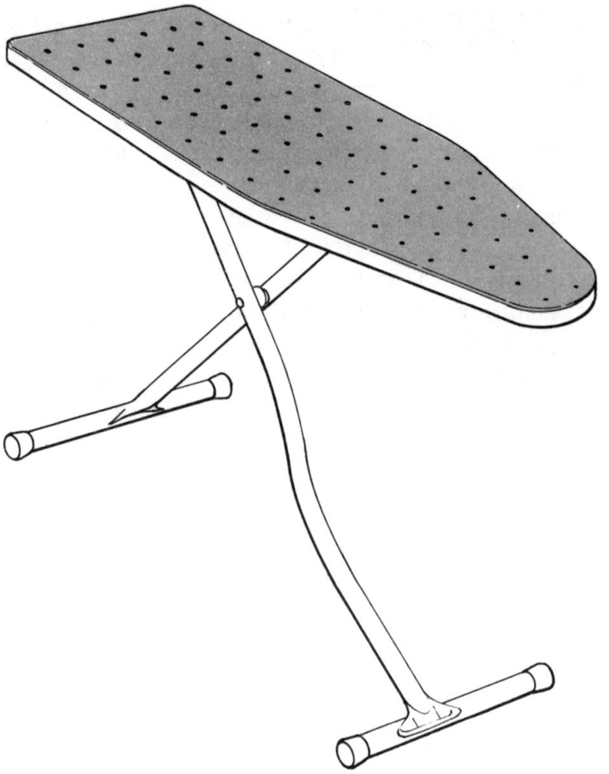

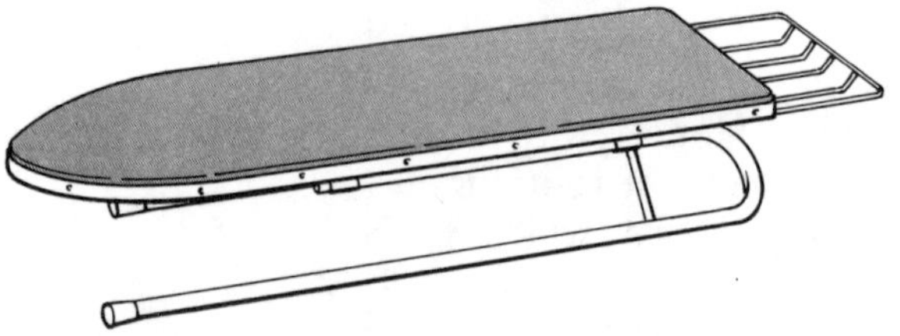

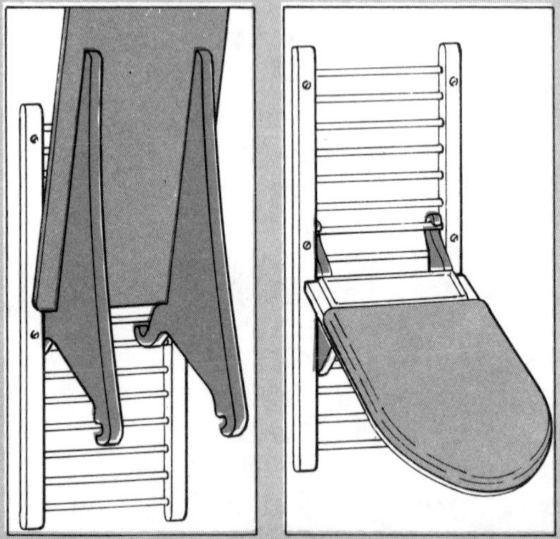

A wall frame with rungs permits the ironing board to be hung at different levels to suit the individual members of the household. The board can also be easily removed when not in use.

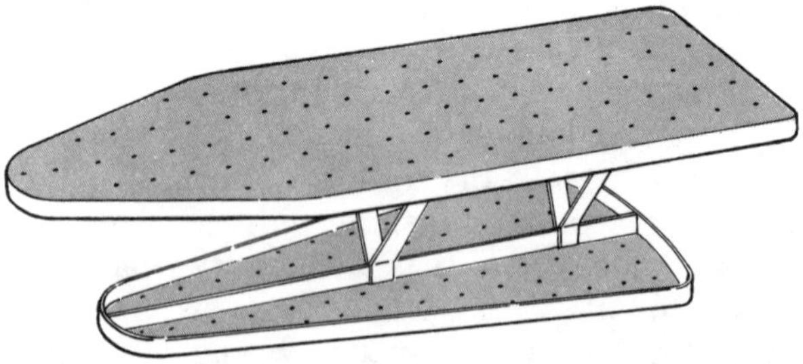

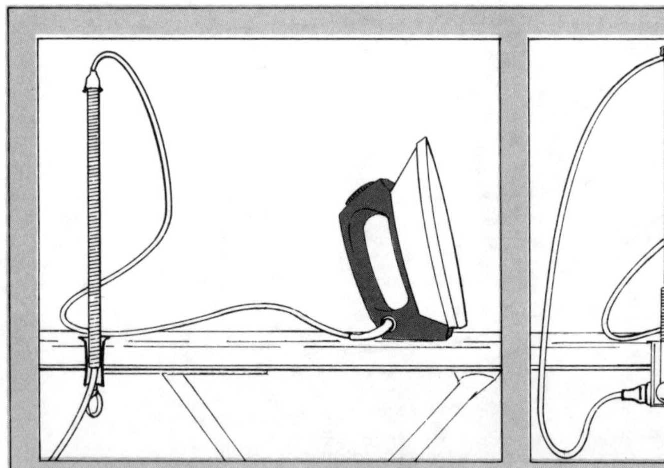

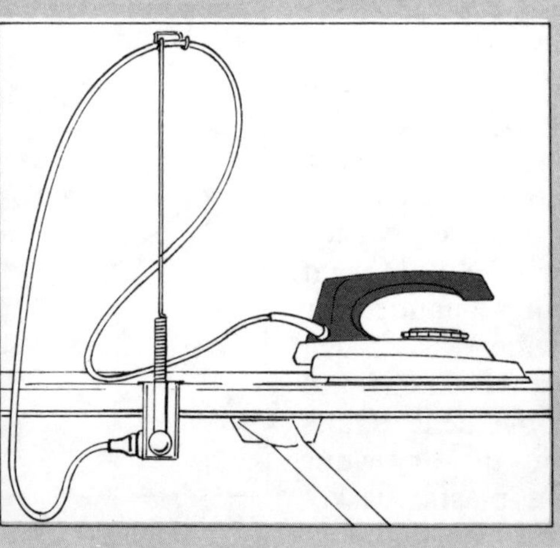

With a cord minder holding the cord out of the way of the ironing surface, the effort of ironing is reduced. It also prevents the cord from tangling by taking up the slack and yet leaves enough cord free to stretch across the board. The two cord minders shown here are among the many types which are available.

and minimizes waste motion and fatigue. On many irons the cord is attached to suit a right-handed person. If you iron with your left hand look for an iron fitted specifically for left-handed ironing or one which has the cord fitted in the center of the handle so that it is suitable for either hand. If the handle is not comfortable to hold, pad it to accommodate your grasp. Be sure the padding does not come near the metal under the handle.

A cord holder helps to keep the cord out of the way while you are ironing, reducing effort as well as wear on the cord. Various models are available from houseware stores and mail order companies. The electric outlet for the iron should be easy to reach at the right of a right-handed person and at the left of someone who is left-handed.

Use the iron set at a lower temperature than would normally be used for the fabric. This will allow you to work at your own speed without fear of scorching the material. It will also permit you to set the iron on the article to hold it while you smooth the fabric.

Starching is rarely required, but if you do want to starch something it is most convenient to use starch from a spray can. If you have trouble with the tiny depresser on top of such cans, a small piece of flat wood glued on the top makes pressing it easier.

Household Chores

Even the most functional home has to be cleaned and maintained. Although careful selection of equipment will make many chores easier, when it comes to conserving energy and saving time, planning of work and the use of efficient methods are most important.

The first step, of course, is to try to organize your home so that a minimum of maintenance is necessary. Work will be lessened if the furnishings, fabrics and finishes are easy to clean. Unquestionably, a neat, sparsely furnished room can be cleaned more quickly and easily than an untidy room and it may be advisable to banish dust-catching knick-knacks and to discard or store non-essential items. But a disability doesn't make an untidy person neat, any more than it makes someone who enjoys being surrounded by bric-a-brac, books and other dust collectors happy to live in Spartan surroundings. There are things everyone can do, however, to make a home easier to clean.

Have pieces of furniture placed so that it's not difficult to clean around them. A couple of inches can make all the difference. A sofa, for example, may be far enough away from a wall to allow dust to collect, but just not far enough away for a broom or vacuum cleaner to get behind it. Any furniture which has to be moved regularly should be fitted with casters.

Learn to simplify your housecleaning chores. A little done every day will be more rewarding and less tiring than a blitz of cleaning once a month. When a little bit is done each day surface dirt will be removed before it becomes embedded and hard to clean. Try to stick to a work schedule and to spread cleaning over a period of time so that some chores are done every day, others every week and others even less often.

The cleaning implements you use should be easy to handle. They should require little or no lifting, nor should you have to stoop, bend or overreach to use them. They should also be as lightweight as possible without detracting from their effectiveness.

New products have eliminated much

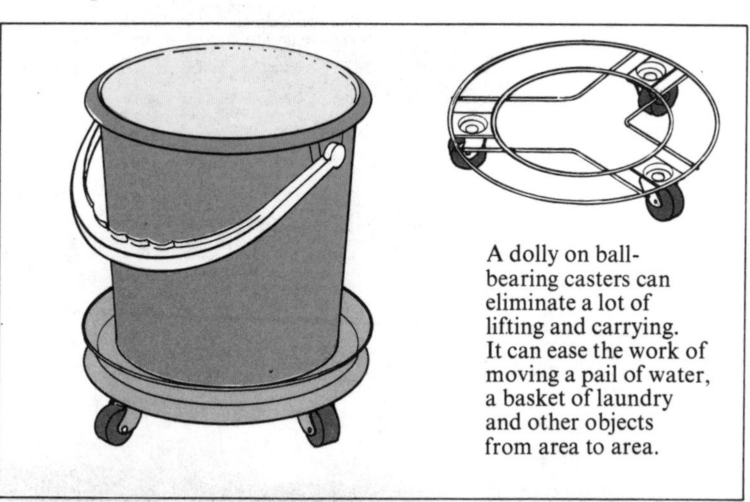

A dolly on ball-bearing casters can eliminate a lot of lifting and carrying. It can ease the work of moving a pail of water, a basket of laundry and other objects from area to area.

of the drudgery of cleaning. Liquid cleansing agents are now available which clean surfaces without scrubbing and don't have to be rinsed off. There are silver polish compounds which retard tarnish and spray-on stain repellents which protect carpets, upholstery and wallpaper. Floor and furniture polishes are available which clean and polish in one step without hard rubbing. Disposable or machine-washable dust cloths are now on the market which pick up and hold dust without rearranging it. And there is an aerosol spray for doormats which "magnetizes" incoming dirt, as well as several types of mats which help to keep the dirt outside. New labor-saving products are continually coming on the market. It's wise to keep up-to-date on them and to try them out.

Cleaning supplies should be stored in a central place and organized so that equipment is easy to get out and to replace. Duplicates of inexpensive items, including dust cloths, sponges and scouring powder, should be kept wherever they are used. If your home is on more than one level have duplicates of as many items as possible on each floor.

Before you begin to clean, plan your work so that you can finish in one room before going on to the next. Get together all the equipment that may be required for a job, instead of going back and forth to get items as they are needed. Save steps by using a wheeled table or cart to carry cleaning supplies, damp cloths, tongs, reacher and a paper bag for trash and into which ashtrays can be emptied. A bicycle basket attached to a walker, or, if you use crutches or canes, a large canvas bag with a shoulder strap, will serve as a carryall for moving cleaning supplies from place to place. An apron with large pockets, in which small items can be carried, saves steps while it keeps your clothes clean.

A home-devised or commercially available dolly, which can be pushed with a foot, a cane or a crutch or pulled with a handle or cord, may be used to transport a pail, vacuum cleaner or other equipment. The dolly should have a raised edge and good-sized casters. A model

Lightweight and easy to move around, this mop pail is actually a large dishpan with handles that has been permanently mounted on a metal frame with swivel casters. It is available from self-help equipment firms.

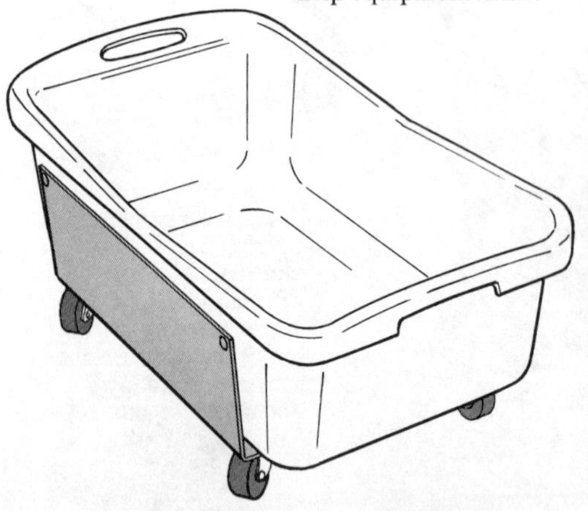

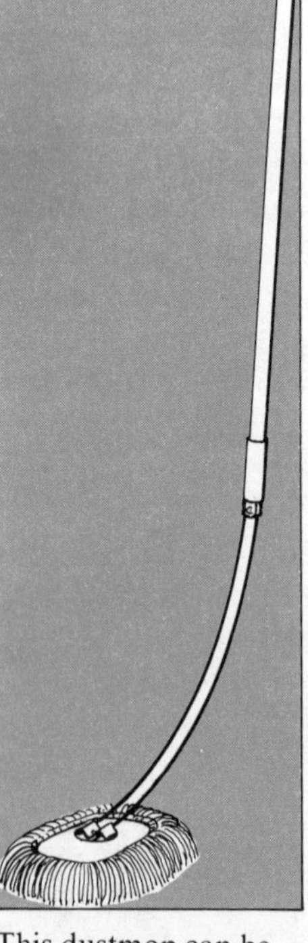

This dustmop can be used without bending; the spring-steel handle flexes to sweep under low furniture.

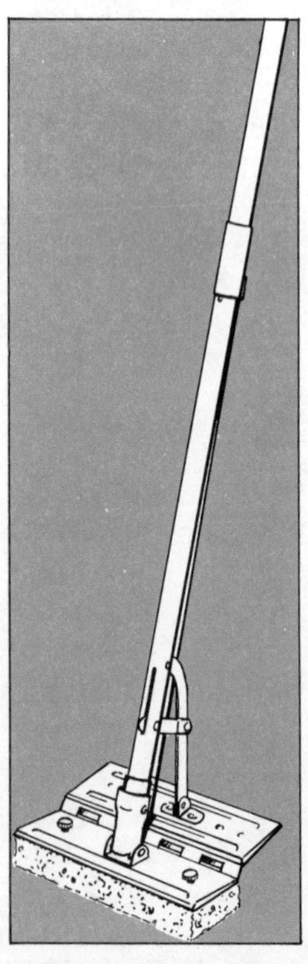

Cellulose sponge mops are available with various self-wringing mechanisms. A large sponge speeds work.

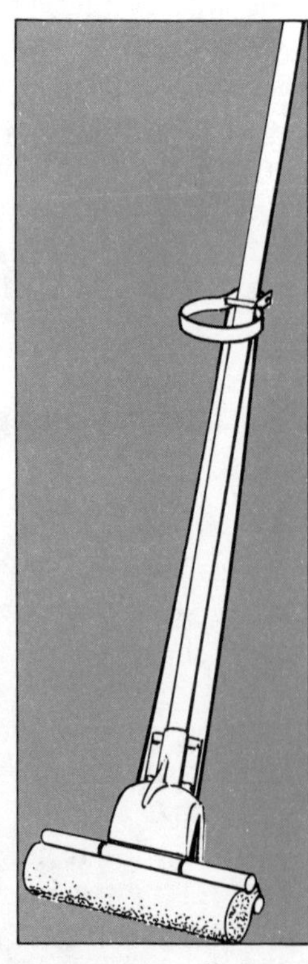

The easy-to-pull wringing lever on this sponge-rubber mop is twenty inches (50 cm) above the floor.

designed for holding and moving large plants will serve this purpose well.

A vacuum cleaner can be used to clean curtains, walls and upholstery as well as floors and carpets. Unfortunately, some models are awkward to handle so if you are buying a vacuum cleaner choose a model that is as lightweight as possible yet has sufficient power. Be sure you can handle the dirt removal apparatus and can change the attachments easily.

The unit should have a long enough cord to permit free movement. An automatic cord rewinder eliminates the need to bend to rewind. Some models have built-in storage for tools inside the cleaner. With others the attachments can be hooked to the sides so that they don't have to be carried separately. If possible test a vacuum cleaner in your home before purchasing it.

There are three types of vacuum cleaners—upright, tank and canister models. The one you choose should depend upon the furnishings in your home and the extent of your disability.

An upright cleaner requires less expenditure of energy than tank or canister models and permits you to remain in a straighter position or to work from a chair. It can also serve as a walking aid, which makes it easier to move around the house. It is, however, more difficult to clean under low furniture with an upright cleaner and fitting the various attachments for other jobs, like cleaning upholstery, can also be more difficult.

Canister and tank models are more convenient for cleaning under furniture and for getting into awkward corners. Maximum suction is provided, however, only if the attachment is making contact with the floor at the correct angle. This can be a problem if grasp is weak or movement limited. An upright model, on the other hand, automatically assumes the right angle.

A canister or tank vacuum cleaner should have wheels or casters to reduce the strain of pulling and permit easy passage over the edges of rugs, over doorsills and the machine's cord, bumpers to protect furniture and mold-

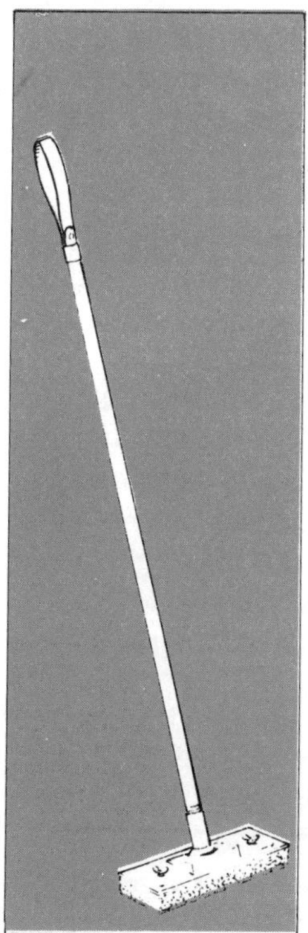

This mop is one of the heads which comes with a combination utility stick available from hospital suppliers.

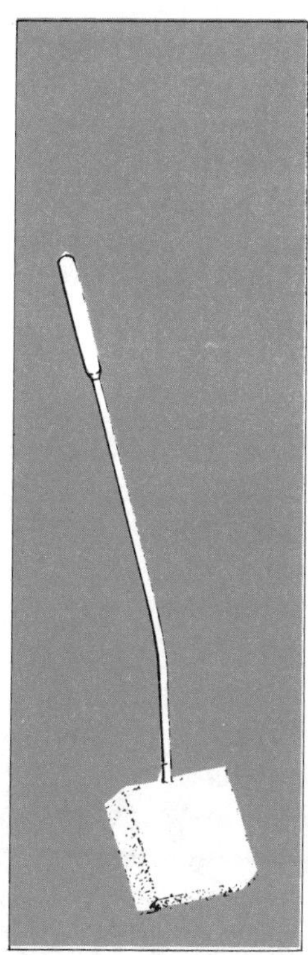

A giant sponge, with a twenty-inch (50-cm), take-apart, metal handle, easily cleans hard to reach places.

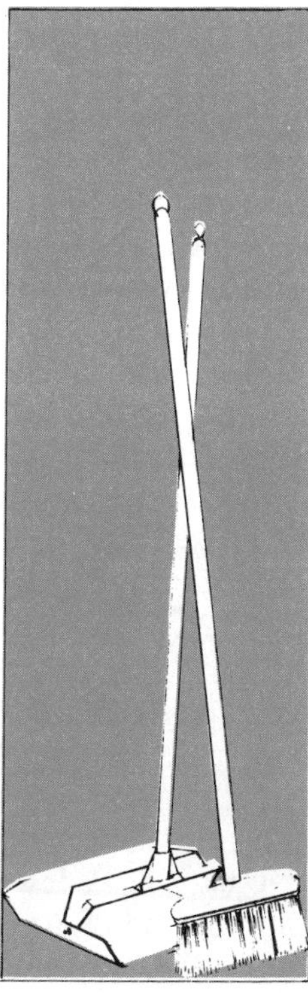

A no-stoop pickup ends dustpan bending. It can be used from a wheelchair or with one hand.

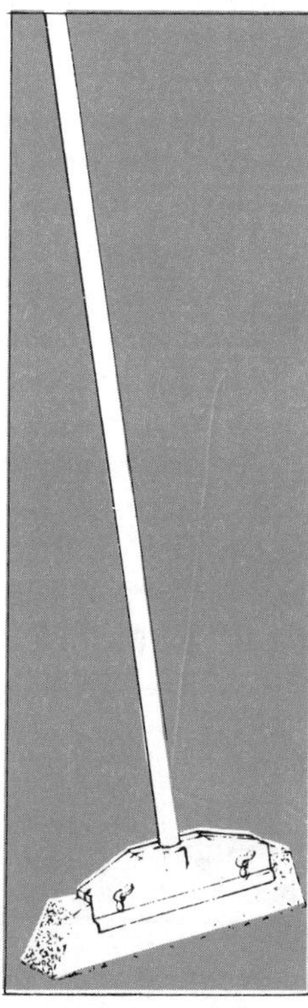

A lightweight magnetic broom is easy to use. Electrostatic action helps the foam head to pick up dirt.

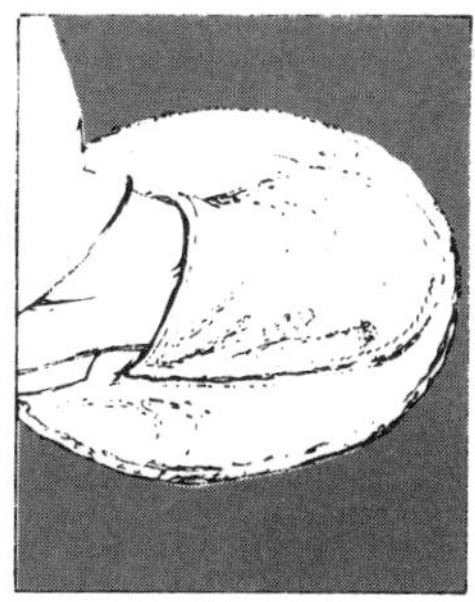

With a foot mop, floors can be dusted and kitchen and bathroom spills can be wiped up without bending down. Just insert your foot into the terry cloth mop and shuffle.

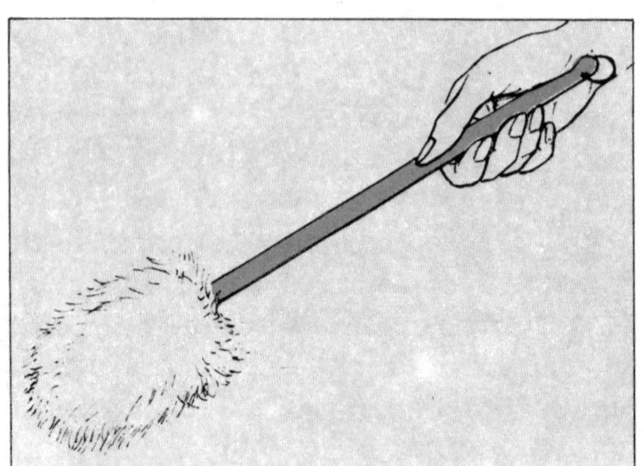

An inexpensive Acrilan duster on a handle is lightweight, extends reach to high or narrow places and picks up dust by magnetic action.

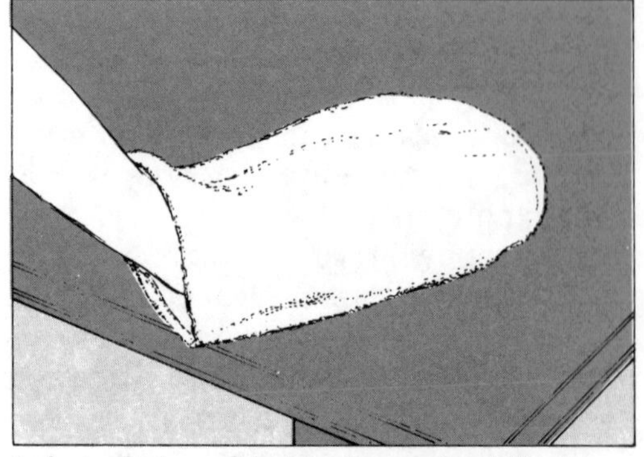

A dust mitt is useful when fingers should be extended or grasp is limited. One mitt on each hand makes quick work of dusting.

ing and disposable dust bags which eliminate the need to empty cloth bags.

If you use a vacuum cleaner from a wheelchair, be careful not to get tangled up in the cord and, most important, don't pull the vacuum up close behind you. It can be worse than painting yourself into a corner. In a tight place you won't be able to turn around if the unit is too close to the back of the chair, nor might you be able to reach around and push the vacuum away.

Light, portable, hand vacuum cleaners are on the market. Although such a unit can be a helpful appliance, because of its lower suction power it usually won't substitute for a full-size vacuum cleaner. An electric broom, however, is a lightweight vacuum cleaner which may be used for floors and upholstery with or without attachments.

A carpet sweeper is lighter and much less expensive than a vacuum cleaner and has the added advantage that it does not have to be plugged into a possibly inaccessible outlet. While a smaller carpet sweeper may be easy to push, it has to be pushed for a longer time to cover the same area.

The handle of a carpet sweeper should be long enough so that there is no need to stoop when pushing it. It should also be designed so that it does not fall over when left in an upright position. A few models have handles made of metal tubes which slot into each other so that a short person or someone in a wheelchair can remove one section and have a shorter handle.

Some carpet sweepers are designed to work on floors as well as carpets. It is important, however, that the lever that adjusts the brushes for use on carpet or floor can be easily operated.

A magnetic broom, which picks up dirt by electrostatic action, is helpful for sweeping uncarpeted floors. To sweep under low furniture, a dust mop with a spring steel rod handle which flexes is very useful. If you work from a wheelchair or find it difficult to bend, a long-handled dustpan and brush should be standard equipment. A balanced tilt-top dustpan, available from department stores and self-help equipment firms, holds dirt until it is emptied over a wastebasket.

Uncarpeted floors should not be polished. Most flooring can be sealed with a finish which has a built-in shine and needs no more than a wipe with a damp mop to keep it clean.

Mopping can be a tiring chore so use cleaners that require no rinsing. If you must do extensive mopping use a dolly to carry the pail and fill the pail only halfway to avoid strain. A cellulose sponge mop is lighter and more maneuverable than a string mop and it is easier to get clean. Models are available which have the squeeze control on the handle. Before buying a mop, look at the models available at your local housewares store and see which is easiest for you to handle.

Most dusting jobs can be done quite easily from a wheelchair. Out-of-reach furniture, windowsills and walls can be cleaned by using the dusting attachment of the vacuum cleaner or a long-handled duster.

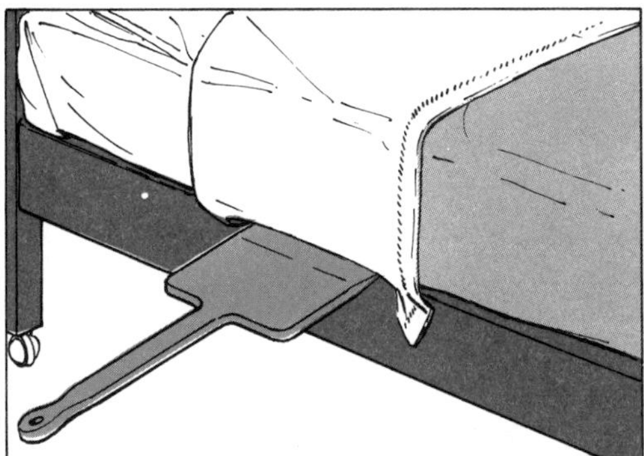

When it is difficult or painful to tuck in the bedclothes, a wooden oven spade can be helpful. If grasp is limited the handle can be built up.

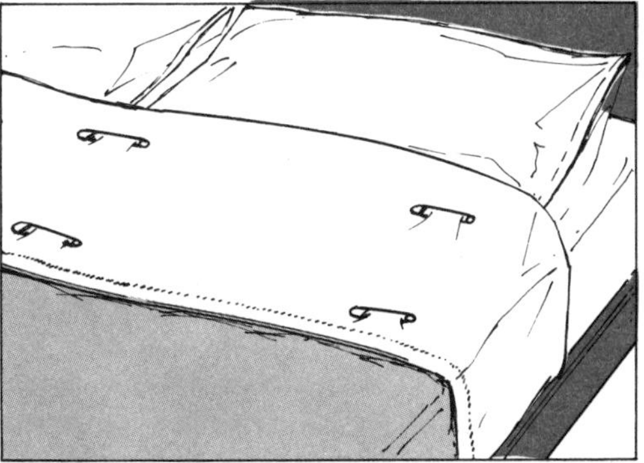

Use large safety pins to keep the top sheet and blankets together. It simplifies bedmaking and keeps bedclothes from slipping during the night.

A long-handled duster can be made by using a reacher with a cloth or by putting a dust cloth over the broom part of a toy broom. The cloth can be stapled to the handle or held in place with a rubber band. Long, lightweight dusters are also commercially available. One unit, which comes in three sections of bamboo poles that fit together, will add seven and a half feet (225 cm) to your reach.

When grasp is limited a dust mitt is often easier to use than a dust cloth.

To clean the bathtub, pieces of stiff nylon dress net, pushed through the head of a sponge-mop holder, makes a lightweight and effective cleaner. A child's mop is just the right length to reach across to the other side of the tub from a wheelchair. (A toy mop is also convenient for cleaning up spills and spots on the floor, and for getting at hard to reach corners, high windowsills and shelves.)

Bedmaking is a heavy, often difficult task. The bed itself should stand away from the wall so that it can be approached from all sides and allow adequate room to maneuver. It should be high enough to reach from a seated position or without bending from a standing position. It is convenient to have a chair or table at one side at the head of the bed on which can be put pillows, covers and clean bedding in the order in which they will be used when the bedclothes are changed.

Top sheets that are large enough so they don't pull out every night make tucking in every day unnecessary, as do contour bottom sheets with elasticized corners which fit snugly over the corners of the mattress. If the bottom sheet fits the mattress so tightly that you have to lift the corner of the mattress to get it on, slit one corner at the foot of the bed and sew in an extra width of material. Then just tuck that corner in.

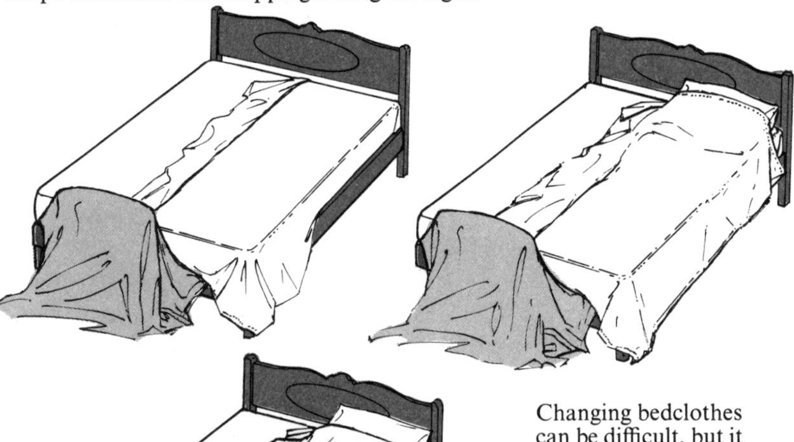

Changing bedclothes can be difficult, but it can be done most easily if the blankets are put back over a chair placed at the end of the bed, the soiled sheets and the pillows are removed and the clean sheets are folded in layers so that half of the bed can be made at one time.

The one-trip method of bedmaking is simple, saves steps and time and should be used even if you can get to both sides of the bed without difficulty. Start at the head of the bed, smoothing the bottom sheet, upper sheet, blanket and cover and place the pillow. Then work your way toward the foot, smoothing as you go. Then go up the other side, straightening the bedclothes and tucking them in and place the other pillow if it's a double bed.

Pillowcases are always hard to put on,

but a pillow cover made of a slippery fabric makes the job easier by cutting down on the friction.

When tucking in bedclothes is difficult or painful, a paddle can be used instead of your hands. A wooden oven spade works very well. About fifteen inches (38 cm) long and made of sturdy wood, oven spades are available from mail order companies and the kitchenware departments of department stores.

Shopping

Planning ahead, having knowledge of local facilities and services and being objective about how much you can manage with or without help will make shopping most successful and least tiring.

Last minute shopping lists invariably omit necessary items, so keep a memo pad with a pencil attached to it in a convenient place in the kitchen. This will make it easy for you to list things as you run out of them, or as they occur to you.

Accessibility guides can be a source of information about stores. Some large department stores, moreover, provide such special services for people with disabilities as guides for blind customers and wheelchairs for those who require them. It's often best, therefore, to call the stores yourself to find out about their facilities, as well as their accessibility, or to ask friends and neighbors to report. When you shop do so at nonpeak hours and early in the week when the stores are uncrowded and the service is best.

Although it's nice to go to a supermarket to see what is available and to be open to on-the-spot inspiration, shopping by telephone to stores that deliver is undeniably useful, particularly for brand-name items and the bulkier staples.

If you're not an enthusiastic shopper you may find that it's far easier and just as gratifying to buy household items as well as clothing from reliable mail order companies. Through their catalogs they often offer a wider range of merchandise than local stores and their prices are competitive.

Safety in the Home

More accidents occur in the home than anywhere else. Some of these accidents are slight, but many of them are serious, even fatal. Most of them could have been prevented. When mobility is limited by disability it is even more important that adequate safety precautions be taken in the home.

In the Kitchen

- Don't wear loose sleeves, dangling scarves or an apron of inflammable material when cooking.
- Always have noninflammable pot-holders near the stove and always keep long oven gloves near the oven and wear them when putting pans in or removing them.
- Always light the match before turning on the gas jets.
- When lighting the oven use long barbecue or fireplace matches.
- Be sure oven racks are steady enough to support filled pans when the racks are pulled forward.
- Turn pot handles so that they don't project over the edge of the stove.
- Cover frying pans with mesh guards to prevent fat from splattering.
- Use long-handled cooking utensils with nonconducting handles.
- Douse a small fat or grease fire heavily with salt or baking powder, which should be kept in a free-flowing container next to the stove. Never pour water on a grease fire—it will make the fire spread.
- If a fire starts in the oven or broiler turn off the heat and shut the door immediately to cut off the air.
- Keep a lightweight fire extinguisher near the stove in the kitchen. The dry chemical charges work well on all home-type fires. A carbon dioxide extinguisher doesn't make a mess or contaminate food. When buying a fire extinguisher be sure you understand how the control works and are able to handle it.
- Keep sharp utensils separate from other implements. Store knives in a covered rack or on a magnetized board.
- Wipe up floor spills immediately.

- Transport hot dishes on a lapboard or wheeled table.
- Inflammable materials, including curtains, paper towels and dish towels, should not be kept near the stove nor near such electrical appliances as broiler, toaster, griddle, waffle iron or electric skillet.
- Never use an electrical appliance near the sink.
- Never use an appliance with a frayed cord.

In the Bathroom

- Install grab bars in the shower, near the bathtub and next to the toilet.
- Use nonslip bath mats in front of the bathtub and shower.
- Use nonslip mats or strips in the bathtub and shower.
- The temperature of the water should be thermostatically controlled.
- Install the kind of lock on the door that can be opened from the outside in case of an emergency.

General

- Be sure stair carpeting is firmly affixed to the steps.
- Anchor all loose rugs to the floor.
- Replace or remove frayed carpeting immediately.
- Don't overload electrical circuits.
- Be sure no electrical cords are lying where they might be tripped over.
- Smoke and fire alarms detect dangerous levels of smoke density or temperature and give a warning in time to allow a safe escape.
- Have a fire extinguisher in every potential danger area, but if anything but a small fire which you can handle without difficulty occurs, get out immediately and call for help.
- Have telephone extensions in as many rooms as possible and keep emergency telephone numbers next to each extension.
- If you live alone arrange for someone to come by or to telephone at least once a day.

Your Personal Needs

Human beings are social creatures, dependent on the warmth, humor, stimulation and affection of others. Almost every aspect of an individual's life is colored by his or her desire to be accepted and admired, to give and to share. For the person with physical disabilities, learning to cope with any obstacles to acceptance is often the first step to a place in society.

Fortunately, more and more aids and techniques are continually being developed which make it less difficult for people with disabilities to deal effectively with this challenge. A great number of aids make eating and drinking, bathing, dressing and grooming easier for people with different kinds of disabilities and these can all contribute to the self-esteem and confidence that make it possible to give and to share socially.

There is no question that the way people look—the way they dress, the effort they make to be well-groomed—strongly influences the impression they make on others. This may seem heartless and narrow-minded, particularly when such adages as "Beauty is only skin deep" and "You can't tell a book by its cover" come to mind. But if you think about it for a moment you realize that the way you look, the outward appearance you present to others, is, after all, a reflection of how you feel about yourself. And if you don't seem to think much of yourself why should other people think much of you? Good grooming is important not only for the sake of appearance, but because it imparts a sense of well-being, reinforces morale and enhances self-esteem.

The person with physical disabilities who is unkempt is even more vulnerable than the able-bodied person who neglects his or her appearance. For the disabled person would in effect be perpetuating the myth that people with disabilities are less attractive, less intelligent, less personable and less worthy individuals than their able-bodied peers. This is where another vicious circle begins. If he or she is treated in accordance with the myth, then self-esteem, already attacked by disability, diminishes further.

Thus, a psychological disability is added to a physical disability. A person who doesn't look presentable doesn't feel presentable and begins to avoid going out and meeting other people and even begins to feel undeserving of friendship, fun and pleasure. All too often the physical handicap is blamed for the lack of friends, the dullness of life, even for the inability to get a job, when actually it may not be the visible physical difference that acts as a barrier, but rather the projected effect of the individual's lack of self-esteem.

To see yourself as others see you can work positively in a reverse way. You can make others see you as you would like to be seen and as you are and have the potential to be. It is only after other people are attracted to you and accept the outside you, however, that they begin to know the real you, the person inside the clothes, beneath the disability.

You don't have to be beautiful or handsome or expensively dressed to be well-groomed. It is necessary, however, to be objective about the best aspects of your appearance and to make the most of them.

For many people with disabilities it's a struggle just to bathe, brush their teeth and get dressed. But it's just as easy, or difficult, to dress in clothes that are flattering as it is to put on the same old sloppy outfit.

It may be easier to skip shaving for a couple of days or to let a beard go untrimmed for several weeks. It may seem unnecessary to go through the hassle of getting a good haircut or to spend time putting on lipstick or mascara. It might seem frivolous to spend money on after-shave lotion or cologne or a bottle of perfume. But these are the extra little touches that make you feel more confident and will make others see you in the light you want to be seen.

Too often attendants or relatives try to persuade a person with disabilities that beyond personal hygiene any time spent on grooming is unnecessary or wasted. Don't be tempted to succumb to such attitudes. The time and effort you spend attending to your personal grooming can help you to achieve many things—not the least of which is self-esteem.

Eating and Drinking

A multitude of aids, which are commercially available, have been designed to make eating and drinking easier, pleasanter and more efficient for people with various disabilities. The principles of some of them—as is true of many other practical aids—can, with a little ingenuity, be applied at home to ordinary utensils which can often be readily and inexpensively adapted to special needs. A therapist's advice should be sought about the suitability of such aids.

Built-up handles on eating utensils are helpful when grasp is weak or limited. Utensils are available from self-help equipment firms which have rounded or molded grip handles, lightweight metal handles that "expand" to accommodate partial grasp and handles padded with closed cell foam rubber that won't absorb moisture and can be put into a dishwasher.

Handles on standard cutlery can be easily built up, but the material used must be lightweight. A rubber bicycle or motorcycle handle, for example, makes a large handle with a good grip. Plastic foam curlers can also be used to increase the diameter of handles; the sponginess is particularly helpful when grasp is weak. Cylindrical closed cell foam padding with a hole down the middle is also available from self-help equipment firms for the purpose of enlarging the handles on all kinds of implements.

Angle-handled utensils are helpful when reach is limited. They are available for right or left hand use.

Using ordinary lightweight cutlery with handles larger than usual may compensate for mild impairment of grasp. A handle of ridged wood or cork will also provide more friction than metal. Attractive, lightweight, bamboo-handled utensils are available from department stores as well as from mail order companies.

When grasp is lacking, or very weak, and an enlarged handle is not sufficient, the spoon or fork can be strapped to the hand. A cuff around the palm makes it possible to use ordinary utensils, which fit into a pocket in the cuff. A plastic cuff, which is available from self-help equipment firms, has a Velcro closure which adjusts to fit around the hand.

Long-handled utensils compensate for lack of reach. These are available from self-help equipment firms, as is a long-handled utensil holder which has a leather pocket into which the handle of an ordinary spoon, fork or knife will fit. Long-handled eating aids are also available with pegs or wing nuts to hold utensils at an angle.

When wrist motion is limited, a swivel-handled spoon, which is self-leveling, can make it easier to eat soup or other nonsolid food. Spoons or forks which are angled serve a similar purpose and are made for right-handed or left-handed use.

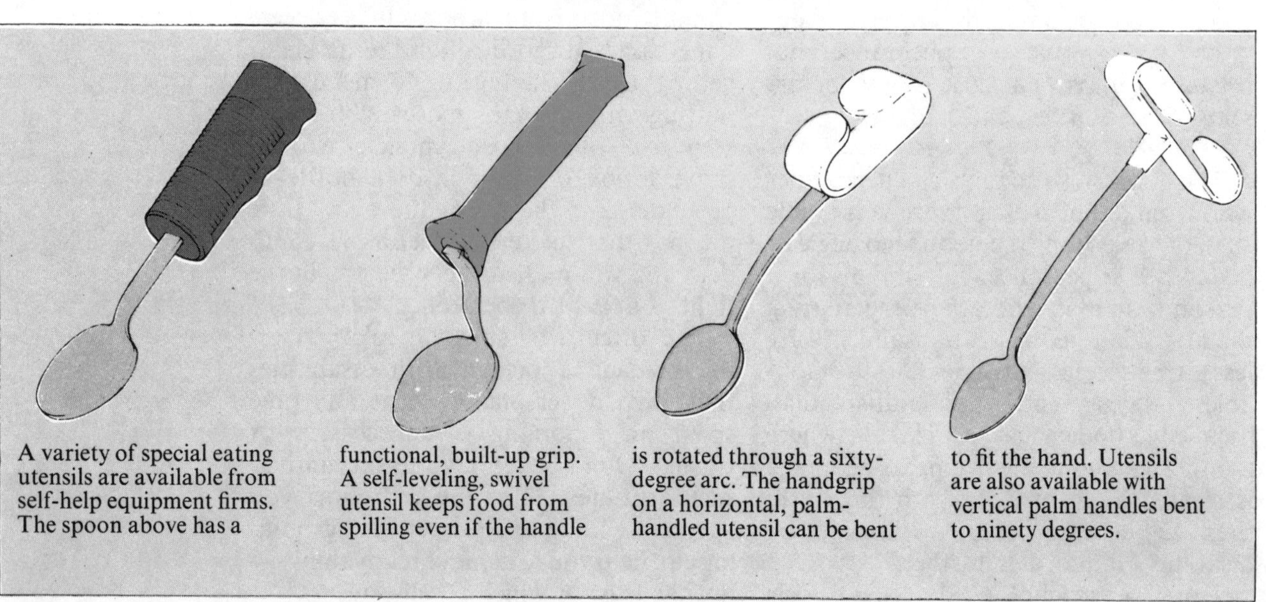

A variety of special eating utensils are available from self-help equipment firms. The spoon above has a functional, built-up grip. A self-leveling, swivel utensil keeps food from spilling even if the handle is rotated through a sixty-degree arc. The handgrip on a horizontal, palm-handled utensil can be bent to fit the hand. Utensils are also available with vertical palm handles bent to ninety degrees.

A rocker table knife makes it possible to cut food with one hand. Since a rocking motion is used to slice through the food it is not necessary to stabilize it with a fork. Some rocking knives are made with prongs at the end so that they can also be used to pick up food. Using such a knife can be dangerous, however, because the sharp edge of the blade near the prongs could cut the mouth. A side-cutting fork is an eating implement which has a cutting edge along one side. The curved blade is only semi-sharp and although it will cut most food, but not all meat, there is little danger of cutting the mouth.

A damp sponge cloth or paper towel or a rubber disc placed under a plate will keep it from sliding. Nonslip place mats made of dimpled rubber or foam are also effective.

It is important to be seated correctly when you eat. The table should be close to you and at elbow height for greatest comfort and to lessen the distance the food has to be brought to the mouth. An adjustable cantilever table can be brought close enough and set at the right height for eating in bed or in a chair.

When it's easier to drink than to eat without help, even soups and stews which need some chewing can be taken from a tumbler. When grasp is weak an unbreakable plastic tumbler is better to use than one made of glass. Besides being lighter, plastic also offers more friction than glass. Terry cloth coasters, which stretch to fit over standard glasses, provide a nonslip grasping surface. A cup with two handles is often easiest to hold.

Flexible or rigid plastic drinking straws are available which can be used over and over again. The holes vary in diameter and some are large enough to use for drinking soups and thick liquids. The longer the straw the harder it is to suck up the liquid, so it's better to raise the tumbler than to use a long straw.

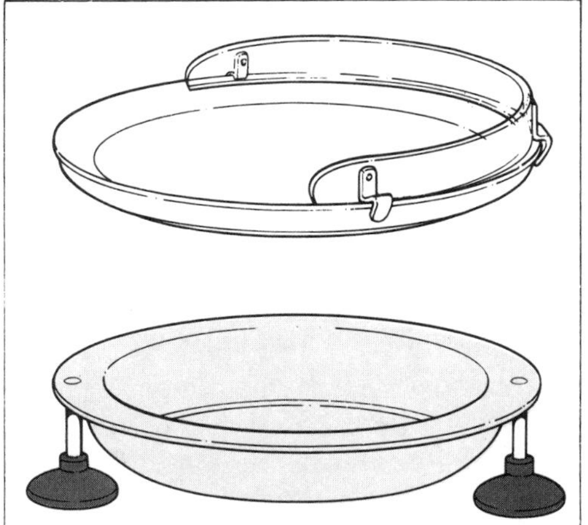

A guard, which clips onto the edge of any plate, keeps food from sliding off and provides a stable area to push against. The special inner lip of the lower plate makes it easy to scoop food into spoon or fork. The suction cups prevent the plate from slipping.

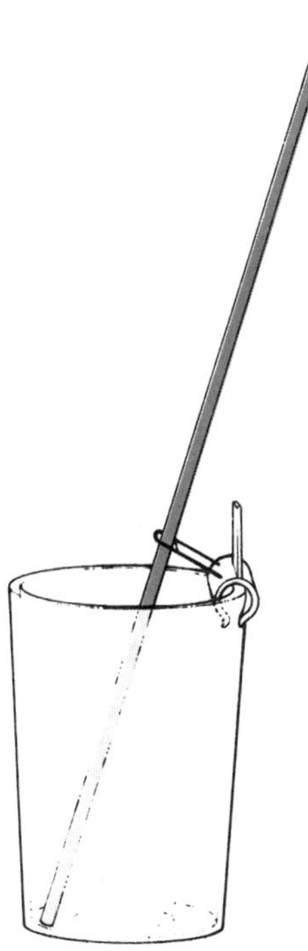

To eliminate lifting a glass or cup, attach a bulldog clip to the side and slip a long plastic straw through the hole.

A side cutter fork, above left, has a semi-sharp curved blade on one side. A rocker knife, above right, makes it possible to cut even tough meat with one hand.

This molded plastic mug has a nontip base and a unique handle which solves a variety of grasping and holding problems.

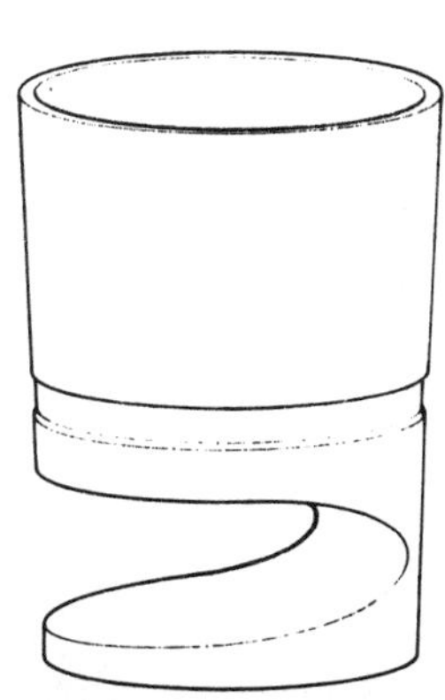

The pedestal cup was designed to accommodate weak finger grasp. It can be easily held with only the thumb and the index finger.

Bathing

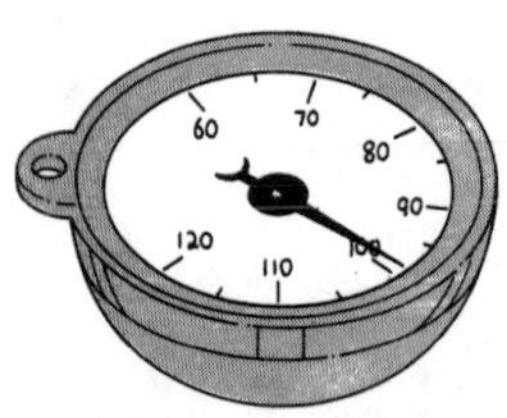

A thermometer that floats or one which fits on the shower head eliminates the danger of scalds.

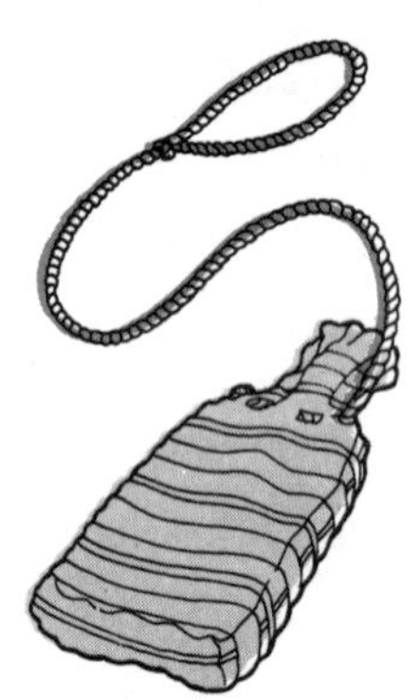

A soapbag makes the soap easier to grasp and can be hung around the neck or looped over the faucets.

Personal hygiene is fundamental to grooming. Bathing should be a pleasure, not an ordeal and there are many ways to make it so. If soaking in a tub is medically advisable it can be an enjoyable and relaxing experience. A bath pillow which supports the head and upper back can make bathing more comfortable. Inflatable cushions that attach to the tub or the tile wall with suction cups are available in different sizes and designs.

To prevent scalding when sensation is lacking, a floating plastic bath thermometer is invaluable. One model indicates the exact temperature of the water in words as well as in numerals.

Various devices are available from department stores and mail order companies which make it possible to have a shower while sitting in the bathtub. Most of these units fit standard faucets and have a shower head which can be attached to the wall permanently or with suction cups at the most convenient height. Most models have the shower head on a swivel socket so that the flow of the water can be directed. Some units have levers which control the flow of water as well.

Another aid to bathing is a bathtub tray which fits across the tub, conveniently holds such necessary items as soap, washcloth and brushes and can be slid close for use and pushed out of the way when getting into and out of the tub. Made in plastic or metal, such trays are available from department stores, as are comparable shelves for use in a standing shower which hang from suction or adhesive-backed hooks.

A cake of soap suspended on a cord around the neck is useful in the bathtub as well as in the shower. Not only is the soap always at hand, but it can be let go of and easily retrieved. Soap which comes on a cord tends to be expensive, however, but a drawstring bag on a cord, into which a cake of soap fits, can easily be made from a dishcloth or other open weave material. The cord can either be looped to hang around the neck or it can have two ends each of which is attached to a faucet in the tub or shower.

Some people find it easier to use a bath mitt than a washcloth. These are available in many materials, including sponge, or can be made from two washcloths. Some terry cloth mitts are made with a pocket

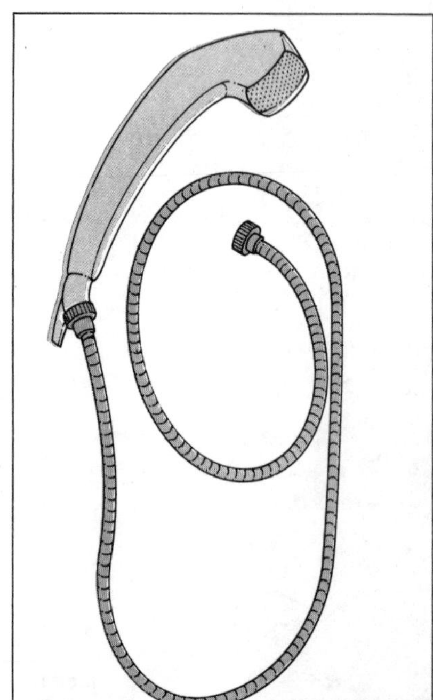

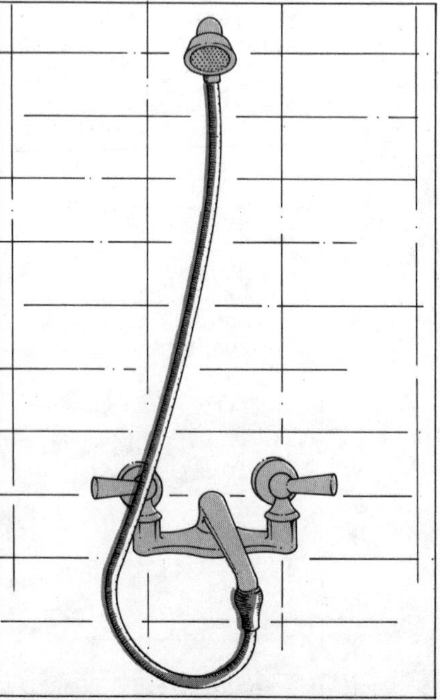

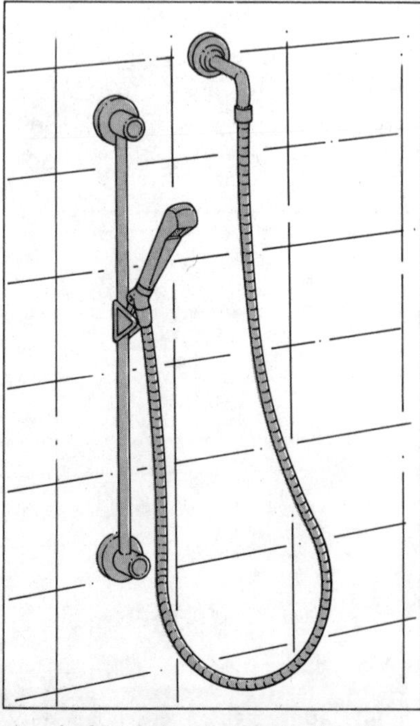

Various devices are available to modify a bathtub for sitting showers. The shower head above contains a valve which controls the water flow without changing temperature adjustment. The simplest and least expensive device is a rubber shower hose, above, which suctions to a tiled wall at the most convenient height.

A swivel socket at the head of the hose permits the flow of water to be directed. The unit above slides up and down the metal bar, has a push-button control for

for the soap. If necessary elastic or a Velcro band can be added so that the mitt fits well around the wrist.

There are various aids, too, for washing parts of the body that are not easy to reach. A long-handled brush or sponge is particularly helpful when reach is limited. A loop can be attached to the handle to make it easier to hold. One long-handled sponge has a hollow into which a cake of soap fits. Many long-handled mops and sponges found in houseware departments and designed for other uses, make excellent bathing aids. Wire handles are often better than plastic since they can be bent to suit individual requirements. Ordinary kitchen tongs or a rustproof reacher can also be used to hold a sponge or washcloth.

It can be difficult to dry yourself, particularly when reach is limited. A large terry cloth bathrobe or a poncho made from a large beach towel will do all the work and keep you warm while it absorbs the moisture. An overhead radiant lamp also warms as it dries. It is often possible to install such a lamp in an existing fixture. An electrician can advise you about doing this.

Mirrors

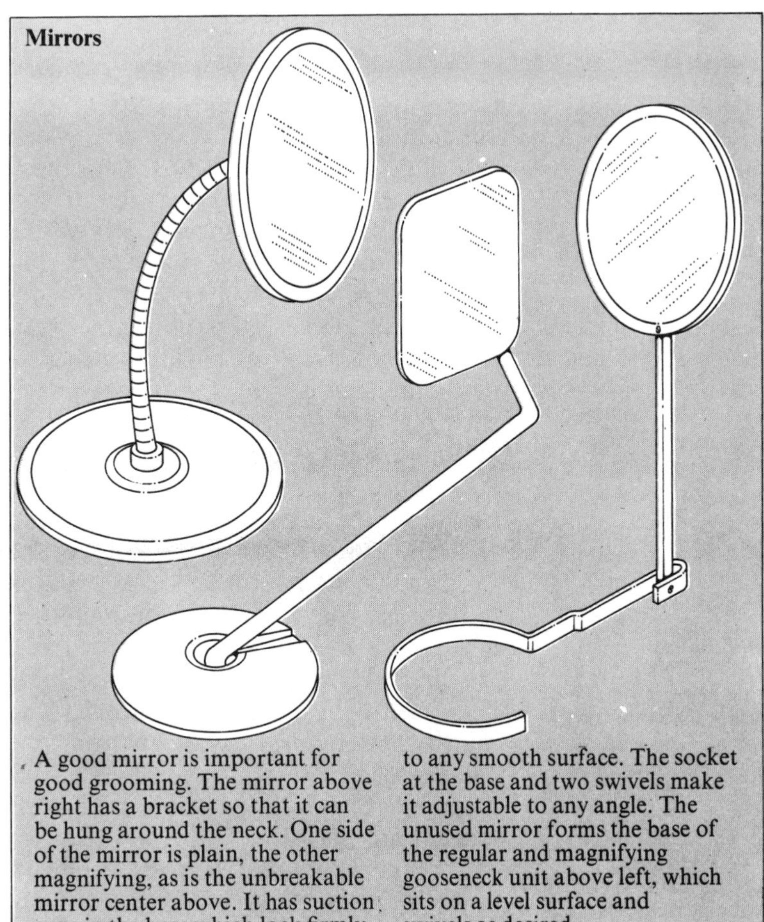

A good mirror is important for good grooming. The mirror above right has a bracket so that it can be hung around the neck. One side of the mirror is plain, the other magnifying, as is the unbreakable mirror center above. It has suction cups in the base which lock firmly to any smooth surface. The socket at the base and two swivels make it adjustable to any angle. The unused mirror forms the base of the regular and magnifying gooseneck unit above left, which sits on a level surface and swivels as desired.

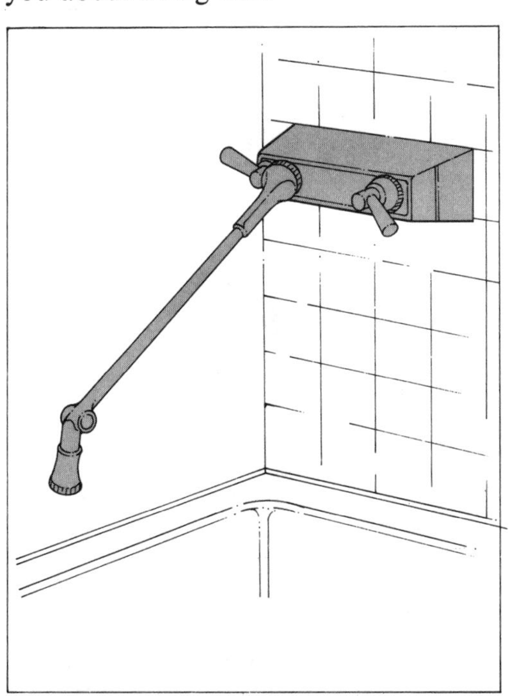

turning the water on and off and a swivel socket to angle the head. The unit above adapts to most bathtub fixtures. The arm pulls down to the desired height.

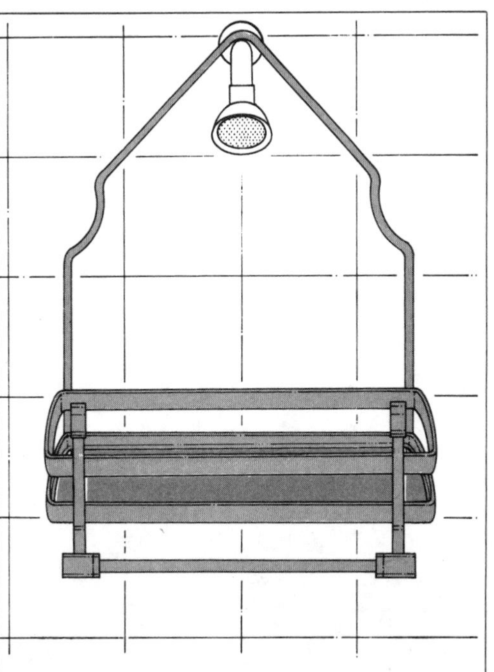

In a stall shower it is helpful to have a unit to hold shampoo, soap and other necessities near at hand. This caddy slips over the shower head and suctions to the wall.

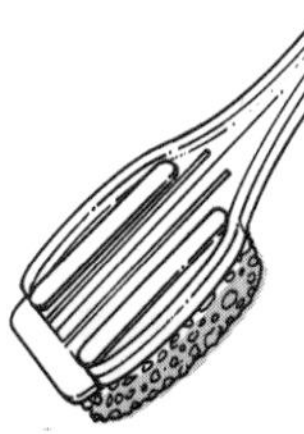

This light, self-soaping bath sponge has a long, contoured handle which is easy to grasp. Lather foams effectively through the sponge into which the soap fits.

Dental Care

Care of teeth and gums can present difficulties to people who have weak grasp or limited reach as well as to those who use only one hand. It is important, however, to devise or buy aids which enable you to look after your teeth and gums properly. Maintenance of oral hygiene can prevent serious dental problems. (There are clinics which specialize in dental care for people who are physically disabled.)

When grasp is weak the handle of a toothbrush can be built up in the same way as the handles of eating utensils. A wide elastic band around the palm of the hand can be made with a loop to hold the toothbrush handle. A long-handled toothbrush which is angled compensates for limited reach. These are available from self-help equipment firms. One model has two brush heads on one handle. The brushes can be adjusted for the best brushing position and then locked into place.

Some people find an electric toothbrush easier to use than one which is manually operated since the handle is larger and easier to hold and less wrist and arm movement are required. Those toothbrushes which have dual motions, moving from side to side and up and down, allow the complete cleaning of teeth and gums. If the toothbrush moves vertically when held upright it can be used despite limited reach. A smaller head on the brush permits greater maneuverability in the mouth.

Dentures can be cleaned with one hand if they are rubbed against the bristles of a brush that is held firm by suction cups. Special denture brushes with suction stands are available from self-help equipment firms.

Reusable metal or plastic keys, which slip on to the bottom of any size tube, help to squeeze out the required amount of toothpaste.

A variety of dental aids are available from self-help equipment firms. The toothbrush center below has a built-up foam handle to accommodate weak grasp. The long-handled toothbrush below left has a double brush head which can be adjusted for the best brushing position and then locked into place. The denture brush below right has strong suction cups which hold it firmly so that dentures can be cleaned with one hand.

Shaving

The handle of a safety razor can be enlarged or extended to accommodate weak grasp or limited reach, but an electric razor, although heavier, is easier to grip, and using one is safer and requires less precision. It also eliminates shaving soap and the need to handle blades. If grasp is weak a holder can be used to keep the razor stable while shaving. A holder can be made from elastic or Velcro and metal holders are available from self-help equipment firms.

Electric razors for women are particularly lightweight and, if necessary, can also be adapted with holders. Many women, however, find it easier to use a depilatory cream than a razor.

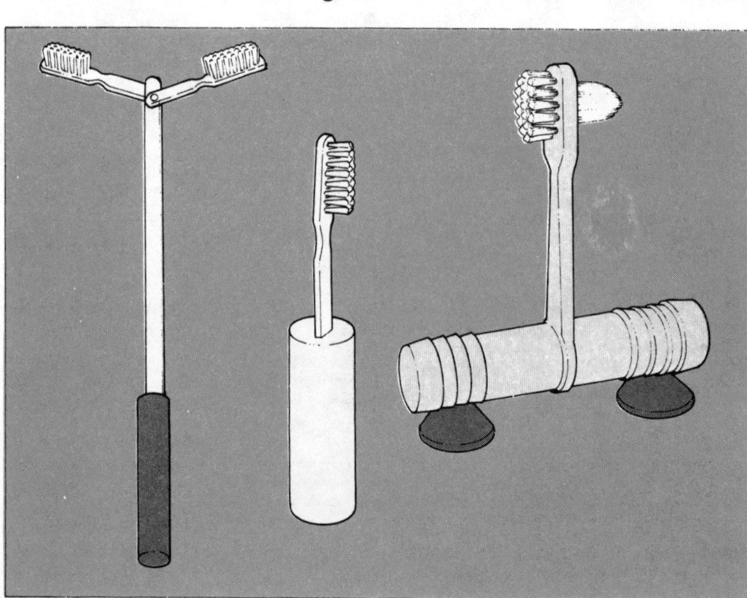

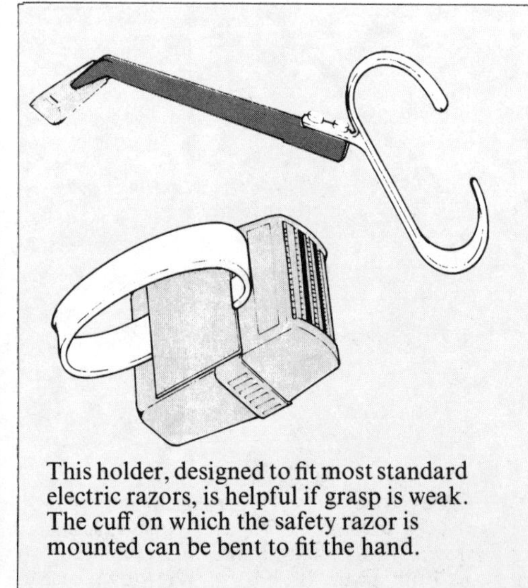

This holder, designed to fit most standard electric razors, is helpful if grasp is weak. The cuff on which the safety razor is mounted can be bent to fit the hand.

Nail Care

Caring for your fingernails can seem impossible if you have limited use of both hands or the use of only one. There are, however, some aids and techniques which make nail care not only possible, but also simple.

A suction-based nailbrush, securely attached to the side of the bathtub or washbasin, can be used single-handed or, if grasp is weak, by rubbing the nails across the brush, rather than the other way around. A plastic nailbrush with a curved handle that fits around the hand can often be used satisfactorily when grasp is impaired.

It's better to file fingernails frequently than to cut them. To file your nails one-handed, tape a nail file or an emery board to the edge of a table—better still, tape down two emery boards, one with the rough side up, the other with the fine side up. A long emery board or file can also be used single-handed when it's jammed into a drawer or held between the knees when you are seated.

Many men prefer to cut their fingernails. Nail clippers are easier to use than scissors. If grasp is weak lay the clippers on a flat, hard surface and use the heel of the hand to press them down. Clippers can be used one-handed by putting them on the floor positioned under the edge of one shoe. Put the fingernail inside the clippers and step gently on the handle.

An electric manicure set can be a great boon. Attachments include files, nail shaper, cuticle loosener and buffer. Some models can be used when grasp is weak but coordination is good. Others can be used single-handed. Some sets operate on batteries.

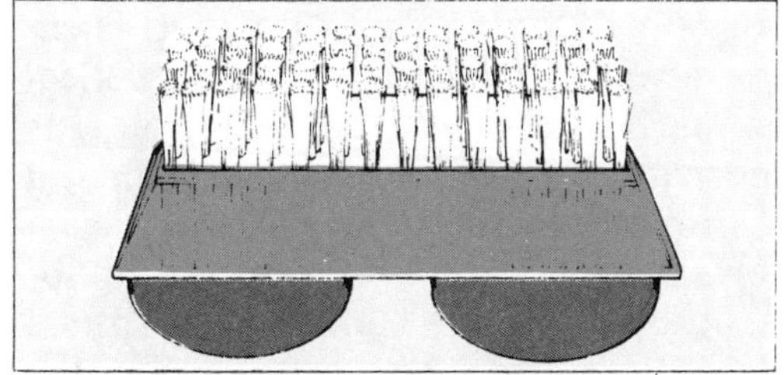

This nailbrush can be used with one hand or with two weak hands for it suctions firmly onto the side of the washbasin.

It's far more difficult to cut toenails than fingernails, even when the feet can be reached. Since a small cut can easily become infected and toenails which are too long can cause problems, if you can't cut your own toenails with ease ask someone else to do it for you.

Hair Care

When selecting or devising aids for hair care, the texture and style of the hair as well as the extent of disability must be considered. A good haircut and a simple style are the first steps in making hair care easier.

When grasp is weak, the diameter of the handle of a comb or a brush can be built up in the same way that handles of other implements can. A cuff around the palm of the hand, into which the handle of brush or comb fits, provides another solution.

It's often less tiring to comb or brush the hair while supporting the arms on a table. A battery-powered hairbrush also makes hair care easier, particularly when the hair is thick or long.

When reach is limited, a long-handled comb which adjusts to various angles is effective. Various kinds of long-handled combs are available from self-help equipment firms.

A hose attached to the faucets makes it easier to wash your hair over a basin or in a bathtub. A plastic shampoo tray is helpful if you can't bend forward and need help to wash your hair. It fits the neck comfortably and keeps water and suds out of the eyes. A conditioner used after the final rinsing eliminates tangles and makes hair manageable. When regular shampooing is inconvenient or difficult a dry shampoo is invaluable.

If hair setting is required, Velcro-covered curlers, which cling to the hair without pins or clips, come in different sizes and can be managed with one hand.

Hairdryers, for men as well as for women, are now available in many styles and weights. Some have brush and comb attachments so that the hair can be styled as it is dried.

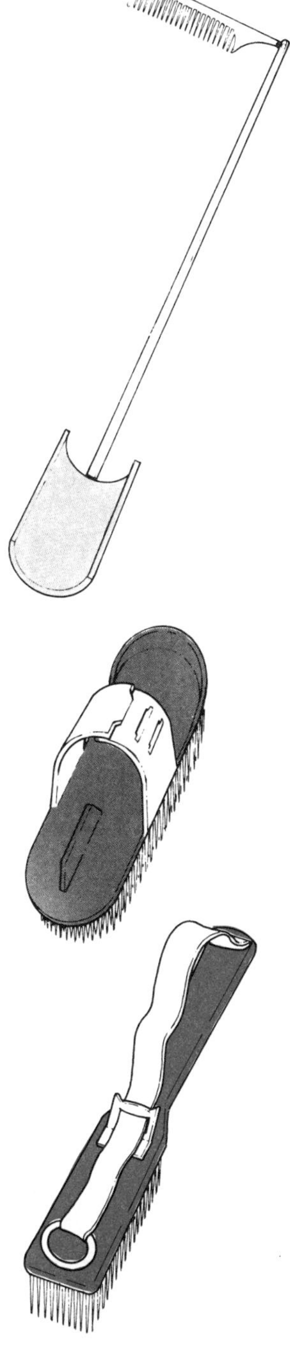

The aluminum shaft on the extension comb top above can be bent to the best angle and the handle can be bent to fit the hand. The hairbrush center has an adjustable handle and a finger divider for better control. The lower hairbrush has an easy-to-fasten handle which locks firmly to the hand.

Cosmetics

There's nothing like a touch of makeup to brighten the face and raise morale. Even women who spend most of their time at home, or even in bed, can look their best and choose for themselves the cosmetics which are most becoming. Several cosmetic companies have representatives who will come to your home with samples of their products. Besides being a convenient and comfortable way to shop this also gives you the opportunity to try before you buy.

To accommodate weak grasp, lipstick tubes can be built up with foam rubber or tape. If reach is limited, the lipstick tube can be mounted in a piece of aluminum tubing.

A mascara wand with a spiral brush is easiest to use and the handle section can be built up or extended in the same way as can a lipstick tube. To be applied properly, however, the extension which holds the mascara should be bent at a right angle. Two loops of fabric taped to the top and bottom of a lipstick tube or a mascara wand make it easier to open.

Many kinds of cosmetics, including eyeshadow, lipstick and blushers are now available in pencil or wand form. These are most easily built up or extended for ease of handling.

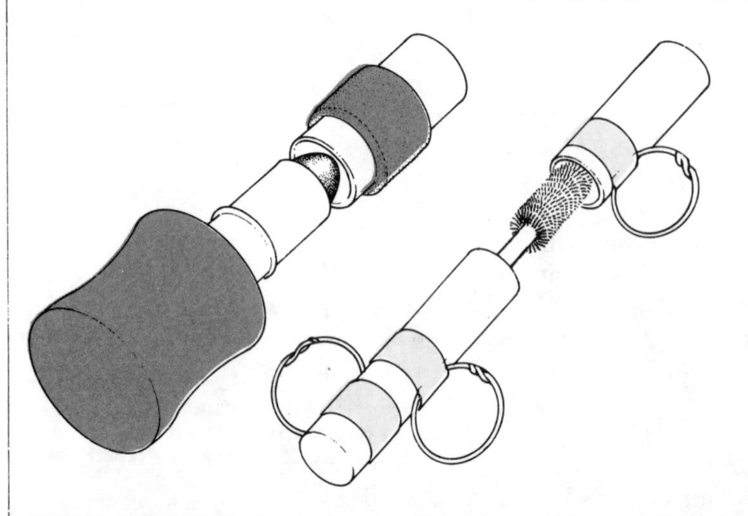

A rounded block of plastic foam can be used to increase the diameter of a lipstick tube. An adhesive-backed silicone strip around the top makes it easier to pull off. Loops of wire taped to the top and bottom of a mascara wand facilitate opening and holding it.

Menstruation

For most women, the menstrual cycle is unaffected by disability. One exception is spinal cord injury which often causes a cessation of periods for several months after the injury.

If grasp is weak or reach limited it can be difficult to handle sanitary pads with their accompanying belt, pins or hooks or to deal with tampons. Pads which tuck into special sani-pants are easiest for some women to change. Others find that the pads which have an adhesive strip on one side, which sticks onto close-fitting underpants, are best. The tab covering the adhesive area is quite easily peeled off.

Today menstruation can be regulated or, if necessary, suppressed. A woman whose periods are heavy or painful or who suffers from premenstrual tension or depression should seek help from her doctor.

Incontinence

Incontinence—loss of bladder or bowel control—is a very common, but not insoluble, problem. The cause can be explained by a doctor and dealt with in a variety of ways. When people who have this condition understand their own type of incontinence there are often ways in which they can help themselves to maintain control or to regain it.

Sometimes some degree of incontinence has to be accepted. In such cases it can be managed by the use of the right equipment. Many younger people who are incontinent as a result of spinal injury, for example, manage this condition so well that it is not apparent. There are various means of protection—collection devices and different forms of pads and pants—which can help to maintain comfort and make it possible to lead a normal life. For such protective equipment to be effective, however, the special physical and social requirements of the individual must be considered. A doctor or therapist should be consulted.

Clothing

Besides being a necessity, the clothes you wear can enhance physical attributes and conceal flaws, can contribute to a sense of self-assurance and can provide a means of self-expression. Modern clothing is designed for comfort and convenience and today's fashions emphasize informality and encourage individual ingenuity. This is, obviously, of great advantage to women and men with disabilities.

When you shop you will, of course, look for clothes which are versatile and are flattering to your skin tone and hair coloring. There are, however, certain additional considerations that should govern your selections.

Choose well-constructed clothing that will withstand extra strain. Seams should be smooth and well finished. There should be adequate seam allowance and double stitching or reinforcements at underarm seams and crotch. Buttonholes should be tightly stitched.

Select garments that are easy to fasten, with openings and sleeves that are simple to manage. Garments which open in front are easiest to get into and out of. A front opening that is three-quarters the length of the garment gives freedom of movement and eliminates the need to reach over the head. Wraparound styles make dressing and undressing easier.

Velcro fasteners, made of tiny polyester hooks and nylon loops which grip tightly and peel apart easily, are ideal. Conventional closures can be changed to Velcro fasteners without changing the appearance of the garment. Velcro can even be hidden under a button closure, with the buttons reattached over the sewn-up buttonholes. There is just one caution: Velcro must be fastened after a garment is removed and during laundering, for it can snag on other fabrics and become fluffed and useless.

Choose garments that are comfortable when you move. Analyze the movements that are involved in your disability. The clothes you wear should not restrict these movements but should move with you. They should never fit so tightly that they bind nor so loosely that they interfere with mobility. Garments that are simply styled and have a minimum of seams are likely to be most comfortable.

Clothing safety is determined by the fabric, the style and the fit. To avoid hazardous situations select clothing made of fabrics with flame-retardant finishes. Check the garment labels for this information. Avoid excess fullness in sleeves, trouser legs and skirts which can catch on wheels or protruding objects, can trip you up and can also be a fire hazard. Avoid fabrics with a loop pile that can catch on rough surfaces.

Select fabrics with care. Choose materials that are nonirritating, lightweight, so as not to increase fatigue, absorbent, resilient enough to respond easily to movement and washable for minimum care.

Sturdy fabrics like denim and gaberdine will take hard wear and won't stretch out of shape. Wrinkle-free materials, such as soft knits or those with a permanent press finish are best since they require a minimum of care and usually look neat. Smooth fabrics make it easier to use a transfer board. Stretch and knit fabrics allow greater freedom of movement.

Although natural fibers have pleasing virtues—cotton is cool and absorbent, wool resilient and insulating and silk elegant and delightful to the skin—they require special care unless they are mixed with synthetic fibers. The new fabrics and finishes greatly decrease care. Drip-dry, crease-resistant, stain-repellent materials are readily available as ready-to-wear garments and yard goods.

Different disabilities and the use of various aids and appliances present concomitant clothing and dressing problems. These can often be solved, or substantially minimized, by selecting suitable garments or by adapting or making adjustments to your existing wardrobe.

The use of crutches, for example, creates friction on fabric. This can be counteracted, so that clothing lasts longer, by adding fabric patches to the underside to reinforce the areas of strain, by lining the garment or by stitching seam tape to the underarm seams. Sometimes, too, the fabric will cause skin irritation from rubbing. The fabric over the sensitive area can be reinforced with a soft, absorbent fabric, such as velour or soft cotton flannel, next to the skin.

It is advisable to choose garments made of knit or stretch fabric and to avoid garments which fit tightly at the waistline or under the arms. Sleeves should, however, be cut high under the arms to avoid distorting the garment and to prevent tearing the fabric.

Walking with crutches makes it difficult to keep a shirt or blouse tucked in. Longer shirttails will help, as will special banding with rubber strips sewn to the inside of the waistband. Women who use crutches find that body shirts are a solution, as are overblouses and sweaters which automatically eliminate the need to tuck in.

Long leg braces make it difficult to put trousers on and to take them off. When buying new trousers choose those with legs loose enough to pull on easily over the braces. A woven fabric will slide over the braces more easily than a knit material. It is often possible to make tighter trouser legs usable by having Velcro or long zippers sewn into the outer or inner leg seams.

By rubbing against the fabric, leg braces also make trousers wear out quickly. Leather guards over the joints and buckles of braces can eliminate some wear and tear, but it is advisable to select trousers that are lined or to reinforce them with an extra layer of fabric at the points of abrasion.

Comfort and neatness when sitting in a wheelchair can be achieved by choosing short jackets or those with side slits or by shortening longer jackets so that the front fits comfortably around the legs and the back is level with the chair seat. Car coats, which are designed for sitting comfort, capes and ponchos are easier to put on and take off than long coats.

Knitted fabrics and looser styles which move with the body, also make for greater comfort. Trousers are most comfortable when they are cut higher at the back and lower at the front. They should not be tight in the crotch or at the knees. The legs of trousers and the hems of skirts should be an inch longer than usual since they ride up a bit.

Sleeves that are long and loose or floppy at the cuff can be hazardous when propelling a wheelchair.

Many women who are wheelchaired find that although trousers are more convenient, skirts or dresses with moderate fullness provide greater comfort. Culottes combine the comfort of a skirt with the convenience of trousers.

Limited elbow or shoulder motion makes it difficult to put clothes on and to take them off. Garments with front openings are easiest to get on and off and action pleats or gussets and raglan or kimono sleeves permit greater maneuverability.

Pockets are extremely practical as well as comfortable. Some people who have the use of only one hand never buy an item of clothing that does not have pockets. Large horizontal or diagonal pockets are easiest to get into when sitting down and are least likely to spill their contents.

Fastening clothing is the greatest problem when only one hand is used or both hands are weak. Wherever possible Velcro fasteners, which require little finger and hand coordination, should be substituted for snaps, hooks and buttons. It is, of course, advisable to select garments which open in front and to use large metal hooks, or Velcro, rather than small hooks and eyes for skirt and trouser closures.

If buttons must be used, medium-sized buttons with rims and, above all, a shank, are most manageable. If the button itself does not have a shank any button can be stitched on with a thread shank. Neck buttons, usually the trickiest to handle, can be fitted with elastic collar extenders which give a little leeway. Buttons sewn on with elastic thread are also easier to deal with. If cuff buttons are sewn on with elastic thread the hand can slip through the already buttoned cuff.

Matching and identifying colors are the greatest dressing problems for people who are visually impaired. Knots of thread stitched to the insides of garments can be used to indicate color. One knot could, for example, mean blue, two knots red and three knots white. Braille clothing tags are available through organizations for the blind. It is a good idea to buy clothing with identifiable features—a blue shirt with one button at the sleeve, for example, and a white shirt with two cuff buttons—and to buy and then store matching outfits together.

For people who are incontinent the choice of clothing is particularly important because it can make the condition more manageable. For women, a full skirt, which can be pulled up quickly and easily, or a wraparound skirt, worn with the opening at the back, are most easily managed.

For men, specially designed trousers with a drop front are available. If an appliance is worn, a zipper in the inside seam of the trouser leg permits easy emptying and changing of the bag.

Women are fortunate in having more fashion leeway today than ever before and many styles have become perennial and are suitable for women of all ages. Smocks, caftans and loose overblouses and dresses, for example, have long been in fashion, are flattering, present no fitting problems, are comfortable and conceal appliances and physical flaws. Many women who are not pregnant find that well-styled maternity clothes are suitable, comfortable and attractive.

Wraparound or front-fastened skirts, blouses and loose overdresses, front-fastened dresses and slacks with elasticized waistbands, are among the obvious choices for comfort and ease of dressing. Tabards that fasten at the waist or at the waist and the shoulder add warmth without weight and are easy to put on. Long sleeveless jerkins have similar advantages. Ponchos and capes are often preferable to conventional coats; they conceal appliances and allow freedom of movement.

Undergarments can present many problems for women with various disabilities. Fastening a brassiere in the back requires great agility and may even be impossible. Bras which fasten in the front are available in many styles and often permit greater independence in dressing. A back-fastening bra can be converted by removing the back hooks and eyes, stitching the opening together and then cutting the center front seam and inserting large hooks and eyes or Velcro, with an underfacing.

Sometimes a bra with stretch straps provides a solution. The bra can be put on backward, fastened in front at the waist, then turned around, the arms slipped in and the straps pulled up into place. Stretch straps are also more comfortable for women who are wheelchaired or use crutches, because they allow greater freedom of movement. Some women find that a completely flexible stretch bra without any fastenings can be put on by pulling it over the head or up from the feet. To prevent straps slipping down the arms, a piece of elastic can be stitched to both straps across the back of a front-opening bra. Foam rubber shoulder pads which slip under the straps on each side distribute pressure and increase comfort.

Pulling a slip over the head can be difficult. Women who are wheelchaired or unable to lift their hips up to slip

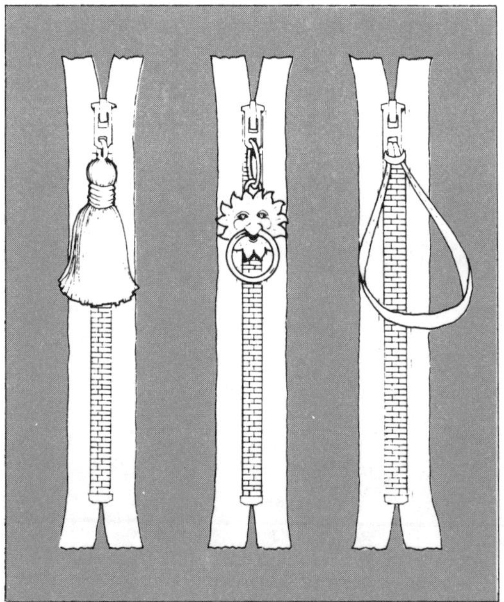

Adding a zipper pull often makes it much easier to open and close a zipper. Zipper pulls can be purchased in sewing departments or can be made from items found around the house.

garments over the buttocks often prefer a camisole top with an elastic waistband. A zipper or Velcro may be added for a front closure. A panty half slip, pulled up from the feet, stays in place and does not tend to ride up.

A full-length slip can be cut down the center front and a fine zipper sewn in. If the zipper extends to the hipline the slip becomes a step-in garment.

A half slip can be pulled on over the head without the complications of straps or pulled up from the feet with a reacher. The elasticized waist should be large enough to slip over the hips easily. Half slips usually have more fullness through the thighs than full-length slips and are often preferred by those who use crutches or are wheelchaired.

Underpants should be large enough to slip on easily over the hips. Band-leg styles of mid-thigh length in such slippery materials as nylon or rayon make sliding transfers easier. Cotton knit briefs are more absorbent, however, and don't hike up. Underpants with seamless seats are best for prolonged sitting.

Women have more difficulty with girdles than with other undergarments. An extra zipper can be inserted into a girdle with a zipper. The second one can open at the bottom so that the garment is easily slipped into. Some models have large hook openings or Velcro closures. A girdle that opens flat can be put on while lying on the bed.

Dressing

Strength, balance, agility and reach are required for dressing and undressing. From long habit an able-bodied person goes through the motions of dressing mechanically. A person who is disabled, however, is aware of every movement required and this awareness can help to bypass those movements which are difficult or impossible.

Many aids and techniques have been devised to accommodate limitations of movement imposed by various disabilities and a therapist should be consulted about which of these would best meet individual needs. Above all, however, patience and practice are necessary. While practice may not make perfect, it does make for greater proficiency.

It is generally easier to undress than to dress. A person who is newly disabled should, therefore, begin by trying to get undressed independently.

Dressing is easiest if it is planned. Have all the garments close to hand in the order in which they are to be put on. Some people can manage their underclothes and lower garments more easily when they are lying down. Others prefer to dress while sitting on the bed or on a chair and then half stand or lean against a sturdy piece of furniture when they are putting on or taking off lower garments.

When arm, elbow or shoulder move-

Dressing Aids

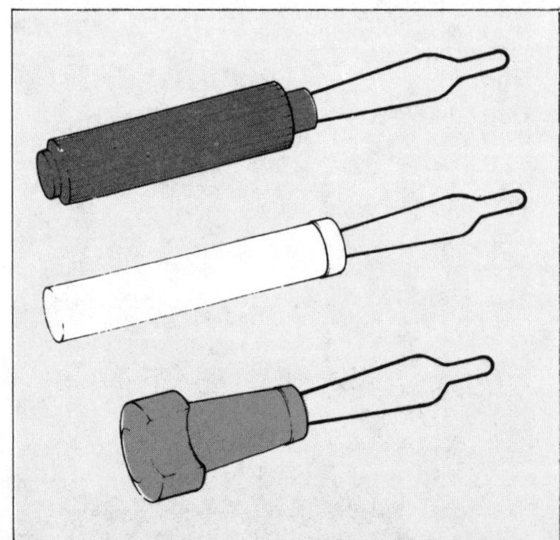

Self-help equipment firms carry a wide range of aids to make dressing easier for people with various disabilities. A long dressing stick, for example, has a large curved pusher to help get clothes off and small and large hooks for pulling clothes on. A short zipper pull with a built-up handle is helpful when it is difficult to hold onto a zipper tab. A buttonhook can be useful for dealing with small buttons. Buttonhooks are available with different types of handles.

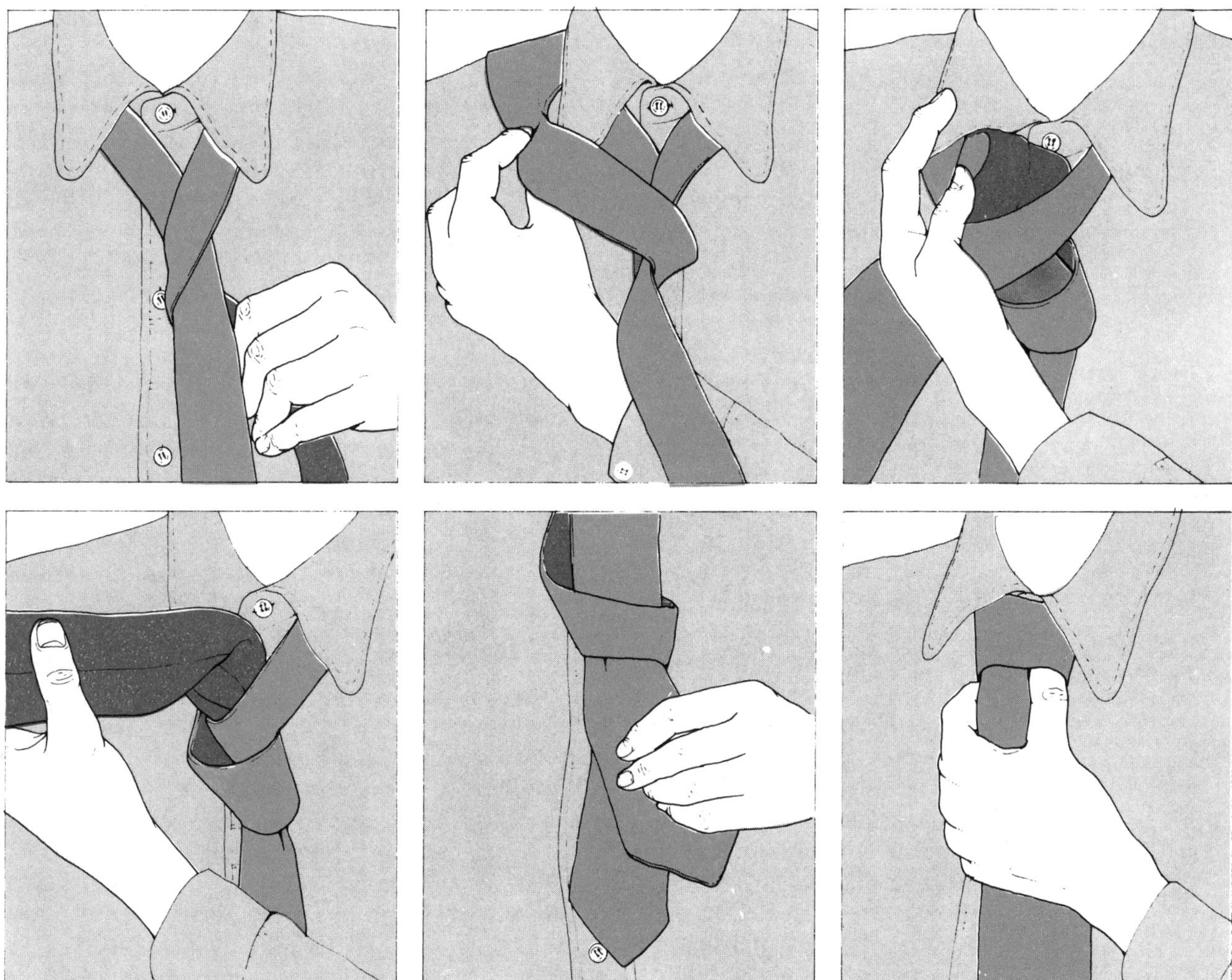

ment is limited, a dressing stick can help to pull an open garment over the shoulders. Dressing sticks are available from self-help equipment firms or one can easily be made from a wooden hanger from which the center hook has been removed. One end may be padded or tipped with a rubber thimble so that the clothes cling to it. A small cup hook can be screwed into the other end for managing zippers or a smooth notch can be cut into the wood for pulling up shoulder straps.

A rubber-tipped cane or stick is useful for hooking clothes upward or for pushing off shoes, socks or garments from below the hips. An elastic or tape loop to go over the palm can be tacked to the top of the stick or it can be built up if grasp is weak.

To facilitate putting on underpants and trousers, when reach is limited or bending difficult, tape loops can be sewn inside the waistband, just in front of the side seams. Two dowel sticks with cup hooks can be used to pull the garment over the feet and up.

Keeping a shirtsleeve down while putting on an outer garment is easier if a tape loop is made to go over the thumb and attached to a clothespin or a stationer's clip, which is then fastened onto the cuff. When the upper garment is in place the taut inner cuff can be released. Alternatively, tape loops can be sewn inside shirt or blouse cuffs. The loop can go over the thumb when it is needed and tucked back out of sight afterward.

Complicated hand movements are involved in tying the knot of a tie. A tie can be left knotted, loosened, so that it will go over the head, and then tightened again. Pre-knotted ties which clip on are available.

To knot a tie with one hand, first secure the tie under the shirt collar with one end hanging longer than the other. Cross the longer end over the other once, then again. Take the upper end and tuck it under and then bring it through the large loop. Insert the end down through the newly formed knot. Pull down firmly on the end to tighten the knot. Raise the knot by holding the back end with the last three fingers and slowly move the knot upward with thumb and forefinger. Then hold both ends firmly and use the thumb to push the knot into place.

Hosiery and Footwear

Putting on stockings or socks and shoes requires agility and involves a number of movements. There are, however, various aids and techniques which make this part of dressing easier.

To put on hosiery, the top of the stocking or sock must be held open to get the foot in and it must then be pulled past the heel and up the leg. A stocking gutter can be helpful since it makes it possible to put on stockings or socks without bending. The stocking is gathered over the stiff gutter, which is about ten inches (26 cm) long. The top of the stocking is attached to garter hooks on tapes. The unit is dropped to the floor, the foot is slipped in and the hose pulled up by the tapes. A variation has two lengths of tape attached to the corners of the gutter at the wider end and two rounded notches cut into the sides at the same end. The stocking is pulled over the gutter so that most of it is gathered into the notches. This type is best for those who have difficulty manipulating garters. Stocking gutters are available from self-help equipment firms or can be made at home from several sheets of cardboard or X-ray film covered with cloth.

Longer, looser-fitting socks are often easier to manage than short stretch socks. Tubular socks, which don't have a shaped heel, are best when it is difficult to put the heel into position. A sock with tape loops sewn on the top can be pulled on by using two wooden dowels with fitted cup hooks. The toes are worked into the sock and the hooks then pull it up.

When bending from the hips is difficult, socks and shoes can be put on while sitting in a chair, the knee bent back and the foot resting on the side rung or on a footstool at the side of the chair.

Some women find that the best way to put on stockings is to use garter tapes—garter hooks sewn to the end of the long tapes. The garters are hooked to the top of the stocking, then the stocking is rolled up and dropped to the floor while the tapes are held. The toes are worked in and the tapes are slowly pulled up.

A foam pad on the floor, used with garter tapes or a stocking gutter, provides a friction surface to help to get the stocking all the way on the foot. The foot is simply rubbed along the pad to force the stocking gently up.

Once stockings are on, however, a

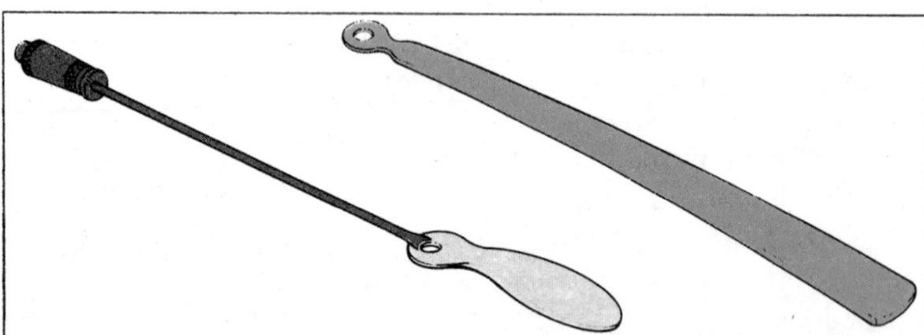

A long shoehorn makes it possible to get shoes on without bending. The upper one is two feet (60 cm) long, the other is eighteen inches (45 cm) long.

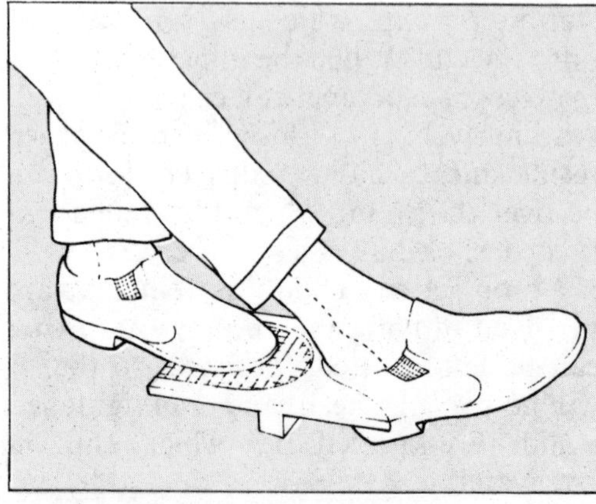

The simple device right eliminates the need to bend to remove shoes. Just insert the heel of one shoe into the notch while holding the unit down with the other foot.

An electric shoe-shiner with a hand hold makes it possible to polish shoes using only one hand. Some units have a variety of attachments so that they can be used for other shining jobs.

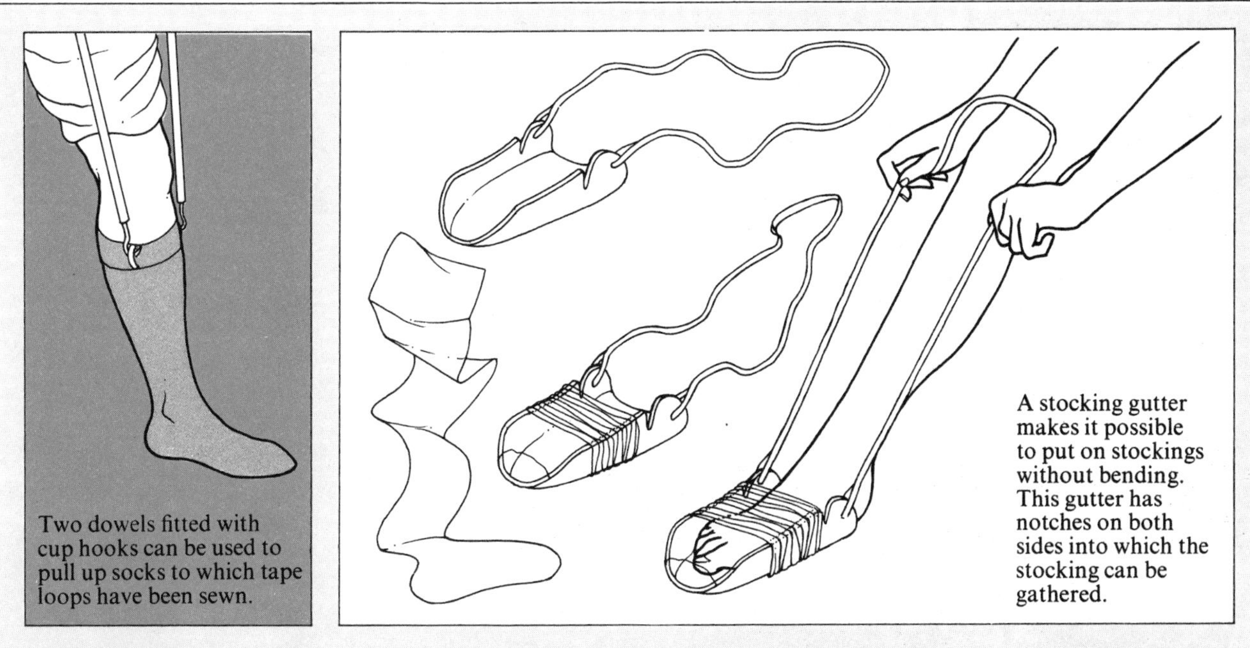

Two dowels fitted with cup hooks can be used to pull up socks to which tape loops have been sewn.

A stocking gutter makes it possible to put on stockings without bending. This gutter has notches on both sides into which the stocking can be gathered.

woman has the problem of keeping them up. (Self-supporting stockings are available, but it is important that they are not so tight that they restrict circulation.) If a simple garment is needed only to hold up stockings a garter belt is a great convenience. A wraparound garter belt that closes with Velcro is easy to put on.

If a garment with more support is required, one which has detachable garters is often desirable since garters are most easily managed if they are attached to the stockings before they are put on. They can then be fastened to the girdle with detachable or clip-on hooks. Another method is to sew buttons to the girdle and fasten to them lengths of elastic which have buttonholes at the free ends. The elastic can then be put through the tops of the garters and buttoned to the girdle.

Panty hose, or tights, do away with the problem of garters. Some women find it easiest to put them on while lying on the bed. Those without a heel are easiest to manage.

Shoes should be kept in good repair. Worn-down heels can affect stability by altering the angle of weight-bearing. Composition soles are hard-wearing and nonslip—an advantage for someone who is wheelchaired since they keep the feet from slipping off the footplates. For someone with a shuffling gait, however, such soles can make walking more difficult, particularly on carpet.

When bending makes reaching the feet impossible, a long-handled shoehorn is invaluable. Some models have a spring at the point where the handle and the horn join, which is helpful if ankles are stiff.

Shoes which give fullest support to the feet are frequently recommended and this usually means that some kind of fastening is involved. When shoes must be specially made by an orthopedic shoemaker, ease of fastening can be taken into consideration.

Elastic shoelaces do not give quite as much support as conventional laces, but they may be laced into a shoe and left at a comfortable tension. A long-handled shoehorn can then be used to get the shoe on. The tongue of the shoe should be stitched on one side so that it stays in place when the foot is pushed in. Easy-to-use shoelace fasteners are available from self-help equipment firms for one-handed use. Laces can be eliminated by having a shoe repair man insert a zipper. The zipper can be opened and closed with a hook on a long handle. It is also possible to have buckle straps changed to Velcro, which can be opened and closed with a long-handled shoehorn.

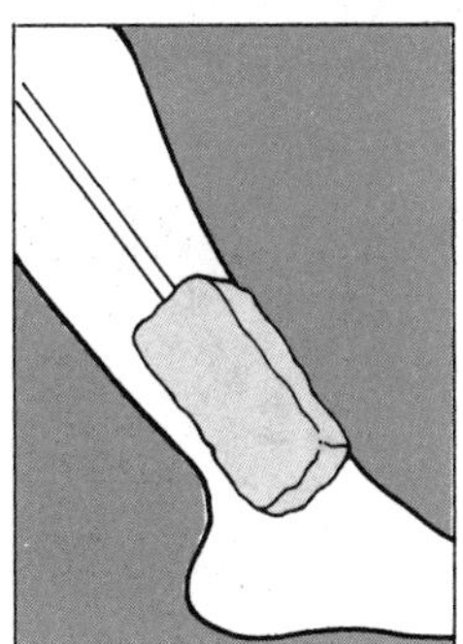

A plastic sponge on a long handle can be used to ease a stocking up. It won't damage the hose or hurt sensitive areas of the leg.

Your Sexuality

In recent years attitudes toward sex have been changing. The sexuality of the individual and his or her needs are now more openly acknowledged and are becoming better understood. Medical advances give people greater opportunity to choose whether or when to have children. Sexual expression has come to be accepted as a valuable and important right of all people, regardless of their intention to have children. Nevertheless, this "sexual revolution" has not fully touched people with physical disabilities who have been persuaded that they are not sexual people.

Sexuality is not earned through work or good deeds, nor is it lost as the result of an injury or illness. Every person regardless of sex, age or disability, is a sexual being. Unfortunately, not only the general public, but also many professional people who work with the handicapped and, certainly, the families of the disabled, frequently ignore or deny the sexual needs of people with disabilities. Consequently, many disabled people continue, without questioning, to attribute asexual natures to themselves. This is another of the vicious circles in which the disabled can get so caught. For if people don't regard themselves as sexual beings others won't either.

Every individual, disabled or able-bodied, has the right to be informed about all aspects of sex, the right to sexual expression and the right to enter into an intimate relationship.

There is evidence that people with physical disabilities know less about sex—and about their own options—than the able-bodied do. Because of problems in techniques of communication the disparity is greatest for people who are blind and deaf.

Those disabled from birth or in childhood are often sheltered by parents and treated as if there were no reason for them even to know about sex. As adults they have to rise above their fears and anxieties before they can even begin to accept their own sexuality and needs. Those who become disabled later in life often discover that sexuality is a neglected aspect of rehabilitation and that they must work out their own reprogramming of their sex lives with an awareness of their disabilities.

Recent efforts to recognize the sexuality of the disabled have been primarily directed toward men with spinal injuries. The sexuality of the disabled woman has been largely ignored, beyond acknowledgement of fertility and a merely passive sexual participation.

Although the disabled have the right to be informed, it's the responsibility of the individual to take advantage of sources of information and counseling to the extent they are available.

Every individual has the right to sexual expression and there is hardly anyone who is too disabled to have some pleasure from his or her sexuality—with a partner if possible, alone if necessary. Sexual expression is versatile and need not be dependent on either an erect penis or a well-lubricated vagina. Each person must discover the kind of sexual expression that works for him or her and the best way to achieve it.

For many people a fulfilling intimate relationship with another human being can be the difference between a lonely, solitary existence and a rich, sharing, rewarding life. Of course, there's always the risk of being hurt when one person gets involved with another. But many relationships provide enough pleasure to offset the pain of their eventual demise.

Marriage obviously does not have to be the aim of every intimate relationship. As is true of everybody, not all disabled people want to marry. For couples who do not feel that they can cope with the demands of married life, a long-term alliance can give them years of pleasure and emotional fulfillment. Most important, a loving and enriching relationship depends on more than sexual capacities.

People's visible disabilities and their own attitudes toward their sexuality can make it very easy indeed for others to consider them sexless, neither thinking nor caring about sex. Personal grooming and hygiene, as well as behavior and attitudes, reflect our attitudes about ourselves. If we consider ourselves sexual beings this is communicated to others.

Your sexuality is your responsibility. What you do with it is up to you.

Sex Counseling

A study recently done in England indicated that most people with physical disabilities have sexual problems at some time—many at all times—and most of these problems are related, directly or indirectly, to the disability itself. In many of these cases, however, it was found that the problems could be solved through sensitive advice and counseling. It is consoling to know that sexual problems are by no means confined to the disabled. According to Masters and Johnson, 50 percent of all married couples have one or another form of sexual dysfunction.

It's not easy to get appropriate sex counseling. Doctors, who might be thought to be the best people from whom to seek advice, often have the same inhibitions about sex as their patients, and many have no knowledge of the sexual aspects of disability. They may either avoid the subject or defensively couch their statements in terms so clinical that they are well beyond the patient's comprehension.

The national organizations for various disabling conditions are often able to put people in touch with sex counselors in their areas who specialize in problems relating to disablement. In the United States only two cities in the country have programs specifically related to disabled sexuality. In San Francisco there is the Human Sexuality Program at the University of California Medical Center, which offers sex counseling to disabled people as part of its comprehensive program. In Minneapolis, at the University of Minnesota Medical School, there is the Physical Disability Program in Human Sexuality run by Dr. Ted Cole.

In the United Kingdom, Sexual Problems of the Disabled (SPOD), a committee established toward the end of 1973 under the auspices of the National Fund for Research into Crippling Diseases, does not directly provide ongoing advice or counseling, but does refer people to counselors in their own localities.

A good place to get counseling, however, is usually from other disabled people or couples who have the same kind of problems and can talk from their own experience and as a result of their own insights. A group of disabled people, once they overcome their initial and natural embarrassment, can often be of the greatest help to each other.

Sexual Satisfaction

For far too long many people with physical disabilities have been deceived into believing that the only satisfaction from sex they can hope to achieve is the pleasure they receive from satisfying their partners. This is nonsense. It's just one of the many myths which society has perpetuated and disabled people are expected to accept.

Nobody could maintain this noble attitude for any length of time. It would be natural to begin soon to feel left out, not want to have sex very often and then, finally, to stop having sex completely.

Certainly it's important to give pleasure to your partner and to want to satisfy him or her. But it's equally important for you to expect and to receive pleasure. A good sexual relationship isn't possible unless there's a balance of giving and receiving between the two people involved. In a one-sided sexual relationship guilt and resentment are inevitable and such negative feelings can make both partners miserable and erode their total relationship.

It's a myth, too, that the only right or satisfactory means of sexual expression is coitus, or sexual intercourse. There are many ways to give and to receive sexual pleasure and satisfaction is possible for anyone who wishes to seek it.

Orgasm

An orgasm is as unique as the individual experiencing it. An orgasm can be achieved through various kinds of stimulation including oral-genital stimulation, masturbation and even fantasy, in addition to coitus, or intercourse. When you have an orgasm you know it, yet no two people describe an orgasm the same way.

Many disabled men and women can achieve a physical orgasm. Others, depending on the disabling condition or the extent and location of their injury, do not have the physical sensation of orgasm but, because the brain can work independently of the genitals in the generation of erotic experience, they do have feelings of sexual fulfillment.

Those who became disabled as adults may remember the sensations they had and can mentally recreate them. Even people who never experienced an orgasm are often able to fantasize one which is both intense and enjoyable. By making love with the lights on, using mirrors to enable them to see their partners' reactions, talking about what they are doing and feeling and then amplifying and integrating all the sensations in their minds, many people are able to achieve a high level of fulfillment.

Other people, including many who are able-bodied, find close personal warmth and body contact without orgasm deeply and fully satisfying. Although the aim of sexual expression may be orgasms for both partners, it's clearly not necessary to have an orgasm to achieve intense sexual satisfaction.

Communication

The essence of all relationships and a necessary ingredient in any mutually gratifying sexual relationship, communication is especially important when one partner is disabled. Sex is usually most pleasurable when it's part of a relationship in which thoughts, feelings and concerns can be openly discussed without embarrassment.

Nobody can know or accurately guess what feels good to someone else, which areas of his or her body are most sensitive, which sensations are most exciting. Your partner isn't a mind reader and must be told what you like, where you have heightened sensitivity and where you lack feeling—just as you must be told what gives your partner pleasure. Both partners share sexual responsibility and should reject old stereotypes of the passive woman and the aggressive man.

If you are embarking on a new relationship it's your responsibility to explain your physical condition to your partner and to tell him or her what you can do, or think you can do, sexually. Don't wait for your partner to initiate the discussion or assume that he or she knows all the

answers. Often someone is justifiably curious, but is afraid to offend by asking questions. It might even be a good idea to ask your partner what he or she wants to know about your limitations. You can alleviate a lot of anxiety for both of you by being open and honest. After all, a healthy sexual relationship is not really possible without trust and communication.

It's not easy to tell someone with whom you want to make love about an appliance, the possibility of a wet bed, muscle spasms, a bad scar on your body or about the sexual positions you can't achieve. But in the long run it's wise to avoid surprises. The chances are that your partner will not only appreciate your honesty, but will also be able to think of ways to solve some of the practical problems and make you feel more comfortable about those you have to live with.

On the other hand, you cannot be a Pollyanna. After you've told it all there is the possibility that your partner might decide that he or she can't confront the situation. As shattering as that might be, it would be better than being rejected later when you've made a greater emotional investment in the relationship. Being open about yourself and your capabilities at the beginning of a relationship avoids the later problems and tensions of unrealistic expectations and consequent disappointments.

Masturbation

A healthy and normal act for any man or woman at any age, masturbation can enable you to fulfill your own needs in a positive and pleasurable way. It feels good, provides release from sexual tension and, equally important, it's a way to explore your own body, to get to know and understand it.

Masturbation can involve parts of the body other than the genitals. Touching and stroking yourself can help you to learn what your body can feel and do. When you know what feels good and gives you pleasure it may help you to communicate your preferences to a partner. Creative mutual masturbation can also be part of lovemaking.

Masturbation used to be the subject of much moral and medical nonsense. Obviously, the way an individual chooses to express his or her sexuality is a very personal decision. But masturbation is a source of sexual pleasure and there is no reason to feel any guilt about it—nor can it do anybody any physical harm. It is a positive and sexually fulfilling act.

Aids to Sexual Pleasure

In the same way that various aids can make such diverse activities as driving, typing, eating, fishing, bathing and cooking easier, or even possible, for people with disabilities, so there are aids and devices which can be used to increase sexual pleasure. Most of these aids, which are readily available from sex stores and mail order companies, were designed for and are extensively used by able-bodied men and women. So there's no stigma attached to buying them or using them.

A vibrator can add a new dimension to sexual enjoyment. There are many types available. Those that fit on the hand can be used for facial or body massage. The battery-powered, penile-shaped vibrators are especially good for vaginal or clitoral stimulation. These are quite lightweight and if necessary can be built up to accommodate limited grasp.

When a man is not able to have an erection he can give his partner the sensation of penetration and penile-vaginal stimulation by using a penis stiffener or a dildo. A penis stiffener, which is usually made of a formed piece of hard rubber, fits over the penis and makes penetration possible. A dildo is an artificial penis made of plastic or rubber which can be strapped on above the penis or held in the hand.

Some couples find that a water bed, by increasing body motion, adds to the pleasures of lovemaking. Water beds have also proved to be excellent for the prevention of pressure sores. A water bed can rest on a sturdy bed frame, but it's extremely heavy so be sure the floor is strong enough to support the weight. A heating unit should accompany any water bed you buy.

Massage oils are available in a variety of flavors and fragrances; they can serve as lubricants and they enhance sensations of smell and taste. Like other aids they can heighten sexual excitement.

Preparations for Lovemaking

Spontaneous sex is not possible for everyone, nor does everyone consider it desirable. For some people a fair amount of preparation is necessary before lovemaking can begin. When joints are stiff, for example, it's often helpful to have a warm shower before making love. And while cleanliness is important for everyone's sexual enjoyment it's particularly so for those who wear catheters or devices to collect urine. (Neither urine collection devices nor catheters, incidentally, need stand in the way of physical intimacy. Depending on your attitude such a device can be a nuisance or no trouble at all.)

If you're not able to do much yourself to get ready for bed, your partner may want to help you. It's your responsibility to let him or her know what has to be done and how to do it. There is much in lovemaking, however, which depends on mental processes and it might understandably be difficult for a partner to feel romantic with someone whose catheter he or she has just changed. The important thing is that you and your partner know each other's feelings about such matters. Then you can decide together how or whether he or she should help you with your personal care.

If you both decide that it's best that your partner doesn't assist you, or he or she can't manage alone, an attendant or another third person can help you to wash and undress, attach any appliances and help you get into bed. This does, of course, intrude upon privacy and it's not exactly convenient to have a third person involved in your sex life. At the same time, the comfort of your attendant must also be considered. With planning and good, honest communication between you, your partner and your attendant, you should be able to work out a happy solution. Many other people have.

Sexual Expression

There are literally hundreds of ways to express sexual feeling and none of them is right or wrong. Any kind of sexual expression that is enjoyable and fulfilling is right, if it is acceptable to both partners.

It's wise to ignore the "marriage manual" formula which views some sexual activities as foreplay, some as after-play and only penile-vaginal penetration as the "real thing." Instead, sexual expression should be regarded as an individual experience without rules or score cards and with the only goal that of pleasure for both partners. Anything is acceptable for however long and in whatever sequence you and your partner prefer. Let things happen at whatever pace is good for both of you. The object is to enjoy yourselves and to get the greatest pleasure by making the most of what you have, and not bemoaning the functions you may lack.

Sexual sensation is possible in areas other than those which are generally regarded as "erogenous zones." There is no area of the body which is not, or cannot become, responsive to erotic stimulation.

It's important to know what your options are and to experiment with various kinds of sexual expression to discover what is most exciting and satisfying. But, again, the key to a good sexual relationship, for any couple, able-bodied or disabled, is communication. You and your partner must convey to each other what feels good and what is and is not pleasurable.

Arousal can begin well before actual sexual activity. Talking and touching while eating or drinking, kissing and caressing each other while watching television or listening to music can be sexually

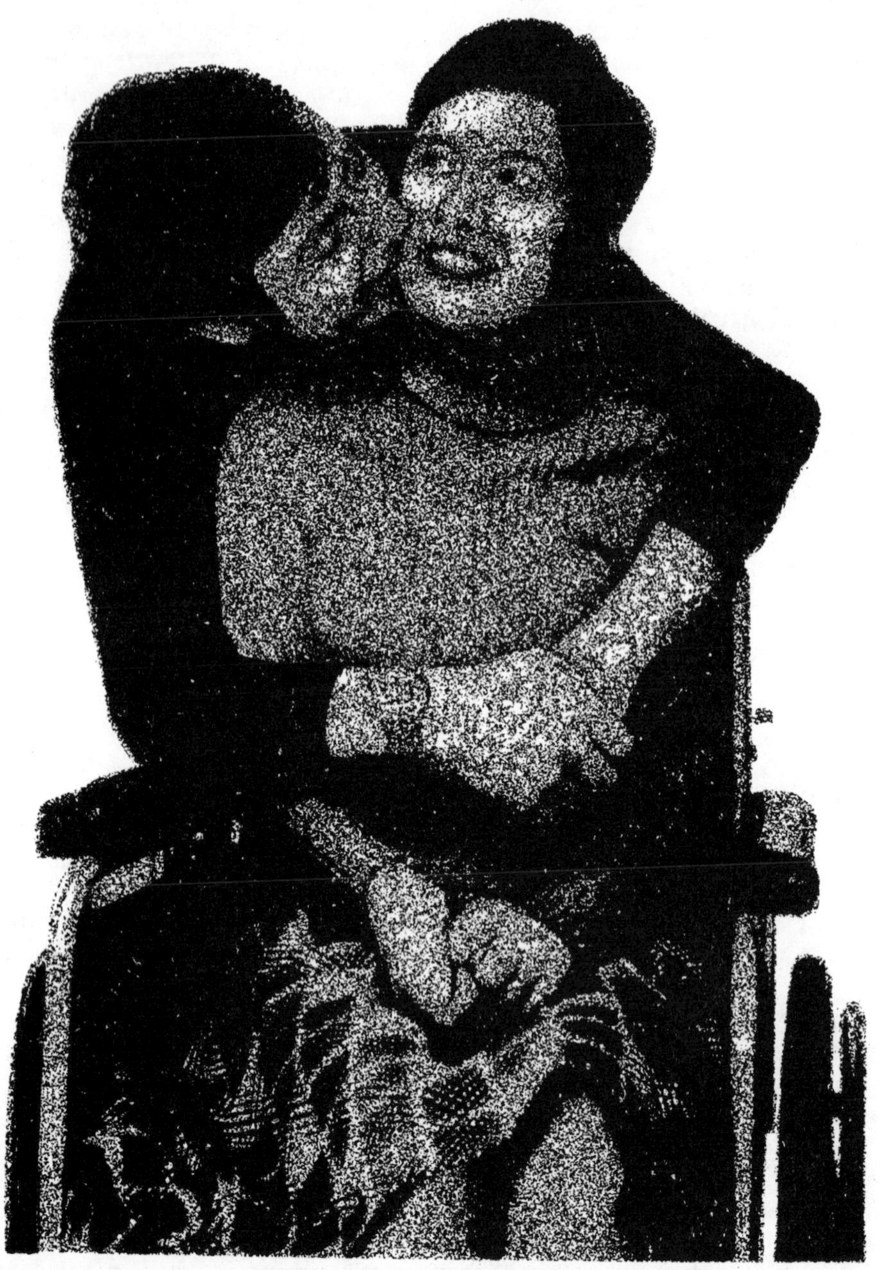

arousing for some people. Others find that they enjoy having their sexual imaginations awakened as a prelude to lovemaking by looking together at erotic pictures or reading erotica (some people might call it pornography, but don't let that influence you) or talking about their fantasies and what they are going to do when they get into bed.

Of course, when one or both partners is disabled it may not be quite so easy, or fast, to get into bed and ready for sexual activity, but many couples find that they can maintain sexual arousal by incorporating some of their preparations into their lovemaking.

Once you're in a position for sexual activity the choice of what to do and how to do it is up to you and your partner; there are no rules. Environmental stimulation can add dimension to lovemaking and heighten enjoyment and should not be overlooked. Some people enjoy total darkness and the scent of incense, for example, while others like to make love by candlelight or soft light and use mirrors so that they can watch each other's reactions.

Simple body contact, the sensation of skin on skin can give both partners great comfort and pleasure. Time spent holding and stroking each other can greatly enhance the feeling of intimacy and increase gratification. Giving a massage can be exciting for both. It can be done with your hands or with a vibrator. It's not necessary to have much manual dexterity if you know where to touch your partner to give him or her pleasure.

Some women can have an orgasm, or can be brought very close to it, by having their breasts stimulated by a partner's hand or mouth. Some men, too, have great sensitivity in their breasts and get intense pleasure when their nipples are licked or rubbed.

You can use any part of your body, including your mouth, to rub and stroke your partner's body and even to stimulate him or her to orgasm. A finger, thumb, wrist, elbow or knee can be used to stimulate the clitoris. The penis can be enveloped by a hand, an armpit, the breasts pressed together, or the buttocks.

Although sexual intercourse is neither the only nor necessarily the most gratifying sexual activity, it is the most common. Penile-vaginal penetration can be accomplished in many positions limited only by individual abilities and inclinations. Obviously, your disability will influence the positions you are able to use. Different positions also have different advantages. Some are better for achieving movement while others are more passive. Some can decrease any inconvenience caused by a urine collection device. You have to experiment to discover which positions are best for you.

A creative approach and time allowed for trial and error will enable you to find comfortable positions. Some couples find that the best way to begin is to find a prone position which is comfortable and then to adapt it for intercourse. Keep various-sized cushions handy. They can make some positions more comfortable or even possible.

Vaginal lubrication, which usually happens naturally during sexual arousal, can be affected by the time needed to become aroused, by a vaginal infection, the Pill or a disabling condition. Sometimes extra lubrication will help to make penetration easier and should always be used when a catheter is left in place. The lubrication used should be water soluble; petroleum jelly, which does not dissolve completely, should never be used.

Even if genital feeling is lacking the anus may remain sensitive and therefore becomes more important in sexual arousal. Men and women often find anal stimulation exciting and some women enjoy the sensation of anal touching and probing during vaginal intercourse.

Anal intercourse is another option. The anus, however, is not as elastic as the vagina and gentleness, gradual entry and extra lubrication are necessary. To prevent the transfer of bacteria from the anus to the vagina, the finger or penis should be washed before coming into contact with the vaginal area.

The mouth is as much a sexual organ as the genitals and can excite and give great pleasure. Some people find that their lips and tongues are more sensitive to touch and temperature than any other parts of their bodies. Certainly the sensations received from the smell, taste and texture of your partner's skin can heighten your pleasure. The tongue or the mouth on a sensitive area such as the ear, neck, wrist or breast can be most exciting.

Some people feel timid about oral-genital stimulation. Fellatio, when the woman uses her mouth and tongue to stimulate the man's penis and surrounding area, and cunnilingus, when the man stimulates the woman's vulva and clitoris with his mouth and tongue, are positive sexual options.

Making love is for every couple, whether able-bodied or disabled, a very private part of their relationship and one that develops and changes to suit their personal choices and needs. Bookstores and libraries are full of books that detail and illustrate an infinite variety of ways to achieve sexual gratification; no practice which is acceptable to both partners should be overlooked.

A loving, determined and resourceful couple, regardless of the disability of one or both partners, can find ways to fulfill their sexual needs and to give them both maximum pleasure.

Homosexuality

Like so many other areas of sexuality rarely discussed openly in the past, homosexuality has now become an acknowledged sexual option. It has been established that one in twenty of the adult population are so inclined and this must obviously include many people with disabilities.

A homosexual relationship can be unrewarding and, perhaps, damaging if one or both partners enter it because they believe heterosexual relationships are unattainable. When there are genuine loving and caring feelings, however, between two men or two women, a happy, satisfying and lasting intimate relationship is as possible as it is for a heterosexual couple.

Many disabled people are involved in the campaign for homosexual equality. Gay Care is a national organization in the United Kingdom which does supportive counseling and helps disabled homosexuals of both sexes to establish social contacts. Gemma is a British group, for disabled lesbians, based in London. In the United States the National Gay Task Force, headquartered in New York, is a national clearinghouse for the gay movement and will give information to disabled homosexuals about local groups which might be of interest to them.

Contraception

Most disabling conditions do not affect a woman's ability to conceive and, according to a recent study, 80 percent of women who use no contraceptive and have sexual intercourse regularly will become pregnant within twelve months. Women with physical disabilities, like all women, must make informed decisions about the contraceptive method best suited to their health needs, their sexual life-style, the limitations imposed by their disabilities and their need for protection from unwanted pregnancies.

Unfortunately, since many doctors make the incorrect assumption that disabled women and men do not, or should not, have any sex life, they often overlook the question of birth control. And some disabled women, who are too timid or embarrassed to initiate the discussion, never receive proper information about contraceptive methods and devices. Doctors, too, are not always aware that certain methods of birth control are incompatible, and sometimes actually dangerous, for some disabled women. A doctor who is uncomfortable discussing a woman's disability may never ask the right questions to determine the best method of contraception for her.

While science is still far from developing the perfect contraceptive there are still several choices available to most women. You and your partner should carefully explore the options which are open to you.

Natural family planning, which is popularly known as the rhythm method, involves abstention from sexual intercourse during the woman's fertile period, the days each month when she ovulates. Three approaches are used to predict ovulation. With the calendar method, prediction of ovulation is based on a year's record of menstrual cycles. The basal body temperature method predicts ovulation based on daily changes in the basal body temperature. Ovulation can also be predicted by observations of changes in cervical mucus.

Although natural family planning involves no medication and there are no health risks, there is a great risk of pregnancy. Even when the method is used correctly and consistently it is only 87 percent effective. An accident, emotional distress or even moving into a new home or starting a new job can change patterns of ovulation and increase the chances of pregnancy. A woman with limited use of her hands might also find the necessary record-keeping, graphing and temperature-taking difficult.

The combination contraceptive method of spermicide foam and condom is 99 percent effective if it is used correctly. The woman uses a spermicide foam, which must be inserted into the vagina immediately before intercourse, and the man uses a condom, or rubber.

This method has several advantages. Both foam and condoms are readily available without prescription. The foam provides vaginal lubrication when it is insufficient or lacking. Condoms are also protection against venereal disease. Special condoms are available for men who are allergic to latex.

To be effective, the condom and the foam must both be used and must be used right before intercourse. While some couples incorporate the insertion of the foam and the putting on of the condom into their lovemaking, others find that it reduces the spontaneity of sex. Some couples find foam messy, others feel that condoms interfere with male or female sensation and the unpleasant taste of the foam can interfere with oral sex.

Manual dexterity is required to insert the foam as well as to put on the condom. This method is not suitable for the woman who uses a catheter since the condom might tear and leak as the result of rubbing against it.

The diaphragm was a widely used contraceptive device before the advent of oral contraceptives. Now that more is known about the side effects of these, the diaphragm is gaining popularity once again.

A diaphragm is a rubber dome with a spring edge which covers the cervix and is used in conjunction with a spermicidal cream or jelly. Since the size of the cervix varies from one woman to another, a diaphragm must be fitted by a doctor or other professional.

Before intercourse, the spermicidal jelly or cream, which comes in a tube, is squeezed into the dome and around the edge and the diaphragm is then inserted into the vagina and in place over the cervix. It can be inserted ahead of time so that it does not interfere with lovemaking, but it must be left in place for six to eight hours following intercourse. If it is used correctly and consistently, checked regularly for holes and replaced every six to nine months, the diaphragm is 97 percent effective.

A diaphragm is not suitable for women with certain disabilities. A fair amount of dexterity and good grasp in one hand is required to insert a diaphragm and then to test to be sure that it has been inserted properly. Emptying the bladder by Credé's method (by putting pressure on the abdomen) could dislodge it. If the pelvic muscles are weak it might slip. When sensation is lacking in the vagina, the discomfort that warns that the diaphragm has slipped or was not correctly inserted would not be felt.

An intra-uterine device (IUD) is a plastic, metal or plastic and metal object which is inserted by a doctor into the uterus. A string hangs from the IUD into the vagina and its presence must be checked regularly to be sure that the device has not been expelled.

An IUD is an effective contraceptive for ninety-seven out of one hundred women. Once it is inserted it works and its use in no way interferes with the spontaneity of lovemaking. While many women experience no side effects or discomfort when using an IUD, others find that it makes their menstrual periods heavier and cramps more severe, especially for the first three months. When periods are very heavy some doctors prescribe iron supplements to prevent anemia.

For women who are physically disabled, insertion of an IUD can be difficult or painful because of pelvic deformities or discomfort in the pelvic examination position. If grasp is limited it may be difficult to check for the presence of the string, although this can be done by the partner. Many women who are spinal injured find the IUD the best kind of contraceptive.

Women who use IUDs do have an increased risk of pelvic inflammatory disease which, if it remains undetected, could lead to fertility problems. The warning signs of the disease include spotting or irregular periods, increased spasticity, pelvic pain or discharge. The disease can remain undetected, as can expulsion of an IUD, if there is a lack of sensation in the pelvic area.

Oral contraceptives are an effective birth control method. The Pill, which stops ovulation and/or causes physiological changes which make pregnancy less likely, is a combination of the hormones estrogen and progesterone. It is taken orally every day for twenty-one days and is then resumed after an interval of seven days.

The Pill, which is extremely easy to use, can decrease bleeding, cramps and the duration of menstrual periods and some women also report a decrease of premenstrual tension. There are, however, medical problems associated with prolonged use of the Pill. Some women feel depressed or anxious while taking it and others find that they gain weight. Most worrying is the fact that there is an increase of thromboembolism, blood clots, in women who are on the Pill. Women who are unusually sedentary, such as those who are wheelchaired, are especially exposed to high risk. The Pill can aggravate symptoms of some disabling conditions.

Circulatory problems can occur with the Pill and when there is loss of feeling a woman may not detect such common warning signs as severe leg, arm or abdominal pains nor notice, even if she inspects her legs regularly, the redness or swelling which might indicate such problems. Heart attacks and strokes have also been associated with the Pill. Symptoms of serious trouble include severe abdominal pain, severe chest pain or shortness of breath, severe heachaches and blurred or double vision. Any woman who is on the Pill should see her doctor immediately if she has any of these symptoms.

Another oral contraceptive, the mini pill, contains only progestin, which changes the cervical mucus to decrease fertility. The mini pill, which is 97 to 98 percent effective if taken at the same time every day, is often satisfactory for women who experience such estrogen-related side effects of the Pill as high blood pressure, nausea and headaches.

Since the mini pill is taken every day it has the advantage that there is no worry about remembering to restart taking it after seven days. Menstrual periods stop after taking the mini pill for a time, which some women might consider a great convenience. Sadly, the problems associated with the Pill are also associated with the mini pill.

Depo-provera, popularly known as the Shot, is an injection of progesterone which is given every three months and is as effective as the Pill—more effective in fact since there's no possibility of forgetting to take a pill each day. It also has all the risks of the Pill, but with the lessened side effects of the mini pill. After the first nine to twelve months menstrual periods often stop. Return of fertility may, however, take longer than with oral contraceptives. After stopping the injections, ovulation often does not begin again for about ten months and some doctors will not give depo-provera to women who want to become pregnant later. Due to estrogen deficiency dryness of the vagina can occur.

The morning-after treatment is an emergency contraceptive. If intercourse has occurred without contraceptives during a woman's fertile period, a high dosage of estrogen, usually diethystilbesterol (DES), is given orally for five days and

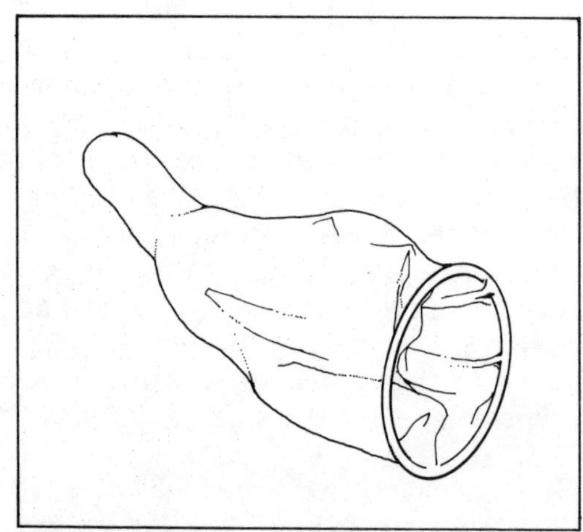

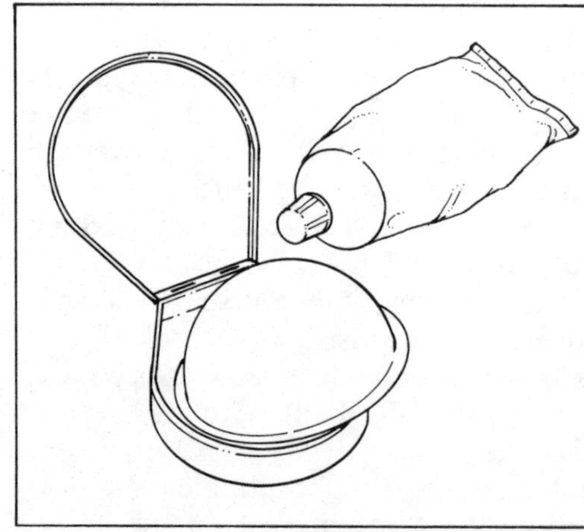

A condom, right, protects against venereal disease and is a highly effective contraceptive method, but only if the woman uses a spermicide foam. A diaphragm, far right, is 97 percent effective if it is used correctly and consistently and in conjunction with a spermicidal cream or jelly. Insertion, however, requires a fair amount of manual dexterity.

prevents implantation of a fertilized egg. To be effective, treatment must begin within twenty-four to seventy-two hours of intercourse. It will not cause an abortion if a woman is already pregnant, but there is evidence that if the fetus is a female, the child will have an increased risk of developing cancer of the vagina or cervix later in life. It is therefore important for a woman to be sure she's not pregnant before starting this treatment.

The course of treatment often results in nausea and vomiting. The same precautions that apply to the Pill apply to this treatment and it is essential before beginning that the doctor be fully aware of a woman's medical history.

No known method of nonpermanent contraception is foolproof and women can and sometimes do become pregnant when they don't want to be. When any woman has an unwanted pregnancy the choices open to her are to continue the pregnancy and to raise the child herself or to relinquish the child for adoption, or to have an abortion to terminate the pregnancy.

Just as disabled women have the same right as able-bodied women to make important decisions concerning their bodies, and their sex lives, they also have the same right to have abortions for unwanted pregnancies. Abortion is now legal in most of the United States and in the United Kingdom.

Before any woman decides to have an abortion, however, she must have her pregnancy medically diagnosed. The earlier an abortion is performed the safer it is. An abortion performed within the first ten weeks is a relatively simple and safe procedure.

Since it eliminates all worry about contraception, sterilization is becoming the most common choice of birth control of couples over the age of thirty. Either the man has a vasectomy (the surgical cutting and tying of the vas deferens, the sperm ducts) or the woman has a tubal ligation (the surgical cutting and tying of the Fallopian tubes).

Until recently, a vasectomy was a far simpler procedure than a tubal ligation, but new methods have now made the operation for women simpler and less expensive than before. Both procedures can now be done on an outpatient basis under a local anesthetic.

Vasectomy and tubal ligations are permanent and irreversible so the decision to undergo such an operation must be seriously considered. Some doctors insist that a couple get counseling before one partner undergoes such an operation, others will not perform surgery if they consider the patient too young or if he or she is childless.

The time, energy and coordination required to use a nonpermanent method of contraception varies with each individual's disability and such methods are only effective when they are used consistently and correctly. Be aggressive about seeking counseling concerning birth control. The choice of an appropriate contraceptive not only avoids unwanted pregnancies but makes for a more satisfying sexual relationship.

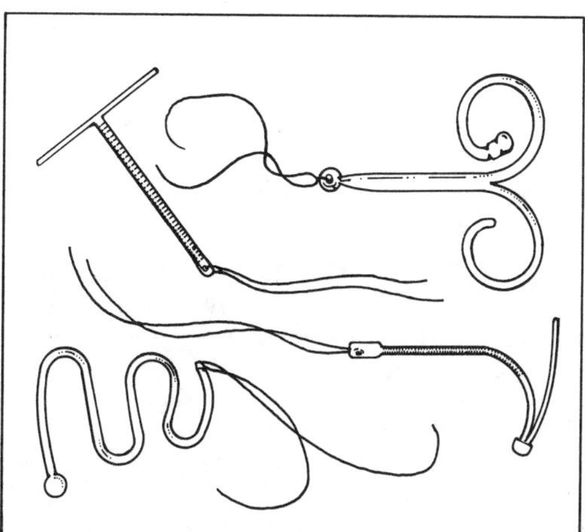

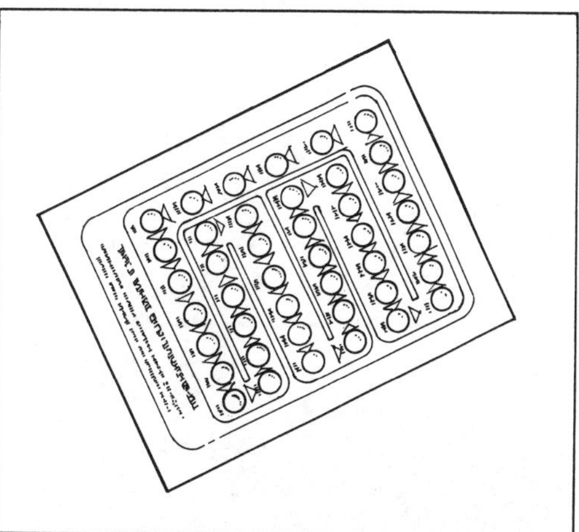

An intrauterine device, which is a satisfactory contraceptive for ninety-seven out of one hundred women, must be inserted by a doctor. Various types of IUDs, far left, are now being used. Although oral contraceptives, left, are very effective, and are simple to use, there are medical problems associated with their prolonged use.

The Disabled Parent

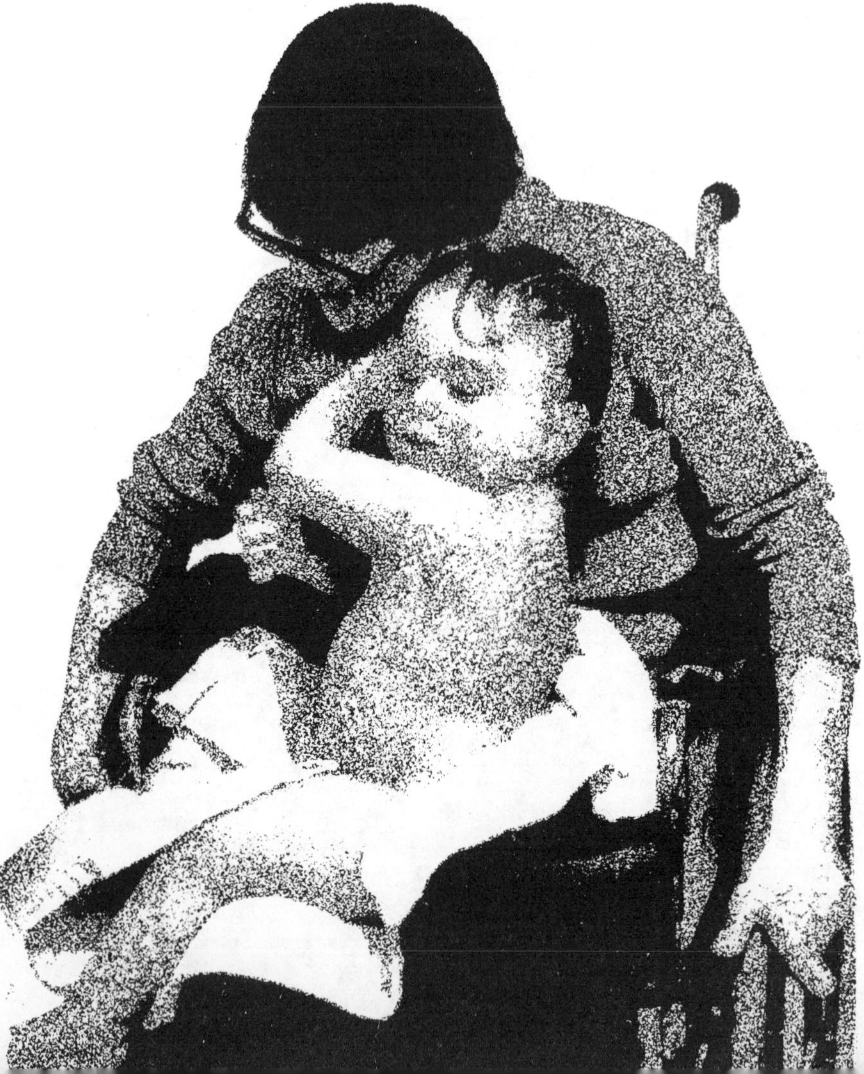

People with physical disabilities are now more than ever before participating actively in community life, pursuing careers, getting married and considering the option of becoming parents. Statistics on childbearing among physically disabled women are not readily available, but the proportion and number who are completing their pregnancies successfully have been increasing in recent years. And more and more disabled mothers and fathers are proving that a physical disability need not be a handicap to being a good parent.

When one or both partners are disabled far more thought is generally given to the question of having children than is the case with the average able-bodied couple. Just as before they married they had to carefully assess their capacity to function in the relationship, so they have to evaluate their ability to meet the physical and emotional demands of child rearing. They realize that the decision to have children or not to have children is a decision that must be made not by anxious relatives, but by the two people chiefly concerned in consultation with their family doctor. Those whose disabilities are related to heredity are aware of the necessity to get the best possible genetic counseling and to act in accordance with the facts as they perceive them. Both husband and wife know how important it is to carefully analyze what they can realistically manage and how much responsibility they can honestly accept.

When a new baby arrives all parents, disabled or able-bodied, no matter how well-prepared they are, have moments of anxiety. Not only are they suddenly confronted with the great responsibility of parenthood, but they have to cope with the new roles that are thrust upon them.

For every parent a new baby means extra work and requires an investment of time and energy. A parent with physical limitation is no different from any other, except for being even busier and more tired because certain tasks will take longer and will require more effort. When it comes to looking after your child, as in so many other areas of your life, various aids and alternative methods of doing things can help you to overcome your handicap, to make your work easier and to care for your child as well as any other parent.

Just as the person with disabilities finds that patience, imagination and ingenuity are required to deal with so many facets of his or her life, so are they necessary in the role of the parent. Often in response to the needs and demands of a growing family new attitudes and different methods of doing things must be adopted. A disabled mother, for example, may realize that despite her own desire to be independent, she has to have help in looking after her home in order to have enough time free to spend with her child. When both parents are disabled, they may find it most convenient to share in the care of the child, with each doing the things that he or she can handle best. Each family is unique and has to find its own solutions to the inevitable day-to-day problems.

Bringing up children is a complex task and the parent who is physically disabled is by no means alone in feelings of inadequacy. Every parent frequently feels that this is a task for which he or she is inadequate and ill-suited. But many of the negative aspects of physical limitations can be positive when it comes to parenting. Limited mobility can give children an increased sense of security because they know their parents are always there when they need them. Because discipline cannot be enforced with physical strength or speed, the establishment of cooperative behavior and basic trust between parent and child becomes an alternative which is not only preferable but is also of lasting merit.

Of course it would be foolish to ignore any specific areas where as a result of your disability you know you may be lacking. Deaf parents of hearing children must, for example, be sure that the children learn to recognize everyday noises, are exposed to music and speak in modulated voices. A mother who cannot cuddle her child in her arms must establish physical contact by using her legs or snuggling up to him on the floor or on her bed. If you recognize your own limitations as a parent you can take the measures necessary to conteract them.

A physical limitation need not in any way affect a parent's relationship with a child, but it is essential that you begin to establish a relationship right from the very start. You and your baby must get to know each other.

Having known no other method of child care, the new baby will automaticcally accept your way of looking after him. Young babies are amazingly adaptable and cooperative. An infant quickly learns to cooperate by clinging to his mother if he feels insecure, by lifting his legs to help when his diaper is changed or by leaning against his father as he carries him in his lap in the wheelchair.

Even older children adapt quickly to a situation. Men and women who have become disabled after having children frequently mention their surprise at their children's ready acceptance of their handicaps. In this regard, as in others, children take their cue from their parents. In most cases the child of a disabled mother or father does not think of her or him as different from his friends' mothers and fathers. One wheelchaired mother overheard her ten-year-old son talking to a friend. "Is your mother a cripple?" the friend asked. "Oh no," her son replied, "she was just in an automobile accident when she was young."

This section, unlike most material on child care, is in large part addressed to both parents, not to the mother alone. Today fathers are increasingly sharing in the day-to-day care of their children. A disabled father should not, and need not, be deprived of this joy.

To avoid the confusion of using "he or she" for the child as well as the parent, the child has been referred to throughout this section as "he" and the parent as "he or she." The material is intended to apply, however, to both girls and boys.

Most of the practical problems of being a disabled parent are limited to the child's early years. This is the period when special equipment may be needed and alternative methods of child care employed. It is those aspects of parenthood that are covered here. Many excellent books on child development and behavior are readily available and they pertain to your child as to any other.

Furniture and Equipment

The ability of disabled parents to care independently for their children is often to some degree dependent on the right choice of furniture and equipment. Although much of the equipment is used for only a relatively short time, it is nevertheless worth the effort to select and adapt items to suit your particular needs.

Furniture and equipment must be chosen with the limitations imposed by your disability in mind. The furniture you select should be sturdy, durable and easy to care for. It should help to encourage the child's early independence. Attention should be paid to safety factors; the latches on the crib, high chair and playpen should, for example, lock securely and be easy for you, but not for the child, to manipulate.

Many pieces of equipment should not be selected as single items, but rather in their relationship to the total performance of a job. They should be part of a work area where all the stages of a specific task can take place. With thoughtful planning and good organization, most of the tasks related to child care can be accomplished safely and with greater ease.

This baby dresser, which has a thick foam changing pad, four deep storage drawers, a towel rack and a shelf for toiletries, is helpful if space is limited since it folds away neatly when not in use. The height, thirty-three inches (85 cm), is most convenient for a wheelchaired parent.

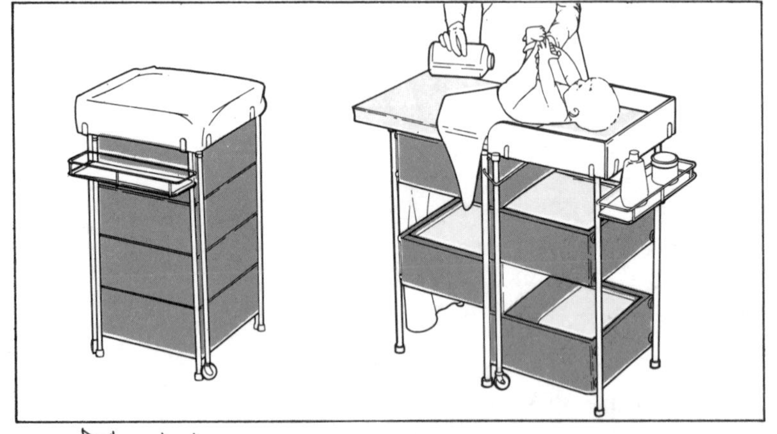

Although you can dress a baby on the floor, on a table or on your bed, it is convenient to have a special dressing area at a convenient height with all the items you need close at hand. There should be a strap on the dressing area to restrain the baby who squirms—and they all do sometimes. The strap can be fastened with Velcro rather than with a clip or buckle.

A continuous work surface on which you can change diapers, dress and undress the baby and even bathe him, is ideal. If you put him on a plastic-covered foam pad he can be slid, rather than lifted, from one area to another.

The height of the work surface must be

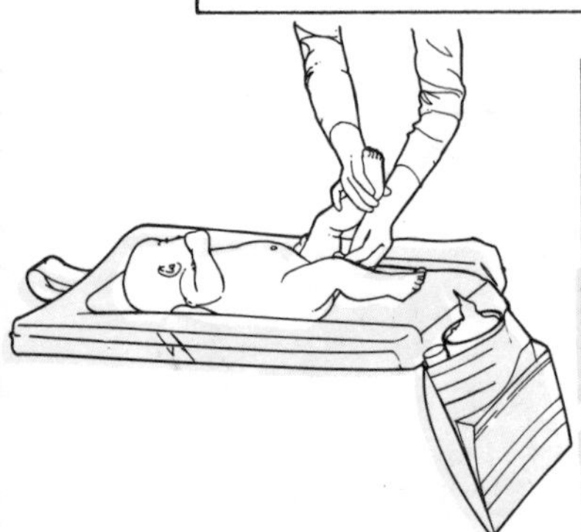

A foam-filled pad, with built-up cushion sides for extra comfort and protection, is useful for changing a baby on a table or even on the floor.

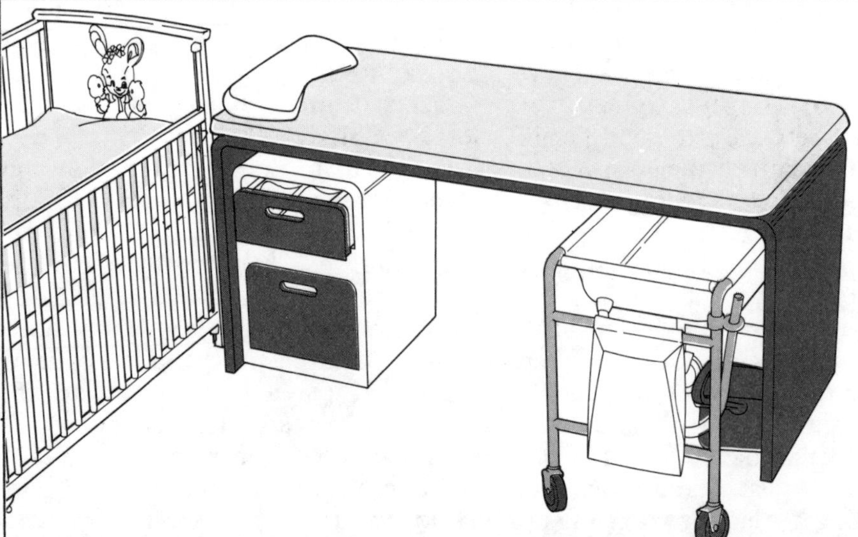

The ideal dressing and bathing area has equipment arranged to permit an easy flow of work. With a minimum of effort the baby can be transferred from the crib, to the dressing table, to the bath. The arrangement above was designed for a parent who sits to work. The drawers are easy to reach and the bathtub stores under the counter when not in use.

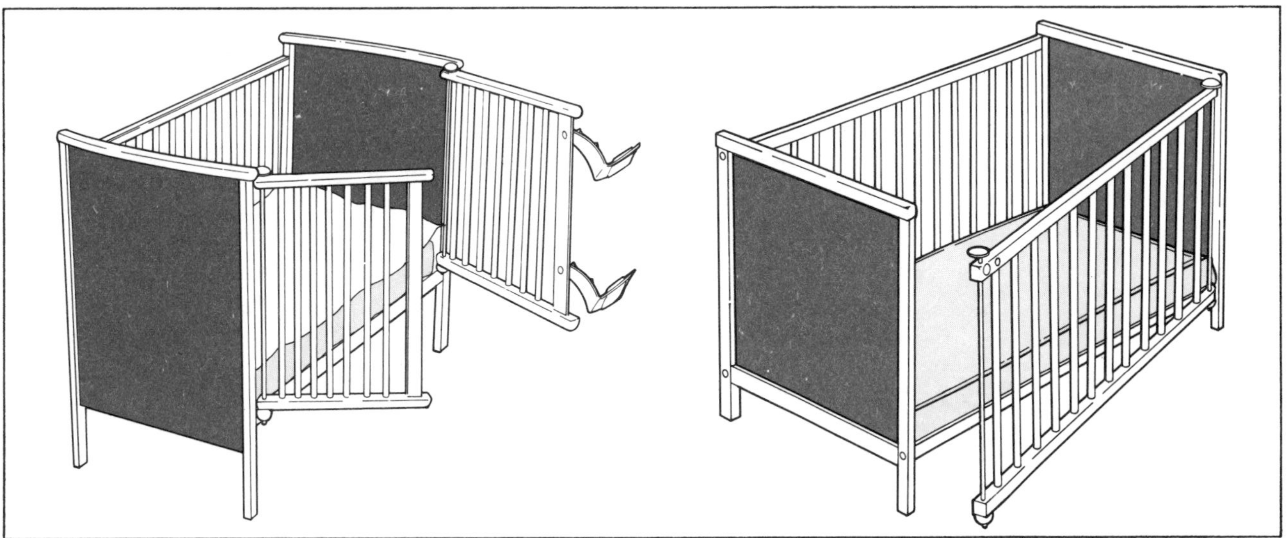

A drop-sided crib with adjustable mattress heights is convenient. The higher level minimizes lifting and can be used until the baby becomes active. A drop-sided crib can be adapted so that the whole side opens outward or opens from the center. This makes it easier to reach the baby anywhere in the crib and permits closer wheelchair approach.

right for you. Someone who is wheelchaired would find a surface of about thirty-one inches (78 cm) high most comfortable. The ambulant parent with one usable arm would, however, want the surface of the dressing area to be higher than usual so that without straining his or her back the upper body and chin could be used to hold the baby and the chin and mouth could be used to help in dressing and undressing.

A wheeled serving table or a tea wagon makes an excellent portable dressing area if the height is right for you. Diapers and other equipment can be stored on a lower shelf and reached with tongs that can be kept hanging on the side.

The crib you buy should have casters on it. For the first few months you will probably want to keep the baby in your bedroom, particularly at night. If you can roll the crib next to your bed you won't have to get up during the night to look after him.

A portable crib is very desirable. Even if you are wheelchaired or walk with crutches you can move the baby from room to room in it. Items that you will need during the day can be put into a bag and hung on the outside of the crib. Portable cribs, which roll easily and are smaller than average, can be pushed through doorways and around corners.

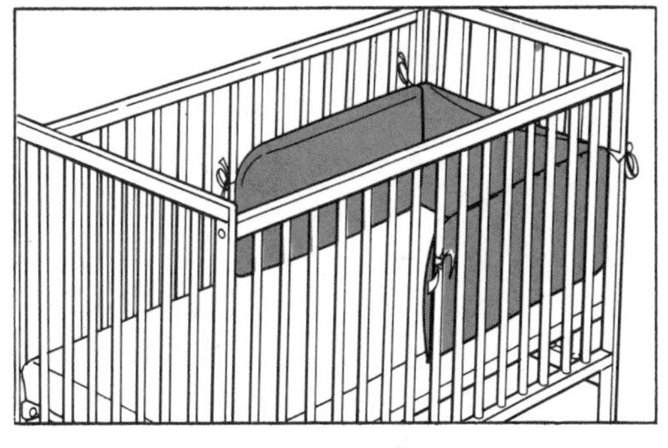

Crib bumpers shield a baby from drafts and also protect his head when he is being lifted out of or lowered into the crib.

Some models are adjustable in height and convert to playpens.

Lifting a baby from a crib is much easier if the mattress can be raised to a comfortable working height and the side of the crib lowered to the various levels of the mattress. If you are wheelchaired there should be enough room beneath the lowered rail for your footrests. If you lack balance, however, a crib with a high rail gives you a support on which to lean. Some parents find that a crib that swings open on one side is more convenient than the type with a rail that goes up and down.

There are cribs available which have rails that swing open on both sides. (These are usually the type from which the rails can eventually be removed completely to make a junior-sized bed.) This permits closer wheelchair approach. If you are ambulant, instead of bending and lifting you can sit on the crib mattress while attending to the baby.

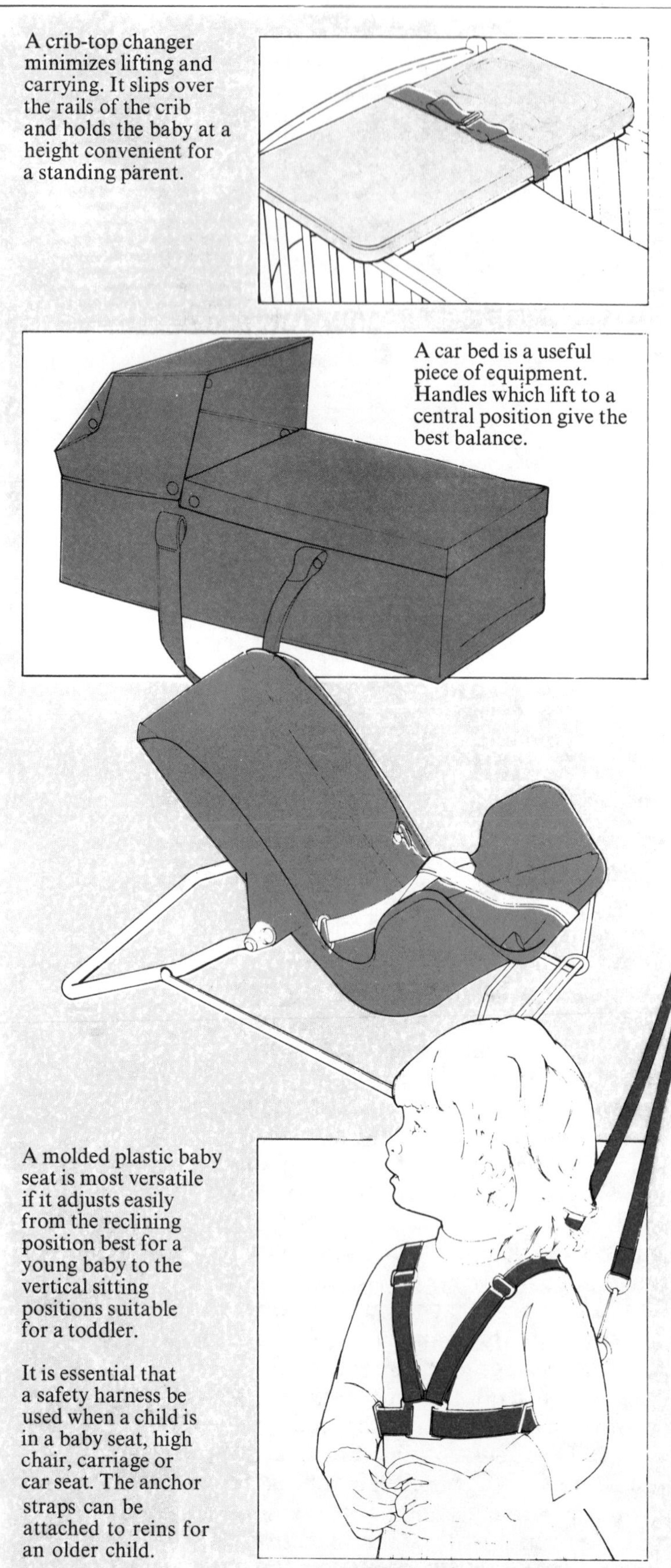

A crib-top changer minimizes lifting and carrying. It slips over the rails of the crib and holds the baby at a height convenient for a standing parent.

A car bed is a useful piece of equipment. Handles which lift to a central position give the best balance.

A molded plastic baby seat is most versatile if it adjusts easily from the reclining position best for a young baby to the vertical sitting positions suitable for a toddler.

It is essential that a safety harness be used when a child is in a baby seat, high chair, carriage or car seat. The anchor straps can be attached to reins for an older child.

If you buy a crib with a rail that drops down be sure you can handle the mechanism which locks it in place. Some have a foot-trip mechanism which can be reached with one hand from a wheelchair. The drop-side mechanism can also be adapted to be balanced by weights and pulleys for fingertip control. It is also possible to rehang the side on bolts and screw eyes so that it can be completely removed.

A plastic cover for the baby's mattress makes cleaning up easier. Fitted sheets are available for cribs. They can be slipped over the corners of the mattress with one hand and need little smoothing. A lightweight foam mattress is easier to lift than one with inner springs. Bumper pads for the crib protect the baby's head when he is being lifted and lowered. It also keeps small toys from falling onto the floor.

Another crib accessory which is handy if you are ambulant is a crib-top changer which slips over the crib rails and makes it possible for you to change the baby at a convenient height and then return him to the crib without having to carry him.

For a small baby a car bed can serve many purposes. Besides being good for taking the baby almost anywhere, it can be placed next to your bed at night on its own stand or on a table of convenient height. For feeding and changing you can then just lift the baby into your bed. A lightweight car bed can be pushed around the house on a dolly, which has large casters, or on a large tea wagon.

When you buy a car bed choose one that has strong handles which lift to a central position to give good balance. This is particularly important if you use only one hand. When you put the baby into the car bed he should be in the center so his weight is evenly balanced.

When the car bed is used in a car it should be kept on the back seat and held in place with straps which are bolted to the car frame.

A molded plastic baby seat is a versatile piece of equipment. It can be used with a padded lining for feeding the baby and playing with him. Without the lining it can be used as a bath seat in the sink or tub. By releasing a safety catch, some models adjust to positions from upright to horizontal and can even be used for sleeping.

Some parents find it helpful to use a playpen, while others don't. A playpen can be used for keeping a toddler out of mischief and out of your way when you have chores to do. Unfortunately, the child who takes most happily to a playpen is usually not the one who gets into trouble.

Conventional, square, wooden playpens are available with or without floors. They tend to be heavy, particularly the models with floors. On the other hand, toddlers will often push those without floors around the room. A gate can be cut in the side of a wooden playpen so the child doesn't have to be lifted over the top and also makes it possible to change or feed him without taking him out. Smaller playpens often have casters so they can be pushed from room to room.

If you have difficulty bending, a playpen can be put on legs so that the height is most convenient for you. A crib-pen, a playpen which converts to crib height, is also helpful for someone who finds bending difficult. One model has nylon mesh sides, fabric covering on the top rail, as well as casters.

Circular playpens, with chrome frames, padded floors and netted sides, have the advantage of being lightweight. They can be folded with one hand, even from a wheelchair.

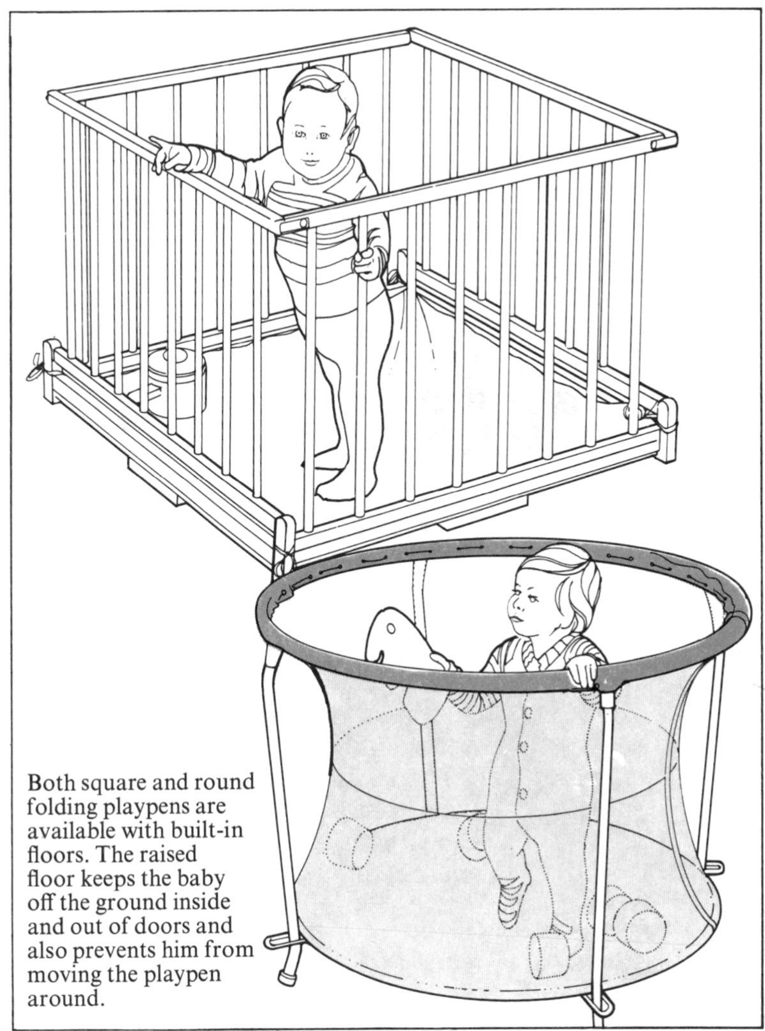

Both square and round folding playpens are available with built-in floors. The raised floor keeps the baby off the ground inside and out of doors and also prevents him from moving the playpen around.

Most disabled parents of small children feel that a harness is indispensable. A harness should be used to keep a child securely in the carriage, high chair, stroller and swing.

Harnesses are available to fit children from the age of six months to three years. Many of them adapt for later use with reins. They are made of leather or nylon webbing. Some have buckles, while others have side clips or back fastenings which are difficult, if not impossible, to manage with one hand, although sometimes a Velcro closure can be substituted.

Several types of harnesses have adjustable anchor straps, to which the harness's side clips attach and can be left permanently looped to the carriage, high chair or parent's wheelchair. Spare sets of anchor straps are often available with a harness. Some parents find it best to keep the harness on the child all the time. They find it easier to grasp the harness than an active child and use it to lift the baby from the floor, the playpen and the crib. They simply keep the anchor straps attached where they will be used and clip the harness's side straps to them as necessary. Other parents find it most convenient to have several sets of harnesses, leaving them in place and just slipping the baby in and out of the one which is appropriate.

Special sleeping harnesses are also available. Such a harness makes it possible for a very young child to sleep in a bed, instead of a crib. One style allows the baby to roll over and sit up freely, but not to stand.

With a toddler securely inside a harness, the reins can be fastened to your belt, a crutch or a walker, enabling him to walk along safely beside you. A longer rein can be used in safe areas, a shorter one on busy streets and in stores.

If you are wheelchaired you can use the side straps, anchored securely to the chair frame at the side of the seat or the back, to keep the child safely in the chair with you, leaving your arms free to maneuver the chair. Or the reins can be attached to the chair and he can walk next to you while you propel the chair. When the child is tired he can climb back into your lap and the side straps can be clipped to the chair.

When choosing a carriage select one that is well-constructed, has good springs and large wheels that will go easily over small obstructions and up and down curbs. The handle must be at the height which is most comfortable for you. As well as considering the height of the handle, when selecting a carriage you should also look at the height of the mattress and be sure it's convenient for lifting the baby in and out. Be sure, too, that you can easily manipulate the brake. If the carriage is in fact a car bed on a chassis the car bed should lift out easily and the lifting handles should meet in the middle so they can be managed with one hand. A carriage can be pushed from a wheelchair, but it must have a hand brake rather than a foot brake. It can also be pushed with only one hand and steered from the center of the handle.

If balance is good, but grasp is weak, the upper body can be used to push the carriage, although the hands should remain on the handle. To aid in downhill propelling and to take the strain off the hands, a belt unit can be attached from the waist to the handlebar. The clips which fasten such a belt must be secure.

As soon as the baby is old enough to sit propped up by a pillow a harness should be used at all times in the carriage.

Regular maintenance of a carriage is a wise precaution. The brake should be checked regularly and the tires should be replaced when they become worn.

A toddler seat should be used on the carriage only with the greatest caution.

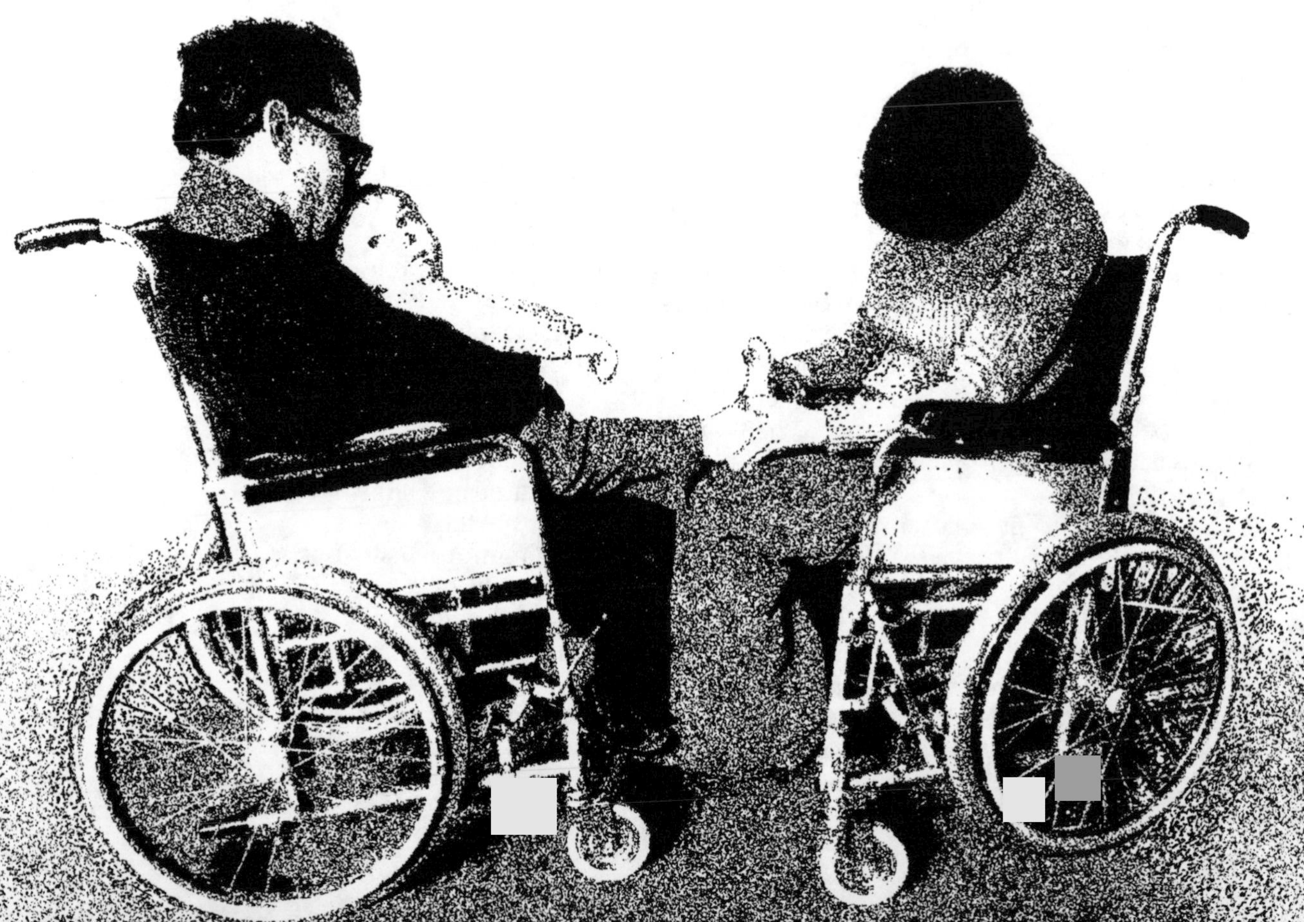

Some manufacturers specifically state that a carriage will be unsafe if laden with heavy packages or another child.

Heavy shopping bags hung from the handle of the carriage can cause it to tip. It is safest to use a shopping tray fitted to the chassis, but these can be difficult to load and unload, and impossible if you can't bend.

A stroller is often hard for the disabled parent to manage since folding and unfolding most models usually requires two hands or one foot and one hand. Many models are light and, therefore, not particularly well-balanced.

Before investing in a stroller carefully check out the available models. Be sure you can open and close the stroller and can manipulate the brake easily. Take into consideration, too, that you will have to lift the child into the stroller or that he will have to climb into it himself.

A child should always be harnessed securely in a stroller.

A car safety seat should always be used from the time the baby can sit up and weighs about twenty pounds (9 kg). If you can't get the child into the car seat yourself you can ask a passerby for help. It's far better to ask for help than to take risks with the child's safety.

Car seats vary in model and in price. This is one case, however, where safety should be the primary criterion when making a selection.

The safest type of car seat is padded, supports the child's head at the back, has built-up side wings for added protection and attaches securely to the frame of the car. The shoulder and waist straps of the harness should be adjustable so that they fit securely and can be lengthened as the child grows.

A car seat should be used for as long as possible. Until a child weighs about forty pounds (18 kg) he is not big enough to be adequately protected by only a harness. When a child graduates from a car seat he should nevertheless use a harness which is bolted to the car frame. A harness which permits a child to stand up is not considered safe. Young children should never be permitted to travel in the front seat of a car.

Feeding

Before her baby is born every mother has to decide whether she wants to breast-feed or bottle-feed. This is a very personal decision and there are many books available on the subject. A disability should not affect a woman's ability to breast-feed but, if she must always be on medication, it must be ascertained whether the drugs would be transmitted in the milk and whether this would, indeed, be harmful to the infant. A doctor can give specific advice.

There are practical advantages to breast-feeding. It eliminates many chores since the milk does not have to be prepared or brought to the right temperature, and there is no equipment to be sterilized. But the greatest advantage is the satisfaction most mothers get from this close physical relationship with their babies.

If the baby cannot be held in the traditional way when he's being breast-fed or bottle-fed, pillows can be used to support him. Sometimes it is best, and most comfortable, to lie on your side facing the baby. Some mothers find it easiest to prop the holding arm and the baby on pillows. In this way a weak arm can be positioned to support the baby.

It is most important, however, that the baby is relaxed when he is being fed—and this is only possible if you are relaxed. If you bottle-feed your baby you may feel most secure and relaxed if you prop him in a baby seat to feed him. If grasp is weak, a cotton sock slipped over the bottle makes it easier to hold. It also helps the baby to learn earlier to hold his own bottle.

There are several ways to burp the baby besides the conventional method of putting him against your shoulder. He can be balanced against one shoulder and the side of a chair or sofa (which should be protected with a towel). Equally effective is laying the baby across your lap, on his stomach, and rubbing and patting his back. You can also sit the baby on your lap, with one hand under his chin to support his head, while the other hand rubs and pats his back.

Plastic bottles are lightweight, virtually unbreakable and can be sterilized by boiling or in a chemical solution. There are various types of screw-on tops, into which the nipples fit. Try different kinds to find the easiest to manage.

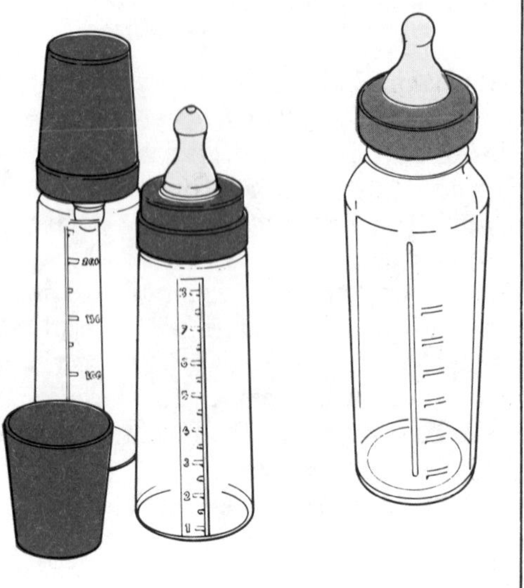

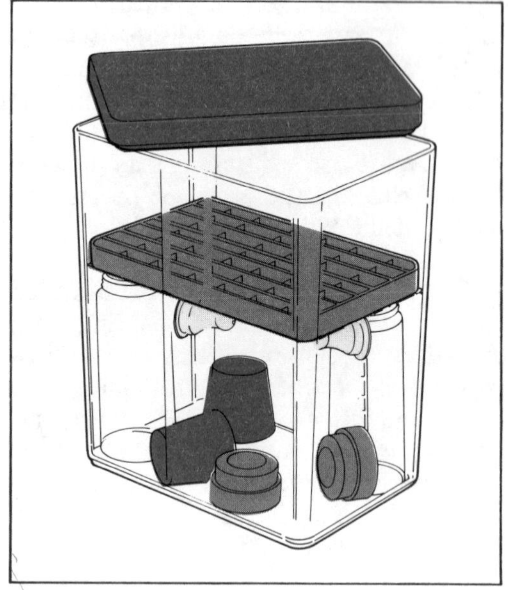

Sterilizing units, such as the one shown above, are available for use with a chemical sterilizing solution. The items to be sterilized are simply washed and then immersed in the solution for at least thirty minutes. An inner float keeps all the items fully submerged to ensure complete sterilization.

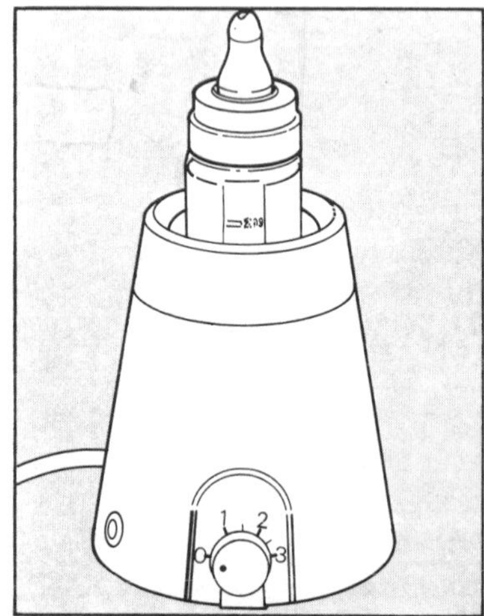

A baby-food warmer eliminates the need to get out of bed at night to warm a bottle. The model above heats cans and jars of baby food as well as bottles.

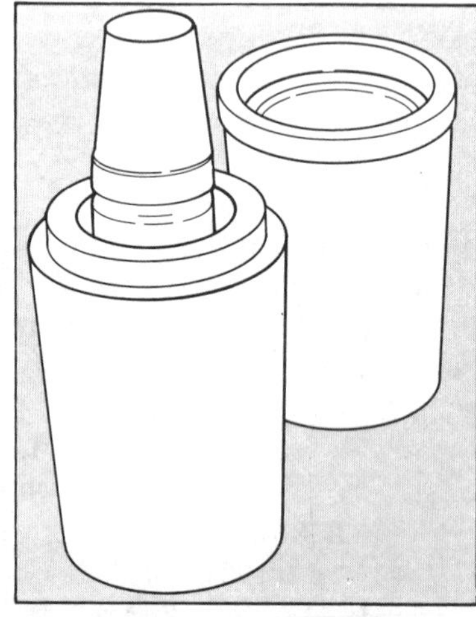

Take the baby's bottle out of the refrigerator and put it into a bottle insulator where it will stay cool for several hours until you are ready to heat it.

When a child begins to drink from a cup, one which has a weighted base and a lid is best. The spillproof cup above is available with one or two handles.

If you decide to bottle-feed your baby you will have to buy various kinds of equipment. (Even if you breast-feed you will need a couple of bottles for orange juice and water.)

Plastic bottles are not only lighter than glass. but they don't break if you drop them. Nipples which fit inside screw-on plastic tops have, fortunately, replaced those that had to be stretched over the rims of the bottles. There are different kinds of screw-on bottle tops available. Before buying bottles, nipples and tops try various kinds in the store to find out which type is easiest for you to handle.

Disposable bottles and nipples eliminate the need to sterilize and are very light, but people with limited manual dexterity often find them difficult to assemble.

Bottles which are not disposable have to be washed thoroughly after they are used and before they are sterilized. To wash the inside of a bottle with one hand or two weak ones, first soak it, then wedge the bottle into a drawer and use a long brush to scrub it. An alternative is to use a bottle brush which is attached to the back of the sink by a suction base, reversing the action by moving the bottle on the brush.

Bottles and other equipment can be sterilized either by boiling or by using a sterilization agent.

For sterilizing by boiling, a lightweight unit with large handles on both sides or across the top is usually easiest to handle. To eliminate lifting the sterilizer when it's full, the bottles can be put into it while it is on the stove and then water can be added, using a lightweight pitcher or a hose attachment from the sink. After the bottles have been boiled for at least five minutes and have cooled, they can be removed one at a time with tongs. An electric sterilizer has the advantage that

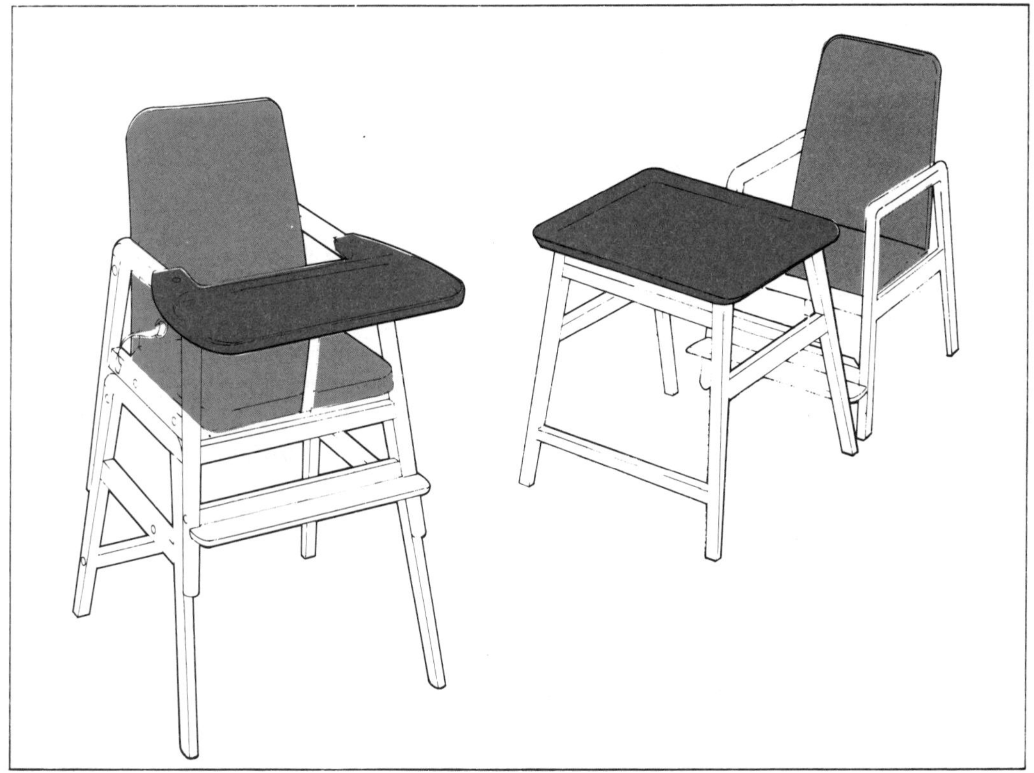

A multipurpose high chair can be used for quite a few years and adapts easily to the needs of a disabled parent. The high chair far left has a seat height of twenty inches (50 cm). The tray can be removed so that the child can eat at a full-size table. It can be converted to a low chair with tray or, for an older child, to a chair and table, left.

it can be permanently left in one place.

Bottles and other equipment can be just as effectively sterilized using a solution of sodium hypochlorite, which is available in liquid or tablet form. After cleaning, the equipment must be immersed in the solution for at least thirty minutes. A bucket or even a large casserole can be used. This method is efficient and less hazardous than boiling.

A bottle which you've taken from the refrigerator can be heated by standing it in hot water. This involves several operations—heating the water, checking the temperature of the milk and then wiping the bottle dry. It may be worth investing in an electric bottle warmer which saves time and is safe since the temperature is thermostatically controlled. Many models can also be used to heat cans and jars of baby food.

When your baby begins drinking from a cup you may find it useful to buy a baby cup which has a cover and a drinking spout. Such a cup is particularly good because it has a gravity-based bottom and will right itself when it's tipped.

An electric blender can save time and money when the baby begins to eat strained and chopped food. You can prepare the food in advance and it will keep in the refrigerator for about four days. One model has a screw top so that the food can be transferred directly into baby food jars.

A baby-food feeder is a good way to introduce the baby to strained food, particularly if you find it difficult to hold a spoon. A feeder is much like a bottle. The strained food is put into it and the baby sucks, at his own rate, through a familiar nipple—but one with a large hole.

A suction-based dish, which won't slip or tip, can be used for strained or chopped food. Such dishes are available with compartments in which hot water is poured to keep the food warm longer. It is easiest to get food up from a dish that has sloping sides.

If coordination is a problem, a plastic or rubber-coated spoon will protect the baby's gums and teeth. The handle of a feeding spoon can be built up if necessary to accommodate weak grasp.

When you're feeding your baby, a plastic apron will keep your clothes clean. For the baby use a plastic bib with sleeves which requires little washing. A plastic bib with a pocket will catch drips and crumbs. The ties on some bibs can be replaced with snaps or Velcro.

A baby can be fed in a baby seat, set on a table of convenient height, for quite a few months, but then the day comes when he needs a proper feeding chair. The height of the chair must suit you. If, for example, you are wheelchaired, it is best for the chair to be on your level. Some parents find that a feeding table, in which the baby sits, is most convenient since the legs can be raised to give knee room underneath.

High chairs come in different heights and some are convertible so that from a high chair you get a chair and table, a low chair and tray and a chair which brings the child to the right height to sit at the family dining table.

If you are wheelchaired, it is probably easiest to put the child into a high chair and to remove him if it has a tray that comes off the front easily and has a locking device which is dependable and is easy to manipulate with one hand. A chair into which the child can simply be lowered is often easiest to manage with one arm or two weak ones. An adjustable footrest adds to the child's comfort and safety.

A baby should always be strapped into a high chair and the chair itself should have attachments for a harness. Some parents find it convenient to have the high chair or feeding table on casters so the child can be pushed around in it.

Lifting and Carrying

Until a baby begins to crawl, and even for several months after this, he has to be lifted and carried from place to place.

Parents who have difficulty bending minimize lifting by having as much equipment as possible at waist height. If arms are weak or only one arm is functional the parent can utilize the natural instinct of a baby to cling to an adult and to clamber. During the day the child should be as free of restricting clothing as possible so that his arms are not hampered in his efforts to hold.

Once a child begins to walk steadily, a sturdy step stool or box should be provided so that he can get up to the washbasin and toilet by himself. If he has steps or a sofa bed next to his crib he can even climb into it and down from it himself after the side has been lowered.

Wheelchaired parents have devised various ways to carry an infant. A tiny baby can be cradled in your lap supported by a soft pillow, the two front corners of which are pinned to the arms of the chair. This leaves your hands free to propel the chair. Another method is to use a baby blanket to make a pouch. Fold the blanket into a V shape. Pin the point of the V to your slacks or skirt and the other two ends behind your back. Then slide the baby between you and the blanket.

As the baby gets older, and squirms too much to be safe lying in your lap, a car bed on a dolly, a portable crib or a carriage can be used to transport him from room to room. Everything needed for the day can be kept on a tea wagon or in a bag and moved with him.

When the baby sits up steadily he can safely travel in your lap again, the side straps of his harness secured to the frame of the chair.

An ambulant parent with one functional arm often finds it best to carry a baby on the hip of the same side as the good arm. The pelvis distributes the weight and reduces arm strain.

This plastic baby's bathtub can be used one-handed since it has a gentle slope to support the baby's back and keep his head well above water level. It can be used with a stand or on a table.

Various child carriers are available which distribute the weight better when carrying the child for some distance, keep the child close and leave the parent's arms free. Carriers are suitable for babies from the time they can fully support their own heads. Some carriers go over one shoulder of the adult and others go over both. To use a carrier a parent must have good balance and at least one strong shoulder.

Bathing the Baby

A baby can be bathed in any of a number of ways and places. You must find the method that works best for you.

No matter how or where you bathe your baby it's essential that before you begin you gather together all the equipment you will need; the paraphernalia necessary for a baby's bath often seems to be in inverse proportion to his size.

It's a good idea to keep shampoo, baby oil and other liquids in plastic squeeze bottles; they won't break and don't need opening. If you find it difficult to handle a cake of soap, add special baby detergent to the bathwater or use a sponge mop on a handle. The sponge can be rubbed on soap held in a dish. A hose makes shampooing and rinsing off soap easier. When grasp is limited, a terry cloth mitt, made by sewing three sides of two washcloths together, makes a washcloth unnecessary and will give you a better hold on the baby.

A plastic-lined, terry cloth bath apron, available from department stores or easily made at home, keeps you dry while you bathe and dry the baby. To dry him, a towel with a hood covers his head and keeps the towel in place while you're handling him. You can make a hood of one corner of a large towel, or buy such a towel in a department store.

Before you undress the baby you should fill the tub. Three or four inches (8 or 10 cm) of water is really sufficient, but you may want to make it warmer than usual so that it will still be warm when he is undressed. If you cannot feel the temperature of the bath water use a floating thermometer.

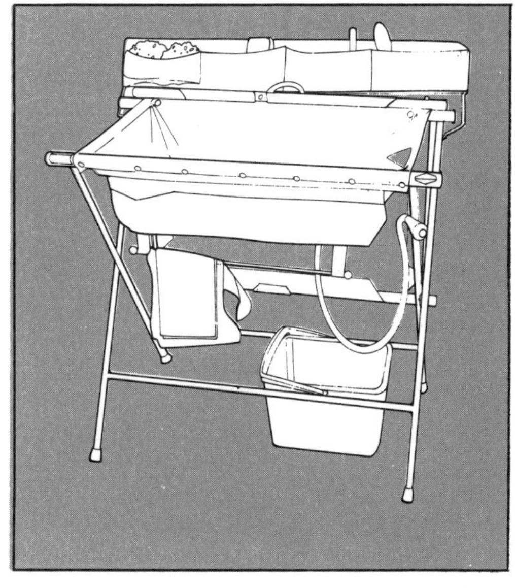

A bathinette is convenient both for dressing and bathing the baby. The removable hammock supports the baby's back and the table top has a safety strap. Items stored on the undershelf can be reached with tongs. Some models have large wheels at one end for easy transporting.

A bathinette combines a dressing-table top and a tub and there is a hammock in the tub which supports the baby. The tub can be filled and emptied using an attached hose—but this means that the bathinette must be used near the source of water or moved back and forth to be filled and emptied. It is also possible, of course, to fill it from a bucket of water, using a light, plastic pitcher and then empty it into the bucket after the baby's bath.

Bathinettes vary in price and, like cars, the cost is related to the "extras." They all have pockets for toilet articles, but the more expensive the model the more pockets it has. Some models have a towel rack as well as a shelf for storing clothes. Some have removable table tops while others have an arrangement whereby the table top can be raised and lowered, rather than removed. A safety strap on the table top of most models is a feature worth having for it keeps the baby secure.

Bathinettes are available in various heights and all have the advantage that they collapse when not in use. Many parents feel that since the tub part itself is usable for only a relatively short time the cost of a bathinette isn't justified.

The kitchen sink is often the best place to bathe a baby and can be used until he's three or four years old. If the sink is the right height for you to wash the dishes, either standing or sitting, it's the right

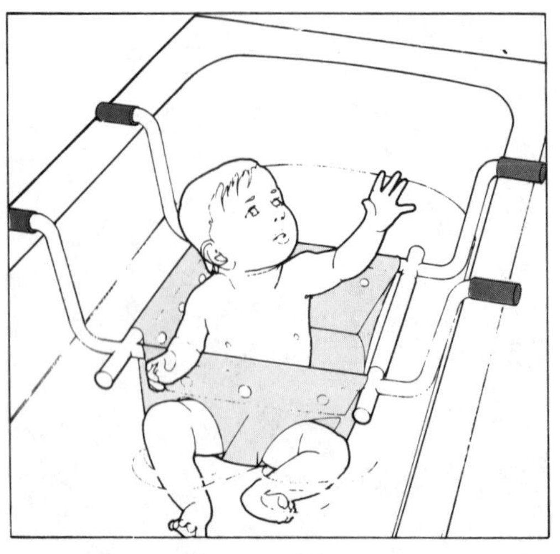

The Safa Bath Seat, right, was designed for disabled children, but some parents with disabilities find it extremely useful for bathing a toddler in the family bathtub. The Safa Bath Seat is available in the United Kingdom through the Spastics Society.

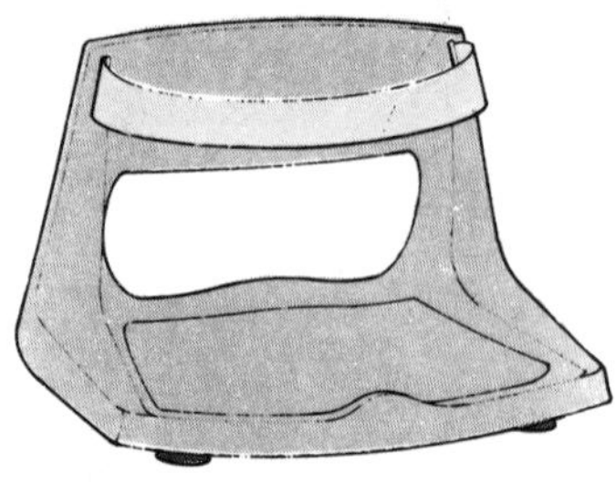

A baby bath anchor is helpful when bathing a child single-handed or with two weak hands. The anchor has a foam cushion, four suction cups under the seat and an adjustable belt which holds the child securely in the sink or bathtub.

height for this job. A sink usually has the advantage that there is space on both sides for keeping the necessary equipment and, padded with toweling, an area on which to dress and undress the baby. The sink is also easier to fill and to drain than a bathinette or a portable tub.

The faucet can be covered with a rubber nozzle to protect the baby's head in case it bumps against the metal. To keep the baby from sliding, the bottom of the sink can be lined with foam rubber. A lining can be easily and inexpensively made from a foam pad cut with a scissors to the exact size and shape of the sink. If you prefer, until the baby is old enough to sit without support, he can be bathed on a plastic baby seat adjusted to a semi-reclining position. A rubber mat should be used under the seat to keep it securely in place.

If the sink is too high, or you can't get close enough to it in a wheelchair, the baby can be bathed in a plastic tub set on its own stand or on a table of convenient height. Plastic bathtubs are available which have a sloping contoured bottom to support the baby's back, with his head well above water level. Such a tub can be filled with a hose attachment from the sink or by ladling water into it from a bucket, but there is, nevertheless, the chore of emptying it later. Some tubs fit into a light frame on casters which does facilitate filling and draining.

Bathing and dressing equipment should be kept on an adjacent table or wheeled cart. If the tub is used on a table, it's helpful if the table is large enough to hold all the bathing equipment and also has enough space for undressing and dressing the baby.

A plastic tub can also be used on your bed to bathe an infant. Protect the bed with plastic sheeting and toweling and have within easy reach everything you will need for bathing, drying and dressing him.

There is no law that says that a baby has to be immersed in water every single day. When it's a hassle to give the baby a tub bath, a sponge bath is an excellent substitute. This can be done on a table, or on your bed, protected by plastic sheeting with toweling on top.

Although it is generally considered hazardous to bathe a baby in a full-size bathtub, some parents find it easiest and most convenient to sit on a stool, a hassock or on the floor and bathe the baby in the family tub. If the baby does not have sufficient balance to sit without support, a plastic tub or a baby seat in a semi-reclining position can be used. A nonskid rubber mat at the bottom of the tub will keep the plastic tub or the seat from sliding. The baby can be undressed and dressed on the floor on several layers of toweling.

It is dangerous to leave a baby or a young child unattended in any bathtub even for the shortest time.

Dressing the Child

A baby not only has to be dressed and undressed, he also has to be changed frequently, his clothes have to be laundered and as he grows they have to be altered. When a child gets older you can buy clothes that encourage him to dress himself, but there are still the early years when you have to do it all.

The first step is to shop carefully, looking for features which will be easiest for you to manage. The advantages of wash and wear fabrics should not be overlooked; they reduce upkeep and make ironing unnecessary. If you cannot go to the stores yourself, shop from the catalogs of large mail order companies. You can study them carefully and then order by telephone or mail. Judiciously selected clothing combined with ingenuity and practice make it possible to dress a squirming infant deftly with only one hand or two weak ones.

Long or full-length openings make it easier to put clothes on and take them off. Those which go over the head should have expandable openings. Babies' nightgowns are available with snap fronts or can be adapted from ties to Velcro closures. Sleeping bags are easy to care for, have full-length zippers and are available in fabrics suitable for winter or summer. Some can be lengthened simply by cutting the stitches which hold the extra hems. Snap or zipper crotches simplify changing. Slip-on booties are easier to put on than those that tie.

In the early months of a child's life changing diapers is a major preoccupation. Fortunately, there are various kinds of diapers available which make this chore a bit easier. When deciding on the type of diapers you want to use, the ease of putting them on, the work involved in their upkeep and the expense are all considerations. Disposal diapers are expensive and have to be bought regularly, while cloth diapers require only an initial outlay, but you have the chore of sterilizing, laundering and folding them yourself. Although a diaper service is an ongoing expense, it is obviously a great boon since the diapers are laundered and folded for you. Usually, however, the diapers belong to the company and special Velcro or snap fasteners may not be added.

Disposable diapers are available with adhesive tapes attached, thus eliminating the need for safety pins. If, however, you prefer a style that does not have tapes a little masking tape will hold them in place. Those which are prefolded in a triangular shape or pleated are easier to fit on an infant. One disadvantage of disposable diapers is that they are not as absorbent as cloth diapers and have to be changed more frequently. Babies with very sensitive skins tend to get a rash when wearing them continuously.

Cloth diapers are available in different fabrics, sizes and shapes. Absorbency is a quality to consider, but for the disabled parent ease of fastening can be of equal importance. Square or rectangular shaped diapers can be folded to give maximum protection, but must be fastened with pins. Some parents find it easiest to pin one side of the diaper first, slip the baby's leg in, pull up the diaper and then pin the other side. Prefolded diapers save time and energy and Velcro or snap fasteners may be added to them. This eliminates the need for pinning and the fastenings can be managed with one hand.

Diaper linings can be used inside cloth diapers. Made of a knitted material that does not hold moisture, they add to the baby's comfort, especially when he is sleeping. Some liners are made of non-woven fabric and are disposable.

Safety diaper pins are available which have recessed plastic heads which always protect the points so there is no chance of pricking the baby. Such pins can be used with one hand.

Use a pincushion to keep diaper pins within reach. If you find it difficult to stick the points through cloth use a bar of soap as a pincushion. The soap will also make the pins glide more easily.

The baby can be changed on a pad on a table that is a convenient height, on a large chair that has closed-in arms, in his carriage or crib or on your bed. If you are ambulant, but have weak arms, you can change the baby on the floor, using your legs to keep him steady.

If you don't change the baby in the same place all the time, a box or bag or a tea wagon which holds all the equipment you will need can be easily moved from place to place.

As long as the baby is light enough to lift easily, one-piece, slip-on protective pants are quite simple to manage even with one hand. Later, lined or unlined snap-on pants can be used. A style that opens flat will make dressing more manageable and diaper changes faster. Velcro strips sewn over the snaps on both sides make fastening easier. Protective plastic pants must be washed by hand.

After rinsing a soiled cloth diaper in the toilet bowl, it can be wrung out with one hand or two weak hands, by twisting it around the spigot of the faucet. A plastic diaper wringer is available, however, which clamps onto the edge of the toilet

A plastic diaper wringer can be used with one hand. It clamps onto the edge of the toilet seat, holds the diaper for soaking and has a spring mechanism which wrings out the diaper as it is pulled through.

seat, has a spring mechanism to hold the diaper for soaking, and squeezes out the excess water as the diaper is pulled through with one hand. The wringer swivels to one side when not in use.

If grasp is weak, a lightweight plastic diaper pail with a large handle can be carried over one arm. When you buy a diaper pail be sure that the knob is large enough for you to grasp and that the cover lifts off easily.

All cloth diapers must be sterilized. This can be done either by boiling or by using a special diaper cleansing agent. Although boiling is an effective way to kill germs and to keep diapers soft and white, it does involve using containers of boiling water and this can be hazardous.

A diaper cleansing agent is simple to use—a solution is made, the diapers are left to soak and then must be thoroughly rinsed in several changes of water. Such cleansers have the disadvantage of hardening the diapers after a while so that they require one or two boilings to restore their softness. If the cleansing agent is not thoroughly rinsed out some babies with sensitive skins will get a rash.

As the child gets older it's important that you select clothes which have features that not only make it easier for you to dress the child, but also encourage him to dress himself.

Garments which open down the front and have large, flat buttons, zippers with large pulls or Velcro closures are easiest to handle. Trousers and skirts with elasticized waists or large hooks on the waistbands simplify dressing as do sweaters and coats with raglan sleeves.

Clothes with ribbons that must be tied, small buttons and open-ended zippers should be avoided. Even if you can manage them the child will probably not be able to.

When manual dexterity is lacking, the shoelaces in a small child's shoes can be replaced with elastic and his foot can just be slipped in and out. When the child is older, slip-on shoes make life easier until he learns to tie shoelaces himself.

It takes time and patience for a child to learn to dress himself. He must be given as much time as he needs to dress and should always be praised for his efforts, even when the result is far from perfect.

Children often don't want to wear, and certainly won't dress themselves in, clothes they don't like. Frequently, the clothes a child takes a dislike to are uncomfortable and interfere with activity. When buying clothes you must consider his comfort and his likes and dislikes.

A training seat, used in conjunction with a step, encourages early independence. Training seats are available with adjustments so they fit securely to most toilet seats. A plastic step, which is light and easy to clean, can be used by a toddler to reach the wash-basin, climb into the bathtub or into bed, as well as to reach the toilet or to get on the toilet seat.

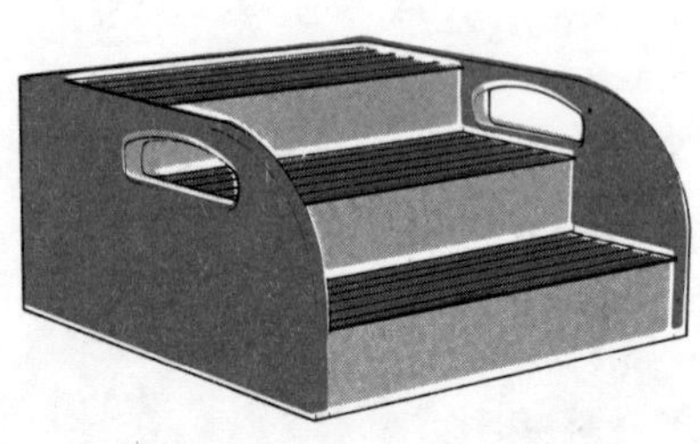

A step stool can be made to exactly the height required. Rubber treads glued to the wood prevent slipping. Handholds cut into the sides make it easier for the child to move the stool himself.

Toilet Training

Whether to toilet train a baby at an early age or to wait until he is a toddler is a decision every parent must make. Some babies are trained easily and quickly, while others balk at the very suggestion.

The decision, therefore, depends to some degree on your child's temperament.

When toilet training is begun early some parents find it best to use a potty chair that gives the baby support. If the baby can sit unsupported it may be more convenient to use a firm-based potty on the floor or a chair. If it's on the floor, the child may be able to get on and off it himself, decreasing the lifting for you and increasing his independence. Since such potties are light, many babies quickly learn to propel themselves across the floor on one, so it's best to choose a nonspill model.

A training seat, which fits over a conventional toilet seat, has the advantage that it takes little space to store, is light to lift and there is no problem of spilling or emptying. The seat you buy should fasten easily and securely without tilting and if the child is very young it should give him the necessary support. Some training seats have safety straps and others have adjustments so that they fit various-sized toilet seats. With the help of steps the toddler should be able to climb up to it himself.

Safety

Although it might be thought that children of disabled parents are at great risk, the fact is that there is no evidence that they have a higher rate of accidents than other children. In part this may be because the children of disabled parents seem to become more cautious. On the other hand, the parents know that they themselves must always be aware of potential danger and cannot afford to neglect practical safety precautions.

It's impossible to make any home completely childproof. Children are curious and imaginative and the trick is to be one step ahead of them. While there are many safety precautions that should be taken when there are small children in the house, it is equally important that a child be taught as early as possible that the stove, electric outlets, a hot iron and sharp knives are dangerous and must not be touched and that he must not eat or drink anything without asking you.

In the kitchen the greatest source of potential danger is the stove. You can buy a guard to fit around the top, but if your arms are weak this can be inconvenient as well as dangerous when you must lift heavy pans over it. Most parents find it best just to turn all the handles of pans away from the front. If the stove and work tops are very low it might be helpful to have a gate at the door of the kitchen to keep the child out, but within sight.

Always keep matches away from children and only have safety matches in the house. Other matches, if by chance they get into a child's hands, are poisonous to suck and have been known to ignite when hit with a heavy object.

It's best to iron when a toddler is sleeping or is safely in a playpen. Put the iron well out of reach when it is cooling.

Bleach, disinfectant, metal polish, turpentine, ammonia, oven cleaner and insecticides are among the substances found in most homes which are poisonous and must be kept in a place where children cannot get at them. It's advisable to keep such things in a high cabinet beyond the reach of prying little hands. If, however, you are wheelchaired and must have these things at a lower level, store them in a locked cabinet.

Medicines should always be kept out of children's reach. Since medicines should be stored in a cool, dry place a bathroom medicine cabinet is not ideal. A cabinet anywhere in the house can be used as long as it locks or is high up.

Weed killers and insecticides should always be locked away and it must be impressed upon every child that he is never to eat berries, fruit or anything else found in the garden.

Electricity is dangerous. Trailing wires are invitations to trouble. Babies try to chew them, toddlers can't resist pulling and playing with them and adults can trip over them. It's best if appliances and lamps are near electric outlets so that long wires are unnecessary. When that is not possible the wire should be attached to the baseboard with insulated staples.

As soon as your child reaches the exploratory stage, electric wall outlets should be safeguarded. Childproof safety outlet covers are available and should always be used to cover outlets which are not in use.

Never leave electrical appliances plugged in when you're not using them. A blender or a washing machine can be fascinating to a small child.

In case of power failures or blown fuses keep flashlights in easily accessible places throughout the house. Check them regularly to be sure that they are in working order.

When a child begins to crawl it is often a good idea to have gates at the top and bottom of a staircase and at the doorways to rooms you don't want him to get into. Expandable gates are available from department stores and mail order companies. Before buying a gate be sure that you can climb over it or open it easily and that the child can't.

If you have a stair lift, extra care will have to be exercised. When the lift is not in use it might be advisable, if it is possible, to switch off the power.

By keeping stools and chairs away from windows a child will not be encouraged to climb onto windowsills. There are, too, various kinds of window locks available for sash and casement windows. Some permit the window to be opened only enough to let in a little fresh air, but not wide enough to be dangerous. Others simply lock the window. Windows which pivot outward can be locked and adjusted so that they will not open more than a few inches.

Keeping your windows locked is fine in the winter, but impractical in warm weather. Open windows can be childproofed by screwing strips of wood or metal across the frames. This is an effective solution, although not a very attractive one. Equally effective, but expensive, are the ready-made frames which adjust to fit over the area of open windows and can be easily removed and stored when not required.

Children love to fool around with keys in locks and can easily lock themselves into a room. It's a wise precaution never to leave a key in a lock, whether the door is locked or not.

Two-way locks, which incorporate various devices so they can be operated from outside in an emergency, can be fitted to a hinged or sliding bathroom door. If you don't have such a lock on the bathroom door it's best to remove the locking device or to put it at a height the child can't reach.

Always use a harness for a small child when he is in a carriage, high chair or stroller.

Young children should never travel in the front seat of a car. The back seat is the safest place for them and, depending on the child's age, a car bed, safety seat or harness should be used.

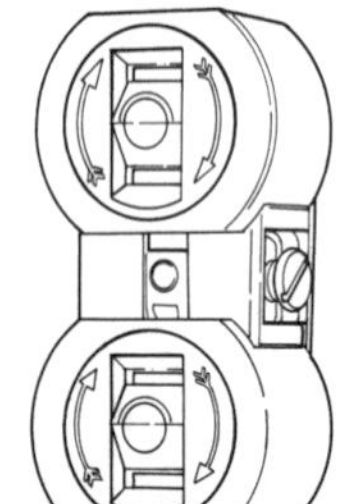

Wall outlets should be safeguarded so that a curious toddler cannot harm himself. General Electric, in the United States, makes a childproof outlet.

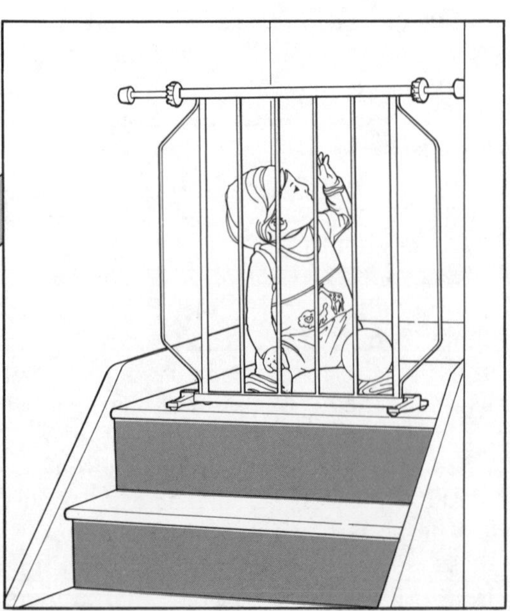

A safety gate used in a doorway or at the bottom or top of a staircase can help to keep a toddler out of mischief. The adjustable-width gate shown here has an easily fitted locking device and rubber buffers to protect the walls.

Cooperative Behavior

Since a parent who is disabled usually cannot rely on physical strength or speed, for the sake of the child's safety and the parent's peace of mind, the child must learn to cooperate and obedience must be stressed from a very early age. Even a baby quickly learns to respond to the tone of his parent's voice. It's a good idea to say "no" firmly, but only when you really mean it, so that the child associates the word with the need for immediate obedience.

It is important that the child learns to

cooperate with you and to be as self-reliant as early as possible. From the time the child is a toddler, he should be encouraged to be independent and helpful. As soon as he is old enough and displays interest in doing things for himself, you should let him try to feed, dress and wash himself with only as much help from you as is necessary. Young children can be taught to put away their own toys and clothes. They love to help with chores and should be permitted to help. It may take longer to get things done, but the time and patience you invest will not be wasted. Giving even a young child opportunities to try to do things for himself and for you lays the groundwork for the cooperation which will be particularly important as he gets older.

Rather than depending on threats of punishment, which a disability can make difficult to implement, it's far better to develop your own powers of persuasion and to rely for obedience on the cooperative behavior of your child. Sooner or later every parent finds that his or her child is too old to be spanked or physically restrained. For an able-bodied parent this point is reached considerably later, when the child is older. You will nevertheless have a great advantage if your child has been accustomed since babyhood to responding to verbal restraint and cooperation has become a way of life.

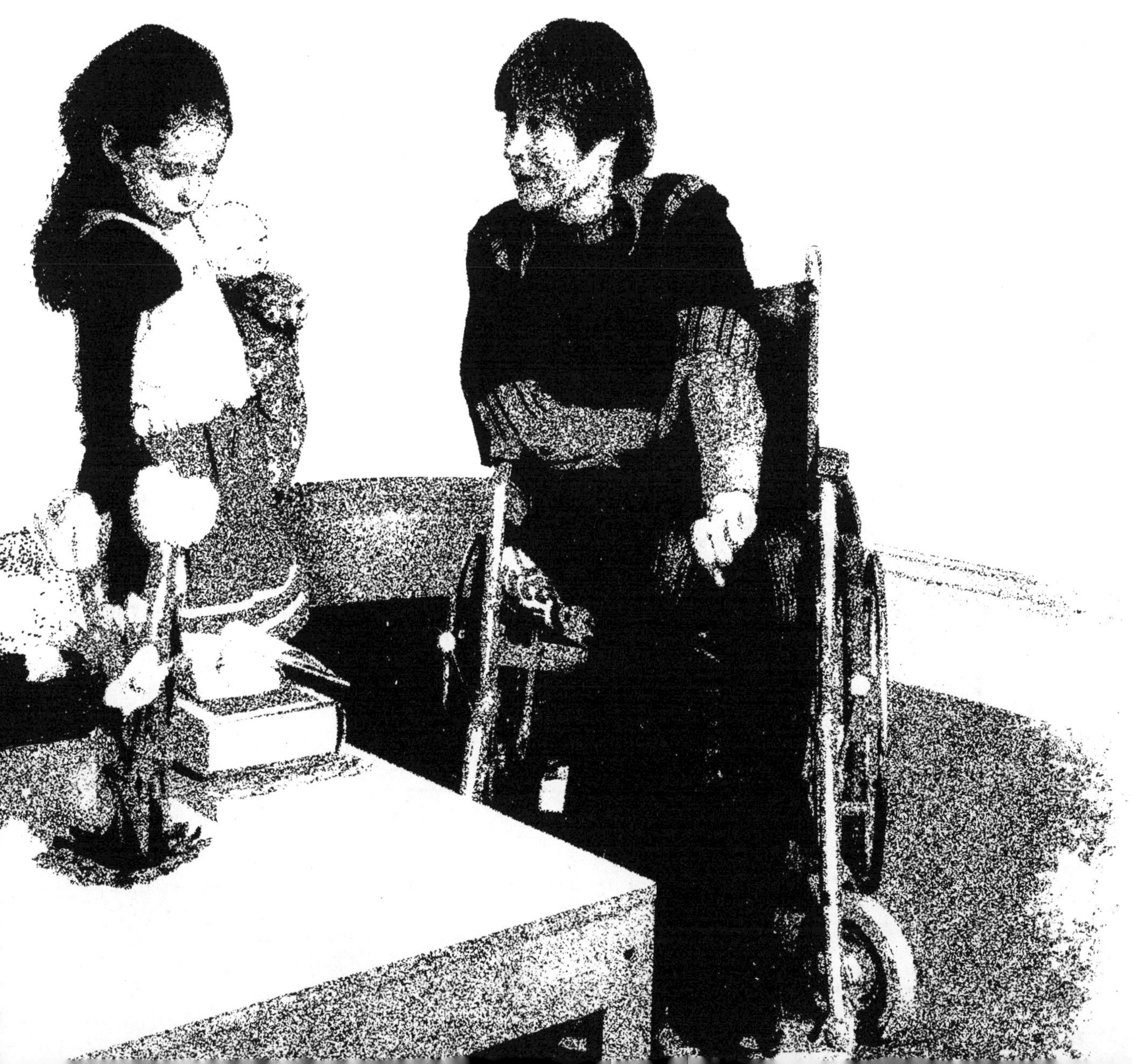

Leisure and Recreation

Leisure is a valuable and important part of life and everyone has the right to choose how it will be used. Some people look upon leisure as the negative of work, as time to be spent passively in activities that require no physical or mental effort and have no aim or object. While this can be very agreeable, and even necessary on occasion, it can become monotonous, blunting both spirit and intellect.

Invested wisely, leisure time can provide stimulation, challenge and enjoyment and can bring freedom from conventional and habitual restraints. It can offer you the opportunity to discover what you can do best and how you can develop your own particular drives, talents and imagination. Often, too, an activity which begins as recreation can become an occupation which not only provides a sense of achievement, but is also financially profitable.

There are also many social advantages to be gained from a positive approach to leisure. The more you can do and enjoy, the more you can give to others. And, invariably, people who involve themselves in a variety of activities are interesting and lively and can communicate with others, while people who have no real enthusiasms find it increasingly difficult to establish good social relationships.

This does not mean that in order to be fulfilled you should feel obliged immediately to join an archery club, go to music appreciation classes, take up basketry or decide to climb a mountain. There are many able-bodied people who don't enjoy competitive sports, have no ear for music or head for heights, are not good with their hands—and go happily through life without doing any of these things. As a person with physical disabilities you have an equal right to choose what not to do. But you also have a right to the same range of opportunities and facilities for learning a skill, for exercise, for creative activity and social participation that are available to the rest of the community.

There is actually a strong case for claiming that the handicapped have more than an equal right. Participation in recreational activities may well be the easiest or even the only way for a person with disabilities to become part of the community, to make new friends, to break out of an institutionalized setting or an overprotected home environment, to give expression to energies and inclinations for which the able-bodied usually have a greater diversity of outlets.

The question of how best to involve people with disabilities in recreational activities still arouses controversy. Until recently, in the United States and Great Britain, the emphasis was on special and essentially segregated provisions—athletic events organized so that those with similar disabilities compete against each other, clubs and leisure centers with specially trained teachers and facilities only for handicapped members, vacations and trips arranged for groups with specific disabilities.

There is, however, a growing body of opinion among handicapped people themselves and those who are closely concerned with their welfare, that these arrangements are not satisfactory because they do not take into sufficient account the desire of the majority of people with disabilities for social integration. They believe, therefore, that at present too great a proportion of available financial and manpower resources is being channeled into segregated provision for a minority of disabled people.

Similar disabilities do not necessarily create a bond of communication or understanding between people who may be disparate in every other way. Indeed some handicapped people positively reject being identified with other handicapped people for the purposes of recreation, sports or travel. To be a member of a "handicapped group" is to be set apart. It is to receive, or to become accustomed to receiving, special treatment and service and to exceptional degrees of protection or restriction. This is not in line with the desires of people with disabilities to live as integrated members of society in all possible contexts—including recreation and leisure.

Nevertheless, there are several arguments in favor of segregation for certain recreational activities and especially for people who are severely disabled. The first is simply one of practicality and convenience. It is undoubtedly easier and cheaper to provide expert instruction and purpose-built facilities for a number of handicapped people to learn riding or pottery together, for example, than for the same number to be given the same amount of instruction and encouragement individually in classes shared with able-bodied students. It is also easier and cheaper to arrange convenient travel and suitable accommodation for a group of thirty vacationers in wheelchairs than to make arrangements for each separately.

Then there is the indisputable fact that some handicapped people greatly enjoy the excitement and challenge of pitting their skills against one another in competitive sports and games. The national and international sports-for-the-disabled programs organized in the United Kingdom and the United States during the past thirty years have been popular and successful, and have proved to be of considerable rehabilitative and therapeutic value.

Often, too, disabled people who may not aspire to highly competitive standards would still like to try a particular sport or leisure activity, but lack the basic skill or sufficient self-assurance to join a group of able-bodied people. In such circumstances there is certainly a place for the "stepping stone" club, class or organization where a person with disabilities can acquire some knowledge and confidence and then, perhaps, move to an integrated setting. Similarly, handicapped people who have rarely traveled may gain initial confidence and know-how by joining a tour that is specially organized for them, before planning independent travel. Although all these arguments are valid, none is strong enough to force people with disabilities to spend their leisure time together if they do not wish to do so.

The ways in which you make use of your leisure and in whose company are ultimately personal decisions. This section explores the diversity of options that are open, or that can be made so, and the ways in which recreation can be, for everyone, a positive, constructive personal "re-creation," a rediscovery of each individual's place in society.

Outdoor Activities

It's not necessary to be able-bodied to enjoy outdoor activities, any more than it's necessary to be a champion. People take up such activities for obvious reasons—they are fun and they make them feel good. Muscular activity, skill, the excitement of competition, the joy of being outdoors, all refresh the body and spirit. Not only can disabled people enjoy these pleasures, but they have every right to share in public recreational facilities. In recent years, more and more people with physical disabilities have in fact begun to take part in a variety of outdoor sports and activities.

Of course, to avoid frustration and disappointment, you must face up to your condition realistically and objectively. You're not likely to decide to play tennis, for example, if you have limited arm movement. You must consider your own strengths and weaknesses and relate them to the activities open to you. That isn't to say that great handicaps haven't been conquered by highly motivated or determined people. There is Norman Croucher, the amazing man who had just begun to enjoy climbing when he lost both legs below the knees in an accident. He has since scaled Mont Blanc and the Matterhorn. His reason is simple. "I know climbing is a risk sport, but if you take climbing away, you take away my life."

To look at the matter positively, many people without the use of their legs can swim perfectly well by using only their arms, and they can also enjoy such activities as fishing or shooting in which strength of one arm and coordination of eye and hand are the most important requirements. And many people with sensory disabilities ski or trek because the emphasis in these activities is on overall body movement. Some sports, including basketball, bowling and archery, have been specially adapted to enable handicapped people to play, and there are many aids, which you can buy or make, that can help you to take part in the sport of your choice.

You may wonder if it's really worth all the effort and the risk of failure, ridicule or even injury just to get a ball over a net or to catch a fish. But outdoor activities have many fringe benefits. They are invigorating and stimulating, especially if you usually spend a lot of time indoors. Even restricted physical exercise improves muscle tone and circulation and helps respiration and coordination. You may even feel encouraged to experiment with new ways of moving—aiming, throwing, holding, reaching—and find that your dexterity or, perhaps, your balance, improves. You discover, or rediscover, the joy of actually moving independently "under your own steam," through water, on horseback or in a boat.

The warm camaraderie, the satisfaction of sharing a common goal with others or of competing against them in a friendly way, are experiences which are open to you. Testing your abilities, either individually or as one of a team, encourages determination, resourcefulness, decision-making and concentration, qualities which some disabled people are slow to develop because they are overprotected in their everyday lives and tend to resist or back away from challenges.

This doesn't mean that you should recklessly disregard the risks involved. There is a slight element of danger in practically every outdoor activity—for able-bodied and disabled alike. It's up to you to decide whether your enjoyment outweighs any risk involved, or whether you are simply being foolhardy by pursuing an activity that could bring trouble upon yourself and others.

Even if you find that there are some sports you cannot manage, or keep up over a long period, it is still worthwhile to try alternative, less strenuous ones. Apart from all other considerations, sports at all levels and of all kinds are an excellent way to make easy and informal social contacts. And once you have mastered the rules of most games, you might have the opportunity to participate as an official, a scorekeeper or an organizer and, of course, you can always go along to help with the refreshments and to cheer your team on.

There are many outdoor activities—water sports, winter sports, horseback riding—in which you can participate at your own speed, in your own way and without concern for the quality of your performance in relation to anyone else's. Such sports, although they may be enjoyed in competition, are especially attractive to some handicapped people who may become self-conscious or anxious in highly competitive situations.

To gain a basic proficiency, it is advisable initially to take lessons from an instructor on a one-to-one basis. The instructor should, preferably, have some experience in teaching the disabled and be conversant with any special techniques that can be helpful while you're learning. Even when you are experienced you should always be accompanied by, or within calling distance of, a capable able-bodied person.

For some people the greatest attraction and stimulus of a sport lies in the pitting of their skill and energies (either individually or as a member of a team) against opponents. Competitive activities give a person who is disabled what may be the first opportunity to interact and cooperate with other people in team situations and to gain a sense of personal accomplishment from actually winning.

Before definitely deciding on any particular outdoor activity it is wise to have a medical reassessment. Discuss with your doctor what you would like to do and find out if it is advisable, or whether you have any secondary disabilities that might cause trouble. Doctors are not always enthusiastic about such activities; they tend to err on the side of caution by keeping people with disabilities in a "cocoon of safety" which some find more restricting than others. Still, certain basic medical factors should be taken into account. They include flexibility and reliability of limbs, efficiency of circulation, susceptibility to loss of physical sensation or balance and a tendency to breathlessness or spasm.

It is impossible, however, to provide positive guidelines because two people with the same handicap might have quite different levels of potential capacity or already-developed compensatory skills. The adverse effects of many disabilities can be mitigated for some by wearing protective clothing when appropriate or by avoiding unnecessary exertion or hazard. As a general rule, the more rigorous the physical demands of a sport the more essential it is to seek sound medical advice first. A written assessment of your medical condition can be valuable to organizers and coaches. Some clubs require a doctor's certificate before accepting a handicapped member.

It is also advisable to talk to an instructor or some knowledgeable person to learn exactly what a particular sport entails before you spend money on expensive equipment or club subscriptions. Initially, try to arrange to participate on a trial basis to discover whether you are able to manage the exertions involved and, even more important, whether you really enjoy them. Some sports organizations and clubs arrange trial courses for all beginners and these are an excellent way to find out if you will be happy with a particular activity. To discover what is available, telephone or write to your local health, welfare, educational or recreational departments or to the national headquarters of the governing bodies of particular sports and recreational activities.

There has been so much emphasis in recent years on the therapeutic and rehabilitative values of sports for the disabled that some people feel that too much pressure is put upon them to become involved in activities for which they have no real inclination and to which they wouldn't be attracted if they were able-bodied. Therapeutic value aside, the prime reason for engaging in outdoor activities is for the sheer fun, pleasure and congenial companionship they provide.

Water Sports

Water is a great equalizer and many people with disabilities are able to achieve a greater freedom and flexibility of movement in or on water than on land. The common denominator of all water sports is swimming, which offers something to practically everyone and can be enjoyed both indoors and outdoors.

The natural buoyancy of water encourages unhindered and easy movement and many people who spend all their time in wheelchairs can nevertheless learn to swim and even to scuba dive. The great majority do not require any aids or special equipment while swimming, although they may while learning and for getting into and out of the water. For the novice there are inflatable cushions to keep the head above the surface and hand paddles to assist movement. Nonambulant people can be lifted into the water in a canvas sling. A self-controlled portable lift which fits onto the side of a pool has been invented to lower and raise swimmers gently.

It is advisable to learn to swim in the controlled conditions of an indoor pool which is not subject to sudden changes of temperature or disturbances of waves and currents. The Halliwick method of teaching swimming, devised by James MacMillan, a British hydraulics engineer, is now widely used in the United Kingdom to teach the handicapped (and the able-bodied, too) to swim and it is being introduced in several other countries, particularly the United States and Australia. This method requires that there be one experienced able-bodied instructor for every student. Learners are taught to experience the basic principle of water's buoyancy through a ten-point program. By this means, even very severely disabled people have learned how to move confidently and freely through water without any aids.

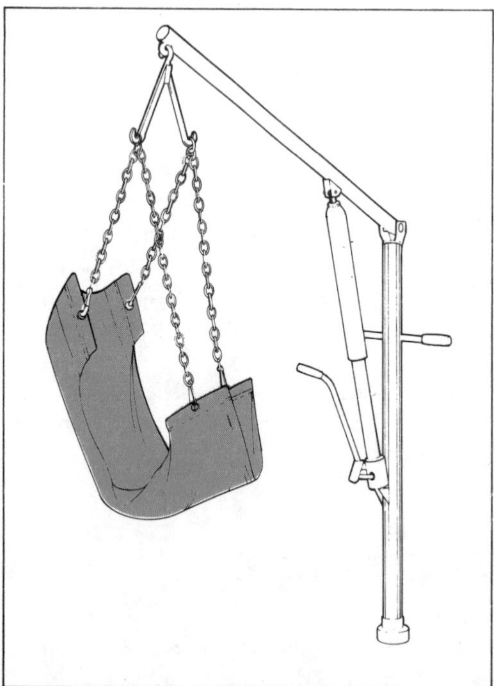

The hydraulic swimming pool lifter above is designed for poolside installation, but the unit could also be installed at dockside for lifting a person into and out of a boat. It has a sixty-inch (150-cm) lifting range and the horizontal swing is ninety inches (225 cm).

Once you can swim, you can enjoy some of the team games that may not be possible for you on land—such as aquatic adaptations of volleyball, baseball and polo. Some disabled swimmers also become good divers. If you want to take up scuba diving be sure to have a medical check-up first and to obey all the normal safety precautions which any qualified instructor will explain. Snorkeling on the surface can be safely enjoyed by anyone who is confident in the water, provided he or she is not too vulnerable to the cold.

Those who find actual swimming too taxing or difficult can learn the technique of drownproofing—a survival technique for nonswimmers that keeps a person afloat with a minimum amount of movement. This could help you feel secure and confident in water—an important first step toward involvement in other water sports.

If in your area there is no swimming pool equipped with support rails or wheelchair access to changing rooms and poolside, write to the municipal authorities or take the matter up with local swimming clubs for the able-bodied. As a member of the community, you have the right of equal access—so don't be fobbed off with the shallow end of the children's pool!

Boating is like driving—your disability is superseded by your functioning role and you are equal to those about you. A young paraplegic says of her newly acquired sailing expertise: "The fact that I am on a par with the next boat pushes the whole idea of being disabled into the background. It becomes unimportant."

The fundamental requirement for everyone taking part in boating activities is, first, the ability to cope with immersion in waters that may be much colder and choppier than those of any swimming pool. And whatever type of craft you are using, be sure to wear the appropriate clothing, such as a properly fitting wet suit or windproof and waterproof outer garments. If any part of your body is vulnerable to friction, bruising or prolonged exposure, it should be protected with extra padding.

The initial problem that faces most wheelchaired boating enthusiasts is that of actually getting aboard. If you are going in a small boat into which you can easily be lifted, then obviously your wheelchair is best left ashore. Yachts or cruisers present greater problems of embarkation. Lifts or tenders that hoist chairs aboard are the best, although not always the most readily obtainable, solution. Should your wheelchair come into contact with salt water, it must be well hosed down and thoroughly dried to prevent erosion.

Many people with disabilities can enjoy sailing in at least one of the many kinds of craft that exist. To control a sailing craft, however, it is necessary to have the use of the arms and at least one hand. There are special seats on the market that enable those with leg disabilities to steer and race sailing dinghies. Anyone who crews in a dinghy must be able to move quickly to keep the boat balanced. In larger sailing craft mobility is less important, but a handicapped crew member should always wear a safety harness that is attached to the boat itself.

To be a proficient rower or canoeist, arm movement and reasonable physical balance is necessary. A twenty-year-old with only the partial use of one leg and a steel rod in his back has crossed the English Channel in a kayak more than once. Rowboats fitted with fixed seats require less leg strength than those with sliding seats. People who must be strapped into a boat should be proficient in emergency procedures in case of the need to release themselves quickly. All canoeists must practice capsize drills in the early learning stages.

Canoes and rowboats can be modified or adapted to provide extra support and balance, but it is quite expensive to have it done. There are now available, however, roomier, flat-bottomed canoes with improved stabilizers that are ideal for recreational use and for fishing. Wheelchairs can sometimes be fitted crosswise between the seats in these boats.

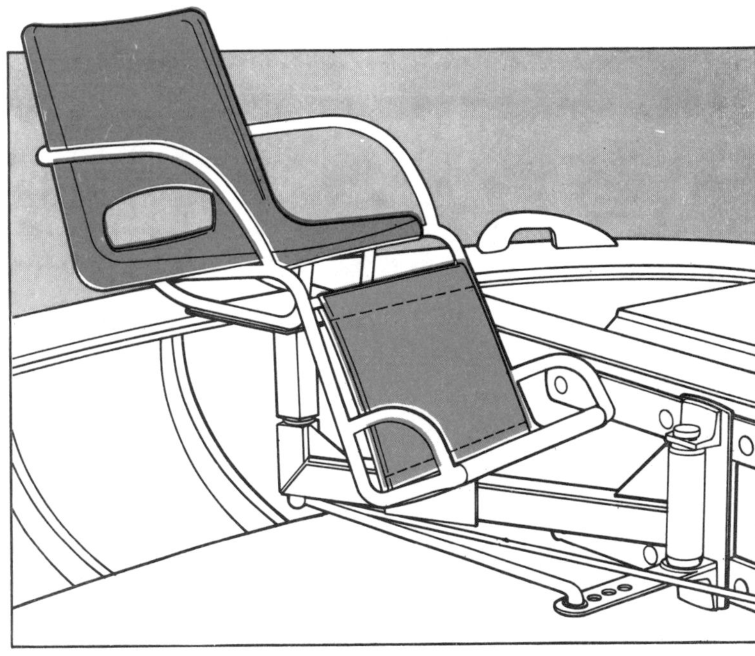

The Sailsafe Sailing Seat enables people who are severely disabled to move from one side of a boat to the other and thus to steer and race sailing dinghies. It is essential that the person using such a device not be restrained or strapped in so that he or she is able to fall free in the event of a capsize.

A physically demanding sport, waterskiing is quite possible for the deaf and the blind (who can be guided by someone with a megaphone in the towboat) and for anyone who has one strong leg and a good sense of balance. Because beginners (able-bodied or disabled) often spend more time in the water than on it, they must wear an approved life jacket or buoyancy aid, and in cold water areas a rubber wet suit. The usual method of teaching a handicapped person to waterski is to start with two tow lines alongside an able-bodied instructor. He holds his tow handle with one hand and, with the other, can steady and help his pupil up into the correct skiing position, which is the most difficult maneuver at first.

Fishing requires little physical strength and can be enjoyed at various levels of expertise. The techniques and tackle required differ—on sea, river, lake or from shore and bank—but anyone who can hold a rod by some means can participate. A major problem for the disabled angler is often access to the water itself,

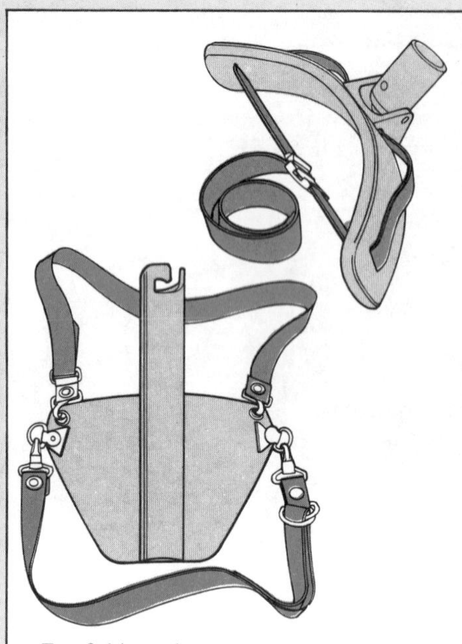

For fishing when arms are weak or with one arm, a fighting belt, above right, stabilizes the rod. The small, light Handi-Gear Harness above is designed to function as a second hand; one adjustable strap is worn over the shoulders, the other around the waist.

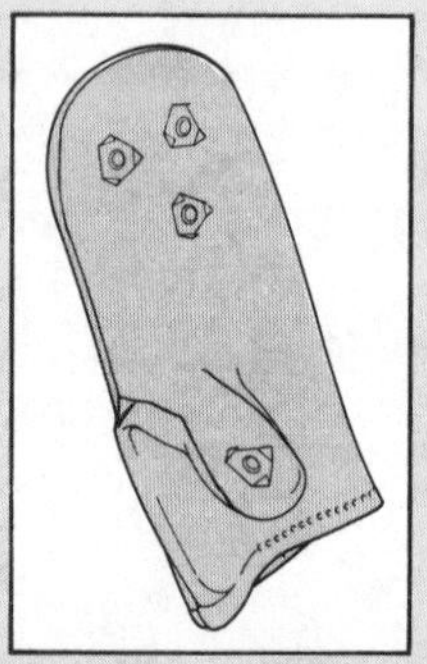

The stainless-steel cleats imbedded in this heavy vinyl Fish-Mitt, give a more secure grip when boating or cleaning fish.

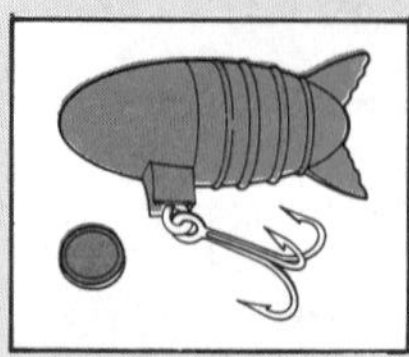

When casting is difficult, a pellet-propelled lure will dive as deep as fifteen feet (4.5 m).

for such natural obstacles as shingled beaches and steep rough banks are difficult to negotiate.

Special facilities for handicapped anglers exist in some recreational areas. The main requirement is a level, railed fishing platform built over the water's edge from which the angler can cast and reel in from a sitting or supported position. The platform should be easily accessible from a car or by wheelchair. If you fish from a chair, be sure the brakes are on and that the chair is not sloping toward the water.

Lightweight aluminum harnesses with adjustable straps are available to aid the angler who has the use of only one arm or hand. People who lack strength in their arms or are easily fatigued should choose a lightweight rod and fish in fresh waters.

For fishing from a boat, a purpose-built swivel-chair can be fitted to a seat to provide back support and to make it possible to change position when casting. And remember, other anglers are invariably friendly and helpful; don't be shy of asking if you need assistance in baiting a hook or untangling a line.

The Land-O-Matic net is an ingenious device, for it is stored in its own handle. When the net is needed, a release is pressed and the tube extends into a three-and-a-half-foot (105-cm) net, which is two feet (60 cm) deep.

Many commercially available devices make fishing easier for the disabled angler. The reel top far right has a trigger handle which is pumped with one hand to take up slack or to retrieve the line. A rod holder, top right, which mounts over the boat rail or on a boat seat, leaves both hands free. The electric reel bottom far right, which operates on a rechargeable battery, makes it possible to spin fish using one hand—either the left or right. A thumb-control button instantly changes the lure-retrieve speeds. If grasp is weak or manual dexterity lacking, a handle, into which the hand fits, attached to a reel, bottom right, often makes the reel easier to control.

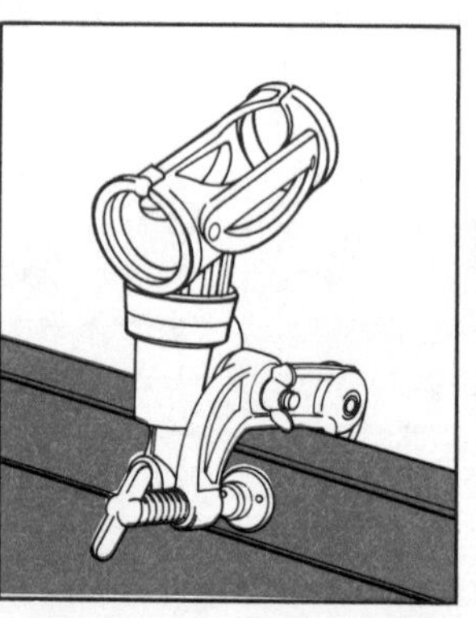

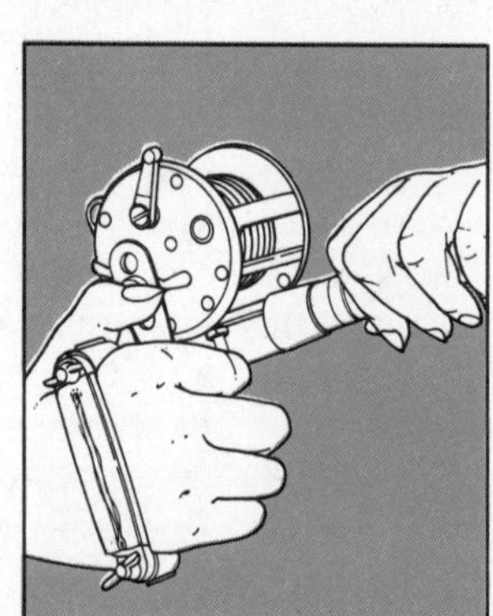

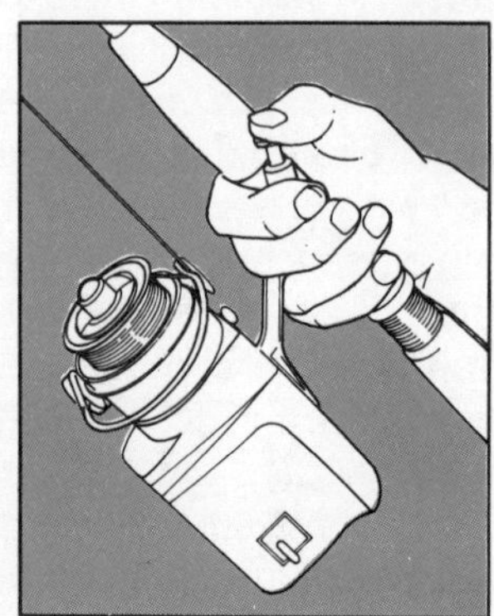

Winter Sports

Skiing might seem out of the question for most people with disabilities, but single-limb amputees often become proficient skiers, as do the deaf, blind and partially sighted. Amputees usually learn three-track skiing by essentially the same methods as able-bodied skiers and often have the advantage of a better sense of balance. It is an individual's choice whether to wear prostheses while skiing; most leg amputees do not.

Amputees must be sure that their instructors are aware of any limitations their condition imposes. They often find ordinary ski poles hard to manage, and the use of one or two outrigger ski guides (rather like crutches with small skis attached) increases support and balance base.

Ski courses specially tailored to the needs of the handicapped have been organized in several states including Colorado, California and Nebraska, and at some winter resorts in European countries including Switzerland, Norway, Austria and France. Colorado and California also have special programs for the blind (as part of BOLD—Blind Outdoor Leisure Development) which feature downhill and cross-country skiing with a sighted guide.

Ice-skating is a wonderful sport for those who can balance upright without any extra support. For some amputees ice-skating has positive therapeutic value and special methods have been evolved to promote participation in this sport. Ankle stabilizers and specially made reinforced boots are widely used by skaters with disabilities.

Many people who can't propel themselves across snow or ice can enjoy the exhilaration of tobogganing. Toboggans can be hired at most winter sport centers in America and Europe where clear runs are established. Fast tobogganing and bobsledding are high-risk sports and usually provide some very bumpy thrills —so be warned. In Scandinavia, however, parties of disabled people, including paraplegics, have traveled in fiberglass toboggans fitted with safety straps.

Horseback Riding

Riding is a splendid way to get into direct contact with the natural world—and to view it from a pleasurably elevated position.

Don't be deterred by misgivings about the difficulty or risk of riding, for a great many people with quite severe disabilities have learned to ride successfully. In Oakland, California, for example, paraplegics and quadraplegics are hitting the trails. Paraplegics are strapped into saddles that have harnesses like seat belts; quads ride on saddles with purpose-built back supports and harnesses.

People who are disabled should have riding lessons from a qualified instructor and may need up to three helpers to aid mounting and to steady them in the saddle. Once the rudiments of the skill have been acquired and complete confidence gained, the individual can progress as far as capabilities and enthusiasm stretch. Some advanced riders even enter show jumping competitions.

Riding is an outdoor activity that combines happily with others—exploring nature trails, camping and hill trekking. And there is an additional bonus—the opportunity to develop a warm and trusting relationship with a particular horse.

The first priority for a rider's clothing is comfort rather than elegance. The standard protective headgear should always be worn and any areas of the body that are susceptible to injury or irritation through friction should be well padded. An adaptive rein-bar used while learning

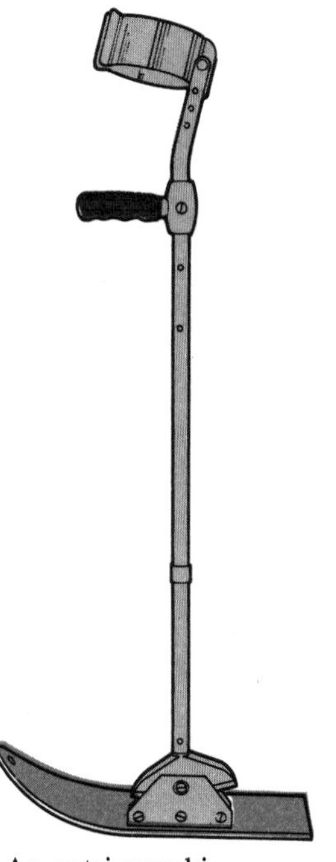

An outrigger ski guide increases the base of support for the amputee skier and, consequently, increases the ease of balance.

An adaptive rein-bar can be helpful to a rider who uses only one arm. The bar, about ten inches (25 cm) long, is attached between the reins. The rider holds the middle of the bar, which then magnifies wrist movement to give the leverage of two hands on the reins.

to ride is helpful to those who have the use of only one arm. For the wheelchaired a ramp helps in mounting and dismounting.

For several decades there have been associations and rehabilitation centers that encourage riding for the disabled in Britain and other European countries. In the United States, permanent equestrian programs and facilities for riders with disabilities were first established in the 1960s. Two principal centers are in Augusta, Michigan and Washington, D.C., with smaller programs in several other states. There is a North American Riding for the Handicapped Association and a similar organization in the United Kingdom. Both associations will give advice on teaching handicapped people to ride.

Flying

The extent of movements and coordination necessary to cope effectively with the controls of an airplane cannot be easily defined. Because of the nature of the risks involved, each individual must be assessed by a qualified instructor who will also take into consideration the kind of craft he or she wants to fly. But with the aid of hand controls for small aircraft, the wheelchaired are taking to the air in ever increasing numbers.

The Wheelchair Pilots Association (International) formed in 1970 and headquartered in Largo, Florida has more than two hundred members in the United States, Canada, Great Britain, Germany, Australia and Japan. In the United States there are now four manufacturers of hand controls. The apparatus fits several Cherokee models as well as Cessna and Grumman aircraft.

All aspiring pilots, handicapped or able-bodied, must have a third-class medical certificate before they are permitted to fly solo. Although disabled pilots-to-be almost certainly encounter more difficulty than average able-bodied applicants, they can rely on an objective appraisal of their physical ability to safely handle a plane.

Athletics

The impetus for the development of wheelchair athletics in the United Kingdom and the United States came from veterans who were severely disabled during World War II, but were not willing to sit on the sidelines for the rest of their lives. Since then the movement has grown until today a considerable number of people with a great variety of disabilities have become involved in competitive athletic sports at local, national and international levels.

The first organized wheelchair sports competitions were held at the Stoke Mandeville Hospital, in Buckinghamshire, England in the late 1940s and the British Sports Association for the Disabled was founded there in 1961. Now there are B.S.A.D. branches in several parts of the country as well as an International Sports Organisation for the Disabled also headquartered at Stoke Mandeville, where there is an excellent sports stadium which offers a wide range of facilities. The Multi-Disabled Games that take place at the stadium annually are open only to organizations affiliated to the B.S.A.D.

The National Wheelchair Athletics Organization, whose headquarters is in New York, has competitive jurisdiction over several sports that have been modified to enable the wheelchaired to participate. The association publishes its own rules and guidebook based on standard national rules, adapted and supplemented where necessary. Regional meets for wheelchaired athletes are held in various states and those who qualify can enter for the association's annual Nationals. At these events the United States team is selected for competition in the International Wheelchair Games and for the Pan American Wheelchair Games. The Paralympics are held every fourth year immediately following the Olympic Games in the host city.

The main competitive athletic events for the disabled are archery, precision javelin, shot put, track events (walking, running, wheelchair racing) discus, fencing, Indian club throwing, weight lifting, swimming, shooting and wheelchair slalom. Anyone who wishes to take part in any of these sports at competitive level must belong to an approved affiliated sports organization, must use a wheelchair which conforms to the standards as defined by the organizing bodies concerned and must be familiar with the rules of the particular sport.

Since 1976 waterskiing and winter sports events for the blind and for amputees have been included in the Olympiad for the Physically Disabled. To promote fair and safe competition, athletes entering most, although not all, the events are medically classified according to type and degree of disability. Competitors are allowed to wear any usual medically prescribed aid, but they must not be strapped into their chairs, although in some events an exception is made for paraplegics.

Archery

Long considered one of the most rehabilitative and satisfying of sports for the handicapped, archery has the advantage that it is played both outdoors and indoors. It requires coordination of the muscles of the back, shoulders and arms, and a wheelchair makes a good solid base from which to shoot. Reliable, good-quality equipment is essential, but it is not cheap—so be sure you are really interested before you invest money. When you do buy it is advisable to go to a specialized archery shop so that you can try various sizes and kinds of equipment.

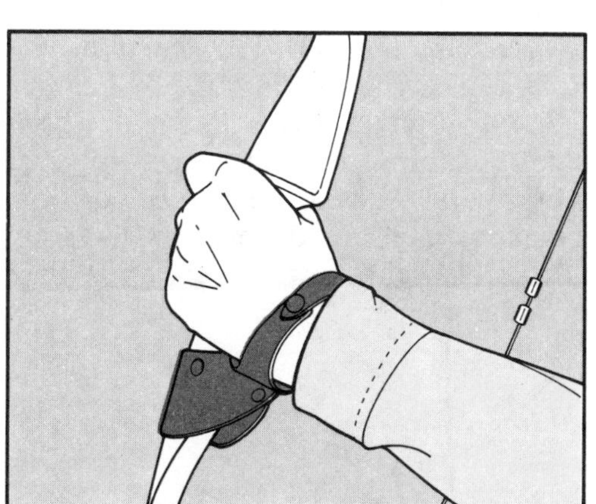

Shooting

For more than twenty-five years shooting with air rifles or pistols has been approved as beneficial therapy for the physically handicapped. The rules of procedure and safety that govern competitions are almost the same for disabled as for able-bodied participants.

The most useful aids for marksmen are tripods or U-shaped holders that support the gun barrel and help to improve the aim of those who shoot from a standing position. For the wheelchaired, a lapboard assists in steadying and coordinating movement. Wheelchair attachments, which can be homemade, hold the weapon when it's not in use. A person with limited arm control can learn to shoot a pistol using a mouthpiece attached to the trigger bar.

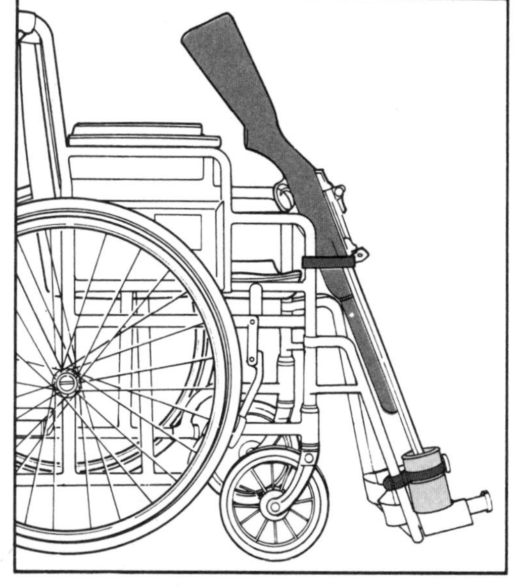

To carry a gun on a wheelchair, a simple attachment can be made. A soup can, the inside padded with foam rubber to protect the barrel, can be temporarily attached to the chair with a metal strap and bolts. A leather strap holds the gun securely in place.

A bow sling, left, available from most sport shops, helps to stabilize the wrist and hand for good control of the bow. To compensate for lack of strength, an adjustable tripod device, right, can be used to balance and hold the forepart of a crossbow stock securely. A camera tripod can be modified for this purpose.

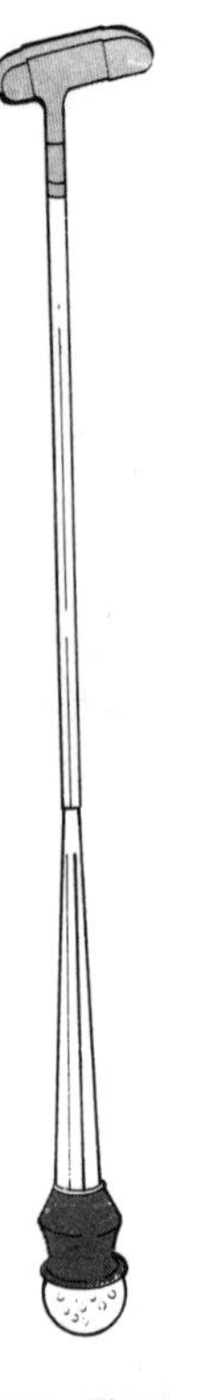

The Putter Finger is a soft, molded rubber suction cup which is designed to fit on the top end of any putter. It eliminates bending or stooping to retrieve a golf ball. The player can recover his ball simply by extending the putter and placing it on top of the ball.

Golf

A golf cart reduces the amount of walking and energy involved in going around a full-sized golf course. Carts come in various sit-down and stand-up models. Now, too, at many golf courses it is possible to rent electric carts that carry both rider and clubs.

In the United Kingdom there is a society of One-Armed Golfers which holds an annual championship tournament—all strokes must be played with only one arm.

Many people enjoy using a backyard golf course or a home putting green. Some of these, available from sporting good stores and mail order companies, can be used on a smooth carpet and have automatic ball returns.

In 1967 a course for putt-putt golf was specially designed for the physically handicapped. A form of miniature golf, the game requires concentration and skill. It has now become highly competitive in the United States where there are two Putters' Associations, one for professionals and one for amateurs.

Indoor Activities

Indoor activities of all kinds have the definite advantages that they can be pursued all year round regardless of weather conditions and some involve less range and vigor of movement than most outdoor pursuits. Like all forms of recreation, they offer opportunities for social interaction within the wider community for, while some of the activities can be happily pursued alone, they are all enriched by being shared on occasion with others. If you want to learn a new game, hobby, art or craft, the quickest and pleasantest way is to contact the appropriate sports organization, hobby or leisure club in your area, and you will invariably be able to draw upon a pool of goodwill and expertise.

Competitive indoor sports can be enjoyed at many different levels of proficiency and in purely recreational fashion. Any of them can be useful for improving such skills as hand-eye coordination and ball handling and becoming part of a team will stand you in good stead for a variety of other activities, both indoors and out. Some indoor games have small-scale versions with lightweight equipment which you can learn to handle first.

Hobbies, arts and crafts have the greatest asset of being almost totally "open-ended." You can do them whenever you feel inclined and become as expert as your talents and capabilities allow, always knowing that there are further avenues to explore, other techniques to master. Activities in this category offer a wide range of choice, a chance to develop individual initiative and the opportunity to put yourself in the position to give as well as to receive.

It is always satisfying to create something new, to make something out of little or nothing and to be able to pass knowledge on to someone else. And there is nothing special about that word "create"; most of us do create, in some way or other, much of the time. It is usually just a matter of finding a form of expression through which you can best and most happily convey your individual experience and ideas about the world.

If you decide to try a new hobby, art or craft, don't immediately buy all the relevant aids that are on the market. They may not be right for you, or you might be able to get something made by a friend, a member of your family or at a handyman shop that will suit your individual requirements much better. But there is some basic equipment that is useful for just about every indoor activity. A bed table is a boon for anyone who is in a recumbent position much of the time, as is a good-sized table that can be worked at comfortably from a wheelchair. Clamps to hold pieces of craft work, paper or board games in position, a compartmentalized work box and good adjustable lighting within easy reach are invaluable.

Indoor Sports and Games

It's not necessary to be ambulant to play wheelchair basketball, which was the first team sport to be specially adapted to the needs of the handicapped player. The National Wheelchair Basketball Association was formed in 1949 and there are now leagues in every state; since 1955 the United States has been sending a team to the International Basketball Championships held in various countries. There is also a Wheelchair Basketball League in the United Kingdom.

Basketball is a fast, action-packed game for all who can catch and throw a ball in whatever way suits them. The general rules covering regular basketball apply to the wheelchair version of the game—players must remain firmly in their seats for a jump ball, for example, and may wheel their chairs while simultaneously bouncing the ball.

Bowling is popular because it is a sport for all ages and participation is possible despite almost any disability. There has been a Wheelchair Bowling Association in the United States since 1962 and league competitions are held in most states. The association's leagues follow the American Bowling Congress rules and national tournaments are held for members every summer. There is also an American Blind Bowling Association with about thirteen hundred members and a National Association for Visually Handicapped Bowlers in the United Kingdom.

The skill of wheelchair bowling lies more in precision than in force or speed. There are several methods of bowling from a chair. The ball can be rolled down by hand in the usual way, but from a stationary position on the bowl line; an adaptive pusher aid or "stick" can be used to send the ball down the lane or the ball can be let down a raised chute positioned on or beneath the arms of the wheelchair. Players using these aids are not, however, eligible for A.W.B.A. competitions. A bowler whose grip is weak or whose finger control is limited can use a ball with a built-in handle that automatically snaps inward on release.

Badminton is a very satisfactory game because the equipment is lightweight and relatively inexpensive and it does not require a great deal of physical strength. It can be played in a sports hall as well as on grass outside, but it is easier to play indoors on a smooth-surfaced floor and without wind the shuttlecock is easier to control. Two useful aids are an extension-handle racket that extends the wheelchaired player's reach for overhead shots and a shuttlecock serving tray for one-handed players, which can easily be made at home.

Fencing is an ancient international sport which in recent years has become popular among people with disabilities because of its excitement and the challenge

With a bowling frame centered in front of the lane, a person who is severely disabled can bowl without lifting the ball. The ball is placed on the highest point of the frame and the bowler need only give it a push for it to roll down the frame and onto the alley. Bowling ramps are not commercially available, but are not too difficult to make.

Available from self-help equipment firms, the Alley Cat bowling aid can be used from a standing position or a wheelchair to propel and guide the ball down the alley.

of direct mask-to-mask competition. Usually the standard fencing court is enlarged to enable those in wheelchairs to maneuver. They are advised to wear safety seat belts. Handicapped people who have good body control and eye-arm coordination can fence with the able-bodied. Lightweight weapons can be inexpensively made for those with inadequate arm strength.

Table tennis is the only table game that is a recognized part of the National Wheelchair Athletic Association's program, and it is conducted according to rules somewhat modified from the standard rules of the United States Table Tennis Association. It can be played very successfully from a wheelchair and by those with limited ambulatory capacity, requires little strength and is easy to learn.

Those unable to play regulation table tennis because of poor vision or lack of muscle or eye coordination can try an adapted form in which the ball is sent across the surface of the table and through an open space in the net, rather than over it. Some players use two-handled paddles for this game.

Pool, with all the variations of the game of billiards, has long been a popular indoor recreation in the United States and in the United Kingdom. A few aids have been devised to help the handicapped player. A wheeled cue rest for teaching people to shoot, a wheeled cue holder and an adapted bridge that steadies the cue in a particular shooting position, can all be made by a home handyman from bits of scrap wood or metal.

Other enjoyable table games include indoor croquet and indoor soccer, quoits, skittles (plastic balls and tennis balls can be used in lieu of a proper skittle set), and finger shuffleboard, a nonstrenuous game for two or four people which is played with checkers on a highly polished surface. There is a home version of bowling on the market called Tally Pin that can be set up on a table, the floor, or even at the foot of a bed. It is portable, lightweight and the pins turn over to show the score when hit.

The only problem the physically disabled cardplayer has is that of actually managing the deck, and there are a number of aids which may help. For those who cannot hold their cards up, there are various grooved holders, available from self-help equipment firms, as well as a tray that hangs out of sight just below the

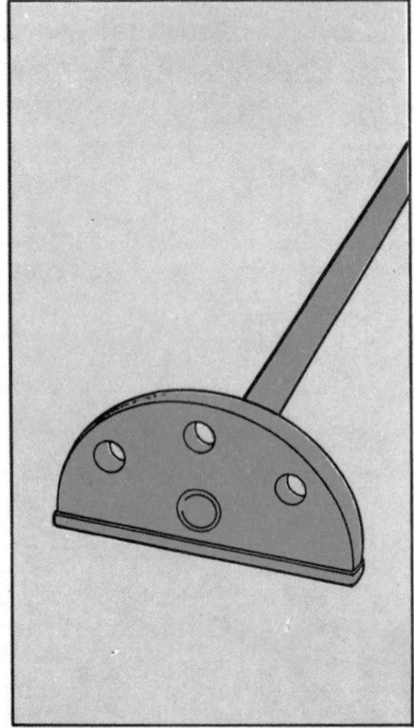

These aids for the billiard player can easily be made in a carpenter's shop. The adapted wooden bridge above steadies the cue in three shooting positions. The steel swivel cue holder above stands over a ball when required.

The wheeled cue rest above is made of a block of wood, a model car's axles and wheels, strips of metal and a cue.

This lightweight solitaire board has nine slots and holds seven cards across. The angled cards are easy to see and to pick up. Available from department stores and mail order companies, it comes with a book of solitaire games.

An effective card holder can be made by sawing slots, which are one inch (2.5 cm) deep, in a piece of solid wood which is at least two inches (5 cm) thick. A piece of felt or pimple rubber glued to the base will keep it from slipping.

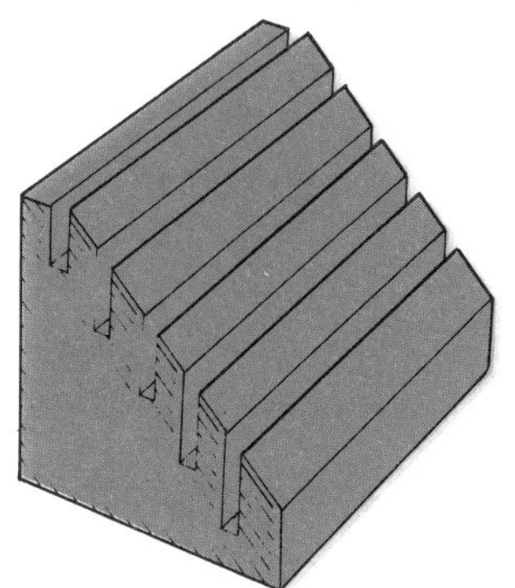

All the cards are visible to the player and can be easily put into and taken out of this wooden card holder rack which is tiered to hold five rows of cards.

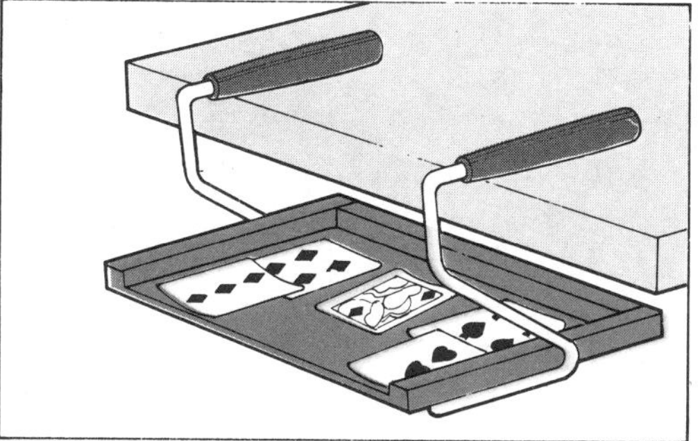

This card tray, which is available from the British Red Cross Society, hangs just below the table for the player who cannot hold cards.

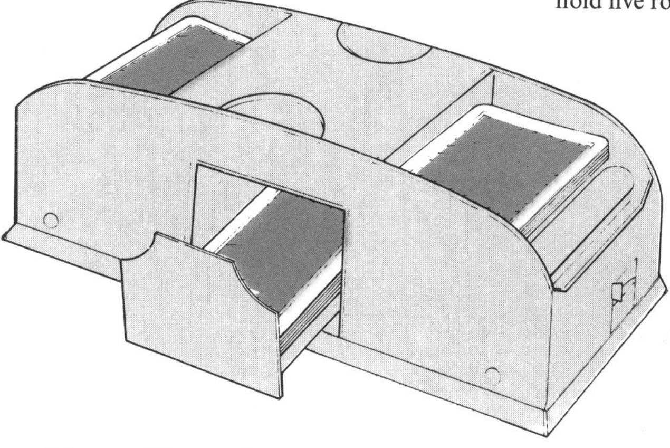

A battery-powered card shuffler can be operated with only one hand. Just divide the deck in half, put it in the shuffler and push the switch. Powered card shufflers are available from mail order companies and department stores.

tabletop. There are also battery-operated card shufflers, automatic card dealers and, for the partially sighted, extra large playing cards with enlarged markings. Braille cards are available for people who are blind.

Bridge players can increase their skill and enjoyment of the game by trying to solve the problems that frequently appear in newspapers and magazines and by joining a local bridge club.

Chess is an ancient, absorbing and complex game. It demands a great deal of concentration, but it is well worth the effort of learning it. The best way to begin is to find a local chess club where you can have the rudiments explained to you. Once you have learned these, there are numerous teaching manuals and chess magazines that can help you to develop your skill by analyzing championship games and solving tactical problems. Chess players are a dedicated and peaceable fraternity, and once you become reasonably skilful many opportunities to take part in club matches and tournaments will arise.

There are, too, Correspondence Chess Leagues in the United States and the United Kingdom which offer library services and advice and also organize tournaments. This is an ideal way for people who are severely disabled to participate, for members conduct games by postcard or on a master scoreboard mailed back and forth between the players. Members can thus be involved in a number of games simultaneously.

Disabled chess buffs have devised many ingenious aids with which to help themselves. These include a hooked mouthpiece to lift wired chess pieces, magnetized boards and electromagnetic mouthpieces for those playing in recumbent positions.

Photography

A versatile hobby that offers great scope for individual imagination and initiative, photography can be expensive. It's a good idea for the beginner to contact a local camera club first for advice about what to buy and where to buy it, for a vast range of sophisticated equipment is available, and prices vary considerably from store to store. Some clubs also keep a pool of used equipment for loan to beginners to practice with.

Many amateur photographers learn to develop their own prints, which is less expensive, and most clubs will give advice on this, too. Indeed, some clubs have darkroom facilities for their members' use. The leading manufacturers of photographic materials issue leaflets on darkroom printing techniques. Black and white film is easier to develop and print than color film. Black and white photographs can also be tinted with translucent oil colors. Details of this process are available from art stores.

If you find it difficult to hold, steady or focus a camera, there are a number of aids on the market that may help—or you may find it best to work out something to suit you and your particular camera. One enthusiastic quadraplegic solved the problem by making his wheelchair into a "rolling tripod" with the help of some metal piping and clamps that fixed the camera to one arm. Cameras can also be mounted on lapboards or trays by means of adjustable rods, to enable those who are recumbent to focus. The shutter can be tripped by means of a cable release held in the mouth.

In addition to recording happy memories of families, holidays and friends, amateur photographers can get many ideas from photography magazines for broadening their horizons in journalistic and artistic directions. Periodicals often run competitions, too, for the best photographs in such categories as action shots, landscapes and portraiture. The more expert you become, the more opportunities open up—for making interesting and informative home movies, for devising slide shows on particular topics, for recording local events in detail. Social organizations of various kinds will often welcome such shows. If you want more ideas or assistance, contact Volunteer Service Photographers Inc., headquartered in New York, which aims to help the disabled through photography and has projects underway for using camera skills in the service of the community.

A small tripod set on a lapboard, below, gives the wheelchaired photographer greater control and flexibility, particularly when working with one hand or if grasp is limited.

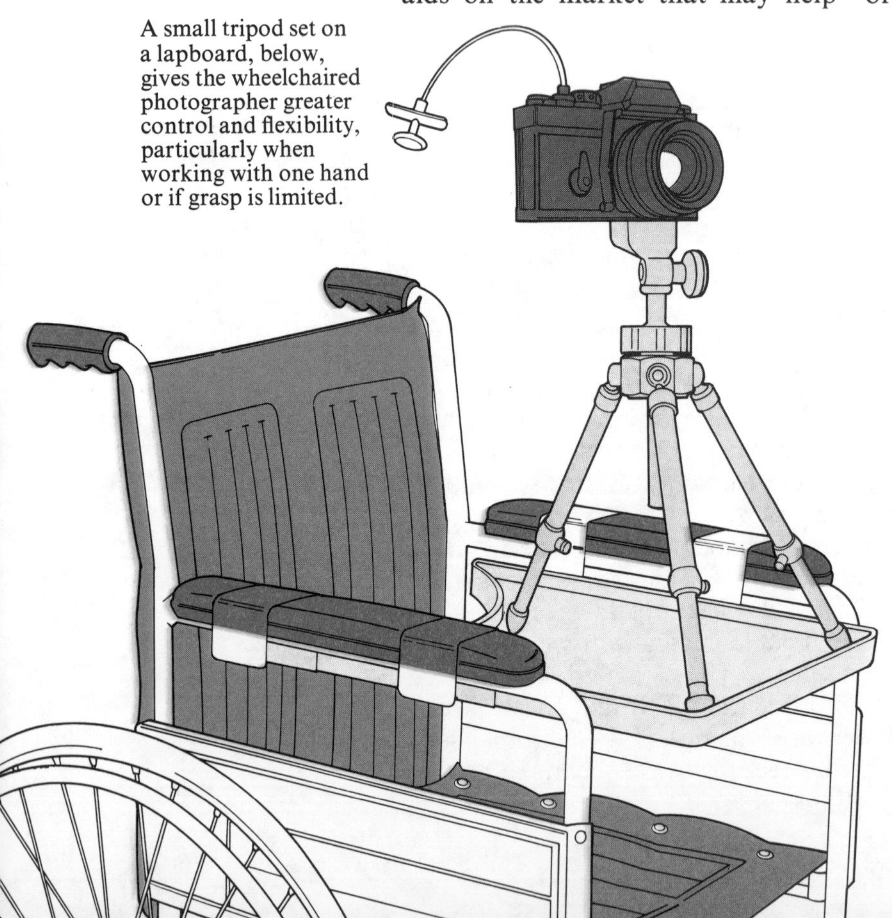

A battery holder, attached to the basic motor unit that has been screwed into the tripod socket of the camera above, makes the advancing of film automatic.

Ham Radio

This is a way of "talking around the world," as one disabled ham put it. And this is true because a ham, a licensed operator of an amateur radio station, can make personal contact on an absolutely equal basis with an indefinite number of other hams living on each of the five continents—all without moving from his or her own room. Any United States citizen who can pass the Federal Communications Commission test qualifies for a license to operate an amateur radio transmitting station. In the United Kingdom the training course for a transmitting license takes about one year and involves a City and Guilds examination. Applicants in both countries must prove their familiarity with basic technical and code knowledge and the regulations governing amateur services. A physical handicap of any kind is not considered a bar and the necessary tests can be taken at home by mail.

The easiest way to find out what hams are all about is to make contact with one of the several regional networks that operate in various parts of America, Britain, most other European countries and Australia. If you don't know a ham personally, try advertising in your local newspaper or inquiring at local radio equipment stores.

Hams may live hundreds, even thousands, of miles apart yet become good friends through an exchange of knowledge and ideas on all kinds of topics. Affiliates of some networks hold companionable "group meets" on certain wavelengths at particular times. Some of the networks maintain a pool of surplus equipment which they lend to newcomers, and experienced hams are always eager to give instruction and help.

Some hams specialize in doing such community services as picking up S.O.S. signals, appealing for unusual type blood donors and relaying personal emergency messages. Fluency in a foreign language can be improved by talking with hams in another country. This unique method of communication can also be used to further other interests. One ham who announced that she was making patchwork quilts was sent scraps of fabric from all over the world.

To help hams who have difficulty with the mechanical operation of the fairly intricate equipment, there are mouthsticks that will move dials and switches, radio controls that function by air pressure and voice-controlled relays that enable even operators who are severely disabled to send intelligible codes. The blind can get initial instruction from records, tapes and braille books on radio operation. There is an International Handicappers' Network, based in California, which is open to all people with disabilities and now has more than three thousand members from every state and almost every country. There are, too, several regional networks operated together by able-bodied and disabled hams.

Collecting

This is a highly pleasurable hobby that can also become quite profitable. Practically everything you can think of is being collected by someone and once a sizable body of people are collecting the same kind of object there is sure to be a magazine on the subject, for collectors are avid writers and readers about collecting. So, if you don't know where to start, buy a variety of collectors' magazines, get some books about the category that interests you from the library and watch the papers for news of local hobby shows.

Many people's collecting obsessions develop from other already established interests. Those who enjoy shooting become fascinated by old rifles, nature lovers collect butterflies, garden catalogs or animal prints, smokers collect book matches. Apart from interest, a factor that should guide your choice is that of expense. It is best to be realistic from the outset; such things as really good paintings, antique furniture, rare books and old silver and china are quite costly to collect. Moreover, there are already many experts (and a number of plausible con men) in the antique world, and the chances of finding a Rembrandt in a local junk shop are slim. But if you have time, enthusiasm and some space to house your trophies, you can do a lot with a little money.

One reason that the collecting of stamps and coins is so popular is that it is possible to begin with a small outlay (for the appropriate containers, albums and reference catalogs), and then expand the collection indefinitely as and when funds allow. Stamps and coins are not only attractive in themselves, but are easy to handle and store. Local stamp and coin collecting clubs or courses usually welcome new members, and there are international networks of philatelists and numismatists with whom knowledgeable collectors can correspond.

Picture postcards, playing or cigarette cards, tickets, theater programs, travel stickers or posters, beer or wine labels, badges and maps are among the many items for similar collections. If you have more space, you could, just for example, collect model soldiers, books, old clocks, dolls, charms, old comic books or movie magazines. People often give their collections focus by building them around a particular theme. They might collect only soldiers of the Civil War, only scenic postcards or only Superman comic books. Part of the joy of collecting is the actual sorting, mounting and cataloging of the finds. As their collections grow, most people like to swap items with other collectors and to buy or sell to complete particular series.

Some collectors are interested in things they can make or renovate into something of real value—seaside pebbles that can be polished and made into jewelry, battered musical instruments that can be repaired, repainted and restrung, bottles that can be made into lamp bases, furniture that can be refinished.

Having a disability really makes no difference from a collecting point of view, except as it limits your going far afield in search of items you want. If that's the case, however, you can advertise any special requirements in the various magazines and bulletins for collectors. You'll probably find others who share interests similar to your own.

Communication Clubs

Joining a club of this kind is an open-ended, essentially social activity that can take as much or as little time as desired, and can lead in a number of new directions. Members of clubs communicate with each other by letter, telephone or tape recordings—and sometimes a mix of all three. Magazines, community newsletters and local radio and television programs often give addresses of principal contacts. In this way people can get in touch with others and share news, views, hints on how to cope with specific problems, descriptions of vacations and travel, stories of families and pets. Tape clubs often send personal greeting messages for members' birthdays and other occasions and offer an exchange or loan service for musical or celebrity recordings.

Some clubs have a large international membership that may be worldwide and, for anyone who wants to know more about a particular foreign country, a good way to further that interest is to correspond with a few resident pen pals. One example is the Voicerespondence Club, with members in forty countries, who contact each other initially through a directory issued by the club which gives members' addresses and such other information about them as their ages and other hobbies. Some clubs organized specially for disabled and housebound people may offer to their members an advice service on financial and practical matters.

Membership in some clubs is restricted to people with a common interest—and that can be anything from ESP to jigsaw puzzles or advertising contests, from astrology to gardening or the breeding of tropical fish. Some clubs circulate a regular magazine featuring members' contributions, raffles, puzzles, recipes, poetry and opinion letters.

There are many variations on the communications club theme, and even if they don't get on the right wavelength immediately, most people find that after a while they have made some congenial and valuable contacts, often some genuine friends.

Art

Many people with disabilities have discovered ingenious ways to overcome or circumvent the barriers which at first seemed to make painting or drawing impossible. Professional artists who have physical disabilities have contributed new insights and dimensions to art through the experience of their disabilities and many disabled people, with no exceptional talent, have learned, as the result of some artistic training, to observe the world with a more sensitive awareness and appreciation. Artistic interest can broaden an individual's social life, too, for amateur artists often get together to discuss each other's work and to visit galleries and museums.

If you have not painted or drawn before, it's best to begin by buying some basic equipment and then experiment by copying a picture you like or painting the scene from your window or an object in your room. If you enjoy the feel of the medium (be it watercolors, oils, pastels or charcoal) then it might be worth getting some technical instruction. There are, too, many books which give step-by-step instruction on drawing and painting. Part-time and evening classes at various levels of ability are organized by institutes of adult education, leisure groups, art colleges and some museums. These courses cover a wide spectrum which includes painting, sketching, creative design, collage, graphics and screen printing.

A person who is unable to attend classes away from home, can advertise for private tutoring or ask about voluntary instruction at a local community service office or art college. In the United States there are art colleges, like other colleges, that offer such facilities as tape-recorded lectures, intercommunicating class-to-home telephones and visiting tutors to enable homebound people to take part in their programs; some also run art-by-correspondence courses. Training and rehabilitation centers for the disabled invariably hold regular art classes. Some people gain more than others from formal art training. Those who find that it does not suit them can often learn a good deal on their own from do-it-yourself books as well as from actual practice.

Because so many people with disabilities have found a creative outlet in painting and drawing there are many aids on the market, as well as many devices that are simple to make at home. Among them are easels fitted with clamps to secure work firmly and electrically operated easels that can be moved to various angles and heights by simply pressing a switch, thus making it possible to paint from a semi-recumbent position. Paintbrushes can be fitted with various mouthpieces for holding between the teeth and with extension devices for working on large areas. These can be made with cardboard tubing or simply by extending new brushes with handles from old ones. People who cannot hold brushes in either the hand or mouth have learned to paint with their feet or toes, or with a brush attached with a band to the forehead. Those who cannot manage fine detailed work can make attractive designs with the palm of the hand, one finger or thumb or by spray painting.

Drawing or coloring skills of any kind can be used in a variety of ways, including greeting cards, calendars, notepaper, posters and postcards. It is also fun to use coloring techniques in conjunction with such other crafts as modeling, pottery and toymaking, and to create interesting pictures by combining paint or pastels with such materials as papier-mâche, mosaic tiles, seashells or scraps of fabric. Another way to use paints is to print designs, making printing blocks from wood, metal, linoleum or even potatoes.

A number of community, cultural and educational organizations in the United States and the United Kingdom sponsor work by handicapped artists at international, national and local levels. The International Association of Mouth and Foot Painting Artists was founded in 1956 to encourage those who cannot use their hands to paint and draw. Artists whose work is of a sufficiently high standard can become life members of the association; they are paid a regular salary and the association undertakes to sell their work. The association also provides allowances to promising handicapped students for further art training.

Many people who don't themselves aspire to paint enjoy art as spectators. Courses in art appreciation, which usually include organized lecture tours, are given by many adult education institutes, art colleges and museums. An increasing number of galleries and museums are now accepting their responsibilities toward handicapped citizens by making their buildings accessible and welcoming. Some exhibitions are designed to accommodate the wheelchaired; some galleries issue braille kits or taped commentaries for the blind and graphic communication symbols for the deaf. There are textile exhibits and "touch murals" which the blind can appreciate by hand, and light-and-color exhibitions with sign-language tours for the deaf. A few cultural institutions arrange traveling exhibitions for the homebound. There has been greater progress in this direction in some parts of the United States than in others; Britain is generally less advanced. If the cultural institutions in your area are not making efforts to reach handicapped citizens, write to the municipal authorities for they have a legal obligation to do so.

Writing

A considerable advantage of writing over most other indoor activities is that it involves a minimum of equipment. Pen and paper are the only basic necessities, although any work submitted for publication has to be typewritten.

Courses in creative writing and journalism are offered by most colleges in the United States and by a few in the United Kingdom; correspondence courses are also available and there are numerous home-study writing manuals. But such instruction can only teach the basics and composition of language structure, help somebody to express his or her ideas coherently and improve the clarity and fluency of writing style. Nobody can be taught to write. Writing, like painting or playing a musical instrument, comes more naturally to some people than to others. But most determined people can achieve considerable literary fluency. If you are an aspiring writer there are many ways to begin.

Try rewriting radio or television news and feature items for newspapers and then try to rewrite newspaper pieces for radio or television. Read everything with critical awareness and analyze other writers' styles. Learn proofreaders' marks and volunteer to do some proofreading; this is a useful skill to acquire and will increase your understanding of language structure. Interview people you know (using a tape recorder if you like) and write up the interviews in various styles. Join a correspondence club which will give you an incentive to write regular and interesting letters.

It is easy to get printed material copied inexpensively, so you might try to produce a news-and-feature bulletin for family and neighborhood consumption —a good way, incidentally, to learn the basics of magazine production and editing. Use your public library, clippings from newspapers and magazines and notes on radio and television programs to build up reference files on topics that interest you and to keep up-to-date the information you already possess on any specialized subject. In such ways you can become something of an expert in a number of different fields.

Before you try to sell your work, carefully study the style and content of the publications you are aiming at and angle your writing accordingly. There is a steady demand for nonfiction—pieces for local newspapers, feature articles for women's, sports, political and hobby magazines, for example, and technical writing for trade and professional journals. There are also a number of excellent magazines produced by the disabled themselves and they welcome articles from their readers. Publications of this kind seldom pay high rates, but they do give you some writing experience as well as the satisfaction of seeing your work in print. Writers' digests, which give information about the requirements and the rates of pay of most current publications, are published annually in the United States and Britain.

It is usually rather difficult to get fiction published. If you decide to try a full-length novel, first send a detailed outline and a few sample chapters to a reputable publisher. Beware of any publisher who advertises for the submission of manuscripts or who assures you that your novel is wonderful and then asks you to contribute toward the cost of its publication, distribution or publicity. Unfortunately, there are many of these "vanity" publishers lying in wait for unsophisticated, aspiring writers. Above all, don't be put off by rejection slips—even famous writers have collected many.

Music

Whether you participate in the making of it or enjoy listening to it, music is a powerful force and can give great pleasure and be a source of comfort and stimulation. People with disabilities affecting their legs often learn to play stringed or small wind instruments. Keyboard instruments can be played by those with some hand or arm control and some players use shoulder slings to support the forearms. Mouthsticks can be used to strike the keys.

There is a small but growing repertoire of piano and organ music written specially for one-handed players. Because organ keys need only be depressed instead of being struck, as piano keys have to be, many people with disabilities find them easy to play and those who cannot use their hands can play small two-octave chord organs on the floor with their toes. These organs can also be fixed to tilt-tables for those in semi-recumbent positions.

Percussion instruments, including tambourines, clappers and triangles are relatively easy to play with limited arm movement and their use develops a sense of rhythm and timing. They are great fun to play in concert with a friendly musical group. Singing is another enjoyable group activity, and for most local choirs a particularly good voice is not necessary—usually just enthusiasm and the ability to read music and to sing in tune are enough.

Music also encourages and gives meaning to movement—and this becomes dancing. The traditional, large-scale figure movements of square and country dancing are particularly adaptable to wheelchair dancing, which the disabled and able-bodied can enjoy together. For the dancers to get the most from it, the caller should give clear instructions on procedure before the dances begin. Some voluntary organizations arrange wheelchair dance festivals and will supply descriptions of dances that have been specially arranged for the wheelchaired. Dancers can also work out their own formations.

If your delight in music is in listening to it, try to acquire a reasonably good stereo phonograph. If you can't afford it organizations concerned with the welfare of the disabled can often supply one. Some phonograph turntables have automatic cueing devices for easier operation and appliances can be fitted to control the lowering and lifting of the pick-up. People with poor hand or arm coordination may find cassettes easier to manage. Most public libraries lend records and some lend cassettes. Braille music scores and records and tape recordings on musical history are available from the Department for the Blind and Physically Handicapped which is headquartered in Washington, D.C., and has branches in every state. A system using vibrating boards, tone boxes and percussion instruments has recently been developed to enable the deaf to perceive and appreciate musical rhythms.

To broaden your musical understanding, you might join a music appreciation class or a club whose members exchange records, tapes, go to concerts together and share musical evenings. Many community organizations welcome people who are knowledgeable enough on musical matters to take part in quizzes or introduce programs of music with a background commentary. Some music enthusiasts create their own musical programs on tape.

Pets

Having a living creature to care for and observe can be a constant source of joy and interest. Some people with limited mobility prefer pets that can be kept within easy viewing range—like tropical fish, caged birds, hamsters or guinea pigs. Others find it fascinating to watch the behavior of ants in a formicarium, worms in a vermarium or newts in an aquarium. Cats and dogs are, of course, more loving and faithful companions, but they must be properly cared for and require access to some outside space. It is not kind to keep as pets active breeds of dog unless they can get regular exercise.

Some dogs can be trained to trot beside a wheelchair, to fetch, carry and pick up dropped objects. Guide dogs are, of course, invaluable to the blind. "Hearing ear" dogs have now been trained to help the deaf by drawing attention to such sounds as telephone and door bells. Animal magazines, books and local associations for animal welfare are good sources of advice on the rearing and keeping of all kinds of pets.

If you want to breed cats or dogs you may find it helpful to join one of the societies of breeders that exist in the United States and the United Kingdom. It is a fairly expensive pastime, however, and the animals may well require more attention than you can easily give them.

Volunteer Work

This is a particularly satisfying involvement for people with disabilities because it puts them on the giving, rather than the receiving, end of the "care package." Sighted people with physical disabilities can do much to help the blind by learning braille (or the braille musical code) so that they can transcribe printed material, by reading aloud to the blind or by acting as "guide eyes" for them on excursions. Older people who have physical disabilities are often particularly successful at establishing warm and trusting relationships with mentally and physically handicapped children and are able to help them to learn some skill, craft or sport.

If you would like to help others who are not physically disabled but have problems of other kinds, you can offer your services to one of the voluntary organizations that exist to help the homeless, the infirm, the isolated or those with such special difficulties as alcoholism, drug addiction and phobias. There are disabled people who are doing extremely valuable personal counseling work in Britain in the field of marriage guidance, in citizens' advice bureaus and with students. Others counsel ex-prisoners and their families or give "language and customs" courses to recent immigrants.

In the United States people with disabilities are active in pressure groups campaigning for environmental or educational improvements, for more cultural or sports amenities, for women's rights—and for better access to public buildings. Organizations of this kind usually also welcome volunteers willing to help with the programming of activities, the keeping of accounts and minutes and the production of publicity material. To find out how and where you could best be of use, get in touch with your nearest voluntary service bureau, neighborhood church or community center—or with one of the many thousands of people already engaged in volunteer work.

Crafts

In recent years a multitude of imaginative ideas have enlivened and enlarged the scope of traditional crafts and many new materials and techniques are used to create a variety of attractive and useful handmade objects. The old-fashioned convention of dividing crafts into "male" and "female" categories has fortunately been discarded: some men are extremely skilful at weaving tapestries; some women are equally good at woodwork.

One of the pleasures of learning a craft is to make something you can give to those you are fond of, or that is appropriate for a certain occasion—such as colored Easter eggs, Halloween masks and Christmas decorations. As you become more proficient at a particular

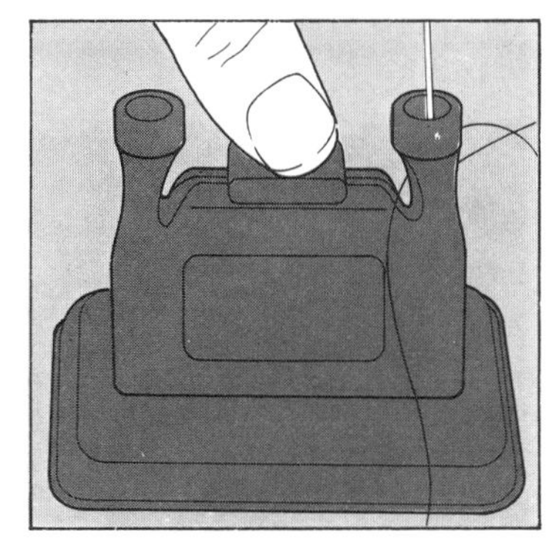

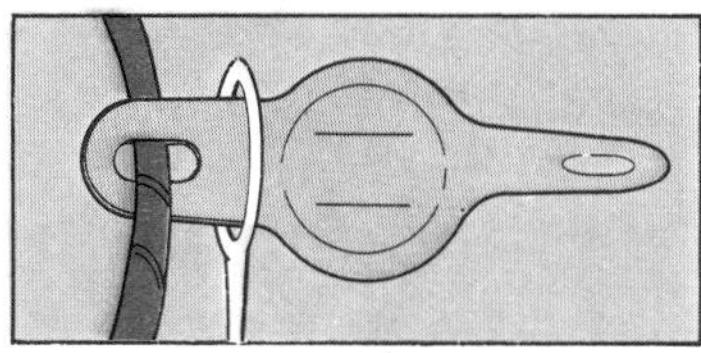

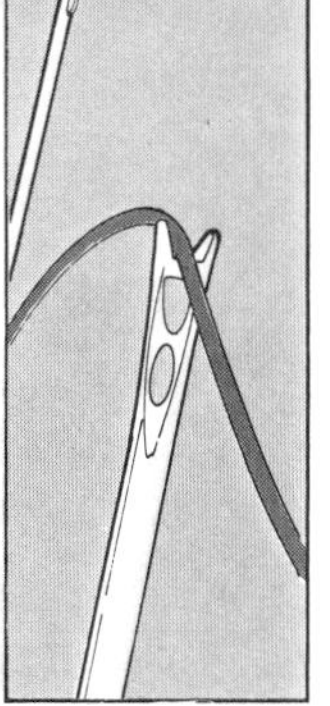

There are many inexpensive aids which make threading needles easier. The automatic threader top left can be managed with one hand. The threader above left makes it simple to thread yarn. With the Redi-Thread needle right a wire loop, not an eye, is threaded. The top groove of the self-threading needle has a spring action.

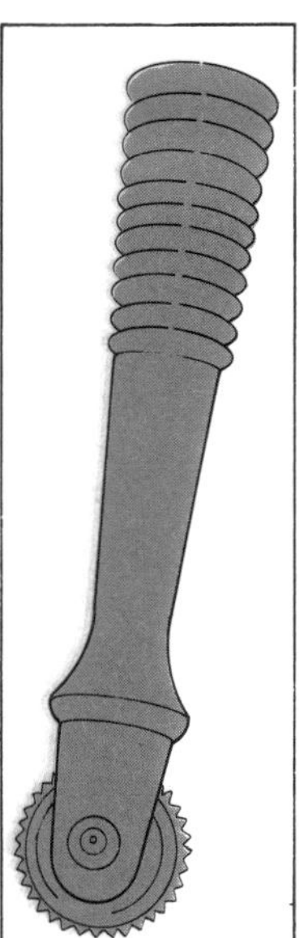

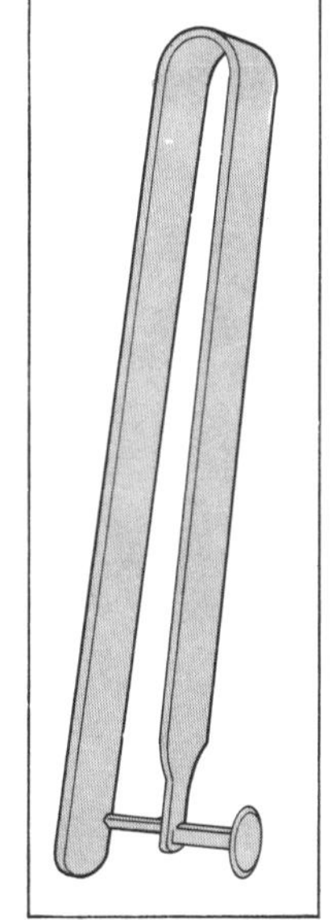

The pattern marker above right marks both pieces of material at the same time. The tracing wheel above left transfers pattern markings onto fabric. Both of these gadgets can be used with one hand.

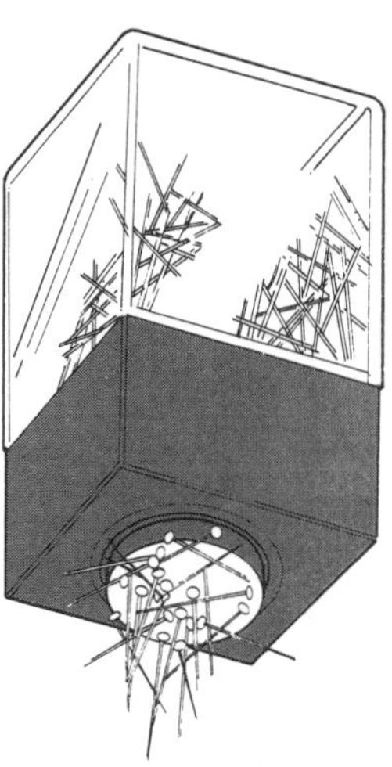

A Pinmaster holder, which magnetically holds pins vertically around a top ring, makes it easier to retrieve pins from a flat surface.

craft you may well be able to make some money by selling your work. Associations that help the disabled can give you ideas for marketing outlets, as can the craft magazines, and there are often opportunities to sell craft work at local bazaars and fairs.

Patchwork and simple crocheting are two of the easiest forms of needlecraft to learn. Patchwork is particularly economical because odd scraps of fabric can be used—as they can for making rag rugs or decorative applique motifs. Once a few basic stitches have been mastered numerous items can be made including bags, mats, aprons and cushion covers. It is often much more fun to undertake larger projects, such as patchwork quilts, rugs or wall-hangings jointly with other people.

There are many aids for doing needlework of all kinds. They include automatic needle threaders and self-thread needles, thimbles with springs attached for easier manipulation, darning boards, special embroidery and tapestry frames, knitting aids for the one-handed and for those with limited grip. Helpful, too, are electric or battery-operated scissors, knitting machines that can be operated by someone with limited arm or hand control, electric sewing machines that can be adapted by the manufacturers to suit individual requirements and small, battery-powered, hand-held sewing machines.

Some dexterity with tools and the ability to handle cutting implements safely are necessary for work with wood, leather and metal. Attractive costume jewelry, belts, wall plaques and junk sculpture can be made fairly easily and can be fashioned from such cheap and readily available materials as old nails, driftwood, curtain rings, tin cans and scraps of wire.

Scale modeling is enjoyed by thousands of people, disabled and able-bodied, of all ages, all over the world. It is a craft which requires manual dexterity, attention to detail and patience. Some modelers specialize in tanks, others in airplanes, ships or soldiers. Many extend their hobby by constructing dioramas which provide a realistic setting for display.

Although models can be made from balsa wood, most people prefer to use the commercial kits, which contain all the

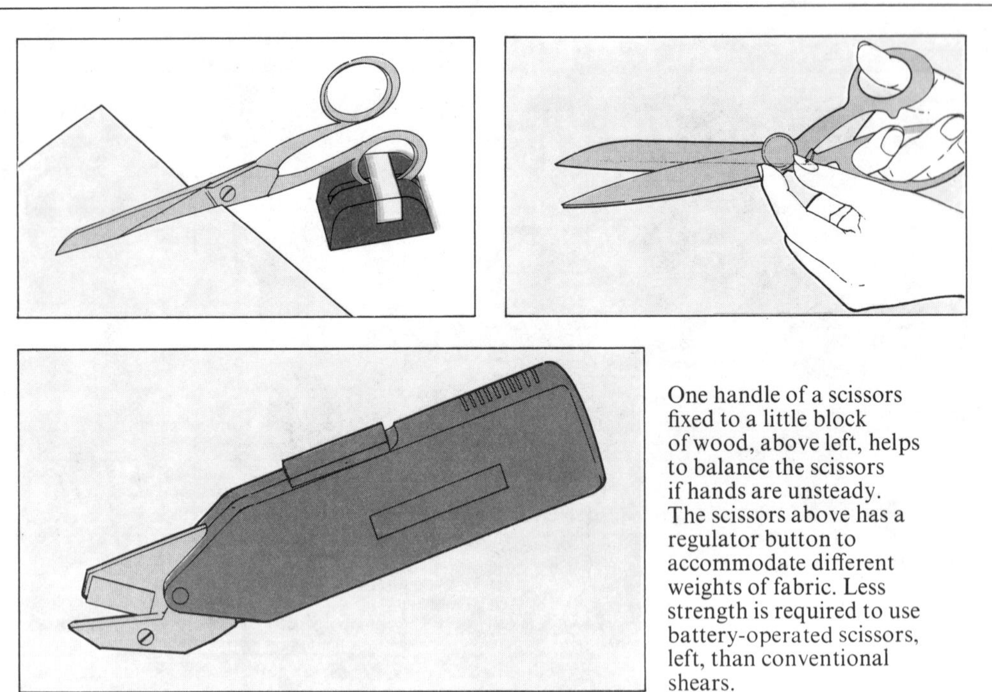

One handle of a scissors fixed to a little block of wood, above left, helps to balance the scissors if hands are unsteady. The scissors above has a regulator button to accommodate different weights of fabric. Less strength is required to use battery-operated scissors, left, than conventional shears.

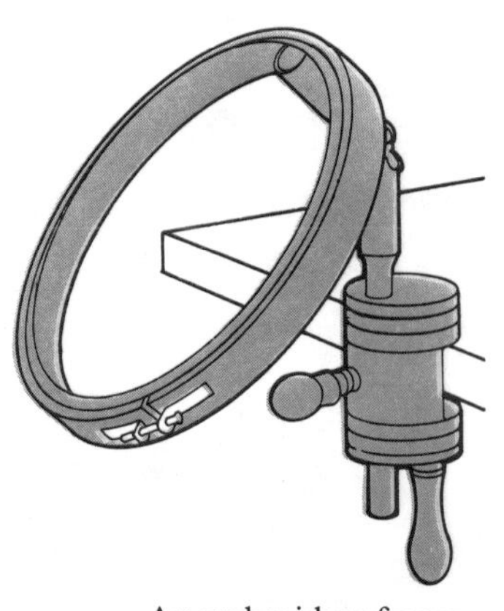

An embroidery frame which can be fixed to a table edge with one hand is not only good for doing needlework, but also makes it possible to sew buttons on a shirt using only one hand.

necessary parts, made of plastic, and instructions for putting them together. The kits, which vary in price in accordance with the complexity and size of the model, are readily available, along with the special glue and paints, in model shops and department stores.

There are societies for scale modelers in the United States and the United Kingdom and the International Plastic Modellers Society offers a technical advisory service.

Scrap paper of all kinds is a versatile and inexpensive craft material and can be used for making papier-mâche sculpture, toys, bowls, masks, kites, Christmas and table decorations and imaginative collages and mobiles. Handmade Japanese art papers are a delight to work with and can be used to make translucent lampshades and attractive floral decorations.

Unusual floral decorations can also be created from dried flowers, seed heads and grasses. When there is sufficient space the plants can be hung to dry in the air, or a dessicant powder can be used. After drying, they can be preserved in a glycerine coating and used for decoration, sachets and pendants.

Beadwork, ropework and macramé are some of the old crafts that have enjoyed a recent revival. Beading is done by threading beads together with a blunt needle and weaving the threads back and forth to produce a pattern. A simple bead-weaving loom can be made by cutting notches in a cardboard box to secure the warp threads.

A loom is not needed for ropework, which can be done simply by cutting lengths of rope, coiling them into shapes and glueing them together. Macramé is a little more complicated. It is done by knotting lengths of yarn at intervals over other lengths to make a decorative design. It is easiest to learn the basic macramé knots using ordinary string; cord, raffia, ribbon or heavy twine can be used when the knots have been mastered. Bags, mats, belts, potholders and necklaces are just some of the things that can be made by using these techniques.

Simple pottery containers are not difficult to produce. To get the feel of the material, the beginner can use compounded self-hardening clay mixtures that become firm after exposure to the air. They are fairly durable, but to work with natural clay a kiln is necessary. There are small kilns on the market that

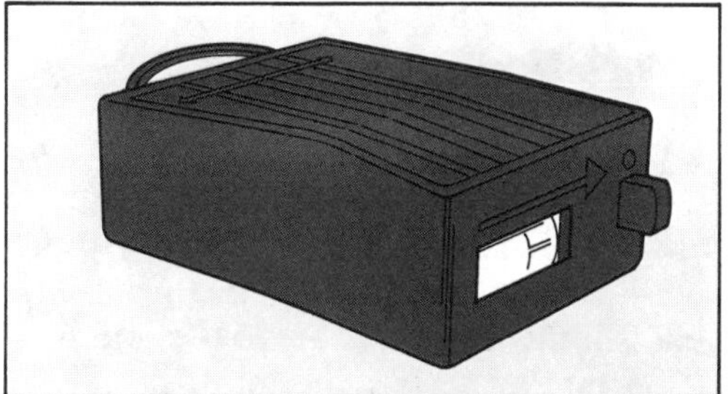

Just turn on the switch of this tapeless measure and run it along any even surface. In the window indicator the measurement is displayed.

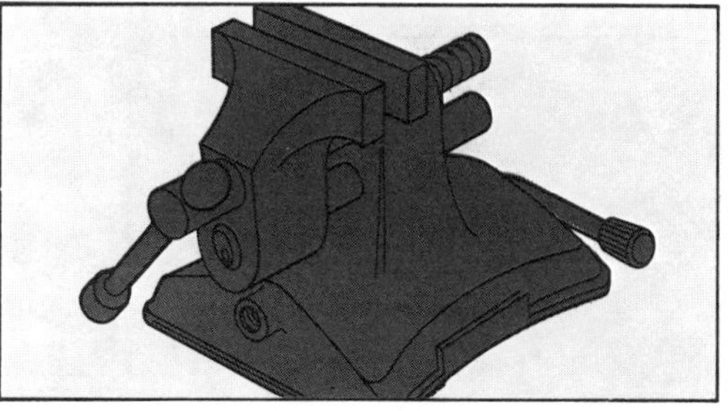

A portable vise with a lever-operated, built-in vacuum cup, anchors firmly at any angle to any smooth surface.

can be operated on ordinary domestic power. Natural clay can be bought from art stores, which also sell colors and glazes in powder form.

Pinch pottery and coil pottery are the traditional methods of shaping clay with only the hands and small bowls, vases and ashtrays can be made. The clay can also be rolled into slabs, painted, impressed with objects and fashioned into relief landscape tiles.

The production of larger, more elegant shapes requires a wheel on which pots can be thrown. Using a potter's wheel is a fascinating skill, but practice and a considerable degree of physical balance and control are necessary. An electric pottery wheel with hand-lever control can be used by the wheelchaired, and wheels with foot controls are available.

Hobby shops and mail order companies carry a range of supplies for every kind of craft. It is often possible to buy cheap leftover scraps from wholesalers or manufacturers and to recycle free materials into decorative and usable craft objects. Scrap paper, cartons, straws, foil, plastic containers, pebbles, buttons, scraps of wood, metal, string, wool and wire can all be put to good use. A disabled craftsman in Cheshire,

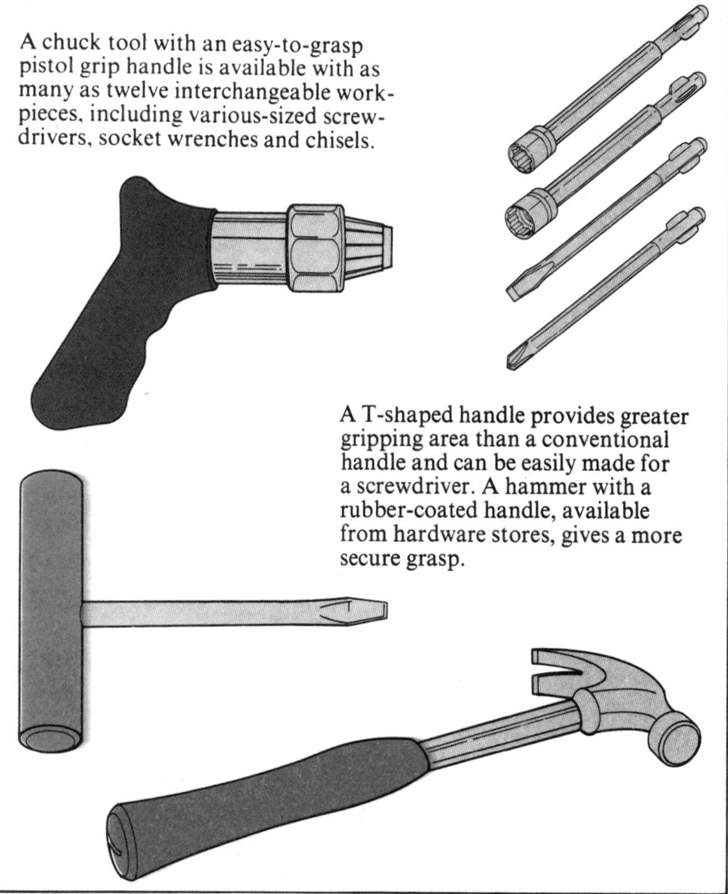

A chuck tool with an easy-to-grasp pistol grip handle is available with as many as twelve interchangeable workpieces, including various-sized screwdrivers, socket wrenches and chisels.

A T-shaped handle provides greater gripping area than a conventional handle and can be easily made for a screwdriver. A hammer with a rubber-coated handle, available from hardware stores, gives a more secure grasp.

England, for example, specializes in abstract wall plaques made of threads stretched between nails on a board, varnished macaroni set in mosaic designs and painted lolly sticks and pipe cleaners on a fabric ground. Some tools can also be improvised from ordinary household utensils.

Many people find that the easiest way to learn a craft is to take some instruction from a qualified teacher. Craft and handwork classes of various kinds are run by adult education departments, by therapy and rehabilitation centers for the disabled and by some voluntary and community groups. In Britain those unable to attend classes can apply to their local welfare authorities for a craft teacher to visit them at home. Help is always available from radio and television do-it-yourself programs and from manuals which give step-by-step instructions and ideas. You can also get ideas from magazine features and from studying craftwork exhibitions in a local museum or art gallery.

Gardening

When you have a physical disability gardening can be both immensely satisfying and frustrating. The satisfaction is in the unique pleasure of dealing with living things—and plants have the advantage of being less persistently demanding than animals. The frustration arises because almost any kind of physical handicap makes the chores of gardening a burden. The greatest satisfaction for the enthusiastic gardner will therefore be achieved by cutting out all work that is too demanding; gardening within your capacity—to the limit if you wish, but never beyond.

Ways of reducing the hard labor will also appeal to those who detest gardening, but are saddled with a garden which they do not want to let run to wilderness. The motive may merely be a desire not to upset the neighbors, or to have a pleasant garden to sit in and admire.

So, enthusiastic or reluctant, handicapped gardeners have a common objective—to make what they do as easy and effective as possible. There are three approaches which together can accomplish this. The first is to adapt the layout of the garden to your disability. The next is to grow only easy-care plants. And the third is to use tools and techniques that lighten inescapable labor.

Most garden designers seem to live in a world in which gardeners stay sound in wind and limb forever. Unhappily, in the real world some of us lose limbs, or the use of them, and all of us grow old. To help overcome such handicaps the workability of a garden must take precedence over conventional design.

The first consideration is accessibility. Design experts go to great lengths to create a garden on different levels "to add interest," as they say. But they also add to the difficulty of getting around if you are in a wheelchair or are unsteady on your feet. However pretty a profusion of steps may look they have no attraction for the handicapped; they are barriers to wheelchairs and treacherous to the infirm. If there are steps, gentle slopes must take their place.

After accessibility comes reachability. Ground level is a long way for those who cannot bend; the solution is to bring "ground level" within reach by raising beds to a height at which they can be cultivated from a chair, or without bending from a standing position. The beds should be made narrow enough to be within arm's reach, and should be surrounded by paved areas for easy access.

Some popular features must be ruthlessly excluded from your garden. Giving them up should not be regarded as a hardship and resented; looking after them would be the hardship. A rockery involves too much bending and painful kneeling if it is to be kept free from weeds. Wide herbaceous borders are hard to work among and demand constant attention in staking, cutting down, dividing, weeding, forking over and replanting. Much the same goes for formal beds of annuals and biennials. Beds of roses require an undue amount of often painful care.

The most wearisome job in a garden can be looking after a lawn. Admittedly an expanse of grass in perfect condition is magnificent, but if it's neglected it looks abominable. Rain quickly turns a trim lawn into a jungle, lack of rain makes it a desert and lack of attention delivers it over to weeds. Since the idea of a raised lawn is both impracticable and ludicrous, the only choice is to eschew grass; there are easier means of providing the areas of restful green that a garden must have.

There is no way to plan a garden which is ideal for all disabled people any more than there is for the halest and heartiest.

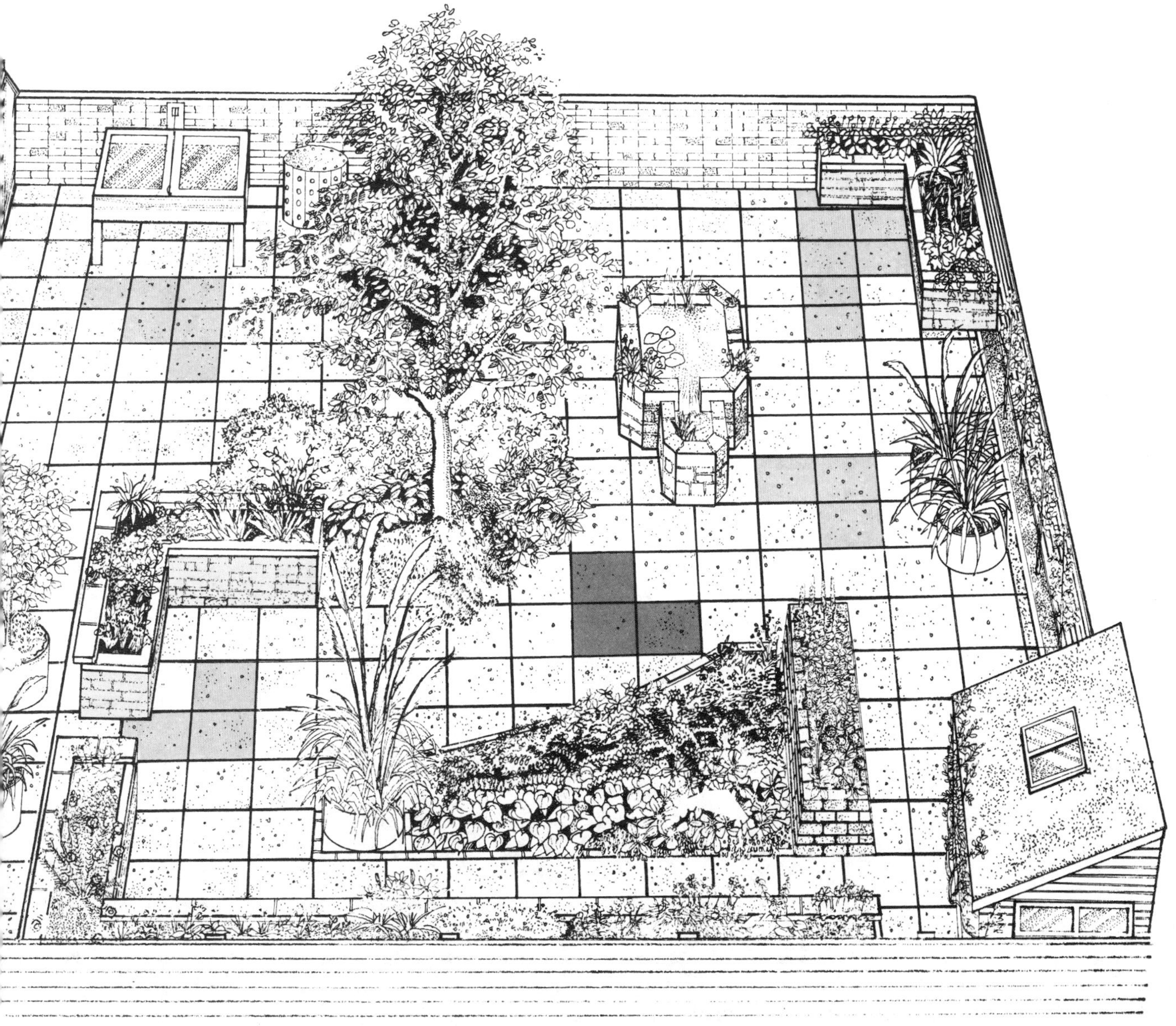

There are too many variables—the climate, soil, siting and shape of the garden, personal tastes and the nature of the disability. Moreover, if the garden is to be used by other members of the family, especially children, their needs have to be considered. Any help they can and are willing to give will be vital in both creating and looking after the garden.

Before a person who is disabled can take over the running of a specially designed, easy-to-run garden it has to be created. And the unwelcome fact is that constructing such a garden may well be beyond the disabled person's strength. He or she, foregoing the pleasures of actually creating a garden, becomes dependent on the goodwill of others or must employ competent workmen to do the job.

If the garden is to be created or converted by other members of the family the work might be spread over a few years, following an overall plan which could nevertheless be adapted when experience suggests how it could be improved. If the work has to be done professionally, it is more economical and satisfying to have as much done as possible in one great spurt at the start.

Obviously not all the ideas which follow would be included in any one garden; they are suggestions for choice. Detailed advice on the constructon of paths, the building of walls and the selection and care of plants will be found in the hundreds of gardening books available in bookstores or at your library.

Paths and Ramps

Concrete is the most serviceable and least expensive material for making paths that are safe to walk on and easy to propel or push a wheelchair over. Concrete may be used in several ways. Laid on the site, the concrete (one part cement, two parts sand, three parts aggregate) should be two to three inches (5 to 8 cm) deep for a path and four inches (10 cm) deep for a drive. To give a firm base if the soil is soft have two inches (5 cm) of well compacted rubble—three inches (8 cm) for a drive—laid under the concrete. The surface of the path should not be left dangerously smooth; it can be roughened a little by taking a stiff broom over it, or by brushing more vigorously as the concrete hardens so that some of the pebbly aggregate is exposed.

Paths can also be made of precast concrete paving slabs, which are cheaper than flagstones. They are laid on a base of sand or mortar. The most common slabs are square or rectangular, but smaller interlocking concrete blocks make more interesting looking paths, and will still stand hard wear.

Many attractive looking paving materials are totally impractical. Loose gravel, pebbles and raised cobblestones set in cement are exhausting to walk over and impossible for wheelchairs. Brick and tiles, even quarry tiles, can be dangerously slippery when wet, and wood is worse. Avoid crazy paving; it settles unevenly and trips you up or the wheelchair wheels can get jammed in the gaps.

Some of these materials, gravel and pebbles especially, may be worth having in the garden just because they are attractive in themselves. They can be used with discretion to add variety to a prosaically paved area, but not in places where there is traffic.

Paths should be between three and four feet (90 and 120 cm) wide to allow room for a wheelchair or for two people to walk abreast, either to give support or just for sociability.

For a person who is disabled, steps can turn a garden into an obstacle course (without the fun) and gentle slopes must take their place. The gradient should be no steeper than one in fifteen. This means a rise (or drop) of one foot (30 cm) in fifteen feet (450 cm) of length. If the garden is on a considerable slope much ingenuity may be needed to plan the course of a path to achieve the desired gradient.

A handrail alongside a path can be helpful, especially if the path is on a slope or if it may become slippery because it runs under trees which shed blossoms, leaves or seed pods. There are chemicals available at garden centers which will get rid of the slipperiness caused by the growth of green algae.

Raised Beds

Although distinction will be given to a garden by raised beds built out of old mellowed bricks, they may be more cheaply built with concrete slabs set into the ground about twelve inches (30 cm) deep. Even wood can be used, but it will be less permanent. For wheelchair gardening, two feet (60 cm) is a convenient height for a raised bed; for the ambulant nonbender the addition of another six inches (15 cm) or so of height will make for more comfortable working. The higher the bed the rather more restricted the choice of plants becomes; for both practical and aesthetic reasons you do not want them towering over you.

Beds which have a path on only one side cannot be more than two feet (60 cm) deep if they are to be tended from a wheelchair. If there are paths on both sides the beds can be four feet (120 cm) deep and this greater depth gives far more scope in planting. Ideally, the paths between these beds should be four feet (120 cm) wide for easy maneuvering of a wheelchair.

The beds must be kept in proportion to the size of the garden, and it is on this basis that their length should be decided. To avoid a barracklike effect they may be of different lengths and widths, with some running at right angles to the others. Curved beds are best avoided; they are difficult to build and to reach for cultivation.

When filling the raised beds it is often an advantage for the sake of drainage to begin with a four-inch (10-cm) layer of broken bricks or stones. On top of this layer the bed should be filled up to the rim with the kind of soil that is best liked by the plants you intend to grow. For general purposes this would be a fertile loamy soil—that is, one made up of a

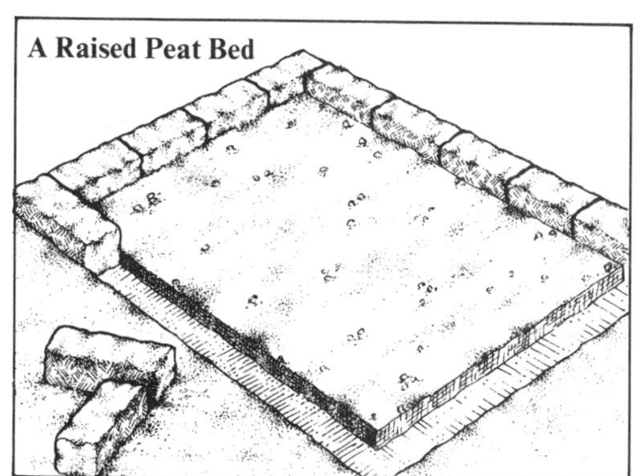

It's easy to make a raised peat bed. It should be sited in partial shade to keep it from drying out. Soak the peat blocks in water for at least twenty-four hours before the bed is built.

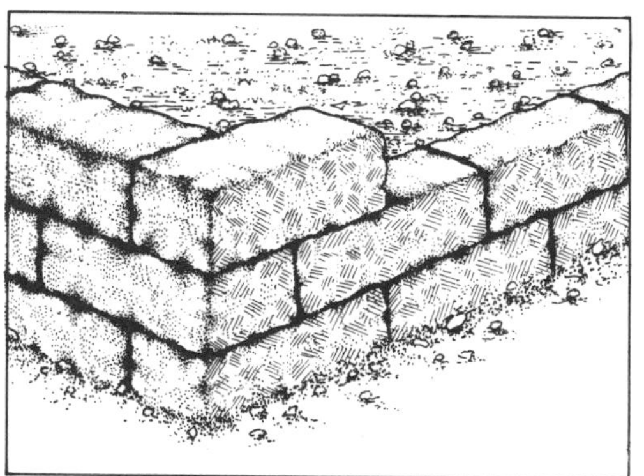

Before laying the first course of blocks, remove soil to half the depth of a block. Then lay the peat blocks in a manner similar to bricks, but leaving spaces for plants.

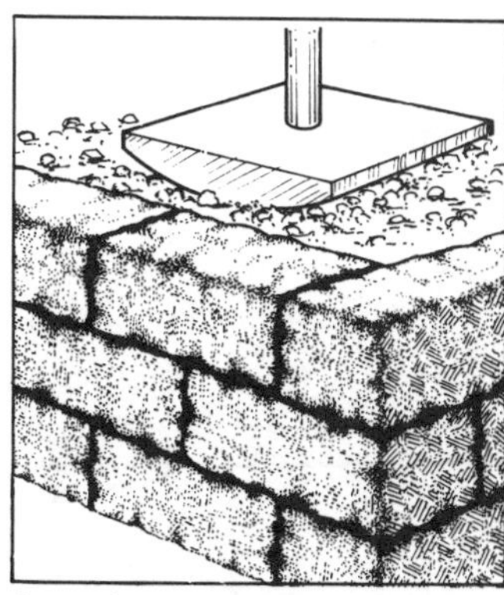

As each course is laid fill the bed with a mixture of half peat and half soil and ram it firm. Such plants as ferns, ericas

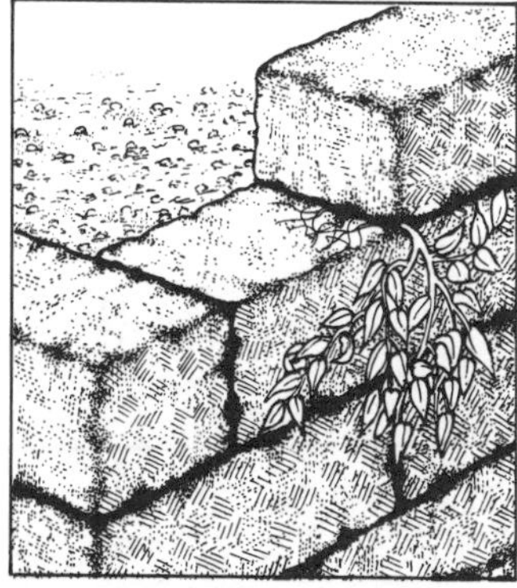

and hederas, planted between the peat blocks, help to bind the bed. Peat beds are usually used for lime-hating plants,

particularly dwarf varieties of azaleas and rhododendrons, but most heathers and many other plants flourish in peat.

greater proportion of sand than clay, and rich in humus. The difficulty may well be getting hold of such soil, and you may have to be content with what is available and improve it by adding manure, compost or peat.

It is far easier in raised beds to accommodate the likes and dislikes of plants than it is in the open garden. If you wanted to, you could create beds of peaty, chalky, clayey, gravelly or sandy soil and grow appropriate plants in each.

What you do grow in raised beds is a matter of personal taste, but there are some things to consider. The plants must appear in proportion to the size of the beds and to each other, especially in their height. Plan the beds so that there is something of interest in at least some of them all year. Do not shy away from favorite plants that are supposed to need a lot of attention. A raised bed makes it so much easier to give them that attention. And if you use the beds for growing vegetables, plant those which mature quickly, especially salad crops, rather than those which occupy the precious space for months before they are ready to eat.

Raised beds make gardening easier except in one respect; the soil dries out more quickly than in the open garden and more frequent watering will be needed in dry weather. Watering with a watering can is such a burden that it will inevitably be neglected. A standpipe and a hose is the least you should have, but trailing a hose around a garden is no fun, and putting it away is even less so. It will probably be left lying around with predictable results.

It is sensible, therefore, while the raised beds are being built and the paving laid to have water piped to all the beds. Each bed will have an outlet from which perforated piping can be made to pro-

A small platform of flagstones, built onto one end of each raised bed not only serves as a seat but, more important, can be used as a workbench for tools and other gardening necessities.

Tubs and large shallow containers supported on pedestals are really small-scale raised beds. They can be planted with alpines, dwarf evergreen shrubs or a variety of herbs. They can also house bulbs in the spring and vivid displays of flowers in the summer.

It is labor-saving to have water piped to each of the raised beds. The perforated piping produces as much water as is required and the only work involved is turning the valve on and off.

duce either a trickle or a spray and the only labor then involved in watering is in turning on and turning off the valve which controls the water supply to each bed. Adding a watering system after the beds have been built is far more costly and it will probably be unsightly. Installing it at the start will prove to be worth all that is spent on it, and at that stage it can be made unobtrusive.

There is not much point in having raised beds if you have to bend down to the ground to pick up tools, fertilizers and the like. This can be avoided by having the beds built with a little platform of flagstones resting on the walls at one end of each bed. This simple labor-saving device will serve both as a workbench and as a seat.

There is a fascination in growing miniature alpines that easily becomes all-absorbing. One of the most satisfactory ways is in a raised bed made with dry stone walling. The mortarless walls ensure that there is no danger of a waterlogged soil (fatal) and allow plants to be grown in crevices between the stones.

Wooden, fiberglass, plastic or concrete tubs are in effect small-scale raised beds and are particularly effective in bringing a paved area to life. The snag is that the soil dries out quickly in hot weather, and since it is impractical to pipe water to each one it has to be taken to them either by watering can or hose pipe. All types of tub must have drainage holes in the base or the soil becomes waterlogged.

Walls

It is sensible to use garden walls to the utmost, for they enable you to garden outside at whatever height is most convenient from a wheelchair or standing. Allow for only a narrow bed—about twelve inches (30 cm)—alongside the wall. A wider bed makes it hard to reach the plants growing up the wall. These plants could be flowering climbers, preferably those without thorns to avoid any vindictiveness, or cordon fruits, or even grape vines. The simplest way to keep climbing plants under control and within reach is to space lines of plastic-covered wire at intervals along the walls up to the appropriate height, fixing them to vine "eyes" driven into the mortar.

Some old brick or stone garden walls are so attractive that it is a pity to cover them completely with vegetation. To these walls you could have fixed (firmly) an arrangement of containers.

A wall may also be used as a background for a stunning display of bonsai. This involves building a sturdy but attractive wooden stand against the wall to accommodate the bonsai at different levels so that each is displayed to best advantage. But all must be accessible, because they may need daily watering. Bonsai may also need shade from the hot summer sun, but they must not be put under trees, for the drip from the leaves will do them no good.

A low wall can be used for a display of bonsai. Adequate shade can be provided by a "roof" of wooden slats fixed to the top of the wall. Nothing need be grown in the border below, although it would be thoroughly in keeping with the aura of bonsai to lay a strip of beautiful pebbles here.

Ground-level Gardening

While raised beds are the best means of growing plants that need a fair amount of looking after, there are many other plants that almost look after themselves. These easy-care plants are the ones to choose for growing at ground level. They will provide areas of green to take the place of lawns or to cover banks which are awkward to reach and they are vigorous enough to smother competing weeds. Such ground cover plants include dwarf evergreen shrubs, trailing ivies, hardy ferns and heathers.

For substitute lawn areas that can be walked over in moderation there are dwarf chamomile and creeping thymes and once they have spread they will need little attention beyond cutting of the dead flowers. There are also many beautiful ornamental grasses with which to create a graceful wild garden that will never need a lawn mower near it.

Family Needs

A garden which has been designed for the sole care and use of a disabled gardener will be without some features that are included in a garden to be used by others. A family garden might include a lawn for lounging or for playing games on, a sand-box for young children, a wading pool or a swimming pool and a vegetable garden. For such features as these you should sensibly disclaim responsibility.

The garden adapted to the needs of the disabled gardener is no ghetto; as much as any conventional garden it can be enjoyed equally by all. Indeed, a garden which is well designed for someone who is disabled can be particularly enjoyable for young children—raised beds might have been invented for playing hide and seek among—and safer with no steps to fall down.

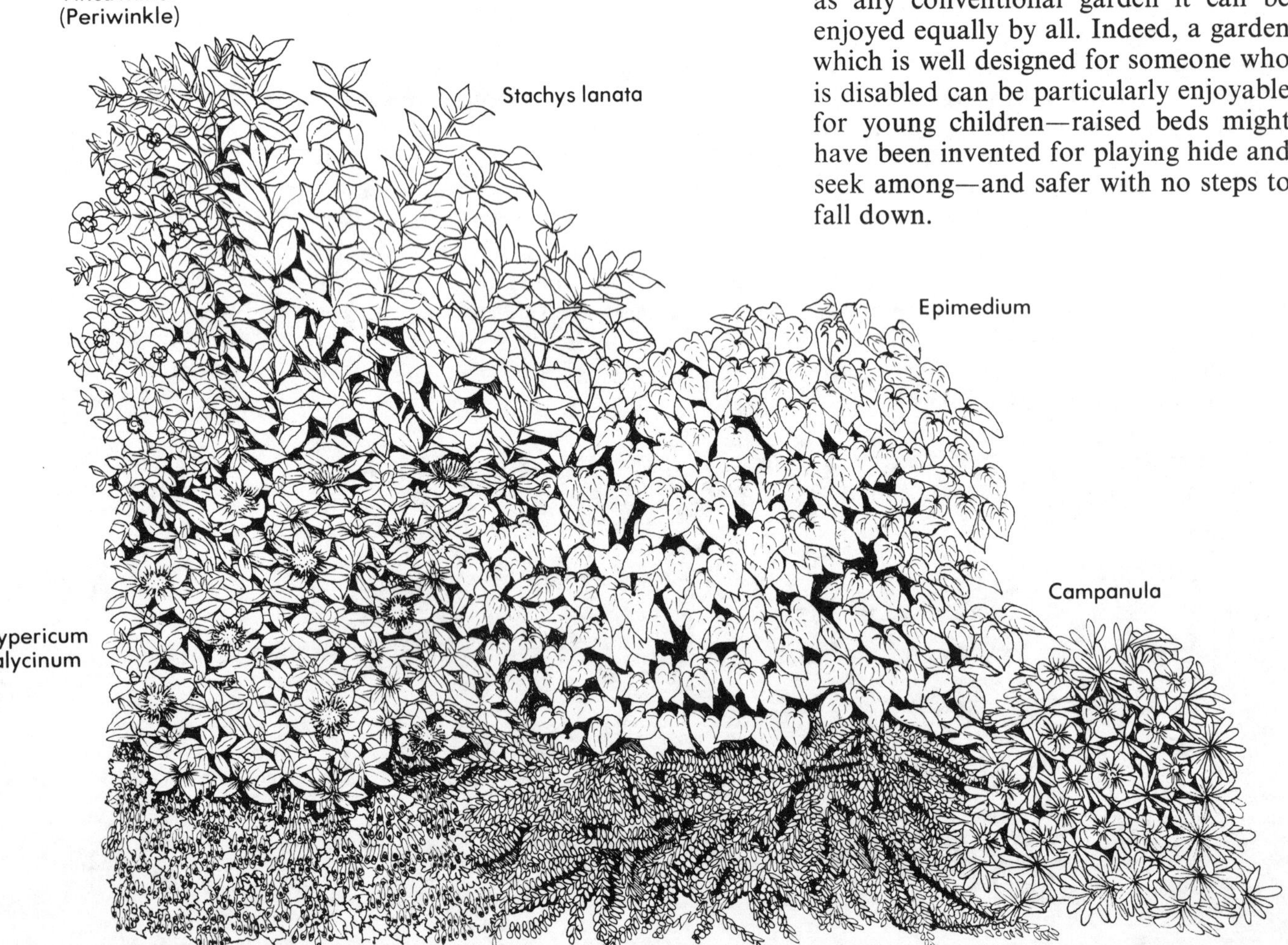

The Raised Pool

For a disabled gardener there are few pleasures more absorbing than a pool. But at ground level a pool is a hazard as well as difficult to look after, so, like the plant beds, a pool should be built raised. It will not look in the least odd; in a garden of raised beds it is thoroughly in keeping. A convenient height is two feet (60 cm). The simplest form of construction is to set a shaped fiberglass pool, about fifteen to eighteen inches (38 to 45 cm) deep, on a concrete base with a two-foot (60-cm) wide stone wall built around it. Plants are grown in gaps left in the wall and aquatic plants will be grown in the pool. The wall itself is topped with smooth flagstones to provide a seat from which the pool plants can be tended or the pool can be admired.

Water is even more fascinating to watch if it moves, and this may be achieved with a small fountain or by the overflow (waterfall would be too grand a word) from an adjoining, slightly higher pool. An electric pump is used to recycle the water, and, for safety's sake, it should be installed professionally.

Tools

In conventional gardening there are four basic implements for cultivating the soil; they are, in diminishing order of the effort they involve, the spade, fork, hoe and rake. Another important range is the cutters—mowers, and pruning shears. With those, plus a wheelbarrow and a broom, an active gardener could manage and could well ignore all the gadgets that flood the market. But handicapped gardeners need a larger number of tools to help them to overcome their disabilities. These may be simple variants of basic tools or tools specifically designed to overcome a specific disability.

There are four main groups of special tools. There are those tools which can be used when the gardener is sitting, either in a wheelchair or in an ordinary chair if standing is exhausting or precarious. Others have been designed for people who find it painful or impossible to bend. A third group is for one-handed gardeners and the fourth is for those whose grip is weak. There are, of course, some tools which people with all types of disabilities find useful.

There are many forks, hoes and rakes suitable for wheelchair use and finding one that best suits you certainly means handling it for some time (and if possible using it) before buying. It is vital that the tool is really lightweight (since all tools have the reprehensible habit of growing heavier the longer you use them), and that the handle is the right length. For raised beds you will need hand tools—trowels,

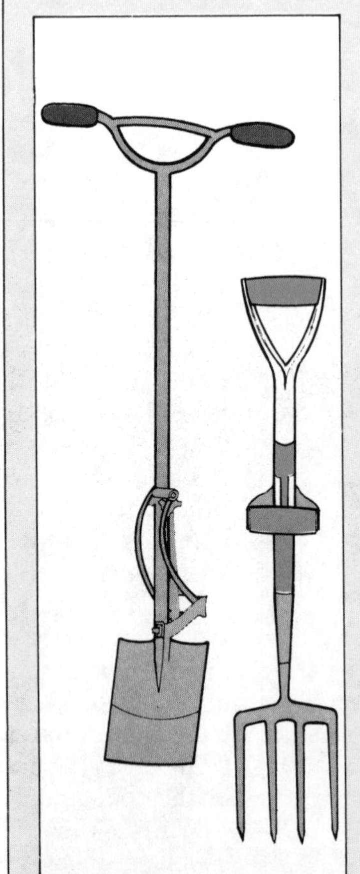

A pedal spade, above left, makes it possible to keep the back straight when digging. A light border fork, above right, fitted with a handle grip, can be used when seated.

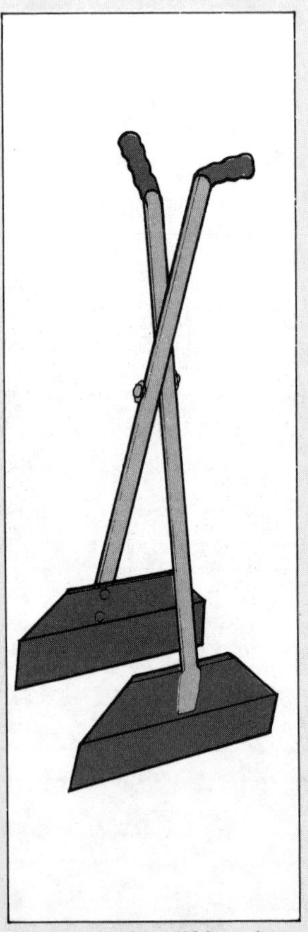

This tool for lifting leaves and garden debris has handles of different lengths requiring minimum effort to pick things up and to dispose of them.

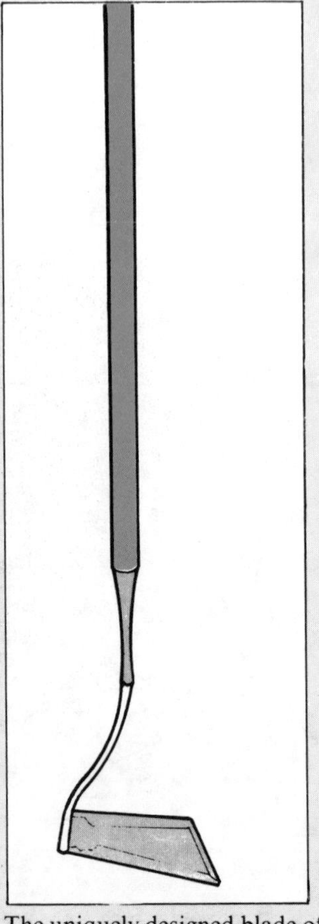

The uniquely designed blade of this "swoe" weeds, cultivates, aerates soil and hoes between plants and in awkward corners. It is available with a long or a telescoping handle.

forks and small hoes—but they must have longer than conventional handles. Some of the tools usually sold for rockery work would be suitable.

Stainless steel, although more expensive, goes through the soil more easily, provided it is kept clean—and it is far easier to keep clean than other metals.

A garden creates an awful lot of rubbish and handling it from a wheelchair is a great chore. It can be made easier by using a lightweight pick-up device which is operated sitting down. This requires patience rather than effort, since only a little can be lifted at a time. The debris is emptied into a low two-wheeled barrow, which is shaped rather like a large dustpan. The barrow hooks onto the back of the wheelchair to be towed away to the compost heap.

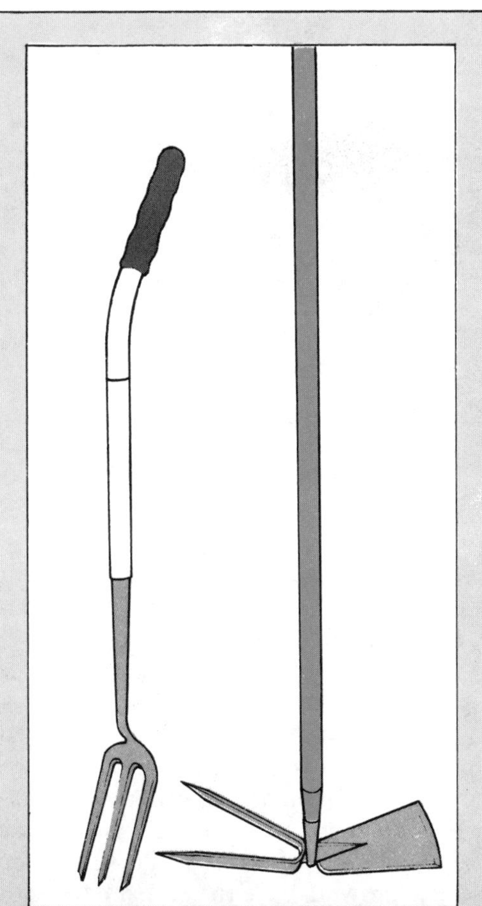

The stainless-steel fork above left is available with an extra-long handle or with a versatile telescopic handle. The double hoe above right was designed as a rockery tool. The blade cuts out weeds and the two-pronged side cultivates.

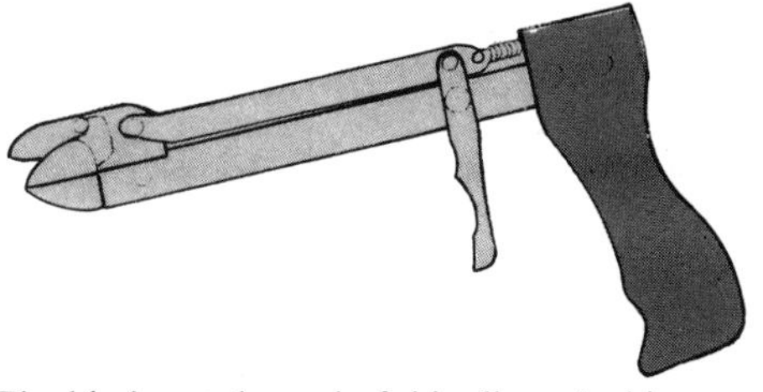

The blades at the end of this clipper's thirty-inch (75-cm) shaft, cuts and holds flowers and leaves. It is a useful tool if reach is limited.

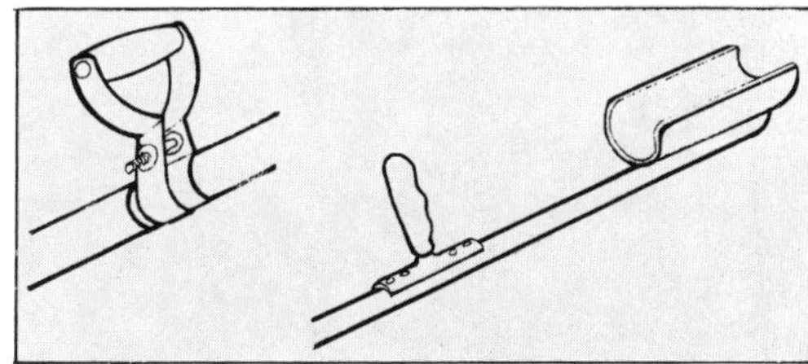

A handle grip, above left, attached to the shaft of a fork or spade makes it easier to work from a seated position. To give single-handed control to a tool, a piece of metal guttering, above right, and a suitable grip can be riveted to the handle.

Digging is a painful operation for those who find it difficult to bend. If there is no other weakness, you can use the type of wedge-shaped shovel with a four-and-a-half foot (135 cm) long handle which is, in fact, the standard spade in many parts of the world. The alternative is a spade operated by a pedal. There are long-handled forks and weeders available, and conventional hoes, rakes and cultivators need involve no bending if they are properly used.

For picking up rubbish without bending there are long-handled pick-up devices and for clearing it away you can use a two-wheeled barrow with a baby carriage handle.

Pedal-operated forks and spades with specially shaped handles are available for use by the gardener who works with only one hand. The lightest of lightweight hoes, rakes and cultivators should be chosen. Some have angled handles which make them easier to control.

There are some forks, hoes and rakes so designed that a strong grip is not necessary for their use. Other handles can be made easier to hold if they are padded with foam rubber, for example, to make them thicker.

The alternative to making soil cultivation easier is to cut it out altogether. The first step is the most onerous—getting rid of vicious perennial weeds;

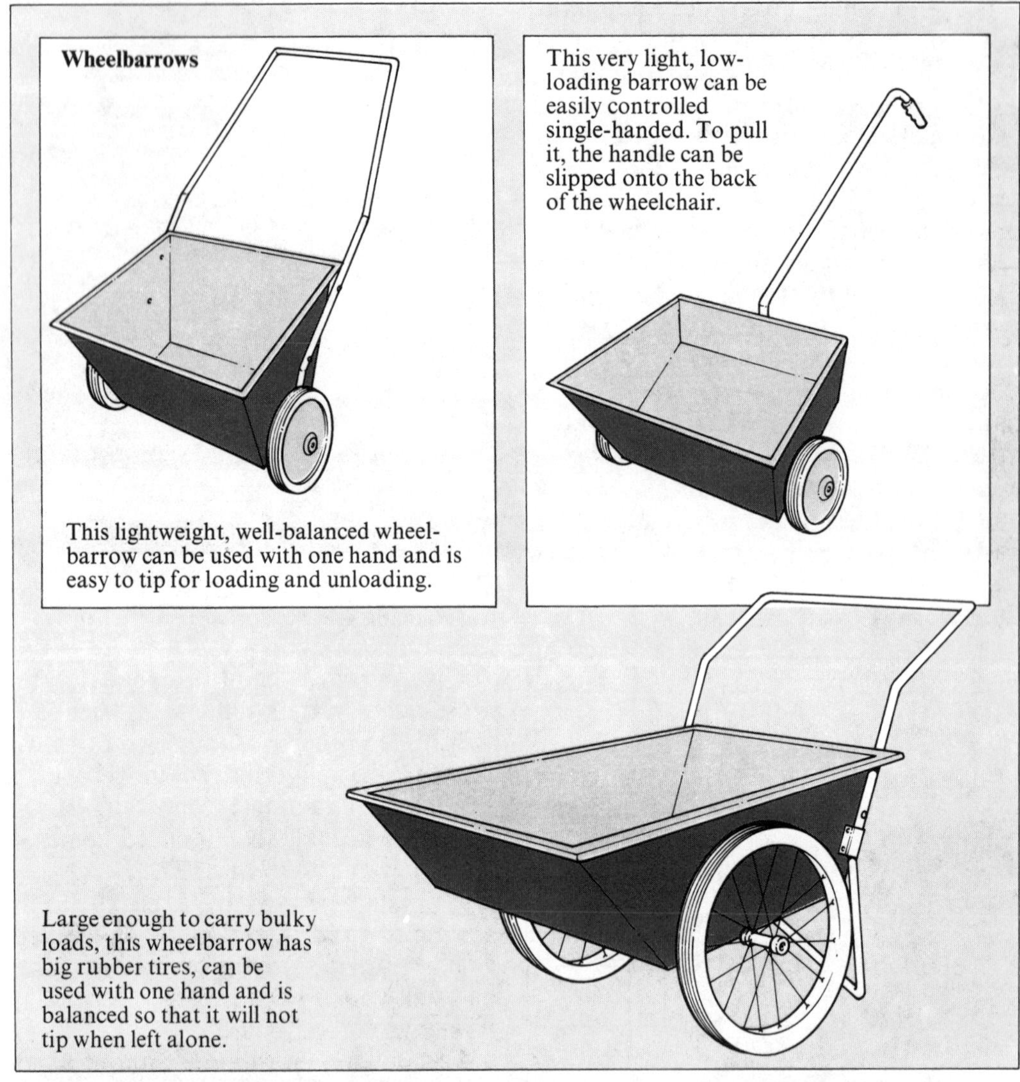

This very light, low-loading barrow can be easily controlled single-handed. To pull it, the handle can be slipped onto the back of the wheelchair.

This lightweight, well-balanced wheelbarrow can be used with one hand and is easy to tip for loading and unloading.

Large enough to carry bulky loads, this wheelbarrow has big rubber tires, can be used with one hand and is balanced so that it will not tip when left alone.

either by digging or by using drastic weed killer (which many gardeners shy away from). But once that has been done no further digging will be needed; instead there is mulching.

Each spring a layer of compost, peat or decayed leaves is spread two or three inches (5 or 8 cm) deep over the soil. While the mulch lies on the surface it suppresses most weeds. Eventually it is taken below ground by worms, is turned into humus and enriches the soil. The richer the soil becomes the more the worm population increases, undisturbed by digging, and the more the soil is aerated. The worms and soil bacteria do the hard work for you.

A drawback to this method in a large garden is the considerable amount of compost that has to be made and spread. Sedge peat is lighter to handle, but it costs more and fertility builds up less quickly than with well-made compost. For a small garden, and especially for raised beds, the no-digging method has everything to commend it.

In theory, mechanized tools should be a great aid in overcoming handicaps, but in practice there are drawbacks. Gasoline-driven lawn mowers may be heavy, difficult to maneuver, smelly and exhausting to keep up with unless their engine speed has been reduced. Power-driven electric mowers have the added hazard of a trailing cable, which may be accidentally cut by the blades or tripped over. (These are additional arguments against having a lawn.) However, if the garden has hedges a lightweight trimmer which works on a rechargeable battery is a must.

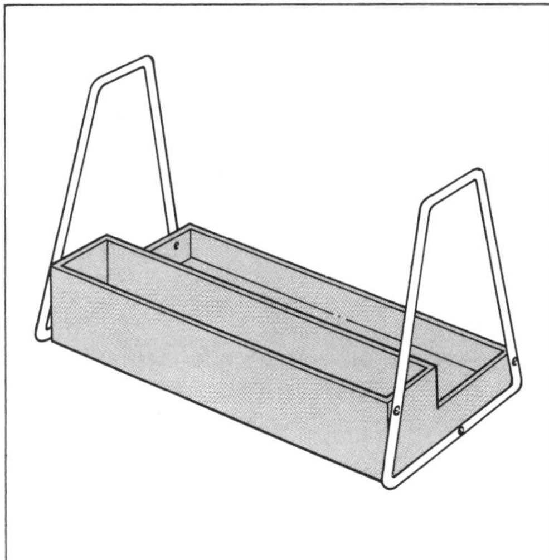

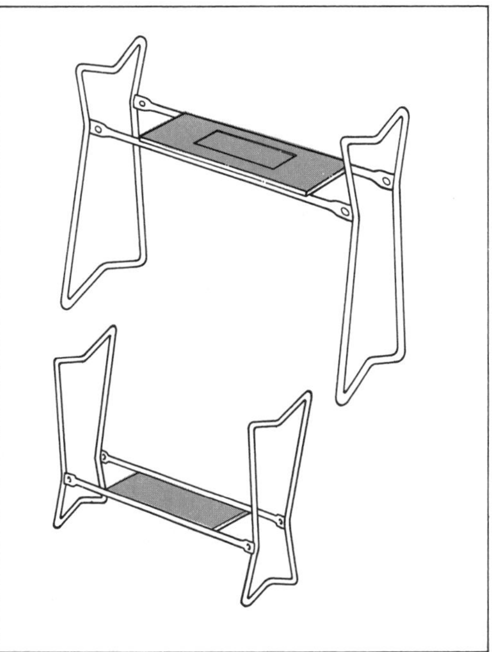

For some jobs, such as weeding among delicate plants, long-handled tools may be clumsy. Instead of bending to hand weed, it is better to kneel with the help of a contraption that allows you to kneel at various heights and has side supports to help in getting up and down. The kneeler above left has foam padding to protect knees. A trough holds small tools and flowers. The kneeler above and right doubles as a stool when it is turned the other way up.

The most important tool remains your own body, handicapped though it may be; without it all the other tools are useless. It must therefore be used with maximum efficiency. Strong and healthy gardeners often wantonly misuse their bodies, but the handicapped cannot afford such waste. The problem is to find the balance between excessive use of vulnerable parts of the body and the fullest use of other joints and muscles which will weaken if they are given nothing to do.

For the gardener who works standing up the most vulnerable area is the spine, especially when bending, lifting and carrying weights and pushing. The spine is often made to do the work that should be shared by the hip and knee joints and the shoulders and arms. Keep the back as straight as possible without holding it rigid. While a lot of back strain can be avoided by using long-handled tools, this is only so if you hold them properly. The advantage of a long handle for a hoe is lost if you grasp the handle low and bend over to push harder. If you mow keep as erect as possible; don't lean over the mower to force it along.

If you have beds at ground level and have no kneeling aid do not kneel down on both knees. In this position your back and head are painfully hunched. Kneel on only one knee and keep your back as straight as you can. Do not stay kneeling for long. And whatever you are doing stop at the first hint of tiredness or boredom.

A garden stool on large wheels makes it possible to remain seated while moving along and working. The seat can be up to two feet (60 cm) from the ground. A shelf under the seat can be used to carry tools.

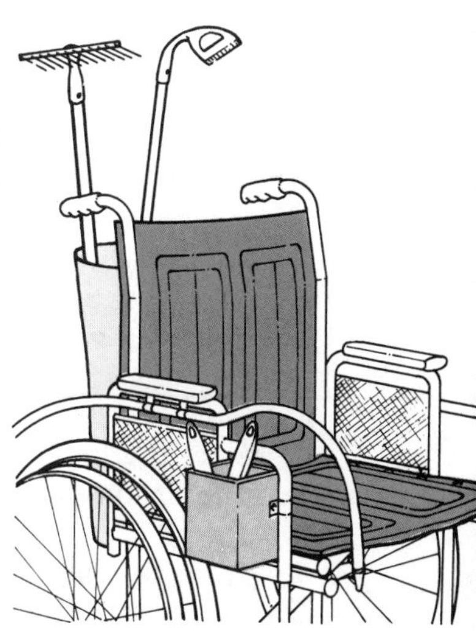

A wheelchair can be equipped to make gardening easier. Removable cloth pockets or spring clips attached to the back of the chair carry large tools, while a small box or pocket attached to the armrest can be used for smaller items. Two hooks on the outside of the armrest hold a hose so that it can be controlled with one hand.

The Greenhouse

For those who live in a fickle climate a greenhouse adds a new dimension for it makes the gardener and his plants less subservient to the weather. In the past there was always the danger of becoming a slave to the greenhouse, compelled to make endless journeys to it each day to see that the plants were not too hot, too cold, too dry or short of ventilation. But today these labors can, at a cost, be taken off your shoulders by equipping the greenhouse with a whole range of automatic controls.

Heating, ventilation, humidity, watering and shading from the sun can all be automated, leaving the gardener free to concentrate as much energy as he or she wishes on the plants. These automatic controls, moreover, have none of the drawbacks which mechanical aids in the garden have. They really do the work themselves. So the greater the individual's disability and the greater his or her enthusiasm the more worthwhile it is to invest in an automated greenhouse.

A heated greenhouse can provide a daily, year round pastime uninterrupted by bad weather. The range of plants that can be grown will depend on how much heat you are willing or can afford to provide. The heat and humidity needed for many palms and orchids would, however, make prolonged working in the greenhouse uncomfortable, even apart from the exorbitant cost. At the other extreme an unheated greenhouse in northern winters would be even more uncomfortable to work in, although less expensive. But at temperatures in between there are enough plants—from exotic flowers to utilitarian vegetables—to provide a lifetime of interest.

For the gardener's convenience the greenhouse should be situated as near to the house as possible, so that it can be reached quickly in bad weather and to reduce the cost of taking water, electricity or gas to it from the house connections. But the needs of the plants have to be considered as well. Therefore, in planning the garden, make sure that you do not site the greenhouse in the shade of the house or of trees. The shorter the days in winter, the most benefit will be derived from the sun if the greenhouse (of the normal rectangular type) is sited from east to west.

Like the garden, the greenhouse must be accessible and easy to work in. For the wheelchair gardener this means that there must be a paved area in front of the greenhouse at least five feet (150 cm) square so that there is adequate space for maneuvering the chair. The path outside should be at the same level as that inside the greenhouse; no step or draft excluder for the wheelchair to negotiate.

A shelf below the staging will provide space for tools, plant pots, seed trays, compost and all the other paraphernalia a gardener accumulates. If you decide to have such a shelf it will have to be solid, rather than slatted, to prevent water from dripping from the plants above.

A greenhouse does not have to be a major interest, but may just be a pleasant minor adjunct to a garden. One attractive-looking model, made of wood, is six-sided. One side is a wide door and there is staging on the other five sides, all within easy reach from a chair in the center. There are no elaborate gadgets and no heating, but such a greenhouse would be excellent, for example, for alpines in late winter and early spring, and for tomatoes, peppers and eggplant later.

Whether or not you have a greenhouse, frames and cloches are invaluable for the protection of plants in cold weather. To avoid having to bend, frames should be raised by placing them on a base eighteen inches (45 cm) high. Conventional wooden framelights are often heavy and clumsy to handle. Aluminum frames fitted with plastic instead of glass are certainly preferable.

Cloches may be used to cover parts of raised beds, as well as any beds at ground level. Always buy plastic cloches; they may not have as long a potential life as those made of glass, but they are light to lift and safer than glass if you drop one or stumble against it.

Besides greenhouses there are other structures which could have a place in your garden plans, but for your comfort

Small plastic garbage cans, set beneath a table in accessible sliding panels, can be used to store small quantities of such materials as peat moss and vermiculite.

Standard galvanized tin cans, angled or hinged under a work bench, can be used to store large quantities of soil and potting mixtures.

more than for the well-being of the plants. If you are lucky enough to have a Victorian-type conservatory built onto the house you can combine many of the advantages of a greenhouse with greater home comforts. Covering part or all of a patio or terrace with corrugated plastic sheeting makes an indoor-outdoor place in which to sit, surrounded by greenery, on wet summer days. And on fine summer days a pergola swathed in climbing plants provides a shady refuge from the hot sun.

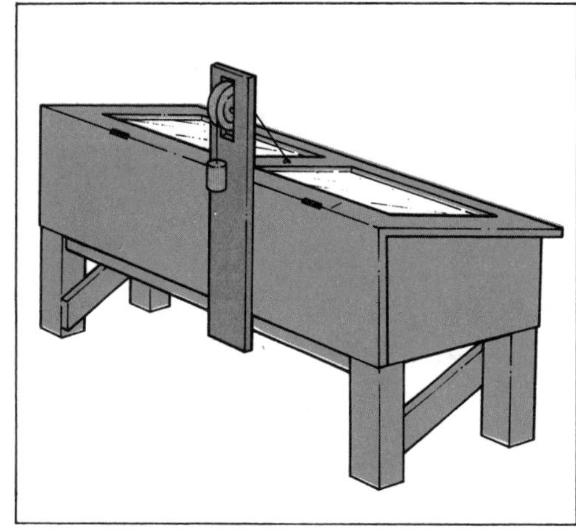

To make a frame manageable, have hinges fitted to the framelight so it can be lifted effortlessly with a pulley and counterweight.

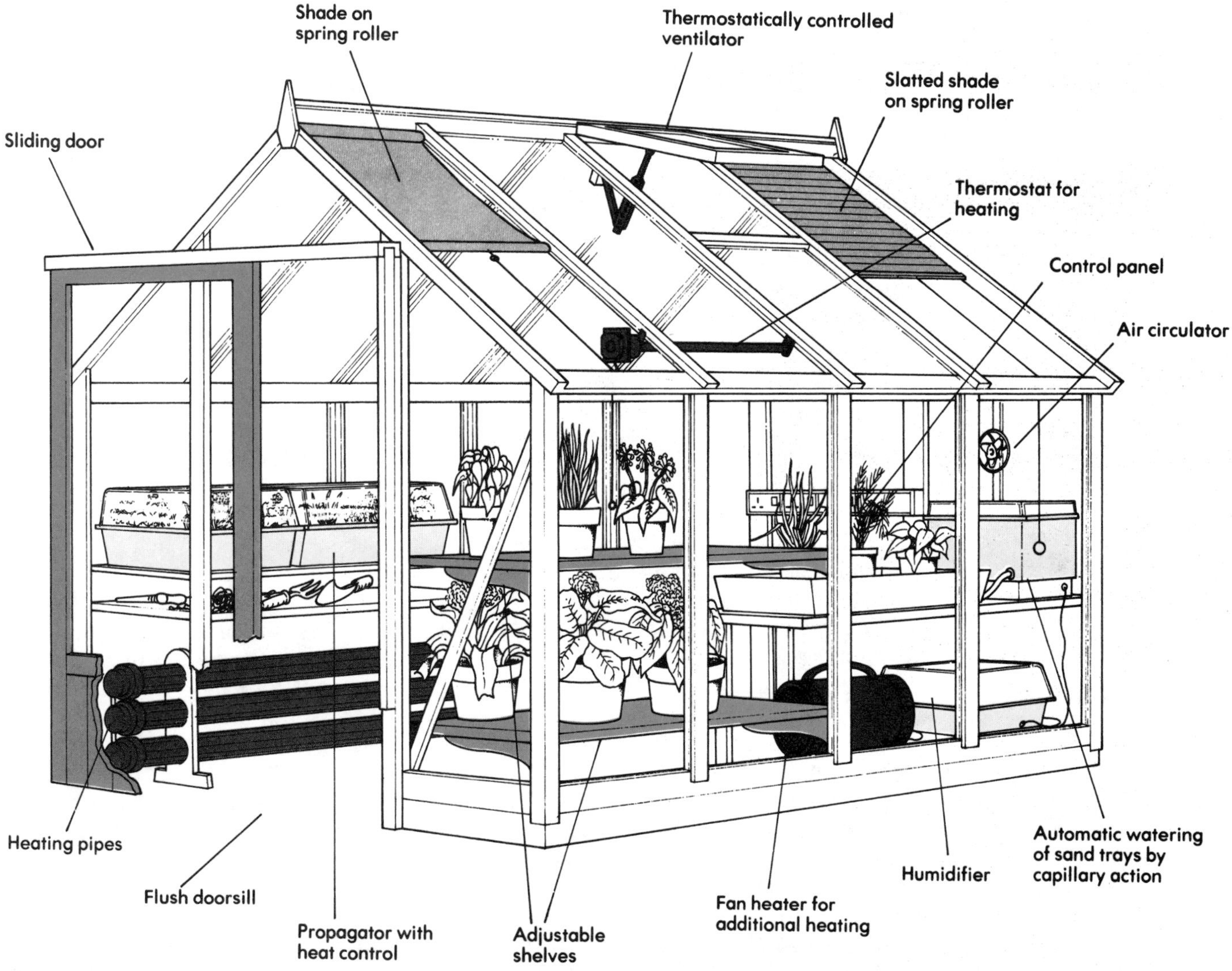

Shade on spring roller
Thermostatically controlled ventilator
Slatted shade on spring roller
Sliding door
Thermostat for heating
Control panel
Air circulator
Heating pipes
Flush doorsill
Propagator with heat control
Adjustable shelves
Fan heater for additional heating
Humidifier
Automatic watering of sand trays by capillary action

Indoor Gardening

Many apartment dwellers or people who are housebound have to indulge their gardening enthusiasms through indoor plants and this can be totally satisfying. Whereas any garden outdoors may at certain times of the year become a burden, a collection of plants indoors can be planned to take up as little or as much time as you wish.

The most effortless way to enjoy indoor plants is to grow them hydroponically. In this method soil and composts are not used. Instead the roots of the plant, anchored in pebbles or granules manufactured from some inert material, draw their sustenance from fertilizer dissolved in the water in which the lower layers of pebbles stand. An indicator in the pot shows when more water, and how much, has to be added, and this may be no more frequently than every three weeks. Additional fertilizer is added only once or twice a year. It is hard to imagine gardening less demanding than that, short of hiring a plant firm to come around and do these slight chores for you.

On the other hand, you can go the whole hog in indoor gardening, using up all the free time and all the energy you have: propagating from seed or cuttings, growing herbs, salad plants, tomatoes and mushrooms as well as the usual ornamental plants, planting and tending window boxes, creating miniature gardens, watering and fertilizing and endlessly puttering until you fall victim to that widespread affliction of gardeners—the plants take over your life.

Indoor gardening has the notable attraction that most of the operations can be carried out while you are sitting at a table. The work has become easier with the introduction of lightweight plastic pots and soilless composts. Clay pots, although beautiful, and soil, although satisfying to handle, did involve a lot of laborious activity. There are also now more varieties of plants available than ever before and there is certainly no lack of expert advice in print and on radio and television.

Tools are no problem Whether you use old kitchen forks and spoons or, doing the thing in style, buy a set of miniature tools, they will be light to handle. The more fervent indoor gardener will probably also want to buy an electric propagator to ensure more success in raising plants from seeds and cuttings than is likely in an ordinary indoor environment.

Deciding which plants to grow involves two things: which plants will grow (and that depends on how cool, warm, light or dark your rooms are) and which plants you want to grow. You should bear in mind how much or how little time you want to devote to them. This is a point often overlooked. Once the fiddling operation of planting a bottle garden has been done, for example, there is little you can do except look at it—admirable if that is what you want, but disappointing if you want to be continuously involved. Cacti and succulents and miniature gardens provide rather more activity, but it tends to come in spurts at certain times of the year.

By growing bulbs for all seasons and not just for spring you can find something to do for much of the year. Window boxes may also need constant care in spring, summer and autumn if they are used for a succession of flowering plants, for salad plants or dwarf tomatoes. Other food crops raised in the kitchen itself, either in the light or in the dark, can keep you busy. They would include beans and other shoots and mushrooms.

The greater variety of plants the more continuous interest they can provide and the more of your time they will take up, if that is what you want. And even if you aim for the absolute minimum of work all plants have to be constantly watched to see that they are not short of water or that pests and disease have not struck.

For someone who is disabled there are fewer obstacles and hazards in indoor gardening than there are outdoors. But always have the plants within easy reach—so have no eight-foot (440-cm) monsters in pots too heavy to move and no pots on high shelves. Above all, never

If you use a capillary watering device plants need little attention. To make the device above, insert a fiber-glass wick through the pot's drainage hole and keep it covered with water in the container below.

Adjustable shelves, top, available from mail order companies, will make an attractive garden in any window. A metal foldaway plant stand, bottom, makes maximum use of floor space. It can hold from fifteen to twenty pots or, if preferred, it can be filled with loam for direct planting.

A tabletop garden gives the opportunity to grow and display a variety of plants. Ready-made or custom built, such a table must be sturdy and have clearance on two sides for the wheelchaired gardener.

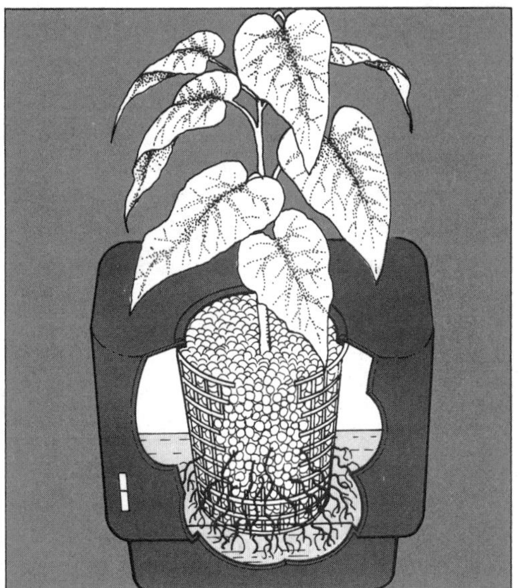

The plant left is grown hydroponically. The outer container is here cut away to show the inner pot with open slotted sides, filled with clay granules, and the water roots which have developed. A water-level gauge tells when to refill.

be tempted to have a hanging basket.

Garden rooms are the ultimate in indoor gardening with the balance further tipped toward human comfort than in a conservatory. The advantage to the plants in a well planned garden room is that they get far better light than they do in an ordinary living room. The dryness of the atmosphere will still limit the choice of plants, but those which do tolerate a certain lack of humidity will be all the healthier because of the good light. You can grow plants in tubs and troughs and plastic or pottery containers, or in raised beds made of wood.

One must accept that some people are better gardeners, indoors or outdoors, than others—in the sense that their plants seem to grow more luxuriantly and die less readily than yours. It's foolish to be disheartened by this, for it's more satisfying to be a contented gardener than a merely successful one. You must cultivate your patience as well as your garden and accept the fact that since plants are living things they do die. Some years the weather will defeat you and pests and diseases will always try to. But there will be another year ahead, and a new generation of plants will not give up trying. Neither should you.

Vacations

Today in the West more people travel further and have more time to do so than was the case even thirty years ago. And there is no reason why people with physical disabilities should be excluded from the modern pleasures of going as far afield as they choose and enjoying interesting vacations. People in the travel and tourist industries are becoming increasingly aware of this, and so are many handicapped people themselves, and they are no longer willing to be restricted by a wheelchair or a physical limitation. An outstanding example is Patrick Segal, a French journalist-photographer, who has traveled thousands of miles overland in China, Vietnam, Australia, California, Brazil and Lebanon—and all in a wheelchair!

While few people, able-bodied or disabled, are as adventurous as this it is becoming more commonplace for handicapped people to visit, either in groups or independently, remote places and faraway countries that were formerly considered quite inaccessible to them.

The social and psychological rewards of traveling are enormous, especially for those people with disabilities who are often forced to live rather confined and uneventful lives. On the whole the able-bodied whom they encounter on their travels are friendly and helpful, although there are some situations in which tact is necessary. People who have difficulty eating can, for example, arouse embarrassment and even hostility in public restaurants. More often, the able-bodied are simply thoughtless. They forget, for instance, that someone who is wheelchaired cannot "see through" them in a crowd of spectators, until they are politely reminded.

Transportation and tourist personnel, guides and hotel staffs are trained to do what they can to help clients who are disabled, but too much must not be expected of them during busy times and it's not always possible to get help just when and how it's wanted. This is a good reason to travel in the middle of the week during off-peak periods if possible.

It would be wrong to suggest that vacationers who are disabled have no special diffculties to contend with; they do, but the difficulties can almost always be overcome. And the greater the number of people who exercise their rights to mobility and to access to all tourist amenities everywhere, the sooner will new travel and vacation facilities be planned with disabled people more in mind and the many inhibiting inadequacies that still exist be remedied.

The vital strategy is to plan ahead and get reliable information in advance about the general accessibility of the mode of transport you plan to use and of the places you want to visit. If you are going to travel abroad, find out well before departure about any visas or immunizations you may need. Check with your doctor about any special precautions to be taken with regard, for example, to sudden extremes of temperature or radical dietary changes.

Blind people who use guide dogs must realize that some countries (the United Kingdom and most of the Commonwealth) impose long quarantines on any imported animal, so that it is not feasible to take one in or out for a short vacation. It is possible to get escort help or other short-term practical assistance by contacting well in advance one of the national or international organizations concerned with disabled people which has volunteers in the places you plan to visit.

It is always advisable to arrange your own baggage insurance and make sure you are covered for health and accident risks wherever you are going. Some vacation insurance policies do not cover, or make special conditions for, people with disabilities and you should check personally with the insurance companies about this.

Among the useful items that seasoned disabled travelers take with them are: a chair-narrowing device for easing a wheelchair through narrow doorways and entrances; a small portable ramp for high curbs; a supply of identity tags for labeling wheelchairs, crutches and baggage; a letter from a doctor explaining the extent of their disability, details of any medication they regularly take and any special health problems they have, in case they should suddenly need medical attention.

Probably the most trouble-free way to go on a vacation is to join one of the groups organized by the few tourist operators or agents who specialize in travel for disabled people. They are all based in the United States and, between them, run tours to all parts of America and practically every country in the world that caters to Western visitors. Recent destinations have included Spain, Japan, Mexico and Morocco. It is possible for people living outside the United States to join these tours *en route*. There are no tourist operators in Britain who deal exclusively with the disabled traveler on the same scale, but some agents have developed great expertise in this area.

Most of the tours include people of all age groups and with a great variety of disability, although some agents specialize in planning trips for people with particular disabilities, such as the blind, the deaf or paraplegics. Recently, agents have begun to organize special interest vacations for the handicapped. These have included skiing tours for the deaf, the blind and amputees and a round-Italy tour for disabled art enthusiasts.

Tour organizers have had years of experience and claim to have "checked the facilities for wheelchairs and arranged for lifters and pushers from one end of the globe to the other." There are usually some able-bodied assistants on hand and, in some cases, a doctor and physiotherapist in attendance. Friends and relatives are usually encouraged to go along, too. Those people who require special help can sometimes arrange for it at extra cost.

A number of voluntary and welfare organizations in both the United States and Britain regularly organize vacations for groups of disabled people who are accompanied by relatives, friends and volunteers. These include vacations centered on such activities are riding, sailing and nature study. There are also international groups which arrange educational exchange trips abroad, usually for younger people and including some who are disabled. Numerous educational institutions organize recreational and study tours every summer which are open to all students, able-bodied and disabled.

If you don't wish to travel with other disabled people you can make arrangements for your own vacations and sightseeing trips through a specialized travel agent. It is also quite possible for a person who is disabled to join any kind of group tour, provided that he or she has some degree of mobility or is accompanied by someone to look after any special needs. (It is, however, sometimes possible to arrange to pay for such attendance.) If you plan to do this, be honest about the extent of your disability with your travel agent or tour organizer from the outset, and don't expect too much extra help and attention from guides who may have about forty people to take care of. You will be most likely to find congenial traveling companions, incidentally, if you choose one of the many special interest tours arranged for those with particular enthusiasms—and they range from archaeology to fishing, from art to gambling.

Getting There

If you are traveling by air it is wise to keep in mind that airlines have different regulations and varying extents of amenities for travelers with disabilities. As a general rule, the smaller the airline and its planes the more difficulties the non-ambulatory passenger is likely to encounter. When you're planning a vacation, allow time to compare the policies and facilities of the various airlines you could use. Some airports are laid out and equipped more conveniently than others, but each airline makes its own provision for the boarding and in-transit transfer of its disabled passengers. Travel agents with experience in arranging group flights for disabled people can offer sound advice.

If you are traveling alone, make your reservation well in advance because some airlines will only accept a certain quota per flight of disabled, and particularly of wheelchaired, passengers. When making reservations be sure that the airline is aware of the physical limitations your disability imposes and of any special dietary requirements—which can usually be met. Also tell them of any equipment you need to carry such as a wheelchair or respirator. As a rule, the wet cell batteries for powered wheelchairs or special oxygen tanks are not allowed. Some airlines provide visual aid instructions for the deaf. Guide dogs can almost always travel with their owners in the passenger compartment. A stretcher-bed passenger is usually accepted if he or she has a medical certificate and gives sufficient prior notice; the fare, however, is expensive because of the amount of space taken up by a bed.

Be sure to arrive at the airport more than one hour before departure time; generally you will be boarded ahead of the other passengers. On arrival, however, you will probably be asked, for reasons of convenience, to disembark last.

Having said this much about regulations, it is amazing how often they can be bent. There have been many charter flights made up entirely of wheelchaired and stretchered passengers and, for one vacation trip, six polio quads all on respirators were carried from Alberta to Hawaii—which required considerable adaptation of the plane's normal power supplies.

For the disabled person traveling overland by car, the major problem is likely to be one of *en route* access to highway rest areas and accommodation. In the United States a booklet, *Highway Rest Areas for Handicapped Travelers*, published by the President's Committee on Employment for the Handicapped, lists barrier-free facilities with such additional conveniences as parking lots with ramps. There are only about four hundred entries for forty-seven states, however, a very small number for so large an area.

Automobile associations in America and Britain also publish information on accessibility of hotels and highway service areas. The British guide includes details of the concessions and exemptions from payment of tolls and ferry charges for which most handicapped drivers are eligible.

Provided that sufficient advance notice is given, hand-controlled vehicles can be hired at little or no extra cost from the major car-rental firms operating in the United States. No facility on a similar scale exists in Europe.

People who cannot comfortably travel within the confined space of ordinary cars often find some kind of recreational vehicle more satisfactory. Most favor a standard truck with interior space converted into a living area or fitted with a roof extension, wide door and ramp or sidelift for a wheelchair.

When suitably equipped inside for all temporary living needs, such vehicles provide disabled vacationers with a considerable measure of freedom of choice by making them less dependent on conventional tourist facilities and enabling them to travel in comfort to otherwise inaccessible areas. One polio quad who needs almost constant respiratory aid has traveled all over Mexico in this way. A variation on the theme are trailers (caravans) or motor-homes that have been specially fitted with adaptations to suit the needs of the individual traveler.

It is also possible for the disabled vacationer to travel overland in the United States using public transportation. The Greyhound Bus Company was a pioneer in aiding handicapped travelers and its Helping Hand Service enables a disabled person and a companion to journey together on a single ticket. People who are disabled are usually given boarding priority and their essential medical aids can be carried free of charge. Reduced fares for blind passengers are also available.

Almost all the national bus companies in the United States now offer similar facilities and concessions for handicapped passengers; whichever one you go by, be sure to alert them in advance. It should be noted, however, that while newly built or modernized bus terminals throughout the United States have good facilities for disabled travelers, there are still hundreds of old, unmodernized ones which leave much to be desired.

No equivalent national networks exist in Europe and individual bus companies offer differing amounts of help. Voluntary organizations and travel agents who specialize in tours for the handicapped in the United States and Europe sometimes use motor-coaches equipped with portable lifts and converted so that the wheelchaired can board them easily and remain in their own chairs while traveling. ACROSS, a British charitable organization, has giant luxury ambulances called Jumbulances equipped with stretcher beds, respirators and other medical equipment to carry people who are severely disabled to various European holiday destinations.

At the other end of the care scale, a few intrepid people in wheelchairs have simply relied on their own wheels and the generosity of others to hitchhike from one city or country to another. One man who has traveled extensively through Europe in this way reports that Britain and Holland are the best bets for the wheelchaired hitchhiker; France is not good and in Sweden the practice is discouraged.

New railroad stock in the United States and parts of Europe has now been designed with the needs of the disabled traveler in mind. In the United States on the short-distance Amfleet trains no passenger is permitted to occupy a wheelchair and must use a train seat, and there are facilities for the handicapped only in the food-service cars.

Every effort is made on Amtrak's nationwide rail network to enable disabled passengers to travel in comfort. The new long-distance Amtrak trains have a ramp entryway and a sleeping car for handicapped passengers. There is a special seat and toilet in every coach car and there are reduced fares for people traveling with attendants. A special reservation system is operated for deaf passengers and guide dogs can travel in passenger compartments. Many of the old-fashioned stations are, however, difficult to negotiate in a wheelchair.

British Rail is making its modern equipment and renovated stations more accessible and there are spaces for wheelchairs in the new Mark III first-class coaches on the Inter-City high speed trains. Disabled passengers pay only second-class fares for these facilities. But the majority of rolling stock and stations are far from new. At major stations, wheelchairs can be borrowed for transfer from a train to another vehicle.

General advice about public-transport travel in the United Kingdom can be obtained from the Department of the Environment; but it is not easy to get detailed information in English about the accessibility of Europe's public transportation systems. Most main line services in Scandinavia and Holland have some facilities for passengers with physical disabilities.

The leisurely and relaxing ambience of life-afloat is ideal in some ways for handicapped people, but, unfortunately, few passenger ships were built to serve special needs. The most satisfactory modern vessel is Cunard Line's *Q.E. II* which has ramps, wide passages and elevators connecting the decks so that the wheelchaired can move around the entire ship with ease. This vessel goes on various extended cruises throughout the year and the company asks only for a medical certificate verifying fitness to travel. A few cruise ships owned by other lines are partially adapted for disabled people.

If you are making an individual booking, discuss the suitability of particular ships and cabins with the reservation staff. Specialist tour operators and some voluntary organizations arrange group cruises that can take you to places as far-flung as Alaska and Indonesia. Numerous disabled people who have gone on cruises testify to the helpful goodwill of ships' crews and other passengers.

On a smaller scale, there are many boats that can accommodate some disabled people on short trips. It is possible, for example, to go through the Everglades in Florida, or on some of the Canadian lakes. In Britain, two canal barges have been specially adapted to carry the wheelchaired along inland waterways and a catamaran large enough to carry ten people in wheelchairs goes on one-day trips from various south coast ports.

Staying There

It's not much fun to arrive somewhere only to find that half your precious vacation time has to be spent figuring out how to get around the architectural barriers separating you from your hotel room, the restaurants or the sights you actually want to see. Apart from the specialists in travel for the disabled, it is unfortunately true that most travel agents have only scant and imprecise information on such matters. Therefore, if you are traveling independently or with a group of mainly able-bodied people, you will be wise to find out in advance just how well you, individually, will be able to cope with the business of actually getting around during your vacation.

SATH, Society for the Advancement of Travel for the Handicapped, a nonprofit, travel industry association based in New York, sends out information about travel and vacation services for people with disabilities. SATH's aim is to integrate the disabled more fully within the conventional tourist industry.

Mobility International, headquartered in London, is a nongovernmental organization whose main objective is to improve the quality of life for disabled people by offering them integration with the able-bodied and equal opportunities to travel, to make exchange visits and to meet with people all over the world. Mobility International offers a comprehensive travel information service as well as a variety of integrated projects which are mainly for young people.

Most large and some smaller cities, some states in the United States and some counties in Britain have access guides for disabled visitors, as do some in Ireland, Canada and Australia. The best bet for information about individual European countries are the Michelin guides which indicate hotel accessibility; there is an English–Danish guide for the handicapped to hotels in Denmark. The American Women's Committee on Employment for the Handicapped publishes a free list of most accessibility guides written in English and tells where they can be obtained.

Some of the guides are much more helpful than others, giving dimensions of hotel rooms and restaurants as well as access information on public buildings, toilets, theaters, churches, civic centers and stores. New York and London have guides of this kind. There are also various travel compendiums published in the United States and Britain by concerned voluntary organizations, tourist authorities and private individuals which can be very useful and there is a guide to France for the physically disabled written in English. If no such information seems obtainable for the places you plan to visit, then write (as always well in advance) to the tourist office of the country or region concerned, to the welfare departments of municipal authorities and to the headquarters of voluntary organizations involved with disablement.

As you will soon glean from the guides, the most difficult and hazardous areas and buildings for the disabled to negotiate are those which are old or historic, created long before the needs of the nonambulatory were given thought. Thus, the charming old inns of Europe and the older American hotels are generally the least convenient. The larger, modern hotels and motels are the most barrier-free—the main reason operators of tours for the disabled opt for first-class modern accommodation.

The major international hotel chains have now established access criteria which include some ground-floor rooms, large elevators, wide doorways, braille menus and bathrooms (invariably the biggest problem in hotels) equipped with grab bars and wall rails. The worldwide Holiday Inn network has long specialized in the provision of comfortable accessible accommodation for its handicapped guests. Of course there are other hotels in the United States and Europe which, although they do not have all the desirable built-in facilities, cater thoughtfully to disabled guests by providing portable wheelchair ramps, bathroom adaptations (taking off doors when necessary) and personnel who are prepared to offer cheerful assistance.

The best way to find out about these establishments is to collect the recommendations of other disabled travelers, some of whom have traveled widely for many years in spite of severe physical limitations. Welfare and voluntary organizations can often provide lists of hotels and small boarding establishments that cater specially to those with disabilities which come within their particular area of concern.

If you do not much care for the idea of an ordinary hotel, there are other alternatives. Vacation centers and camps are popular with some people because of their extensive on-the-spot entertainment and recreational facilities. They are usually recently built on level terrain, often with lovely natural scenery close at hand, all of which minimizes problems of access and transportation. They almost always have swimming pools, dance halls and game rooms. Some have recreational or study programs, too.

Some of these centers and camps are specifically designed to accommodate people with disabilities and have cottage-type, one-level rooms, or adapted motor-homes. Some people prefer to live in their own converted recreational vehicles. Other conveniences include wide, hard-surface connection ways, adaptive aids for sporting equipment and some resident medical care. In many of the camps some voluntary help is on hand, but campers who are severely disabled usually need to be accompanied by attendants.

Most of the open-air adventure camps cater to handicapped children, but there are several where young adults are also welcome. A Directory of United States Camps for the Handicapped is available from the Easter Seal Society.

Those people who are unable to spend very long in the relative inconvenience of an outdoor environment because of their disabilities, can still arrange day or week-end stays at some of these camps. Voluntary organizations and welfare service departments in the United States and Britain regularly organize summer vacations for groups at these centers.

There is a leisure center in Cornwall, England run by the Spastics Society which features an original mix of sporting and outdoor activities, courses in the natural sciences and various handicrafts. An Adventure Centre in the Lake District offers to those with varying disabilities the opportunity to enjoy such outdoor activities as sailing and riding, indoor hobbies and nearby nature trails—some with wheelchair access, others which are particularly aromatic, for blind people.

There are a number of international Handi-camps in European countries, including Britain, in which about one-third of the campers are handicapped. All the campers join together to carry out particular work projects. Everyone contributes as much as he or she is able.

If you are planning a vacation in one of the fine American National Parks, get a copy of the *National Park Guide for the Handicapped* which covers historic monuments as well as areas of natural beauty. The guide states that almost all architectural barriers within the park system have been eliminated so that wheelchaired visitors "are free to move almost any place" in all but thirteen of the two hundred and forty-two listed areas. Most parks have raised contour maps, audio programs, braille markers and tactile exhibits for blind visitors.

Those who find both conventional hotel accommodations and an outdoor environment difficult to cope with, but who badly need a vacation change-of-scene may welcome a short-term rest-stay in one of the many residential homes and centers for the disabled that are run by the welfare authorities and voluntary organizations in the United States and Britain. To find out about this possibility, contact the organizing service concerned.

Another alternative is to arrange a vacation home-swap on an individual basis with someone who has a disability similar to your own. In this way, you can enjoy a pleasant stay in a different environment, but be based in a home that is already adapted to suit your special needs—such as barrier-free access or a rocking bed. The best way to find a suitable person with whom to exchange is to send details of your own requirements and accommodation to the headquarters of concerned voluntary organizations or to one of the periodicals published for disabled people.

The Disabled Child

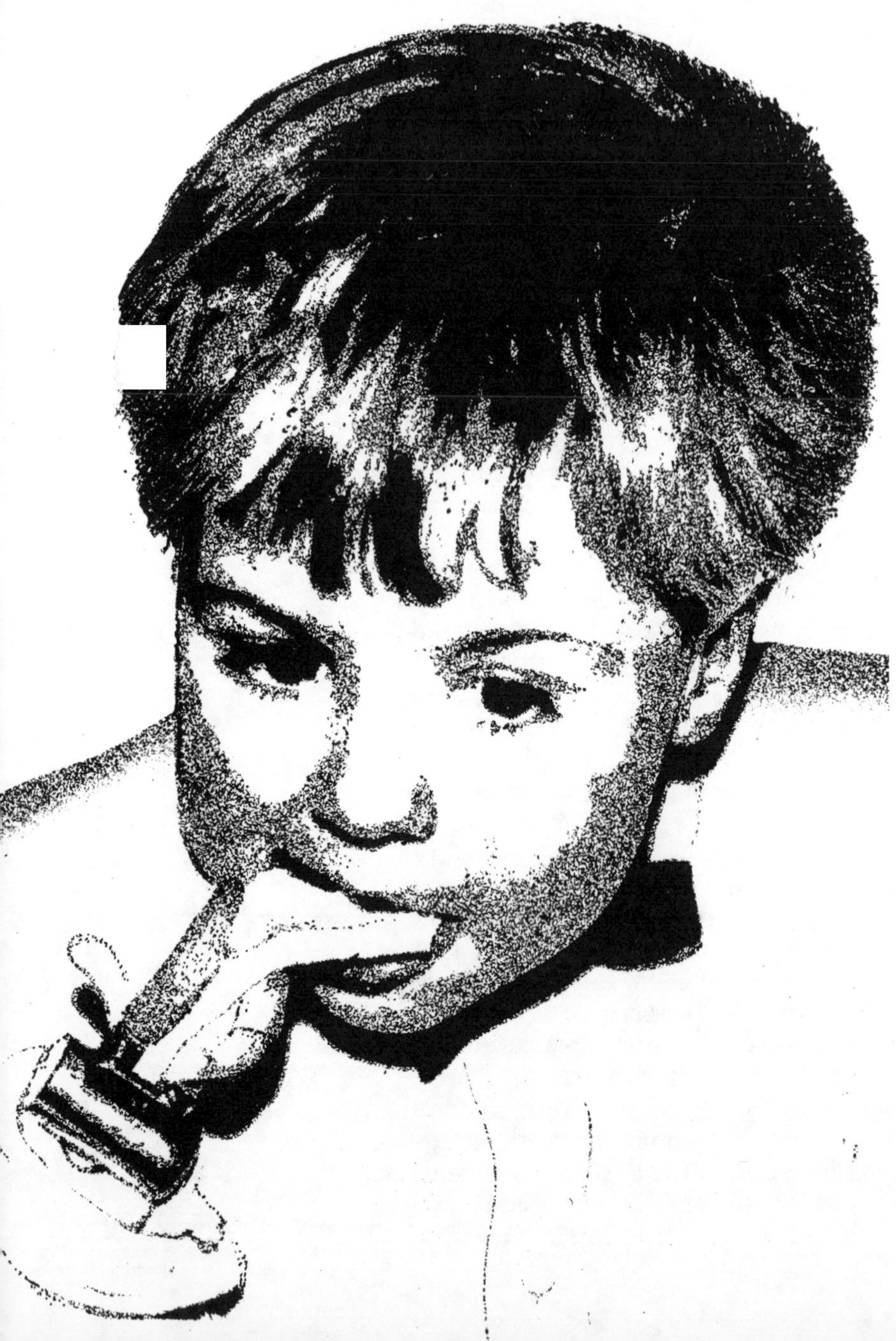

A few words thrust you into a totally alien world, one for which no adequate preparation is possible. Perhaps suddenly, maybe after an anxious period of medical testing, you are told by your doctor that your child has a handicapping condition and for you—and your family—nothing will ever be the same again.

Most parents who have experienced this trauma believe that this is the worst time, the period when the knowledge is still raw and unassimilated; the days and weeks and months after the doctor has explained that a child who was injured in a skiing accident will never regain the use of his legs, or the baby, imbued with so many hopes, is unlikely ever to be able to feed herself or to sit unaided.

However minor or severe your child's disability, the emotional shock of discovery is devastating. Our society places so much emphasis on physical perfection and achievement that you will look far into the future, even if the child is an infant. And in your distress and confusion it may seem terribly bleak. What job will this child, for whom you both wanted and dreamed of so much, be able to hold? Will he be able to live independently? Will she be able to bear children? There is profound disappointment and concern.

Doctors and therapists who have worked with parents of physically handicapped children tend to believe that although each case and each family is unique, there are similarities in the ways in which families react and attain gradual acceptance. Broadly, psychiatrists speak of a sequence of three stages, which may overlap, and which can be compared to coming to terms with a deep loss or bereavement.

During the early stage, emotional shock and confusion may be accompanied by denial. Parents simply refuse to hear what they are told by the doctors; they just do not want to hear what is being said—and therefore they do not. It is common for parents to say later that after the first shock they cannot remember a word of the doctor's subsequent explanation. So in addition to the strong emotional reaction, there is also likely to be ignorance on the parents' part concerning their child's condition, its treatment and the possible outcome. A mutually supportive and trusting relationship between doctor and parents is of the utmost importance. For at this time many parents are susceptible to doctor or clinic shopping, hoping to hear a different or more optimistic diagnosis, but in fact probably exposing themselves to further anguish and increasing the strain on their child.

Conscientious and loving parents of a physically disabled child often develop strong feelings of guilt which are quite irrational. This stage is likely to follow that of initial bewilderment. On one level it may arise because of their lack of understanding of their child's condition and its cause. When they realize that it happened through chance—and are given realistic guidance and advice—the feelings of guilt may be lessened. But some nagging questions may nevertheless persist. What did we do wrong? Are we being punished? If the child was involved in an accident or was injured on the playing field, both parents may reproach themselves bitterly for not ensuring that their child had stricter supervision. If it is discovered that there is a hereditary factor in the child's disability, the parents may blame themselves, even if they could not have known about this when they decided to have a baby.

When parents are unable to resolve these inner anxieties they may become hostile—toward doctors, friends and neighbors, and, most destructively, toward each other. Struggling with acceptance and the fatigue of daily care, most parents of a disabled child will experience bouts of despair. Often professional guidance is needed to help them to express, and to learn to cope with, these ambivalent feelings of love, of guilt and of anger as well as sheer physical exhaustion.

Sooner or later, most parents reach the final stage of acceptance, of marshaling their inner resources so that they are ready to cope. As one parent puts it, "There comes a moment when we can pull ourselves together and go on." Then expectations for a child are modified and the struggle for the best care, education and aids is begun.

A recent series of interviews with parents of physically disabled children showed that most of them coped successfully. The psychiatrist who conducted the interviews was Dr. Jerome Schulman of Children's Hospital in Chicago. He concluded that the parents who managed best were those who did not still believe, not even deep down, that they were in any way responsible for their child's condition, who had an objective view of themselves and who were open about their child's disability with each other, with their family and friends and with their doctors. These parents had attitudes of realistic hopefulness. And, above all, in speaking of these parents, Dr. Schulman reported how impressed he was by "the extent to which essentially terrible problems can precipitate personal growth."

This section deals specifically with children—their care, their clothes, their discipline and their education. Although the line is often difficult to draw with certainty, it has been written essentially for parents whose children have some physical disability, but who are not mentally impaired; children who, perhaps with appropriate aids, may be able to attend the local school and will one day take their places as independent men and women in the community. Parents should also refer to other sections of the book in which the information and creative ideas may well be relevant.

Throughout this section the child is referred to as "he." This is purely for convenience; to continually say "he or she" is awkward.

Finally, as every parent knows, the daily care of any child is full of ups and downs. Raising a child who has a physical disability is likely to be altogether more demanding. And yet, as has been said by many parents, the special needs, and the achievements, of such a child also bring special joys.

Coping as a Family

However well a handicapped child is assimilated into family life, the fact of his disability can create exceptional physical and emotional strains on all those who are close to him. If a great deal of physical care is needed, his parents' fatigue becomes a problem which can affect everyone. Taking the child to the doctor, the therapist and the clinic is time-consuming. Concern for the child's future is an ever present anxiety.

An obvious strain which affects the entire family is the financial one, particularly in the United States where there is no national health service. A recent study, made in New York City of families of children with rheumatoid arthritis, showed that during the first year of the illness more than one-quarter of these families went into debt. All of them found it necessary to cut every possible financial corner. In some cases, the fathers took on second jobs; in others, the mothers were forced to go out to work. This was despite the fact that two-thirds of these families did get some help in mitigating the costs of the illness—by fee reductions in clinics and day care centers, camps and visiting nurse services. The study also showed that about one-third of the mothers who were questioned experienced serious physical and emotional strain because of all the care their children required.

There is no easy answer to the question of how much an entire family should sacrifice financially to meet the needs of a child who is disabled. Obviously, if a child would truly benefit from a sophisticated and expensive aid—to give him greater mobility perhaps, or a means of communication—most parents would do their utmost to obtain it for him, regardless of cost. Yet, despite the child's special needs, he is one of a family—of three or four or more. Whenever possible, his needs should be weighed against those of the rest of the family. If there is a choice between extra therapy for the child or a family holiday it is often necessary for the parents to remember that their child benefits most from having a happy and relatively tranquil home. His greatest resource is his family—and families, and all their members, need nurturing.

Perhaps even more pervasive of family life than the financial considerations is the amount of time and energy the child's disability may demand, particularly of his mother who is likely to be with him most. A child may need to be fed very slowly and carefully because of poor muscular control. If he is in a wheelchair he may need help transferring onto crutches and getting into and out of the car. A severely disabled child requires constant lifting. Although to a parent this may become routine, a brother or sister may begin to resent what he or she comes to believe is too much parental attention. And because older siblings may understand the disabled child's need for physical care, their natural resentment may be further complicated by guilt feelings. Intellectually, they know that their disabled brother or sister cannot help needing so much attention, but there are times when they resent it all the same.

Discussing these feelings within the family can prevent resentment from building up. It makes sense to talk about essential daily chores, aiming at a more equitable distribution of responsibility throughout the family. Perhaps, for example, an older child can start helping to get a disabled brother or sister up in the mornings or be put in charge of the going-to-bed routine. It might be possible to change swimming therapy to Saturday mornings when the father is free to help and to spend a little more time alone with the child. This kind of adjustment of routine is invaluable in lessening the work load on the mother, and constructively involving the father and brothers and sisters in the child's care.

It is helpful to remember—and all too easy to forget—that a disabled child is more like than unlike any other child. Yet many parents find it extremely difficult to discipline their disabled child, perhaps because of a residual guilt that his life is necessarily limited. But this is not a realistic approach to preparing the child for the disciplines of life outside the family. He needs to be set limits at home like those set for his brother or sister. He needs, just as much as his brother or sister, to grow up with respect for parental authority. So it is right that parents insist on standards of manners and behavior. Set regular bedtimes on school nights. See that the child helps to pick up his toys and keep his room neat. Making reasonable rules and seeing that they are kept are essential for the child's development and also lessen the resentment of siblings who will quickly and rightly question why he seems to have special privileges.

Whatever a child's disability—and however positively parents and siblings learn to cope with it at home—accommodation must also be made to the outside world. You and your child will become more comfortable among other people if he is included in family outings from an early age and is involved when friends visit the house. Most families find that the attitudes of others are sympathetic and helpful. Nevertheless, there are, inevitably, occasional upsetting experiences. It can happen anywhere, out of the blue. A chance remark may be overheard while shopping: "They shouldn't wheel a child like that around in public. . . ." "Disgraceful letting the poor little thing struggle with crutches. . . ." Or perhaps nothing is said—there are just stares and whispers.

To you, who love him, the wound goes deep. It cannot alleviate the immediate hurt but it might help to remember that, when confronted by a disability, many people unfamiliar with handicapping conditions simply do not know how to react. While most respond with kindness and thoughtfulness, others, out of ignorance, can be bigoted and cruel. Most families seem to find their own ways of coping with occasional hurt and embarrassment. There are times when humor or sharp anger can help to deal with feelings of outrage. Encourage the children to talk about bad experiences they may have had or thoughtless remarks they may have overheard. If you suspect that one of the children is avoiding certain people or not bringing friends home from school, try tactfully to get him to share his feelings with you.

Stresses differ from family to family and depend on the extent of the disability, but a family can deal with all of them better if they are acknowledged and openly discussed. The moment there are signs that the pressures are too great on one or both parents or on another child, professional counseling should be sought through the family doctor. A family must not be disabled because a child has a disability.

Independence

The greatest gifts you can give to your child are the desire to be as independent as possible and the determination to work toward that goal. When parents have a realistic belief in their child's ability to do things for himself, the child is likely to develop realistic expectations of his own abilities. The more secure he feels about himself, the more independent he is encouraged to be in his own home, the more confidence he will have to explore the world around him. This can also increase his motivation to use the various aids his disability requires.

At birth all babies are totally dependent on their mothers. After the first six months, the moves toward autonomy begin—holding his own cup, trying to pull off a sock or deciding to eat peas and not potatoes for lunch one day. Achieving independence is an uneven process for all children. One day the three-year-old wants to put on his own coat, the next day he insists on his mother doing it for him; soon, he will automatically do it by himself. The child who has physical disabilities wants to be independent just as much as any other child, but it may take longer to achieve—and some children may only be able to achieve it in a limited way.

Parents always have ambivalent feelings as they watch their child struggle toward independence. There are regrets that babyhood is over and the desire to keep the child a baby for just a little bit longer is mixed with pride in seeing him gain more skills. A child who is disabled makes particularly powerful demands on the parental instinct to protect, but this instinct is only justified as long as it is beneficial to the child.

Although the right balance between dependence and independence is hard to gauge, too much protection can prevent a child from tackling those tasks he is capable of accomplishing and from reaching out for more challenges. Many disabled adults who are dependent on others for even their most trivial needs were restricted more than their disabilities required by loving, but overprotective, parents. It won't hurt any child to try and to fail—to pick up his own toys with a reacher, perhaps, or to undress himself—as long as you support him in his efforts and applaud them.

According to many studies, children who are physically disabled do not have the everyday experiences which lead to independence—trips to the supermarket, the library, to restaurants—that are usual for children who are able-bodied. There are many understandable reasons for this. It is often difficult to transport a child with heavy braces; many public buildings are still inaccessible. And there is the embarassment which some families

feel when they must confront stares or questions from strangers. Nevertheless, depriving the child of such experiences hampers his desire for independence.

Children with impaired hearing live in an isolated world and have their special needs, although their disability is often not visible and it doesn't restrict their mobility. Because it is hard to communicate with a deaf child in words, other ways must be found to reward his efforts at independence—perhaps through the warmth of physical closeness and hugging. Blind children also need tactile reassurance as they master a new skill or make an obvious effort to do things for themselves. Children who are deaf or blind tend to suffer, understandably, from parental overprotection which, although lovingly intended, is counterproductive. Allowed reasonable opportunities, a child who is congenitally blind can acquire enormous self-confidence and the ability to do things competently for himself while still very young.

All children, whatever their disabilities, benefit from being given some domestic responsibilities around the house. Most children can be of some help in the kitchen—setting the table, timing eggs, helping to wash the salad and vegetables. A weekly allowance, a token amount at first, gives a child the opportunity to handle change and to make decisions.

As all children near adolescence they begin to think about the future. The more self-confident and independent the child is, the better able he will be to see a place for himself in the adult world.

From a child's earliest school years it is the responsibility of parents to see that homework is done neatly and submitted on time. This prepares the child for the discipline of higher education or job training. The more realistic the independence that is expected of him when he is young, the higher the degree of self-support he is likely to attain as an adult. Of course, some children are so severely handicapped that they will always be in need of physical care and financial support. This can be extremely depressing to the child as he enters adolescence and becomes more and more conscious of the limitations his disability imposes. The situation and its uncertainties are also desperately worrying for his parents. At this time, the best possible vocational counseling is often advisable.

Aids

Today a wide range of aids is available to help even severely disabled children to perform such ordinary activities of everyday life as feeding themselves or picking up dropped toys. These aids range from variations of the simple utility stick, which can be used in a hundred different ways—for reaching objects, in playing or dressing or grooming—to the sophisticated electronic devices which give the deaf the ability to communicate. Of course, such specialized equipment as communication and mobility aids must be prescribed by professionals. A therapist's advice should always be sought, too, about other aids because it is often possible, and preferable, to teach a child an alternative method of doing things so that he will not have to rely on aids. Remember also, that when learning alternative methods children have the advantage of being more adaptable than adults and have less to unlearn.

Parents' knowledge of their own child, his daily routine, his particular likes and dislikes, do put them in the best position to know what frustrates the child and what small bit of independence would make him happier and less anxious. Specific aids are being invented and refined all the time; parents should keep up-to-date through the appropriate national organization. But your own imagination and ingenuity are important, too. Many self-help aids have been devised by parents of disabled children. A visit to the hardware store with your child's particular problem in mind can result in a happy solution. A pair of ordinary kitchen tongs could, for example, be the perfect way for a small child to move toy cars and trucks.

Mobility

Most of us have no concept of how limiting and frustrating it is for a child to be unable to get up and choose a toy or run to see what's going on in another room. The child whose mobility is severely delayed or limited is cut off from the joys of exploration and discovery. As a result, emotional and intellectual development may suffer. It is vitally important for parents of a physically disabled child to do everything they can to help him to compensate for this basic limitation.

Some wheelchairs for children, like the one left, are designed to accommodate growth. With the back mounted forward the seat is eleven and a half inches (29 cm) deep and fourteen and a half inches (36 cm) wide. Changing the upholstery and the seat's position make it two and a half inches (6.5 cm) deeper and wider. The height of the removable armrests is adjustable.

The baby who is disabled needs the stimulus of being moved around, indoors and out, so that he experiences different surroundings. Frequent outings are an essential part of his life, and if you prop him in a baby seat (strapped in and with padded sides if necessary) he can be with the rest of the family. A baby who is unable to turn his head or support himself needs to be carried from room to room, to be taken outdoors to hear children playing, to watch the clouds and to see trees bend in the wind. Bright mobiles attached to the crib and playpen make the baby's limited view more exciting.

Carrying the baby in a sling that hangs around the neck, or in a piggy-back contraption over the shoulders, will leave the parent's hands free as he or she goes about daily activities. Shopping or housework can be done while the baby gains a feeling of closeness and the sensation of movement that will prepare him for using mobility aids later. To simulate the sensation of crawling, a baby can be placed on a blanket on the floor or the lawn with a pillow under his stomach for support.

There are many aids which are designed to increase mobility and are fun to use for a child from about the age of two. Such modifications as padding to

A carryall of denim or similar sturdy fabric, above, attaches over the wheelchair arm and has several roomy compartments. Held in place with Velcro tabs it does not interfere with the wheel.

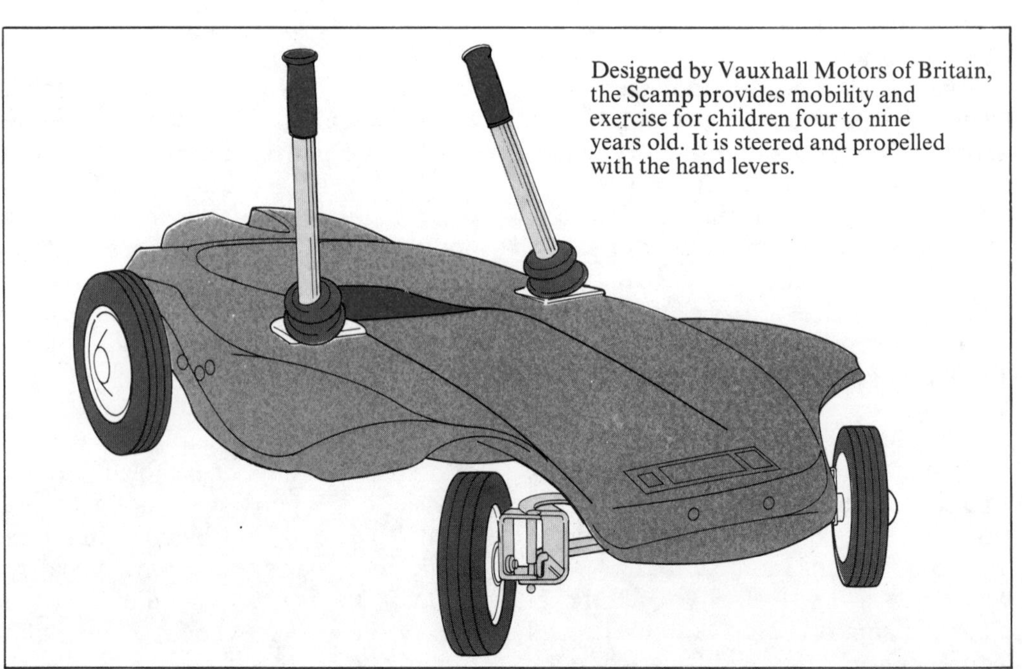

Designed by Vauxhall Motors of Britain, the Scamp provides mobility and exercise for children four to nine years old. It is steered and propelled with the hand levers.

give extra support can be made to most of these aids.

A child who is to become as mobile as possible with whatever range of walking aids is prescribed, needs realistic parental encouragement and support. If, for example, the parents' attitude toward crutches or braces or a walker is positive, their child's feelings about them are likely to be positive, too. If, on the other hand, a parent has not fully accepted the fact of the child's disability and questions the need for a walking aid or feels embarassed about it, the child will be the first to sense it. He will then not regard a walking aid as a passport to greater independence—as the means of being able to go to the neighborhood school, to get his own coat from the closet or to play with other children. At the slightest setback—and all children have setbacks when they begin to use walking aids—his parents' negative feelings, which he may only sense, will discourage him.

However much parents may anticipate their child's need for a wheelchair, they may nevertheless become depressed when the doctor initially suggests that it is time for the child to get one. It is natural for parents to feel some anxiety when a child faces new, and perhaps difficult, experiences. People who have a strong emotional reaction to the thought of their child using a wheelchair often find on examination of their feelings that they have a fundamental unwillingness to accept their child's disability and therefore cannot understand that to the child a wheelchair can prove to be a magic carpet.

Walking aids can be prescribed for children as young as two. A four-legged, rubber-tipped, light chrome walker, for example, is designed for children from two to six who have limited use of their legs. A lightweight metal frame gives somewhat older children sturdier support when walking. Also helpful for the child who walks with difficulty are adjustable tubular steel walkers which have wheels with rubber tires outside the frame and nonslip handgrips. Such aids must be prescribed by a doctor or therapist.

Many children with little use of their legs can learn to walk with braces and crutches. Walking confidently with such aids, however, is usually achieved only after a good deal of training. Children, particularly if they are very young, need a lot of practice in the use of crutches and braces before they become adept. But young children are also highly adaptable and with consistent guidance and encouragement they learn quickly.

A child's individual needs must be carefully assessed before any walking aid can be prescribed. It is vital that he is fitted with the aids which best suit him, and that modifications are made to the aids as the child develops. This can only be done by a skilled professional, a doctor or a therapist, who must also regularly review the child's needs, his growth patterns and his capabilities. A child's progress with walking aids depends on many factors—the extent of his disabilities, his motivation and the attitudes and encouragement of family, friends and teachers.

Since the child who is just beginning to walk with aids needs expert training and regular practice, it's important that parents get adequate instruction so that they can help their child effectively at home. Parallel bars are frequently used in teaching a child to walk. They are not difficult to make and a doctor

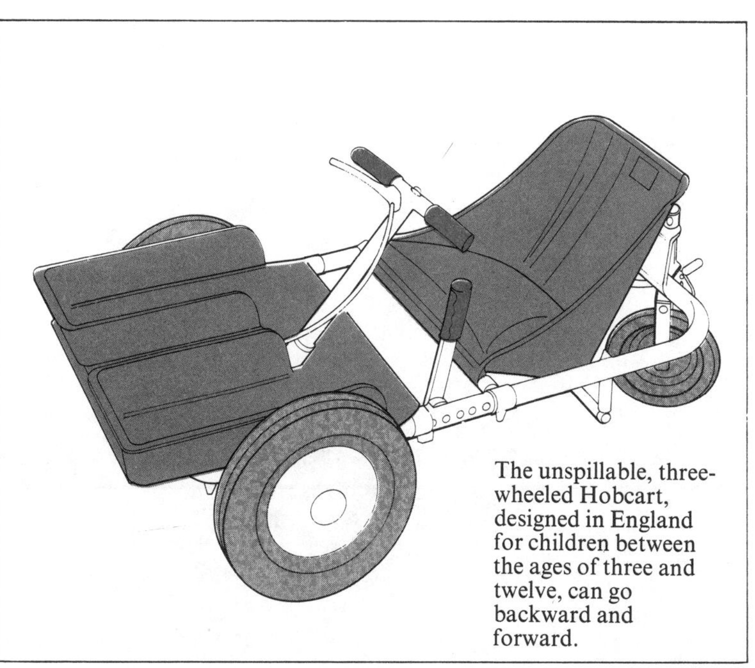

The unspillable, three-wheeled Hobcart, designed in England for children between the ages of three and twelve, can go backward and forward.

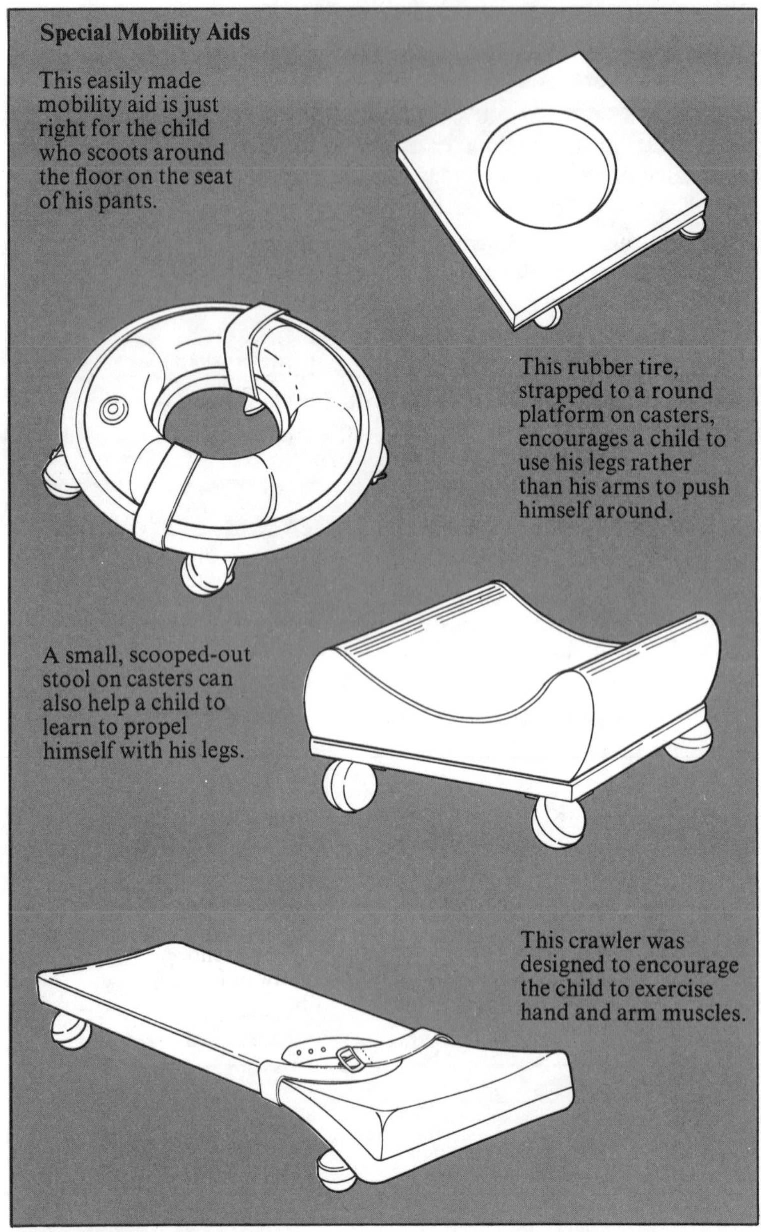

Special Mobility Aids

This easily made mobility aid is just right for the child who scoots around the floor on the seat of his pants.

This rubber tire, strapped to a round platform on casters, encourages a child to use his legs rather than his arms to push himself around.

A small, scooped-out stool on casters can also help a child to learn to propel himself with his legs.

This crawler was designed to encourage the child to exercise hand and arm muscles.

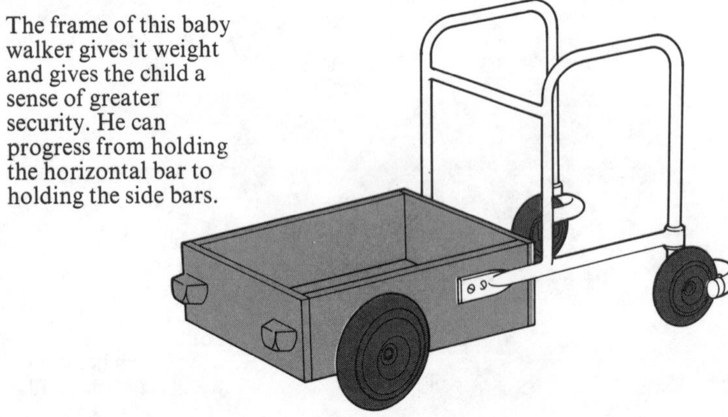

The frame of this baby walker gives it weight and gives the child a sense of greater security. He can progress from holding the horizontal bar to holding the side bars.

or therapist often advises that they be used at home for additional practice. Parents should also be given instructions about caring for braces. When a child uses crutches the rubber tips must be checked regularly and replaced as soon as they show signs of wear. Some children are better able to keep the crutches in an upright position if the handbars are covered with rubber.

A wheelchair can greatly increase the scope of a child's mobility and doctors and therapists often recommend one for a child who uses braces or crutches efficiently because it enables him to cover greater distances. A wheelchair can give a child more independence at home, at school and with his friends. Used sensibly, it also helps to prevent the excessive fatigue to which physically disabled children are prone. Many children are able to propel a wheelchair so skilfully that they become the envy of their able-bodied friends.

Choosing the right wheelchair for a child is the job of a specialist. You can help considerably in the selection of the correct chair, however, by telling the therapist as precisely as possible the conditions under which your child will probably use it. For the child who uses a wheelchair in school, for example, removable arms often make it easier to slide the chair under a desk. Removable arms also make it possible for the child to transfer from the wheelchair to the toilet, bathtub and bed. If you will have to carry the chair up and down stairs or transport it in a car be sure it folds easily and is light enough for you to carry. It is helpful if the child can try several models before the final selection is made.

The size of the wheelchair prescribed depends on the child's height and weight. The very smallest wheelchair is suitable for children of preschool age. There are adjustable wheelchairs available which are designed to grow with the child from the age of six to sixteen. There is a four-inch (10-cm) leeway from seat to footrests.

Useful wheelchair accessories include a crutch holder, a bag to hold books, toys and school lunch, and a lap tray which fits onto the armrests. A transfer board is also helpful.

Eating and Drinking

By the time most children are two years old, and sometimes earlier, they want to feed themselves and to drink from a mug without help. Self-feeding is a symbol of independence and means that a child is ready to take his place at the center of family life—the dinner table.

Simple finger foods, like crackers and carrot sticks, are the best preparation for self-feeding. This should be started during the last part of the first year, or whenever you feel your child is ready to manage it. Some disabled children, however, need to be taught how to bite, chew and swallow before they are ready to learn to feed themselves. If a child needs this kind of training, the therapist will show the parents how to feed the child at home.

It is important that a child feel comfortable and secure when he is eating. A footrest will give additional support if his feet do not reach the floor. A young child in a high chair should be strapped in with a harness to keep him from falling forward. A high-backed chair is essential if the head and neck need support.

A tray with grooves to hold plate, bowl and cup may be practical for a child with poor coordination. Nonslip place mats keep plates from slipping as do suction bases placed beneath plates and bowls. It's wise to use unbreakable plates and cups and plastic glasses for the whole family. It will cut down on breakage and prevent the child from feeling that he is clumsier than other members of the family. An insulated plate with a suction base keeps food hot for a long time and is useful when the child is learning to feed himself and is still rather slow.

Long-handled utensils are practical when reach is limited and implements with built-up handles are valuable aids when grasp is weak. A flexible rubber spoon is easy and safe to manipulate in the mouth. A rocker knife makes it possible for an older child to cut food using only one hand. All these eating aids are available from self-help equipment firms.

For drinking, a mug with two handles is easiest to hold. A weighted mug, which cannot tip over, helps to prevent spills, as does a flexible jumbo straw stuck through the lid of a plastic food container. Remember, however, that the longer the straw the more effort required to suck.

When a child is learning to feed himself it's a messy—if rewarding—business. An apron or smock which is easy to wash will keep clothes clean and a plastic sheet under the child's chair will save you lots of cleaning up afterward.

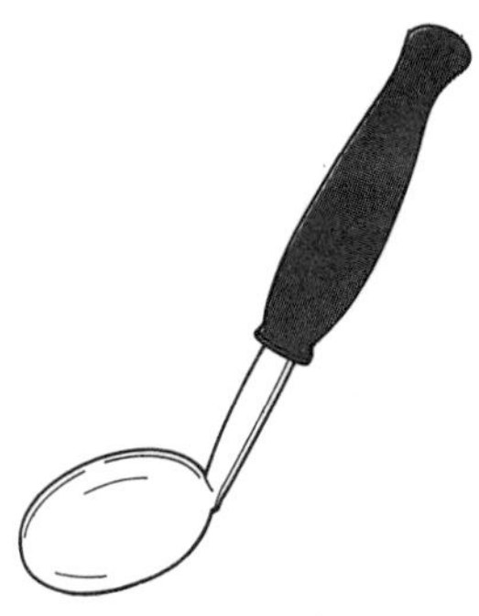

Available for either hand, this spoon has a molded handgrip and is angled for a child.

Eating and Drinking Aids

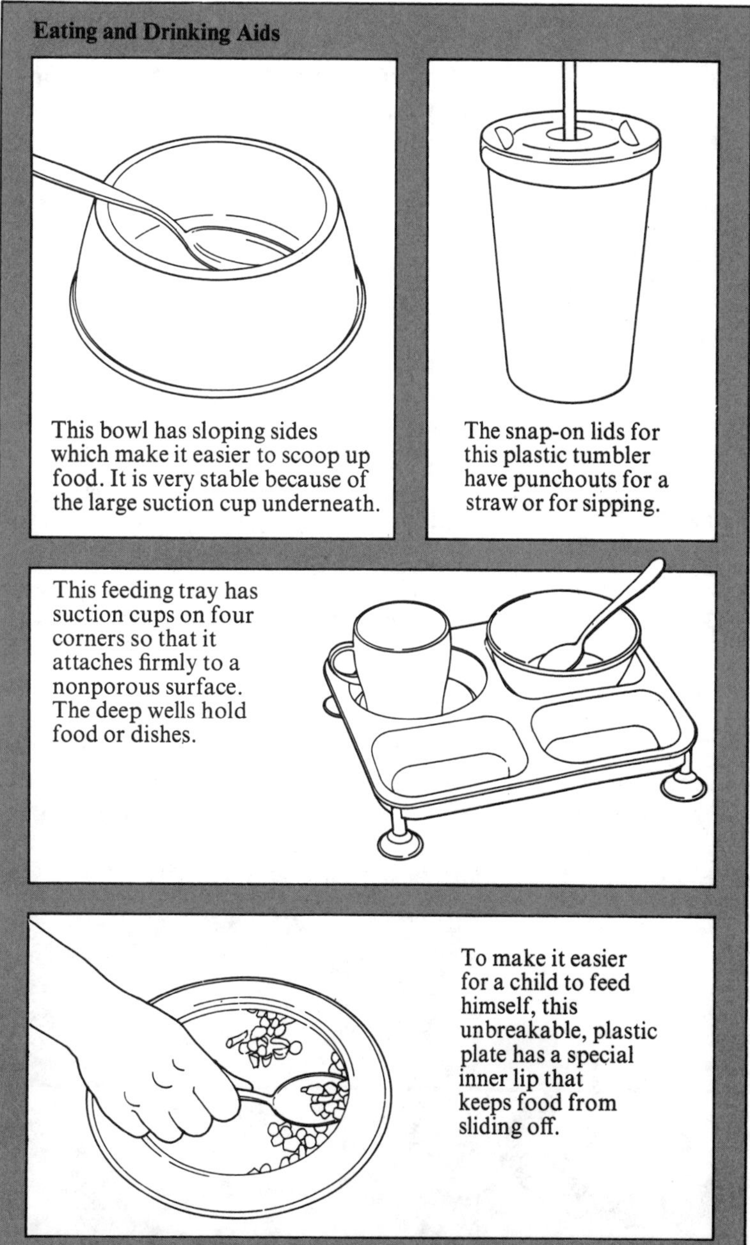

This bowl has sloping sides which make it easier to scoop up food. It is very stable because of the large suction cup underneath.

The snap-on lids for this plastic tumbler have punchouts for a straw or for sipping.

This feeding tray has suction cups on four corners so that it attaches firmly to a nonporous surface. The deep wells hold food or dishes.

To make it easier for a child to feed himself, this unbreakable, plastic plate has a special inner lip that keeps food from sliding off.

Toilet Training

Many children with disabilities are able to take care of their own toilet needs. The ability to do so often dictates whether or not a child must go to a special school.

As with any child, toilet training should be started gradually without creating too much anxiety in parent or child. The right time to begin depends on the individual child and the handicapping condition. Most children start to be aware of their body functions from about eighteen months, so this is usually a logical time to make the child aware of the connection between bowel movement and potty seat. If your child becomes balky and seems to feel overmanaged, you can stop the training for a time and start again when he seems more amenable. It is best to try to ignore failures—and to reward successes.

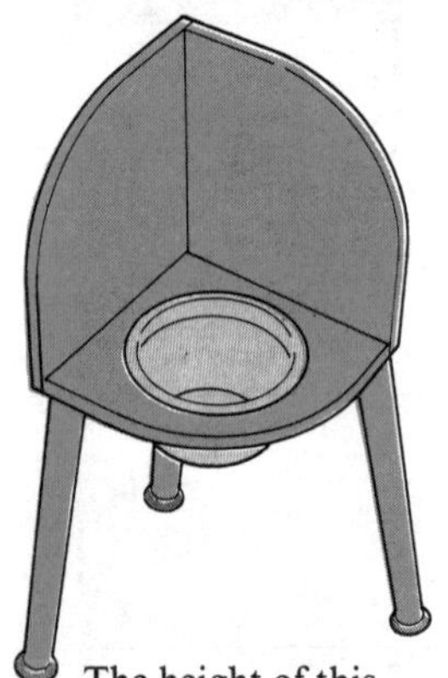

The height of this potty chair enables the child to sit with his feet flat on the floor. The triangle shape of the chair's back is designed to keep the shoulders and arms forward.

The potty chair below right has a solid base and gives good support at the back and sides. The seat and lid can be removed, below, and fitted to any adult toilet seat.

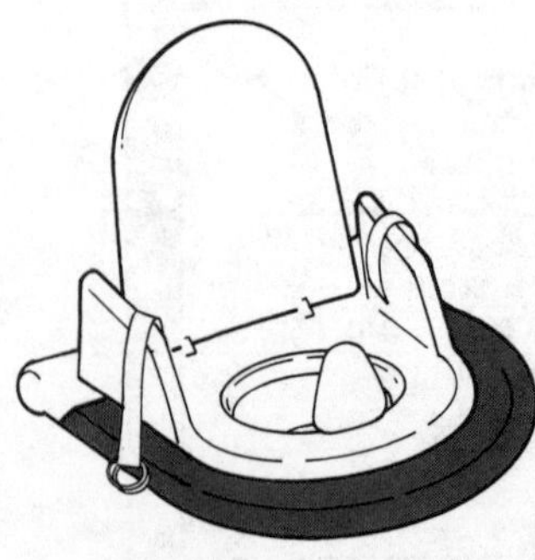

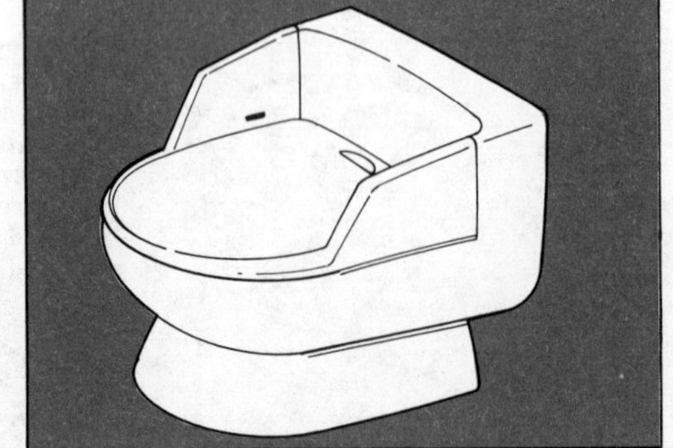

Most children begin toilet training on a potty seat and progress to an adult toilet with a training seat fitted onto the toilet seat. A disabled child may feel more secure if his feet are firmly supported while he is using the toilet. Either potty or training seat can be taken on trips away from home if this makes the child more confident. A nontip potty seat with a splashguard for boys is available, as is a potty chair with high sides and a restraining front bar to give support to the child who needs it.

Some children who use wheelchairs find it easiest to transfer and to manage by themselves if they straddle the toilet seat back to front. To facilitate transfer from wheelchair to toilet, the height of the toilet seat may need to be raised. The easiest and least expensive way to do this is to use a removable seat which fits onto the existing one. Padded toilet seats are available to help prevent pressure sores. Grab bars next to the toilet give support and are also an important safety measure. A step in front of the toilet is also useful.

For a child who lacks bladder or bowel control, a program to suit his condition may be devised by the doctor or therapist. To be successful, such programs require the parents' patience, understanding and cooperation.

Bathing and Grooming

The need for personal cleanliness and good grooming must be impressed upon all children from the time they are very young. The better groomed a child is, the better he will feel about himself and the more outgoing he will tend to be. This is especially true if a child has a visible disability which immediately sets him apart from his peers and can make him self-conscious about his appearance.

Cleanliness is the basis of good grooming. All very young children must be bathed, and most need adult supervision until they are about ten. A child who is severely disabled will, of course, always require help. Depending on the extent of the child's disabilities, you will want to encourage him to take over as much of his own bathing as possible as soon as he is able to.

Although it is easiest to bathe a baby or young child in a sink or baby bathtub, if the child is too large, or if only an adult-sized tub is available, there are several aids which will make the child feel secure and enable you to wash him thoroughly. A bath hammock can be made which supports the child who is not able to sit properly and leaves your hands free to get to work with a sponge or face cloth. An inflatable chair made from strong waterproof canvas is available which gives support in the water when weighted down by the child. A simpler device for a young child is a plastic basket, foam-lined at the bottom,

Sometimes, in order to develop self-help skills, a child who is disabled requires a specially designed aid, such as the simple strap above.

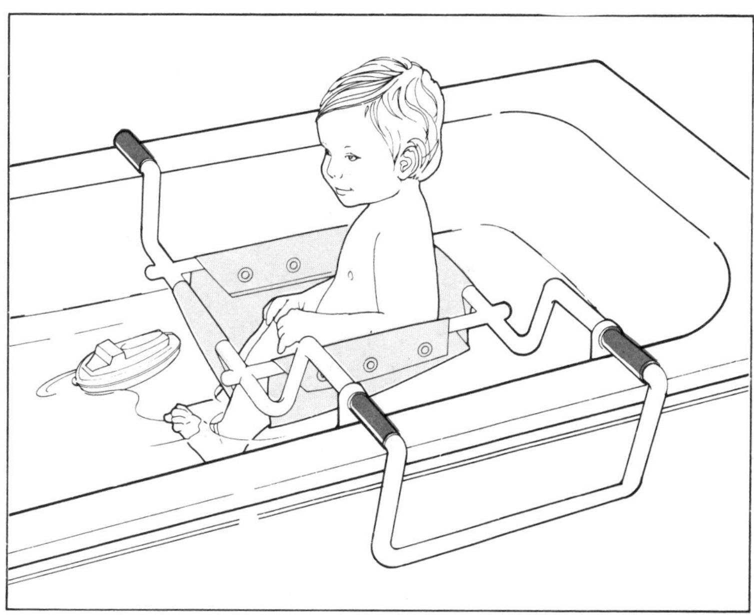

with part of the side cut out for the legs. All these aids serve the same purpose.

To make a physically handicapped child's bathtime happier and encourage independence, various devices may be helpful. A bath seat gives a child a sense of security and makes it easier to get into and out of the bath, as does a sturdy chair placed next to the tub. A child can wash himself with only one hand using a sponge or bath mitt which has a pocket for the soap. A horseshoe-shaped inflatable bath pillow can be used to support the neck and keep the child's head above the water. A hand shower, which attaches to the faucet, makes shampooing as well as washing easier. A long-handled brush extends reach and makes it simpler to wash back, legs and feet. A toweling bathrobe or poncho keeps the child warm and does the drying at the same time.

Nonslip bathmats next to the tub and nonslip strips in the tub are essential for safety, as are strategically placed grab bars. A therapist's advice should be sought before grab bars are installed.

A simple routine for grooming should be established when all children are very young so that it becomes second nature. It is best if the child can learn to brush his teeth, wash his hands and face and comb his hair by himself, even if he must use some aids; but of course the extent of his independence depends on his disability. With guidance, and constant reminders from parents, most children are gradually able to take over such tasks.

If a child who is disabled finds some aspect of grooming particularly difficult, a bit of thought and ingenuity can often overcome the problems. When reach is limited, a long piece of aluminum tubing can, for example, be curved and fixed onto a rattail comb or round-bristled brush. A nailbrush can be attached to the side of the washbasin with suction cups so that the child need only rub his nails against it. If grasp is limited, an electric toothbrush, a Tippee toothbrush, which stays upright and rings a bell when correctly positioned in the mouth for brushing, or a toothbrush which has been firmly screwed onto a long stick, may be easy to manage.

A child will be encouraged to keep himself neat and clean if toilet articles are kept together on an open shelf within easy reach. It is also important that a child have a mirror placed at a convenient height so that he can see into it when he combs his hair. Seeing his own face looking clean, or being able to admire a new haircut, are the biggest boosts of all to good grooming.

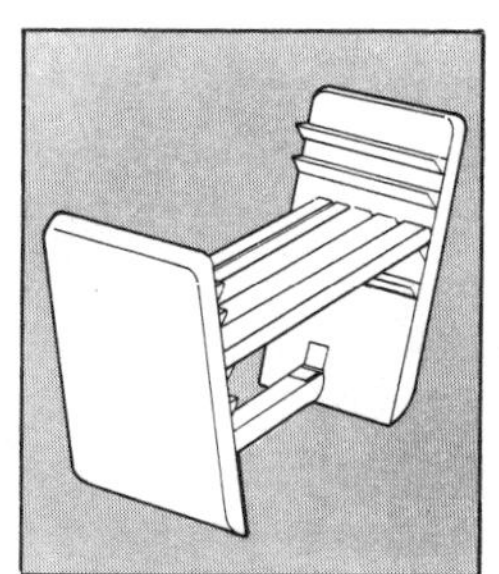

These bath seats were designed for the child who has reasonably good sitting balance but who cannot bend his hips sufficiently to sit with his legs in front of him. The seat above can be easily made. The Safa Bath Seat, top, is available through the Spastics Society of Great Britain.

The long handle on this tube squeezer can be slid between the fingers to be turned.

Clothing and Dressing

Everyone feels happier and more self-confident when he or she is attractively and comfortably dressed. It is particularly important to a disabled child who is often concerned about how he looks to other people. Little children enjoy the admiring looks they get when they wear new clothes; older children want to wear the same kind of clothes as the other kids in school.

From a very young age, all children like some say in what they wear. A three-year-old may suddenly prefer the blue sweater to the red—and refuse to wear one shirt altogether. He is not just being difficult; he is asserting a healthy independence. As he gets older he will show more and more clothes preferences. If it is difficult for him to go shopping with you he might be able to participate in the selection of his clothes from store catalogs.

It is important that even a young child learn to dress himself to the extent he is able, both for his own independence—and for your convenience. The timing will depend on the individual child, and will of course be affected by his disability. Most children learn to undress before they can dress; in fact, undressing—at appropriate and inappropriate times—can become quite a game.

A good way to teach a child to dress himself is to start with outer clothing and work inward, so that the child first learns to take off his own coat or sweater and works back to underwear, shoes and socks as he becomes able to do so. Don't be too quick to rush to the child's aid as you see him struggling with a sleeve or a sock, even if it does mean that getting him dressed to go out takes longer than if you dressed him yourself. On the other hand, don't expect a child to do more than he is capable of. He could become so frustrated that he loses the will to try.

The child's age, everyday needs and the extent of the disability are all considerations when buying clothes. If your child is not able to go shopping with you, take careful measurements. A good, easy fit is particularly important for the child who uses crutches or a wheelchair. Buying clothes for any child is a hit-or-miss proposition, however, so be prepared to make exchanges.

Look for garments which give with movement, open down the front and have wide or expandable necklines that go easily over the head. Full sleeves are simpler to put on. All-in-one jumpsuits with crotch fastenings are warm and comfortable for the very young child who has limited mobility and is on the floor much of the time. To cut down on wear, reinforce clothes at pressure points—padded knees for the child who crawls a lot; an extra layer of material below the armholes for the child who uses crutches. A child who uses a wheelchair will find a short coat less bulky and easier to put on than a long one, and capes and ponchos are practical for girls. Wherever possible, try to find, or put in yourself, elasticized waistbands; these are comfortable and eliminate the need for fastenings in skirts and slacks. Above all, choose fabrics which don't wrinkle and are easy to care for.

Openings and fasteners may present problems when the child begins to dress himself. Front openings are easiest to manage and almost every kind of closure can be replaced with Velcro. Long tabs sewn on either side of a waistband can make it possible for a child to pull on pants and jeans by himself. Buttons should always have a shank and an old-fashioned button hook can be a valuable aid. Zippers sewn along the inner seams of trousers can also make dressing easier. For pulling up zippers, a stick with a cup hook attached to the end can be made or purchased. Many of the tips on clothing and dressing for adults (pages 143 to 149) are also applicable to children.

A triangle chair, right, with two posts attached to the base to keep the legs apart, was designed for children who tend to straighten their hips and fall backward when lifting their arms to use their hands. The chair and variations of it should be used, however, only on the advice of a doctor or therapist.

The Child at Home

For the first years of every child's life home is his universe. When the family includes a child who is physically disabled, it may be necessary to make certain adaptations to enable him to live as efficiently as possible despite the limitations imposed by his disabilities. Many of the aids and modifications suitable for an adult who is physically disabled will be of equal value to a disabled child. (See the section You and Your Home.) The more secure and independent a child becomes in his own home, the better prepared he will be for the widening world of school and friends as he grows older.

Furniture may have to be moved to make mobility easier and safer. Leaving the center of the room uncluttered, with lots of space between pieces of furniture, allows a child to move around more freely. It makes sense to put away small objects that can be easily broken and delicate pieces of furniture which cannot be used for support. A child who is learning to walk, or who walks or "cruises" with difficulty, needs sturdy furniture to lean on. A blind child is most secure when furniture arrangements become familiar and are not changed. For a child who has impaired vision, good lighting is essential; it is also necessary for a child with hearing loss who depends on lipreading for comprehension.

Wheelchairs and crutches are used most easily and safely on smooth flooring; if there is carpeting, it should not have deep pile. Loose rugs can be a hazard, as can trailing electric cords. Sturdy grab bars in the bathroom and on all stairways will not only aid the child but will give an adult additional balance if the child has to be carried.

A special chair, and sometimes a table, which suit a child's needs and can be easily moved from room to room as required, can be very helpful for some children. For a very young child who needs support when sitting, propping devices allow him to join in family activities and to see what is going on around him. An automobile tire or a sturdy box with a cushion behind the child's back can be used. A corner chair permits the young child to sit, supported, and to play on the floor with other

The arms of this birchwood chair can be adjusted vertically to suit a child from the age of one to ten years. Some chairs of this kind also have seats which can be adjusted.

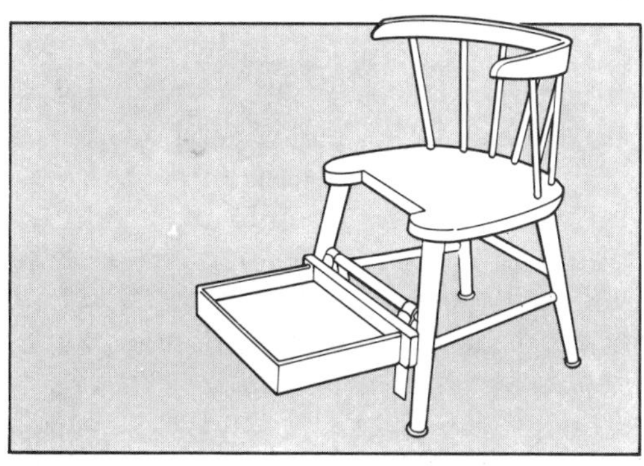

Adding a footrest and cutting into the seat of this captain's chair provide support and security.

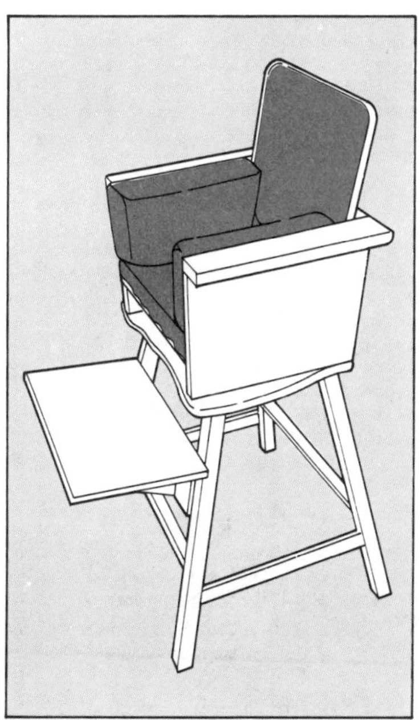

A commercially available high chair, above, can if necessary be modified to make the support for the feet wider and deeper, to provide much wider armrests and to elevate the seat itself.

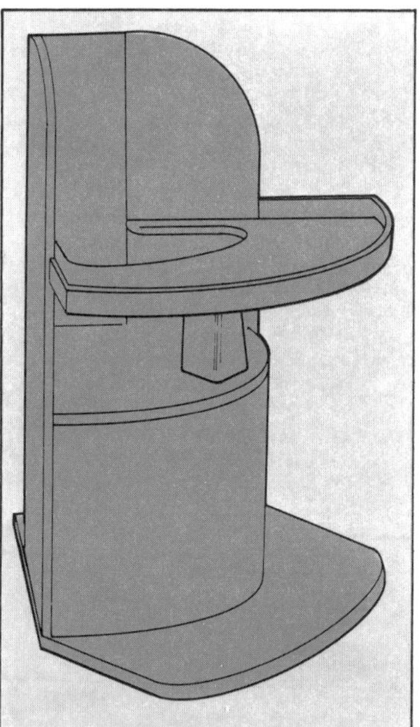

The sturdy, homemade corner seat above has a large tray for feeding and playing which does not upset the balance of the chair. A similar corner seat can be made level with the floor.

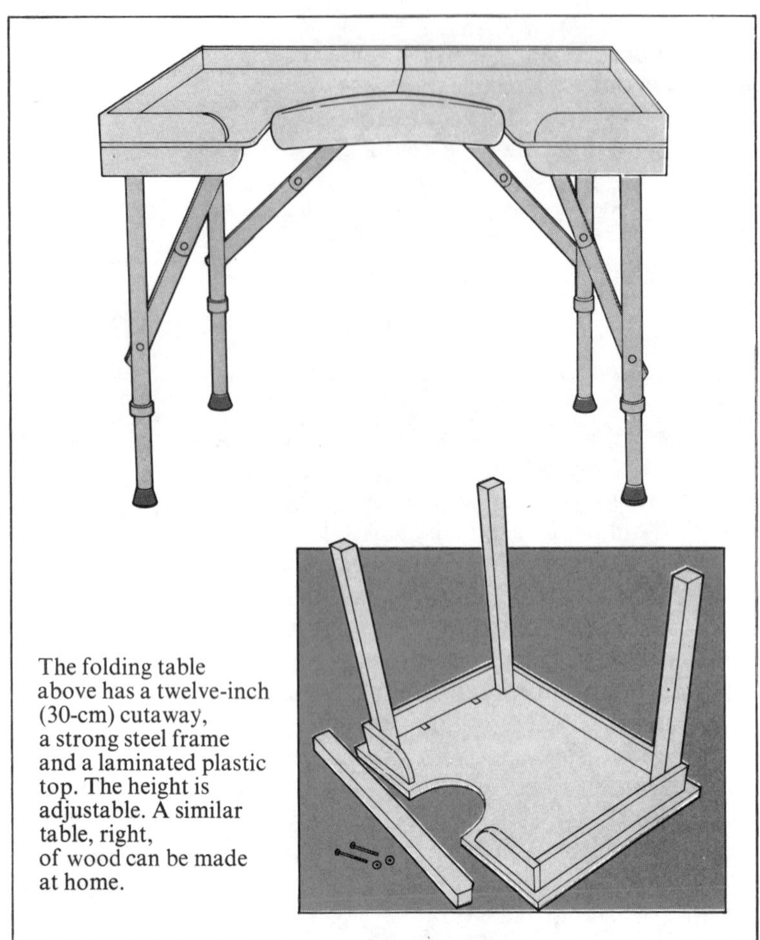

The folding table above has a twelve-inch (30-cm) cutaway, a strong steel frame and a laminated plastic top. The height is adjustable. A similar table, right, of wood can be made at home.

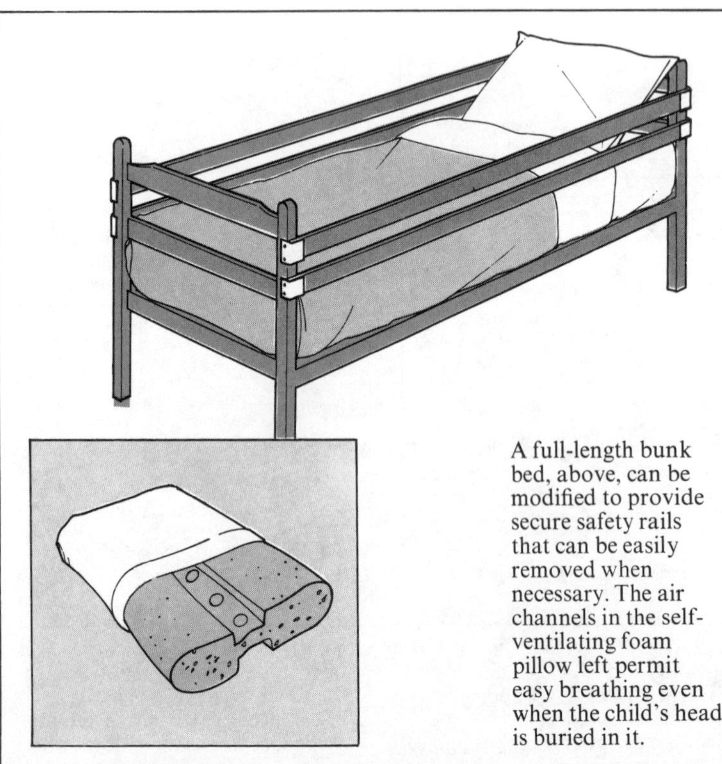

A full-length bunk bed, above, can be modified to provide secure safety rails that can be easily removed when necessary. The air channels in the self-ventilating foam pillow left permit easy breathing even when the child's head is buried in it.

children. A somewhat older child may need a sturdy chair that cannot tip and with sides for support if necessary. If the chair is painted, be sure lead-free paint is used. When the chair is not being used at a table, a fitted tray provides armrests and a surface on which to draw or to play with small toys.

Many children are most comfortable and feel most secure if their legs do not dangle when they are sitting. Nonskid footrests are available which attach to most chairs. For children between the ages of one and ten, a plastic-topped play table is available which adjusts to four different heights, as does the matching chair. Some children prefer a cut-out desk or play table at which they can sit or stand supported. Of course, blocks can be used to raise a table or chair to a suitable height for working, eating or playing.

Every child needs some privacy, and a room of his own is ideal. It makes the routine of bedtime and naptime easier to maintain and, as the child gets older, allows him space to pursue his own hobbies and to be by himself or with his friends away from the rest of the family.

For easier independent transfer a child who uses a wheelchair should have a bed which is about the same height as the chair seat. If the child has to be lifted in and out, a higher bed is also preferable. Safety rails can be fitted onto the sides of a bed to keep the child from falling. Foam rubber bumpers, the kind used in cribs, will ensure that a child who has poor muscular control will not bruise himself against the sides. A self-ventilating pillow allows a child to breathe freely even if his head appears to be buried in it. For the child who must spend a good deal of time in bed, a sheepskin or a ripple pad, which consists of rows of air cells, will help prevent pressure sores. An intercom system is valuable; it permits parents to hear the child at night and when he is alone in his room. The more expensive systems permit two-way communication.

Especially in his own room an older child needs light switches that he can reach and turn on and off by himself. A night light which plugs into an electric outlet makes many children feel more secure. Open shelves for toys and books, as well as for clothes are most accessible. Large clothes hooks within easy reach help to keep the room neat.

Stimulation and Play

Because the everyday experiences of most handicapped children are to some degree limited by their disabilities, parents have yet another responsibility—that of exposing the child to experiences which stimulate the imagination and increase knowledge. Many disabled children are in the house a good deal of the time and often have few friends. Their lives may be quite rigidly divided between home and school with little opportunity for broadening activities. Whatever your child's disability, he will respond to, and his life will be enriched by, the most stimulating environment you are able to provide.

Throughout childhood, and especially while a child is still very young, close and caring family relationships are vitally important to healthy emotional development. Studies of children in institutions have shown how seriously deprived a child becomes if he is denied the ordinary give-and-take of one-to-one relationships. What every child needs most is to be talked to, played with, laughed with, read to—and to be generally included as a member of the family. This kind of continuing interaction provides a child's most important and constant stimulation.

From babyhood onward, a child needs to be made aware of different textures, to have opportunities to touch sand and grass, velvet, feathers, stones and smooth plastic. Even children who lack manual dexterity can learn to enjoy rolling clay, crayonning and finger painting. (Thick crayons may be easier to grasp; aprons

and a waterproof sheet under the table help to prevent too much mess.) Most children love sand and water play. With plastic containers and practical floor covering, this can be indoor play as well as a garden activity.

Different sounds are important, too. Sound is one of the main ways in which a child who is blind learns about the world. Most babies and young children respond to music. Familiar tunes encourage even a very young child to clap and sing to himself. If the rhythm is strong enough a child who has some hearing loss may be able to learn to move in time to music. For a child who is particularly musical, a drum or cymbals or a tambourine will provide splendid entertainment. Homemade instruments —bells to shake or a comb covered in tissue paper—are fine for improvisation. Daily shopping trips and, perhaps, drives in the country or to the seaside will enable a child to recognize the sounds of different kinds of traffic, waves breaking on the shore and cows and horses in the fields. Imitating sounds is a good way for young children to pass the time on long car journeys.

Make believe is a key factor in the development of a child's imagination. Given a little fantasy, the most familiar toys and pieces of furniture are transformed into ships and dragons and haunted houses. Old clothes are worth saving for dressing up. Odd gloves can be used to make finger puppets and sheets strung up on wires make perfect curtains for pretend play staging.

All children love being read to and from a very young age start to show a preference for one story over another. The habit of looking at books and reading is more likely to be acquired early by a child who has been encouraged to point to words and pictures as he is being read to. For a child who is disabled, books can provide a marvelous window on the world and give him vicarious experiences which are difficult—or impossible—for him to have otherwise. Most libraries have an area set aside for children and most young children enjoy making their own selections.

Television, watched with discretion, can provide entertainment, information and relaxation after a tiring day at school or while recovering from an illness. But the amount of television young children watch, and the content of the programs, must be supervised. Too much time in front of the television set is not good for any child. For all its value, it is essentially passive entertainment, and children need to be encouraged to do those things in which they are actively involved.

It has only recently been understood how important play is for children, particularly during the early, formative years. It is through play—by touching, seeing, tasting and smelling—that a child explores his environment and learns. A child has fun as he splashes in the bathtub or rides his tricycle, but he is is also observing the results of his own movements and is steadily improving his coordination. Pulling and pushing trucks and cars exercises his muscles and teaches him how familiar objects really work. By playing house with another child he is learning how to get along with someone else and putting into practice some of the domestic tasks he watches his mother and father performing.

The child who is physically disabled has all the same needs for play as any other child, but because of his disability he may get fewer opportunities to meet these needs. Research has shown that physically handicapped children tend to have fewer outings, trips and toys than children who are not disabled. And therapists have found that parents often need to be encouraged to play with their disabled child in ways that come quite naturally with a child who does not have a disabling condition. Concerned and anxious parents may feel, understandably, that their child has less ability to cope with toys and games and play situations than is actually the case. In fact, because of his disability, a child may need earlier and stronger stimuli than his able-bodied brother or sister needed when they were his age.

A baby who cannot learn to crawl toward the end of his first year and who must spend a lot of time immobile, needs to be presented with lots of changes of scenery. He should be moved to different

rooms and given different toys to grasp and look at, things he could get for himself if he was able to move easily alone. As he grows up he may need extra help and encouragement in his play in order to make the fullest use of his abilities.

The sheer enjoyment of play can be the biggest incentive to try just a little bit harder. It gives another, pleasurable dimension to the life of a child whose horizons are limited by his braces or who has known a good deal of isolation and discomfort. The benefits of play are inestimable. Even in small ways like learning to build a house out of blocks or, despite his wheelchair, joining in a ball game with the neighborhood children, success in play helps to bolster self-confidence and independence.

Toys

Selecting the right toy for any child is always a challenge to parents, and a source of great satisfaction when one is chosen which seems exactly suited to a child's interests and abilities. Children always seem to go for the old standbys —rattles and furry animals, wooden blocks, dolls and doll houses, Lego, pull and push toys and sturdy trucks and cars. Such toys are especially good because they can be played with imaginatively for several years as a child grows and develops and are always the best loved and longest lasting toys on any child's toy shelves.

Balls, another all-time favorite, can be used in some way by most children, whatever their disability. They can be bowled as well as thrown; an attached string makes a ball easier to retrieve. Bean bags make splendid balls, landing—flop!—right where they are thrown and not further away.

All the toys a child plays with must be safe. Button eyes on toy animals should be securely attached so they cannot come off. There should be no sharp edges and all paintwork must be nontoxic. If a child uses larger toys for support or to move himself around, it is essential that these are sturdy and well made. You should be guided in your choice of toys by your doctor or therapist. Some toys can help to strengthen limbs or encourage balance as well as improve coordination, so it makes sense to harness fun to therapy.

Most disabled children can use outdoor equipment—although some of it

Available from self-help equipment firms, this large, polished wood tic-tac toe board has large circles and crosses which fit onto pegs.

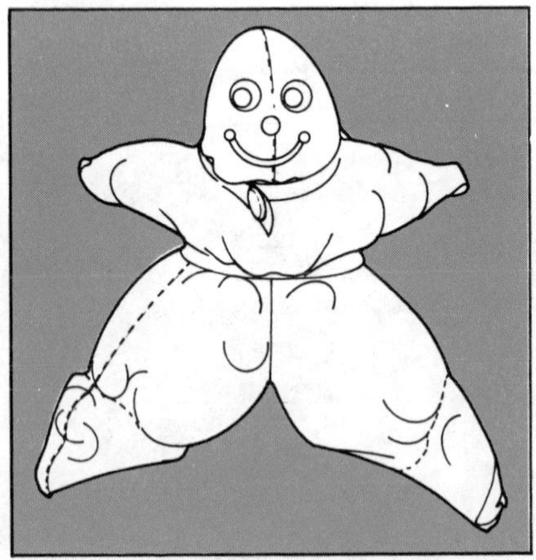

Tossing a bean bag provides good fun for young children. This star bean bag is simple to make. Its points make it particularly easy to grasp.

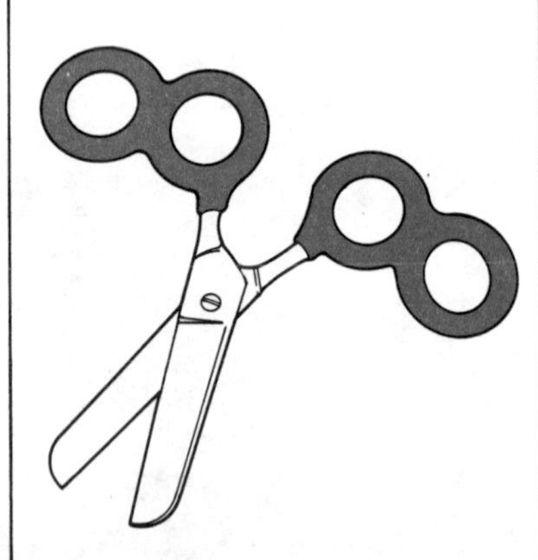

With training scissors, which are available for right or left hand, an adult can place a hand over the child's to reinforce the pattern of motion.

Bright-colored, giant foam blocks, made in a variety of shapes, are lightweight, safe and delight young children.

A blackboard which is hinged to the wall at the top and has one extension bar on each side which can be attached to the wall, can thus be sufficiently angled to provide adequate clearance for a child in a wheelchair.

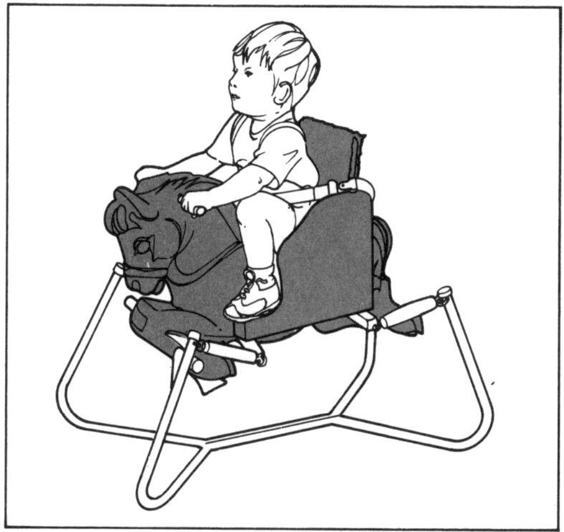

Modifications can often be made to a rocking horse to accommodate a child's special needs. A sturdy wooden seat, which incorporates a footrest and a padded backrest, can be built to fit snugly around the horse's body. A seat belt can be added to hold the child securely.

Based on the design used by the Chailey Heritage Craft School and Hospital in England, the Chailey Trolley is a sturdy play trolley and mobility aid for children under the age of five. It has two large wheels and three casters, two at the rear and one at the front, so it is easy to maneuver and can be propelled by children from about nine months old. This simple device makes it possible for many children to join in games and play with toys at floor level.

must be adapted to a child's special needs. A chair swing with built-up sides and a bar in front to prevent falling can be used by a child who needs support. A chair placed in a sandbox or wading pool allows a child to sit, supported, while playing. A doll's carriage or a wheelbarrow can be weighted, giving added stability to help the child who walks with difficulty. Tricycles and other large toys which can be sat on and maneuvered may need such modification as built-up sides, a back support or padding.

Around the house, too, there are many substitute toys for days when the familiar ones seem boring. Pots and pans and wooden spoons from the kitchen always provide good fun. A further look into kitchen cabinets may produce an egg beater, measuring cups and empty cans with lids. Desk drawers contain paper clips, tape, half-used notebooks and a selection of pens, pencils and erasers. The blessing of such items is that they can be put to use by children of widely differing ages and abilities.

You may find, as your child gets older, that although he would like to play with the same toys as other children of his age, because of his disability he cannot manage them. Jigsaw puzzles, a perennial favorite with most children, are a good example. A child who has very limited grasp may not be able to do the more difficult puzzles which have lots of small pieces and require considerable manual dexterity; yet the puzzles with large pieces which he can manipulate are probably too babyish. A good solution is to make puzzles, with pictures geared to his interests, with large pieces which he can handle. If he enjoys playing with electric trains but cannot easily operate the switches, hooks or pieces of wood attached to them may make them easier for him to grasp. A little ingenuity can enable your child's play to keep up with the level of his mental development.

Whatever a child's disability, the trick is to find those toys which suit his interests and abilities and give him some challenge, but are not so difficult for him that he starts to feel a sense of failure if he cannot use them very well. He should be shown how a new toy works, or have some of the endless possibilities of a toy explained, and then be left to get on with it. A bit more assistance may be needed, but it is much more important to admire his progress. It is always a temptation to give too much help to a child who has special difficulties, but it is really best if he learns to reach out and grasp a toy on his own, or starts to build, to the best of his ability, with the wooden blocks he was given for his birthday.

Friends

Although a child needs to develop his own interests and inner resources so that he can play quite happily alone, every child needs friends. The most attentive parent cannot compensate for the companionship of other children or for the give and take of playing with others of the same age.

No child really plays with another child before the age of three or four. It's unrealistic to expect a child to share toys before that; sharing comes naturally when he is old enough to understand the pleasures of cooperation. Before a child reaches this stage, however, he will certainly benefit from parallel play—sitting on the floor near another two-year-old as they grab toys separately. This might not seem at all constructive, but it is actually good preparation for the genuine play that comes later.

Is it best for disabled children to seek friends exclusively among other handicapped children? Although parents always have this question very much in mind, there is no hard and fast rule as to whether it's better to encourage a child to play with other disabled children or to have friends who are not handicapped. The answer depends very much on the child's disability, his personality and the opportunities he has for meeting other children.

Some children are naturally outgoing and make friends easily. Others tend to be "loners" no matter how much encouragement they get. Ideally, when a child is mature enough he will associate quite happily with other children who are disabled as well as with those who are not. How well he gets along with a friend will be the deciding factor, not whether the friend is also disabled. It may take a long time before a child gains this kind of confidence and in the case of a severely disabled child there may be little possibility of choice.

When children are very young, it is probably easiest for them, in terms of achievement and self-confidence, if they play mostly with children who are also disabled. When a child is still coming to terms with his disability it can be depressing to play constantly among others who can do so much more than he can, and to be left behind when they go skating or bike riding. But studies have shown that when other children have joined groups which are not solely for the handicapped, they gradually learn to participate, although it may take them a long time to feel relaxed in the situation.

Able-bodied children have a natural curiousity about a disabled child's aids, appliances and inability to do some of the things that they take for granted. Most parents find it best to anticipate curious questions before embarrassing situations arise. When able-bodied children meet a disabled child for the first time, it helps to explain that he cannot hear very well and therefore he must wear a hearing aid or that he uses crutches because his legs are not strong enough to support him. When parents are reasonably matter-of-fact about their child's disability and the limitations it imposes, the more naturally he, and other children, are likely to accept it. As a child gets older, parents should discuss how the child himself can best explain his disability to others.

It may take a lot of courage for a parent to permit a disabled child to join in appropriate games with other children in the neighborhood, but it is important for a child to learn to be part of a group and to feel that his parents treat him like other children his age. It will do much for a child's self-confidence if he can take part in some activities with other children and feel that he is part of the gang.

Education

All parents want their children to have an education which will enable them to make the most of their abilities, help to fulfil them as people and teach them to get along in the world. As a disabled child approaches school age, however, there are many questions that parents ask which would not occur to them if the child were able-bodied.

Most parents will wonder, above all, whether a child must be educated in a special school which caters exclusively to the needs of the disabled or whether he can be educated in a regular school, perhaps with additional supportive therapy and some specialized teaching. Depending on the child's disability, parents may also have questions concerning access in a neighborhood school. They will wonder whether the child will be able to manage the stairs and, if he needs help in the bathroom, whether there will be someone to assist him. All parents hope that their children will make a good social adjustment to school life and make friends among their classmates.

The way the education of a handicapped child is planned depends both on the extent of the child's disability and the educational facilities available in the local school district. Although getting the right kind of schooling for each disabled child may seem a formidable task, parents now have the law firmly on their side in the United States as well as in the United Kingdom. Parents have the right to demand the same standard of education for a disabled child as for one who is able-bodied. Never before have so many educational opportunities been available to disabled children—from preschool through college.

It is only recently that the value of early education has been properly understood. Educators now believe that it is when children are very young that their learning capacity is greatest. Preschool takes advantage of this intellectually and, equally important, helps to develop social skills. Children who are disabled often lack the daily opportunities to play with other children that are taken for granted by able-bodied children. Experience of some kind of nursery school or play group can be especially valuable for a disabled child, giving him the chance to try out new and different toys, to learn songs and listen to stories. This may be his only opportunity to form relationships with other children and it will accustom him to a classroom setting. It is believed that preschool classes can directly affect a child's performance later when he starts regular school. It is essential that a child who is congenitally deaf begins special schooling very early—between the ages of three and four.

The local branch of the appropriate national organization will certainly have a list of preschool classes which might be suitable for your child. These may include therapy groups in hospitals or clinics as well as special classes in the neighborhood.

In the United States, 10 percent of the participants in Head Start must be disabled children. Head Start is run by the Office of Child Development, Office for Human Development Services of the Department of Health, Education and Welfare in Washington D.C. They have also funded fourteen experimental projects to develop a variety of models for serving disabled children in an integrated preschool setting.

Many regular nursery schools will include one or two handicapped children in each class, providing the disability is not too severe. If you find there are no local facilities suitable for your child, and if you have enough space indoors and a garden, you may consider joining with three or four other parents to start your own preschool group two or three mornings a week.

Today there is a far greater sensitivity among the general public to the problems of people with disabilities. It is now accepted that most disabled people must be integrated into the community and to do this they must be enabled to achieve the greatest possible degree of independence. Due in part to this growing awareness, the trend has emerged during the past decade to educate children with disabilities, wherever possible, in regular schools. This educational process is described as mainstreaming. While many parents welcome the fullest possible educational integration for their children, others feel that their children need the protection of special schooling.

Although the Children's Act of 1944 guaranteed that every child in the United Kingdom should receive an appropriate education, the concept of mainstreaming dates from 1954 when a circular from the Ministry of Education stated that "No handicapped child should be sent to a special school who can be satisfactorily educated in an ordinary school."

In the United States the Education for All Handicapped Children Act was passed in 1975. This act commits the federal government to providing free public education for all handicapped children and gradually increases the fiscal role of the federal government in the education of the disabled. At the time the act was passed, a member of the Senate rightly commented that "this promises handicapped children the educational opportunity that has long been considered the right of every other American child." The law, which is administered by the Department of Health, Education and Welfare's Bureau of Education for the Handicapped required that by 1978 all disabled children from the age of three to eighteen (to be raised to twenty-one by 1982) have available to them "a free, appropriate public education and related services designed to meet unique needs."

Many educators believe that after the vital establishment of the basic right of a handicapped child to receive the same standard of public education as any other child, the law's other very valuable contribution is its insistence on treating the disabled child as an individual. It states specifically, for example, that labeling of children in terms of specific disabilities should be discouraged because of the stigma it imposes. The act requires an educational program tailored to the disabled child's unique needs—these needs to be evaluated by a team of professionals—which may include supervised transportation, supportive classes in regular public school, a special school or even a program of home education.

As with all innovative ideas, the concept of educating physically disabled children in the same schools as children who are able-bodied is controversial. It is of course dependent on each child's disability and the educational facilities available within the local school system, including class size, proximity to home, physical layout of the school and the availability of specially trained teachers and support services.

Mainstreaming does not signal the end of all special schools, nor should it. There are many severely disabling conditions which preclude a child's being educated satisfactorily in any school which is not geared to meet his special needs. Yet study after study has shown that most disabled children who are not mentally impaired do better academically when educated in regular schools than when they are isolated in special schools.

Children with certain handicapping conditions clearly can adapt more easily to mainstreaming than others. Many disabled children are bright and motivated and have the ability to hold their own in a classroom with able-bodied children. Although it is difficult to make definitive judgments about the adjustment and progress of disabled children who are mainstreamed, tentative findings suggest that teasing from schoolmates is not generally a problem and that overall social relationships are adequate and are related to the child's personality rather than to his disability.

Strong support services are the key to successful mainstreaming. Many schools in which disabled children are enrolled have "resource rooms" where a child can receive coaching from a special education teacher, make up notes from classes he may have missed or have access to braille textbooks.

Some teachers in regular schools feel, however, that they are now being expected to carry out professional tasks for which they have not been trained. Many disabled children do require extra time and attention from the teacher if they are to keep up with the rest of the class. For a teacher already stretched to the limit by a large class of students of mixed abilities, this can prove overwhelming, however much that teacher may agree with the concept of educating disabled children in the same schools as able-bodied children. A solution may be to decrease the size of classes in which disabled children are included.

Whether it is decided that your child

should attend the local school or that his needs will be better served in a special school, it will be helpful to the child, the teacher and to you if you can establish an open relationship with his teacher before school begins. The teacher will be better prepared to deal with the situation if he or she has a knowledge of the child's condition and understands what he can and cannot be expected to do for himself. You know your child best and your observations are important, so be as honest with the teacher as you can.

A teacher will want to know of a child's likes and dislikes and special interests which can be encouraged. It's also wise to tell the teacher whether or not you think he will get along well with the other children or needs time to make friends. Of course, both the school authorities and his teacher must be informed of any specific medical difficulty and given exact instructions if any medication is to be administered.

School systems are legally responsible for special transportation for children who are unable to use the regular school bus. Introduce your child to the driver who will be taking him to school every day and explain your child's handicap.

These are some additional practical considerations to keep in mind before entering a child in a new school. If he has braces or uses a wheelchair be sure doorways are wide enough and the approach to the building is level. Be sure that there is an elevator as an alternative to stairs between floors. If the child can use stairs, but needs support, check that the handrails are stable and of the correct height.

Be sure, too, that there are bathroom facilities within easy reach of the child's classroom—not two floors away or in the next building. If a child uses a wheelchair he should be able to enter the lavatory independently and transfer himself onto the toilet, using grab bars if necessary. Washbasins should be of the type that is fixed to the wall with room for wheelchair clearance underneath. Faucets, soap and hand towel should be within easy reach.

If a child must be lifted, it will benefit both teacher and child if the parents can pass on the techniques which they have found work best. Aids such as a canvas bag attached to a wheelchair and a pick-up stick will enable the child to keep track of his schoolbooks and other possessions.

It is vital that fire drills are worked out and practiced. In a regular school the teacher should be particularly careful that the disabled children in the class know and understand fire drill instructions and that the other children are also aware of any special instructions in the event that they may be required to give assistance.

Working out as many practical details as possible before a child starts in a new school will help him to adapt more comfortably to his new surroundings—and will give you, and your child, greater confidence in his ability to cope away from home.

There are broad implications in the concept of educating the disabled with the able-bodied. Education is a two-way street. At the same time as a child with braces or impaired hearing is educated, so, in a different way, are his peers. In the United States as thousands of disabled children who were formerly relegated to special schools are now entering regular classrooms, a movement has begun to try to prepare the students to cope with these new classmates.

In Rhode Island concerned teachers and parents of disabled children have developed a program to aquaint able-bodied children with the effects of various handicapping conditions. Able-bodied students are required to take a preparatory course so that wheelchairs, braces and hearing aids become less frightening. Disabled guest speakers are also asked to the schools and children are invited to question them frankly about their handicaps. This program has created considerable interest throughout the United States and, as mainstreaming becomes more common, it seems likely that such courses will at some stage be required in all schools in which the disabled and the able-bodied are educated together.

Perhaps the most significant aspect of

mainstreaming is the implications it has for better understanding in the future between the disabled and the able-bodied. It has been shown with all minority groups—and the disabled are certainly a minority group—that contact with the community in general during the formative years tends to remove the fear and distrust which leads to later segregation. It seems reasonable to assume that mainstreaming will lead to more open attitudes and more opportunities for the disabled in every aspect of life—jobs, friendships and every kind of social activity.

Recreation

Leisure is as important an aspect of a young person's life as education. A child should be exposed to as many potential pastimes as possible in order to find those which are of greatest interest. Some children are drawn to hobbies which they can pursue alone. Others enjoy the stimulation of competitive activities. It is all a question of individual temperament and ability, but the child should be aware of the many recreational options which are open to him.

The appreciation of art, in all its forms, should be part of every child's life, adding extra dimensions and making him aware of the creativity which surrounds him.

Whenever a child shows a desire to express himself artistically and in any medium, he should be encouraged. The fun and the creativity of trying is really more important than the finished product. It helps any child when his parents show a genuine interest in whatever it is he has made, whether it's a simple finger painting, a crayonned illustration of a favorite nursery rhyme, a clay pot or a wire sculpture.

There are many aids available which make it possible for people with various disabilities to do all kinds of creative work. These are detailed in the section on Leisure and Recreation (pages 182 to 227), which also describes many imaginative activities which are as suitable for children as they are for adults.

Music is a marvelous bonus in life and can be enjoyed by almost anyone. Even if a child has impaired hearing, he may learn, in time, to respond to familiar rhythms.

Music on the radio, on television, on records and tapes can enrich the daily life of any child and may lead to a lifelong interest as his appreciation deepens and develops. An involvement in music can also broaden a child's social life as he meets others who share his interest.

The range of music available to children is enormous. It begins with nursery tunes and then goes on from rock and pop music, to folk songs and semi-classical, to encompass the riches of instrumental and vocal classical music. Tapes and records can be borrowed from many libraries, making it possible to sample different kinds of music at no expense.

Today most schools encourage an interest in music through appreciation classes, concerts and, often, their own bands. If a child enjoys singing and has a good voice, the school choir, as well as local choral groups, may give him an opportunity to sing. Children who like to sing often find it an advantage to be able to read music.

Despite disability, many children are able to learn to play musical instruments. A child who is wheelchaired can support a guitar or a stringed instrument on his lap. Exercises on the piano can strengthen weak fingers and improve coordination. No matter what standard a child is able to achieve, he will benefit in increased confidence, and gain pleasure, from his accomplishment.

Just as there has been a trend toward educating children with disabilities in regular classes, so there has been a similar move for integration in recreational activities. Today it is possible for handicapped children to become involved in various recreational activities without being labeled "different."

Scouting is among the many clubs and activities available to youngsters with disabilities. In the United States and the United Kingdom the strongest efforts have been made to promote integrated scouting for disabled boys and girls. In both countries national scouting organizations have similar policies of fitting youngsters who are disabled into regular units whenever possible; only those who are severely disabled are placed in special groups. The labeling of children by their disability is also discouraged because it tends to make them feel separate from their peers.

In 1977 the Boy Scouts of America Scouting for the Handicapped Program included eight hundred scouting units of physically disabled scouts, involving a total of eleven thousand boys. In addition, there are disabled scouts in many of the nearly one hundred and fifty thousand regular units. The Girl Scouts of America have the same kind of program. In the United States, Camp Fire Girls also have a policy of including girls with disabilities in regular units, and many councils across the country have special programs for the handicapped. In the United Kingdom about 2 percent of the total enrollment in Boy Scouts and Girl Guides are disabled.

In the United States the Boy Scouts Camping and Engineering Services supplies technical advice to local scout councils on accessibility standards. The service also supplies councils with *Camp*

Facilities for the Handicapped, a booklet which gives practical information on accommodation for disabled boys on nature trails, in activity areas, swimming pools and rest rooms. In addition, Boy Scouts of America puts out books to help leaders develop or adapt programs for disabled scouts, as well as specialized books on scouting for youngsters who are physically disabled, visually handicapped and have impaired hearing.

In the United Kingdom, PHAB is a highly creative effort to promote integration among young people from the ages of sixteen to twenty-four. PHAB is an acronym of Physically Handicapped, Able-bodied and the keynote of the organization is the integration of the disabled with the able-bodied. PHAB was inspired by the belief that disabled young people should be encouraged to join in community activities and get together with able-bodied youngsters in the neighborhood. There are now almost one hundred and fifty PHAB clubs operating throughout the United Kingdom which have weekly meetings in various centers.

Each year throughout the summer PHAB sponsors holidays abroad and one-week residential courses. The physically handicapped and the able-bodied have the opportunity to live together and to participate together in a wide range of activities.

Sex Education

Sex education is important for all children. Information about reproduction and human sexuality should be imparted matter-of-factly and at levels appropriate to the child's age and understanding. This enables the child to grow up with an acceptance of sex as an integral, and pleasurable, part of life.

For children who are disabled, sex education is particularly important because they may have fewer opportunities to mix, unsupervised, with their peers outside the home or school and thus to join in the usual exchange of information about sex. Another factor which makes early sex instruction for the disabled crucial was found by Dr. Katharina Dalton, in her British study, to be that the sexual development of most disabled boys and girls is earlier than of those who are able-bodied.

It can be frightening, and possibly emotionally damaging, for a girl to begin to menstruate or for a boy to experience a nocturnal emission without an understanding of what is happening to her or his body. Misconceptions and a lack of knowledge in the early years can result in lifelong sexual problems.

Professionals working with people with disabilities have found that they are not, generally, as informed about sex nor as well prepared to cope with their sexuality as are their able-bodied peers. This is undoubtedly a legacy of unenlightenment, of centuries of refusal by the able-bodied to accept the sexuality of the disabled. To a lesser degree, this attitude persists.

Even some sympathetic and well-meaning parents do not speak to their disabled children about sex because of a misguided desire to protect them. Of course, if a parent must bathe a child and help him to dress, way beyond the age when this would be necessary if he were able-bodied, there is a natural tendency to continue to regard him as a child despite his age and development. Parents may almost hope that if it is ignored their child's sexuality will simply go away.

While most schools now include sex education as part of the curriculum, professionals, parents and educators still believe that responsibility for sex education is essentially in the home. It should begin when children are very young and ask "Where did I come from?" or "Why has he got a penis and I don't?" If these first simple questions are answered correctly and casually children will be encouraged to ask questions that are more pointed and pertinent to their own sexuality as they develop toward manhood and womanhood.

If your child seems to ignore all reference to sex, don't assume that he's not interested. He may feel that you do not want, or expect, him to ask questions. Giving him the opportunity to read books, listen to tapes and, in the case of a blind child, feel models, may encourage open discussion.

Many teenagers find it easier to discuss sex with an older brother or sister, an older friend, teacher or therapist, than with a parent. An older person who is also disabled and whom a child trusts could be the ideal confidant. Some schools encourage discussions with a teacher or counselor so that specific problems and anxieties can be talked about freely.

For all teenagers, stimulated by the disturbing new sensations in their bodies, sexual interest starts to involve the emotions. It is natural for a teenager to wonder whether he or she will be able to attract a girl friend or boy friend, to have fun on dates and to enjoy sexual experimentation. A teenager who is disabled will experience all these desires—but with more uncertainty. It is important that he understands that people with disabilities are able to have rewarding sex lives. To what extent this will be possible for a particular child depends much less on the disabling condition than on how he has been encouraged to regard his own sexuality.

All children tend to take their sexual attitudes from their parents. It is essential, from the disabled child's earliest years, that his parents understand and accept that he is a sexual being and that he will have the right to express his sexuality responsibly. It is this that will give him as an adult the freedom to take risks, to make mistakes, as well as to have positive relationships. Wise parents will encourage a disabled child to expect sexual fulfilment. This is the ultimate aim of sex education.

Puberty

As parents have always recognized, the transition from child to adult—the teenage years—is never smooth. Adolescence begins at the onset of puberty with its profound, and to the child often disturbing, signals of physiological changes.

The word puberty comes from the Latin *pubetas* meaning "age of manhood," and it describes the first phase of adolescence—roughly from eleven to fifteen—when sexual maturity becomes apparent. In the medical sense, puberty begins with the gradual enlargement of the ovaries of the female and the prostate gland and the seminal vesicles of the male. It is more convenient, however, to date puberty from the beginning of breast development and the menarche, the onset of menstruation, in girls, and the sprouting of pubic hair in boys. The timing is individual, however, and a recent study undertaken in Great Britain by Dr. Katharina Dalton has shown that physical maturity of boys and girls with a broad range of physical disabilities, including congenital deafness and blindness, occurs considerably earlier than of children who have no handicapping condition.

The physiological changes that occur at puberty are due, in part, to an increased output of hormones by the pituitary gland which is situated immediately below the brain. Pituitary hormone stimulates the activity of the gonads, or sex glands, which in turn increase the production of hormones and the growth of the mature sperm in males and the release of ova, or eggs, in females. These sex hormones, including testosterone in males and estrogen in females, combined with other hormones of the body, encourage the growth of bone and muscle and direct the rapid adolescent growth spurt. The accelerated increase in total body size that comes during adolescence, the age at which the growth spurt begins, its duration and its intensity, vary widely.

For boys the first sign of puberty is usually an acceleration of the growth of the testes and scrotum. A slight growth of pubic hair may appear at the same time, but generally it is a little later. Increase in height and penile growth begin about a year after the first testicular acceleration. Along with the growth of the penis there is an enlargement of the seminal vesicles, where the sperm is stored prior to ejaculation. Erections of the penis are harder and become more frequent. Erections are controlled by the body's hormones; extra blood rushes to the penis, fills up its spongy holes and makes it firm and enlarged. When the sperm have been ejaculated, the blood drains away and the penis becomes small and soft again.

During puberty a boy will start to have nocturnal emissions, or "wet dreams," to cope with the production of sperm. The first ejaculation of seminal fluid is likely to occur about one and a half years after the accelerated penis growth. Facial hair begins to appear about two years after the start of pubic hair growth. Hairs of mustache and beard appear first. Hair on the chest does not grow until late adolescence or early adulthood.

The breaking of the voice, caused by the enlargement of the larynx and the lengthening of the vocal chords, may begin early or late in adolescence; as in all aspects of physical development there is a wide individual variation. It may crack quite gradually, and almost imperceptibly to both the adolescent and his parents; it may happen suddenly.

All boys who are entering puberty need a factual understanding of what is happening to their bodies as well as emotional reassurance, preferably from their fathers. For every boy, and particularly for one who is disabled, these emerging signs of manhood reinforce his sense of self and his awareness that he is becoming a man. Self-conscious as he is, he should not be teased by the family when his voice starts to break or the beginning of a beard appear. Incidentally, since boys tend to compare notes, parents should point out at this time that the size of a penis is not related to sexual performance. Boys who have not been circumcised should also be told that unless they follow thorough, routine hygiene, smegma may gather under the foreskin which can become irritated and infected.

Boys can find puberty an extremely trying time. Aroused by the slightest provocation, and often none at all, a boy's body in adolescence can seem completely out of control. He will be comforted if he knows that he is not the first boy to be embarrassed by erections while at the swimming pool. He must also be prepared for wet dreams, and understand that they are harmless and natural although they may occur as frequently as two or three times a week. They are, in a sense, outward proof of his natural development.

In a girl the first sign of sexual maturity is usually when her breasts begin to enlarge, although the growth of pubic hair sometimes precedes this. The uterus and the vagina mature at the same time as the breasts. The first menstrual period, the menarche, occurs quite late in the sequence of puberty. While able-bodied girls are on average in their fourteenth year at menarche, girls with physical disabilities are likely to be at least a year younger—and perhaps as young as ten. (Girls with diabetes are an exception, usually developing later than average.) It is thought that early menarche occurs in girls whose physical disorders have affected the hypothalamus.

Although the onset of menstruation signifies that the womb has probably reached a mature stage of development, it does not necessarily follow that the full reproductive cycle has been attained. Early menstrual periods are often unaccompanied by ovulation. There is frequently a period of adolescent infertility lasting a year or eighteen months after menstruation begins, but this cannot be relied on.

The same study by Dr. Dalton also showed that while the duration of each menstrual period for an able-bodied adolescent tends to be six to seven days, gradually shortening during the twenties to an adult pattern of three to five days, in the case of disabled adolescents the duration was about five days. It was found that disabled adolescent girls tended to have regular periods without the painful menstrual cramps which are common in other teenage girls.

Before puberty begins, every girl should have a good understanding of such words as womb (or uterus), Fallopian tubes and vagina. She should have been told by her mother, and perhaps shown diagrams, that the vagina is the passageway between the outer sexual organs, which include the clitoris, and the inner sexual organs, which include the womb. A girl is then ready to absorb the knowledge that at any time between the ages of nine and sixteen, the two small round ovaries inside her start to release tiny eggs—usually one each month. The egg moves slowly into the open end of the nearby Fallopian tube and rolls gently along the tube toward the womb. The egg also signals a chemical messenger ahead to let the womb know that it is coming; the womb then grows a thick, spongy lining to make a comfortable growing place in case a baby is started. But this requires fertilization by the male sperm; so unless this happens, the egg dies and the uterine lining breaks up into a few spoonfuls of blood which are expelled through the vaginal canal.

It is essential that a girl know the biological facts of menstruation before her periods begin. Don't rely on bits of knowledge she may have picked up from friends. As soon as you feel the subject can be broached, it is important to tell your daughter about menstruation so that when her periods start she will feel confident about looking after herself. Several leading manufacturers of sanitary products put out booklets, available on request, which give sensible, sympathetic information. This gives additional guidance, and is particularly useful when a mother finds communication a bit difficult.

The onset of menstruation is an essential stage of development in any girl's life, but it is particularly important to the disabled girl because it demonstrates that no matter what her disability she has normal ovaries and uterus and has become a woman. At this time it must also be pointed out to her that a disabling condition rarely affects fertility or precludes successful pregnancy.

A girl will be closely influenced in her attitude toward her periods by her mother. A sensible, informed attitude can affect, in a positive way, her feelings about her own sexuality and about the reproductive process. Feelings of shame, of being "unwell," talk of "the curse," unfortunately still persist. But if a mother is relaxed and natural about menstruation, it is likely that her daughter will be.

It will help your daughter, however young, to know that there are several kinds of sanitary protection available. There are pads which are used with a belt, pads which adhere to underpants and tampons which are worn internally. Both pads and tampons come in different sizes. She will be able to decide herself which kind is most comfortable.

However well prepared she is, a first period is still something of a jolt for a young girl. It is easy for a mother, who is accustomed to having periods, to forget how inexpert a girl is when she first has to cope. Understandably, most young girls have certain fears regarding menstruation. It is common for them to worry about excessive bleeding. Largely for her reassurance, you can tell your daughter that waterproof panties are available should she need them. She may have additional anxieties related to her disability. She may worry about changing a pad at school if she needs help; or whether it will "show" if she uses crutches. It is healthy if she can express these fears so that you can reassure her or, if necessary, make special arrangements with her teacher. Although a disabled girl may be very young when she begins to menstruate, it is important that her initial experience is as pleasant as possible. Her early attitude toward menstruation can affect how she will feel about her sexuality.

When a girl's breasts first start to develop, they may be tender. This is quite normal and will stop as soon as they have grown, but the breasts will always be sensitive to touch. Adolescent girls are very aware of breast size, and often become self-conscious if they believe their breasts are very large or very small compared with their friends'. When breast development becomes obvious, a tactful mother will prevent teasing from the girl's father and brothers.

Buying her first bra is an exciting experience for a young girl and reinforces her growing sense of womanliness. Bras with front fastenings, which may be easier for her to manage herself, are now widely available.

All teenagers experiencing the physiological changes of puberty need matter-of-fact reassurance and empathy from their families and teachers. The physiological changes of puberty are exciting and frightening. The girl's menarche and developing breasts or the boy's facial hair and nocturnal emissions, give the disabled child, just as any other, the most basic affirmation of womanhood or manhood. In this way at least, if not in many others, most disabled teenagers are the equals of their able-bodied peers; and many indeed mature physically ahead of them.

At the same time, questions about the future, particularly those concerning sexual relationships, marriage and children, are raised. Even more than able-bodied children, those who are disabled need the greatest possible understanding of their parents, and perhaps professional counseling, if they are to emerge from childhood into sexually independent adulthood.

Masturbation

Even very young children find comfort and pleasure in touching their genitalia. When the physiological changes of puberty take place, it is only to be expected that these feelings become accentuated.

Virtually all adolescent boys and the majority of teenage girls masturbate. Children who are disabled are no different, except that too often circumstances rob them of rightful privacy.

Masturbation is natural and harmless and gives a greater understanding of the body's sexual responses, which will be important later within the context of sexual relationships. Unfortunately, lingering myths that masturbation can cause illness or insanity may, even today, make an adolescent feel guilty and depressed. It will help if you are able to indicate, casually, that masturbation is normal and continues to some degree throughout a lifetime.

The Disabled Teenager

All young adolescents begin to wonder how they will take their places in the adult world. It is during these relatively few teenage years that so many decisions and changes have to be made. The options of higher education and vocational training have to be explored. Special interests develop, the circle of friends widens and emphasis shifts from parents and the home to the peer group; what the adolescent's friends say and do become very important.

In these years the teenager must also make difficult social adjustments which involve getting along with the opposite sex on a more mature level. Heterosexual friendships and dating begin, and these relationships start to take on sexual connotations. The adolescent also begins to develop a unique sense of self, to ask the questions: What do I think of myself? Who am I? What do other people think of me? Will I be able to hold down a job and marry and raise children of my own? Such questions are pondered by all adolescents, and all are frequently confused and anxious as they realize that they are about to assume new roles and will have to accept responsibility for themselves as adults.

It is no wonder that most adolescents experience the typical wide mood swings, the "highs" and "lows." And while parents continue to be the chief models for future behavior and relationships, there is also the adolescent's strong tendency to rebel against parental guidance. It is a rare parent-child relationship that does not suffer periods of stress during adolescence.

These phenomena of adolescence are as natural for the teenager with disabilities as for any other. But for the disabled teenager there are exceptional needs and stresses. All teenagers have strong feelings of being different. The fifteen-year-old girl whose breasts have suddenly blossomed may, for example, be extremely self-conscious, while a teenage boy with gangling arms and legs is painfully aware of what he imagines is his clumsiness. The disabled teenager experiences all these uncertainties brought about by physical growth and maturation, and they are magnified because to some extent he feels different from his peers anyway.

During these years, more than ever, the child needs realistic guidance and support. Often professional guidance can be invaluable in deciding on a possible career or a suitable college or how to make the most of a particular talent. As with all adolescents, it is essential that the disabled teenager have realistic goals to strive for, concrete aims that are not impossibly high, as he matures.

An understanding professional, a therapist or school psychologist, may also give help in broadening the teenager's social life by putting him in touch with social clubs or hobby groups which interest him, and in which he feels comfortable. This is necessary because disabled children tend to have fewer opportunities to meet people. They may have to be encouraged to be socially active. During these years of adolescence, social activities become especially important. It is damaging for any child to feel out of the social swim just at the time when boy-girl relationships begin to flower. It is at this time in their child's life that parents have to realize that he is on the brink of adulthood and is entitled to privacy and a social life of his own.

During adolescence it is particularly important that the child is able to speak about his disability. Talking it through will do much to mitigate his concerns and his often unconscious fears. Yet parents find teenagers notoriously difficult to talk to. Often it is desirable if they can turn to someone outside the family—perhaps a sympathetic teacher—to whom they can speak more freely. The better your child understands the physical implications of his condition the more likely he is to come to terms with the limitations it imposes—and be less hesitant about mixing with other people, explaining his disability to friends and asking for help when he needs it.

Achieving independence is described as a vital task of adolescence. Never easily accomplished, it is essential if the child is to assume adult responsibility for himself, to whatever extent he is able. However minor or severe your child's disabling condition, gaining this independence is likely to be difficult, both for you and for him. As a young child, he will almost certainly have had more done for him physically than the average child. If his condition is severe, you will have accepted the responsibility for organizing his daily routine. Whatever his disability, it is probable that you have protected him much more than if he could walk without a brace or did not have impaired sight or hearing. But once he reaches adolescence, it is part of your job to help him to be as independent as his disability permits. The balance between his independence and his genuine need for assistance is a hard one to strike. You must help him to accept his capabilities as well as his limitations.

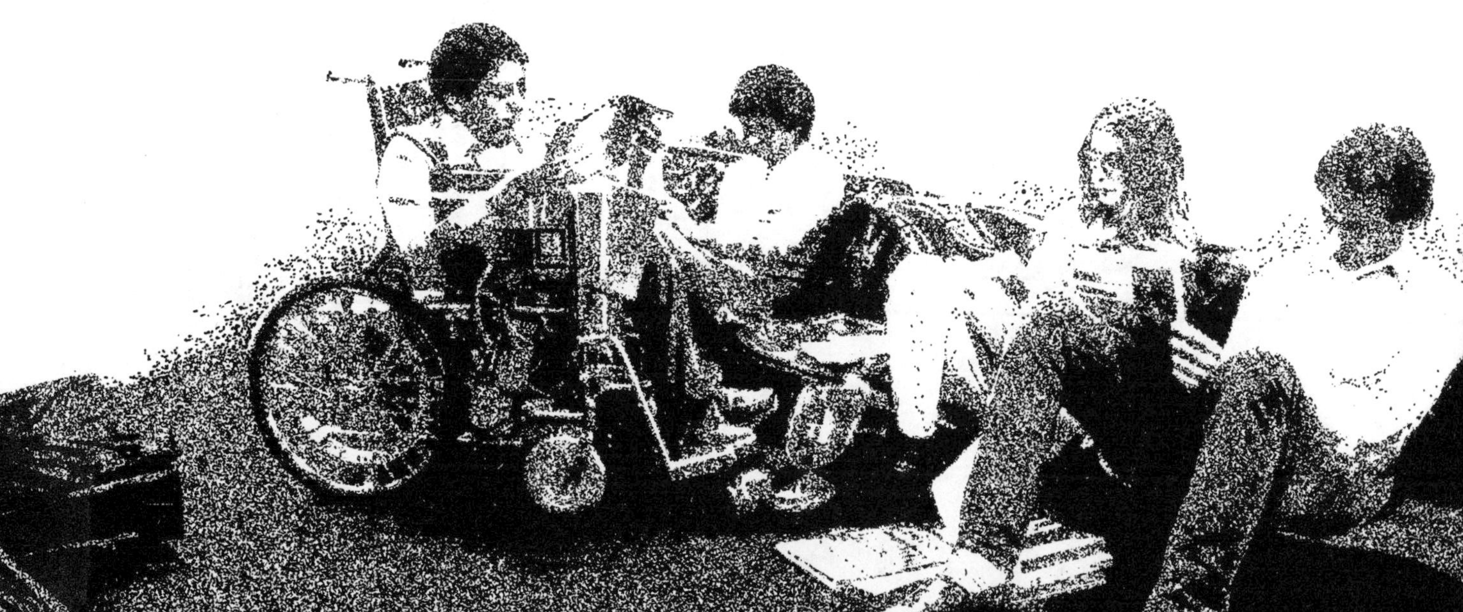

The Disablers

Amputation. The complete surgical removal of any limb or part of a limb from the body, undertaken only when there is damage or disease beyond hope of recovery. Industrial and road accidents are major causes of severe damage, but the necessity for amputation may also arise as the result of such diseases and conditions as cancer, gangrene, frostbite and hardening of the arteries.

Amyotrophic Lateral Sclerosis. A rapidly progressive neuromuscular disorder of adults, resulting from degeneration of the motor nerves in the spinal cord and brain stem, and leading to atrophy of the muscles controlled by these nerves in the hands, arms, feet, legs and tongue. The cause is unknown, but a genetic factor possibly makes some individuals more susceptible than others.

Ankylosis. The condition of a joint that has restricted movement because of fibrous bands, malformation or the actual fusing together of the bones, due to injury, prolonged immobility or such disease as rheumatoid arthritis.

Aphasia. Caused by brain damage, sometimes resulting from a head injury and often occurring after a stroke, aphasia is loss or impairment of the power of speech. A person who is severely affected may be unable to speak or write, to understand speech or writing or to communicate by signs.

Arthritis. Inflammation of one or more joints. The two chief forms are osteoarthritis and rheumatoid arthritis; gout is a related disorder. In osteoarthritis there are painful degenerative changes in the joints but, in most cases, except those involving the hip, there is no disability.

Rheumatoid arthritis can be crippling. It affects people of all ages, but is most common among the middle-aged and is about four times as prevalent among women as it is among men. The disease usually begins in the small joints of the hands or feet, later involving other joints, including the shoulders and hips, with increasing inflammation and pain and gradual destruction of joint cartilage. Early treatment can avoid the disablement caused by stiff and painful joints.

Ataxia. Failure to coordinate the actions of the various muscles involved in performing a movement. The conscious brain directs a movement, but the choice of muscles and the balance of their actions depend on unconscious reflexes. Ataxia is a disturbance of these reflexes. The ataxic gait is clumsy and falls are common.

Athetosis. Uncontrolled, purposeless movements, often a symptom of cerebral palsy. There is frequently a loss of direction during simple movements and fine movements are difficult.

Benign Congenital Hypotonia. A neuromuscular disorder of infants, characterized by weak and floppy muscles. A genetic defect causes deterioration of the motor nerves and this results in atrophy of the muscles supplied by these nerves. In some cases, the condition does not progress and may improve considerably. In other cases, the muscles will remain small and comparatively useless throughout life.

Blindness. The partial or total loss of vision. One definition is the "inability to perform any work for which eyesight is essential." Blindness may result from injury to the eye itself or from some abnormality or lesion in the brain or the optic nerve or it is sometimes due to a systemic disorder such as diabetes. Other causes include cataract, detached retina, glaucoma, iritis, keratitis, opthalmia and various forms of trachoma. Some people are born blind.

Brittle Bones (Fragilitas Ossium). This is a rare hereditary disease that can cause severe deformity. During childhood trivial falls can result in serious fractures. The liability to fracture diminishes with age. If there have been repeated fractures, the lower limbs may not develop normally and the person affected may have to rely totally on a wheelchair.

Cardiovascular Diseases. The most common types of chronic disability are caused by these diseases associated with the heart and circulatory system. They include arteriosclerosis, coronary heart disease, high blood pressure and rheumatic carditis. The degree of heart disorder varies from conditions where ordinary physical activity causes no discomfort to those where any activity causes discomfort.

Cerebral Hemorrhage. Bleeding from a rupture of a blood vessel in the brain, usually from an artery weakened by arteriosclerosis. A cerebral hemorrhage may cause aphasia if it takes place in the speech center of the brain, hemiplegia if it involves the motor pathways.

Cerebral Palsy. A group of medical conditions characterized by nerve and muscle dysfunction caused by damage to the part of the brain which controls and coordinates muscular action. According to the location of the damage, varying disabilities occur. The most common are spasticity, athetosis and flaccidity and there is sometimes difficulty with speech.

Defective development of brain cells before birth, injury during delivery, an accident or infectious disease may result in cerebral palsy. The effects are permanent and regular treatment is necessary to prevent disabilities and deformities from becoming more severe.

Colostomy. An artificial opening in the abdomen to enable the large intestine, or colon, to empty into a plastic bag that is held in place by adhesive and a belt worn across the abdomen. The operation is often performed when there is cancer of the rectum and sometimes when there is bowel incontinence as the result of spina bifida, for example, or spinal injuries.

Congenital Disability. A disability, not necessarily hereditary, which is present at birth or manifest soon after. A child may, for example, suffer an injury before birth which is congenital although not hereditary.

Contracture. The permanent or temporary shortening of a muscle or ligament which limits normal joint movement. Contractures may occur in arthritic and neurological conditions, especially when there is spasticity.

Cystic Fibrosis. An uncommon disease of young children which can cause progressive lung damage.

CVA. The abbreviated term for cerebrovascular accident, caused by cerebral hemorrhage, thrombosis or embolism, the consequence of which may be hemiplegia or aphasia.

Deafness. Total or partial loss of hearing is of either of two types. In the conductive type something interferes with the passage of sound to the inner ear; in perceptive deafness there is damage or defective development of the inner ear, the actual organ of hearing. The effect depends on the type and extent, the age at which deafness began and the training subsequently received. A person who is born deaf and therefore has never heard speech is more handicapped than is a person who becomes deaf after learning to speak and to read.

The terms "deaf-mute" and "deaf and dumb" are inaccurate descriptions. Most people who are deaf have nothing wrong with their vocal chords. They cannot speak, or cannot speak clearly, because they cannot hear.

Diabetes. A disorder in which the body is unable to control the use of sugar as a source of energy. In severe cases, nerve degeneration may impair the ability to walk. In extreme cases, gangrene may develop and a leg amputation become necessary. Diabetes can cause progressive impairment of sight.

Dwarfism. The condition of being abnormally small. Achondroplasia is the most familiar type; the growth of the long bones is defective, but in all other respects there is normality. A much rarer type is due to disorders of the pituitary gland and the lack of the growth hormone. Some chronic diseases of childhood may also interfere with normal growth.

Embolism. The blockage of an artery by a fragment of a blood clot, or similar obstruction. Embolism of a small artery in an area with a good network of arteries has no ill effects. Embolism of an artery of the brain is one cause of stroke, resulting in aphasia or hemiplegia. It usually occurs as the result of a blood clot arising from disease in the wall of an artery or vein elsewhere in the circulatory system.

Encephalitis. Acute inflammation of the brain, most commonly caused by a virus infection. The residual effects may be slowness of movement, shuffling gait, slow speech and difficult articulation. Mental faculties are not usually affected.

Epilepsy. A nervous disorder due to a sudden unusual release of energy in the brain. The severe form, known as *grand mal*, is characterized by sudden loss of consciousness and convulsions. The much less marked manifestations of *petit mal* are a few fleeting seconds of unconsciousness with no falling and occasionally with some slight twitching or eye-blinking. Between attacks there is usually no evidence that the individual is epileptic. In the great majority of cases the condition is not handicapping.

Friedreich's Ataxia. A rare, progressive disease of the nervous system which appears in childhood or early adolescence. In the early stages of the disease standing and walking are unsteady. As it progresses, muscles become weak, there is loss of control of movement and vision may be impaired. The disease is hereditary, but the cause is unknown.

Gout. A constitutional disorder in which there is an excess of uric acid in the blood, manifested by inflammation of joints and the deposit in them of urate crystals. About one patient in five has a near relative with gout. Some people have high blood levels of uric acid without developing the disease. In an acute attack, usually only one joint is affected, often a big toe, which becomes swollen, red and extremely painful. After many attacks a joint can become permanently deformed because of large deposits of uric acid crystals in the bones. Gout can often take the form of chronic arthritis without acute attacks.

Hemophilia. A hereditary disease in which the blood clots only very slowly, so that a minor cut or bruise can cause prolonged bleeding and there is a tendency to bleed internally without any obvious cause. It affects only males, but is transmitted in the genes of females. The genetic defect is the inability to synthesize a protein needed for normal clotting of the blood. In severe cases internal bleeding can erode the joints of arms or legs.

Hemiplegia. Paralysis on one side of the body, usually referred to as a stroke. It may be caused by damage to the brain (on the side opposite the affected side), occurring from thrombosis, embolism or cerebral hemorrhage, or, less commonly, from a head injury or brain tumor.

Huntington's Chorea. A rare hereditary condition in which degenerative changes occur in the cortex, the outer layer of the brain. Symptoms, which usually appear between the ages of thirty and fifty, include involuntary jerky movements, ataxia, slow slurred speech and mental deterioration.

Hydrocephalus. The term applied to the abnormal accumulation of cerebrospinal fluid in the skull due to failure of circulation of the fluid. The causes may be congenital (it is frequently associated with spina bifida), meningitis or a tumor. Often present at birth, the condition can be arrested by surgery. If not alleviated, it can result in spasticity of the legs and, less frequently, of the arms, ataxia, imbalance, clumsiness of fine finger movements and mental impairment.

Ileostomy. A surgical operation similar to a colostomy, involving an opening at the end of the ileum, or small intestine, instead of the colon.

Incontinence. The inability to retain the evacuations of the bowels or bladder, or both, sometimes caused by a disorder of these organs, but more often by injuries to or diseases of the spinal cord and brain, including traumatic paraplegia and spina bifida.

Meningitis. Inflammation of the meninges, the membranes enclosing the brain and spinal cord, caused by infection by bacteria or by viruses.

Monoplegia. Paralysis of a single leg or arm.

Motor Neurone Disease. A rare condition of the central nervous system which causes rapid and progressive physical deterioration. Onset is usually in middle age, with weakness and wasting of the arms and weakness of the legs. There may be incontinence, but there is no sensory loss and mental faculties are not affected.

Multiple Sclerosis. Perhaps the most common organic disease affecting the nervous system, it almost invariably attacks young people, most often adults between the ages of twenty and thirty-five. Multiple sclerosis affects many parts of the nervous system and is often characterized by relapses followed by remissions of partial and, occasionally, complete recovery. The spinal cord tends to be most frequently involved, causing periods of partial to complete paralysis of the legs and, at times, of the trunk and arms. Numbness, tingling and sensory changes may occur.

The disease's name stems from the scar (sclerotic) tissue which forms on the myelin sheath covering nerve fibers of the brain and spinal cord, weakening the nerve impulses. If the nerve fibers themselves become destroyed, impulses can no longer be carried and there can be no restoration of muscle function. The basic causes of multiple sclerosis are as yet undiscovered.

Muscular Dystrophy. A group of chronic hereditary diseases with the common characteristic of progressive weakening and degeneration of the muscles, due to a genetic defect in metabolism. Of the three main types, pseudo-hypertrophic (Duchenne) is the most common and most severe. It occurs only in males, sometimes at birth but usually between the ages of two and six, with rapid progression and no remission. It starts with the muscles of the pelvic area, waddling gait and difficulty climbing stairs and rising from the floor, then spreads to the shoulders and other parts of the body.

The Landouzy-Dejerine type, probably the most benign, usually appears in late adolescence. It affects the face and shoulder muscles first, sometimes progresses very slowly with plateaus of significant duration and with minimal disability.

Myotonic dystrophy strikes in young adulthood and, unlike the other types, affects the muscles of the extremities first, with disability progressing steadily and becoming very severe within fifteen to twenty years.

Myasthenia Gravis. A chronic neuromuscular disease thought to result from a defect in the transmission of nerve impulses to voluntary muscles because of a blockage at the nerve-muscle junction. It can occur at any age, but most commonly affects women in their twenties and men past forty. It begins with weakness of the eye muscles and often progresses to the limbs.

Osteomyelitis. Acute infection in a bone, sometimes following a compound fracture but more usually deriving from a site of infection elsewhere in the body.

Paget's Disease. A disease of unknown cause, seldom occurring under the age of forty, in which one or more bones gradually becomes thick and soft and occasionally fractures spontaneously.

Paraplegia. Total or partial paralysis of both lower limbs. Paraplegia is caused by injury or disease involving the spinal cord. Below the level of the lesion, or damage, there is locomotor paralysis and sensory loss. Bladder and bowel functions can be affected. About half of the people whose paraplegia is the result of an accident have a complete lesion, meaning that paralysis is symmetrical and complete below the level of the injury. For the other half the lesion is incomplete and paralysis is uneven so that, for example, one leg may be more severely affected than the other.

Parkinson's Disease. A chronic disease of the brain, principally affecting older people, characterized by tremors and muscle rigidity causing slowness of movement, shuffling gait and impaired speech. Mental faculties are not affected.

Peroneal Muscular Atrophy (Charcot-Marie-Tooth Disease). This is a progressive neuromuscular disorder which affects both children and adults, is hereditary in most cases and causes degeneration of cells of the spinal cord and peripheral nerves. As a result, atrophy and weakness usually occur first in muscles of the feet, spreading to the legs and, after some years, to the hands and arms.

Poliomyelitis. A virus disease which affects the anterior nerve cells of the spinal cord and brain stem causing paralysis of the muscles. The polio virus does not strike in any regular pattern. In some cases, it may result in complete or partial muscular paralysis. When the lungs and breathing system are affected, dependence on a mechanical breathing aid may be necessary.

Polio vaccine was developed during the 1950s and its use is now almost universal. As a consequence, polio has been virtually obliterated and there is little possibility that it will recur in the West, except in cases of failure to be immunized. There are, however, many thousands of people who were disabled by polio.

Polyneuritis. General inflammation of the nerves of the peripheral nervous system, extending from the spinal cord and brain to the skin, muscles and other parts of the body. It may be caused by a virus infection, diabetes, alcoholism, chemical poisoning, an allergy or malnutrition. Varying degrees of paralysis are associated with the condition.

Progressive Spinal Muscular Atrophy. A group of progressive neuromuscular disorders, classified as infantile, juvenile and adult. The infantile type (Werdnig-Hoffman Disease) is severe and rapidly progressive, beginning before or at birth or in the first few months, characterized by a general weakness and atrophy of the muscles. The juvenile type, afflicting children and adolescents, is only slowly progressive, with a relatively benign course permitting walking as long as twenty years after onset. The adult type (Aran-Duchenne Disease) initially affects the hands, but with slow progression there may be complete paralysis of the arms and spastic paralysis of the legs. Infantile and juvenile types are of genetic origin; the cause of adult cases is unknown.

Quadraplegia. Paralysis of all four limbs, caused by traumatic injury or disease to the nerve cells of the spinal column in the neck. The most common causes of injury are diving accidents, falls, traffic accidents, where the head is thrown forward following deceleration of the body, and war injuries.

Rubella. The medical term for German measles which causes little discomfort to adults. If contracted by a woman during the first three months of pregnancy, however, the baby born subsequently can be massively affected, with disabilities including blindness, deafness, mental incapacity and associated physical impairments of incontinence and immobility.

Spina Bifida. A congenital condition in which the vertebrae of the spine of an unborn baby have failed to develop properly, leaving a gap into which the spinal cord protrudes. This may cause paralysis varying in different cases from a small patch of numbness to complete paralysis from the waist down, incontinence and, quite commonly, hydrocephalus and consequent brain damage.

Sickle-cell Anemia. This hereditary disease gets its name from the sickle shape, rather than the normal round shape, of the red blood cells. These cause the production of an abnormal form of hemoglobin, resulting in insufficient oxygen to body tissues and consequent pain and chronic fatigue, with limitations on ordinary physical activity. This disease occurs primarily in individuals of Negro ancestry; it is estimated that more than two million black Americans have some form of sickle-cell anemia.

Spondylitis. A form of arthritis affecting the spine. Ankylosing spondylitis, the commonest form, is most prevalent among men between the ages of twenty and forty. In severe cases, complete fixation of the spine may occur.

Stroke. Cerebral hemorrhage, thrombosis or embolism, resulting in hemiplegia and aphasia.

Syringomyelia. A rare and slowly progressive disease of the nervous system which affects adults. A cavity forms in the spinal cord, causing loss of sensation of heat, cold and pain. The sense of touch is not affected. As the disease progresses, the legs may become spastic and extensive deformity and paralysis develop. In some cases, the disease spontaneously stops worsening and the person affected is left with a moderate to severe physical disability. Mental faculties are not affected.

Tetraplegia. Another term for quadraplegia, paralysis of all four limbs.

Thalidomide. A sedative drug prescribed in Europe in the late 1950s and early 1960s. A side effect was severe physical deformity among some babies born to mothers who used it.

Thrombosis. The blocking of an artery or vein by a blood clot, or thrombus, that has formed in the vessel, as distinct from an embolism which is blocking by part of a clot formed elsewhere in the circulatory system. Thrombosis in an artery of the brain, or in a neck artery leading to the brain, can cause stroke.

Resources

The aim of this section is to give you a meaningful sampling of available resources which are themselves likely to lead you to others. A definitive list of resources would itself fill a large book and would encompass organizations and services which operate locally as well as nationally.

This section includes national organizations and agencies, general reference books, directories and periodicals, as well as organizations and services, further reading and sources of information pertaining to specific disabilities, aids, communication, housing, mobile homes, home adaptation, home management, personal needs, sex, the disabled parent, education, employment, getting around, rights and entitlements, leisure activities, the disabled child and the disabled teenager—and a listing of hospital suppliers, self-help equipment firms and mail order companies.

For Specific Disabilities

Amputees

Amputees' Service Association
Suite 1504, 520 N. Michigan Avenue
Chicago, Illinois 60611
Publishes a monthly newsletter.

The National Amputation Foundation, Inc.
12–45 150th Street
Whitestone, New York 11357
Publishes a free newsletter, *The Amp*.

UNITED KINGDOM
British Limbless Ex-Servicemen's Association
Frankland Moore House
185–187 High Road
Chadwell Heath, Essex RM6 6NA
Publishes a magazine *BlesMag*.

AUSTRALIA
Civilian Maimed and Limbless Association
159 Princes Highway
St. Peters, N.S.W. 2044

Limbless Soldiers Association S.A. Inc.
Hayward Buildings
24 Charles Street
Adelaide, S.A. 5000

Arthritis

The Arthritis Foundation
1212 Avenue of the Americas
New York, New York 10036
Publishes *Arthritis Foundation News* quarterly and *Bulletin on the Rheumatic Diseases* nine times a year.

UNITED KINGDOM
British Rheumatism and Arthritis Association
6 Grosvenor Crescent
London SW1X 7ER
Publishes *The Review*, a quarterly magazine.

CANADA
The Arthritis Society
Suite 420
920 Yonge Street
Toronto, Ontario M4W 3J7
Publishes *Arthritis Information Bulletin* quarterly.

AUSTRALIA
Australian Arthritis and Rheumatism Foundation
G.P.O. Box 1444
Sydney
N.S.W. 2000

Birth Defects

The National Foundation/March of Dimes
P.O. Box 2000
White Plains, New York 10605
Originally established as the organization for polio, The National Foundation is now concerned only with the prevention of birth defects and has three thousand chapters throughout the United States and Canada. Publishes *National Foundation News*, a monthly.

AUSTRALIA
Foundation 41
Crown Street Women's Hospital
Crown Street
Sydney, N.S.W. 2000
Concerned with the prevention of birth defects Foundation 21 has units which do research in the areas of foetal biology, child development, pharmaceuticals, genetics and environmental factors.

Blind and Partially Sighted

American Council of the Blind
1211 Connecticut Avenue, N.W.
Washington, D.C. 20036

Runs the National Blindness Information Center, a national hotline service to assist with needs and to give information on social, legal and educational problems. The toll-free number is 800–424–9770.

American Foundation for the Blind
15 West 16th Street
New York, New York 10011
A service organization for the blind, publishes *New Outlook for the Blind* in print, braille and recorded editions ten times a year. Also publishes and revises annually *International Guide to Aids and Appliances for Blind and Visually Impaired Persons.*

American Printing House for the Blind
1839 Frankfort Avenue
Louisville, Kentucky 40206
Publishes and distributes talking books and books in braille, in large type and embossed.

Guiding Eyes for the Blind
Yorktown Heights, New York 10599
and The Seeing Eye, Inc.
Morristown, New Jersey 07960
Contact for information on guide dogs.

National Association for Visually Handicapped (Partially Seeing)
3201 Balboa Street
San Francisco, California 94121

> *Where Do I Go From Here?* is a talking book for newly blind people. It is available from *Dialogue Magazine*, 3100 Oak Park Avenue, Berwyn, Illinois 60402.

United Kingdom
Guide Dogs for the Blind Association
Alexandra House
113 Uxbridge Road
London W5 5TQ

National Federation of the Blind of the United Kingdom
20 Cannon Close
Rayners Park
London SW20 9HA
A nonpolitical consumer pressure group concerned with education, employment and other matters of importance to blind people.

The National Library for the Blind
35 Great Smith Street
London SW1P 4BU *and*
1 St. John Street
Manchester M3 4DL

Partially Sighted Society
40 Wordsworth Street
Hove, East Sussex BN3 5BH
Publishes a magazine *Oculus.*

Royal National Institute for the Blind
224–6–8 Great Portland Street
London W1N 5AA
Involved with all facets of education, training, rehabilitation and employment of blind people. Provides information and source material. Publishes a monthly magazine, *New Beacon*, and *Monthly Announcements*, both of which are available in braille editions. Publishes *Apparatus and Games for the Blind*, an illustrated catalog of all kinds of aids for employment, communications and recreation.

Canada
Canadian Council of the Blind
96 Ridout Street South
London, Ontario M6C 3X4

Quebec Federation of the Blind
1172 St. Matthew
Montreal H3H 2H5

Australia
National Federation of Blind Citizens
P.O. Box 2130
Richmond, South Victoria 3121
Publishes *Buff*, a quarterly, in braille, extra large type and on cassette.

Royal Guide Dogs for the Blind Association of Australia
P.O. Box 162
Kew, Victoria 3101
Publishes a quarterly, *Mobility.*

Cardiovascular Disease

Cardio-Vascular Disease
The American Heart Association
44 East 23rd Street
New York, New York 10010
Publishes a magazine, *Heart Facts.*

> *Self-Care for the Hemiplegic,* practical, highly illustrated manual which explains how to cope with dressing, eating and personal hygiene after a stroke and *About Stroke,* basic facts about strokes, their cause and effects, are available from the Sister Kenny Institute, Minneapolis.*

Stroke Clubs of America
805 12th Street
Galveston, Texas 77550
Publishes a free newsletter.

United Kingdom
British Heart Foundation
57 Gloucester Place
London W1H 4DH

The Chest, Heart and Stroke Association
Tavistock House North
Tavistock Square
London WC1H 9JE
Publishes *Hope*, a magazine of general interest, and the more technical *Chest, Heart and Stroke Journal.*

Canada
Canadian Heart Foundation
1 Michelas Street, Suite 1200
Ottawa, Ontario KIM 7B7

Australia
National Heart Foundation
P.O. Box 2
Woden, A.C.T. 2606
Publishes *National Heart News,* a monthly.

Cerebral Palsy

Dental Guidance Council for Cerebral Palsy
122 East 23rd Street
New York, New York 10010
Send one dollar for their information packet on dental care.

United Cerebral Palsy Associations Inc.
66 East 34th Street
New York, New York 10016
Seeks solutions to the health, personal, social and employment problems of people who have cerebral palsy. Publishes *Crusader* ten times a year and will send on request a list of public information literature.

United Kingdom
Spastics Society
12 Park Crescent
London W1N 4LQ
Provides a wide range of services including facilities for assessment, holidays, treatment, education training and residential care and operates a mobile exhibition of aids that travels around the country. Publishes information material, many booklets and the monthly magazine *Spastics News.*

Canada
Canadian Cerebral Association
1 Yonge Street
Toronto, Ontario M5E 1E8

*For complete address see listing under General Organizations and Agencies, pp. 268–269.

AUSTRALIA
Australian Cerebral Palsy Association
5 Blake Street
North Perth, W.A. 6006

Cystic Fibrosis

National Cystic Fibrosis Research Foundation
521 Fifth Avenue
New York, New York 10017

UNITED KINGDOM
Cystic Fibrosis Research Trust
5 Blyth Road
Bromley, Kent BR1 3RS

CANADA
Canadian Cystic Fibrosis Foundation
51 Eglington Avenue, E., Suite 401
Toronto, Ontario M4P 1G7

AUSTRALIA
Cystic Fibrosis Association of N.S.W.
21–23 Belmore Street
Burwood, N.S.W. 2134

Cystic Fibrosis Association of S.A.
1 Sleeps Road
Belair, S.A. 5052

Deaf and Partial Hearing

Alexander Graham Bell Association for the Deaf
1537 35th Street N.W.
Washington, D.C. 20007
Information center on deafness. Publishes books and a newsletter.

American Humane Association
P.O. Box 1266
Denver, Colorado 80201
Trains hearing dogs.

The Better Hearing Institute
1430 K Street, N., Suite 600
Washington, D.C. 20005
Nonprofit organization which gives information on the medical, surgical and amplification help that is available for people with hearing problems. Toll-free hearing and help line—800–424–8576

Council of Organizations Serving the Deaf
P.O. Box 894
Columbia, Maryland 21044
Visual aids, printed material, services for the deaf, including legal counseling, adult education, driver safety, vocational training and public information programs. Write for publications lists.

National Association of Hearing and Speech Agencies
919 18th Street, N.W.
Washington, D.C. 20006
Makes referrals to one of its 169 member affiliates where a person with hearing or speech difficulties can receive appropriate help including diagnosis, evaluation, preschool hearing instruction, counseling and rehabilitation.

National Association of the Deaf
814 Thayer Avenue
Silver Spring, Maryland 20910
A clearinghouse and citizens' advocate in matters related to deafness and impaired hearing. Publishes a monthly magazine, *The Deaf American*.

Readings on Deafness (Deafness Research and Training Center, New York). A collection of articles which represent a repudiation of practices and thinking which have historically restricted deaf people from realizing their full potential. The book is intended for deaf people, their families, the professional community and laypeople.

UNITED KINGDOM
Royal National Institute for the Deaf
105 Gower Street
London WC1 6AH
Publishes a monthly magazine, *Hearing*, and a free booklet, *Special Aids to Hearing*, which tells about services and devices (not hearing aids) which are available to help the hard of hearing.

AUSTRALIA
Australian Federation of Adult Deaf Societies
101 Wellington Parade South
Melbourne East, Victoria 3002

Diabetes

American Diabetes Association, Inc.
18 East 48th Street
New York, New York 10017
Publishes bimonthly magazine, *ADA Forecast*.

UNITED KINGDOM
British Diabetic Association
3–6 Alfred Place
London WC1I 7EE
Publishes a bimonthly newspaper.

CANADA
Canadian Diabetic Association
1491 Yonge Street
Toronto, Ontario M4P 1A6

Epilepsy

Epilepsy Foundation of America
1828 L Street, N.W.
Washington, D.C. 20036
Advocates for people with epilepsy.

UNITED KINGDOM
British Epilepsy Association
3–6 Alfred Place
London WC1 7EE
Publishes the quarterly magazine *Epilepsy News*.

CANADA
Canadian Epilepsy Association
90 Eglington Avenue, Suite 405
Toronto, Ontario M4P 1A6

Friederich's Ataxia

Friedreich's Ataxia Group in America, Inc.
Box 1116
Oakland, California 94611
Publishes a free newsletter.

UNITED KINGDOM
Friedreich's Ataxia Group
Bolsover House
5–6 Clipstone Street
London, W1

Hemophilia

National Hemophilia Foundation
25 West 39th Street
New York, New York 10018
Publishes a newsletter, *Hemofax*.

UNITED KINGDOM
Haemophilia Society
P.O. Box 9
16 Trinity Street
London SE1 1DE

CANADA
Canadian Hemophiliac Society
Chedoke Center
Patterson Building
Box 2085
Hamilton, Ontario L8M 3R5

Multiple Sclerosis

ATOMS (Association to Overcome Multiple Sclerosis)
79 Milk Street
Boston, Massachusetts 02109
This action group, which is open to anyone with MS, lobbies for progressive legislation for disabled people and disseminates information.

National Multiple Sclerosis Society
205 East 42nd Street
New York, New York 10010
Supports research, educates lay and professional people and coordinates

information dissemination about the condition. Publishes *MS Keynotes* irregularly and *MS Messenger* quarterly.

UNITED KINGDOM
Multiple Sclerosis Action Group
71 Grays Inn Road
London WC1X 8TR
Represents the interests of people suffering from MS. Watchdog on current legislation and medical research. Has a twenty-four hour telephone counseling service: 01–568 2255

The Multiple Sclerosis Society
4 Tachbrook Street
London SW1V ISJ
Publishes a quarterly magazine, *MS News*, and a monthly information bulletin, *MS Bulletin*.

CANADA
Multiple Sclerosis Society of Canada
130 Bloor Street, W., Suite 700
Toronto, Ontario M5S 1S5

AUSTRALIA
Multiple Sclerosis Society of Australia
239 Mowbray Road
Chatswood, N.W.S. 2067
Publishes *The Key*, a quarterly.

Muscular Dystrophy

Muscular Dystrophy Associations of America, Inc.
810 Seventh Avenue
New York, New York 10019
The scope of MDA's patient service program includes many related neuromuscular disorders including Friedreich's ataxia and myasthenia gravis. The association publishes the quarterly *MDA News*.

UNITED KINGDOM
Muscular Dystrophy Group of Great Britain
Nattrass House
35 Macaulay Road
London SW4 0QP
Publishes the quarterly *The Muscular Dystrophy Journal* and *The Muscular Dystrophy Handbook*, a comprehensive directory which covers a wide range of services and activities and lists information to help people with muscular dystrophy and their families.

CANADA
Muscular Dystrophy Association of Canada
Suite 1014, 74 Victoria Street
Toronto, Ontario M5C 2A5

Myasthenia Gravis

Myasthenia Gravis Foundation, Inc.
2 East 103rd Street
New York, New York 10029

UNITED KINGDOM
Myasthenia Gravis Council of the Muscular Dystrophy Group of Great Britain
Nattrass House
35 Macaulay Road
London SW4 0QP

Ostomies

The United Ostomy Association
1111 Wilshire Boulevard
Los Angeles, California 90017
Publishes *Ostomy Quarterly*.

UNITED KINGDOM
Colostomy Welfare Group
38–39 Eccleston Square
London SW1V 1PB

AUSTRALIA
Colostomy Rehabilitation Association of N.S.W.
First Floor, 243 Elizabeth Street
Sydney, N.S.W. 2000

Ileostomy Association of N.S.W.
4th Floor, 254 George Street
Sydney, N.S.W. 2000

Parkinson's Disease

American Parkinson's Disease Association
147 East 50th Street
New York, New York 10022

UNITED KINGDOM
Parkinson's Disease Society of the U.K. Ltd.
81 Queen's Road
London SW19 8NR

Poliomyelitis

UNITED KINGDOM
British Polio Fellowship
Bell Close
West End Road
Ruislip, Middlesex HA4 6LP
Publishes *The Bulletin*, a quarterly magazine.

Spina Bifida

Spina Bifida Association
c/o The Texas Medical Center
2333 Moursund
Houston, Texas 77025

Spina Bifida Association of America
104 Festone Avenue
New Castle, Delaware 19720
Publishes a free newsletter.

UNITED KINGDOM
Association for Spina Bifida and Hydrocephalus (ASBAH)
30 Devonshire Street
London W1 2EB
Has 80 local associations throughout England, Wales and Northern Ireland. Publishes *Link*, a bimonthly magazine.

Spinal Injuries

National Paraplegia Foundation
333 N. Michigan Avenue
Chicago, Illinois 60601
Publishes *Paraplegia Life*, a bimonthly magazine, and many books and pamphlets including *Handbook for Paraplegics and Quadriplegics* and *How to Get Help if You're Paralyzed*. Write for their Basic Library of Publications list.

Paralyzed Veterans of America
7315 Wisconsin Avenue, N.W.
Washington, D.C. 20014
Focuses upon improving medical and rehabilitation programs for veteran and nonveteran adults with spinal cord injuries. Publishes a monthly magazine, *Paraplegia News*.

UNITED KINGDOM
National Spinal Injuries Centre
Stoke Mandeville Hospital
Aylesbury, Bucks. HP21 8PP
Publishes the quarterly magazine *The Cord: International Journal for Paraplegics*.

Spinal Injuries Association
120–126 Albert Street
Camden, London NW1 7NE
Publishes newsletter and has published two excellent books, *So You're Paralyzed* and *Able to Work* both written by Bernadette Fallon and available from the association.

CANADA
Canadian Paraplegic Association
520 Sutherland Drive
Toronto, Ontario M4G 3V9
Publishes a quarterly magazine, *Caliper*.

AUSTRALIA
Australian Paraplegic and Quadriplegic Council
20 Amherst Avenue
Trinity Gardens, S.A. 5068

Australian Quadriplegic Association
P.O. Box 83
Coogee, N.S.W. 2039
Publishes a quarterly, *Quad Centre*.

General Organizations and Agencies

American Coalition of Citizens with Disabilities, Inc. (ACCD)
1346 Connecticut Avenue, N.W.
Washington, D.C. 20036
A nationwide umbrella association of sixty-five organizations, including many activist groups, of and for disabled people. The coalition has assumed a major role in promoting equal opportunities and civil rights for individuals with disabilities. Members receive information on these activities and a monthly newsletter, *ACCD Action.*

American Genetic Association
1028 Connecticut Avenue, N.W.
Washington, D.C. 20036

Disabled American Veterans
National Headquarters
P.O. Box 1403
Cincinnati, Ohio 45214
Promotes the welfare of service-connected veterans and publishes *DAV*, a monthly magazine.

Human Resources Center
Willets Road
Albertson, New York 11507
This private nonprofit organization provides vocational and educational training for severely disabled children and adults and conducts research, evaluation and training programs. Send for publication list.

The Library of Congress
Division for the Blind and Physically Handicapped
Washington, D.C. 20542
Provides a variety of free library services, through 140 cooperating libraries, for blind and physically disabled people.

National Association of the Physically Handicapped
2810 Terrace Road, S.E.
Washington, D.C. 20020
Membership is open to anyone with a physical disability who will join forces to fight to eliminate barriers and solve problems common to all disabled people.

The National Easter Seal Society for Crippled Children and Adults
2023 West Ogden Avenue
Chicago, Illinois 60612
Operates service programs for disabled children and adults in every state and Puerto Rico. Publishes the free bimonthly news bulletin *Easter Seal Communicator*. Write for catalog listing booklets and informative leaflets.

National Congress of Organizations of the Physically Handicapped, Inc.
6106 North 30th Street
Arlington, Virginia 22207
This strong lobby group promotes employment, education, equal rights and rehabilitation of people with physical disabilities, as well as legislation and social integration. Publishes the *COPH Bulletin*.

National Rehabilitation Association
1522 K Street, N.W.
Washington. D.C. 20005
Facilitates communication between professionals working with the disabled. Membership is open to everyone concerned with the problems common to all disabled people. Publishes bimonthly *NRA Newsletter*, a quarterly legislation newsletter, a magazine, *The Journal of Rehabilitation*, and many pamphlets.

Developmental Disabilities Office
Office of Human Development
Department of Health, Education and Welfare (HEW)
330 C Street, S.W.
Washington, D.C. 20201
This agency coordinates programs provided for by the Developmental Disabled Assistance and Bill of Rights Act, a law to help people with cerebral palsy, epilepsy, autism and other disabilities defined as developmental, which require special services and provisions.

Office for Handicapped Individuals
Department of Health, Education and Welfare (HEW)
200 Independence Avenue, S.W.
Washington, D.C. 20201
A coordinating and advocacy unit which runs a clearinghouse to disseminate information to individuals and organizations on all matters pertaining to the handicapped community. OHI will answer questions on the many federal programs for the handicapped and direct individuals to the appropriate federal or private organization. The Office for Handicapped Individuals is represented in the ten regional HEW offices throughout the country.

President's Committee on Employment of the Handicapped
1111 20th Street, N.W.
Washington, D.C. 20036
Established in the mid 1940s, this agency publishes many useful booklets and leaflets. Write for their publication list.

Rehabilitation International
The International Society for Rehabilitation of the Disabled
432 Park Avenue South
New York, New York 10016
A nongovernmental federation of national organizations, agencies and groups in more than sixty countries which are involved in worldwide problems of rehabilitation. Publishes *The International Rehabilitation Review.*

Rehabilitation International, U.S.A.
20 West 40th Street
New York, New York 10018
Independent national organization affiliated to Rehabilitation International. Membership includes annual subscriptions to *Rehabilitation World* and the *International Rehabilitation Review.*

Sister Kenny Institute
Chicago Avenue at 27th Street
Minneapolis, Minnesota 55407
A rehabilitation institute, education center and an important source of helpful publications and audiovisual materials. Write for publication list.

Federal Information Centers in seventy-seven major cities will direct you to the correct federal, state or local agency you need. Look in your telephone directory under U.S. GOVERNMENT, FEDERAL INFORMATION CENTER or write to General Services Administration, Washington, D.C. 20405 for the leaflet *Federal Information Centers.*

UNITED KINGDOM
Age Concern
Bernard Sunly House
60 Pitcairn Road
Mitcham, Surrey CR4 3LL

British Red Cross Society
9 Grosvenor Crescent
London SW1X 7EJ
Many involvements with services for disabled people in the community. Publishes *Red Cross News.*

The Centre on Environment for the Handicapped
120–126 Albert Street
Camden, London NW1 7NE
A clearinghouse on environmental problems, buildings, housing, access and education. Has a reference service and a library.

Disabled Living Foundation
346 Kensington High Street
London W14 8NS
Provides a permanent exhibition of equipment and aids to assist with every aspect and type of disability. Nothing is on sale, but information on sources of supply is available. Visits by appointment only. Publishes information sheets on more than twenty aspects of disability as well as many excellent books.

National Fund for Research into Crippling Diseases (Action Research for the Crippled Child)
Vincent House
Springfield Road
Horsham, West Sussex RH12 2PN
Sponsors research projects in many areas of concern to disabled people. Publishes quarterly magazine *Action*.

The Royal Association for Disability and Rehabilitation
25 Mortimer Street
London W1N 8AB
Formerly the Central Council for the Disabled, this is an umbrella organization, coordinating the work of most groups working in the disability field. Useful source of information on access, housing, mobility and travel. Publishes annual *Holiday Guide*, many access guides and a helpful publications list as well as *The Bulletin*, a monthly newsletter, and a quarterly magazine, *Contact*.

AUSTRALIA
Australian Council for Rehabilitation of Disabled (ACROD)
Bedford and Buckingham Streets
Surry Hills, N.S.W. 2010
The national federation of voluntary bodies conducting programs for disabled people, ACROD provides an information service and publishes the excellent, comprehensive *Directory of Services for Disabled People*.

General Reference Books

ABC—An ABC of Services and Information for Disabled People by Barbara McMorland (Disablement Income Group Charitable Trust, Attlee House, Toynbee Hall, 28 Commercial Street, London E1 6LR). This compact and comprehensive handbook lists benefits, facilities, organizations, services and sources of further information available to disabled people in the United Kingdom.

Access—The Guide to a Better Life for Disabled Americans by Lilly Bruck (David Obst Books, Random House, New York). A compendium of valuable information on ways that people with disabilities can get into the mainstream of American life. With emphasis on consumer protection, the book covers physical access, media images, consumer movements, communication, civil rights, recreation and travel and explains how to take action to achieve what is needed and wanted from government agencies and private organizations.

Designing for the Disabled by Selwyn Goldsmith (RIBA Publications, Ltd., London). An important book for anyone concerned with the design of buildings to be used by disabled people. Invaluable for professionals, it will also be of great interest to concerned laypeople.

Directory for the Disabled compiled by Ann Darnborough and Derek Kinrade (Published by Woodhead-Faulkner, Cambridge, in association with the Multiple Sclerosis Society of Great Britain and Northern Ireland). A handbook of information and opportunities with helpful addresses and extremely detailed information.

General Information to Help the Recently Disabled (The Insurance Company of North America and the Human Resources Center, New York*). A helpful resource booklet.

A Good Age by Alex Comfort (Crown Publishers, New York and Mitchell Beazley Publishers Ltd., London). Attacks some common myths about age and offers guidance to positive strategies as well as supportive and realistic advice.

The Handicapped Person in the Community edited by David M. Boswell and Janet M. Wingrove (Tavistock Publications in association with the Open University Press, London). Informative material about the situation, services and needs of people with disabilities, this book is intended primarily for students and for those in professional contact with disabled people, but it should be of interest to the concerned layperson.

Handicapping America: Barriers to Disabled People by Frank G. Bowe, Ph.D. (Harper and Row, Publishers, New York). An important book which is concerned with the attitudes toward disabled people that handicap their ability to be productive citizens. It is a hard-hitting inspiring study.

Integrating the Disabled, the Report of the Snowden Working Party (National Fund for Research into Crippling Diseases, Surrey*). An important study of how far disabled people are integrated into the community and their status in such areas as education, employment, housing, community and personal relationships.

The One-Hander's Book by Veronica Washam (The John Day Company, New York). Detailed illustrated guide to the techniques of mastering the activities of daily living single-handed.

Physical Disability, a Psychological Approach by Beatrice A. Wright (Harper and Row, Publishers, Inc., New York). An examination of social-psychological problems common to people with all types of physical disabilities and of all ages—and their possible solutions.

What You Can Do for Yourself by Patricia Galbreath (Drake Publishers, Inc., New York). Practical tips and ideas for achieving independence inside and outside the home.

You Can Do It From A Wheelchair by Arlene E. Gilbert (Arlington House, Publishers, New Rochelle, New York). Written by a wheelchaired mother of four, this book is full of practical first-hand advice.

*For complete address see listing under General Organizations and Agencies, pp. 268–269.

Periodicals

There are many monthly, quarterly and annual magazines, newsletters and bulletins published in English for, and often by, people with disabilities. Those periodicals which are produced by national health organizations or are directed toward people with specific disabilities are mentioned in the section dealing with specific disabilities. The list which follows is of periodicals of general interest. The cost of a subscription is not mentioned except when it is free and the address to which to write concerning subscriptions is given in parentheses.

Accent on Living (P.O. Box 700, Bloomington, Illinois 61701). This pocket-sized quarterly is full of practical information about transportation, housing and other aspects of disabled living.

Disabled U.S.A. (The President's Committee on Employment of the Handicapped, Washington, D.C. 20201). Formerly called *Performance* and now revamped and enlarged, this free monthly magazine reports progress in the nationwide program to provide employment opportunities for people with disabilities and gives general information about developments in rehabilitation and placement and about new promotional and educational ideas and activities.

Green Pages (Winter Park, Florida 32789). This quarterly news magazine for the disabled includes a useful National Buyer's Directory of Products and Services.

The Independent (2539 Telegraph Avenue, Berkeley, California 94704). Subtitled A New Voice for the Disabled and Blind, this well-written and informative action periodical is published quarterly by the Center for Independent Living.

Rehabilitation Gazette (4502 Maryland Avenue, St. Louis, Missouri 63108). This excellent international journal and information service for disabled people is published once a year by a volunteer staff. The aim of Editor Gini Laurie and her husband Joe is to reach, to inform and to dignify the disabled throughout the world.

Aids

Sources of Information

Accent on Information
P.O. Box 700
Bloomington, Illinois 61701
A computerized retrieval system, run by the publishers of *Accent* magazine which provides information on a variety of subjects. Send for a Search Request form which lists categories. Basic research costs six dollars, returned if the requested information is not available.

Institute of Rehabilitation Medicine
400 East 34th Street
New York, New York 10016
This outstanding rehabilitation center publishes many books, leaflets and periodicals dealing with aids for daily living. Write for publication list.

United Kingdom
Disabled Living Foundation Information Service
364 Kensington High Street
London W14 8NS
A comprehensive information service on aids and equipment which provides information to individuals or, on a regular basis, to subscribers who receive up-to-date and back-dated information sheets and bimonthly bulletins. The information sheets cover many areas including beds, chairs, communication, eating and drinking aids, hoists and lifting equipment, leisure activities, personal toilet, transport, walking appliances, wheelchairs, household equipment, children's aids and equipment and clothes for adults.

Rehabilitation Engineering Movement Advisory Panels (REMAP)
Thames House North
Millbank, London SW1P 4QG
REMAP, a voluntary organization of engineers, working through forty different regional panels, offers technical expertise to solve specific problems encountered by individual disabled people when standard equipment and approaches fail.

Further Reading and Reference

Aids for the Ill and Disabled is a free booklet available from Vocational Guidance and Rehabilitation Services, 2239 East 55th Street, Cleveland, Ohio 44103.

Aids to Independent Living—Self-Help for the Handicapped by Edward W. Lowman, M.D. and Judith L. Klinger, O.T.R., M.A. (McGraw-Hill Book Company, Inc., New York). This now classic compilation of aids and advice is the fruit of more than twenty years of research and practical experience in rehabilitation at the Institute of Rehabilitation Medicine, New York University School of Medicine. More than seven hundred pages and fully illustrated with photographs and drawings, the book covers almost every area of daily living.

Independent Living for the Handicapped and the Elderly by Elizabeth May, Eleanor Hotte and Neva R. Waggoner (Houghton Mifflin Co., Boston). A comprehensive and helpful book which covers aids and techniques to cope with the problems of daily living

Physically Handicapped. Aids to self-help in homemaking, grooming and clothing. Available from Extension Service, U.S. Department of Agriculture, North Carolina State University at Raleigh, Raleigh, North Carolina 27607.

Self-Help Manual for Arthritis Patients by Judith L. Klinger, O.T.R., M.A. (The Arthritis Foundation, New York**). A booklet which includes a selection of the self-help devices shown in *Aids to Independent Living* and of use to people with various disabilities.

Sources of Information on Self-Help Devices for the Handicapped, an annotated bibliography, free from The National Easter Seal Society, Chicago.*

United Kingdom
Aids for the Disabled—HB2 (Department of Health and Social Security, London). Summary of all types of aids available from government and Social Services sources. Includes useful resource material. Available from the Royal Association for Disability and Rehabilitation, London.*

Coping with Disablement (Consumers' Association, London). Practical advice about most aspects of disabled living. Discusses aids as well as alternative techniques.

Equipment for the Disabled. Compiled and edited at Mary Marlborough Lodge, Nuffield Orthopaedic Centre, Oxford (Oxford Regional Health Authority on behalf of the Department

**For complete address see listing under For Specific Disabilities, pp. 264–267.

of Health and Social Security). A series of well-illustrated manuals on aids for various aspects of daily living. Appropriate aids are suggested for particular situations and specific disabilities. Homemade adaptations as well as commercial sources, approximate prices and lists of relevant addresses are given. The titles in the series include: *Clothing and Dressing for Adults, Communication, Disabled Child, Disabled Mother, Hoists and Walking Aids, Home Management, Housing and Furniture, Leisure and Gardening, Personal Care, Wheelchairs* and *Outdoor Transport*. The manuals can be ordered separately and are available with or without a binder from Equipment for the Disabled, 2 Foredown Drive, Portslade, Sussex BN4 2BB.

Electronic Aids

For information about electronic reading equipment, print-to-speech machines, variable speech control systems and talking calculators, write to The Library of Congress, Division for the Blind and Physically Handicapped, Washington, D.C.*

Possum, Inc., 700 North Valley Street, Suite B, P.O. Box 4424, Anaheim, California 92803, will provide information about the availability of the Possum system in the United States.

United Kingdom
Possum Controls, Ltd., 63 Mandeville Road, Aylesbury, Bucks HP21 8AE, furnishes information about this system in Great Britain.

Possum Users Association, Copper Beech, Parry's Close, Stoke Bishops, Bristol BS9 1AW, assists users of Possum equipment. The association is run on a voluntary basis by severely disabled people who themselves use Possum and is dedicated to the financial and social improvement of conditions of its members and other disabled people. Publishes a magazine, *Possibility*.

Communication

Reading

The Braille Forum (190 Lattimore Road, Rochester, New York 14620). A free monthly available in braille, large print, on cassette, open reel tape and sound sheet.

Choice Magazine Listening (14 Maple Street, Port Washington, New York 11050). Bimonthly audio anthology for the blind, the visually impaired and the physically handicapped. The best writing from outstanding popular periodicals is recorded on 8 rpm records. Subscriptions are free.

Division for the Blind and Physically Handicapped of the Library of Congress* publishes many reference circulars including *Aids for Handicapped Readers, Braille Instruction and Writing Equipment, Closed Circuit Television Reading Devices for the Visually Handicapped, Commercial Sources of Spoken Word Cassettes, Directory of Local Radio Services for the Blind and Physically Handicapped, Library Services to the Blind and Physically Handicapped, Reading Materials in Large Type, Braille Book Reviews* and *Talking Book Topics*, a bimonthly publication. Write for further information and a list of publications and services.

The New York Times Large Type Weekly (229 West 43rd Street, New York, New York 10036).

Projected Books, Inc., 300 North Zeeb Road, Ann Arbor, Michigan 43103, is a nonprofit organization which sells ceiling projectors and microfilmed books.

United Kingdom
Microfilm Library, the National Fund for Research into Crippling Diseases, Sussex,* will photograph books for use with a microfilm projector free of charge.

Writing

Type With One Hand by Nina K. Richardson (South-Western Publishing Co., New Rochelle, New York and available in Great Britain from Quill's International Book Service, Amersham, Bucks., HP6 5BZ).

Special Typewriter Keyboard Charts and Instructions for Handicapped Typists prepared by Maxwell Crooks (National Fund for Research into Crippling Diseases, Sussex*).

Speaking

Blissymbolics Publications, P.O. Box 222, Coogee, Sydney, Australia 2034 will provide information about Blissymbols.

Write to Sign Language Programs, Gallaudet College, Washington, D.C. 20002, for information about sign language, sign language classes, textbooks and interpreting for deaf people.

Registry of Interpreters for the Deaf, Inc. (RID), P.O. Box 1339, Washington, D.C. 20013, will furnish information about learning sign language, acquiring interpreting skills, establishing an interpreter training program and securing interpreting services at local and national levels. RID publishes a directory which lists members and suggests reimbursement for professional services.

Hearing

How to Buy a Hearing Aid, Consumer Report, June 1976 (Reprint and Book Department, Consumer's Union, Orangeburg, New York 10962). This is reading recommended by the American Speech and Hearing Association.

Making Sure Hearing Aids Help. A leaflet which is available free from Food and Drug Administration, 5600 Fishers Lane, Rockville, Maryland 20852.

Paying Through the Ear. This study on hearing aids was undertaken by, and is available from, the Public Citizens Retired Professional Group, 3700 Chestnut Street, Philadelphia, Pennsylvania 19104.

Hearing Aids (Royal National Institute for the Deaf, London*). Booklet with detailed advice on aids, their use and care and answers to questions of concern to the partially deaf.

*For complete address see listing under General Organizations and Agencies, pp. 268–269.

Telephoning

Services for Special Needs. Free from local Bell Telephone Business Offices, this booklet describes devices developed for people with problems of communication.

For a free list of equipment and devices (other than teletypewriters), to assist telephone communication between speech or hearing impaired people, write to *The Deaf American*, 5125 Radner Road, Indianapolis, Indiana 46226.

Telephone Services for the Handicapped (Publications Division, Institute of Rehabilitation Medicine, New York). Illustrated manual of aids, devices and equipment which permit disabled people to use the telephone.

Teletypewriters for the Deaf, Inc., P.O. Box 28332, Washington, D.C. 20005 publishes a directory of TTY subscribers in the United States and abroad.

Your local Western Union (toll-free number) will send messages in braille (ask for a Braillegram) or in large print.

UNITED KINGDOM
Help for the Handicapped—Telephone Aids (DLE 550). This leaflet is available free from local telephone sales offices. It provides information on aids to assist disabled or partially hearing people to use the telephone.

Housing

Further Reading and Sources of Information

Architectural and Transportation Barriers Compliance Board, Washington, D.C. 20201, will furnish information and bibliographies listing current literature on housing for disabled people.

Housing and Handicapped People by Marie McGuire Thompson is a summary of problems, programs and legislation. Free from The President's Committee on Employment of the Handicapped, Washington, D.C.*

Housing and Home Services for the Disabled—Guidelines and Experiences in Independent Living by Gini Laurie (Harper & Row, Hagerstown, Maryland). This is an invaluable in-depth survey, by the editor of *Rehabilitation Gazette*, of housing options for disabled people in the United States and abroad. It is very readable and an important book.

Housing for the Handicapped and Disabled: A Guide for Local Action by Marie McGuire Thompson (National Association of Housing and Redevelopment Officials, 2600 Virginia Avenue, N.W. Washington, D.C. 20037). Required reading for any group planning a housing project, for Ms. Thompson discusses the way to achieve community cooperation among building, financial and disability groups.

Housing or Housing Options? by Marie McGuire Thompson and Edward H. Noakes (National Easter Seal Society, Chicago*). Reprint of an article which appeared in the 1977 issue of *Rehabilitation Gazette* which summarized papers presented at the 1978 Easter Seal Society Convention by these two well-known authorities on the housing problems of the disabled.

National Center for a Barrier-Free Environment, Information Clearinghouse, 8401 Connecticut Avenue, Washington, D.C. 20015, is a source of information and bibliographies on housing and architectural barriers.

Office for Independent Living for the Disabled, The Department of Housing and Urban Development (HUD), 7th and D Streets, S.W., Washington, D.C. 20410, will provide information on HUD housing programs for disabled people and will refer specific inquiries to the appropriate local authority. Write for the free leaflet *HUD Programs That Can Help the Handicapped*.

UNITED KINGDOM
Housing Grants and Allowances for Disabled People. A guide for disabled individuals to assistance with home improvements and housing costs. Available from the Royal Association for Disability, London.*

Mobile Homes

Buying and Financing a Mobile Home and *Mobile Homes—Alternative Housing for the Handicapped* are free leaflets available from Office for Independent Living for the Disabled. The Department of Housing and Urban Development (HUD), 7th and D Streets, S.W., Washington, D.C. 20410.

Manufactured Housing Institute, P.O. Box 201, 14650 Lee Road, Chantilly, Virginia 22021, will provide the name and address of your state mobile home association as well as up-to-date lists of parks in areas as requested. Choosing a good park is as important as the choice of a mobile home.

Tips on Buying a Mobile Home is a free pamphlet from the Council of Better Business Bureaus, Inc., 1150 7th Street, N.W., Washington, D.C. 20036.

UNITED KINGDOM
Donnington Mobile Homes for the Handicapped, 52–60 The Broadway, Didcot, Oxfordshire, will provide information about specially designed mobile homes.

Home Adaptation

Handicapped at Home by Sydney Foott. (A Design Centre Book, published in association with the Disabled Living Foundation, London*). This attractive, illustrated book offers concise, practical advice on ways to plan and equip the home for maximum independence.

Home in a Wheelchair by Joseph Chasin (Paralyzed Veterans of America, Washington, D.C.**). Information about wheelchair homes, based on the personal experiences of PVA members who have designed, built or modified homes for themselves.

Wheelchair Bathrooms by Harry A. Schweikert, Jr. (Paralyzed Veterans of America, Washington, D.C.**). This amusingly written book is full of good ideas on bathroom design and equipment.

**For complete address see listing under For Specific Disabilities, pp. 264–267.

Home Management

Further Reading and Reference

Adaptations and Techniques for the Disabled Homemaker by Karen Hodgemen, O.T.R. and Eleanor Warpeha, O.T.R. (Sister Kenny Institute, Minneapolis*). A helpful manual which illustrates adaptive devices and special techniques to simplify household chores.

Cookbook in Extra Large Type and *Cookbook in Braille* are available free from Volunteers for the Blind, 332 South 13th Street, Philadelphia, Pennsylvania 19107.

Easy-to-Use Kitchens and *Easy-to-Use Sink Center* are helpful, clearly written leaflets available free from Cooperative Extension Service, University of Nebraska, Lincoln, Nebraska.

Mealtime Manual for the Aged and Handicapped by Judith L. Klinger, O.T.R., M.A., Fred Frieden, M.D. and Richard A. Sullivan, M.D. (Simon and Schuster, Inc., New York). A valuable step-by-step, illustrated guide to simplifying cooking and kitchen activities for people with different needs and physical limitations. The book covers commercial equipment, self-help devices, planning and designing the kitchen and menu suggestions.

Planning Kitchens for Handicapped Homemakers by V. H. Wheeler (available from the Publications Unit, Institute of Rehabilitation Medicine, New York University Medical Center, 400 East 34th Street, New York, New York 10016). The Institute's kitchen-planning consultant advises on the planning of a new kitchen and explains how to make the best of an old one. This is a basic guide for professionals and laypeople. It is full of good ideas and includes a source list for equipment.

The Wheelchair in the Kitchen—A Guide to Easier Living for the Handicapped Homemaker by Joseph Chasin and Jules Saltman (Paralyzed Veterans of America, Washington, D.C.**). This well-illustrated, readable little book tells how to plan, build, remodel or adapt the kitchen for most efficient wheelchair use. The tips on refrigerators, sinks, storage and appliances are practical and particularly helpful.

United Kingdom

Electrical Aids for Disabled People a free booklet, available from the Marketing Department of the Electricity Council, London, which deals with the use of specialized equipment and adaptations of electrical appliances available for people with disabilities.

Gas Aids and the Disabled and *How Gas Makes Life Easier for Disabled People* are leaflets, available free from the British Gas Home Service Department, London, which describe aids and adaptations available to assist disabled and partially sighted people to use standard gas appliances.

If You Can't Stand to Cook by Lorraine Gifford (Marshall, Morgan & Scott, London). A book of simple recipes for the handicapped homemaker.

Kitchen Sense for Disabled or Elderly People by Sydney Foott, Marian Lane and Jill Mara (The Disabled Living Foundation, London*). This is the British equivalent of *Mealtime Manual* and gives detailed, illustrated, expert advice on all aspects of kitchen planning, equipment, food preparation, menus and shopping, as well as sources of equipment.

Personal Needs

Dental Care

Write to National Foundation of Dentistry for the Handicapped, 1121 Broadway, Suite 5, Boulder, Colorado 80302, for free booklet: *Dental Care for Handicapped Persons: An Important Health Issue.*

Toothbrushing and Flossing, A Manual of Home Dental Care for Persons who are Handicapped and *Helping Handicapped Persons Clean Their Teeth* are both available from the National Easter Seal Society, Chicago.*

United Kingdom

For information about dentistry for the Handicapped in the United Kingdom write to General Dental Council, 37 Wimpole Street, London W1.

Incontinence

Incontinence: A Guide to the Understanding and Management of a Very Common Complaint by Dorothy Mandelstam (Disabled Living Foundation, London*). This well-written book covers a wide range of appliances, special clothing and aids and offers practical and reassuring advice.

Clothing and Dressing

Adapt Your Own Clothing (Office of Independent Study, Division of Continuing Education, University of Alabama, University, Alabama 35486). This book is an excellent guide for people with special needs. It costs one dollar.

Braille Color Clothing Tags, to permit blind people to make their own clothing selection, are free in the United States from the American Foundation for the Blind, New York.**

Clothes Sense for Handicapped Adults of All Ages by P. Macartney (Disabled Living Foundation, London*). A practical, illustrated guide to the best kind of clothing for people with various disabilities, together with tips for dressing and the adaptation of an existing wardrobe.

Clothing for the Handicapped (Sister Kenny Institute, Minneapolis*). An illustrated manual of designs and tips for clothing suited to various situations and conditions. It includes information about children's and adults' clothing.

Convenience Clothing and Closures prepared by Talon Consumer Education and Velcro Corporation, 41 East 51st Street, New York, New York 10022. This is a sensible booklet which discusses the kinds of clothing and closures most easily managed by people with disabilities.

*For complete address see listing under General Organizations and Agencies, pp. 268–269.

Dressmaking for the Disabled (Disabled Living Foundation, London*). This booklet explains how paper patterns can be adapted to the needs imposed by physical disabilities.

Flexible Fashions. This booklet is free from the Arthritis Foundation, New York,** and explains how to turn ready made clothes into functional fashions to suit the individual with disabilities.

Functionally Designed Clothing. Free leaflet from Vocational Guidance and Rehabilitation Services, 2239 East 55th Street, Cleveland, Ohio 44103.

How to Adapt Existing Clothes for the Disabled (Disabled Living Foundation, London*).

Footwear

Footwear for Problem Feet by M.D. England (Disabled Living Foundation, London*). This illustrated book deals with general problems relating to foot health. It is not intended for people who need orthopedic or specialist help.

In the United States for information about getting odd or different size shoes write to Handicappers of America, R.R.2, Box 58, Camby, Indiana and The National Odd-Shoe Exchange, 1415 Ocean Front, Santa Monica, California 90401. For lightweight or extra large shoes write to King Size Company, Brockton, Massachusetts 22402.

Sex

Further Reading

Entitled to Love by Wendy Greengross, M.D. (Malaby Press, London, in association with National Fund for Research into Crippling Diseases). A doctor's highly readable and practical approach to the sexual and emotional needs of people with disabilities.

Forum by Nicole Davoud (free booklet from Multiple Sclerosis Society of Great Britain and Northern Ireland, London**). A collection of articles written by the founder of CRACK, an MS group of young people, on social and sexual problems as related to people suffering from multiple sclerosis, but of equal value to those disabled from other causes.

Let There Be Love by Gunnel Enby (Taplinger Publishing Company, Inc., New York and Elek Books Ltd., London). This is an absorbing and human story which describes sex-related problems, sex education and social attitudes and policies in Sweden, as experienced by the author who is disabled by polio.

Not Made of Stone, The Sexual Problems of Handicapped People by K. Heslinga, Ph.D., A.M.C.M. Schellen, M.D. and A. Verkuyl, M.D. (Charles C. Thomas, Publisher, Springfield, Illinois and Woodhead-Faulkner (Publishers) Ltd. Cambridge, England). An explanation of the anatomy and physiology of human reproduction, genetics and contraceptives and helpful information on the positive value of sexual aids. This illustrated book also considers family relationships and sexual options for those with specific disabilities. It is intended essentially for professionals, but can be useful to laypeople.

Sexual Adjustment, A Guide for the Spinal Cord Injured by Martha Ferguson Gregory (Accent Special Publications, Accent on Living, Inc., Bloomington, Illinois 561701). Written by a vocational rehabilitation counselor who is married to a quad, this little book is practical and down-to-earth.

Sexual Options for Paraplegics and Quadriplegics by Thomas O. Mooney, Theodore M. Cole, M.D. and Richard A. Chilgren, M.D. (Little, Brown & Company, Inc., Boston, and available in the U.K. through Quest Publishing Agency, 145a Croydon Road, Beckenham, Kent BR3 3RB). This unusual sex manual is written by a spinal cord injured person with the assistance of two physicians experienced in human sexuality research and rehabilitation. It includes photographs showing spinal injured people preparing for sex and participating in various kinds of sexual expression with special attention devoted to the problems of people who must wear catheters or ileostomy bags and who cannot move their arms or legs or both. It is a unique source of explicit and medically reliable information for people who are disabled (and not necessarily spinal injured) and their partners.

Sexual Rights for the People Who Happen to Be Handicapped by Sol Gordon (Human Policy Press, Syracuse, New York). A sensitive and helpful little book.

Sexuality and the Spinal Cord Injured Woman by Sue Bregman. (Sister Kenny Institute, Minneapolis*). This small book offers frank advice on social and sexual adjustment and counters stereotyped attitudes toward the sexual potential of women with spinal injuries.

A Small Wind of Change by William Stewart, for the Committee on Sexual Problems of the Disabled (SPOD) (National Fund for Research into Crippling Diseases, Sussex*). Report of a project which investigated sexual problems among 212 disabled people in England.

Towards Intimacy—Family Planning and Sexuality Concerns of Physically Disabled Women by the Task Force on Concerns of Physically Disabled Women (Human Sciences Press, New York). A practical and positive approach to the problems of women with physical limitations. This book is clearly written and is as supportive as it is informative.

Within Reach—Providing Family Planning Services to Physically Disabled Women (Human Sciences Press, New York). The result of a survey of the relevant literature, discussions with professionals in family planning, rehabilitation and sexuality, this book explains the needs and experiences of disabled women so that the relevant services for them can be improved.

Sources of Advice and Information

Sex and Disability Project, Institute on Attitudinal, Legal and Leisure Barriers, 1828 L Street, Washington, D.C. 20036, is a project which has been set up to provide a model for sexual adjustment counseling services for people with disabilities. Write for further information.

National Gay Task Force, 80 Fifth Avenue, New York, New York 10011, offers information about supportive counseling to homosexuals of both sexes and all ages.

**For complete address see listing under For Specific Disabilities, pp. 264–267.

Sex Information and Educational Council of the United States (SIECUS) 1855 Broadway, New York, New York 10023 is a nonprofit resource center which provides information on all aspects of human sexuality and publishes a bimonthly newsletter *SIECUS Report*. Write to Human Sciences Press, 72 Fifth Avenue, New York, New York 10011 for their publications catalog which includes books of particular interest to people with disabilities.

United Kingdom
Family Planning Association, 27–35 Mortimer Street, London W1A 4QW, offers family planning advice, which is free under the National Health Service as are contraceptive supplies prescribed. The FPA will send a book list and free information leaflets upon request.

Gay Care, 84 Burton Road, London SW9 6TQ, offers supportive counseling and helps disabled homosexuals of both sexes and all ages to establish social contacts.

Gemma, BM Box 5700, London, WC1 V6XX is a group for disabled lesbians.

Sexual Problems of the Disabled (SPOD), Brook House, 2–16 Torrington Place, London WC1 7HN, is an organization whose aim is to encourage public and professional awareness of the sexual needs and difficulties of disabled people. Provides practical information and makes referrals for help.

The Disabled Parent

Early Years by Morigue Cornwell (Disabled Living Foundation, London*). Written by a physiotherapist, this handbook for disabled parents draws upon the experiences of parents with a variety of handicaps from pregnancy through their children's early school years. The book is illustrated, practical and eminently helpful.

Motherhood: How to Cope by Morigue Cornwell (Disabled Living Foundation, London*). A sensible book which discusses the problems of mothers with physical disabilities, including those who are deaf or blind.

Education

Sources of Information

Bureau of Education for the Handicapped, Department of Health, Education and Welfare, Washington, D.C. 20202. Within this bureau there are the divisions of Educational Services, of Training Programs, of Research, of Library Programs and of Special Education, each of which can be contacted for specific information.

Council of Better Business Bureaus, Inc., 1150 17th Street, N.W., Washington, D.C. 20035 will send on request a list of private companies that offer correspondence courses in many fields. Send for *Tips on Home Study Schools.*

Gallaudet College, 7th Street and Florida Avenue, N.E., Washington, D.C. 20002 provides higher education for deaf people and features model preschool, elementary, secondary and continuing education programs.

National Braille Association, Inc., 85 Godwin Avenue, Midland Park, New Jersey 07432, has a Braille Book Bank—college textbooks in braille in the sciences, mathematics and foreign languages.

National Home Study Council, 1601 18th Street, N.W., Washington, D.C. 20009 publishes *Directory of Accredited Private Home Study Schools.*

National University Extension Association, 1 DuPont Circle, N.W., Suite 360, Washington, D.C. 20036 will furnish information about home study courses.

> If you wish to file a complaint against a college or university for discrimination, the Office for Civil Rights, Department of Education and Welfare (HEW), Washington, D.C. 20201, will advise you and explain the relevant legislation that can make this possible.

Write to Production Center for Hearing Impaired, University of Nebraska, 301 Barkley Center, Lincoln, Nebraska 68583, for educational resource material.

Union for Experimenting Colleges, Antioch College, Yellow Springs, Ohio, will furnish information about the University Without Walls program.

United Kingdom
Association of Disabled Professionals, The Stables, Banstead, Surrey, has members from a wide variety of professions. It aims to improve employment and educational opportunities for disabled students and further career prospects for disabled professionals. The association gives advice on training and employment problems and publishes a quarterly newsletter and a house bulletin.

Association of British Correspondence Colleges, 4 Chiswell Street, London EC1Y 4UR, and Council for the Accreditation of Correspondence Colleges, 27 Marylebone Road, London NW1 5JS, are both organizations which seek to ensure that correspondence colleges conform to high standards of tuition and service. Both will supply lists of correspondence colleges and relevant information concerning them.

The Open University, Walton Hall, Milton Keynes MK7 6AA, will send free *Guide for Applicants* which gives information about the facilities and support services provided for disabled students. The Senior Counsellor for Disabled Students will provide more detailed information.

National Bureau for Handicapped Students, City of London Polytechnic, Calcutta House Precinct, Old Castle Street, London E1 7NT, will furnish information on educational opportunities for further, adult and higher education, on financial assistance and on accessibility.

The National Institute of Adult Education, 35 Queen Anne Street, London W1M 0NL, provides information on a variety of courses and day and evening classes offered through local Education Departments, Workers' Educational Associations and university extra-mural departments.

Royal National Institute for the Blind, London,** has a students' library which will lend books free of charge and transcribe examinations into braille.

*For complete address see listing under General Organizations and Agencies, pp. 268–269.

Further Reading and Reference

Accessibility of Junior Colleges for the Handicapped is a survey of more than 375 junior colleges and is free from the President's Committee on Employment of the Handicapped, Washington, D.C.*

Home Study Educational Opportunities is a booklet which provides information about home study courses for high school or college credit. It is free from The President's Committee on Employment of the Handicapped, Washington, D.C.*

The College Guide for Students with Disabilities by Elinor Gollay and Alwina Bennet (Abt Publications, Cambridge, Massachussetts). This is a valuable directory of higher educational services, programs and college facilities.

A Guide to College/Career Programs for Deaf Students (Gallaudet College and the National Institute for the Deaf, Washington, D.C.) covers most of the colleges in the United States and Canada that have programs for deaf students.

Look Out for Yourself: Helpful Hints for Selecting a School or College. This leaflet is available from Public Documents Distribution Center, Dept. 10, Pueblo, Colorado 81009.

Mobility for Handicapped Students is free from Rehabilitation Services Administration, Department of Health, Education and Welfare, Washington, D.C. 20201.

Some Colleges and Universities with Special Facilities to Accommodate Handicapped Students. Free from National Easter Seal Society, Chicago.*

Vocational and Educational Opportunities for the Disabled. This free booklet, which includes information on home study, is available from Human Resources Center, New York.*

United Kingdom

Access to Universities and Polytechnic Buildings is available from the Royal Association for Disability and Rehabilitation, London.*

The Disabled Living Foundation, London,* has an information leaflet on higher education for physically disabled people. It is free on request.

Employment

Sources of Information

American Vocational Association, 1510 H Street, N.W., Washington, D.C. 20036, can give helpful information on careers.

Association of Rehabilitation Facilities, 5330 Wisconsin Avenue, Suite 955, Washington, D.C. 20015, will give information on vocational rehabilitation.

Bureau of Apprenticeship and Training, Manpower Administration, U.S. Department of Labor, Washington, D.C. 20210, will furnish on request literature and information on career opportunities. They can also provide you with the address of the regional office which will supply the names of companies in your area that offer apprenticeship training.

Department of Human Resources Development, 800 Capital Mall, Sacramento, California 95814, will furnish free literature on a wide variety of occupations.

The Electronic Industries Association, Electronic Industries Foundation, 2001 I Street, N.W., Washington, D.C. 2006, has launched a program in association with HEW to develop training and career employment opportunities for disabled people in the electronic industries. Write for further information.

Employment and Training Administration, U.S. Department of Labor, 600 D Street, S.W., Washington, D.C. 20201, sponsors state employment services, sheltered workshops and public service employment programs for disabled people.

> Federal Job Information Centers, maintained by the Civil Service Commission, are located throughout the country and provide information on local federal jobs. Dial 800– 555–1212 for the toll-free number of the nearest Federal Job Information Center.

The Interagency Committee on Handicapped Employees, Civil Service Commission, 1900 E Street, N.W., Washington, D.C. 20415, will send free and useful publications on request. These include: *Employment of Physically Handicapped Persons in the Federal Service, Employment of the Deaf in Federal Service* and *Employment of the Blind in Federal Service.*

National Vocational Guidance Association, 1607 New Hampshire Avenue, N.W., Washington, D.C. 20009, offers assistance on career decisions.

Office of Public Information, Small Business Administration, Washington D.C. 20416, will supply free leaflets on the way to start a small business.

Project for the Handicapped in Science, 1776 Massachusetts Avenue, Washington, D.C. 20036, sponsored by the American Association for the Advancement of Science, aims to help disabled students participate fully in college and university science programs and to help disabled scientists find suitable employment. They publish a quarterly, *Access to Science.*

United Kingdom

The British Computer Society, 29 Portland Place, London W1N 4HU, has a Specialist Group for the Disabled which will furnish information on opportunities for disabled people in the computer industry.

Home Opportunities for Professional Employment (HOPE), Oakwood Further Education Centre, High Street, Kelvedon, Essex, is an organization of disabled professionals established to investigate the field of home employment. Write, enclosing stamps, for advice and detailed information about a variety of occupations that can be pursued from home.

Royal National Institute for the Blind, Commercial Training College, 5 Pembridge Place, London W2, has courses for computer programmers and for commercial employment in shorthand and typing, audiotyping and telephoning.

Further Reading and Reference

Disabled? Vocational Rehabilitation Can Help, Vocational Rehabilitation

**For complete address see listing under For Specific Disabilities, pp. 264–267.

for the Blind and Disabled and *Services for the Visually Handicapped* are leaflets which can be had free from local State Education Departments or Offices of Vocational Rehabilitation.

Fact Sheet on Handicapped Assistance Loans is free from U.S. Small Business Administration, 1030 15th Street, N.W., Washington, D.C. 20416.

Careers for the Homebound and *Employment Assistance for the Handicapped, a Directory for Federal and State Programs to Help the Handicapped to Employment* are among the many free publications on employment which are available from the President's Committee on Employment of the Handicapped, Washington, D.C.*

On Your Own: 99 Alternatives to a 9-to-5 Job by Kathy Matthews (Vintage Books, New York).

Working Together—The Key to Jobs for the Handicapped. A guide from the AFL-CIO, 815 Sixteenth Street, N.W., Washington, D.C. 20006.

United Kingdom
Able to Work by Bernadette Fallon (Spinal Injuries Association, London**). A guide aimed at the young, newly disabled man and woman. Covers preparation for work, statutory help available (with details of numerous services and schemes), training schemes, further education, self-employment and working from home.

Earning Money at Home and *Making Extra Money at Home.* These leaflets are free on receipt of self-addressed envelope from *Woman's Own* Reader Service, King's Reach Tower, Stamford Street, London SE1 9LS.

Get Yourself Going the Work-Easy Way by Henry Mara and Penny Thrift (Disabled in the City, 40 Etherly Road, Tottenham, London N15 3AJ). Both authors of this action handbook for the handicapped office worker are disabled by multiple sclerosis.

Make a Fresh Start with the Training Opportunities Scheme (TSA L6). This free leaflet, available from DROs at local Employment Offices or Job Centres, describes the Training Opportunities Scheme (TOPS) which offers further training to people who wish to develop new skills in order to improve their job prospects.

Getting Around

By Public Transportation

Access Travel: A Guide to Accessibility of Airport Terminals. Lists sixty-nine accessibility features of more than two hundred airport terminals around the world and includes information on the way to make advance arrangements if vou have special needs. Free from U.S. General Services Administration, Washington, D.C. 20405.

Air Traveler's Fly Rights is free from Office of Consumer Affairs, Civil Aeronautics Board, Washington, D.C. 20428.

Consumer Information About Air Travel for the Handicapped. Free from TWA, 605 Third Avenue, New York, New York 10016.

Seeing Eye Dogs as Air Travelers. Information for airlines personnel. Free from The Seeing Eye, Inc.,**

Tips on Dealing with Deaf Passengers. Free from Gallaudet College, Washington, D.C. 20002. How to tell airlines personnel how to help you.

Helping Hand Service for the Handicapped. Free leaflet from Greyhound Lines, Greyhound Towers, Phoenix, Arizona 85077. (In Great Britain contact Greyhound International, 199 Regent Street, London W1R 8PJ.

The Disabled and the Elderly: Equal Access to Public Transportation. Free from The President's Committee on Employment of the Handicapped, Washington, D.C.*

By Private Transportation

American Automobile Association, 1712 G Street, N.W., Washington, D.C. 20015. Membership includes automobile insurance, travel planning information and aid in the event of automobile trouble. Will send free on request a list of automobile hand-control manufacturers. Publishes *The Handicapped Driver's Mobility Guide,* a directory that lists and describes more than five hundred transportation services for disabled drivers, including driving schools, manufacturers of driving aids and publications.

United Kingdom
The British School of Motoring Disabled Drivers Training Centre, 102 Sydney Street, London SW3, provides a helpful service to disabled people who want to achieve travel independence. The centre assesses each individual's requirements and will also make necessary conversions to vehicles.

Disabled Drivers Association, Ashwellthorpe Hall, Ashwellthorpe, Norwich NR16 IEX, will help and advise any disabled person on all matters of mobility. Publish quarterly magazine, *The Magic Carpet.*

Disabled Drivers Motor Club, 39 Templewood, London W13 8UD. The aim of the club is to protect the interest and welfare of disabled drivers. Publishes the magazine *The Disabled Driver.*

Motability is a government-sponsored organization set up to enable recipients of the Mobility Allowance to lease automobiles for a limited period (possibly four years) in exchange for their cash allowance. For details, contact one of the Disabled Drivers Associations or the Royal Association for Disability and Rehabilitation, London.*

By Wheelchair

Wheelchair Selection: More Than Choosing a Chair with Wheels, is an excellent book available from Sister Kenny Institute, Minneapolis.*

How to Push a Wheelchair by David Griffiths and David Wynne. A helpful and practical booklet for the wheelchair user and helper. Available from The Royal Association for Disability and Rehabilitation, London.*

People in Wheelchairs—Hints for Helpers (British Red Cross Society, London*). Illustrated booklet full of helpful information.

Travel

Mobility International, 2 Colombo Street, London SW1 8DP. Based in London but serving disabled travelers worldwide, this organization is a

*For complete address see listing under General Organizations and Agencies, pp. 268–269.

clearinghouse for information on travel in Europe, North America and the Middle East. Provides contacts and opportunities for international travel and exchange visits. Furnishes travel information or makes referrals.

SATH (The Society for the Advancement of Travel for the Handicapped), 26 Court Street, Brooklyn, New York 11242, is a nonprofit organization established to assist members of the travel industry to better serve the disabled traveler. SATH will provide, free of charge, a list of travel agents experienced in arranging trips for people with disabilities and, for one dollar, a bibliography of material concerning travel for the handicapped.

Travel Information Center, Moss Rehabilitation Hospital, 12th Street and Tabor Road, Philadelphia, Pennsylvania 19141, provides free information on accessibility of national and international cities, hotels, motels, cruise ships and airlines to help disabled people plan trips at home or abroad.

Access to the World. A Travel Guide for the Handicapped by Louise Weiss (Chatham Square Press, Inc., New York). An outstanding book which gives information to facilitate travel in many countries by all means of transportation, explores access in major cities, and includes an invaluable listing of international hotels as well as tips on travel and health care.

Rights and Entitlements

Organization and Sources of Information

Center for Concerned Engineering
1707 Q Street, N.W.
Washington, D.C. 20009
A watchdog group, sponsored by Ralph Nader, which applies its engineering expertise to advise on the improved design of wheelchairs and other devices used by disabled people.

The Disability Rights Center
1346 Connecticut Avenue, N.W.
Washington, D.C. 20036
A nonprofit organization run by disabled people working closely with consumer advocate Ralph Nader. Publications include *Medical Devices and Equipment for the Disabled* and *Consumer Warranty Law: Your Rights and How to Enforce Them.*

National Center for Law and the Deaf
Gallaudet College,
7th Street and Florida Avenue, N.E.
Washington, D.C. 20002
Set up by Gallaudet College and the National Law Center of George Washington University to represent people who are deaf and hearing-impaired and give them legal advice. Send for their publications list.

National Center for Law and the Handicapped, Inc.
1235 North Eddy Street
South Bend, Indiana 46617
Gives active support for the legal rights of people with disabilities through legal assistance, research and public and professional education. Publishes a newsletter and *Amicus*, a bimonthly magazine which gives information about current litigation on issues of concern. Both are free.

United Kingdom

Disability Alliance
96 Portland Place
London W1N 4EX
A pressure group whose main aim is to achieve a comprehensive incomes scheme for disabled people. Publishes *Disability Rights Handbook*, a guide to income benefits and certain aids and services for disabled people.

Disablement Income Group (DIG)
Attlee House, Toynbee Hall
28 Commercial Street
London E1 6NS
Pressure group campaigning for a National Disability Income and an allowance to cover the extra costs of disabled living. The Disablement Income Group Charitable Trust researches and publishes information on the economic aspects of disability. and a quarterly journal *Progress.*

National Council for Civil Liberties
186 Kings Cross Road
London WC1 9DE
Gives legal advice to protect the rights and liberties of the private citizen, especially minority groups.

Further Reading and Reference

Into the Mainstream: A Syllabus for a Barrier-Free Environment by Stephen A. Kliment (free from National Easter Seal Society, Chicago*). Covers the development of legislation, basic barrier conditions, solutions for their removal and techniques of organizing action groups. Includes a list of information sources and concerned agencies. The American Institute of Architects considers this publication important enough to distribute it to every member of its organization.

Checklist of Income Tax Deductions for Medical Expenses. This helpful leaflet is free from United Cerebral Palsy Association, Inc., New York.**

ALPHE—Assistance in Law for Physically Handicapped Elders (624 University Avenue, Palo Alto, California 94303) is a new periodical which deals with the legal rights of older people with disabilities.

Medicaid—How Your State Helps When Illness Strikes is a free leaflet which explains very clearly the difference between Medicare and Medicaid. Available from Medical Services Administration, Social and Rehabilitation Services, U.S. Department of Health, Education and Welfare, Washington, D.C. 20201.

The Rights of Physically Handicapped People and *Rights of Hospital Patients* are published by Civil Liberties Union, 22 East 40th Street, New York, New York 10016.

Social Security and Supplemental Security Income (SSI) information is available in free leaflets from local Social Security Offices—*Disabled? Find Out About Social Security, If You Become Disabled, Disability Benefits for Blind People, Pocket History of Social Security, Supplemental Security Income for the Aged, Blind and Disabled, Pocket Guide to Supplemental Security Income, Helping the Aged, Blind and Disabled.*

> Social Security notices can be sent to blind people in braille. If desired, a printed letter, which can be read by a sighted person, will be enclosed. Make the request to: Department of Health, Education and Welfare, Social Security Administration, Baltimore, Maryland 21235.

What You Should Know About Health Insurance is a booklet available free

**For complete address see listing under For Specific Disabilities, pp. 264–267.

from Health Insurance Institute, 277 Park Avenue, New York, 10017.

Word from Washington. This free monthly newsletter summarizes and evaluates the current legislation relevant to disabled people and lists new publications and reports. It is available from United Cerebral Palsy Association, Inc., Government Activities Office, 425 Eye Street, N.W., Washington, D.C. 20001.

UNITED KINGDOM
Accidents and the Law by N. D. Vandyk (The Law Society and Oyez Publishing Co., London). Explains how to go about claiming compensation in the United Kingdom for accidents and the legal procedures involved.

Consumers' Guide to the British Social Services by Phyllis Willmott (Pelican Books, Middlesex). A handy guide to the complex social services and organizations that meet the needs of the population. Contains an exhaustive directory of organizations.

Provision for the Disabled by E. Topliss (Basil Blackwell and Mott, Oxford). A comprehensive book about facilities for the disabled provided by the social services.

Leisure Activities

Sports

American Association for Health, Physical Education and Recreation Program for the Handicapped
1201 16th Street, N.W.
Washington, D.C. 20036
Send for free information sheet of contacts, organizations and publications in the United States.

National Wheelchair Athletic Association
40–24 62nd Street
Woodside, New York 11377

National Wheelchair Basketball Association
University of Illinois
Rehabilitation-Education Center
Oak Street and Stadium Drive
Champain, Illinois 61820

UNITED KINGDOM
The British Association of Sporting and Recreational Activities of the Blind,
5 Curzon Road
Thornton Heath, Surrey

British Deaf Sports Council
140 Green Lane
Cookridge, Leeds LS16 7JQ

British Sports Association for the Disabled
Stoke Mandeville Stadium for the Disabled
Harvey Road
Aylesbury, Bucks. HP21 8PP
Coordinating and advisory body for all statutory and voluntary organizations in the field of sports and recreation in Great Britain.

Great Britain Wheelchair Basketball League
18 Wroxall Drive
Grantham, Lincs. NG31 7WQ

CANADA
Canadian Wheelchair Sports Association
Room 7127, Aberhart Hospital
Edmonton, Alberta T6G 2J3

EIRE
Irish Wheelchair Sports Association
Arus Chuchulain
Blackheath Drive
Clontare, Dublin 3

Flying

The Federal Aviation Administration,
Department of Transportation
Washington, D.C. 20591
Provides information about flying for disabled pilots, as well as the portable hand controls which can be installed in general aviation aircraft for paraplegic pilots.

Wheelchair Pilots Association
1101 102 Avenue N.
Largo, Florida 33452
Membership is open to any disabled person who is interested in flying. The association has chapters throughout the United States and abroad.

Horseback Riding

North American Riding for the Handicapped Association
Box 100
Ashburn, Virginia 22011
Publishes a newsletter.

UNITED KINGDOM
Riding for the Disabled
National Headquarters
National Agriculture Centre
Stoneleigh, Kenilworth
Warwickshire CV8 2LY

Skiing

National Amputee Skiers Association
863 United Nations Plaza
New York, New York 10017

For information about outrigger ski guides write to Pauls Sports, Inc., Route 1, Box 615P, Excelsior, Minnesota.

CANADA
Canadian Association for Disabled Skiing
Box 2077
Banff, Alberta T0L 0CO

Water Sports

UNITED KINGDOM
Sports Council
70 Brompton Road
London SW3
The coordinating committee on swimming and water sports for people with disabilities.

Recreational and Competitive Wheelchair Sports, published annually and available free from Paralyzed Veterans of America, Washington, D.C.,** is a summary of qualifications for and classifications of wheelchair sports.

Sports 'n Spokes, the bimonthly magazine for Wheelchair Sports and Recreation (6043 North 9th Avenue, Phoenix, Arizona 85013).

Outdoor Pursuits for Disabled People by Norman Croucher (Disabled Living Foundation, London*). The author, a double-amputee who climbed the Matterhorn, describes various sports and their suitability to different disabilities, urges the reader on enthusiastically and includes details of active programs throughout the U.K.

Art

Arts, Box 2040, Grand Central Station, New York, New York 10017, is an information service, sponsored by the National Endowment for the Arts and Educational Facilities Laboratories, which aims to make arts programs and facilities more accessible to people with disabilities. Write for list of free publications.

*For complete address see listing under General Organizations and Agencies, pp. 268–269.

Sister Kenny Institute Art Show for Disabled Artists is held annually. There are two categories—artists who work with mouth, foot or forehead and artists with disabled arms and hands. For details write to: Art Show Chairperson, Sister Kenny Institute, Minneapolis.*

Chess

British Correspondence Chess Society, 90 Headstone Road
Harrow, Middlesex HA1 1PE

Communication Clubs

Accent Pen Pals, Box 726, Bloomington, Illinois 61701, is run by *Accent* magazine. Write for information, enclosing a stamped, self-addressed envelope.

People to People, International Headquarters, 2201 Grand Avenue, Kansas City, Missouri. An international pen pal association.

The Voicerespondence Club, P.O. Box 207, Shillington, Pennsylvania 19607, has members from all over the world who correspond by tape.

United Kingdom
Braille Correspondence Club, Social Services Department, Civic Centre, Newcastle-upon-Tyne NE1 8PA, has an international link-up. Write, giving personal particulars and standard of braille.

Inter-Nations Friendship Club, 30 Wellington Parade, Blackfen Road, Sidcup, Kent. Write for worldwide membership list and quarterly newsletter. There is no charge, but voluntary donations are welcomed.

Dancing

Wheelchair Square Dancing Instructions on a thirty-minute cassette. Three dollars from Colorado Wheelers, 525 Meadowlark Drive, Lakewood, Colorado 80226.

Diagram of action and main turns for twelve dances adapted for wheelchaired dancing are available from The Librarian, The Spastics Society, London.**

Ham Radio

The American Radio Relay League
225 Main Street
Newington, Connecticut 06111.

The Handicapped Air Program, 804L N. Hamlin Avenue, Skokie, Illinois 60076, will provide information on shortwave listening.

United Kingdom
Associated for Blind and Disabled Radio Amateurs, Radio Society of Great Britain, 45 Doughty Street, London WC1N 2AE

Gardening

Gardening for the Disabled, a free leaflet from Rehabilitation International, New York.*

United Kingdom
The Easy Path to Gardening. (The Reader's Digest Association in conjunction with the Disabled Living Foundation, London*). Subtitled "For all who want to go on enjoying a rewarding hobby," this comprehensive and attractive book is an excellent guide to gardening for people with physical limitations.

Music

Music Services Unit, The Library of Congress, Division for the Blind and Physically Handicapped,* lends free of charge, music scores, textbooks and instructional material in braille, disc recordings, cassettes, open-reel tapes and large print music. Write for information, a book list and catalogs–all available in print, braille or on tape.

United Kingdom
British Society for Music Therapy, 48 Lanchester Road, London N6 4TA, is concerned with music for adults and children as an aid in treatment, education and rehabilitation for emotional, physical or mental handicaps.

Nature Study

The National Audubon Society, 950 Third Avenue, New York, New York 10022. Write for information about birdwatching.

United Kingdom
The Royal Society for the Protection of Birds, The Lodge, Sandy, Bedfordshire, SG19 2BR, publishes the magazine *Birds* and an access guide to nature reserves.

Photography

Volunteer Service for Photographers, Inc., 111 West 57th Street, New York, New York 10019. This organization was established to advise and assist disabled photographers. Publishes a newsletter, *Vignette*.

The Disabled Child

Sources of Information

"Closer Look"
The National Information Center for the Handicapped
1201 16th Street, N.W.
Washington, D.C. 20036
Funded by HEW, this is an information service for parents of children with mental, physical and emotional handicaps. Five coalitions throughout the country provide information and make referrals when necessary. *Practical Advice to Parents,* a booklet published by Closer Look, is a guide to finding help for handicapped children and teenagers.

Coordinating Council for Handicapped Children
407 South Dearborn Street
Chicago, Illinois 60605
Write for publications list. The booklets the council publishes include *Your Rights as Parents of a Handicapped Child* and *Your Guide to Services for Handicapped Children*.

United Kingdom
Voluntary Council for Handicapped Children
National Children's Bureau
8 Wakely Street
London EC1V 7QE
An umbrella organization for all groups dealing with handicapped children. Provides information and has an advisory service.

Further Reading and Reference

The Art and Science of Parenting the Disabled Child. (National Easter Seal Society, Chicago*).

Building an Estate for a Crippled Child by George M. Rideout and John D. Riordan (National Easter Seal Society, Chicago*). This booklet is a guide for parents who want to build an estate as a protection against an uncertain future for a handicapped child. Insurance, savings, stocks and real estate are among the topics covered.

Caring for Your Disabled Child by Benjamin Spock, M.D. and Marion O. Lerrigo, Ph.D. (The Macmillan Company, New York and Collier-MacMillan Limited, London). A guide to understanding and helping the mentally, physically or emotionally handicapped child.

**For complete address see listing under For Specific Disabilities, pp. 264–267.

Clothing for the Handicapped Child (Disabled Living Foundation, London*). A practical, well-written book.

The Exceptional Parent (Room 708, Statler Office Building, 20 Providence Street, Boston, Massachusetts 02116). This is an excellent bimonthly magazine which publishes articles on a wide range of subjects of interest to parents of disabled children and teenagers.

Functional Aids for the Multiply Handicapped edited by Isabel P. Robinault, Ph.D. (Harper and Row, Publishers, Hagerstown, Maryland). A resource book for physicians, therapists and rehabilitation specialists which was written in response to questions about what to buy, how to use or construct aids specifically applicable to the cerebral palsied child. The book could be, however, of interest and use to parents of children with other handicapping conditions. But be warned that the photographs of children with blanked out faces are unfortunate —and may be disturbing.

Handbook for Parents with a Handicapped Child by Judith Stone and Felicity Taylor (Arrow Books, London). Encyclopedic handbook includes directory of services for children with specific disabilities, relevant organizations and information on schools, holidays and recreation.

A Handicapped Child in Your Home (available from Superintendent of Documents, Government Printing Office, Washington, D.C.). This booklet is written for parents who have a severely disabled child at home and deals with the problems, hardships and rewards they encounter.

Handling the Young Cerebral Palsied Child at Home by Nancie R. Finnie. U.S. Editor Una Haynes (E. P. Dutton, New York and William Heineman Medical Books, Ltd., London). This guide for parents and others involved in the care of young children with cerebral palsy includes chapters written by a psychologist, a psychiatrist and a speech therapist as well as a section which covers community resources and suppliers of aids and equipment. The book is charmingly illustrated and much of the material would be helpful to parents of children with any physical disability.

Help for the Handicapped by Florence Weiner (McGraw Hill Book Company, New York). This is a valuable resource book. It's divided into sections, each dealing with a specific disability.

How to Build Special Furniture and Equipment for Handicapped Children by Ruth B. Hofmann (Charles C. Thomas, Publisher, Springfield, Illinois). This illustrated book gives simple and easy-to-follow directions for building furniture for disabled children at a fraction of the retail cost and with more satisfactory results.

How to Organize an Effective Parent Group and Move Bureaucracies by Charlotte Des Jardines (Coordinating Council for Handicapped Children, Chicago). The title of this book is self-explanatory. It encourages assertion, persistence and the use of mass action to exert meaningful pressure.

Self-Help Clothing for Handicapped Children by Clari Bare, Eleanor Boetike and Neva Waggoner (National Easter Seal Society, Chicago*). This book is designed to aid parents and professional personnel in the selection and adaptation of clothing for children with disabilities.

Special People by Arnold Sackmary and Roger Zeeman (New Jersey A.C.L.D., Convent Station, New Jersey). Written for siblings of disabled boys and girls, this booklet is designed to help them understand the special problems involved at home and at school for their disabled brothers or sisters.

Recreation

Handicapped Adventure Playground Association, Central Office, Fulham Palace, Bishops Avenue, London SW6 6EA. HAPA is internationally recognized as the pioneer in the field of adventure playgrounds for disabled children. They run four imaginative playgrounds in London and publish *Adventure Playground for Handicapped Children*, an illustrated booklet which explains their philosophy and methods.

The National Easter Seal Society, Chicago,* publishes *Toys, Games and Apparatus for Children with Cerebral Palsy* by Gladys Rogers and Leah Thomas, *Your Child's Play* by Grace Langdon, Ph.D., and *Let's Play Games!* an illustrated booklet on games that children with physical handicaps can play with or without adaptations. It includes instructions, lists of materials needed and rules for fifty-six games for children from the ages of five to eight.

Education

The Council for Exceptional Children, 1920 Association Drive, Reston, Virginia 22091, is an organization which conducts research and training on education of disabled children and works for improved education, legislation and services.

Office for Child Development, Office for Human Development Services, Department of Health, Education and Welfare, Washington, D.C. 20201, will provide information on the Head Start program and assistance if necessary.

Your Rights Under the Education for All Handicapped Act is a pamphlet available from the Children's Defense Fund, 1520 New Hampshire Avenue, N.W., Washington, D.C. 20036.

United Kingdom

The National Council for Special Education, 17 Pembridge Square, London W2 4EP, is concerned with education of handicapped children in both special and ordinary schools.

The Disabled Teenager

Living Fully by Sol Gordon (The John Day Company, New York). An excellent book which takes a practical and honest look at the problems which must be faced by young people with disabilities and explores how they can best achieve full and happy adult lives.

Facts About Sex for Today's Youth by Sol Gordon (The John Day Company, New York). Straight talk in simple language for the adolescent with disabilities.

View of Life by Henry Henscheid (The National Easter Seal Society Chicago*). A lovely and inspiring booklet written for disabled teenagers about the problems they might encounter. The author, who writes in the first person, is a young man who is disabled by cerebral palsy.

United Kingdom

Physically Handicapped Able bodied (PHAB) Association, 42 Devonshire Street, London W1N 1LN. A national organization established to promote integration of physically handicapped young people through social and recreational activities.

*For complete address see listing under General Organizations and Agencies, pp. 268–269.

Where to Get It

Throughout this book we have referred to hospital suppliers, self-help equipment firms and mail order companies as the sources for various aids and gadgets. The Publications Office of the Institute of Rehabilitation Medicine, 400 East 34th Street New York, New York 10016, will send on request a list of commercial sources for adaptive equipment. *Accent on Living's Buyers Guide* is a seventy-page booklet which lists the names and addresses of manufacturers of products for the disabled and related publications. It is available from Accent Special Publications, Box 700, Bloomington, Illinois 61701. The companies in the list which follows will all send catalogs on request.

Hospital Suppliers

Accurate Medical Service
8004 West Chester Pike
Upper Darby, Pennsylvania 19082
This is one of the distributors of a nationwide group operated under the name MED (Medical Equipment Distributors). Accurate Medical Service will supply, on request, a list of their distributors.

E. F. Brewer Company
13282 West Carmen Avenue
P.O. Box 711
Butler, Wisconsin 53007

S. H. Camp and Company
P.O. Box 89
Jackson, Michigan 49204
This company has branches in Australia, the United Kingdom, the Netherlands, New Zealand, Sweden and Switzerland.

Ted Hoyler and Co., Inc.
2222 Minnesota Street
Oshkosh, Wisconsin 54901

G. E. Miller, Inc.
484 South Broadway
Yonkers, New York 10705

Nelson Medical Products
5690 Sarah Avenue
Sarasota, Florida 33581

J. A. Preston Corporation
71 Fifth Avenue
New York, New York 10003

Rehabilitation Equipment Inc.
1556 Third Avenue
New York, New York 10028

Rehabilitation Equipment and Supply
1823 West Moss Avenue
Peoria, Illinois 61606

United Kingdom
Renray Products (UK) Ltd.
75 Woolvale Road
Belfast BT13 3PB
Northern Ireland

Self-Help Equipment Firms

Cleo Living Aids
3957 Mayfield
Cleveland, Ohio 44121

Fashion-Able
Rocky Hill, New Jersey 08553

Maddak, Inc.
Pequannock, New Jersey 07440

J. T. Posey Company
39 South Santa Anita Avenue
Pasadena, California 91107

Fred Sammons, Inc.
P.O. Box 32
Brookfield, Illinois 60513

Canada
Down Brothers and Mayer & Phelps Ltd.
410 Dundas Street West
Toronto 2B

United Kingdom
British Red Cross Society
Aids for the Disabled
9 Grosvenor Crescent
London SW1X 7EJ

Carters (J. and A.) Ltd.
Alfred Street
Westbury, Wilts. BA13 3DZ

Aids for the Disabled
Homecraft Supplies (Fleet Street) Ltd.
27 Trinity Road
London SW17

Llewellyn Living Aids
Carlton Works
Carlton Street
Liverpool L37 ED

Mail Order Companies

Alsto Company
1384 Third Avenue
Cleveland, Ohio 44107
General mail order firm specializing in garden and home workshop equipment.

Bancroft's
251 East Fifth Street
St. Paul, Minnesota 55101

L. L. Bean, Inc.
248 Main Street
Freeport, Maine 04032
Specializes in recreational and outdoor activities equipment.

Breck's of Boston
401 Summer Street
Boston, Massachusetts 02210

Creative Playthings, Inc.
Princeton, New Jersey 08540
and
5757 West Century Boulevard
Los Angeles, California 90045
Specializes in children's toys, educational aids and furniture.

J. W. Holst
2470 Brittannia Road
Sarasota, Florida 33581

Miles Kimball
Kimball Building
41 West Eighth Avenue
Oshkosh, Wisconsin 54901

Montgomery Ward
Albany, New York 12201

Mothercare by Mail
P.O. Box 228
Parsippany, New Jersey 07054

Sears Roebuck and Co.
4640 Roosevelt Boulevard
Philadelphia, Pennsylvania 19132

Sunset House
12800 Culver Boulevard
Los Angeles, California 90066

United Kingdom
Mothercare by Mail
Cherry Tree Road
Watford, Herts. WD2 5SH

Index

References in italics denote illustrations.

C

D

E

F

Acknowledgements

A great many individuals, organizations, institutions and local and national agencies have given invaluable help and advice during the preparation of this book. The publishers, editor and contributors wish to extend their thanks to them all, and in particular to the following individuals who gave so generously of their time and counsel:

IN THE UNITED STATES

Mary Adams, O.T.R., Rehabilitation–Education Center, University of Illinois
Cynthia Allen, Victor Valley Community College, California
Laurie Bean
William J. Bean, HEW
Frank Bowe, Ph.D., American Coalition of Citizens with Disabilities, Inc.
Susan Daniels, Ph.D., Institute on Attitudinal, Legal and Leisure Barriers, Washington, D.C.
Rose Elfinbein, O.T.R., Institute of Rehabilitation Medicine, New York
Sandi Enders, O.T.R., Center for Independent Living, Berkeley
Anna Fay, National Paraplegia Foundation, Inc.
Eunice Fiorito, Mayor's Office for the Handicapped, New York
Ann Frank
Thomas Freebairn, Deafness Research and Training Center, New York
Harriet Griswald
Sylvia Glickman, *Worcester Sunday Telegraph*
Robert M. Goldenson, Ph.D.
Alan Hartman
Judy Heumann, Center for Independent Living, Berkeley
Ralph Hotchkiss, Center for Concerned Engineering, Washington, D.C.
Jan Ellen Jacobi, American Coalition of Citizens with Disabilities, Inc.
Lois Sachs Johnson, Governor's Committee for the Handicapped of Du Page County, Illinois
Debby Kaplan, Disability Rights Center, Washington, D.C.
Jean Kaiser, The California Association of the Physically Handicapped, Inc.
Rose Fadul Kardashian, O.T.R., Institute of Rehabilitation Medicine, New York
Dr. Jose Lafitte, Gallaudet College
Mary Ann Lang, New York Association for the Blind
Peter Lasson, Architectural and Transportation Barriers Compliance Board
Gini and Joe Laurie, *Rehabilitation Gazette*
Nancy Loeb, Moss Rehabilitation Hospital, Philadelphia
Carr Massi, O.T.R., Institute of Rehabilitation Medicine, New York
Sharon Mistler, Institute on Attitudinal, Legal and Leisure Barriers
Jeff Moyer, Center for Independent Living, Berkeley
Dr. Timothy J. Nugent, Rehabilitation–Education Center, University of Illinois
Margaret Parsons (deceased), Department of Health, Education and Welfare
Jim Pechon, Center for Independent Living, Berkeley
Rami Rabby, American Federation of the Blind
Micky Rachlis
Judi Rogers, O.T.R., Center for Independent Living, Berkeley
Robert H. Ruffner, President's Committee on Employment of the Handicapped
Sieglinde Shapiro, Disabled in Action of Pennsylvania
Renah Shnaider, The California Association of the Physically Handicapped, Inc.
Jo Ann Smith, Moss Rehabilitation Hospital, Philadelphia
Wesley Sprague, The New York Association for the Blind
Angela Thompson, Disabled in Action, New York
Norman L. Tulley, Gallaudet College
Anna Waltz, Seattle Department of Human Resources
Peter D. Waters, Possum, Inc.
Douglas Watson, Ph.D., Deafness Research and Training Center, New York
Freida Zames, Disabled in Action, New York

IN THE UNITED KINGDOM

Stephen Bradshaw, Spinal Injuries Association
Norman Croucher
Winifred Dale
Dr. Katharina Dalton
Steve Dwoskin
Elizabeth Fanshaw, M.A.O.T., Disabled Living Foundation
Vic Finklestein, The Open University
Pat Gilliland
Selwyn Goldsmith, Department of the Environment
Mary Greaves
Lady Hamilton, Disabled Living Foundation
Judith Hillelson, O.T.R.
David Hyde (deceased), Possum User's Association
Nick Johnson
Felicity Lane Fox
Peter Large, Association of Disabled Professionals
Susie Large
Sarah Lomas, M.A.O.T., Disabled Living Foundation
Barbara Meredith, Disablement Incomes Group
Tony Northmore
Diana Staples, Mary Marlborough Lodge
Dorothy Whittaker
Rosalie Wilkins, *Link*
Bernice Wood, Spinal Injuries Association

ARTISTS

Patricia Capon/Joan Farmer Artists: 104–23

Chris Forsey: 15, 17 top right, 82–3, 90–1, 140–2, 145–7, 160–1, 208–9, 218–19

Richard Johnson: Cover design

Stuart Perry: 58–9

Len Roberts: 92–3, 204–5, 210–13

R. A. Sherrington/B. L. Kearley Ltd.: 22–30, 34, 94–103, 124–31

Alan Suttie: 13, 16, 17 bottom left, 19, 84–9, 136–9, 148–9, 206–7, 214–17

Craig Warwick/Linden Artists: 31–3, 164–7, 170–4, 176, 178, 184–94, 201–3, 232–37, 239–40, 244–5

PHOTOGRAPHERS AND AGENCIES

Malcolm Aird/The Employment Service Division of the Manpower Services Commission: 134, 153

Central Office of Information, London: 41

Lew Dakan: 1

John Drysdale/Camera Press: 230, 243

Keystone Press Agency: 226

President's Committee for the Employment of the Handicapped: 42

Tedde Kast Scharf: 45

Sybil Shelton: 60, 67, 70, 257

David Sperling: 49

Homer Sykes/The John Hillelson Agency: 2/3, 6–8, 35, 74, 77, 80, 133, 150, 156, 162, 168, 179

U.S.A.F.: 251

David White/Camera Press: 241